British Novelists, 1890-1929: Traditionalists

Dictionary of Literary Biography

1: *The American Renaissance in New England,* edited by Joel Myerson (1978)
2: *American Novelists Since World War II,* edited by Jeffrey Helterman and Richard Layman (1978)
3: *Antebellum Writers in New York and the South,* edited by Joel Myerson (1979)
4: *American Writers in Paris, 1920-1939,* edited by Karen Lane Rood (1980)
5: *American Poets Since World War II,* 2 parts, edited by Donald J. Greiner (1980)
6: *American Novelists Since World War II,* Second Series, edited by James E. Kibler, Jr. (1980)
7: *Twentieth-Century American Dramatists,* 2 parts, edited by John MacNicholas (1981)
8: *Twentieth-Century American Science-Fiction Writers,* 2 parts, edited by David Cowart and Thomas L. Wymer (1981)
9: *American Novelists, 1910-1945,* 3 parts, edited by James J. Martine (1981)
10: *Modern British Dramatists, 1900-1945,* 2 parts, edited by Stanley Weintraub (1982)
11: *American Humorists, 1800-1950,* 2 parts, edited by Stanley Trachtenberg (1982)
12: *American Realists and Naturalists,* edited by Donald Pizer and Earl N. Harbert (1982)
13: *British Dramatists Since World War II,* 2 parts, edited by Stanley Weintraub (1982)
14: *British Novelists Since 1960,* 2 parts, edited by Jay L. Halio (1983)
15: *British Novelists, 1930-1959,* 2 parts, edited by Bernard Oldsey (1983)
16: *The Beats: Literary Bohemians in Postwar America*, 2 parts, edited by Ann Charters (1983)
17: *Twentieth-Century American Historians,* edited by Clyde N. Wilson (1983)
18: *Victorian Novelists After 1885*, edited by Ira B. Nadel and William E. Fredeman (1983)
19: *British Poets, 1880-1914*, edited by Donald E. Stanford (1983)
20: *British Poets, 1914-1945*, edited by Donald E. Stanford (1983)
21: *Victorian Novelists Before 1885,* edited by Ira B. Nadel and William E. Fredeman (1983)
22: *American Writers for Children, 1900-1960,* edited by John Cech (1983)
23: *American Newspaper Journalists, 1873-1900,* edited by Perry J. Ashley (1983)
24: *American Colonial Writers, 1606-1734,* edited by Emory Elliott (1984)
25: *American Newspaper Journalists, 1901-1925,* edited by Perry J. Ashley (1984)
26: *American Screenwriters,* edited by Robert E. Morsberger, Stephen O. Lesser, and Randall Clark (1984)
27: *Poets of Great Britain and Ireland, 1945-1960,* edited by Vincent B. Sherry, Jr. (1984)
28: *Twentieth-Century American-Jewish Fiction Writers,* edited by Daniel Walden (1984)
29: *American Newspaper Journalists, 1926-1950,* edited by Perry J. Ashley (1984)
30: *American Historians, 1607-1865,* edited by Clyde N. Wilson (1984)
31: *American Colonial Writers, 1735-1781,* edited by Emory Elliott (1984)
32: *Victorian Poets Before 1850,* edited by William E. Fredeman and Ira B. Nadel (1984)
33: *Afro-American Fiction Writers After 1955,* edited by Thadious M. Davis and Trudier Harris (1984)
34: *British Novelists, 1890-1929: Traditionalists,* edited by Thomas F. Staley (1985)

Documentary Series:
1: *Sherwood Anderson, Willa Cather, John Dos Passos, Theodore Dreiser, F. Scott Fitzgerald, Ernest Hemingway, Sinclair Lewis,* edited by Margaret A. Van Antwerp (1982)
2: *James Gould Cozzens, James T. Farrell, William Faulkner, John O'Hara, John Steinbeck, Thomas Wolfe, Richard Wright,* edited by Margaret A. Van Antwerp (1982)
3: *Saul Bellow, Jack Kerouac, Norman Mailer, Vladimir Nabokov, John Updike, Kurt Vonnegut,* edited by Mary Bruccoli (1983)
4: *Tennessee Williams,* edited by Margaret A. Van Antwerp and Sally Johns (1984)

Yearbooks:
1980, edited by Karen L. Rood, Jean W. Ross, and Richard Ziegfeld (1981)
1981, edited by Karen L. Rood, Jean W. Ross, and Richard Ziegfeld (1982)
1982, edited by Richard Ziegfeld; associate editors: Jean W. Ross and Lynne C. Zeigler (1983)
1983, edited by Mary Bruccoli and Jean W. Ross; associate editor: Richard Ziegfeld (1984)

Dictionary of Literary Biography • Volume Thirty-four

British Novelists, 1890-1929: Traditionalists

Edited by
Thomas F. Staley
University of Tulsa

A Bruccoli Clark Book
Gale Research Company • Book Tower • Detroit, Michigan 48226

Manufactured by Edwards Brothers, Inc.
Ann Arbor, Michigan
Printed in the United States of America

Library of Congress Cataloging in Publication Data
Main entry under title:

British novelists, 1890-1929: traditionalists.

(Dictionary of literary biography: V. 34)
"A Bruccoli Clark book."
Includes index.
1. English fiction—20th century—History and criticism. 2. English fiction—19th century—History and criticism. 3. Novelists, English—20th century—Biography—Dictionaries. 4. Novelists, English—19th century—Biography—Dictionaries. 5. English fiction—20th century—Bio-bibliography. 6. English fiction—19th century—Bio-bibliography. I. Staley, Thomas F. II. Series.
PR881.B724   1984 [985 823'.912'09   84-18723
ISBN 0-8103-1712-5

To
Gordon Taylor
colleague and friend

Contents

Plan of the Series

. . . Almost the most prodigious asset of a country, and perhaps its most precious possession, is its native literary product—when that product is fine and noble and enduring.

Mark Twain*

The advisory board, the editors, and the publisher of the *Dictionary of Literary Biography* are joined in endorsing Mark Twain's declaration. The literature of a nation provides an inexhaustible resource of permanent worth. It is our expectation that this endeavor will make literature and its creators better understood and more accessible to students and the literate public, while satisfying the standards of teachers and scholars.

To meet these requirements, *literary biography* has been construed in terms of the author's achievement. The most important thing about a writer is his writing. Accordingly, the entries in *DLB* are career biographies, tracing the development of the author's canon and the evolution of his reputation.

The publication plan for *DLB* resulted from two years of preparation. The project was proposed to Bruccoli Clark by Frederick G. Ruffner, president of the Gale Research Company, in November 1975. After specimen entries were prepared and typeset, an advisory board was formed to refine the entry format and develop the series rationale. In meetings held during 1976, the publisher, series editors, and advisory board approved the scheme for a comprehensive biographical dictionary of persons who contributed to North American literature. Editorial work on the first volume began in January 1977, and it was published in 1978.

In order to make *DLB* more than a reference tool and to compile volumes that individually have claim to status as literary history, it was decided to organize volumes by topic or period or genre. Each of these freestanding volumes provides a biographical-bibliographical guide and overview for a particular area of literature. We are convinced that this organization—as opposed to a single alphabet method—constitutes a valuable innovation in the presentation of reference material. The volume plan necessarily requires many decisions for the placement and treatment of authors who might properly be included in two or three volumes. In some instances a major figure will be included in separate volumes, but with different entries emphasizing the aspect of his career appropriate to each volume. Ernest Hemingway, for example, is represented in *American Writers in Paris, 1920-1939* by an entry focusing on his expatriate apprenticeship; he is also in *American Novelists, 1910-1945* with an entry surveying his entire career. Each volume includes a cumulative index of subject authors. The final *DLB* volume will be a comprehensive index to the entire series.

With volume ten in 1982 it was decided to enlarge the scope of *DLB* beyond the literature of the United States. By the end of 1983 twelve volumes treating British literature had been published, and volumes for Commonwealth and Modern European literature were in progress. The series has been further augmented by the *DLB Yearbooks* (since 1981) which update published entries and add new entries to keep the *DLB* current with contemporary activity. There have also been occasional *DLB Documentary Series* volumes which provide biographical and critical background source materials for figures whose work is judged to have particular interest for students. One of these companion volumes is entirely devoted to Tennessee Williams.

The purpose of *DLB* is not only to provide reliable information in a convenient format but also to place the figures in the larger perspective of literary history and to offer appraisals of their accomplishments by qualified scholars.

We define literature as the *intellectual commerce of a nation*: not merely as belles lettres, but as that ample and complex process by which ideas are generated, shaped, and transmitted. *DLB* entries are not limited to "creative writers" but extend to other figures who in this time and in this way influenced the mind of a people. Thus the series encompasses historians, journalists, publishers, and screenwriters. By this means readers of *DLB* may be aided to perceive literature not as cult scripture in the keeping of cultural high priests, but as at the center of a nation's life.

DLB includes the major writers appropriate to each volume and those standing in the ranks immediately behind them. Scholarly and critical counsel has been sought in deciding which minor figures to include and how full their entries should be.

*From an unpublished section of Mark Twain's autobiography, copyright © by the Mark Twain Company.

Wherever possible, useful references will be made to figures who do not warrant separate entries.

Each *DLB* volume has a volume editor responsible for planning the volume, selecting the figures for inclusion, and assigning the entries. Volume editors are also responsible for preparing, where appropriate, appendices surveying the major periodicals and literary and intellectual movements for their volumes, as well as lists of further readings. Work on the series as a whole is coordinated at the Bruccoli Clark editorial center in Columbia, South Carolina, where the editorial staff is responsible for the accuracy of the published volumes.

One feature that distinguishes *DLB* is the illustration policy—its concern with the iconography of literature. Just as an author is influenced by his surroundings, so is the reader's understanding of the author enhanced by a knowledge of his environment. Therefore *DLB* volumes include not only drawings, paintings, and photographs of authors, often depicting them at various stages in their careers, but also illustrations of their families and places where they lived. Title pages are regularly reproduced in facsimile along with dust jackets for modern authors. The dust jackets are a special fea-

ture of *DLB* because they often document better than anything else the way in which an author's work was launched in its own time. Specimens of the writers' manuscripts are included when feasible.

A supplement to *DLB*—tentatively titled *A Guide, Chronology, and Glossary for American Literature*—will outline the history of literature in North America and trace the influences that shaped it. This volume will provide a framework for the study of American literature by means of chronological tables, literary affiliation charts, glossarial entries, and concise surveys of the major movements. It has been planned to stand on its own as a vade mecum, providing a ready-reference guide to the study of American literature as well as a companion to the *DLB* volumes for American literature.

Samuel Johnson rightly decreed that "The chief glory of every people arises from its authors." The purpose of the *Dictionary of Literary Biography* is to compile literary history in the surest way available to us—by accurate and comprehensive treatment of the lives and work of those who contributed to it.

The *DLB* Advisory Board

Foreword

The forty years between 1890-1929 were the most fertile and diverse period of the British novel. During these years, marked as they were by the Great War and by sweeping and revolutionary changes in the social, political, and economic structures of Britain, the novel became a much broader reflector of the aims, confusions, concerns, ideas, and attitudes of all classes of the British people, effectively mirroring forces of change in the culture. The British novelists of the nineteenth century shaped what F. R. Leavis has termed "The Great Tradition," but it was during the years after 1890 that the novel in Britain established itself as the dominant literary genre. More than any other literary form, it most completely absorbed and pointed to the fundamental changes in consciousness that were taking place.

These changes were so substantial and unalterable that Virginia Woolf proclaimed, "in or about December 1910 human character changed." This phrase is remembered more for its dramatic quality than its historical accuracy, but, nevertheless, it points with psychological accuracy to the profound changes in the way man was beginning to think about his universe, his social and governmental structures, and, most profoundly, about himself and his place in the world. In her choice of date, Woolf was referring specifically to the first postimpressionist exhibition in England, but her announcement serves as a summation of the developments that were to take place during the next twenty years.

It is simplistic and therefore rash to look for an exclusive periodicity in literature, just as it is arbitrary and naive to divide a period's literature into discrete categories; however, during the years from 1890 to 1929 there were two strong but not mutually exclusive impulses among novelists—first, to write largely out of the tradition that immediately preceded them at the same time that they confronted the changing shape of the world; and second, to attempt to break sharply from the traditions and values that they inherited and reflect in form, technique, and subject matter an altered vision of the world and the self. Such divisions are, however, obvious only on the surface. For example, the works of Joseph Conrad contrasted with those of James Joyce demonstrate this division, but there are important similarities in their fiction as well. Among minor writers these distinctions blur. One point is clear: the British novel, as a whole, reflected the great transitions of the society and the nation itself.

This volume of the *Dictionary of Literary Biography* includes those novelists whose works by and large reflect affinities in form and content with the earlier novel, or, perhaps more accurately, novelists whose work is not preoccupied with what we have come to term the modernist temperament; this group will be included in *DLB 36, British Novelists, 1890-1929: Modernists.* Although many of the novelists included in this present volume reveal a new awareness in their fiction in both subject matter and theme, they did not view innovation or radical change as their primary purpose. That the novels of the period are so divergent is a tribute to the resilience and adaptability of the genre.

Conrad, the most imposing figure in this volume, retained the frame of the traditional realist novel, but his work reflects from the outset his preoccupation with the moral self. The shift from individual to social principles in the moral world lies at the center of his work, hence the sea, the jungle, the remote in general provide the contexts in which he studies his characters. It is important, too, to remember that despite the crucial influence of Conrad's fiction on the British novel, he was not British by birth or upbringing.

Closer to the tradition of the nineteenth-century realist novel in Britain were Arnold Bennett and John Galsworthy, whose novels reveal the changing social conditions in England. Both looked with irony at the unquestioned goals of progress, the iniquities and even injustices in society, but their work seldom transcends the period because of their failures to impose social consciousness needed to provide moral force. H. G. Wells, on the other hand, was the best-known popularizer of progressive thought in England. He was aware of thinkers such as Marx long before most other writers, yet his methods for conveying his ideas in fiction were conventional.

Ford Madox Ford and E. M. Forster have achieved greater stature than Bennett and Galsworthy, because, rather than embodying a distant or lofty moral objectivity, they brought to their novels a controlled subjectivity which gave them immediacy as well as a moral perspective. Forster's *Howards End,* centering on the liberal values of the

Schlegel sisters and the more "progressive" commercial values of the Wilcoxes, suggests through its symbolism and themes an optimistic alliance. Ford's *The Good Soldier,* with its complex perspective on moral behavior, probes deeply the question of human deception and the relative nature of truth, a distinctly modern theme. While his fiction looks forward to the modernists, it owes much to earlier French fiction as well.

A number of the writers included in this volume were enormously popular in their own time, but their themes and concerns have limited their reputations. Kipling's position is an interesting one. He frequently wrote from a distinctively modernist disposition with its allusive qualities and its economy of style, and, while his imperialist values are clearly reflected on the surface of his fiction, there is also in Kipling's work an attempt to prick the social conscience of the country. Yet he is remembered as the preeminent nationalistic writer. G. K. Chesterton, also an enormously popular public figure in his day, reveals in his work well-recognized liberal values of the period, but, in fact, his broad engagement with current issues has left much of his work dated. The writings of Oscar Wilde represent an important strain in the literature of the period with his concern with art for its own sake, a characteristic of so much of the writing of the 1890s that fell out of favor with the advent of modernism.

That the tradition of the well-wrought realistic novel remained strong even as the great modernists were expanding the genre attests to the novel's vitality and flexibility.

—Thomas F. Staley

Acknowledgments

This book was produced by BC Research. Karen L. Rood is senior editor for the *Dictionary of Literary Biography* series. The editorial staff includes Philip B. Dematteis, Jean W. Ross, and Margaret A. Van Antwerp.

Art supervisor is Claudia Ericson. Copyediting supervisor is Joycelyn R. Smith. Typesetting supervisor is Laura Ingram. The production staff includes Mary Betts, Rowena Betts, Kimberly Casey, Patricia Coate, Kathleen M. Flanagan, Joyce Fowler, Judith K. Ingle, Vickie Lowers, Judith McCray, and Jane McPherson. Jean W. Ross is permissions editor. Joseph Caldwell, photography editor, did photographic copy work for the volume.

Walter W. Ross did the library research with the assistance of the staff at the Thomas Cooper Library of the University of South Carolina: Lynn Barron, Daniel Boice, Sue Collins, Michael Freeman, Gary Geer, Alexander M. Gilchrist, Jens Holley, David Lincove, Marcia Martin, Roger Mortimer, Jean Rhyne, Karen Rissling, Paula Swope, and Ellen Tillet.

The following booksellers provided invaluable assistance in providing illustrations for this volume: Bertram Rota Ltd., Clearwater Books, Guildhall Bookshop, Ian McKelvie Books, and Sylvester & Orphanos Booksellers & Publishers.

The editor also acknowledges with gratitude the significant contributions of Scott Simpkins, Charlotte Stewart, and Mary O'Toole.

British Novelists, 1890-1929: Traditionalists

Dictionary of Literary Biography

Maurice Baring

(27 April 1874-14 December 1945)

Peter M. Irvine
University of Tulsa

SELECTED BOOKS: *Hildesheim: quatre pastiches* (Paris: A. Lemerre, 1899; London: Heinemann, 1924);

The Black Prince and Other Poems (London & New York: John Lane, 1903);

Gaston de Foix and Other Plays (London: Richards, 1903);

Fifty Sonnets (London: Privately printed, 1905);

With the Russians in Manchuria (London: Methuen, 1905);

Mahasena (Oxford: Blackwell, 1905);

Sonnets and Short Poems (Oxford: Blackwell, 1906);

Desiderio (Oxford: Blackwell/London: Simpkin, Marshall, Hamilton, Kent, 1906; revised, 1911);

A Year in Russia (London: Methuen, 1907; revised, 1917; New York: Dutton, 1917?);

Proserpine: A Masque (Oxford: Blackwell, 1908);

Russian Essays and Stories (London: Methuen, 1908);

Orpheus in Mayfair and Other Stories and Sketches (London: Mills & Boon, 1909);

The Glass Mender and Other Stories (London: J. Nisbet, 1910); republished as *The Blue Rose Fairy Book* (New York: Dodd, Mead, 1911);

Landmarks in Russian Literature (London: Methuen, 1910; New York: Macmillan, 1912);

Dead Letters (London: Constable, 1910; Boston: Houghton Mifflin, 1910);

The Collected Poems of Maurice Baring (London & New York: Lane, 1911; enlarged, London: Heinemann, 1925; Garden City: Doubleday, Page, 1925);

Diminutive Dramas (London: Constable, 1911; Bos-

Maurice Baring (photo by Bertram Park)

ton & New York: Houghton Mifflin, 1911);

The Russian People (London: Methuen, 1911);

The Grey Stocking and Other Plays (London: Constable, 1911);

Letters From the Near East, 1909 and 1912 (London: Smith, Elder, 1913);

Lost Diaries (London: Duckworth, 1913; Boston & New York: Houghton Mifflin, 1913);

What I Saw in Russia (London & New York: Nelson, 1913; enlarged, London: Heinemann, 1927);

Palamon and Arcite: A Play for Puppets (Oxford: Blackwell, 1913);

Round the World in Any Number of Days (Boston & New York: Houghton Mifflin, 1914; London: Chatto & Windus, 1919);

The Mainsprings of Russia (London & New York: Nelson, 1914);

An Outline of Russian Literature (London: Williams & Northgate, 1914; New York: Holt, 1915);

In Memoriam: Auberon Herbert (Oxford: Blackwell, 1917);

Poems 1914-1917 (London: Secker, 1918); enlarged as *Poems 1914-1919* (London: Secker, 1920);

Manfroy: A Play in Five Acts (London: Privately printed, 1920);

R.F.C., H.Q., 1914-1918 (London: Bell, 1920); republished as *Flying Corps Headquarters, 1914-1918* (London: Heinemann, 1930);

Passing By (London: Secker, 1921);

The Puppet Show of Memory (London: Heinemann, 1922; Boston: Little, Brown, 1922);

Overlooked (London: Heinemann, 1922; Boston & New York: Houghton Mifflin, 1922);

A Triangle: Passages From Three Notebooks (London: Heinemann, 1923; Garden City: Doubleday, Page, 1924);

His Majesty's Embassy and Other Plays (London: Heinemann, 1923; Boston: Little, Brown, 1923);

C, 2 volumes (London: Heinemann, 1924; Garden City: Doubleday, Page, 1924);

Punch and Judy and Other Essays (London: Heinemann, 1924; Garden City: Doubleday, Page, 1924);

Half a Minute's Silence and Other Stories (London: Heinemann, 1925; Garden City: Doubleday, Page, 1925);

Cat's Cradle (London: Heinemann, 1925; Garden City: Doubleday, Page, 1926);

Daphne Adeane (London: Heinemann, 1926; London & New York: Harper, 1927);

Catherine Parr: or, Alexander's Horse (Chicago: Old Tower Press, 1927);

French Literature (London: Benn, 1927);

Tinker's Leave (London: Heinemann, 1927; Garden City: Doubleday, Doran, 1928);

Cecil Spencer (London: Privately printed, 1928; London: Heinemann, 1929);

Comfortless Memory (London: Heinemann, 1928); republished as *When They Love* (Garden City: Doubleday, Doran, 1928);

The Coat Without Seam (London: Heinemann, 1929; New York: Knopf, 1929);

Poems 1892-1929 (London: Privately printed, 1929); republished as *Selected Poems* (London: Heinemann, 1930);

Robert Peckham (London: Heinemann, 1930; New York: Knopf, 1930);

In My End Is My Beginning (London: Heinemann, 1931; New York: Knopf, 1931);

Friday's Business (London: Heinemann, 1932; New York: Knopf, 1933);

Lost Lectures: or, The Fruits of Experience (London: P. Davies, 1932; New York: Knopf, 1932);

Sarah Bernhardt (London & Edinburgh: P. Davies, 1933; New York & London: Appleton-Century, 1934);

The Lonely Lady of Dulwich (London: Heinemann, 1934; New York: Knopf, 1934);

Unreliable History (London & Toronto: Heinemann, 1934);

Darby and Joan (London: Heinemann, 1935; New York: Knopf, 1936);

Have You Anything to Declare? A Notebook with Commentaries (London: Heinemann, 1936; New York: Knopf, 1937).

OTHER: Leonardo da Vinci, *Thoughts on Art and Life,* translated by Baring (Boston: Merrymount, 1906);

English Landscape, compiled by Baring (London: Humphrey Milford, 1916);

Translations, Ancient and Modern (with Originals) (London: Secker, 1918);

The Oxford Book of Russian Verse, edited by Baring (Oxford: Clarendon, 1924);

Last Days of Tsarskoe Selo: Being the Personal Notes and Memories of Count Paul Benckendorff, translated by Baring (London: Heinemann, 1927);

Algae, an Anthology of Phrases, collected by Baring (London: Heinemann, 1928);

Alfred Musset, *Fantasio, A Comedy in Two Acts,* translated by Baring (New York: Pleiad, 1929);

Russian Lyrics, translated by Baring (London: Heinemann, 1943).

Maurice Baring, a prolific writer of wide artistic range, belongs in the category of English Catholic authors with G. K. Chesterton, Hilaire Belloc, Evelyn Waugh, and Graham Greene. His publications, numbering over fifty books, ranging

Ethel Smyth and Maurice Baring in Copenhagen, 1900

from poetry and drama to literary criticism and parody, included an autobiography and some fifteen novels. The novels, easily his greatest achievements, are unassuming portraits, written in the barest and most lucid of styles, of the star-crossed loves and spiritual quests of sensitive and cultivated members of the cosmopolitan elite. Remarkably consistent in subject, theme, and technique, they read almost as separate chapters of a single, continuous work. Although Baring's fictive world is a closed one, it is painstakingly realistic. The lives of princesses, lords and ladies, diplomats and writers strike one as being very ordinary. None of his protagonists, with all their flawed decisions and disappointments, are exceptional or strong enough to qualify as tragic figures. Yet their desperate search for love, their sensitivity and cultivation, their gentle melancholy, and above all their credibility as human beings make them worth getting to know.

The fifth son of Edward Charles Baring, a prominent London banker, and Louisa Emily Charlotte Bulteel, and kinsman of several English dignitaries, Maurice Baring began his elaborate education under a succession of governesses and tutors. In his early years he acquired a familiarity with French language and literature which rivaled his knowledge of English. When he was sent to school in 1884 his masters were amused at his broken English, and at Eton College, nearly a decade later, he won the Prince Consort's French Prize with little difficulty. Thereafter he spent a few years abroad and at Cambridge and Oxford training for the diplomatic service, perfecting his knowledge of languages and refining his taste for the arts. In 1898 Baring was nominated attaché to the Paris embassy. For the next six years he held posts in several countries; during this time he visited Russia, learned the language, and wrote with authority on the land, the people, and the literature. By 1904 he had decided that he was better suited for a literary career than for diplomacy, and, upon the outbreak of the Russo-Japanese War, accepted a position as military correspondent for the *London Morning Post*. When, in 1909, he reached a spiritual crisis, he converted to Catholicism—"the only act in my life," he states in his autobiography, "which I am quite certain I have never regretted." At the end of World War I, having distinguished himself as a staff officer in the Royal Flying Corps, he devoted himself entirely to his writing. It was not until 1921, however, at the age of forty-seven, that Baring saw publication of his first novel, *Passing By*. A steady run of novels followed at the rate of nearly one per year in the ensuing decade, among which the most notable are *C* (1924),

"Mr. Maurice Baring, testing carefully the Russian sense of humour" (1908), caricature by Max Beerbohm (© Eva Reichmann, courtesy of Miss Elizabeth Williamson)

Cat's Cradle (1925), and *The Coat Without Seam* (1929).

The fourth of Baring's novels, *C* chronicles the brief, troubled life of Caryl Bramsley ("C."), who, misunderstood and disapproved of by his parents and educators, leads a repressed childhood, alternating between a London home and one in the country. After acquiring the standard education of an English gentleman, during which period his love for literature propels him in the bohemian world of artists and intellectuals, he resigns himself to a career in diplomacy. While studying in England and abroad he falls simultaneously in love with two young women who are to preoccupy him for the rest of his life. The one, Leila Bucknell, is a stunning worldly beauty for whom men are little more than playthings; the other, Beatrice Lord, is a more

ethereal beauty of Catholic upbringing for whom love is altogether sacred. Without becoming mere types or symbols, the two women effectively embody the conflict in C.'s character, which culminates, at his death, in a poignant effort toward an affirmation of faith.

C is typical of Baring's novels in many ways. It is written in the tradition of the Bildungsroman, tracing patiently and meticulously the spiritual, intellectual, and emotional movement of a character on the fringes of the beau monde. It is narrated by an omniscient voice, in the straightforward, unpretentious style that characterizes all of the author's fiction. And it treats many of the themes that pervade the other novels: the search for meaning in life, typified as a conflict between a pagan sense of fate and retribution and the Christian concept of grace and redemption; the vicissitudes of earthly love, as much a curse as it is a blessing, doomed from the outset to failure; and the loneliness and unsurety of the eternal exile.

One could complain that Baring amasses more material than necessary in his detailing of character and event. At times he merely skates along the surface, routinely cataloguing the traits of new characters only to drop them pages later and reintroducing old ones of no consequence. The protagonist is occasionally forgotten in a flurry of parties, theatergoings, and country outings. Yet there is a reason for all this. If the reader is left feeling jaded and impatient, then he is experiencing a very real aspect of the milieu which Baring is striving to depict. One is made to feel, in such instances, the very numbness or deadness of heart that the protagonist is suffering.

Baring's 1925 masterpiece, *Cat's Cradle,* surpasses *C* as a Bildungsroman. It presents the long, stirring history of Blanche Clifford, who, after spending years of unhappiness married to an Anglo-Italian prince, Guido Roccapalumba, falls in love with and eventually marries a young English Catholic gentleman, Bernard Lacy, who is fifteen years her junior. Never able to find fulfillment in life, she punishes herself for the misery and deaths of a succession of admirers whom she is never guilty of encouraging. She struggles against jealousy for her younger cousin and protegée, Rose Mary Clifford, Bernard's one real love. And she even blames herself for Guido's death, though it occurs long after she has left him. In a supreme act of self-sacrifice, she resigns herself to Bernard's love for Rose Mary and dies of "heart starvation."

Unlike *C, Cat's Cradle* employs a central metaphor as a unifying device, which Baring goes so far as to have two of his characters explain: "our lives are like the pattern in a game of cat's cradle, as if someone was playing cat's cradle with us . . . as if we were the threads," one says. "Yes," agrees the other, "it's a funny pattern they make. . . . the same threads get changed into different patterns and combinations." The image describes in simple terms the complex relationships of a half-dozen characters whose cross-loyalties, reversals, and frustrations in love result in a number of unhappy unions and broken hearts. And it embodies, as well, the author's curious strain of determinism, in which happenstance and fate are conceived as playing equally important roles in human destiny.

Though Baring's story of Princess Blanche is his only full-scale portrait of a woman, it is told with sensitivity and skill. In portraying the tragedy of

wrongheaded self-commitment—of unrequited love—through the medium of a woman of exceptional beauty and charm, Baring scores his greatest triumph in the novel. Blanche, as the center of consciousness, provides him with the essential degree of distance which he fails to achieve in *C,* with its numerous semiautobiographical digressions.

In 1929 Baring produced *The Coat Without Seam,* a novel which combines many elements of the two earlier ones. It is, predictably, a personal history, tracing in this case the unhappy life of Christopher Trevenen, a "dreamy, obstinate, inattentive" young man born of the upper classes but forced into a life of poverty. Yet another one of Baring's many self-defeating protagonists, Christopher, laboring under a persecution complex, ruins chance after chance for advancement in life and botches one love affair after another. At the moment of his death in battle at the end of World War 1, he realizes that the fate of his soul is more important than his life in the world.

Baring again uses a controlling image in this novel, though less subtly than in *Cat's Cradle.* "The coat without seam" is the holy coat for which the Roman soldiers bartered on the day of Christ's death. Interpolating passages from old letters, legends, and other Church memorabilia, Baring traces the coat's history through the ages as it passes from hand to hand, symbolically correlating it with the worldly career and spiritual development of Christopher Trevenen. "Perhaps everybody's life is really a Coat Without Seam," says Christopher at one point. "But mine seems like a patchwork full of holes, and seamed and darned and ragged and tattered and dirty." Each time Christopher happens upon a new chapter to the legend, he invariably experiences a disappointment; the coat, so to speak, receives another tear.

At the worst, Baring's method seems contrived. As well-constructed a novel as it is, *The Coat Without Seam* lacks the careful balance between realism and symbolism found in *Cat's Cradle,* and it is marred, though to a lesser extent, by the same sort of bland semiautobiographical lapses which make *C* such plodding reading in places. Yet in spite of the flaws, Christopher Trevenen remains an interesting and convincing study of a troubled, obstinately proud and sensitive personality.

Although Baring was censured in his time by his non-Catholic readers for his seeming Tractarianism, he deserves credit for the sincerity and delicacy with which he treated his religious themes. He is never overbearing or complacent in his belief, even in a novel as overtly religious in tone as *The*

Conversation Piece, by James Gunn: G. K. Chesterton, Maurice Baring, and Hilaire Belloc (National Portrait Gallery, London)

Coat Without Seam. If his picture of life is bleak, it is devoid of bitterness or condemnation. As Paul Horgan aptly notes in *Maurice Baring Restored* (1970): "It is Baring's triumph that, in a literary world generally oriented to skepticism, he is able to make religion a matter of reality and importance in his writing. . . . He is never bantering or patronizing, like Chesterton, or rude, impatient and contemptuous, like Evelyn Waugh, or glumly rebellious, like Graham Greene." Regardless of one's leanings, one can appreciate how intelligently and candidly Baring examines so many of the important religious questions which continue to perplex humankind.

Most of Baring's critics look upon his novels as minor masterpieces in character study and social depiction. Limited as they are in subject and theme,

the novels are no longer in vogue except among a few readers who prefer a realistic but tame version of upper-class life to one that is overly romanticized or sensationalized. They can be read and appreciated today for the accuracy with which they reproduce the extinct world of the late Edwardian elite, for the purity and simplicity of their style, and for the erudition and sensitivity which they display.

References:

Princesse de Bibesco, "Mes admirables compagnons de voyage. II: Maurice Baring," *Revue de Paris,* 76 (March 1969): 9-16;

Ian Boyd, "Maurice Baring's Early Writing," *Downside Review,* 92, no. 3 (1974): 160-170;

Manuel D'Almeida, "Maurice Baring," *Broteria,* 62 (1956): 31-46;

Selim Ezban, "Maurice Baring et la France," *PMLA*, 60 (June 1945): 503-516;

Frank C. Hannighan, "The Art of Maurice Baring," *Bookman*, 75 (August 1932): 321-326;

Paul Horgan, ed., *Maurice Baring Restored* (New York: Farrar, Straus & Giroux, 1970);

Raymond Las Vergnas, "Maurice Baring," in his *Chesterton, Belloc, Baring,* translated by C. C. Martindale (Folcroft, Pa.: Folcroft Library, 1975), pp. 88-133;

David Lodge, "Maurice Baring, Novelist: a Reappraisal," *Dublin Review*, 234 (Fall 1960): 262-270;

Dame Mary Ethel Smyth, *Maurice Baring* (London & Toronto: Heinemann, 1938).

Papers:
Collections of Baring's papers are in the Houghton Library at Harvard University, the Humanities Research Center at the University of Texas, Austin, and the libraries of Colby College and Temple University.

Max Beerbohm
(24 August 1872-20 May 1956)

Ann Adams Cleary
University of Tulsa

SELECTED BOOKS: *The Works of Max Beerbohm* (New York: Scribners, 1896; London: John Lane, 1896);

Caricatures of Twenty-Five Gentlemen (London: Smithers, 1896);

The Happy Hypocrite: A Fairy Tale for Tired Men (New York & London: Lane, 1897);

More (London & New York: Lane, 1899);

The Poets' Corner (London: Heinemann, 1904);

A Book of Caricatures (London: Methuen, 1907);

Yet Again (London: Chapman & Hall, 1909);

Zuleika Dobson; or An Oxford Love Story (London: Heinemann, 1911; New York: Lane, 1912);

Cartoons: "The Second Childhood of John Bull" (London: Swift, 1911);

A Christmas Garland (London: Heinemann, 1912; New York: Dutton, 1912);

Fifty Caricatures (London: Heinemann, 1913; New York: Dutton, 1913);

Seven Men (London: Heinemann, 1919; New York: Knopf, 1920); republished as *Seven Men and Two Others* (London: Heinemann, 1950);

And Even Now (London: Heinemann, 1920; New York: Dutton, 1921);

A Survey (London: Heinemann, 1921; New York: Doubleday, Page, 1921);

Rossetti and His Circle (London: Heinemann, 1922);

A Defense of Cosmetics (New York: Dodd, Mead, 1922);

A Peep Into the Past (New York: Privately printed, 1923);

Things New and Old (London: Heinemann, 1923);

Around Theatres, 2 volumes (London: Heinemann, 1924; New York: Knopf, 1930);

The Guerdon (New York: Privately printed, 1925);

Observations (London: Heinemann, 1925);

Leaves from the Garland (New York: Privately printed, 1926);

A Variety of Things (London: Heinemann, 1928; New York: Knopf, 1928);

Lytton Strachey (Cambridge: Cambridge University Press, 1943; New York: Knopf, 1943);

Mainly on the Air (London: Heinemann, 1946; New York: Knopf, 1947);

Max in Verse: Rhymes and Parodies, edited by J. G. Riewald (Brattleboro, Vt.: Stephen Greene, 1963; London: Heinemann, 1964);

A Peep into the Past and Other Prose Pieces by Max Beerbohm, edited by Rupert Hart-Davis (London: Heinemann, 1972; Brattleboro, Vt.: Stephen Greene, 1972);

Beerbohm's Literary Caricatures: From Homer to Huxley, edited by J. G. Riewald (Hamden, Conn.: Archon, 1977).

OTHER: *Herbert Beerbohm Tree: Some Memories of Him and of His Art,* edited by Beerbohm (London: Hutchinson, 1920; New York: Dutton, 1920).

"My gifts are small," Max Beerbohm once observed. "I've used them very well and discreetly, never straining them; and the result is that I've made a charming little reputation." Beerbohm, a well-known caricaturist, drama critic, and essayist, wrote only one novel, *Zuleika Dobson* (1911), but that fantasy of Edwardian undergraduate life at Oxford is a classic.

Henry Maximilian Beerbohm was born in London on 24 August 1872. He was the youngest child of Julius Ewald Beerbohm and his second wife (and former sister-in-law), Eliza Draper Beerbohm. One of Beerbohm's half brothers was the noted actor-manager Herbert Beerbohm Tree (eighteen years his senior), who was later to introduce Beerbohm to Oscar Wilde and other theatrical personalities of the time, as well as to supply Beerbohm with a succession of fiancées from his acting troupe.

Beerbohm was educated at Charterhouse and Merton College, Oxford. He drew on his experiences from this time for his comic satires, most notably in *Zuleika Dobson*. During his years at Oxford (1890-1894), the precocious undergraduate published caricatures and essays in the *Strand* and other periodicals. Beerbohm was very much the young dandy, dining with Oscar Wilde and his friends, attending the theater, music halls, his clubs, and occasional lectures. He met artists Aubrey Beardsley and William Rothenstein and was invited to contribute to the *Yellow Book,* a fin-de-siècle aesthetic house organ. "The Pervasion of Rouge," an ironically precious history of artifice, duly appeared in the periodical's first issue, in April 1894. In the essay, Beerbohm refers to Cissy Loftus, a young music-hall performer. During the previous year he had written a number of letters to his friend Reggie Turner about his infatuation with Miss Loftus, his "Mistress Mere." The purely epistolary affair from afar with this "Small Saint" had led Beerbohm to look briefly with disgust at his life, and traces of the experience appear in his later fiction.

Beerbohm left Oxford without a degree. In 1895 he made a four-month tour of American cities with Herbert Beerbohm Tree's theatrical company. Beerbohm, hired as his half brother's secretary, was soon relieved of duties because he took too much time composing and polishing the business letters. While on the tour, he met and later became unofficially engaged to an American actress in Tree's group, Grace ("Kilseen") Conover. After his return to London, Beerbohm lived with his mother and

Self-caricature by Beerbohm, circa 1893 (© Eva Reichmann, courtesy of Merton College, Oxford)

sisters and continued to contribute caricatures and articles to the *Savoy,* the *Saturday Review,* and the *Yellow Book.*

In 1896, an audaciously slender volume appeared. Its cover bore the formidable title *The Works of Max Beerbohm with a Bibliography by John Lane* (publisher of the *Yellow Book*). The twenty-three-year-old author had collected seven of his sixteen published articles for the book. Replete with mock-scholarly footnotes and biographical information, the *Works* epitomizes Beerbohm's penchant for deflating pretentiousness with satiric imitation. Anything large—ideas, ideals, literary works, London crowds—caused him dismay. The concluding essay in *Works,* "Diminuendo," contains a wry reminiscence of Oxford ("The townspeople now looked just like undergraduates and the dons just like townspeople") and a spurious notification of retirement: "I shall write no more. Already I feel myself to be outmoded. I belong to the Beardsley period." He will leave the literary scene "to the younger men with months before them." By 1899, *More* had appeared. This second collection of essays was followed by *Yet Again* (1909), *And Even Now* (1920), and *A Variety of Things* (1928). Most critics agree that Beerbohm is a master of the personal essay—a form not favored by modernists.

"The Happy Hypocrite" (1897) was Beerbohm's first fiction and final contribution to the *Yellow Book,* where it appeared before it was published separately as a book. It is an archly moralistic tale indebted to Oscar Wilde's "The Happy Prince" and *The Picture of Dorian Gray.* In it Lord George Hell, a Regency rake, dons a magical mask in order to seduce Jenny Mere, a music-hall performer who can only love a man who has "the face of a saint." The ploy succeeds, and the couple moves to a cozy forest hut far from vice-ridden London. When a jealous woman from Lord Hell's past unmasks him, he is surprised to find that his reform, undertaken in pretense, has caused all marks of dissipation to disappear. His natural features, reflected in the pupils of Jenny's eyes, are those of a saintly man. The impetus for the story, which has only biographical interest today, may well lie in Beerbohm's earlier infatuation with Cissy Loftus and in the cautious distress he displayed during the scandals involving his friend Oscar Wilde.

In 1898 George Bernard Shaw bestowed upon Beerbohm both his epithet "the incomparable Max" and his post as drama critic for the *Saturday Review.* "Why I Ought Not To Have Become a Dramatic Critic" was Beerbohm's introductory piece, and throughout the twelve years he held the position, he retained the attitude of an intelligent amateur who took "neither emotional nor intellectual pleasure" in theater. Because of family ties to the theatrical world, Beerbohm had never held performers in awe. His impressionistic criticism, always entertaining, was often wittily contemptuous of the pretensions of players, playwrights, and playgoers

alike. He especially disliked Shaw's "straitjackets of panacea" and suggested that Shavian comedy was far superior to Shavian reform. Almost a third of Beerbohm's 453 critiques can be found in *Around Theatres* (1924).

During the twelve years Beerbohm was a working journalist, he enjoyed an active social life and was much sought after as a conversationalist and wit. He discovered the pleasures of Italy when the *Daily Mail* sent him there in 1906 to write a travel series. Beerbohm's relationship with Grace Conover had ended amicably in 1903; he immediately asked another of his brother's actresses, Constance Collier, to be his fiancée. By the time she broke their engagement in 1904 in favor of a leading man, Beerbohm had met his future wife, Florence Kahn, an actress from Memphis, Tennessee, who was touring England in Ibsen roles. She became his fiancée in 1908.

Beerbohm continued drawing and arranged four exhibitions of his work during his *Saturday Review* years, 1898-1910. Caricature, an exquisitely efficient form of criticism, perfectly suited Beerbohm's tastes: the drawings cost him small effort; they were elegantly pretty; and they could be appreciated only by a well-informed elite.

The year 1910 was a time of change for Beerbohm. He gave up his post as drama critic, married Florence Kahn, and moved with his bride to the Villino Chiaro in Rapallo, Italy. Except for occasional trips to London to arrange exhibitions of his drawings and for longer periods associated with the war years, the Beerbohms led a comfortably placid existence in Rapallo, where for a time they had Ezra Pound as a neighbor. (Max once remarked that "Pound's treacle of praise, don't you know, was always tinctured with the vinegar of envy.") Beerbohm's move to Italy was not inspired by political disaffection. Social demands and expenses were lighter in Rapallo than in London. In the nearly fifty years Beerbohm lived in Italy, he never learned to speak the language.

Most of Beerbohm's fiction was written during the decade following his move to Rapallo. Released from the demands of producing a weekly column, Beerbohm began working on his comic fantasy, *Zuleika Dobson.* (As early as 1898, he had sketched out elements of the novel.) Finally, Zuleika (rhymes with Eureka) took form: her hourglass Edwardian figure enchants and ultimately destroys the entire student body of Oxford in Beerbohm's appalling little story.

The characters and plot are patently preposterous: Zuleika Dobson, a world-renowned but

Photo inscribed to Beerbohm's friend Reggie Turner after Beerbohm read Turner's light novel The Steeple, *published by Greening and Company in 1903*

inept performer of magic tricks, visits her grandfather, the warden of Judas College. She can only love a man who is impervious to her charms and therefore rejects the marriage proposal offered by the love-smitten young duke of Dorset, member of an Oxford club so exclusive that for two years running he was the sole member. Dorset gallantly decides that death is his only honorable alternative and plans to drown himself in Zuleika's honor at the conclusion of the annual boat races. Zuleika thinks this would be a lovely gesture. The duke later reconsiders, and Zuleika is miffed. Fate intervenes with a message from home informing Dorset that two black owls, his family's traditional portent of death, had hooted on the ancestral battlements at dawn. He resignedly telegraphs a reply: "Prepare vault for funeral Monday." The other students, who are also in love with Zuleika, learn of the duke's impending suicide and decide, as in everything else, to follow his example. The absurd plot slips through thickets

Max Beerbohm in London, 15 January 1908 (photo by Alvin Langdon Coburn)

Although the characters of Zuleika and the handsome dandy of a duke would seem to be tailor-made dramatic roles, attempts to adapt the novel to the stage or cinema have been unsuccessful. Only the allusive intricacies of Beerbohm's prose give the story life: the novel is a former drama critic's revenge.

In 1912, following the enthusiastic reception given *Zuleika Dobson,* Beerbohm again turned to material he had generated during the 1890s. He selected eight of his earlier literary parodies, wrote nine new ones, and had the collection published as *A Christmas Garland.* Hilaire Belloc, G. K. Chesterton, Joseph Conrad, Thomas Hardy, Maurice Hewlett, Henry James, Rudyard Kipling, George Bernard Shaw, and H. G. Wells were some of his targets. The literary parodies are closely related to Beerbohm's caricatures. Drawing was always easier for him than writing, but through the years, written captions took on an increasingly important function in Beerbohm's art: words compensated for his public's growing unfamiliarity with visual clues. It is a subtle change in what is otherwise an almost static body of work. Beerbohm never dramatically changed his style. His pictures became wordier and his prose less wordy; the attitudes informing his art remained constant. Both the caricatures and his literary parodies depended for their effect on exaggeration of a physical characteristic and a diminution of all other features. Thus Beerbohm could caricaturize Henry James by emphasizing an enormous bulk balanced on tiny feet, whereas his literary parody would feature James's convoluted syntax within a trivial context: in one of Beerbohm's more famous parodies, "The Mote in the Middle Distance," Jamesian children lengthily consider the moral ramifications of peeking in Christmas stockings.

In 1915, the Beerbohms returned to England for the duration of World War I. Herbert Beerbohm Tree died, and Beerbohm supervised the compilation of a memorial volume, adding an essay of his own to those contributed by other family members and friends. By 1919, Beerbohm was back in the small house overlooking the Mediterranean. Another essay collection, *And Even Now* (1920), was made; his reputation as a caricaturist was at its height.

Beerbohm's only important fiction other than *Zuleika Dobson* was collected and published in 1919 as *Seven Men.* Five narrative sketches about six men are stitched together by observations of the narrator persona, Max Beerbohm, the seventh man of the title. (Max had allowed himself only a cameo appearance in his novel—Zuleika explains that the

of irony and patterned gardens of parody, pauses for a couple of chapters of diverting authorial intrusion, then hastens the duke into an untimely drowning (he had to leap into the river before the boat race had ended because a rain shower threatened to spoil his outfit). The other Oxonian love-lemmings are disposed of with great splashes (and one tardy and unaesthetic death by defenestration). The novel concludes with the sprightly Zuleika wondering where next to go, now that Oxford has palled. She decides to visit Cambridge.

Zuleika Dobson was an immediate success when it appeared in 1911, and its remarkable stylistic surface has helped the novel retain a respectable measure of interest through the years. Although some critics think the work is a seamless parodic delight, others admit to a less complete enchantment. The tragedy of mass suicide; the sentimental realism of Katie Batch, the landlady's daughter; and the awkward Americanisms attributed to the Rhodes scholar, Mr. Abimilech V. Oover, are commonly cited flaws. The novel's virtues reside in its impeccable narrative structure and in its lyrical evocation of an Oxford delicately skewed by satire.

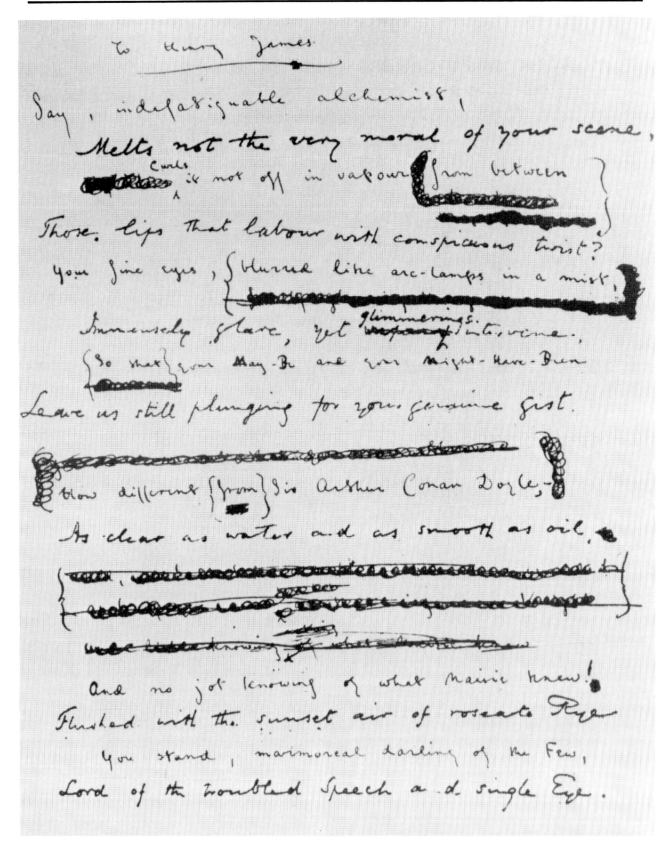

Draft for a sonnet with odd-numbered lines by Beerbohm and even-numbered lines by Edmund Gosse (© Eva Reichmann, courtesy of Melville E. Stone)

Max and Florence Beerbohm in the early 1930s (courtesy of Morris Kahn)

offer of free second-night tickets to the first reader who can provide a suitable fifth act. "A. V. Laider" is a quieter study of a deranged imagination. In "James Pethel," the only story not dealing with some aspect of the craft of writing, Beerbohm draws on past holidays at Dieppe. Pethel, "a great character" to his acquaintances, is an irresponsible risk-taker who exposes the narrator's own weaknesses. A prominent theme in these stories is failure.

The next few years (1922-1928) saw the publication of a ten-volume collection of Beerbohm's writings, and two important series of caricatures appeared: *Rossetti and His Circle* (1922) and *Things New and Old* (1923).

After a 1925 exhibition of caricatures (*Observations*), Beerbohm entered a pronounced retirement. He wrote no more fiction of any consequence. "The Dreadful Dragon of Hay Hill," a story published in the 1928 collection *A Variety of Things,* was an allegory using his favored theme of appearance and reality. It was dismissed as dreadful by critics and public alike. No new caricatures were published, although Beerbohm continued for the rest of his life to make sketches for his own amusement. Books in Beerbohm's private library had title pages mercilessly improved with sly alterations and caricatures. Beerbohm's only new venture was a successful series of BBC broadcasts made during 1935 and collected with later broadcasts in *Mainly on The Air* (1946). (Beerbohm was in England in 1935

"literary flavour" of her speech "is an unfortunate trick which I caught from a writer, a Mr. Beerbohm, who once sat next to me at dinner somewhere.") The stories in *Seven Men* range from exuberant fantasy to social realism. "Enoch Soames" is the sad tale of a singularly unappreciated 1890s author who sells his soul to the devil for the privilege of time-tripping to the British Museum reading room of 1997. He wishes to see how posterity has received his works—a volume of poetry, *Fungoids,* and some collected essays, *Negations.* He should never have gone, of course. "Hilary Maltby and Stephen Braxton" is a send-up of Edwardian literary infighting. "Savonarola Brown" provides a mad parody of an Elizabethan drama featuring Saint Francis, assorted Borgias and Medicis, Dante, and Leonardo da Vinci. Narrator/Beerbohm casts himself in the unenviable position of trying to complete an unfinished play by Brown, a playwright who insists that the law of probability should be inoperative in drama. The sketch ends with Beerbohm's desperate

Sir Max Beerbohm in Rapallo (Camera Press-Blau Pix)

so his wife could appear in a revival of *Peer Gynt* at the Old Vic.) The couple again stayed in England through and beyond the war years from 1938 to 1947.

Beerbohm reaped the rewards of genial survival: honorary degrees from Edinburgh and Oxford, a knighthood in 1939. Merton College made him an honorary fellow; he gave the 1943 Rede lecture on Lytton Strachey; the Maximilian Society was formed on the occasion of his seventieth birthday, and retrospective exhibits of his work were held in New York and London on his eightieth. His Villino Chiaro was "on the circuit"—a stopover point in Italy for younger writers making their literary pilgrimages to Majorca to visit with Somerset Maugham and Robert Graves.

After Florence Beerbohm died in 1951, Beerbohm asked a longtime friend, Elisabeth Jungmann (whom the Beerbohms had first met as Gerhart Hauptmann's aide in 1928), to come to Rapallo. She cared for Beerbohm until his death; they were married a few weeks before he died on 20 May 1956. His ashes were placed in St. Paul's Cathedral.

Beerbohm's work is still a focus for critical attention in the fields of art, criticism, and literature. Half a dozen major biographies and critical studies have been published since his death, with J. G. Riewald's scholarship and bibliographical studies foremost in thoroughness. Beerbohm's contemporary critics were often simply eulogistic; modern essays frequently display a sense of bemused apology. Examination of Beerbohm's work, as yet, tends to be inseparable from examination of "the incomparable Max" himself. His own comment from an 1896 essay has been prophetic: "For to be outmoded is to be a classic, if one has written well."

Letters:

Max Beerbohm: Letters to Reggie Turner, edited by Rupert Hart-Davis (London: Rupert Hart-Davis, 1964; Philadelphia: Lippincott, 1965).

Bibliographies:

A. E. Gallatin, *Sir Max Beerbohm: Bibliographical Notes* (Cambridge, Mass.: Harvard University Press, 1944);

Gallatin and L. M. Oliver, *A Bibliography of the Works of Max Beerbohm* (Cambridge, Mass.: Harvard University Press, 1952);

Catalogue of the Library and Literary Manuscripts of the Late Sir Max Beerbohm (London: Sotheby, 1960).

References:

S. N. Behrman, *Portrait of Max: An Intimate Memoir of Sir Max Beerbohm* (New York: Random House, 1960);

David Cecil, *Max* (Boston: Houghton Mifflin, 1965);

Bruce R. McElderry, Jr., *Max Beerbohm* (New York: Twayne, 1972);

J. G. Riewald, *Sir Max Beerbohm, Man and Writer: A Critical Analysis with a Brief Life and a Bibliography* (The Hague: Nijhoff, 1953; Brattleboro, Vt.: Stephen Greene, 1961);

Riewald, ed., *The Surprise of Excellence: Modern Essays on Max Beerbohm* (Hamden, Conn.: Archon, 1974).

Arnold Bennett

Anita Miller

See also the Bennett entry in *DLB 10, Modern British Dramatists, 1900-1945.*

BIRTH: Hanley, Stoke-on-Trent, England, 27 May 1867, to Enoch and Sarah Ann Longson Bennett.

MARRIAGE: 4 July 1907 to Marguerite Soulie; child: Virginia (born to Dorothy Cheston).

AWARD: James Tait Black Memorial Prize for *Riceyman Steps,* 1924.

DEATH: London, England, 27 March 1931.

BOOKS: *A Man from the North* (London & New York: John Lane/Bodley Head, 1898);
Journalism for Women: A Practical Guide (London: John Lane/Bodley Head, 1898);
Polite Farces for the Drawing Room (London: Lamley, 1900);
Fame and Fiction: An Enquiry into Certain Popularities (London: Richards, 1901);
The Grand Babylon Hotel: A Fantasia on Modern Themes (London: Chatto & Windus, 1902); republished as *T. Racksole and Daughter: Or, the Result of an American Millionaire Ordering Steak and a Bottle of Bass at the Grand Babylon Hotel, London* (New York: New Amsterdam Book Company, 1902);
Anna of the Five Towns (London: Chatto & Windus, 1902);
The Gates of Wrath: A Melodrama (London: Chatto & Windus, 1903);
The Truth About an Author, anonymous (London: Constable, 1903; New York: Doran, 1911);
How to Become an Author: A Practical Guide (London: Pearson, 1903);
Leonora: A Novel (London: Chatto & Windus, 1903);
A Great Man: A Frolic (London: Chatto & Windus, 1904);
Teresa of Watling Street: A Fantasia on Modern Themes (London: Chatto & Windus, 1904);
Tales of the Five Towns (London: Chatto & Windus, 1905);
The Loot of Cities: Being Adventures of a Millionaire in Search of Joy (A Fantasia) (London: Rivers, 1905); enlarged as *Loot of Two Cities: Being the*

Arnold Bennett, 1928 (courtesy of Richard Bennett)

Adventures of a Millionaire in Search of Joy (A Fantasia) and Other Stories (London: Nelson, 1917);
Sacred and Profane Love: A Novel in Three Episodes (London: Chatto & Windus, 1905); republished as *The Book of Carlotta* (New York: Doran, 1911);
Hugo: A Fantasia on Modern Themes (London: Chatto & Windus, 1906);
Whom God Hath Joined (London: Nutt, 1906);
The Sinews of War: A Romance of London and the Sea, by Bennett and Eden Phillpotts (London: Laurie, 1906); republished as *Doubloons* (New York: McClure, Phillips, 1906);

Things That Interested Me: Being Leaves from a Journal (Burslem: Privately printed, 1906);

The Ghost: A Fantasia on Modern Themes (London: Chatto & Windus, 1907; Boston: Turner, 1907);

The Reasonable Life: Being Hints for Men and Women (London: Fifield, 1907); revised as *Mental Efficiency, and Other Hints to Men and Women* (New York: Doran, 1911; London: Hodder & Stoughton, 1912);

The Grim Smile of the Five Towns (London: Chapman & Hall, 1907);

The City of Pleasure: A Fantasia on Modern Themes (London: Chatto & Windus, 1907);

Things Which Have Interested Me: Being Leaves from a Journal, Second Series (Burslem: Privately printed, 1907);

The Old Wives Tale (London: Chapman & Hall, 1908; New York: Doran, 1911);

The Statue, by Bennett and Phillpotts (London: Cassell, 1908; New York: Moffat Yard, 1908);

Buried Alive: A Tale of These Days (London: Chapman & Hall, 1908);

How to Live on 24 Hours a Day (London: New Age Press, 1908; New York: Doran, 1910);

The Human Machine (London: New Age Press, 1908; New York: Doran, 1911);

Things Which Have Interested Me, Third Series (Burslem: Privately printed, 1908);

Literary Taste: How to Form It (London: New Age Press, 1909; revised edition, London: Hodder & Stoughton, 1912; New York: Doran, 1927);

Cupid and Commonsense: A Play in Four Acts (London: New Age Press, 1909);

The Glimpse: An Adventure of the Soul (London: Chapman & Hall, 1909; New York: Appleton, 1909);

What the Public Wants: (A Play in Four Acts) (London: Duckworth, 1909);

Helen with the High Hand: An Idyllic Diversion (London: Chapman & Hall, 1910);

Clayhanger (London: Methuen, 1910);

The Card: A Story of Adventure in the Five Towns (London: Methuen, 1911); republished as *Denry the Audacious* (New York: Dutton, 1911);

Hilda Lessways (London: Methuen, 1911; New York: Dutton, 1911);

The Honeymoon: A Comedy in Three Acts (London: Methuen, 1911);

The Feast of St Friend (London: Hodder & Stoughton, 1911; New York: Doran, 1911); republished as *Friendship and Happiness: A Plea for the Feast of St Friend* (London: Hodder & Stoughton, 1914);

The Matador of the Five Towns and Other Stories (London: Methuen, 1912; with different contents, New York: Doran, 1912);

Milestones: A Play in Three Acts, by Bennett and Edward Knoblock (London: Methuen, 1912);

Your United States: Impressions of a First Visit (New York: Harper, 1912); republished as *Those United States* (London: Secker, 1912);

The Regent: A Five Towns Story of Adventure in London (London: Methuen, 1913); republished as *The Old Adam: A Story of Adventure* (New York: Doran, 1913);

The Great Adventure: A Play of Fancy in Four Acts (London: Methuen, 1913; New York: Doran, 1913);

The Plain Man and His Wife (London: Hodder & Stoughton, 1913); republished as *Married Life: The Plain Man and His Wife* (New York: Doran, 1913);

Paris Nights and Other Impressions of Places and People (London: Hodder & Stoughton, 1913; New York: Doran, 1913);

The Price of Love: A Tale (London: Methuen, 1914; New York: Harper, 1914);

Liberty: A Statement of the British Case (London: Hodder & Stoughton, 1914);

From the Log of the Velsa (New York: Century, 1914; London: Chatto & Windus, 1914);

The Author's Craft (London: Hodder & Stoughton, 1915; New York: Doran, 1915);

Over There: War Scenes on the Western Front (London: Methuen, 1915; New York: Doran, 1915);

These Twain (New York: Doran, 1915; London: Methuen, 1916);

The Lion's Share (London: Cassell, 1916);

Books and Persons: Being Comments on a Past Epoch, 1908-1911 (London: Chatto & Windus, 1917);

The Pretty Lady: A Novel (London: Cassell, 1918);

The Title: A Comedy in Three Acts (London: Chatto & Windus, 1918);

Self and Self-Management: Essays About Existing (London: Hodder & Stoughton, 1918);

The Roll Call (London: Hutchinson, 1918);

Judith: A Play in Three Acts, Founded on the Apocryphal Book of "Judith" (London: Chatto & Windus, 1919);

Sacred and Profane Love: A Play in Four Acts Founded Upon the Novel of the Same Name (London: Chatto & Windus, 1919);

Our Women: Chapters on the Sex-Discord (London: Cassell, 1920);

Body and Soul: A Play in Four Acts (London: Chatto & Windus, 1920);

Things that Have Interested Me (London: Chatto & Windus, 1921);

The Love Match: A Play in Five Scenes (London: Chatto & Windus, 1922);

Mr. Prohack (London: Methuen, 1922);

Lilian (London: Cassell, 1922);

Things That Have Interested Me, Second Series (London: Chatto & Windus, 1923);

How to Make the Best of Life (London: Hodder & Stoughton, 1923);

Don Juan de Marana: A Play in Four Acts (London: Laurie, 1923);

Riceyman Steps (London: Cassell, 1923);

London Life: A Play in Three Acts and Nine Scenes, by Bennett and Knoblock (London: Chatto & Windus, 1924);

The Bright Island (London: Cockerel Press, 1924);

Elsie and the Child: A Tale of Riceyman Steps and Other Stories (London: Cassell, 1924); republished as *Elsie and the Child and Other Stories* (New York: Doran, 1924);

The Clayhanger Family. I. Clayhanger. II. Hilda Lessways. III. These Twain. (London: Methuen, 1925);

Things That Have Interested Me, Third Series (London: Chatto & Windus, 1926);

Lord Raingo (London: Cassell, 1926; New York: Doran, 1926);

The Woman Who Stole Everything and Other Stories (London: Cassell, 1927);

The Vanguard: A Fantasia (New York: Doran, 1927); republished as *The Strange Vanguard: A Fantasia* (London: Cassell, 1928);

Accident (New York: Doubleday, Doran, 1928; London: Cassell, 1929);

The Savour of Life: Essays in Gusto (London: Cassell, 1928);

Mediterranean Scenes: Rome –Greece –Constantinople (London: Cassell, 1928);

The Religious Interregnum (London: Benn, 1929);

Piccadilly: The Story of the Film (London: Readers Library, 1929);

Imperial Palace (London: Cassell, 1930);

Journal 1929 (London: Cassell, 1930); republished as *Journal of Things Old and New* (New York: Doubleday, Doran, 1930);

Venus Rising from the Sea (London: Cassell, 1931);

The Night Visitor and Other Stories (London: Cassell, 1931);

Dream of Destiny: An Unfinished Novel and Venus Rising from the Sea (London: Cassell, 1932); republished as *Stroke of Luck and Dream of Destiny: An Unfinished Novel* (New York: Doubleday, Doran, 1932);

The Journals of Arnold Bennett, 1896-1928, 3 volumes, edited by Norman Flower (London: Cassell, 1932-1933; New York: Viking, 1933);

Florentine Journal, 1st April –25 May 1910, edited by Dorothy Cheston Bennett (London: Chatto & Windus, 1967);

Arnold Bennett: The Evening Standard Years. Books and Persons, 1926-1931, edited by Andrew Mylett (London: Chatto & Windus, 1974).

Straw was laid in the streets outside Chiltern Court, to deaden sounds, while Arnold Bennett lay dying in his flat there. It was the last time the city of London was to pay such respect to a public figure. To some extent this respect was nostalgic because by 1931 Bennett's reputation was already considerably frayed. He had been too successful; he had written too much. His short stories and his journalism were appearing in magazines and newspapers on both sides of the Atlantic; his novels *The Old Wives Tale* (1908) and the Clayhanger trilogy—*Clayhanger* (1910), *Hilda Lessways* (1911), and *These Twain* (1915)—were considered to be masterpieces; *Riceyman Steps* came close to being a best-seller and in 1924 won the James Tait Black Memorial Prize for fiction published in 1923. His book reviews, which appeared each Thursday in the London *Evening Standard,* were so influential that he was at his death far and away the most important literary critic in Europe.

If all this success were not enough to invite envy and spite, Bennett was also a member of the establishment: he served in 1918 as Director of Propaganda for the Ministry of Information, his opinion on political matters was sought and given, and he visited Checquers with Lord Beaverbrook, his close friend. He lived well, traveled extensively, often in his own yacht, and kept servants. He was thus a target for ambitious young writers; Virginia Woolf in particular attacked him in her essay *Mr Bennett and Mrs Brown,* published as a pamphlet in 1924. He was made to look old-fashioned by Woolf and was caricatured as the philistine Mr Nixon by Ezra Pound in his poem *Hugh Selwyn Mauberley* (1920). Pound admitted decades later that he had never read Arnold Bennett's work and knew nothing about him, except that he was rich and owned a yacht.

This reputation for good living damaged Bennett's credibility as a writer. The Bloomsbury set ridiculed him because he came from the pottery district and retained his Northern accent throughout his life. His father had kept a pawnshop before qualifying as a lawyer in early middle age. This sort of thing was used as a weapon against Bennett by people too young or too careless to remember that he had fought the good fight against English philistinism all his life; his tastes were sophisticated, encompassing painting, music, architecture, and interior decoration, and especially French literature. Long before Pound discovered Verlaine, Bennett was attempting to bring his work to the attention of the English public.

Enoch Arnold Bennett was born on 27 May 1867 in Hanley, one of the six Staffordshire towns which were later to become federated into Stoke-on-Trent, and which he was to make famous as—for purposes of euphony—the Five Towns. He was the eldest of nine children of Enoch and Sarah Ann Bennett, the son and daughter, respectively, of a potter and a tailor. Enoch Bennett, a pawnbroker, was a man of iron will and strong ambition: he studied law at night and in 1876 he became a solicitor and moved his family to Burslem, another of the six towns. In 1878 they moved to a larger house at 205 Waterloo Road in the Cobridge neighborhood of Burslem. Until recently this house was the site of the Arnold Bennett Museum.

In 1883 Enoch Arnold Bennett left school (Middle School, Newcastle-under-Lyme) to clerk in his father's law office. It was his father's wish that the boy become a lawyer. Enoch Arnold had literary interests, however; he continued his studies at night at the Wedgewood Institute and in 1885 passed matriculation examinations for London University. His father did not wish him to attend university. In 1888 Enoch Arnold twice failed his legal examinations; in November of that year he began to write weekly columns for two Staffordshire newspapers. He read voraciously and taught himself to read French. He admired Balzac and Flaubert, and among English writers, he was impressed with the works of George Moore and Thomas Hardy. He often said that it was Moore's *A Mummer's Wife* which awakened him to the "romantic" possibilities of the pottery district in which he had spent his formative years.

After Bennett secured a position as a shorthand clerk in a London law office in 1889, his father reluctantly consented to his move to London. Once there he began to move in "cultural" circles and to put his considerable knowledge of books to use: he collected and sold, by mail order, old and rare books and sent his stories to London periodicals.

In 1894 he gave up the law, which held little interest for him, and, with his father's help, became assistant editor of the weekly ladies' magazine *Woman*. The following year the *Yellow Book* pub-

Bennett's birthplace, 90 Hope Street, Hanley, over his father's pawnshop, and the bigger house at 205 Waterloo Road, Burslem, where the Bennett family moved in 1878, two years after Enoch Bennett became a lawyer

lished his short story "A Letter Home," which he had written in 1893; and he began work on a serious novel, *A Man from the North* (1898), a realistic picture of the attempts of a young man from the pottery district to adjust to life in London as an office clerk. Carefully and sensitively written, without sentimentality or self-conscious passages, the book is an impressive debut.

His first London publication had been in *Tit-Bits* magazine: a prizewinning parody of Grant Allen's *What's Bred in the Bone* (1891). Critics have been fond of contrasting *Tit-Bits* and *Yellow Book* as examples of a striking split in Bennett's intellectual processes between serious literary and crass commercial production. The impression they give is that these stories appeared at the same time: in fact the *Tit-Bits* parody appeared in December of 1891, nearly three and one half years before the *Yellow Book* story. In any case Bennett saw no difficulty in writing serious fiction, light or sensational fiction, and journalism, all at more or less the same time. In 1898 *Journalism for Women* was published in March, a month after John Lane brought out *A Man from the North*; in the same year he began a series of critical articles (published in 1901 as *Fame and Fiction*) for the literary weekly the *Academy,* and he began work on a series "Love and Life" (published as *The Ghost* in 1907), which was to run in 1900 in the English woman's magazine *Hearth & Home.* Thus at the outset of his career Bennett set a pattern of work: he financed his elegant style of living and his serious work by journalism and light popular work. This is not to say that he did not respect his popular pieces; he took great pride in his journalism and enjoyed writing it, and his sensational or light novels as well.

In 1900 he gave up the editorship of *Woman,* to which he had succeeded in November of 1896, in order to concentrate all of his considerable energies on writing. The following year he began his association with the literary agent J. B. Pinker, which was to last until Pinker's death in 1922. While he continued to contribute signed and unsigned pieces of journalism (book and play reviews and comments on literature, art, travel, and social phenomena such as insurance companies) to various London periodicals, he continued also his pattern of publishing both serious and sensational fiction by producing in 1902 his second serious novel, *Anna of the Five Towns,* and his second sensational novel, *The Grand Babylon Hotel. Anna of the Five Towns* is written in the same restrained, unsentimental style as *A Man from the North,* but it is a more ambitious and interesting book, the first to be written in the Five Towns setting. Here is Bennett's first use of the Northern

characters he knew so well: their materialism and the narrowness of their lives. The restraint and meticulous craftsmanship of the novel were undoubtedly Bennett's legacy from George Moore, Turgenev and de Maupaussant, the Goncourts, and Flaubert. There is strength and vigor as well in the portrait, for instance, of Anna's father, Ephraim Tellwright: the first of many such portraits in Bennett's gallery of grotesques. Both *Anna of the Five Towns* and *The Grand Babylon Hotel,* a lively, amusing thriller, received good critical notices.

In 1902 Bennett's father died at the farm in Bedfordshire which Bennett had rented for himself, his parents, and his sister Tertia. A year later Tertia became engaged to be married, and Sarah Ann Bennett returned to Staffordshire to live. Bennett had long wanted to live in France, the home of his literary mentors, and he felt free to move there. Before he left England he wrote his autobiographical book *The Truth About an Author,* which appeared anonymously in 1903. The tone of the book is light; Bennett's intention was to tease literary pomposity and pretentiousness. But the effect was unfortunate: Bennett's biographer Reginald Pound says that this book "struck a bounderish note in the ears of critics . . . because it linked the sanctities of authorship with the crudities of commerce." The book hurt Bennett, just as Anthony Trollope's *An Autobiography* (1883) hurt Trollope (with its revelation that the Victorian novelist wrote every day for a set number of hours and went on to begin a new novel if he finished writing one before his time was up). After its appearance Bennett's book was taken by critics to be a literal description of his attitude toward his craft and not at all as what it was: an amusing fragment by a cocky and insecure neophyte of twenty-seven.

Bennett lived in France, with intermittent trips to England and elsewhere abroad, from 1903 to 1912. This was a crucial period in his life. He continued his journalism, contributing long series of articles to the English periodicals *T. P.'s Weekly, PTO,* the *London Evening News,* and the *Manchester Daily Dispatch.* He continued his examinations of life in the Five Towns, which he had marked out as a territory for himself, with his third serious novel *Leonora* (1903), the story of a middle-aged wife and mother and the second in an intended series of books about women, of which *Anna of the Five Towns* was the first. He contributed also a series of stories to the *Windsor Magazine,* which were collected and published in 1905 as *Tales of the Five Towns.* His third novel about a woman—this one a singer—also appeared in 1905. *Sacred and Profane Love,* which has a

Marguerite Soulie Bennett, whom Bennett married in Paris, 4 July 1907 (photo by H. C. Murcott)

inspired period of his life: in October of 1907 he began to write *The Old Wives Tale* (1908), his most ambitious novel to that time; he interrupted work on it for a few weeks in early 1908 to write *Buried Alive* (1908), one of his most popular light novels, which has been adapted to the stage and the screen. In March 1908 for the weekly *New Age* he began his series "Books and Persons," a *causerie* which he signed Jacob Tonson. For the next three years he used this series to discuss books, painting, publishing, magazines, newspapers, travel, theater, censorship, ballet, and European news of cultural significance. These articles created a stir; through them Bennett became known as erudite and knowledgeable, a writer who had broken through the crust of rather smug insularity that surrounded most of his British colleagues. The year 1908 saw the publication of *The Old Wives Tale*, the novel which he felt had to make his reputation—he was now over forty years old—and which succeeded to his complete satisfaction. In the same year he produced *How to Live on 24 Hours a Day*, the most successful of his "pocket philosophies," and began to see some success on the stage. The Stage Society produced his *Cupid and Commonsense*, a dramatization of *Anna of*

Bennett in Paris, 1907. Marguerite Bennett kept this photograph, inscribed "A son coeur, Marguerite. Arnold," on her dressing table until her death

Five Towns setting, suffers from a melodramatic heavy-handedness. It is probably Bennett's least attractive serious novel.

By 1906 his career had begun to blossom. In June of that year he became engaged to Eleanor Green, the sister of the novelist Julian Green, but in August the engagement was broken off. No more than this is known, but Eleanor Green later chose to describe the affair as a ridiculous misunderstanding on Bennett's part: this explanation was accepted by Bennett's biographers and repeated by Dorothy Cheston, who had her own reasons to present Bennett as a clumsy provincial, frightened of women, whose marriage to Marguerite Soulie was a reaction to his rejection by Eleanor Green. This story too hurt Bennett's reputation. He met Marguerite Soulie in January 1907 and married her in July. She was a tall, dark, striking woman who worked in a dressmaker's shop but had theatrical ambitions.

Despite implications that he was reacting to a broken heart, Bennett's marriage heralded a most

Bennett at work on his 1908 novel The Old Wives Tale

terviewed, often by writers who were celebrities themselves, photographed, caricatured, honored at banquets, luncheons, parties, autographing sessions, and mobbed by women. Doran said that no English author since Dickens had had such an American reception. Serial rights to his next three novels were sold at figures from twenty to twenty-five thousand dollars (Doran had not been able, immediately after publication of *The Old Wives Tale,* to sell any serial rights to Bennett's work, even for four thousand dollars—so much had his reputation grown since 1908).

In 1912 Arnold Bennett, an assured success, came home to England to live. *Milestones,* his most successful play, which he had written with Edward Knoblock, had settled into a long run at the Royalty Theatre. In June he bought his yacht, the *Velsa,* actually a large barge, and went sailing in Holland. The following February he and Marguerite moved into a house, Comarques, at Thorpe-le-Soken, Essex. In 1913, the last year before World War I, the *English Review* published Bennett's serious discussion of his profession, which appeared in 1915 as a book called *The Author's Craft. The Great Adventure,* a play based on *Buried Alive,* opened in March for a long run at the Kingsway Theatre in London. Until the fall of 1914 Bennett wrote, traveled on the Continent, and sailed the Mediterranean. Then, in August 1914, the world abruptly changed.

He was not a flag-waving patriot but he was an activist by nature, and he could not avoid being swept up in the war. At forty-seven he was too old for active service. He believed that the war was a mistake, but he thought it was an inevitable mistake; and he expected positive social revolution to come from it. Looking forward to the destruction of the autocracies of Germany and Russia, he believed it was essential that the Allies win.

The war cost him money immediately: the *Daily News* dropped the serialization of his newest novel,*The Price of Love* (1914); his receipts from his plays dropped dramatically. Nevertheless he instructed Pinker to give money to any writer less fortunate than he who might need it. He himself began to write a series of political articles for the *Daily News* that were to run more or less for the duration of the war. He pointed out inefficiencies in recruiting, mistreatment of soldiers and their families by the government, and attacked the mandarins at the War Office, the jingoistic Harmsworth Press, and the supporters of conscription. His articles were read by the Liberal cabinet, and he was summoned to London for consultations "on the war." He spent much time in London, not only for

the Five Towns, at the Shaftesbury Theatre in London.

In 1909 his work appeared in the prestigious *English Review:* "The Matador of the Five Towns" in April, and in July the script of his play *What the Public Wants,* which had been produced by the Stage Society in May to excellent reviews and was running at the Royalty Theatre. September 1910 saw the publication of *Clayhanger.* It had been written in five months, from January to June, and it received immediate, positive critical attention on both sides of the Atlantic. *Hilda Lessways,* the second Clayhanger novel, appeared in 1911, as did *The Card,* a light novel which achieved much the same success as *Buried Alive.*

Arnold Bennett had now an enviable position as a successful man of letters. His literary popularity was confirmed in 1911 during his only trip to America, where in six weeks he visited six cities, going as far west as Chicago and being received everywhere with eager enthusiasm. Because of his crippling stammer, he could not make public speeches. But everywhere he went, shepherded by the American publisher George Doran, he was in-

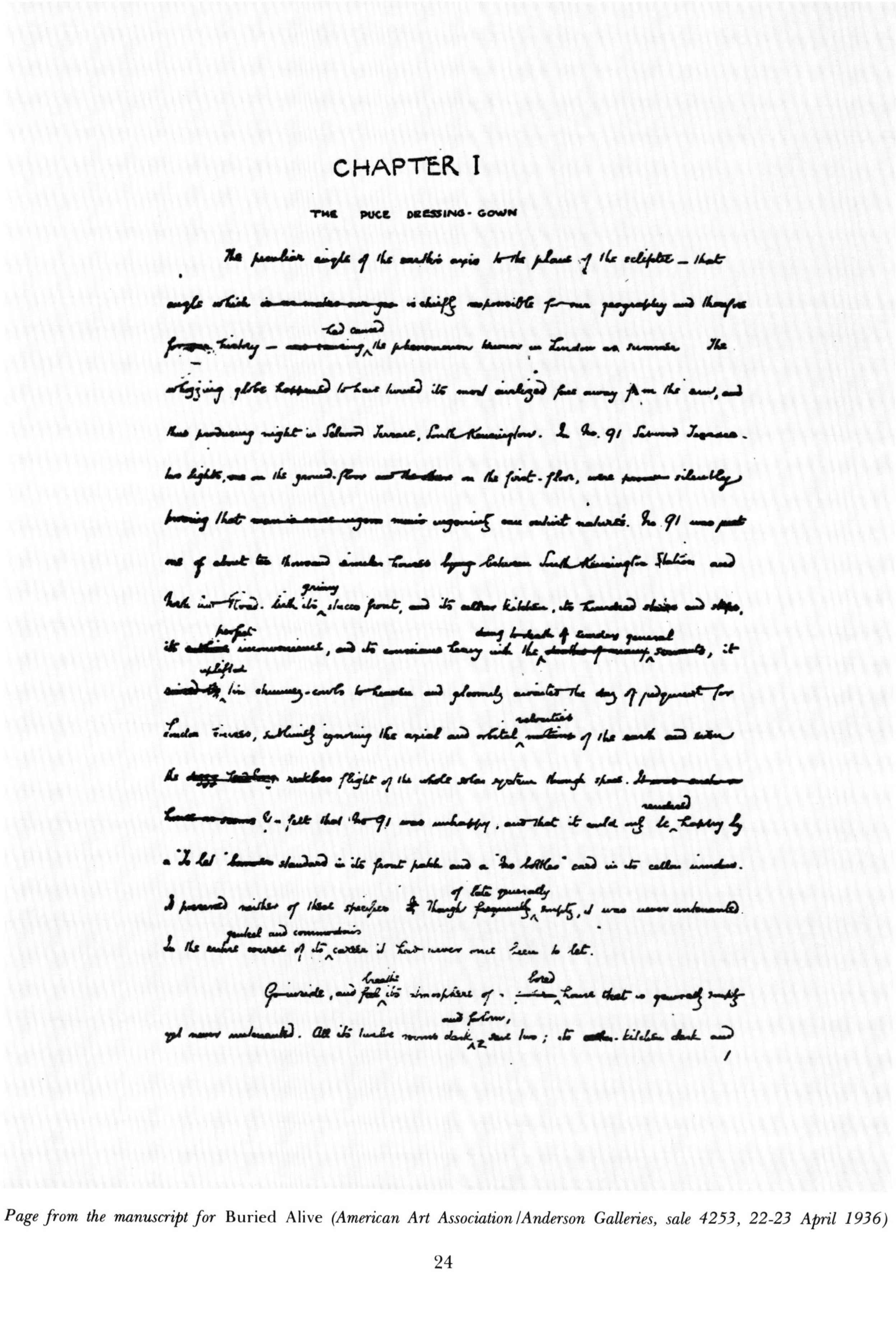

CHAPTER I

THE PUCE DRESSING-GOWN

The peculiar angle of the earth's axis to the plane of the ecliptic — that angle which [illegible] is chiefly responsible for our geography and therefore for [illegible] history — [illegible] had caused the phenomenon known in London as summer. The whizzing globe happened to have turned its most civilized face away from the sun, and thus producing night in Selwood Terrace, South Kensington. In No. 91 Selwood Terrace two lights, one on the ground-floor and [illegible] on the first-floor, were [illegible] silently proving that [illegible] man's ingenious can outwit nature's. No. 91 was just one of about ten thousand similar houses lying between South Kensington Station and Putney Road. With its grimy stucco front, and its cellar kitchen, its hundred stairs and steps, its perfect [illegible] inconvenience, and its conscious beauty with the doing to death of countless general [illegible] servants, it uplifted [illegible] its chimney-cowls to heaven and gloomily awaited the day of judgment for London houses, sublimely ignoring the axial and orbital rotations [illegible] of the earth and even the [illegible] reckless flight of the whole solar system through space. [illegible] You felt that No. 91 was unhappy, and that it could only be rendered happy by a "To let" [illegible] standard in its front patch and a "No bottles" card in its cellar window. It possessed neither of these specifics. Though of late generally [illegible] empty, it was never untenanted. In the entire course of its genteel and commodious career it had never once been to let.

Go inside, and breathe its atmosphere of a [illegible] bored house that is generally empty yet never untenanted. All its twelve rooms dark and forlorn, save two; its cellar-kitchen dark and

Page from the manuscript for Buried Alive (American Art Association/Anderson Galleries, sale 4253, 22-23 April 1936)

conferences and fundraising but also because his relations with his wife were increasingly strained. In 1915 he became a director of the *New Statesman*, traveled to the front as a propagandist for the government, and published in America *These Twain*, the third Clayhanger novel, and his last set in the Five Towns. British publication came the following year.

The *Clayhanger* trilogy is the largely autobiographical story of a family in the Five Towns. The first novel, *Clayhanger,* deals with the rivalries and tensions that exist between generations—a theme Bennett dealt with in *Anna of the Five Towns*—presented from the viewpoint of Edwin Clayhanger, who longs to be an architect and struggles with the strong will of his father, Darius. The second novel in the trilogy, *Hilda Lessways,* retells much of the action of the first book, but this time from the point of view of Hilda, who will become Edwin's wife. This novel continues Bennett's strong interest in the psychological situation of women. The technique Bennett uses in these two novels foreshadows Joyce's method in *Ulysses* (1922): the same events seen from two separate points of view gain depth and significance. Finally, in *These Twain,* the strains of marriage are examined and the author struggles to maintain impartiality while he uses points of view of both husband and wife. *The Roll Call* (1918), which continues the Clayhanger story with the son of Hilda and Edwin, is set in London and is not considered part of the *Clayhanger* series.

In 1918 Bennett was appointed first director of British propaganda in France and then director of propaganda for the Ministry of Information under Lord Beaverbrook. He also produced *The Pretty Lady*, his first novel since 1916. Set in London, it struck a new note for Bennett: its atmosphere is nightmarish; the characters appear to have been wrenched from their normal grooves of behavior by the horrors of the war. The leading female character is a French prostitute with a primitive faith in the Virgin Mary. An interesting aspect of the book is its dialogue: when the characters speak French, Bennett uses almost literal translation, a device later used by Hemingway. Although most reviewers praised the book, some were shocked at what they considered its cynicism; there were threats of legal action against it from the Catholic Federation of Westminster, but these came to nothing. Despite such distractions and the organization work he was required to do at the ministry, Bennett continued his journalism during the last year of the war, writing series not only for the *Daily News*, but for the *New Statesman, Nash's and Pall Mall Magazine,* and *Lloyd's*

Sunday News, as well. In addition, *The Roll Call* ran from April to October in *Munsey's Magazine.*

During the next three years Bennett separated formally from Marguerite Bennett and occupied himself with theater matters and travel. He replaced the *Velsa,* which had been commandeered by the government, with a new yacht, the *Marie Marguerite.* The amount of journalism he produced fell off markedly, rising again in 1922, when he met Dorothy Cheston. At the end of 1922 Bennett began to write *Riceyman Steps,* arguably his most impressive work since *Clayhanger,* and moved with Dorothy Cheston into a house at 75 Cadogan Square in London. She eventually took the name Bennett by deed poll, but the two were never married.

When *Riceyman Steps* was published in 1923, response to it, both critical and popular, was gratifying. H. G. Wells, Joseph Conrad, and Thomas Hardy all praised the book highly, Wells maintaining that it was better than *The Old Wives*

Dorothy Cheston, with whom Bennett began living in 1922 (photo by Sasha). Cheston, who took the name Bennett by deed poll, is the mother of Bennett's daughter, Virginia, born in 1926.

Tale. Bennett was delighted, but annoyed that the character of the maid, Elsie, had attracted so much positive attention. The book, he felt, contained a good deal more than Elsie. And in fact *Riceyman Steps* differs from Bennett's other novels: it is a dark, Dostoevskian tale; its symbolic framework is almost Freudian. Despite the absorbing charm of its realistic detail, it is not a realistic novel. Bennett intended far more than that and realized his intention, although readers were not accustomed to reading his work in that way.

Although he deplored the popular sentimental attitude toward his character Elsie, Bennett brought her to life again in a short story "Elsie and the Child," which he liked well enough to make it the title story of his 1924 collection and to have it published in 1929 in a limited edition illustrated by McKnight Kauffer, whose work Bennett greatly admired.

Nineteen twenty-six was another year of importance: his daughter Virginia was born to Dorothy Cheston in April, *Lord Raingo* was published in October, and in November at Lord Beaverbrook's request he began his review column "Books and Persons" in the *Evening Standard. Lord Raingo* created a considerable stir, largely because it was based on real people in the war office; Bennett consulted closely with Beaverbrook for his working notes, and the novel has been called one of the great political novels in English. Like *The Pretty Lady* and *Riceyman Steps*, it is a dark book: the entire last third of it describes Raingo's lingering death from pneumonia—or from his own death wish. The novel deals not only with power, but with the relationship of a middle-aged man with his young mistress. Raingo himself is a rounded character, unlike Earlforward in *Riceyman Steps.* Frank Swinnerton has said that Raingo is Bennett himself.

Over the next three years, Bennett continued to travel and to write articles, fiction, and plays. Difficulties had arisen in his household, and the relationship with Dorothy Cheston was no longer pleasant. Toward the end of 1929, using the Savoy in London as his model, he began writing *Imperial Palace* (1930), his last completed novel, about the interior working of a great hotel. He wrote in his journal that he had been fighting against writing this long novel for years. Thirty years earlier, he said, he had been taken to the Savoy Hotel for tea and had gone home and written *The Grand Babylon Hotel* in three weeks of evenings. But *The Grand Babylon Hotel* was "a mere lark"; this novel was to be a serious study of "the big hotel de luxe." Some of the frustrations which had built in him over the

critical reception of his work were expressed in this journal entry: "And when I have finished it [*Imperial Palace*] and corrected the manuscript and corrected the typescript and corrected the slipproofs and corrected the page-proofs, and it is published, half the assessors and appraisers in Britain and America will say; 'Why doesn't he give us another "Old Wives Tale" '? I have written between seventy and eighty books. But also I have written only four: 'The Old Wives Tale,' 'The Card,' 'Clayhanger' and 'Riceyman Steps.' All the others are made a reproach to me because they are neither 'The Old Wives Tale', nor 'The Card', nor 'Clayhanger', nor 'Riceyman Steps.' And 'Riceyman Steps' would have been made a reproach too, if the servant Elsie had not happened to be a very 'sympathetic' character. Elsie saved 'Riceyman Steps' from being called sordid and morbid and all sorts of bad adjectives. As if the 'niceness' of a character had anything to do with the quality of the novel in which it appears!"

Imperial Palace, a massive novel, sold well, but critical reactions to it were mixed. In the same year that it appeared, Vicki Baum's *Grand Hotel* was published. Also about the workings of a large luxury

Dust jacket for Bennett's 1930 novel, which was overshadowed by Vicki Baum's Grand Hotel, *published the same year*

hotel and dealing with many characters, it was not as ambitious a novel as *Imperial Palace,* nor did it have the complexities of Bennett's novel; but *Grand Hotel* became an international best-seller, and *Imperial Palace* was to some extent swept aside by it.

Bennett's investments were hurt somewhat by the market crash of 1929. He fretted about money and about the amount of money which Dorothy Cheston insisted on investing in theatrical ventures (she had always had the ambition to become an actress). Despite these financial worries he became fascinated by new apartments at Chiltern Court, above the Baker Street Underground Station, where H. G. Wells had taken a flat. Part of his reason for giving up Cadogan Square was that he wished to cut down somewhat on his servant staff (Dorothy could not get along with them).

Two flats were converted into one; McKnight Kauffer was engaged as an interior designer; and Bennett eagerly looked forward to living in a modern Bauhaus-influenced interior (he had always surrounded himself with antique furniture, although he bought modern paintings). Miles of steel shelving were ordered for his seven thousand books. In her biography Dorothy Cheston gave the impression that this move to Chiltern Court was a reflection of a mind at the end of its tether. Certainly it reflected a desire for change, which was in fact characteristic of Bennett. Frank Swinnerton, who became one of the executors of Bennett's will, has said that his financial affairs were in relatively good order; and he was not squeezed for money. In January of 1931 Bennett and Dorothy Cheston went to France for a holiday, and she later wrote that there Bennett contracted the disease from which he was to die two months later.

After his death both Cheston and Marguerite Bennett wrote memoirs about him. Both women had axes to grind; both provided a picture of Arnold Bennett which each wished the world to remember. Reginald Pound, Bennett's first biographer, trod warily, since both women were still alive when he wrote his book. Although Pound's book is thus far the most reliable biography of Bennett, it is not in the last analysis an attempt at the whole truth; and the picture of Bennett's last years is heavily colored by Dorothy Cheston's narrative. When Pound's book appeared in 1953, Bennett's reputation rested on *The Old Wives Tale,* the only book of his still in print in America.

The second biography appeared in 1966. Written by Dudley Barker, its title is *Writer by Trade,* which recalls the attitude of Bloomsbury toward Bennett. Called into being undoubtedly by the death of Marguerite Bennett, the book contains a good deal of information about the collapse of Bennett's marriage which until then had not been publishable. It also contains many errors, and the picture that emerges is the picture that Dorothy Cheston has carefully shaped: a good man but befuddled, talented but not of the first rank, and, in his last years, not quite responsible for his actions. The evaluation of the novels is, however, stronger than Pound's evaluation. Despite its slanted view of Bennett himself, Barker's book suggests that *Clayhanger, Riceyman Steps, Lord Raingo,* and even *Imperial Palace,* a book Dorothy Cheston particularly disliked, are powerful novels. The third biography of Bennett, by Margaret Drabble, is heavily influenced by Dorothy Cheston and contains little that is new except fresh errors.

However, there has been some revision of the condescending attitude toward Bennett. The most important was the publication in 1963 of James Hepburn's *The Art of Arnold Bennett,* which attempted to examine seriously work that had been dismissed because of the peculiar attitude of critics toward Bennett as a man. Barker's more respectful approach to the work in 1963 reflects this revision of attitude. Of great importance was the publication of Bennett's letters in three volumes edited by James Hepburn, in 1966, 1968 and 1970. Also of great importance, although as yet perhaps generally unappreciated, is Frank Swinnerton's *Arnold Bennett: A Last Word,* which was published in 1978, shortly after the death of Dorothy Cheston Bennett, and in which Frank Swinnerton, the last of Bennett's friends, attempts to tell the truth at last about this writer and his unfortunate private life. A consensus seems to be growing, despite the mass of negative comment which grew during Bennett's last years and for three decades or so after his death, that he was in fact a great novelist, and that ignorance of his work impoverishes the body of English literature.

Letters:

Arnold Bennett's Letters to His Nephew, edited by Frank Swinnerton (New York: Harper, 1935);

Arnold Bennett and H. G. Wells: A Record of a Personal and a Literary Friendship, edited by Harris Wilson (London: Hart-Davis, 1960);

Correspondence André Gide-Arnold Bennett: Vingt Ans D'Amitié Littéraire (1911-1931), edited by Linette F. Brugmans (Geneva: Librarie Droz, 1964);

Letters of Arnold Bennett, edited by James Hepburn: volume 1, *Letters to J. B. Pinker* (London: Oxford University Press, 1966); volume 2, *1889-1915* (London: Oxford University Press, 1968); volume 3, *1916-1931* (London: Oxford University Press, 1970);

Arnold Bennett in Love, edited and translated by George and Jean Beardmore (London: Bruce & Watson, 1972).

Bibliography:

Anita Miller, *Arnold Bennett: An Annotated Bibliography 1887-1932* (New York: Garland, 1977).

Biographies:

Marguerite Bennett, *Arnold Bennett* (London: Philpot, 1925);

Bennett, *My Arnold Bennett* (New York: Dutton, 1932);

Dorothy Cheston Bennett, *Arnold Bennett, a Portrait Done at Home* (New York: Kendall & Sharp, 1935);

Margaret Locherbie-Goff, *La Jeunesse d'Arnold Bennett* (Avesne-sur-Helpe: Editions de l'Observateur, 1939);

Reginald Pound, *Arnold Bennett* (New York: Harcourt, Brace, 1953);

Dudley Barker, *Writer by Trade: A View of Arnold Bennett* (London: Allen & Unwin, 1966);

Margaret Drabble, *Arnold Bennett: A Biography* (London: Weidenfeld & Nicolson, 1974);

Frank Swinnerton, *Arnold Bennett: A Last Word* (London: Hamish Hamilton, 1978).

References:

Walter Allen, *Arnold Bennett* (Denver: Swallow, 1949);

William Bellamy, *The Novels of Wells, Bennett and Galsworthy, 1890-1910* (New York: Barnes & Noble, 1971);

F. J. Harvey Darton, *Arnold Bennett* (New York: Holt, 1915);

James Winford Hall, *Arnold Bennett: Primitivism and Taste* (Seattle: University of Washington, 1959);

James Hepburn, *The Art of Arnold Bennett* (Bloomington: Indiana University Press, 1963);

L. G. Johnson, *Arnold Bennett of the Five Towns* (London: Daniel, 1924);

Georges Lafourcade, *Arnold Bennett: A Study* (London: Muller, 1939);

J. B. Simons, *Arnold Bennett and His Novels* (Oxford: Blackwell, 1936);

Patrick Swinden, *Unofficial Selves: Character in the Novel from Dickens to the Present Day* (London: Macmillan, 1972);

Frank Swinnerton, *Arnold Bennett* (London: Longmans, Green, 1950);

Louis Tillier, *Studies in the Sources of Arnold Bennett's Novels* (Paris: Didier, 1949);

Geoffrey West, *The Problem of Arnold Bennett* (London: Joiner & Steele, 1932);

Virginia Woolf, *Mr Bennett and Mrs Brown* (London: Leonard & Virginia Woolf, 1924);

Walter F. Wright, *Arnold Bennett: Romantic Realist* (Lincoln: University of Nebraska Press, 1971).

Papers:

The largest collections of Bennett's papers are housed at University College in London, at the University of Texas in Austin, at the Northwestern University Library, and at the Berg Collection in the New York Public Library.

John Buchan

(26 August 1875-11 February 1940)

Barbara B. Brown
Marshall University

SELECTED BOOKS: *Sir Quixote of the Moors* (London: Unwin, 1895; New York: Holt, 1895);

Scholar Gipsies (London: John Lane, 1896; New York: Macmillan, 1896);

Sir Walter Ralegh [sic]: *the Stanhope essay* (Oxford: Blackwell/London: Simpkin, Marshall, Hamilton & Kent, 1897);

John Burnet of Barns (London: John Lane, 1898; New York: Dodd, Mead, 1898);

The Pilgrim Fathers: the Newdigate prize poem, 1898 (Oxford: Blackwell/London: Simpkin, Marshall, Hamilton & Kent, 1898);

Brasenose College (London: F. E. Robinson, 1898);

Grey Weather (London: John Lane, 1899);

A Lost Lady of Old Years (London: John Lane, 1899);

The Half-Hearted (London: Isbister, 1900; Boston & New York: Houghton Mifflin, 1900);

The Watcher by the Threshold and Other Tales (Edinburgh & London: Blackwood, 1902; enlarged, New York: Doran, 1918);

The African Colony (Edinburgh: Blackwood, 1903);

The Law Relating to the Taxation of Foreign Income (London: Stevens, 1905);

A Lodge in the Wilderness, anonymous (Edinburgh & London: Blackwood, 1906);

Some Eighteenth Century Byways and Other Essays (Edinburgh & London: Blackwood, 1908);

Prester John (London: Nelson, 1910); republished as *The Great Diamond Pipe* (New York: Dodd, Mead, 1910);

Sir Walter Raleigh (London: Nelson, 1911; New York: Holt, 1911);

The Moon Endureth: Tales and Fancies (Edinburgh & London: Blackwood, 1912; New York: Sturgis & Walton, 1912);

The Marquis of Montrose (London: Nelson, 1913; New York: Scribners, 1913);

Andrew Jameson, Lord Ardwall (Edinburgh & London: Blackwood, 1913);

Nelson's History of the War, 24 volumes (London: Nelson, 1915-1919); republished as *A History of the Great War* (4 volumes, London: Nelson, 1921-1922; 8 volumes, Boston & New York: Houghton Mifflin, 1922);

Salute to Adventurers (London: Nelson, 1915; Boston

John Buchan, 1906 (Radio Times-Hulton)

& New York: Houghton Mifflin, 1915);

The Thirty-Nine Steps (Edinburgh & London: Blackwood, 1915; New York: Doran, 1916);

The Power-House (Edinburgh & London: Blackwood, 1916; New York: Doran, 1916);

Greenmantle (London: Hodder & Stoughton, 1916; New York: Doran, 1916);

Poems, Scots and English (London & Edinburgh: T. C. & E. G. Jack, 1917; revised and enlarged, London: Nelson, 1936);

Mr. Standfast (London: Hodder & Stoughton, 1918; New York: Doran, 1919);

These for Remembrance (London: Privately printed, 1919);

The Island of Sheep, by John Buchan and Susan Buchan as Cadmus and Harmonia (London: Hodder & Stoughton, 1919; Boston & New

29

York: Houghton Mifflin, 1920);

The History of South African Forces in France (London: Nelson, 1920);

Francis and Riversdale Grenfell: A Memoir (London: Nelson, 1920);

The Path of the King (London: Hodder & Stoughton, 1921; New York: Doran, 1921);

Huntingtower (London: Hodder & Stoughton, 1922; New York: Doran, 1922);

A Book of Escapes and Hurried Journeys (London: Nelson, 1922; Boston & New York: Houghton Mifflin, 1923);

The Last Secrets (London: Nelson, 1923; Boston & New York: Houghton Mifflin, 1924);

Midwinter (London: Hodder & Stoughton, 1923; New York: Doran, 1923);

Days to Remember: The British Empire in the Great War, by John Buchan and Henry Newbolt (London: Nelson, 1923);

The Three Hostages (London: Hodder & Stoughton, 1924; Boston & New York: Houghton Mifflin, 1924);

Lord Minto: A Memoir (London & New York: Nelson, 1924);

The History of the Royal Scots Fusiliers, 1678-1918 (London & New York: Nelson, 1925);

John Macnab (London: Hodder & Stoughton, 1925; Boston & New York: Houghton Mifflin, 1925);

The Man and the Book: Sir Walter Scott (London & Edinburgh: Nelson, 1925);

The Dancing Floor (London: Hodder & Stoughton, 1926; Boston & New York: Houghton Mifflin, 1926);

Homilies and Recreations (London: Nelson, 1926; London & New York: Nelson, 1926; Boston: Houghton Mifflin, 1926);

Witch Wood (London: Hodder & Stoughton, 1927; Boston & New York: Houghton Mifflin, 1927);

The Runagates Club (London: Hodder & Stoughton, 1928; Boston & New York: Houghton Mifflin, 1928);

Montrose (London & Edinburgh: Nelson, 1928; Boston & New York: Houghton Mifflin, 1928);

The Courts of the Morning (London: Hodder & Stoughton, 1929; Boston & New York: Houghton Mifflin, 1929);

The Causal and the Casual in History (Cambridge: The University Press, 1929; New York: Macmillan, 1929);

The Kirk in Scotland, 1560-1929, by John Buchan

and George Adam Smith (London: Hodder & Stoughton, 1930);

Castle Gay (London: Hodder & Stoughton, 1930; Boston & New York: Houghton Mifflin, 1930);

The Blanket of the Dark (London: Hodder & Stoughton, 1931; Boston & New York: Houghton Mifflin, 1931);

Sir Walter Scott (London & Toronto: Cassell, 1932; New York: Coward-McCann, 1932);

The Gap in the Curtain (London: Hodder & Stoughton, 1932; Boston & New York: Houghton Mifflin, 1932);

Julius Caesar (London: P. Davies, 1932; New York: Appleton, 1932);

The Magic Walking Stick (London: Hodder & Stoughton, 1932; Boston & New York: Houghton Mifflin, 1932);

The Massacre of Glencoe (London: P. Davies, 1933; New York: Putnam's, 1933);

A Prince of the Captivity (London: Hodder & Stoughton, 1933; Boston & New York: Houghton Mifflin, 1933);

The Free Fishers (London: Hodder & Stoughton, 1934; Boston & New York: Houghton Mifflin, 1934);

Gordon at Khartoum (London: P. Davies, 1934);

Oliver Cromwell (London: Hodder & Stoughton, 1934; Boston: Houghton Mifflin, 1934);

The King's Grace (London: Hodder & Stoughton, 1935); republished as *The People's King: George V* (Boston: Houghton Mifflin, 1935);

The House of the Four Winds (London: Hodder & Stoughton, 1935; Boston & New York: Houghton Mifflin, 1935);

The Island of Sheep (London: Hodder & Stoughton, 1936); republished as *The Man from the Norlands* (Boston & New York: Houghton Mifflin, 1936);

Augustus (London: Hodder & Stoughton, 1937; Boston: Houghton Mifflin, 1937);

Memory Hold-the-Door (London: Hodder & Stoughton, 1940); republished as *Pilgrim's Way* (Boston: Houghton Mifflin, 1940);

Comments and Characters, edited by W. Forbes Gray (London & New York: Nelson, 1940);

Canadian Occasions (London: Hodder & Stoughton, 1940);

Sick Heart River (London: Hodder & Stoughton, 1941); republished as *Mountain Meadow* (Boston: Houghton Mifflin, 1941);

The Long Traverse (London: Hodder & Stoughton, 1941); republished as *The Lake of Gold* (Boston: Houghton Mifflin, 1941).

OTHER: *Essays and Apothegms of Francis Lord Bacon,*
   edited with an introduction by Buchan (London: W. Scott, 1894);

Izaak Walton, *The Compleat Angler, or the Contemplative Man's Recreation,* edited with an introduction and notes by Buchan (London: Methuen,
   1901).

Many contemporaries knew John Buchan, or
Tweedsmuir, only as journalist and statesman.
Some readers knew him as historian and biographer. But most readers in both England and
America knew Buchan best for his fiction, as the
writer of the exciting adventures of Sir Edward
Leithen, Dickson McCunn, and Richard Hannay.
Hannay is the gentleman-hero of the popular
spy-thriller—or "shocker" as Buchan called his adventure novels—*The Thirty-Nine Steps,* which sold
over a million copies in English, has been translated
into many other languages, and in 1935 was made
into a popular film by Alfred Hitchcock.

But Buchan was also a serious novelist in the
tradition of Sir Walter Scott and Robert Louis
Stevenson, both important influences on his early
works. Buchan's literary output is prodigious. He
wrote thirty novels, seven books of short stories,
sixty-six other books, seven full-length biographies,
several short biographies and memoirs, and many
articles. He also produced twenty-six pamphlets
and contributed to more than seventy books. Yet
astonishingly, Buchan was not primarily a man of
letters. He was also a barrister, publisher, war correspondent, wartime director of information, director of Reuters, member of Parliament, diplomat,
high commissioner for the Church of Scotland, and
from 1935 until his death, governor-general of
Canada as the first Baron Tweedsmuir of Elsfield.

Buchan was born at Perth, Scotland, the eldest
child of John Buchan, minister of the Free Church
of Scotland, and his wife, Helen Masterson Buchan.
Buchan's childhood was spent along the Fife coast
and at Kirkcaldy, and his boyhood in Glasgow.
Summers were spent with his Masterson grandparents in the Tweed valley, where the rugged natural
scenery was to become a powerful influence on his
writing. Other early influences were the Bible and
Pilgrim's Progress. He attended Hutcheson's Grammar School at Glasgow and later Glasgow University, and, in 1895, won a scholarship to Brasenose
College, Oxford. His first book, an edition of the
Essays and Apothegms of Francis Lord Bacon (1894),
had already been published. At Oxford, Buchan
increased his literary reputation by having four
more books published, including the historical ro-

mances *Sir Quixote of the Moors* (1895) and *John Burnet of Barns* (1898), by contributing to the *Yellow
Book,* reading manuscripts for John Lane, publishers, and writing the history of his college.

From Oxford, Buchan went to London to
study law at the Middle Temple, supporting himself
by contributions to the *Spectator* and *Blackwood's.* His
first attempt at a contemporary novel, *The Half-
Hearted* (1900), was only moderately successful, but
it introduced a theme that appears in the later
books. Lewis Haystoun, the novel's introspective
hero, is engaged in "making" his soul, deliberately
choosing to play an active role in the universal war
between good and evil, and triumphing over his
feelings of futility and cowardice by sacrificing his
life in a heroic rearguard action. Additional treatments of the theme of soul-making are found in *A
Prince of the Captivity* (1933), *The Island of Sheep*
(1936), and *Sick Heart River* (1941).

After his admission to the bar in 1901, Buchan
spent two years on the staff of Lord Alfred Milner,
high commissioner for South Africa. Deeply moved
by the history and beauty of South Africa, Buchan
later wrote *The African Colony* (1903), a lengthy survey of South African history and politics; *A Lodge in
the Wilderness* (1906), a symposium detailing his
political faith in imperialism; and *Prester John*
(1910), a boys' book of high adventure. Buchan
joined Nelson publishers as chief literary advisor in
December 1906. In 1907 he married Susan Gros-
venor, granddaughter of Lord Ebury and great-
great-niece of the Duke of Wellington. Three of
their four children survive: Alice (Lady Fairfax-
Lucy), John (second Baron Tweedsmuir), and William.

In the early years of the twentieth century
Buchan was little known as a writer of fiction. But a
collection of tales, *The Moon Endureth* (1912), included "Space," which introduces the popular
Buchan hero Edward Leithen, eminent London
lawyer and member of Parliament. In *The Power-
House,* an early shocker serialized in 1913 and separately published in 1916, Leithen uncovers and successfully prevents a malevolent conspiracy to destroy civilization. Buchan develops two important
themes that recur in later, more artfully plotted
books: the chase or "hurried journey" and "how
thin is the protection of civilisation." As the destructive Lumley tells Leithen in *The Power-House:*
"You think a wall as solid as the earth separates
civilisation from barbarism. I tell you the division is
a thread, a sheet of glass. A touch here, a push there,
and you bring back the reign of Satan." For Buchan
the power of evil was both real and ever-

Angling in Still Waters

To some men angling comes as a recreation to others as a business and to others as a toil. Some men, notably those who have been arrant poachers in their youth, can be seen sallying out morning after morning at the appointed time, with the usual paraphernalia of the fisherman. They reach the water and begin work. Hour after hour as if their life depended on it, they will whip the stream, and return at night, worn out with their exertions only to renew them on the next day. Such men have no thought above their catch; if they have made a specially large basket their spirits will be exuberant for a week. Times and seasons are remembered by them only in connection with some piscatorial exploit, and their talk savours strongly of their rod and basket. The last class is still more amusing. There are people who think that it is the right thing to do when they get a holiday, to array themselves in waterproofs, take their stand in the middle of a stream and try an art of which they know nothing. To such men troubles come thick and fast. They usually begin by choosing the wrong fly, and the frantic manner in which their lure splashes down on the water are directly the

First page of the manuscript for Buchan's first published article, which appeared in the Gentleman's Magazine, *August 1893 (courtesy of Lady Fairfax-Lucy, Lord Tweedsmuir, the Hon. William Buchan, and the National Library of Scotland)*

of a plot by a secret international organization to assassinate a prominent European politician. Before details can be discovered, Scudder is murdered in Hannay's rooms. Hannay's "hurried journey" filled with danger and suspense begins. Disguised, he flees to Scotland, where he is soon hunted by police and enemy agents alike. Beyond the protection of the law, he comes to comprehend the thinness of civilization. Aided at last by Sir Walter Bullivant of the foreign office, Hannay realizes that the plot is more far-reaching than the assassination. The conspirators hope to steal secret naval plans from the British Admiralty and use them to cripple the British fleet. Hannay's final dramatic thwarting of the conspiracy brings the suspenseful narrative to a satisfactory climax. John Cawelti, in an essay entitled "The Joys of Buchaneering," considers *The Thirty-Nine Steps* the most successful of the Hannay books, and millions of readers would doubtless agree.

Partially recovered from his illness, Buchan served as war correspondent for the *London Times* and as major (later lieutenant colonel) in the Intelligence Corps. In 1917 he was appointed director of information and the following year director of intelligence in the new Ministry of Information. In 1919 he was made a director of Reuters. Buchan now felt what he described as "an intense craving for a country life" and "sense of continuity." He settled in the manor house of Elsfield, a Cotswold village four miles from Oxford, and, in addition to his adventure tales, began writing a new type of historical romance, foreshadowed by such earlier novels as *A Lost Lady of Old Years* (1899) and *Salute to Adventurers* (1915). A major purpose was an attempt to unite time and space, to select the historical moment which would best reveal the character of a particular landscape.

The Path of the King (1921), the first of these historical romances, is a fantasy that traces the flow of "kingly blood" from a young Viking to Abraham Lincoln. Following this came *Midwinter* (1923), *Witch Wood* (1927), *The Blanket of the Dark* (1931), and *The Free Fishers* (1934). The vivid descriptions in these novels reflect Buchan's own deeply felt responses at various periods of his life to particular locales and countrysides.

But it was the adventure story that guaranteed Buchan's ever-growing popularity. Richard Hannay and his associates—Peter Pienaar, a Dutch hunter; Sandy Arbuthnot; Sir Archie Roylance; John S. Blenkiron, the American industrialist—continue their escapades in *Greenmantle* (1916), *Mr. Standfast* (1919), *The Three Hostages* (1924), and *The*

Buchan as a lieutenant colonel in the British army, 1916 (courtesy of Lady Fairfax-Lucy, Lord Tweedsmuir, and the Hon. William Buchan)

threatening, and the theme of the constant battle between good and evil is a basic one in his canon.

At the start of World War I Buchan was seriously ill with a duodenal ulcer. Bedfast and restless, he began writing the monumental *History of the War* (1915-1919) for the publisher Thomas Nelson; and to amuse himself, he completed another shocker, *The Thirty-Nine Steps* (1915). In the dedication to Nelson, Buchan defined the shocker: "the romance where the incidents defy the probabilities, and march just inside the borders of the possible." It was a definition Buchan was to elucidate repeatedly.

Buchan's hero of *The Thirty-Nine Steps* is Richard Hannay, who has made his fortune in South Africa and retired in England. He is bored, but he is soon drawn into adventure. In a chance encounter with Franklin P. Scudder, an American newspaperman and amateur sleuth, Hannay learns

Elsfield Manor, near Oxford, where Buchan settled in January 1920 to satisfy the "intense craving for a country life" he described in Memory Hold-the-Door *(1940)*

Courts of the Morning (1929). Hannay also appears in the short-story collection *The Runagates Club* (1928) and *The Gap in the Curtain* (1932). Edward Leithen reappears in *John Macnab* (1925), *The Dancing Floor* (1926), *The Runagates Club,* and *The Gap in the Curtain.* Other novels feature a third and quite different Buchan hero, Dickson McCunn, the retired Glasgow grocer with the romantic heart and adventurous spirit. McCunn and the Gorbal Diehards, a group of ragamuffin boys from the streets of Glasgow, are seen in *Huntingtower* (1922), *Castle Gay* (1930), and *The House of the Four Winds* (1935), lively books but marred somewhat by lack of unity of plot and of tone.

From 1927 to 1935 Buchan was a member of Parliament representing the Scottish universities. In 1933 and 1934 he served as lord high commissioner to the General Assembly of the Church of Scotland, and in 1935 he was raised to the peerage as the first Baron Tweedsmuir and appointed Governor-General of Canada, a post he held until his death in 1940. Buchan had visited the United States and Canada in 1924, but now he traveled extensively, visiting Washington as the guest of President Franklin Roosevelt, receiving honorary

degrees from Harvard and Yale. His writings during these last five years of his life were, as usual, varied: a final Hannay adventure, *The Island of Sheep* (1936); *Augustus,* a life and times biography of the emperor Augustus (1937); a boy's book, *The Long Traverse* (1941), using once more the theme in the historical romances of the sense of continuity in history; the autobiographical memoir *Memory Hold-the-Door* (1940); and *Sick Heart River* (1941), Sir Edward Leithen's last and greatest adventure, considered by some critics Buchan's masterpiece and by other reviewers a disappointment.

The number and variety of Buchan's works make assessment challenging. Certainly he holds a significant position in the historical development of English-American biography. His fictional works sold widely throughout the world, but, with the exception of perhaps three or four books, they are customarily assigned to the second rank. Critics have attacked Buchan for what they perceive as his snobbishness and attitude of "clubland" provincialism. But such critical interpretations misread the essential Buchan and overlook his most significant achievements.

The continuing development of the spy novel

Bookplate with the motto "Following nothing base" that Buchan used on his coat of arms when he became Lord Tweedsmuir in 1935 (courtesy of Lady Fairfax-Lucy, Lord Tweedsmuir, and the Hon. William Buchan)

in the twentieth century throws light on Buchan's distinctive contributions. In action there is mystery and a series of adventures, hurried journeys full of danger. In theme there is a sense of cosmic good and evil. In character, Hannay is typical: he is no professional governmental agent but a gentleman amateur, drawn into international intrigue by a love of adventure and a strong sense of duty. In setting there is a deep love of the outdoors and an awareness of man's affinity with nature. Finally, in style there is clarity, dignity, and ease. "His own style," says A. L. Rowse, "was vigorous and natural, athletic and spare; running beautifully clear like one of his own Border streams. . . . Since style is one of the most preservative elements in literature, his best books will continue to be read so long as we care for good standards in letters."

Bibliographies:
Archibald Hanna, Jr., *John Buchan, 1875-1940: A Bibliography* (Hamden, Conn.: Shoe String Press, 1953);

B. C. Wilmot, *A Checklist of Works By and About John Buchan in the John Buchan Collection, Douglas Library, Queen's University* (Boston: G. K. Hall, 1961);

J. Randolph Cox, "John Buchan, Lord Tweedsmuir: An Annotated Bibliography of Writings about him," *English Literature in Transition,* 9, no. 5 (1966): 241-291; 10, no. 4 (1967): 209-211; 15, no. 4 (1972): 67-69;

Robert G. Blanchard, *The First Editions of John Buchan* (Hamden, Conn.: Archon Books, 1981).

Biographies:
Janet Adam Smith, *John Buchan: A Biography* (London: Rupert Hart-Davis, 1965);

Smith, *John Buchan and his World* (New York: Scribners, 1979).

References:
Barbara B. Brown, "John Buchan and Twentieth-Century Biography," *Biography,* 2 (Fall 1979): 328-341;

John Cawelti, "The Joys of Buchaneering," in *Essays in Honor of Russel B. Nye,* edited by Joseph Waldmeir (East Lansing: Michigan State University Press, 1978), pp. 7-30;

David Daniell, *The Interpreter's House, A Critical Assessment of John Buchan* (London: Nelson, 1975);

Francis R. Hart, *The Scottish Novel from Smollett to Spark* (Cambridge: Harvard University Press, 1979), pp. 169-181;

Gertrude Himmelfarb, "John Buchan, an Untimely Appreciation," *Encounter,* 15 (September 1960): 46-53;

M. R. Ridley, "A Misrated Author?," in his *Second Thoughts* (London: Dent, 1965), pp. 1-44;

Arthur C. Turner, *Mr. Buchan, Writer* (London: SCM Press, 1949);

Susan Tweedsmuir, *John Buchan By His Wife and Friends* (London: Hodder & Stoughton, 1947);

Richard Usborne, *Clubland Heroes* (London: Constable, 1953).

Papers:
Buchan materials are in the John Buchan Collection, Douglas Library, Queen's University, Kingston, Ontario; in the National Library of Scotland, Edinburgh; and in the Edinburgh University Library.

G. K. Chesterton

(29 May 1874-14 June 1936)

Brian Murray
Youngstown State University

See also the Chesterton entries in *DLB 10, Modern British Dramatists, 1900-1945* and *DLB 19, British Poets, 1880-1914.*

SELECTED BOOKS: *Greybeards at Play: Literature and Art for Old Gentlemen, Rhymes and Sketches* (London: Johnson, 1900);

The Wild Knight and Other Poems (London: Richards, 1900);

The Defendant (London: Johnson, 1901);

Twelve Types (London: Humphreys, 1902); enlarged as *Varied Types* (New York: Dodd, Mead, 1908);

Robert Browning (London: Macmillan, 1903);

G. F. Watts (London: Duckworth/New York: Dutton, 1904);

The Napoleon of Notting Hill (London & New York: John Lane/Bodley Head, 1904);

The Club of Queer Trades (London & New York: Harper, 1905);

Heretics (London & New York: John Lane, 1905);

Charles Dickens (London: Methuen, 1906; New York: Dodd, Mead, 1906);

The Man Who Was Thursday (Bristol: Arrowsmith/London: Simkin, Marshall, Hamilton, Kent, 1908; New York: Dodd, Mead, 1908);

All Things Considered (London: Methuen, 1908; New York: John Lane, 1908);

Orthodoxy (London & New York: John Lane/Bodley Head, 1908);

George Bernard Shaw (London & New York: John Lane/Bodley Head, 1909);

Tremendous Trifles (London: Methuen, 1909; New York: Dodd, Mead, 1909);

The Ball and the Cross (New York: John Lane, 1909; London: Wells Gardner, 1910);

What's Wrong With the World (London, New York, Toronto & Melbourne: Cassell, 1910);

Alarms and Discussions (London: Methuen, 1910; enlarged, New York: Dodd, Mead, 1911);

William Blake (London: Duckworth/New York: Dutton, 1910);

Appreciations and Criticisms of the Works of Charles Dickens (London: Dent/New York: Dutton, 1911);

G. K. Chesterton, 1925 (courtesy of Aidan Mackey)

The Innocence of Father Brown (London, New York, Toronto & Melbourne: Cassell, 1911; New York: John Lane, 1911);

The Ballad of the White Horse (London: Methuen, 1911; New York: John Lane, 1911);

Manalive (London, Edinburgh, Dublin, Leeds, New York & Paris: Nelson, 1912; New York: John Lane, 1912);

A Miscellany of Men (London: Methuen, 1912; enlarged, New York: Dodd, Mead, 1912);

The Victorian Age in Literature (London: Williams & Norgate, 1913);

Magic (London: Martin Secker, 1913; New York: Putnam's, 1913);

The Flying Inn (London: Methuen, 1914; New York: John Lane, 1914);

The Wisdom of Father Brown (London, New York, Toronto & Melbourne: Cassell, 1914);

Poems (London: Burns & Oates, 1915);

Wine, Water and Song (London: Methuen, 1915);

The Crimes of England (London: Palmer & Hayward, 1915);

A Short History of England (London: Chatto & Windus, 1917);

Utopia of Usurers (New York: Boni & Liveright, 1917);

Irish Impressions (London, Glasgow, Melbourne & Auckland: Collins, 1919);

The Superstition of Divorce (London: Chatto & Windus, 1920);

The New Jerusalem (London: Hodder & Stoughton, 1920);

Eugenics and Other Evils (London, New York, Toronto & Melbourne: Cassell, 1922);

What I Saw in America (London: Hodder & Stoughton, 1922);

The Ballad of St. Barbara and Other Verses (London: Palmer, 1922);

The Man Who Knew Too Much and Other Stories (London, New York, Toronto & Melbourne: Cassell, 1922; abridged edition, New York: Harper, 1922);

Fancies Versus Fads (London: Methuen, 1923; New York: Dodd, Mead, 1923);

St. Francis of Assisi (London: Hodder & Stoughton, 1923; New York: Doran, 1924);

Tales of the Long Bow (London, New York, Toronto & Melbourne: Cassell, 1925);

The Everlasting Man (London: Hodder & Stoughton, 1925; New York: Dodd, Mead, 1925);

William Cobbett (London: Hodder & Stoughton, 1925; New York: Dodd, Mead, 1925);

The Incredulity of Father Brown (London, New York, Toronto & Melbourne: Cassell, 1926);

The Outline of Sanity (London: Sheed & Ward, 1926);

The Queen of Seven Swords (London: Sheed & Ward, 1926);

The Return of Don Quixote (New York: Dodd, Mead, 1926; London: Chatto & Windus, 1927);

The Collected Poems of G. K. Chesterton (London: Palmer, 1927; revised, 1933; New York: Dodd, Mead, 1966);

The Secret of Father Brown (London, Toronto, Melbourne & Sydney: Cassell, 1927);

Robert Louis Stevenson (London: Hodder & Stoughton, 1927);

Generally Speaking: A Book of Essays (London: Methuen, 1928);

The Poet and the Lunatics: Episodes in the Life of Gabriel Gale (London, Toronto, Melbourne & Sydney: Cassell, 1929; New York: Dodd, Mead, 1929);

Four Faultless Felons (London, Toronto, Melbourne & Sydney: Cassell, 1930; New York: Dodd, Mead, 1930);

The Resurrection of Rome (London: Hodder & Stoughton, 1930; New York: Dodd, Mead, 1930);

Come to Think of It . . . (London: Methuen, 1930);

All Is Grist: A Book of Essays (London: Methuen, 1931; New York: Dodd, Mead, 1932);

Chaucer (London: Faber & Faber, 1932; New York: Farrar & Rinehart, 1932);

Sidelights on New London and Newer York and Other Essays (London: Sheed & Ward, 1932);

All I Survey: A Book of Essays (London: Methuen, 1933);

St. Thomas Aquinas (London: Hodder & Stoughton, 1933; New York: Sheed & Ward, 1933);

Avowals and Denials. A Book of Essays (London: Methuen, 1934; New York: Dodd, Mead, 1935);

As I Was Saying (London: Methuen, 1936; New York: Dodd, Mead, 1936);

Autobiography (London: Hutchinson, 1936; New York: Sheed and Ward, 1936);

The Paradoxes of Mr. Pond (London, Toronto, Melbourne & Sydney: Cassell, 1937; New York: Dodd, Mead, 1937);

The Coloured Lands (London: Sheed & Ward, 1938);

The End of the Armistice (London: Sheed & Ward, 1940);

The Common Man (London: Sheed & Ward, 1950);

A Handful of Authors, edited by Dorothy Collins (London & New York: Sheed & Ward, 1953);

The Glass Walking-Stick and Other Essays from the Illustrated London News, 1905-1936, edited by Collins (London: Methuen, 1955).

G. K. Chesterton was a writer of volcanic intelligence and gentle wit, who, over a forty-year career, produced hundreds of essays and over one hundred books. Approximately a dozen of these books have been described as novels, but they are as frequently called romances, extravaganzas, fantasies, parables, or allegories. For while they are thick with the details of everyday life, Chesterton's hastily written book-length fictions are outlandishly plotted and, in the main, unabashedly didactic.

These books are often dismissed as trifling and incomprehensible, but the best of them, which are quite brilliant in their way, have always had their advocates and analysts and are often republished.

Chesterton was born in London. His father, Edward Chesterton, a well-off house agent, was accessible, witty, and, as Chesterton put it in his *Autobiography* (1936), "full of hobbies." Indeed, "Mr. Ed" spent less time at his place of business than in his study, where he painted, whittled, took photographs, built "magic lanterns," and manufactured toffee. He also constructed toy theaters for which he composed extravagant dramas that were produced for the pleasure of his and the neighborhood's children. In his autobiography, Chesterton admitted that his love of "romantic things" had been instilled by his "Pickwickian" father.

Chesterton's mother, Marie Louise Grosjean Chesterton, was, like her son, genial and untidy. His younger brother Cecil, who later became a well-known polemical journalist, was quick-witted, sharp-tongued, and devoted to debating with his brother. Summarizing his relationship with Cecil, Chesterton once wrote: "We really devoted all our boyhood to one long argument, unfortunately interrupted by meal times, by school times . . . and many such irritating frivolities." Even at mealtime "We shouted at each other across the table, on the subject of Parnell or Puritanism or Charles the First's head." As Chesterton's biographer Dudley Barker notes, "the incessant youthful arguments trained the adult Chesterton to be as sharp, vigorous and swift a public debater as any man alive; a debater who could stand on a platform against Bernard Shaw and give as good as he received."

At the age of thirteen Chesterton began as a day boy at St. Paul's Preparatory School in London. Here Chesterton became well known as an eccentric, a designation he kept, and no doubt later cultivated, for the rest of his life. At St. Paul's, Chesterton was dreamy, squeaky-voiced, and comically lanky. As a man he was much the same, though—at more than 300 pounds—hardly lanky. Certainly, as a man, as at St. Paul's, Chesterton was an unflagging reader. By the time he was twelve, he could recite long sections from Dickens, Scott, and Shakespeare. He read, he said, "for the mere brute pleasure of reading," for "the sort of pleasure a cow must have in grazing all day long."

From 1893 to 1895, Chesterton attended London's Slade School of Art, where he devoted as much time to writing verse as he did to sketching and painting. At twenty-one Chesterton went to work for the publishing firm of Fisher Unwin and

spent the next five years there reading and editing manuscripts and writing blurbs. In his spare time, he contributed poems and commentaries to many London-based periodicals, including the politically liberal, anti-imperialist *Daily News.* Chesterton first became known as "a man who might write something good one day"—as Compton Mackenzie later remembered—when his book *Twelve Types,* which featured essays on Byron, Tolstoy, and Savonarola, was published in 1902. In fact, by the summer of that year Chesterton, a colorful figure in his black cape and slouch hat, was one of Britain's most widely read columnists and reviewers and would retain the distinction for three decades to come. Of his Fleet Street origins Chesterton was consistently proud: he liked to think of himself as a happily hardworking journalist even when, midway in his career, several critics ranked his poem *The Ballad of the White Horse* (1911) and his play *Magic* (1913) among the best of the post-Victorian era.

Chesterton had a great many interests, and he produced essays on an impressively wide range of subjects. For example, *All I Survey,* a 1933 collection of his journalistic prose, contains such pieces as "On Education," "On Monsters," "On Eyebrows," and "On the Solar System." In *As I Was Saying* (1936), Chesterton writes with his usual gusto "About

Chesterton as a young man (Marion E. Wade Collection, Wheaton College)

Inscription to Father John O'Connor on the fly leaves of Chesterton's 1909 novel The Ball and the Cross. *O'Connor was the model for the priest-detective of Chesterton's many Father Brown stories (G. K. Chesterton 1874-1974: An Exhibition of Books, Manuscripts, Drawings and Other Material, National Book League, 14-31 May 1974; courtesy of Miss D. E. Collins).*

Shirts," "About Voltaire," "About Relativity," "About Blondes," and "About Modern Girls," among other things. These pieces, though slight, do exhibit the central strengths and weaknesses of Chesterton's distinctive prose style. Often, they shimmer with graceful rhythms, apt aphorisms, and arresting metaphors. But almost as often they suffer from verbosity—from an avuncular long-windedness. One recent critic has suggested that "the cumulative effect" of reading long stretches of Chesterton's *Orthodoxy* (1908) and his *The Everlasting Man* (1925) is "intensely tiring, like being force-fed unchewable candy."

It is probable that much of the credit for Chesterton's contentment—and success—belonged to his wife, the former Frances Blogg, whom he married on 28 June 1901. Frances helped counter the potentially disastrous effects of G. K. C.'s notorious absentmindedness: she scrupulously kept track of his date book and his bank account and more than once quite literally pointed him in the right direction. She also helped Ches-

terton shape his religious beliefs—beliefs that would eventually inform nearly everything he wrote. In 1901, when Frances was a devout High Church Anglican, Gilbert was still groping for a viable religious creed. By 1910, Chesterton was openly and prolifically defending Christian orthodoxy. In 1922, Chesterton converted to Roman Catholicism; six years later Frances followed.

Chesterton's first novel, the futuristic fantasy *The Napoleon of Notting Hill* (1904), concerns itself with political, not religious, issues. Set in 1984, it depicts an England that has become so crazily democratic that she elects her leaders by lot. As a joke, King Auberon Quin transforms London's boroughs into a series of medieval cities, complete with "armour, music, standards, watch fires" and "the noise of drums." But the joke curdles when a young poet named Adam Wayne triumphantly leads the good citizens of Notting Hill into battle against Kensington and Bayswater because aggressive property developers in those suburbs seek to level Notting Hill's Pump Street and its quaint shops

G. K. and Frances Chesterton aboard the Aquitania *at the end of Chesterton's 1921 American tour (courtesy of Joan Newcomb)*

for a "great thoroughfare." For, unlike most Londoners, Adam takes Quin's League of Free Cities seriously. And using his army, he succeeds in expanding his Notting Hill empire before meeting his demise in a dramatic but comic-bookish manner.

The Napoleon of Notting Hill sets forth a number of Chesterton's political principles. Throughout his career, he repeatedly backed the small neighborhood shop over the chain store, the tiny colony over the empire with expansionist aims. He supported any small and colorful entity that fought absorption into an amorphous mass. Thus, as long as Adam Wayne strives to protect the integrity of his own locality, he is a true hero—the prototype, in fact, for several Chesterton protagonists. In later book-length fictions such as *Tales of the Long Bow* (1925) and *The Return of Don Quixote* (1926), Chesterton again focuses on likable, adventure-loving fellows who plunge into battle against imposing, unjust foes. In fact, these later works tend to advertise the biases of Distributionism, a neo-medievalist political program also championed by Cecil Chesterton and Hilaire Belloc, among others. Essentially, the Distributionists condemned industrial capitalism and the monopoly of economic power that came in its wake. But they also condemned George Bernard Shaw's brand of Fabian socialism, believing that it would inevitably produce a state too intrusive and a bureaucracy too unwieldy. Drawing some inspira-

tion from Pope Leo XIII's 1891 encyclical *Rerum Novarum,* the Distributionists called for a massive reapportionment of property so that smaller, family-run farms and cottage industries could proliferate and, through friendly competition, flourish.

Chesterton's third novel, *The Man Who Was Thursday* (1908), is appropriately subtitled *A Nightmare.* Like most dreams, it is diffuse, bizarre, and fascinating. Its protagonist, Gabriel Syme, is a poet-turned-detective who has been recruited by a mysterious figure to infiltrate a group of anarchists, each of whom is named after a day of the week. But as Syme—assigned the name Thursday—soon discovers, these convincingly jaded terrorists are all investigators on the same mission: all, that is, but the mountainous, enigmatic Sunday, the kingpin. In the end, after a wonderfully zany chase, the six detectives locate Sunday at his country mansion, where he provides them with exquisite food, drink, and entertainment and admits that he is the dark-shrouded figure who sent them on their weird hunt in the first place.

Like any dream, *The Man Who Was Thursday* is not easily fathomed. But then, neither is life or nature or God—any of which, it can be argued, is symbolized by the whimsical, protean Sunday. In his autobiography, Chesterton insists that he wrote the book in order to demonstrate to the pessimists—the nihilists—of his generation that the world was "not so black" as they would believe. Sunday "appears brutal," notes Chesterton, "but is also cryptically benevolent." Indeed, at the close of the work, Syme announces that he has discovered "the secret of the world." "We," he says, "see everything from behind, and it looks brutal. That is not a tree, but the back of a tree. That is not a cloud, but the back of a cloud. Cannot you see that everything is stooping and hiding a face? If we could only get round in front. . . ."

Eight months after the publication of *The Man Who Was Thursday,* Chesterton's *Orthodoxy* appeared, squarely setting forth the religious beliefs that had been implicit in earlier works. Here, as in much of his fiction, Chesterton argues that the world is too full of foolish ideas competing with other foolish ideas for the attention of a gullible public. Among the prominent idea-sellers are the militant rationalists, the fact-mongers, who relentlessly measure, weigh, and scrutinize the world and solemnly proclaim it wanting. Too, there are the hedonists, the Lawrentians, who seductively counsel fleeing from despair by yielding to instinct and emotion. For Chesterton, reason alone will never illuminate the mysteries of the universe. In fact, true knowledge and raw ecstasy result only when one ceases to regard the world as an enor-

mous machine and sees it as a complex of recurring "miracles" conjured by an exuberant God. The Christian church, Chesterton concludes, is of incalculable value for it patiently reminds man of these truths.

The Ball and the Cross (1909) shows Chesterton freely exhibiting his faith and mocking the spiritual indifference of the modern world. Evan MacIan, a Catholic, and James Turnbull, an atheist, begin an argument that leads to the challenge of a duel—a duel that is constantly interrupted by policemen, judges, journalists, and other good citizens who find it both astonishing and amusing that two grown men should want to fight over an irrelevance like religion. As MacIan and Turnbull try to find a place where they can kill each other in peace, Chesterton presents their lengthy and intense debate, which ends with MacIan getting the last significant words. "Left to itself," he says, "the world"—which he refers to as "the Ball"—"grows wilder than any creed." It "cannot stand by itself," it "staggers" and "will go quite lop-sided" without the cross to hold it "upright."

Chesterton's critics tend to agree that *The Ball and the Cross* is his last major novel, for in such works as *Tales of the Long Bow* and *The Return of Don Quixote,* polemics too easily get the best of plot. And as W. W. Robson suggests, works such as *The Poet and the*

In 1930 Chesterton lectured at the University of Notre Dame on the Victorian age. These cartoons with self-caricatures were published in the December 1930 issue of the student humor magazine, Juggler *(© Dorothy Collins).*

November 1936 advertisement for Chesterton's posthumously published autobiography

Lunatics (1929) and the posthumously published *Paradoxes of Mr. Pond* (1937) "seem often childish" rather than "childlike." Moreover, the works Robson names, as well as *The Man Who Knew Too Much* (1922) and *Four Faultless Felons* (1930), are made up of interlinking short stories and perhaps should not be classified as novels at all.

Chesterton died in the summer of 1936, apparently the victim of an edematous condition aggravated by several years of heart and kidney trouble. As his later autobiographical musings reveal, Chesterton assumed that he would never be considered a novelist of enormous importance; that, as a writer of fiction, he would always remain best known for the long series of Father Brown stories he began with *The Innocence of Father Brown* in 1911—stories he sometimes tossed off in a day or two. Undoubtedly, Father Brown, the unassuming priest who drops typical Chestertonian quips as he solves ghastly transgressions not with Holmes-sharp logic but by "getting inside" the criminal mind, is Chesterton's greatest fictional creation. As Kingsley

Amis suggests, Father Brown stories such as "The Sins of Prince Saradine" and "The Perishing of the Pendragons" also contain "some of the finest, and least regarded, descriptive writing of the century." But then, Chesterton's genius for description is equally evident in the early *Napoleon of Notting Hill*, in which, for example, London is described as being "really herself" at night, "when her lights shine in the dark like innumerable cats, and the outline of the dark houses has the bold simplicity of blue hills." Indeed, though he was as wildly imaginative as any writer of his generation, Chesterton was primarily—as Robson puts it—"fascinated by the romance of the prosaic": a fact which best explains the endurance of his art.

Bibliography:

John Sullivan, *G. K. Chesterton: A Bibliography* (London: University of London Press, 1958).

Biographies:

Maisie Ward, *Gilbert Keith Chesterton* (New York:

Sheed & Ward, 1943);

Dudley Barker, *G. K. Chesterton: A Biography* (New York: Stein & Day, 1973);

Alzina Stone Dale, *The Outline of Sanity: A Life of G. K. Chesterton* (Grand Rapids: Eerdmans, 1982).

References:

Hilaire Belloc, *The Place of Gilbert Chesterton in English Letters* (London & New York: Sheed & Ward, 1940);

Ian Boyd, *The Novels of G. K. Chesterton: A Study in Art and Propaganda* (New York: Barnes & Noble, 1975);

Cecil Chesterton, *Gilbert K. Chesterton: A Criticism* (London & New York: John Lane, 1909);

Laurence J. Clipper, *G. K. Chesterton* (New York: Twayne, 1974);

Christopher Hollis, *Gilbert Keith Chesterton* (London: Longmans, Green, 1954);

Lynette Hunter, *G. K. Chesterton: Explorations in Allegory* (New York: St. Martin's, 1979);

Hugh Kenner, *Paradox in Chesterton* (New York: Sheed & Ward, 1947);

Rufus William Rauch, *A Chesterton Celebration* (Notre Dame: Notre Dame University Press, 1983);

John Sullivan, ed., *G. K. Chesterton: A Centenary Appraisal* (New York: Harper & Row, 1974).

Joseph Conrad

Kingsley Widmer
San Diego State University

BIRTH: Berdyczów (now Berdichev), Russia, 3 December 1857, to Apollo and Ewa Bobrowska Korzeniowski.

MARRIAGE: 24 March 1896 to Jessie George; children: Borys, John Alexander.

DEATH: Bishopsbourne, England, 3 August 1924.

SELECTED BOOKS: *Almayer's Folly: A Story of an Eastern River* (London: Unwin, 1895; New York: Macmillan, 1895);

An Outcast of the Islands (London: Unwin, 1896; New York: Appleton, 1896);

The Children of the Sea: A Tale of the Forecastle (New York: Dodd, Mead, 1897); republished as *The Nigger of the "Narcissus": A Tale of the Sea* (London: Heinemann, 1898);

Tales of Unrest (London: Unwin, 1898; New York: Scribners, 1898);

Lord Jim: A Tale (Edinburgh & London: Blackwood, 1900; New York: Doubleday, McClure, 1900);

The Inheritors: An Extravagant Story, by Conrad and Ford Madox Hueffer (New York: McClure, Phillips, 1901; London: Heinemann, 1901);

Youth: A Narrative, and Two other Stories (Edinburgh & London: Blackwood, 1902; New York: McClure, Phillips, 1903);

Typhoon (New York & London: Putnam's, 1902; London: Heinemann, 1912);

The Nigger of the "Narcissus": Preface (Hythe & Cheriton: Privately printed by J. Lovick, 1902); republished as *Joseph Conrad on The Art of Writing* (Garden City: Doubleday, Page, 1914);

Typhoon and Other Stories (London: Heinemann, 1903);

Romance: A Novel, by Conrad and Hueffer (London: Smith, Elder, 1903; New York: McClure, Phillips, 1904);

Nostromo: A Tale of the Seaboard (London & New York: Harper, 1904; New York: Harper, 1904);

The Mirror of the Sea: Memories and Impressions (London: Methuen, 1906; New York: Harper, 1906);

The Secret Agent: A Simple Tale (London: Methuen, 1907; New York: Harper, 1907);

A Set of Six (London: Methuen, 1908; Garden City: Doubleday, Page, 1915);

Under Western Eyes (London: Methuen, 1911; New York: Harper, 1911);

Some Reminiscences (London: Nash, 1912); republished as *A Personal Record* (New York: Harper, 1912);

'Twixt Land and Sea: Tales (London: Dent, 1912;

New York: Hodder & Stoughton/Doran, 1912);

Chance: A Tale in Two Parts (London: Methuen, 1913; Garden City: Doubleday, Page, 1913);

Within the Tides (London & Toronto: Dent, 1915; Garden City: Doubleday, Page, 1916);

Victory: An Island Tale (Garden City: Doubleday, Page, 1915; London: Methuen, 1915);

One Day More: A Play in One Act (London: Privately printed, 1917; Garden City: Doubleday, Page, 1920);

The Shadow-Line: A Confession (London, Toronto & Paris: Dent, 1917; Garden City: Doubleday, Page, 1917);

The Arrow of Gold: A Story between two Notes (Garden City: Doubleday, Page, 1919; London: Unwin, 1919);

The Rescue: A Romance of the Shallows (Garden City: Doubleday, Page, 1920; London, Toronto & Paris: Dent, 1920);

Notes òn Life and Letters (London & Toronto: Dent, 1921; Garden City: Doubleday, Page, 1921);

The Secret Agent: Drama in Four Acts (Canterbury: Privately printed by H. J. Goulden, 1921);

The Rover (Garden City: Doubleday, Page, 1923; London: Unwin, 1923);

Laughing Anne: A Play (London: Bookman's Journal Office, 1923);

The Nature of a Crime, by Conrad and Ford Madox Ford (London: Duckworth, 1924; New York: Doubleday, Page, 1924);

Suspense: A Napoleonic Novel (Garden City: Doubleday, Page, 1925; London & Toronto: Dent, 1925);

Tales of Hearsay (London: Unwin, 1925; Garden City: Doubleday, Page, 1925);

Last Essays (London & Toronto: Dent, 1926; Garden City: Doubleday, Page, 1926).

Collections: *The Works of Joseph Conrad,* The Uniform Edition, 22 volumes (London: Dent, 1923-1928); reprinted and enlarged, 26 volumes (London: Dent, 1946-1955);

Collected Works of Joseph Conrad, The Memorial Edition, 21 volumes (Garden City: Doubleday, Page, 1925).

Joseph Conrad is now widely accepted as one of the modernist masters of serious narrative fiction. Historically placed, he is a major figure in the transition from Victorian fiction to the more perplexed forms and values of twentieth-century literature. Now, unlike in his lifetime, he is one of the most read British novelists of his period. However, his twenty volumes of novels and stories vary

Beinecke Library, Yale University

greatly in quality and interest. Since he was primarily a commercial storyteller aiming at the popular market, only a limited part of his work will bear much serious response and intellectual consideration. A handful of fictions, such as "Heart of Darkness," *Nostromo,* "The Secret Sharer," and *The Secret Agent,* are generally acknowledged to be outstanding. But since there is disagreement about some of the others, and since the larger context of his works might be illuminating, it may be useful to survey most of his fiction.

Conrad's life, explored in a spate of recent biographies, is also distinctive for its drastic fracturing. Several times exiled, with major changes of scene, nationality, and language, he seems to have suffered from a powerful sense of loss and alienation. This may have encouraged his emphatic pessimistic skepticism. Though writing in a time and culture often characterized as optimistic and affirmative, Conrad displays senses of defeat shading into a cosmic malignancy and an anxiously heavy ideological conservativism. With his exilic sense of foreignness—including the English he wrote in, learned relatively late in life (after Polish, German, and French)—he inclined to elaborately self-conscious writing and tendentious moralizing. A pervasive sense of anxiety about his roles, and other psychological involutions relating to considerable physical illness and repeated periods of great depression, may have further encouraged this elaborateness of manner and a rather un-British ideological insistence. Yet seeking popular acceptance in a foreign land and language, Conrad yoked ornate narrative methods with sentimental tales and lush descriptive rhetoric with harshly narrow moral reflections. The resulting ideological melodramas have had considerable influence on major later novelists, such as Graham Greene and William Faulkner. Conrad's exotic scenes, stereotyped romantic figures, heavily adjectival poetic rhetoric, and moralistic male codes appear to have greatly influenced many other writers. There is considerable disagreement about the value of Conrad's rhetorical exoticism and pyrrhonistic conservativism.

Born Józef Teodor Konrad Korzeniowski, Conrad was the only child of ardent Polish nationalists in the mid-nineteenth-century Russian empire. His parents were of impoverished landed-gentry background and romantic outlook. Besides rather unsuccessfully managing other people's estates, his father was a literary man (a minor conventional poet and translator). Conrad's parents were harshly exiled to Northern Russia in May 1862 for rebellious political activities preliminary to the Polish nationalist uprising of 1863. His mother died when he was seven, his father when he was eleven. Exile and the related orphaning appear to have had traumatic effects on the young Conrad.

Supported and raised by various relatives (most important, by a maternal uncle, Tadeusz Bobrowski, a prosperous lawyer who nagged his nephew but also indulged him and continued to provide financial aid until Conrad was in his thirties), he had a sickly childhood and irregular schooling in Russian exile, then in Polish Russia, and then in the Polish area of Austria. Information on Conrad's childhood and youth is limited—unlike many authors he never wrote directly about his early years. He did report that, in spite of sporadic schooling, he was a voracious reader of romantic novels and adventure accounts. In mid-adolescence, he carried his traumatic legacy, which apparently included considerable sexual and other emotional repression as well as orphaning and other displacement, even further into self-chosen exile.

Conrad had early developed a romantic

yearning to go to sea, though he had no firsthand knowledge of sea life. In September 1874, when he was sixteen, with his uncle's help he moved to Marseilles, France, which became his home for nearly four years. From there, he gained work experience on sailing ships, including voyages to the West Indies as an apprentice and steward. He may also have engaged in smuggling operations, perhaps transporting weapons from France to Spain for the Spanish Carlists (an unsuccessful right-wing monarchical restoration conspiracy). He may also have become involved in a romance with an older woman in the Carlist movement. While the evidence is uncertain, he apparently failed in several of these affairs, desperately lost more of his uncle's money gambling at Monte Carlo, and attempted suicide. (Suicide was to become a recurrent crux in Conrad's fictions.)

Having soon recovered from the bullet wound in his chest and having been financially rescued by his uncle, he started his maritime career over again, leaving France for England and shipping out in 1879 as an ordinary seaman on a British steamer. In the following years he acquired English (though he always retained a heavy accent), worked on various British sailing ships, especially in the Far East, and with considerable ambition but some difficulty passed various maritime officers' examinations,

Konrad Korzeniowski, 1874 (photo by W. Rzewuski; Beinecke Library, Yale University)

culminating in a Master's Certificate in the British Merchant Service in November 1886. He had become a naturalized British citizen the previous August. The romantic Polish exile appeared to have become before the age of thirty a solid Britisher with a settled traditional vocation.

But Captain Conrad was not really very successful in the merchant marine: he had only one small regular command (in 1888), spent periods without a berth and briefly tried his hand at river steamboat captaining in the Congo, continued to live beyond his salary (with his uncle's help), suffered repeated physical and temperamental difficulties in his vocation, and worked in a dying industry—sailing ships. While his sea experiences and his travels in exotic foreign scenes provided much of the material for his later writing and fame, and while the role of sea captain was partly appropriate for one identifying with exile and hierarchy, the life of a minor maritime officer was not steady enough, remunerative enough, and gentlemanly enough. (Throughout his life, Conrad, from a

Konrad Korzeniowski in Marienbad, 1883 (photo by Otto Bielefeldt; National Library, Warsaw)

proud gentry background, was rather snobbish, and in appearance and manner rather a dandy.) His later accounts of sailing ships make clear that in spite of his efforts at romantic and moral exaltation of a sea career it was a boring, lonely, fearful, and harsh way of life. After nearly twenty maritime years, when he was in his late thirties, he entered another career—as an English commercial writer of fiction.

Conrad's efforts to be a British novelist were arduous and anxious. He was writing in a language not learned until he was in his twenties. He chose not just to write of his experiences and concerns but to make a commercial career as an English storyteller. Vehemently not a bohemian, he saw the writing career as a settled and orderly way of life, in contrast to his maritime career. He married Jessie George, a pleasantly dull and submissive younger woman, in 1896 and settled into conventional British middle-class family life, eventually with two sons born in 1898 and 1906. For many years he was burdened with debts, with physical and psychological illnesses, and with considerable anguish over writing. But with the aid of several outstanding English editors, including Edward Garnett and Ford Madox Hueffer (who later changed his surname to Ford), he established himself not only as an exotic novelist and a moderately popular magazine storywriter but as a gentlemanly artist, friend of Henry James, R. B. Cunninghame-Graham, H. G. Wells, and other well-known contemporaries. In his last years (from 1913 until his death) he finally had a considerable commercial success and a worldwide reputation. After a Polish childhood and youth, partly in exile, then some years as a French sailor and adventurer, and then after spending the larger part of two decades as a British merchant mariner, Conrad had successfully achieved a career as a famous British writer. It may be viewed as a striking Victorian-Edwardian success story.

He started out by writing exotic romances, a highly commercial-popular form of late-nineteenth-century literature—many of his sources appear to be French—and at times brought rather more moral seriousness to it than Kipling, Stevenson, and other romancers writing in English during the period. His three linked novels placed in Malaya—*Almayer's Folly* (1895), *An Outcast of the Islands* (1896), and *The Rescue* (1920; begun in 1896, partly written in later years)—fancifully expand upon some episodes and characters drawn from his maritime experiences, and stories he heard, around Malayan commercial outposts. The first was slowly started in the 1880s when Conrad was still a

First page of the manuscript for Conrad's first book (Anderson Galleries, sale 1768, 12-14 November 1923)

merchant-marine officer. The lushness of the exotic materials is heightened by an often ornate descriptive style, strong in portentous atmospheric detailing. This suggests a Westerner's anxieties with the threatening tropical jungles and the alien native psyches, as well as the moral ambiguities of colonialism.

Though Conrad's later writing became more disciplined and polished in manner, it continued some of the oddity of style, especially a high-flown rhetoric of considerable redundancy (and perhaps an underlying Polish and French syntax). The heightening provided a persisting tone of ominousness, mysteriousness, and ironic reflectiveness, which partly distinguishes some of Conrad's fiction from simpler commercial exoticism. There is usually an anxious moralist in his intense undergrowth.

The lush rhetoric seems appropriate to the broad theme of the Malayan fictions: the destructiveness of debased romantic idealism in weak colonialist characters in an alien environment. The background pattern for the three early novels includes the ambitious plans of a paternalistic European trader, Tom Lingard, who aims at the restoration of a native kingdom and great colonial wealth. The awkwardly ordered *Almayer's Folly* is the first novel finished, but it describes episodes late in the chronology of political manipulations and wars

Jessie George, 1896 (courtesy of Borys Conrad)

Joseph Conrad, 1896 (Beinecke Library, Yale University)

among the Malayans, Arab traders, jungle tribes, and European colonialists. The trading station that gives the novel its title belongs to Almayer, Lingard's ambitious, but weak and corrupt, protégé. Married to a native woman (who reverts to local allegiances), he sentimentally adores his grown daughter. His deceitful treatment of Lingard and others and his incompetent and ill-fated greed direct the melodramatic actions in which he loses his daughter to a native leader (the rhetorical erotic scenes show Conrad at his weakest), his defeat in the complicated maneuvers of political control and commercial exploitation, and finally the loss of his despairing life. Romantic fantasies, such as Al-

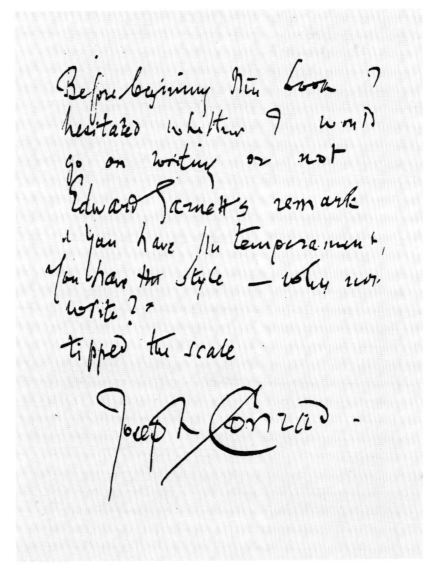

Inscription in a copy of the first edition of An Outcast of the Islands *(American Art Association, 28 April 1927)*

mayer's, ending in weakness, failure, and despair, are nuclear Conradian fictional experiences.

An Outcast of the Islands, somewhat more clearly ordered, concerns earlier periods of this colonial history. Willems, another vain and corrupted European weakling, betrays his patron Lingard, becomes an outcast, and finally is killed by his native mistress (proper reward in the nineteenth-century-European perspective for having gone "native"). *The Rescue,* completed only after several decades and marked by the less energetic handling of the late Conrad, focuses on yet earlier episodes of the colonial history. The paternalistic Lingard, a figure of more gentlemanly stature than Almayer and Willems, goes down to defeat because of his idealistic megalomania for commercial-political power. He was the victim of a "fixed idea"—a favorite phrase of Conrad's—which results in the loss of reality and in pathetic retribution. Perhaps the main interest in these early fictions, besides the exoticism, rests in the curious combination of the conventions of popular romance and an antiromantic, pessimistic analysis of moral corruption, which was to characterize many of Conrad's novels.

As a writer with commercial ambitions, Conrad early on eagerly sought the publication of his stories in magazines which paid better proportionately than the publication of novels. Several of the first five of his shorter fictions, later collected as *Tales of Unrest* (1898), were simply variations on the

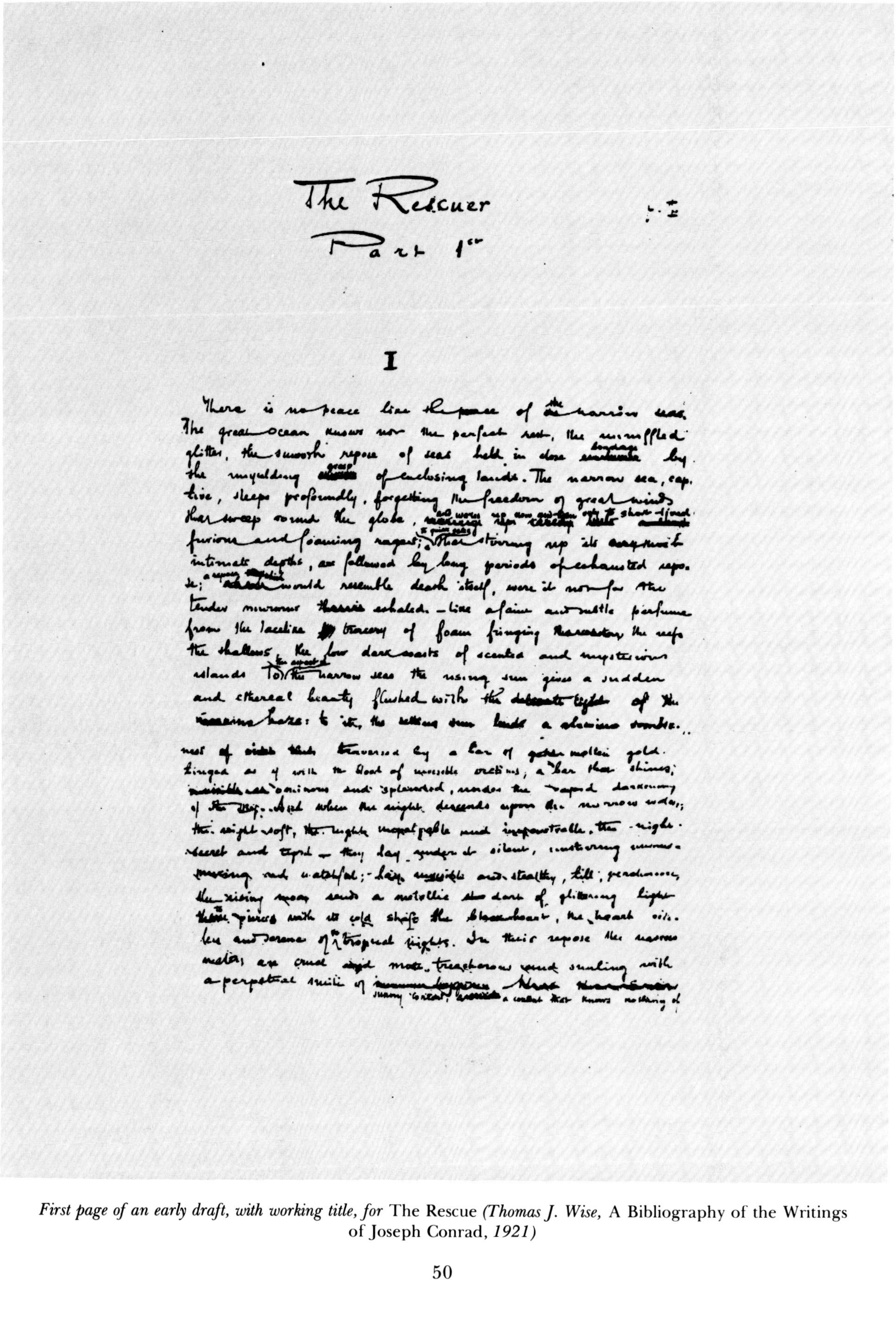

The Rescuer
Part 1st

I

[handwritten manuscript text]

First page of an early draft, with working title, for The Rescue *(Thomas J. Wise,* A Bibliography of the Writings of Joseph Conrad, *1921)*

Inscription in a copy of the first edition of Tales of Unrest *(American Art Association, 28 April 1927)*

Far East materials of the early novels. "The Lagoon" (1897) rather awkwardly and unbelievably has a Malayan tell a European of his stealing a beloved but forbidden woman with the loyal help of his brother. But while the three are being pursued, and for motives which are not altogether clear, he abandons his brother and makes his escape with the woman. His brother is killed. During the telling of this story to the European, the beloved woman is reportedly dying of an illness. The main thrust of the skittishly exotic tale seems to be that bitter guilt is the final dark product of romantic "illusions."

The longer "Karain: A Memory" (1897) more elaborately uses the distancing narrative frame characteristic of many of Conrad's tales. The story-within-a-story technique has been one of Conrad's most influential bequests to later writers. In having a narrator tell a tale at one or more removes from the action, a more complex view is often suggested. Besides the substance of the tale, the reader sees the narrator's view of, and reflections on, the events. Here a somewhat perplexed European attempts to explain the mysterious native actions. The evidence also suggests that Conrad saw multiple narration as a "distancing" device to help him avoid what would otherwise be painfully intense subjectivity and to provide ambivalent moral separation from the action. In "Karain: A Memory" a European trader retrospectively tells the story of a Malayan native ruler who had become obsessed with his best friend's sister, who had violated native taboos and run away with a European. After Karain and his friend had vengefully pursued the couple for many months, Karain finally kills his friend instead of the lovers, apparently out of some obscure romanticism. Guiltily haunted for many years by the ghost of his friend, he becomes increasingly deranged until his burden is exorcised by a totem made up by some sympathetically condescending Englishmen. Yet the English narrator finally reflects that the story, in spite of its oddity, has a deeper reality (a greater passion?) than the ordinary English scene he is now in. Such garrulous ambivalence in the antiromantic telling of romantic melodrama becomes essential Conradianism.

While the materials and narrative mode of Conrad seem set in these early fictions, he did experiment with some varying subject matter. The crudely overwritten "The Idiots" (1896), produced during his honeymoon in Brittany (as biographers have psychologically made much of), makes a macabrely violent tale of a French peasant couple who have produced four idiots. In an action quite unprepared for in the story, the wife kills the husband during sex in order to stop producing yet more idiots. Then in a guilty frenzy she destroys herself. Polar in subject matter yet parallel in the theme of domestic hatred is the novella "The Return." The characters, unusual in Conrad, consist of a contemporary upper-class London husband and wife. The wife starts to run off with a literary man but quickly returns to her husband. Conrad's early analysis of that stolidly obtuse stock gentleman of English society shows sardonic perceptivity, emphasizing the insularity, rigidity, and smugness. But the story gets muddled midway with absurd domestic dialogue, erratic shifts in point of view, and Conrad's pervasive inability to present a believable woman. The final reversal has the husband leaving the wife, supposedly never to return. Essentially, the story argues that the upper class, of both sexes, lacks loving faithfulness. The hunger for "fidelity" persists through all of orphaned-and-exiled Conrad's writings, though usually in the maritime and colonial materials in which he seems to have felt greater assurance and in which he was rather entrapped by his commercial writing role.

Clearly the best, and best known, of the early stories is the satiric "An Outpost of Progress" (1897). Here Conrad makes his first fictional use of

the brief period he spent in the Belgian Congo nearly a decade earlier. Perhaps because of his great anger at what he saw there, this story shows little moral ambivalence. With harsh irony, Conrad directly recounts the disintegration of two lower-middle-class European incompetents during a few months at an isolated jungle trading post. They let their native workers be enslaved in exchange for ivory, and they lose most connection with their surroundings. In a petty rage over precedence, culminating in a fight over some sugar when supplies run low, one murders the other and then, a bit improbably, guiltily commits suicide by hanging himself on the cross marker on the grave of the previous manager. The mocking tone savages not only the Great Civilizing Company's colonial exploitation and its hypocritical pretenses at progress but the representative weak fools of modern mass society.

Committed to prolific writing, Conrad was extending the range of his subject matter. He drew on his job in 1884 as second mate on the British sailing ship *Narcissus,* and on some related experiences, for his third published novel, *The Nigger of the "Narcissus,"* first published as *The Children of the Sea* in 1897. This is the work that launched his reputation as a noted writer about the sea. Favorably commented upon by literary contemporaries, it also brought him some artistic recognition. While it is better written, more stylistically disciplined, than the Malayan novels, it is hardly the "masterpiece" that some later critics have called it, marred as it is by a confused narration and irascible bigotries. The telling gets muddled with a mixture of detached omniscience and reminiscence by an unidentified crew member, who grossly identifies with the officers and simplemindedly exalts them. Much of the treatment of the crew alternates between contempt for their overwhelmingly "childish" ways (and for any touches of dissidence), and sentimentalization of their endurance. Their stoicism is mystifyingly ennobled in Old Singleton, a seaman for fifty years, powerful, inchoate, and stupid, who stays at the helm for thirty hours during a devastating storm. His spare revelations consist of stock superstitions and, ultimately, a "chilling . . . resignation" to endless work, obedience, brutalization, and death. The narrative view insists that such are about all that the ordinary humans can plausibly expect.

Fortunately for the narrative, the old royalist sea peasant plays only a small role, compared with the storm and other troublemakers. Nearly capsized in a gale on the run from Bombay to London, the *Narcissus* luckily survives in spite of apparently

Inscription in a copy of the first English edition of The Nigger of the "Narcissus" *(American Art Association, 28 April 1927)*

faulty design, an overconfident and rigid captain, and a terrified crew. The lengthily developed storm scene is often praised for its "realism" when what is really meant is its intensity. Some of the scene is quite powerful. The lavish visualization of the storm-wrecked ship depends less on verisimilitude than on the nearly surreal play upon the grotesque. Comic-horrific scenes include the descriptions of the frenzied fraternal rescuing of the dying black, which creates solidarity, and the lunatic preaching of the evangelical cook, which provides absurdity. The intense descriptions of the crew's suffering suggest a nearly hysterical vision of human misery. This vision achieves an absurdist poetry with the "acrid savor of existence" in a hostile universe.

The central totemic figure of the "nigger"—un-able-bodied seaman James Wait, a West Indian black—is partly presented in a racist rhetoric which may now appear less nasty than quaint: his "pathetic and brutal" face has "the tragic, the mysterious, the repulsive mask of a nigger's soul." In Conrad's fascinated repulsion (he almost always presented alien ethnic types as ominously mysterious), the black himself, as well as much of the crew, is uncertain if he is resentfully shamming illness or really dying. He serves as the love-hate image of the crew's own emotional "extremity." We are told that their identification with him becomes the "sentimental lie" which provides the maintaining "common bond" under extreme duress. This childish transcendentalism energizes their common endurance, producing what Conrad elsewhere describes as his ultimate simple value of "fidelity."

In one episode, responding to a miscalculated insult to Wait by the captain, the crew nearly mutinies, but their rebellion peters out under coolly harsh authority because, the reader is told, they have confused their political revolt against bad treatment with their symbolic revolt against death. In other episodes, the crew's sympathetic bond with the black man makes them, as one of Conrad's· rhetorical flights has it, "highly humanized, tender, complex," which is also to be "excessively decadent." In Conrad's ideology, the miserable laborers in the world must remain miserable and laboring, aspiring only to a stupidly stoical manliness, like Old Singleton.

The unstoical black man finally dies and is buried at sea. Even his corpse seems to resist burial for a moment—an apt touch. The poignant but futile rebellion against death is also exploited by the tale's other troublemaker, Donkin, a complaining cockney slacker. Conrad disproportionately loads the descriptions of him with epithets: he is ugly, lazy, whining, dishonest, parasitic, violent, and mutinous. He even robs the black man as the latter is dying. Early on, he is also set up as an ideological strawman, defined (but not shown) as representative "pet of philanthropists and self-seeking landlubbers." And in the penultimate paragraph he is described as one "who never did a decent day's work in his life" but now "no doubt earns his living by discoursing with filthy eloquence upon the right of labor to live." In this view, laborers, including those whom Conrad contemptuously called the "children of the sea," had the right to live, barely and submissively, but they should be quiet about it. "Pity," as we are told here (and elsewhere in Conrad), is socially dangerous. Joseph Conrad undoubtedly long held this view, though just possibly he is emphasizing it here to accord with the bigotries of the middle-class British readers of his time.

In spite of the contemptuously overloaded denigration of Donkin, which constitutes a crude, ad hominem political polemic of Conrad's, the character does stand for demands for decency and justice. At one point, for example, he incites one of the seamen to suggest that the crew should eat as well as the officers—a practice now widely accepted in Western maritime services. Conrad did seem to be somewhat aware of a moral dilemma: when the system is vicious, humanizing claims tend to

undermine "the unspoken loyalty that knits together a ship's company" in the only solidarity that keeps a drastically arbitrary and exploitative system going in a malign cosmos. So false and precarious is the shipboard order that any complaint—such as the one about food—or any other dissidence must be treated as outrageous blasphemy. Conrad, a drastically pessimistic ideologue, seems to hold that misery for most is so inevitable that it can only be quietly endured, at its best achieving a heroic submission, and not much ameliorated or changed. Otherwise, the whole top-manipulated illusionary fidelity will collapse, sinking storm-wracked ship and the cosmically ill-fated human community.

It is this insistent heightening of the issue, this surreal ideological pressuring of the rhetoric and the scene, which produces the enlarged anxiety and exceptional intensity of some of Conrad's sea writings. However, direct ideologizing is skittishly avoided in the next novella, "Youth" (1898), which was also based on Conrad's earlier maritime experience. Here Conrad first employed part of a perspective and narrative device for somewhat distancing the anxiety and pessimism, the garrulous retrospective narrator Captain Marlow, who was to be employed as a persona of the author in novel after novella for many years.

In "Youth" Captain Marlow gives, with nostalgic high spirits, a generation-later account of his first berth as a second mate at twenty. His ill-fated sailing bark, on a coal run from London to Bangkok, is rammed at the start. Although it is repaired, it repeatedly leaks and must be returned for more repairs. Then it is storm-beaten, then catches fire, and then explodes and sinks in the Indian Ocean. The young officer's first command is of a small lifeboat. In the story's odd disproportion, the fear, pain, frustration, and exhaustion of a multiple ill-fated voyage, ending with an unsympathetic shore society, is treated as a genial initiation rite. The disparity between the harsh events and Marlow's burbling tone in recounting them produces an emphasis upon the absurd. The far-distancing narration allows amoral bemusement at the futility and produces a work of grotesquerie.

To follow the sequence of sea tales is to see the varied uses Conrad made of the limited set of incongruities of his maritime experiences. He explored artistic variations on a few themes. The bumbling captain in "Youth" was earnestly foolish. The bumbler captain in the longish novella *Typhoon* (1902) comes out heroic, in spite of himself. Captain MacWhirr, master of a small steamship trading the China coast, is a totally dutiful creature of very limited intelligence, imagination, and responsiveness—"ignorant of life to the last, without ever having been made to see all it may contain of perfidy, of violence, and of terror." But his very lack of sympathy and insight, his very literalism, is also his virtue. Unlike his second mate, who goes out of his mind in the typhoon, and unlike his responsive first mate, whose imagination and despairing sensitivity make him ineffective in the storm, the captain stolidly endures the worst, which he perhaps could have avoided. His stupidity and literalism, and his vague "sense of the fitness of things," ironically work out to be a fundamental practicality and decency. The ship survives. Furthermore, the two hundred Chinese indentured workers, carried in the hold and brutally beaten around in the storm, are treated with a crude approximate justice in dividing up their jumbled possessions because of the captain's dutiful simplicity. Conrad, apparently to maintain his underplaying of the emotional intensity of the material, employs displaced descriptions (pieces of letters, logs, and comments by other people) in order to praise the captain's stupid literalism and hard Protestant virtues. By background and temperament, Conrad was not such a person, but he was making—not without some irony—a paean to the traditional unemotional English character.

In such an intriguing performance as *Typhoon* we might recognize Joseph Conrad as countering his own much more anxiously emotional responses, a self-reversal of his own romanticism, which in his life took the form of the romantic Polish exile's becoming an imitation English gentleman. The duality takes more subtle form in Conrad's most famous maritime tale, the later novella "The Secret Sharer" (1910). Drawing on his experience in the 1880s of suddenly being given an emergency first command of a strange ship in an Eastern port, Conrad, in an unusual form for him, has his first-person narrator tell his own tale rather than musing over the actions and motivations of others in a story that is not preceded by a frame narrative. The emotional split within the young captain becomes the subject of the story by way of the doppleganger device and theme. The "secret self" takes form as the captain's double, a look-alike fugitive first mate the captain takes on board his first night, secretes with endless anxiety, and finally aids in flight. At the level of conventional characterization, the captain's immediate and full identification with the criminal mate—though they are of the same age and physique, social class, maritime school, and of similar experience—is inexplicable. And it remains so,

leaving the story fundamentally ambiguous, for Leggatt, the mate with whom the earnest captain identifies to an extreme degree, is a murderer. In a rage, though with some provocation in a storm, Leggatt killed a seaman under his command. The murderer shows no remorse for his action, and weeks later he still thinks of his victim as a "snarling cur" who deserved to die. The captain immediately agrees with this attitude. Thus his aid to the murdering mate is neither justice nor charity but secret identification, which he does not fully understand. The captain's narration emphasizes his immediate anxieties but does not treat the deeper sources of his identification, his near mergence with the fugitive. Suggestively, the young captain rejects sea authority (the fugitive's captain) and law and order (the fugitive's return for trial) as responses for what is identified as the Cain-cursed dark side of the self.

The "secret self" of Conrad's account need not be allegorized as the Freudian id or the Christian demon—as some critics would have it—since the author maintains the surface verisimilitude of the fiction. To stay with Conrad's issue: for a young man to achieve his own identity—"that ideal conception of one's own personality every man sets up for himself secretly," as the captain announced early in the story—he must dispose of the dark secret self without either total repression or total mergence. Yet the anxious captain must avoid probing the deeper sources of his secret identification with the violent mate. What the captain does is aid the fugitive to escape by a dangerous testing of himself, drifting his becalmed sailing ship close to a desolate rocky island under the somewhat plausible guise of picking up the off-land breeze. The testing of his command, it should be noted, is made quite drastic: as the new captain, he knows little of the ship, the officers, the crew, and the place, and he outrageously risks the lives of all. Furthermore, on a dark night he goes much closer to the rocks than needed (the fugitive is an expert swimmer who did a greater distance originally to arrive at the captain's ship). By a mixture of daring and luck, the young captain succeeds in dropping the fugitive and getting the ship underway. The captain then feels he has achieved a sense of mastery, overcome some hidden "shadow" on himself, and arrived at "the perfect communion" of his first command, and his ideal fantasy of himself. But the final words of the story are his for his fugitive "second self," outcast "to take his punishment: a free man, a proud swimmer striking out for a new destiny." The curious mergence of freedom and punishment, and of new destiny as fugitive outcastness, may give the

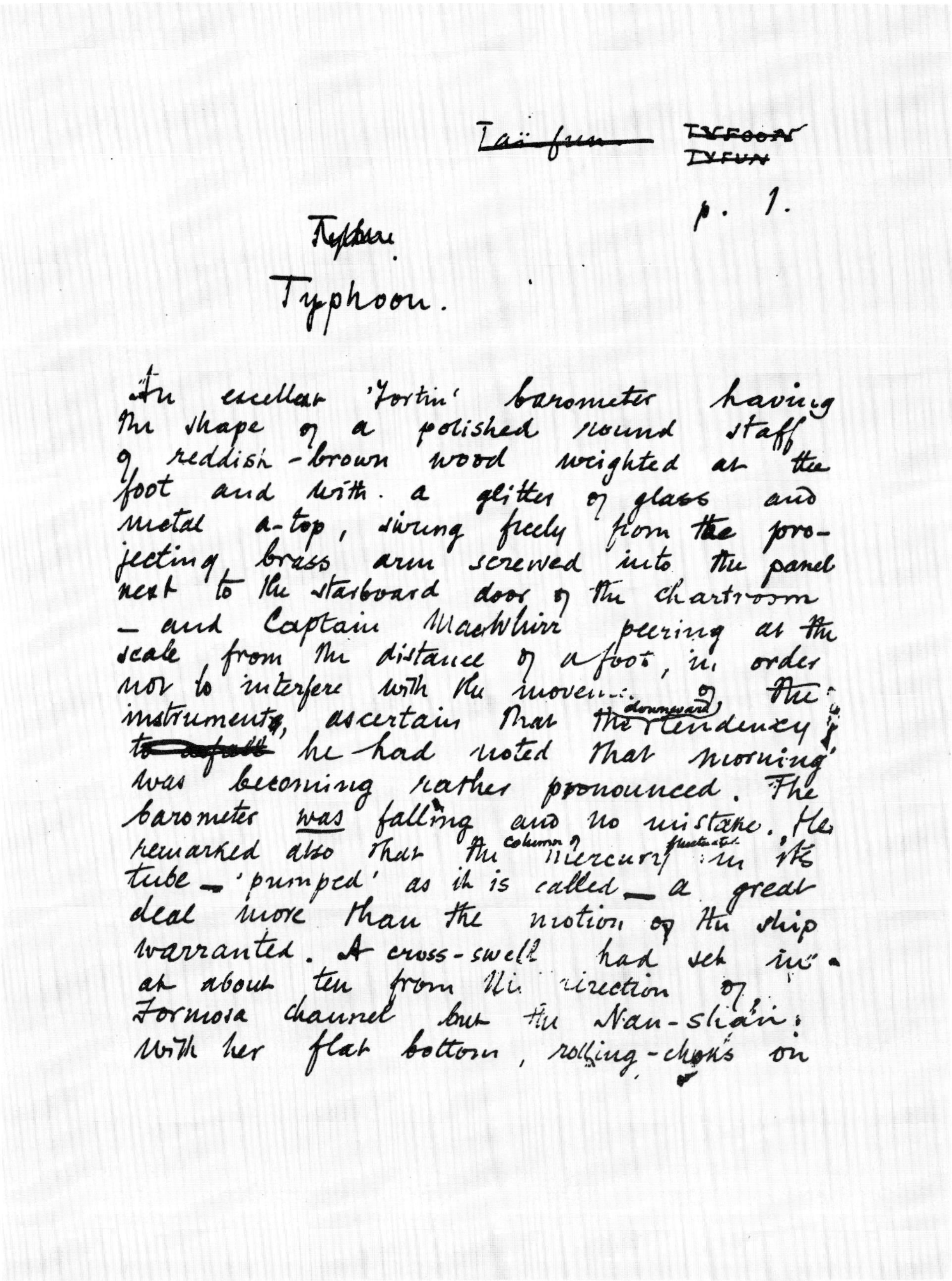

~~Taï-fun~~ ~~TYFOON~~
~~TYFUN~~
p. 1.
~~Typhoon~~.
Typhoon.
An excellent 'Fortin' barometer having the shape of a polished round staff of reddish-brown wood weighted at the foot and with a glitter of glass and metal a-top, swung freely from the projecting brass arm screwed into the panel next to the starboard door of the chartroom — and Captain MacWhirr peering at the scale from the distance of a foot, in order not to interfere with the movements of the instrument, ascertain that the downward tendency ~~to a fall~~ he had noted that morning was becoming rather pronounced. The barometer was falling and no mistake. He remarked also that the column of mercury fluctuated in its tube — 'pumped' as it is called — a great deal more than the motion of the ship warranted. A cross-swell had set in at about ten from the direction of Formosa channel but the Nan-shan, with her flat bottom, rolling-chocks on

First page of the manuscript for Conrad's 1902 novella (Anderson Galleries, sale 1768, 12-14 November 1923)

reader the deepest tropes for Conrad's perplexed views in this somewhat overwrought tale around obscure ambivalences about playing authority figure.

In the pattern of Conrad's fictions and ideology, the antimoral story "The Secret Sharer" is a breakthrough to the romanticism that Conrad usually attacks. He could not often maintain the artistry of the split psyche, the balancing of the violent fugitive and the young master making the desperation gamble. When in the late novel *The Shadow-Line* (1917) he attempts to repeat the initiatory "first command" experience, including some of the same metaphors, the same scene (the ship becalmed off Koh-ring in the Java Sea), and the same testing, it loses the narrative immediacy and precariously balanced doubleness in a mixture of the skittish and the sentimental. Introduced with an elaborately redundant jocularity, the story becomes another exercise in endurance in which the young captain must deal with a becalmed ship, and, this time, a sick crew as well. In a tale that is dialectically as well as stylistically flat, the only double for this captain consists of the dead master he has replaced, a man who went mad in his final days and disposed of the needed shipboard medicine. Conrad dallies a bit with the ex-captain—the sick mate is obsessed with the sense of a ghost—but supernaturalism is essentially uncongenial to Conrad and the motif is dropped. The only aid on the ship for the young captain is a heroically submissive invalid, Ransome, a sailor with a bad heart. He saves the ship. But since he is only mawkishly presented, that service is not very interesting. What strength the tale has is (as in *Typhoon*) the vivid descriptions of the malignant weather, but the heavily jocular opening, the belabored theme of endurance, the sentimental handling of character, and a very paltry sense of what constitutes maritime maturity make the whole slight stuff.

Conrad several times commented that he felt entrapped in the public expectations of him as a producer of sea tales. His best work usually does lie elsewhere. To move back to chronological sequence: after "Youth" Conrad wrote what is now his most famous novella, "Heart of Darkness" (1899). In 1890 Conrad had spent a few months under contract to captain a river steamer in what was then the relatively new and brutally exploited Belgian colony of the Congo. He commanded one for only a few days, after lengthy travel in central Africa, and in serious illness and disgust invalided out and returned to Europe. He briefly drew on the materials in "An Outpost of Progress," then several years later made more complex use of the scene in "Heart of Darkness," with the retrospective narration of his recurrent persona Captain Marlow. It has been suggested that some of the special intensity of the story derives from Conrad's own near-death in the Congo, an experience given to Marlow. Certainly Conrad's moral rage at what he saw of colonialism in Africa also informs the novella.

But the thrust of the tale is yet wider. A shadowy narrator describes Captain Marlow's telling the story, some years after the events, to four solid citizens on a pleasure yawl in the Thames estuary one evening. As darkness closes in, multiple parallels are suggested: Congo and Thames, Belgian and British colonialism—indeed, European imperialistic history back to the time when Roman legions brutally conquered primitive Britain which has, like "darkest Africa," also "been one of the dark places of the earth." There are further elliptical ironies in a damning account of imperialism being told to its representative London profiteers (a corporate director, etc.). Marlow grants partial exemption of the British colonial exploitation to the usual brutality because of British "devotion to efficiency." Otherwise colonialism is mostly "robbery with violence" of those "who have a different complexion or slightly flatter noses," and, says Marlow, the viciousness of colonization of other peoples can be redeemed only by an unselfish dedication to a larger "idea." However, the rest of the story undercuts that pious hope by shadowing forth a large darkness at the heart of things.

Throughout Marlow's account of his obtaining the Congo job through family connections in the "whited sepulchre" capital city where the company has its headquarters reverberates the hypocrisy of the "noble cause" and the ominousness of the "philanthropic pretense" disguising the exploitation. Conrad's play upon metaphoric and atmospheric effects in this scene are famous. The brutal absurdity—"the merry dance of death and trade"—also appears in striking images on Marlow's sea trip to Africa and then the journey inland, where not only crazy inefficiency but "rapacious and pitiless folly" get annotated with descriptions of chained, dying, and murdered natives. The colonialists, high and low, provide satiric images of callous exploiters and apathetically demoralized brutes. An odd partial exception is a company chief accountant, meticulously starched and turned out in the jungle like a "hairdresser's dummy." His books are in "apple-pie order." While he may maintain efficiency and a moral image of keeping up appearances, he is cruelly indifferent to sick

87.

More than justice! I rang the bell
before a door on the first floor and
while I waited he seemed to stare
at me out of the polished panel, stare
with that wide and immense stare
embracing, condemning, loathing all the universe — I seemed
to hear the whispered cry "Oh! the horror!"

The dusk was falling. I waited had
to wait in a lofty drawing room with
three long windows from floor to ceiling that
were like three luminous and
be-draped columns. The bent gilt
legs and backs of the furniture shone
in indistinct curves. The tall white marble
mantelpiece fixture fire place had
a cold and heavy whiteness. A
grand piano stood massively in a
corner with dark gleams on the flat surfaces like a
sombre and polished sarcophagus. A
door high door opened — closed. I rose.

She came forward in the dusk
all in black with a pale head, floating
towards me in the dusk. She was in mourning. It
was more than a year since his death.

whites as well as dying natives. But he is the first to inform Marlow of a larger possibility, of Kurtz, a "remarkable" man and unusually successful trader far up the river. Through gradual, though ambiguous, disclosures to Marlow, Kurtz comes to represent some larger conception of value, even "pity, and science, and progress," thus some positive purpose beyond brutal greed. A man "with moral ideas of some sort," sent out by a reforming group, Kurtz becomes the focus of Marlow's Congo quest, his hope for some redeeming "idea" in the moral darkness of what he sees as the colonial "nightmare."

The conception of Kurtz, the source evidence suggests, is largely a product of Conrad's moral imagination. Moral indignation certainly dominates the delineation of most of the other Europeans, who are sarcastically described as fraudulent "pilgrims" and "sordid buchaneers." To counter any sense of romantic adventurism, for example, Conrad epitomizes one typical enterprise, the Eldorado Exploring Expedition, as "reckless without hardihood, greedy without audacity, and cruel without courage." Marlow sardonically surveys such efforts while he is delayed by the broken-down steamboat, the general inefficiency, and the machinations of the jealously mediocre manager and the others plotting in "imbecile rapacity." Captain Marlow maintains some sense of values, Conrad insists, only by his work. The effort is presented as not just dutiful repair of the boat but as an article of larger faith in the personal redemption of disciplined labor. The only positively described Europeans are the few mechanics. Later, work is linked to a "deliberate belief" which commands reality and resists the reversion to savagery. Work becomes a larger dedication, as with the primitive native whom Marlow has trained to religious devotion to the steamboat's boiler. Another instance of the moral penumbra of "efficiency" cited in the early part of the story comes with Marlow's discovery of a carefully annotated handbook on seamanship, belonging to a romantic wandering trader. This book illustrates, Marlow says, "an honest concern for the right way of going to work" (regardless of however irrelevant in the middle of the jungle), and thus an implicit moral ordering "luminous with another than a professional light." Whether this exalted work ethic can adequately counter the overwhelming evil of the exploitative order must remain doubtful, but Conrad does make it the clearest moral affirmation of the tale.

In this context, Marlow's fascination with and affirmation of Kurtz must remain ambiguous. Kurtz, Marlow insists, has been corrupted by his solitude from "civilization" and lost the absolutely essential "restraints" that keep one human, and which Marlow finds even in the cannibals. Kurtz's charismatic qualities, usually attributed to a powerful rhetoric (little heard by the reader, as many critics have noted), subordinate to his ruthlessness. Of course, much about Kurtz remains dark, enigmatic; what we know of him comes from the refractions of other consciousnesses (as is usually true when Conrad presents puzzling characters). Even one of the greatest admirers of Kurtz, the quixotically devoted romantic wanderer (owner of the redeeming sea manual) has been taken gross advantage of by Kurtz. But apparently representative of Kurtz's moral contradictions is the report, given to Marlow, that Kurtz wrote for a European committee on civilizing the natives. It is full of highfalutin benevolent rhetoric, but it ends with Kurtz's scrawled "Exterminate all the brutes!"

Though claiming the rhetoric of idealist and reformer, Kurtz is consumed with greed and power. He has accumulated vast quantities of ivory not by trade but by theft and warfare, made himself ruler (with a native queen—a subject for Victorian shivers) of a native tribe and army, and let himself be worshipped as a god. He has systematically engaged in conquest, terror, executions, and other undescribed "horrors." Confused about returning to the colonial order, in which he retains large ambitions, he has both ordered the steamboat attacked by his native army and boarded it, critically ill, to leave. He slips away in the night to be worshipped by the natives but is easily persuaded by Marlow to come back because of his European commercial-political ambitions, about which he continues to rant egomaniacally. He obviously lacks all character, which is later confirmed by Marlow in details about Kurtz's manipulative European past.

At the river scene, Marlow decides that Kurtz is morally "mad" and "hollow at the core." Just why Marlow takes Kurtz so seriously, other than as an exemplum of the "powers of darkness" unrestrained, may be puzzling to the reader. For Marlow sees Kurtz even on his ideal side as a devotee of "sham" fame and power and "childish" in his cult of himself. Yet Marlow still credits Kurtz with endless struggles of conscience and with being a "remarkable man." He is, of course, desperate Marlow's chosen "nightmare" in a rather perverse defiance of the prevailing petty nightmares. Kurtz, then, is less morally real than a reflection of Marlow's moral needs. Thus Marlow elaborately rationalizes Kurtz's last dark words, "The horror! The horror!," taking them as an "affirmation, a moral victory paid for by innumerable defeats, by abominable horrors, by abominable satisfactions." Kurtz had the courage, Marlow fervently insists, to make a judgment on himself, to achieve moral insight. However vicious, then, Kurtz had the redeeming larger "idea" which Marlow has been looking for as a saving grace in the European colonial evil.

But the moral claim is entirely the good captain's, not the nasty colonialist's; considering the gross viciousness and futility of Kurtz, Marlow's entirely private affirming interpretation remains at best a pyrrhic value. The rest of the narrative skeptically suggests that value may be all there is. After recovering from his own near-fatal illness and returning to Europe, Marlow, still dedicated to his idea of Kurtz, learns that he was not only a megalomaniac colonialist but a rootless semi-intellectual, all manipulation and no value—the type now recognized as a demagogic seeker of power and celebritydom. The hollow evil in the colonies is also the evil hollow at the heart of Western culture.

Marlow concludes his sense of obligation to his myth of Kurtz by visiting Kurtz's middle-class fiancée who romantically continues to idealize Kurtz as a great man. Moralist Marlow decides it would be "too dark altogether" to disillusion her. Though he hates lies, he accedes to hers, and even assures her that Kurtz's last words (actually "The horror!") were her name spoken lovingly. For Marlow, this saving lie is justified because he is speaking to a female idealist, a Victorian lady, that is, someone he views as less than humanly intelligent and responsive. This bigotry has been prepared for by Marlow's playing the sycophant to his powerful aunt (while he thinks, "It's queer how out of touch with truth women are") and with later chauvinist remarks ("women . . . are out of it," necessarily dreaming in a "beautiful world of their own"). Many readers have found this pseudoidealization of the pure lady (insistently recurrent in Conrad) to be, along with the sometimes footloose moral rhetoric (as with the description of Kurtz's end), and the portentous atmospherics (such as the endless play on metaphors of darkness and Marlow's Buddha-like wisdom), considerable flaws in an otherwise powerful story. But they may be integral to the Conradian point of view and values. Nor do they altogether obscure the real corrosive moral of the story, as with the final scenic metaphor back in London where Marlow, described again as Buddha-like, and all else flow into the heart of an immense darkness. Whatever Captain Conrad's conscious intentions may have been with "Heart of Darkness," his Captain Mar-

low's revelations in this harsh tale must be seen as verging on moral nihilism. Half camouflaging it for a Victorian audience by saving lies for the ladies, and by more involuted ones for the captains of this colonialist world should not mislead as to where vivid impressionism of scene (a redeeming artistic "efficiency"?) and the moral ironies darkly flow.

Kurtz was only a "sham" idealist, his fiancée only a pathetic romantic, Marlow a romantic turned ironist. Exposing romantic idealism remained an obsessive subject with the disenchanted romantic author, as his first successful long novel, *Lord Jim* (1900), shows. This somewhat bifurcated narrative links what so far had been Conrad's two main sources of subject matter, his maritime and his colonial experiences. The first part centers on the decrepit steamship *Patna,* which is carrying eight hundred Muslim pilgrims across the Indian Ocean. When the ship is damaged, stopped, and in danger of sinking, the cowardly officers—including, after a sensitive delay, the young mate-protagonist Jim—abandon the ship, making no provision for the passengers. But the *Patna* survives and is safely towed to port by another ship. Jim is tried and convicted of patent dereliction of duty, though he loses only his mariner's certificate and his good name. Full of romantic "exalted egotism," he rationalizes away his cowardice and goes in pursuit of his fanciful "honor."

Eventually, with the help of several old men (fatherly Captain Marlow and his businessman friend Stein), who themselves yearn for romance, Jim ends up a trader on a far-distant colonial island, Patusan. In this parallel second "trial" of character he seems successful, befriending the native ruler by leading an expedition against predatory Arabs and becoming the paternalistic colonialist Lord Jim. But though supposedly faithful to the natives, he later comes to identify with the devil in the guise of the predatory Gentleman Brown—a fellow white outcast and egotist—when he arrives with a marauding gang. Jim does not protect the natives, though he easily could have; the son of the chief is murdered by Brown, and Jim suicidally expiates his repeated guilt by letting the chief kill him in vengeance. His final dishonor is his abandoning the native woman, Jewel, who adores him. Thus romantic idealism—really a fantasy of self-importance and a male code of honor—shows its unredeemable price.

But such a summary of the exotic scenes and stereotyped characters leaves out many of the distinctive Conradian qualities. After the early chapters of omniscient narration (though some information is withheld), much of the story is told by,

an end.

It was a great peace, I was thinking
mostly of the living who buried in its remote
places are lost to life as we conceive it and
yet
its
places out of the knowledge of mankind still
are fated to share its tragic or grotesque
miseries. In its noble struggles too — who knows.
The human heart is great enough to contain
all the
all its
beyond the reach of every

all the world and strong enough to carry within
its palpitating walls into the most dumb and
deserted wilderness all the unrest, all its perplexities and — O verily believe — the solution of all
its innumerable problems. This enough to
bear the burden but where is the courage that
cast it off!

sentimental mood for I stood there a long
time

Page from the manuscript for Lord Jim *(Wise)*

again, Captain Marlow. Conrad's elaborate reflex-ive method allows for both mystification of motives and ambiguous moral responses to the events. For example, what seems a digression by Marlow be-comes ideologically central: Captain Brierly, the highly regarded and successful young master of the fine ship *Ossa,* seems to old Marlow to be an ultimate in "self-satisfaction" and a totally "complacent soul," yet he kills himself shortly after sitting as maritime assessor at Jim's trial for dereliction of duty. Marlow asserts that Brierly "never in his life" showed "self-mistrust," much less made a "mistake," and that he was exceptionally competent and sure and solid; he even states (in one of the most trite bits of rhetoric) that he was totally loved by one of the "most wonderful" of dogs. Yet the good captain must have been led during Jim's trial to examine himself for contemptible fear and lack of decency—the issues with Jim—and his self-verdict "must have been of unmitigated guilt." To justify the character improbability, Marlow eliminates other motives (money, drink, age, incompetence, madness, women, and irrational impulse). Captain Brierly went to his death calmly, carefully providing for the future of his ship and his first mate, re-checking the navigation and even oiling the log, carefully saving his dog and gold watch (an award for brave dutifulness), and efficiently preparing himself to sink in the sea with four weights attached to his body. Since many suicides, probably including Conrad's own attempt as a young man, show ambiv-alent muddle, what the author typically does here is not pose probabilities of character but paradoxes of moral ideology.

Conrad's manner in presenting this story shows an ideological emphasis and not, contrary to some critics, psychological analysis and dramatiza-tion of probable character. Brierly had quite implausibly—given his character, success, and the circumstances—identified with romantic-loser Jim during Jim's trial. Conrad gives him a doctrinal conclusion, contrary to character and psychology, that the conventions of duty by which the captain lived did not work, and so concluded himself. Brierly had believed in "professional decency": the mariner's fidelity not to goodness or intelligence or people but to a role and routine (even if it be caring only for a shipload of old rags). Since "simple" of-ficer Jim, from a proper background, also belonged within this convention—we are repeatedly told and then retold in the conclusion to the later "Author's Note" that Jim "was of the right sort; he was one of us"—his case should exemplify the adequacy of the mariner's convention of duty, "the sovereign power

enthroned in a fixed standard of conduct." Conrad seemed to believe that a professional ethic was the only basis of what little modern moral community there is. Brierly is reported to have held that "the only thing that holds us together is just the name . . . for decency." But Jim's behavior, the trial, and Brierly's state of mind, show this ethic as not only insufficient but irrelevant. The "name" of decency, the appearance of a code of values and its "sense of dignity" and all that is "supposed to be," have again been revealed as sham. The moral conventions do not really work, and so Conrad ideologically pushes Captain Brierly to a suicide which is improbable for the character and his role but that logically ex-presses the moral fear in Conrad's own extreme doubt.

Finding it unbearable that the inadequacy of conventional decency and dignity should be re-vealed, sternly righteous Brierly, we are told, even offered to bribe Jim to skip out on the rest of the trial and hide. When Jim, pursuing his romantic fantasy of honor, does not flee underground, Brierly puts himself under the sea. This Dostoevski-like acting upon the logic of an idea is not, surely, the probable behavior of a young, con-fident, obtuse, successful British Master Mariner. Conrad imposes on his representative captain what he described elsewhere as the excesses of "reflec-tion," leading to the terrors which come from the radical idea that all may be illegitimate. Marlow also gives what he calls the "last word of amazing pro-fundity" on the suicide, Brierly's first mate's epitaph: "neither you nor I, sir, had ever thought so much of ourselves." Nor apparently so much of conventional appearances. Seasoned doubters, like the mate and Marlow—and Conrad—can live on, skeptically holding to the "name" of simple ideas and faiths in which they humbly do not believe. Without such life-lies (as Conrad's contemporary Ibsen called them), a self-respecting man (much less an ideal lady) can hardly live with the terrifying truth that claims to disciplined routines, civilized pretenses, finally amount to very little, though there is not, in Conrad's alien world and pessimistic view, much else.

In the ornate structure of *Lord Jim,* Captain Brierly's suicide provides an aslant parallel to Jim's self-sacrificial death for an egotistical fantasy of self-importance. Jim, too, repeatedly appears as the "simple" mariner who indeed thinks much of him-self and his "shadowy ideal of conduct." Jim's case is complicated by his guilt over previous failure, by chauvinistic pretenses to masculine "honor," and by his ambivalent role as colonial autocrat arrogantly

James Lingard, the Berau trader who was the inspiration for the character Lord Jim

doing good for his natives while playing out a debilitating different role. In a much-quoted passage, philosophical Stein advises Jim to follow out his romantic dream, "in the destructive element immerse." True enough, the destructive dream allows the only possibility of heroic shape and meaning, however fatal to himself, and others.

Carried into the reflective depths, the Conradian sea-captain morality of simple ideas and fidelities will hardly do for humane purpose, though several die well by them. The sly moralizing of another, Marlow, must again be recognized as peculiarly ironical, as when he says: "For a moment I had a view of a world that seemed to wear a vast and dismal aspect of disorder, while, in truth, thanks to our unwearied efforts, it is as sunny an arrangement of small conveniences as the mind of man can conceive." Ah, yes, sunny indeed, and the next paragraph echoes "Heart of Darkness" again in that "it had grown pitch-dark where we were."

Conrad's writing in these most productive years was not confined to the dark moral riddling of exotic maritime and colonial scenes. For some years he attempted to collaborate on popular fictions with his younger close friend Ford Madox Hueffer. Probably Conrad's contribution was the smaller

part of the artistically poor but still commercially unsuccessful collaborations, *The Inheritors* (1901), *Romance* (1903), and *The Nature of a Crime* (not published until 1924). Ford was almost surely a more general intellectual source for Conrad, and may have contributed to, as well as influenced, some of Conrad's other writings, including his best.

Conrad also wrote more short fictions. "Amy Foster" (1901) is another attempt to deal with the more obscure land (rather than sea) peasants. Yanko, a poor Carpathian lad washed ashore from a wrecked emigrant ship on a rural English shore is harshly mistreated because of his simplicity and inability to communicate to the cold English peasants. Though always the alien, eventually he marries a homely and dumb local girl, Amy Foster. But in fear and misunderstanding she abandons him when he is ill. Yanko dies, the story concludes, of "the supreme disaster of loneliness and despair." This moral, and the narration, comes from an intelligent local doctor. What is he doing there? In a characteristic charge, Conrad says that the man's intellectuality, "like a corrosive fluid, had destroyed his ambition." Amy Foster, we are also told, though dull has just enough "imagination" to fall in love, but not enough to go on loving the alien. These curious distinctions of Conrad's anti-intellectualism, which marks much of his work, serve here as ideological rivets for one of his most bathetic templates of loneliness and outcastness.

"To-Morrow" (1902) is an awkward and redundant effort at writing a pathetic comedy about a retired and lunatic coastal captain whose fantasy of what his son will be like when he returns denies the actual son when he does come back. (Freudian critics relate this to obsessive parent-child fantasies in the orphaned Conrad's work.) The novella "Falk" (1903) is an awkwardly rambling story around a mock-heroic Scandinavian tugboat captain in an Eastern port and his elaborate efforts to marry a German shipowner's niece. Curiously, Falk's sexual hunger is displaced into his digressive story of when he committed cannibalism in order to survive on a long-disabled ship. But Conrad's Victorian-shocker deployment of the primordial passions seems undercut by the skittish handling. Sheer will to endurance, quite beyond moral decorum, wins in hunger and in lust.

"The End of the Tether" (1902) is a sentimental short story inflated into near-novel length (apparently, as happened several times with Conrad, to meet the demands of a publishing contract). A once superior sailing captain, Whalley attempts in his late sixties to keep up the facade of a fastidiously proud gentleman and master, though actually impoverished and with a leeching married daughter. Whalley successfully connives for a petty steamboat command and pretends to captain, though really almost blind. A hysterically malicious owner (Conrad's suggestive portrait of a compulsive gambler) tricks the captain, and the ship ends up on a reef for the insurance money. Captain Whalley goes down with the ship. Though Conrad apparently meant to mock his old captain as an optimist who does not believe in "evil," and who with dangerous sentimentality went on too long, the maudlin repetition of his virtues and the crude melodrama undercuts the pessimistic idea.

While these tales have implicitly powerful themes—obtuseness of the aging, voracious sexuality, egotistical fantasy, alienated loneliness—and touches of graphic rhetoric, they are poor. Some of the mawkishness and forced melodrama may, of course, be attributed to the popular magazine audience for which they were written.

But Conrad was doing partly more serious work as well. *Nostromo* (1904) is Conrad's largest novel in size, scope, and ambition. The first half engages the reader, by a back-and-forth movement in time and focus, in a broad nineteenth-century world of diverse characters and politics. While the mosaic is thin and stereotyped on subjective experience, it is rich on mythic history. In the central action, the town of Sulaco, Coastaguana (placed in South America) turns its province into a separate country, the Occidental Republic, in a conservative counterrevolution after a long period of misrule by a psychopathic tyrant, a weak traditional oligarchy, and a debased military-populist coup. Finally, in the Conradian disenchantment, the controlling politics "rest in the development of material interests," that is, standard colonial capitalism.

Specifically, the "material interests" are those almost "mystically" idealized by a local self-aggrandizing upper-class Englishman, Charles Gould (this stick figure certainly represents the traditional gentlemanly "solid English sense not to think too much"), whose San Tomé silver mine is backed by a prudent and pious American millionaire. Lesser roles are played by a foreign railroad and a shipping company. While the machinations, bribery, and finally even the military power of the Gould Concession bring commercial modernization and an appearance of order, a choral character (Dr. Monygham) insists at a crucial point near the end that it is all based on "inhuman" expediency, not moral principle and continuity, and so will again result in "barbarism, cruelty, and mis-

rule." Conrad shows considerable political intelligence.

But this intelligence does not extend to his handling of his already disenchanted idealists, such as Mrs. Gould, another high-minded Victorian lady devoted to charity who feels that the obsessive faith in "material interests" has alienated her from her husband and kinder purposes. Conrad's prescient and tough-minded reflections on historical change in exploited countries should not be misread as skeptical evenhandedness. There are bad and worse. The "better class" traditionalists, such as the sentimentalized Avellanos, appear as foolish, patriotic "constitutionalists" but individually are given bravery and other nobility. Fatuous, they nonetheless avoid "the somber imbecility of political fanaticism." In contrast, the "liberal" demagogues, such as the savagely caricatured Monteiros, come out only as greedy and brutal scoundrels leading the "scum" of the revolting populace. Only the cool opportunistic capitalists, and their devotedly obtuse servitors (Major Pépé, Captain Mitchell, the engineers) show effectiveness, with a redeeming efficiency but no faith in better values. Again Conrad combines an extreme conservativism with a drastic skepticism.

The novel's entitling figure, Nostromo, is also one of the servitors. An Italian ex-sailor become "captaz de cargadores" (port foreman—Conrad's shrewd conviction that the foreman, sergeants, chiefs, keep the institutions going) turns out to be a courageous man and a "prodigy of efficiency." But he is also consumed by vanity and a lust for fame and popularity. Another of Conrad's figures trapped in the romantic fantasy of himself, he is supposedly incorruptible but in the end is totally dominated by his obsession with a secreted load of silver. Conrad's slow exposure of this corrupted romantic overbalances the larger events. The last part of the novel is an ornately manipulated melodrama in which Nostromo pretends to love and becomes engaged to a lighthousekeeper's frigid daughter (he is actually in love with her more responsive sister) in order to retrieve his cache of silver. He is shot by the women's father, a man Nostromo has looked on as his own father, who does not know whom he is shooting. Thus the twentieth-century novel of political skepticism reverts to earlier popular romance and moralizing, with strange psychological undertones.

But more intriguing things appear. A late-introduced character, upper-class journalist Martin Decoud, poses some of the Conradian dilemmas of mind in an indifferent universe. As so often in Con-

Don Pépé very calm stroked his grey and pendent moustache, whose fine ends hung below the clean cut line of his jaw, and spoke with conscious pride in his reputation.

"So padre I don't know what will happen. This I know that Don Carlos can speak to that macaque Pedrito Montero and threaten the destruction of the mine with perfect assurance that he will be taken seriously. For people know me."

He turned the cigar in lips a little nervously and went on

"But that is talk — work for the politicos. I am a military man. I do not know what may happen but I know what ought to be done. The mine should march upon the town with guns, axes, knives tied up to sticks, por Dios. Only.... on hill."

His hand twitched. The cigar turned faster in the corner of the lips.

"And who should lead but I? Unfortunately — observe — I have given my word not to let the mine fall into the hands of these thieves, and In war — you know, mi padre — the fate of battles is uncertain — and whom could I leave here. The explosives are ready. But it would require a man of honour, of intelligence, of judgment, of courage. Another old officer of Paez — or — or — perhaps one of our old chaplains ..."

He got up long, lank, upright with his martial moustache and the bony structure of his face from which the sunken eyes seemed to tremble the priest who stood still an empty snuff box held upside down in his hand and glared back at the governor of the mine.

→ to recto

Page from the manuscript for Nostromo *(Wise)*

rad, the intellectual is a suicide: "The brilliant Costaguanero of the boulevards had died from solitude and want of faith in himself and others." For this urbanely cultivated ex-Parisian and "the spoiled darling of the family, the lover of Antonia [stock highfalutin lady of the dominant upper-class family] and journalist of Sulaco, was not fit to grapple with himself single-handed." In three days of isolation, after spiriting to a desert island with Nostromo (who leaves) a crucial load of silver needed to maintain a coup, he reached a "state of soul in which the affectations of irony and skepticism have no place." Skeptical Conrad is punishing his skeptical alter ego, as several critics have noted.

Decoud (in an unusually direct narrative for Conrad) is described as being driven into an "exile of utter unbelief" so great that he started losing "his own individuality." This includes passively merging into "nature," which for sea-fearful Conrad seems horrible. Decoud has by chance been separated from the usual social conspiracy for active illusions against a destructive cosmos. By the seventh day of anxiously sleepless solitude in "waiting without faith," he "beheld the universe as a succession of incomprehensible images" and sank into despair.

Conrad argues that Decoud's values have been "intelligence" and "passion." But these are antithetical to saving illusions. By the tenth day the silence of his natural solitude has become "a still cord stretched to breaking-point, with his life, his vain life, suspended to it like a weight." He attempts to break this cord of despair with a pistol shot, at himself, yet never hears "the cord of silence snap aloud in the solitude" as, weighted down with four bars of silver (as Brierly in *Lord Jim* with four weights), he falls to his death in the sea, "swallowed up by the immense indifference of things." It is such intense images of precarious existence and lack of human meaning which give Conrad much of his modernity in his Victorian romances.

Conrad rather pushes his anti-intellectual ideological issue with the figure of Decoud. We are told he is a "victim of the disillusioned weariness which is the retribution meted out to intellectual audacity." Yet the hyper-simple Nostromo also reaches disillusion as "the reward of audacious action," and in a few hours of isolation is overwhelmed by a "sense of loneliness, abandonment, and failure," and so also finds himself in Decoud's state of "universal dissolution." If both the ironic intellectual and the vain man of action end up the same, temporarily, discrimination has been submerged in Conrad's ideological obsession with despair and his prose-poem on universal meaninglessness.

But the contrast between action and intellectuality did not really exist anyway, in spite of the assertions. While Decoud has been described as a Parisian *flaneur*, a striking "dandy," and a "cosmopolitan" ironist, he has also been dramatized as a man of action: he purchased and arranged for the improved rifles finally crucial to the defense of the new state; he was founder and editor of the local bombastic conservative newspaper; he was an energetic fighter against the populace in the Sulaco riots and activist organizer of the provincial separatist movement; and he was partner in the daring night removal of the crucial lighter load of silver. To see this figure as primarily the skeptical intellectual, as some critics have, is to accept foolishly Conrad's assertions against his dramatizations. Conrad feared intellectuals.

Early in *Nostromo* Conrad repeats an obsessive moral: "Action is consolatory. It is the enemy of thought, the friend of flattering illusion. Only in the conduct of our action can we find the sense of mastery over the Fates." This reversal of the traditional emphasis on the power of contemplation takes form in Conrad's other fictions in the glorification of work and the fidelity to simple sea routines. Our maintaining illusions depends on keeping idle minds away from devilish awareness of our futile condition as men. (Women are exempt from the need for action because they do not, and he insists should not, think—women who do, we are told in *Nostromo,* are "barren and without importance.") A forced indolence and solitude ostensibly bring out the faithlessness of Decoud's skeptical intellect, but the case really seems to be against his "habit of universal raillery" and his modern intellectual's mockery of vanity, stupidity, sadism, usual politics, English hypocrisy, the "virtues of material interests," conservative propaganda (including his own), and vulgar patriotism. Such men are dangerous. Can it be that Decoud was not stupid and dull enough, like the blandly complacent official Captain Mitchell, not "insane" enough like Charles Gould with his "fixed idea" of the absolute virtue of capitalist enterprise, not bitterly enough "crushed" as was Dr. Monygham who ended up a ruthless sycophant of the rich Mrs. Gould, and not vicious enough, like a good many other characters in *Nostromo?* A sensible reading of the novel requires some awareness of Conrad's most peculiar arguments. Conrad desperately feared the effect of radical skepticism, perhaps including his own, on the simple ideas and illusionary faiths necessary for social order and the pretenses at moral meaning.

A good example of Conrad's will-to-meaning

appears in his "A Familiar Preface" to *A Personal Record*. There he says that those who read his fictions know "my conviction that the world, the temporal world, rests on a very few simple ideas. . . . It rests notably . . . on the idea of Fidelity." No casual statement, this is contrasted in the following paragraph with the ideas involved in the "revolutionary spirit," which he condemns for optimism, intolerance, and unscrupulousness; and, he insists, the revolutionaries' "claim to special righteousness awakens in me . . . scorn and anger." Conrad's politics, then, are less a skeptical detachment than a counterrighteousness to the radical thinking which he feared. *Nostromo* should be partly read as a counterrevolutionary critique, a radical conservative.

Elaborately reflective Conrad, for that is the nature of his better fictions and the premise of the refracted narrations (when not, as often later, just moral mannerism), nonetheless tended to fear all reflection for its radical potentialities. Elsewhere in the preface to his memoir: "Nothing humanly great . . . has come from reflection." Thus he presents his successful functionaries (such as Captain Mitchell of *Nostromo* and Captain MacWhirr of *Typhoon,* who lack fear because of "the lack of a certain kind of imagination") as mostly stupid. As endlessly ruminative Captain Marlow of *Lord Jim* says, "it is this very dullness that makes life to the incalculable majority so supportable and so welcome"; elsewhere he repeats the Conradian credo that what is necessary is the "belief in a few simple notions that you must cling to if you want to live decently."

No doubt this anti-intellectualism is itself an important idea, but we may do Conrad an injustice if we do not recognize it usually working as a defiant commonplace, a practical barring of ideas (and intellectuals) by disallowing them. This accords with an ancient fideistic method by which drastic skepticism despairingly encourages simple faith, or at least the pretense of it, though the contradiction seems obvious (and can become mean) in answering the largest questions of human meaning and conduct by refusing to answer and yet claiming the refusal as the answer.

The one specific value Conrad claims in his personal preface, "Fidelity," must remain perplexed because of the exilic situation of the author and of so many of his characters, who often lack the friends to be faithful with, or the homeplace to be faithful to, or the communion to be faithful in. In desperation, the fideistic modernist would short-circuit the issue by often using an unworthy purpose or petty routine or illusory honor as the

cord to save one from darkly solitary chaos. His "faithful seamen" holding to "fixed standards of conduct" and "simple routines of the sea," or similar subserviences, can attempt to answer large perplexities with small loyalties. But even they often require rather special human limitations. As Conrad wrote of a storm-wracked, real-life captain in *The Mirror and the Sea,* the man was fortunately "too simple to go mad, too simple with manly simplicity which alone can bear man unscathed in mind and body" against annihilating forces. (What fear pursued Conrad!) Those not quite simple enough — Kurtz, Brierly and Jim, Decoud, among others — are driven to suicide. Conrad's political and moral conservativism is unusual in claiming neither religious absolutes nor organic order, only fear and fragility.

A combination of ideological obsession and the romantic fictionist's desire for extreme situations led Conrad even in his crude commercial stories to touch on nineteenth-century radicalism, as in *A Set of Six* (1908). "Gaspar Ruiz" (1906) awkwardly tells of a simple strong-man South American guerrilla leader repeatedly switching from the republican to the Spanish royalist sides in the endless brutal confusions of the war of independence. He dies absurdly holding up a cannon. His coldly superior wife then commits suicide, apparently revealing her romanticism.

"An Anarchist" (1906) is pathetic but less maudlin. A simple French mechanic is convicted as an anarchist, mostly because of accidental circumstances, then sent off to a French penal colony in South America. He escapes but ends up as practically a slave on a colonial ranch. While the arch narration seems somewhat ambivalent in attitude, that being reached for is contempt for anarchists' wicked silliness. "The Informer" (1906) also utilizes contemptuously distant narration to tell of a London revolutionary group with an upper-class patroness (a role which repeatedly enraged Conrad). She is disillusioned when, through a tricky plot, her anarchist lover turns out to be a police informer. He commits suicide; she withdraws from life. The reader is provided little internal sense of the characters but is to realize from external evidence that such sad results must be inevitable to revolutionary posturing.

Other stories of the period include "The Brute" (1906), an elaborately empty pub anecdote about a repeatedly ill-fated ship. "The Duel" (1908) lengthily retells a legendary tale of two French officers of the Napoleonic period who repeatedly duel over minor points of honor in their juvenile

Inscription in a copy of the first edition of The Secret Agent *(American Art Association, 28 April 1927)*

homoerotic love. "Il Conde" (1908), a simpler but more ominous account of a Neopolitan aristocrat repeatedly held up by the same gentleman mugger, and caught in paranoid delicacy, is the best of these stories of implicit but unrecognized complicity in an irrational fate.

The Secret Agent (1907) is of quite a different order; indeed, it may be Conrad's most powerful novel. With criminal "mystery" in the purlieus of London political terrorism, he may have found especially suitable material for his harshly ironic melodrama. The confirmation may be seen in the more disciplined and direct style, which achieves a heightened fusion of vivid description and sardonic reflectiveness. Gone is the garrulity and digressive lushness; only rarely (a bit in the final chapter, and a few other passages) does Conrad fall back on narrative indirection and redundant portentousness. Subtitled *A Simple Tale,* the novel is both infernally complicated in its neatly savage plotting and yet devastatingly simple in the fixed (obsessional) ideas of all the characters. With several of them, Conrad reaches a degree of intense subjectivity beyond that of his other fictions.

Perhaps this resulted from the negative political milieu. There is little place for romantic inflation and Victorian sentimentality, except mockingly, in this absurdist tale of a bumbling agent provocateur, grotesque marginal terrorists, conniving police officials, and the yellow journalism fears of the time.

While Conrad's grimly conservative ideology permeates the fiction, the impassioned disdain also allows some acute impartiality (for example, "terrorist and policeman both come from the same basket"). The perspective demands law and order yet insists on its inadequacy.

The most ardent admirer of law and order is Adolf Verloc, a longtime petty secret agent of an east European government and an informer to British police who passes for a passive member of an ostensibly revolutionary group in London. In temperament and character, the double agent is a "highly respectable" petit bourgeois shopkeeper—prudent, regular, domestic, anxiously complacent—an occupation which is also his secret agent cover. Driven by his diabolical foreign employer to carrying out a nihilistic provocation in order to bring repression down on the radicals, the bombing of a scientific symbol (the Greenwich Observatory), he anxiously messes it up—a shopkeeper with too big a deal. The disproportions come out macabre. Verloc's bomb-carrying dupe is his wife's mentally retarded brother, his surrogate son, who stumbles and blows himself to bits. Verloc is sorry about that. Now he will have to sell his shop and make various other prudent domestic rearrangements.

With ponderous self-pathos, the put-upon murderer tries to explain the arrangements to his devoted wife, revealing his one "amiable weakness: the idealistic belief in being loved for himself." Conrad's cynical analysis cuts deep and wide. But Winnie Verloc, from a mean and abused childhood, has only one passion, her devotion to her retarded brother; indeed, she married fat, crude little Verloc solely in order to provide a protective family. When the obtuse agent of others' needs concludes his self-pitying display with a sexual demand, the outraged Winnie sticks the family carving knife in him. Fearfully fleeing, the desperately simpleminded woman latches on to comrade Ossipon, a compulsive womanizing radical who has been after her. He robs her of Verloc's savings and in his fright of the police deserts her. She throws herself over the railing of a channel boat, another of Conrad's suicides from solitude and thought. Ossipon, glib ex-medical student, is left to disintegrate in guilt. No wonder the story concludes with a savage description of yet another terrorist, the lunatic bomb-making "professor" with the "simplicity of his idea calling madness and despair to the regeneration of the world." Conrad, of course, has deployed madness and despair for the simplicity of his idea of *not* trying to change an impossible world.

Using political images popular at the turn of the century, the author calls his revolutionaries "anarchists." But they are not: the "professor," a resentful failure acknowledged to have talent, avows nihilism with an elitist neo-Nietzschean hatred of mediocrity and the masses; another revolutionary spouts the clichés of antianarchist Marxian economic determinism; the most noted caricature is a gentle, crippled ex-convict (police-protected and supported by an eccentric wealthy patroness) whom even the author views as a pathetically quaint religious utopian. Stevie, Winnie Verloc's witless brother, in his anguished sympathy for both a beaten horse and its miserably poor cabdriver, and his stuttering moral indignation that it is "bad world for poor people," appears to be the only libertarian, though unrecognized as such, in the story. Possibly Conrad thought he was exposing, as he claimed, the "criminal futility" of anarchists, but it is rather more an ideological psychodrama of simple crippled people carried into despair.

Not that Conrad does not play upon conservative bigotries. The radicals and double agent Verloc are repeatedly charged with "indolence" and self-indulgence, though mostly shown in frenzied efforts and puritanic asceticism. But such prejudices are submerged in the brilliantly heightened misconfrontation of Winnie and Adolf Verloc. Almost equally acute is the bureaucratic infighting of class-separated types, the callous Chief Inspector and the opportunistic Assistant Commissioner of Police, though Conrad skimps on completing the disillusioning action with the officials, a parallel to the radicals, perhaps in fear of too obviously exposing the establishment nihilism.

Conrad's denigration of political-moral ideas and his often astutely cynical ironies against all (including a "great" MP) make this ostensibly political novel quite antipolitical. All ideals—as with retarded Stevie's desperate and fatal fidelity to Verloc, the professor's "frenzied puritanism of ambition" soured to destructiveness, and Verloc's complacent respectable-husband misjudgment of his wife—get reduced to small, private desperations and illusions. Rightly enough, the shrewd police official sees the main action of the story as less a political than a "domestic drama" (and further demonstrates his shrewd insight by partly subverting the investigation in ways to please his socially ambitious wife). No one can play a larger scene. Showing that all political theater quickly reduces to private needs and vanities and resentments, the nihilistic conservative author has dissolved politics into fatal charades.

Again, as with Decoud in *Nostromo,* the real terrorism is solitary thinking, though here the desert island is modern anomic urban life. Winnie Verloc "felt profoundly that things did not stand much looking into," and it was her "distant and uninquiring acceptance of facts which was her force and safe guide in life." She "did not allow herself to fall into the idleness of barren speculation" (intellectual "speculation" may be really what Conrad means by radical "indolence"). We might see Mrs. Verloc's failure as similar to Captain Brierly's in *Lord Jim.* Solid citizens driven to reflection—she by Stevie's death—end in despair at the bottom of the sea.

Granted, Conrad sometimes loads the analysis; for example, he gives Winnie a quite improbable association of ideas: three minutes after she kills her husband she starts obsessively to visualize herself dropping from the gallows (the conservative's dubious, and irrelevant, idea of the efficacy of capital punishment). But rather more interesting is the implicit authorial self-irony. Conrad has given simple Winnie a "singleness of purpose" and simple solidarity, the maternal devotion to her brother, as he has given Verloc his simple respectable faith in his wife's domestic love and as he has given simpleminded Stevie his unquestioned fidelity to Verloc and his bomb. Yet in all the cases the intellectual simpleness and virtue and fidelity become a "fixed idea" with an "insane logic." Conrad's own credo of "simple ideas" and ordinary virtues and "Fidelity" is devastatingly shown as fatal.

Some of Conrad's power in *The Secret Agent* of thought shows the distinctive modernist artistry of rendering ironic one's own values. The ostensible antinihilist nihilistically makes his most powerful case against himself. Intensely entering the minds of pathetically repulsive characters, yet maintaining the dialectics of the sardonically anti-intellectual fable, Conrad brings the reader to a conservativism totally radical in which there are no bedrock values (religion, tradition, community) and the examined life is not worth living. "The force of sympathy," Conrad cynically notes by way of a policeman, is a "form of fear." He has made the fear palpable as the "impenetrable mystery" of despair at the heart of human affairs.

Under Western Eyes (1911), Conrad's other and longer novel employing the materials of political revolutionism, seems considerably lesser work than *The Secret Agent* in style, artful ordering, subjective intensity, and insightful paradoxes. Part of the difficulty is the use of a rather Jamesian narrator, an obtusely lofty-mannered teacher of languages and English literature. While the figure may have been psychologically desirable to Conrad for distancing himself from the painful revolutionism, which is almost as hopeless as that of his father, the narrative creaks badly and sometimes breaks down, as with the sentimental old Englishman who defensively provides the entitling perspective. This excuses Conrad from understanding or sympathetically presenting the revolutionaries.

Most of the story is set in Geneva—although the protagonist's absurdly improbable diary and some other two or three times removed reports give some St. Petersburg scenes—which allows further denigration of the whole Russian madness when contrasted to the bland Swiss order. Given such removed scene and narration, the exiled revolutionaries come out mostly as pathetic grotesques. The English teacher, and apparently the author, naturally see them as ill-mannered, theatrical, badly dressed, extreme, bombastic, dangerous, and providing a most slovenly tea. The leading figure, an heroic escapee from Siberia, is caricatured as a pompous, mystic feminist and sycophant to a rich, hysterical, and ugly refugee woman. He in fact exploits women. But the women, from their adolescent fixations on, have been horrendously, even comically, self-exploited. The authorial contempt rests heavily. While Conrad despises the "lawless autocracy" of Czarist Russia, which exiled his parents and from which he was a refugee, the reactive ideological conservative insists that the equally lawless revolutionaries are utterly incompetent, false, and ugly, and provide no answer other than another form of mystic nastiness.

For the true answer, as with the seamen of the *Narcissus,* is suffering endurance. Its main, though not only, exemplification is protagonist Razumov, orphaned bastard of a Russian prince. A depressive, ambitious, conformist, isolato university student, Razumov is imposed upon by young revolutionary fellow student Victor Haldin. The romantic idealist, only son of a small-landowning widow of mildly liberal sentiments, Haldin has been the back-up assassin in a plot against a repressive minister. (Conrad's details here obviously draw on the high-minded Russian nihilist movement of a generation earlier.) Fleeing the police, Haldin, inexplicably lacking an escape plan, somewhat fortuitously goes to the apartment of Razumov, whom he knows only slightly but has been romantically impressed by as a high-minded solitary. He asks Razumov to carry a message to a driver with a team, asking the driver to meet him that night for his flight. Fearful and resentful, Razumov finds the driver, but he is in a

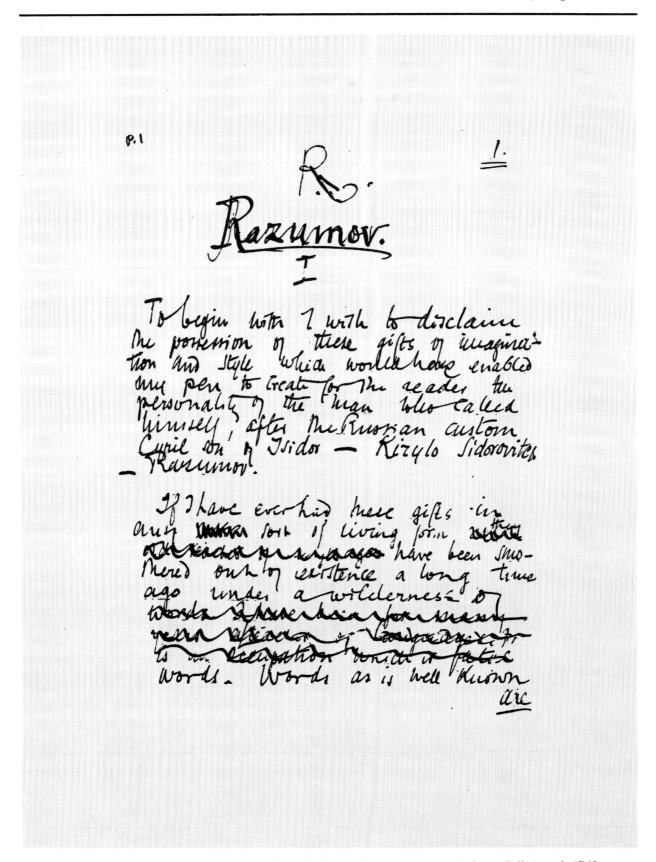

First page of the first complete draft, with working title, for Under Western Eyes *(Anderson Galleries, sale 1768, 12-14 November 1923)*

drunken stupor, and Razumov ragingly beats him without arousing him. Feeling trapped, Razumov goes to his putative father and then to the secret police, trying to prove his orphan self to authority by betraying his supposed friend and his own uncertain sentiments. Then he goes back to deceive Haldin, who is captured and secretly executed. A police official persuades Razumov to exploit for his own and the government's advantage his erroneous reputation as a revolutionary friend of Haldin's by going to Geneva to spy on the revolutionary refugees. Most of the narrative presents Razumov's anguish leading to his self-exposure as a police spy and the denouncer of Haldin, a version of the outcast's betrayal-and-repentance suicidal pattern earlier established in Conrad's fictions, as in *Lord Jim*.

Since assassin Haldin has been only slightly (and inadequately for the story) presented, and even then as mostly a phantom of guilt in Razumov's bad conscience, the idealistic counterpole takes the form of Haldin's sister Nathalie (who, with her dying mother, is a refugee in Geneva). This totally virtuous and beautiful young lady believes in the eventual reign of love and concord but not in any lesser revolution. Blandly presented by the covertly lusting English teacher, Conrad's trite vaporings about the idealistic Victorian lady (effectively presented Winnie Verloc was no lady) further weaken the style.

Razumov's irritable relations with the despised revolutionaries reveal piecemeal his bad conscience. When he fortuitously establishes revolutionary credentials, his rage at acceptance drives him to confess his betrayal of Victor Haldin to Miss Haldin. Shortly later, he concludes "it was myself, after all, whom I have betrayed most basely." Just how remains unclear since he does not apparently change his fearful conformist and self-serving politics. In spite of Conrad's stiff elaboration of his protagonist, many readers have difficulty in sympathizing with him since his was an endless pathological betrayal, not simply the aberration of a single night. He has even meanly gotten a fellow student to gratuitously rob his own father. And the spying is part of an elaborate and long-term viciousness. But Razumov's intelligence is rather thin and fatuous, as in the political credo he writes emphasizing anti-intellectual patriotism and submissiveness.

Razumov also confesses to all at a party of revolutionists. A terrorist (later revealed as a secret police agent) vengefully breaks his eardrums—a rather small punishment belying the charges of extremism leveled against them but reinforcing those of ineffectiveness against the revolutionaries.

Perhaps realizing this, Conrad later has the deaf Razumov fail to hear a tram bell so that he is run over and permanently crippled. Perhaps his further longing for punishment gets gratified by the Good Samaritan devotion of a revolutionary woman, heavily described as ugly and bedraggled and masochistic, who returns with Razumov to Russia as his caretaker as he slowly dies. These matters are all summarized by a twice-removed narrative that flattens their impact.

Miss Haldin also returns to Russia, we learn in a vague and roundabout way, to do loving charitable work. The police official who set Razumov to spying is reported as having been later purged for another offense—the extremist autocracy like the extremist revolution devouring its own. The revolutionaries remain as ineffective as ever. The great feminist revolutionary, financially betrayed by his rich patroness, has covertly returned to Russia and inspirationally "united himself to a peasant girl." The madness and viciousness go on as usual. Apparently only a fool or a scoundrel would be active for either side. Politics is impossible. One must go on lovingly enduring the inevitable suffering, without thinking about it.

Why this rather inferior imitation of Dostoevski should be treated with high seriousness as a political fable is puzzling. Perhaps the lesser political moral, presented with deprecating, sententious asides by the old English teacher, that Russia failed in not having gentle, law-abiding, anti-intellectual, decently conservative English history behind it, is comforting. Certainly the awkward earnestness of a conservative author exposing the excesses of his protagonist, a sickly conservative in his fear and solitude and lack of love, provides some poignancy. And the strained narrative distancing also suggests more ambiguity than the moralistic melodrama really offers. Unlike the provocative *The Secret Agent* with its pyrrhonistic conservativism, *Under Western Eyes* is a poor but curious work of an unusual cast in the tradition of the English novel.

Conrad's stories of this period include "The Secret Sharer." The novella "A Smile of Fortune" (1911), collected in *'Twixt Land and Sea* (1912), also concerns a young merchant marine captain, but the scene this time is set mostly in port. The central action turns about a sly ship chandler who wishes to peddle both potatoes for marketing and his illegitimate daughter, an outcast in the bigoted European caste society of the Eastern port. Sexually excited by the resentful and eccentrically mannered girl (treated with embarrassed caricature in the narration), the captain hangs around and finally kisses

Joseph Conrad, 1912 (photo by William Cadby; courtesy of John Conrad)

her in an aroused manner (something quite unusual in Conrad). Guiltily, he buys potatoes he does not want; inexplicably, he also turns cold toward the girl. By chance, the burdensome potatoes acquired because of the expensive kiss are sold at his next port for a substantial profit—"the smile of fortune." But, without reason or understanding, the captain cannot bear to go back to the first port (where the girl awaits him) as his shipowners insist and thus is forced to resign his command, which he considers a large misfortune. But the real misfortune, of course, which Conrad could suggest but could not really confront in this awkward fiction, was the captain's overwhelming sexual and social fear.

The intolerably dragged out "Freya of the Seven Isles" (1912) turns about suitors competing for a bumbling farmer's young daughter—a romantic English trading captain and a gross Dutch naval officer, in the Eastern islands. The rejected naval officer manages to wreck the beloved captain's fine bark. Since his beautiful ship gave him his romantic "power" over the woman, as well as his livelihood, the young captain despairs and quickly

degenerates into sickly madness. The abandoned heroine, who oddly makes no effort to see her lover again, dies of pneumonia and love. Conrad's lovers oddly engage in the most ornate evasions. The obtuse father is one of the inconsistent narrators of this romantic melodrama which switches between repetitious descriptions, absurd dialogues, and sheer bombast. No doubt commercial magazine intentions partly explain the badness.

Conrad's next long novel, *Chance* (1913), was, after American serialization, a moderate best-seller. After years of financial anxiety and commercial hackery, he made considerable money from his writing, generally in inverse proportion to the quality of the fiction. Now the refracting narrator, Marlow, becomes a tiresome mannerism, with involuted strategies by which somebody tells somebody who tells somebody who tells Marlow, who tells the unidentified narrator. This narrative device furthers plot trickery (withheld information), and the unfortunate avoidance of subjective immediacy and understanding, and also provides a vehicle for redundant sententiousness. Much of the skittish moralizing seems to be done in response to a contemporary issue, the women's movement of the time. The aged sentimentalist bachelor Marlow offers numerous smug denigrations, often contradictory, of female idealism and lack of idealism, toughness and weakness. Perhaps his clearest point is that feminism turns women "into unscrupulous sexless nuisances," while true femininity is always and necessarily "passive."

A pathological passivity, male as well as female, informs the plot. Sixteen-year-old Flora de Barral is cruelly dumped by her governess when her father, a naive and fixated speculative financier with a pyramid scheme, goes bankrupt and gets seven years for fraud. Thus traumatized and unloved by her various brutal lower-middle-class relatives—in one of Conrad's few sharp social comments: they are petty and righteous with "all the civic virtues in their very meanest form"—Flora grows up self-denigrating, suicidal, "painfully forlorn." Captain Anthony, a merchant marine master in his mid-thirties, meets her. Oversensitive (we know that because we are repeatedly reminded that he is the son of a poet), he legally marries Flora out of pity, but out of idealism he does not consummate the marriage. Out of need and her sense that she is unlovable, the twenty-three-year-old child accepts the arrangement. For many months she and her crazed and jealous ex-convict father live separately aboard Captain Anthony's ship. And for many skittish chapters the reader repeatedly learns what an impossible situation it is.

Amid the run of dully garrulous prose and tiresome narrative maneuvers, Conrad does make several serious points. The obvious one is about sexual repression: since pairing is natural, the denial of "the embrace" is unnatural and "a sin against life" which results in a "forcibly tortuous involution of feelings." But for Conrad this problem is less sexual-psychological than misguided moral idealism, again, though this time unegotistical. What Captain Anthony in his "delicacy" has stirred up are "the troubles of transcendental good intentions, which, though ethically valuable . . . cause often more unhappiness than the plots of the most evil tendency." But since all the main characters are stupidly passive, the transcending goodness remains obscure.

A concluding series of melodramatic chance happenings resolve the situation. The ex-convict father, apparently gone mad in incestuous paranoia, poisons Captain Anthony's brandy. The decent young second mate, who got his job by sheer chance and by even more farfetched chance happens to see the potion, rushes to save his master. But the captain despairingly gives up. That takes Flora a little out of her passivity, and she leans against him. Seeing this betrayal, the evil father takes the poisoned drink and dies, though this is hidden from the sensitive Flora. Apparently the marriage is then consummated. But sometime later the ship sinks and, after saving his wife and second mate, the captain goes down with it. After passively hanging around Flora-the-widow for four more years, the second mate (encouraged by Marlow, who has also encouraged Flora), acts finally as if he is going to have his turn with flowery, passive femininity.

Melodrama, of course, has been interestingly employed by some serious writers (Euripides, Balzac, Dostoevski, Sartre), but Conrad's here is not only exceptionally mechanical, it mostly lacks compensatory social and psychological perceptions and ideas, except clichéd prejudices, such as the antifeminism. His earlier melodramas at least had stronger ideological arguments and more exotic scenes to enliven them. Like the one-sided notion of "chance" in *Chance,* the whole novel is rather shoddy.

Chance marks Conrad's not-so-fortuitous financial success (pushed by friends, publishers, and the press, and his own eagerness) as well as a wider celebrity. So after a few more stories he gave up his hack magazine writing, though he continued with popular novels. The stories, collected in *Within the Tides* (1915), include "The Planter of Malta" (1914). The entitling figure is another of Conrad's solitaries, visiting in an Eastern port. Meeting a celebrated society beauty searching for her missing fiancé whom she had wronged, he develops an obsessive passion for her. Under false pretenses—her missing lover was his assistant, dead for some time—he lures her and her family to his island plantation. Eventually he reveals the death of the unworthy drug-addict lover and his own passion. The lengthy early sections concern plot manipulations and skittish comments on stereotyped figures (the manipulative and hypocritical philosopher-father, the pretentiously vain and empty woman, the irredeemably snobbish aunt, the pontificating newspaper editor, the superior protagonist suffering from vague despair and anxiety). The love scenes show such a gross self-parody of inflated language as to sink any story. Rejected by the woman who is unable to love, the solitary planter neatly commits suicide in the sea. This compulsively repeated pattern in Conrad of the superior solitary descending into despair and suicide in an artificial and false world can be taken as the author's nuclear trope. But the writing, as well as being sentimental melodrama, suggests obscured motives of anxious impotence, guilt, and self-hatred.

The shorter "The Partner" (1910) is better. In this simple story, a conniving businessman gets his partner to plant a crooked first mate on his brother's ship in order to help sink it for the insurance money, which they want to use for a patent medicine scheme. The connivance works, but chance complicates matters when the criminal mate robs and kills the captain who, in the necessary cover-up, must be treated as a suicide. Thus the partners do not get sufficient insurance money to carry out their scheme, and all end in failure. The ex-stevedore, who is the partner in the telling with the commercial writer-narrator, is treated denigratingly for his "raw" and ruffianly insistence on de-romanticizing the tale by placing it in the real world of cowardice, cupidity, and chance. While the story is not really probing of motives or other meanings with its stereotyped characters, its melodramatic action is presented well and with an appropriately cynical morality (perhaps traceable to Maupassant, a main influence on Conrad, along with Daudet and less meritorious French fictionists). Defensively, the narrating commercial writer admits that he failed "to cook it for the consumption of magazine readers," that is, give it the ornate exoticism and inflated rhetoric that Conrad exploited in many of his fictions. That is its rare advantage.

The also short "The Inn of the Two Witches" (1913) has been all too cooked for commercial magazine readers. Drawing, as he frequently did in his later years, on his hobbyist's interest in the Napoleonic wars, Conrad places the scene a hundred years earlier in the Peninsula Campaign. A brave trusted seaman on a secret mission disappears at a Spanish country inn run by several old crones and a wicked Gypsy. About to undergo the same fate, a young English officer accidentally discovers the fatal device, a murderous mechanical bed. He escapes and a Spanish band punishes the witches and those related to them. The whole is an empty piece of heavily atmospheric costume flummery.

The shortly following story "Because of the Dollars" is a return to the romantic Eastern material. Captain Davidson, a *really* good man" (the same benign figure appears later in *Victory*), is victim of a conspiracy to rob him of government dollars he is transporting on his trading route steamboat in the islands. Warned by a kindly prostitute he has platonically befriended, he successfully defends himself, but the woman is brutally killed. With a sense of

decent obligation to the dead woman, he brings her young son to his wife to raise. She, a stupid and righteous petite bourgeoise with a "mean little soul," uses the questionable propriety of the situation as an excuse to leave the captain for good. His foster son trained by missionaries to become one of them, the good captain is left "without a single human affection near him." In this mean and malicious world, Conrad's sentimental tale insists, the reward of virtue is sad solitude.

Conrad's remaining short fictions were collected posthumously as *Tales of Hearsay* (1925). Included was "The Black Mate," apparently his first story, rewritten many years later, about an aging white-haired mate who finds employment difficult and so dyes his hair and beard deep black to get a job on a sailing ship captained by a mean spiritualist. In a tricky plot, the mate, after an accident, claims to have been attacked by an apparition in order to explain his hair turning white. This ruse works in this tiresome bit of magazine dalliance.

A much graver trick is at the center of Conrad's one story drawing on World War I materials, "The Tale" (1917). In a vague and portentous manner, a British naval captain recounts his boarding an anchored neutral merchant vessel on the suspicion that it had been supplying German submarines. In spite of careful examination, he can find no confirmation of neutrality violations by its Scandinavian master, who claims simply to be lost in the fog with no clear idea of his location. The British officer orders him to leave on a certain course; if he fails to do so, it means he knows where he is; if he follows the order he will smash on a reef in the fog. He follows the British order and the ship goes down with all hands. The British officer concludes that he will "never know" whether he had "done stern retribution—or murder." While this may seem like a Conradian tale of moral ambivalence (and has been so misread), it is as given a tale of malicious murder committed under the guise of "duty." If the neutral captain had been supplying submarines, he would have known where he was and either refused to go or corrected course (suicide is ruled out by the characterization). Since he does neither, the British captain, by his own logic, is a mass murderer. His claim to uncertainty, not to "know," and his woman auditor's claim that he is a man of virtue and "humanity" (yet another example of feminine illusion?) are bitter ironies of self-deceit. Is Conrad muddled on the logic of the story, or is he exposing vicious moral illusion? While there appears to be no way of being certain of authorial intention, the story may be both. In the apparent muddle, Conrad may be claiming a conservative-moral gesture while simultaneously dramatizing its falsity—the essential self-illusory nature of most human values.

"Prince Roman" (1917) seems to be the only time Conrad directly used Polish material in his fictions. He had perhaps been released into it by his visit as a noted English author to Russian Poland just before World War I. The entitling figure is an exalted Polish nobleman—suffering from melancholy over the death of his young wife—who joins as a common soldier a Polish military rebellion against the Russians (1830s). Sternly dutiful both during and after the war, he is sent to Siberia and serves a twenty-five-year sentence. But even as a completely deaf old man he is noted for his patriotic charity. The tale is a simpleminded paean to continuing Polish aristocracy and patriotism, Conrad's origins, somewhat awkwardly done, and of no larger interest.

"The Warrior's Soul" (1917), another tale of the Napoleonic period, is recounted years later by an old Russian officer and tells of an adolescent Russian officer of supposedly tender sensitivities. He had once been done a great favor in Paris by a French officer, an outstanding figure of love and nobility, and had fervently promised any return favor any time. During the Napoleonic army's retreat from Moscow, the same French officer, ill and hopeless, makes himself the prisoner of the young Russian. The prisoner demands that the youth carry out his warrior's pledge of honor and kill him. After some pained hesitation, the young Russian carries out the promise and shoots the French officer. We are told that he later resigns from the army and becomes a recluse in apparent melancholy. Though the story is handled in an awkward and clichéd way, and there is little probing into character and psyche, we do sense again Conrad's feeling for impossible moral dilemma and the pyrrhic affirmations of a traditional code of honor—his Polish legacy.

In the discriminating criticism there seems general agreement that Conrad's later fictions magnify the earlier weaknesses and that the late works are more weary in style and tendentiously sentimental. *Victory* (1915), the most earnest of the later works, is a sometimes disputed case. Its protagonist, Axel Heyst, is yet another isolated intellectual whose defeat comes from his failure at simple commitment to life. His double appears as an allegorical Mr. Jones—diabolical gentleman, homosexual, gambler, and killer—with whom Heyst forms an implicit Faustian pact. The plenitude of evil is enhanced by the presence of

Dust jacket for the British edition of Conrad's 1915 novel

Jones's two bestial assistants and a malicious hotel keeper. The minor moral virtues, as so often in Conrad, are embodied by several ship captains, one the delicate-prudent part-narrator Davidson. But Conrad attempts to go beyond their stoical virtues by providing a figure of transcendental goodness, Lena, a pathetic but exalted heroine reminiscent of some of Dickens's heroines. It is a heavy morality play.

Conrad's allegory becomes more insistent here than in his earlier fictions while the background has become much thinner. Basic information about Heyst, thirty-five-year-old aristocratic wanderer in the Indies, is withheld through three-fourths of the narrative and then consists of a few summary paragraphs. Reportedly, he once believed in "progress" and seems "mysterious"— "Enchanted Heyst," a romantic finally disenchanted by a predatory society. But Conrad also insists that Heyst's failure really goes back to his fixation at eighteen in a "profound mistrust of life" and a "pitilessly cold" intellectuality that denies human affirmation (a more absolute Decoud of *Nostromo*). Heyst's deficiencies are related to his father, a Schopenhauerian "romantic" philosopher who indoctrinated his son with a pessimistic skepticism and bequeathed the world a book "that claimed for mankind the right to absolute moral and intellectual liberty of which he no longer believed them worthy." By a logical rather than psychological deduction, Conrad has Heyst guiltily follow his father's spoiled romanticism and become an unemployed isolato, with a private income, a disdainful intellectual. He neither works to change the world nor submits to it.

The two times Heyst slightly ventures out of his romantic withdrawal, he gets into disproportionate trouble. The first time his "sceptical mind was dominated by the fullness of his heart," pity leads him to lend money to a desperate captain to save his brig. His charity results in his acquiescing to the insistently grateful captain's invitation to take part in an abortive coaling scheme, the captain's death on a business trip, and Heyst's guilty remorse and further withdrawal. A later chance departure from his abandoned coaling station on a deserted East Indian island includes a chance visit to a malicious German's hotel. There Heyst makes his second fall into common humanity when, out of pity, he rescues Lena, a poor orphan girl, and takes her back to his island refuge. As with Lord Jim, Heyst's romantic act resulted from "undisciplined imagination." For Conrad, romantic love is but an extension of romantic skepticism. But the guilty pity produces impotence, and Heyst cannot love. Even when alone with Lena on his tropical island he treats the adoring woman as a stranger, and he continues to believe that "he who forms a tie is lost," continues to follow his father's nihilistic philosophy and "remain free from the absurdities of existence." But such avoidance results in the greatest absurdity of all. Conrad brings the grim outside world to the island retreat in the form of simple allegorical figures of evil. Misled by the malicious hotel keeper's fantasy (a Dickensian *idée fixe* of sexual jealousy), three crooks go to rob Heyst. Pedro, savage ape and unimaginative Caliban, serves as Conrad's metaphoric argument against positive natural law. The "feral" Ricardo serves as Conrad's image of the renegade, an ex-ship's officer reverting to the wild and thus exemplifying the danger of removing quasi-military restraints. Just as supposed anarchism belongs to cripples in *The Secret Agent,* and claims to equality and workman's rights to a liar, thief, and coward (Donkin) in *The Nigger of the "Narcissus,"* so avowals of "independence" and "freedom" belong to the predatory Ricardo in *Victory.* He lives by the rule of competitive egoism in which "man depended on himself as if the world were still one great, wild jungle without law." The leading third crook, Mr. Jones, is simply the devil himself. It is all unrelievedly tendentious.

After an animalistic attack on Lena, Ricardo falls adoringly in love with her. The simple Victorian girl uses this to embark on an elaborate deception to save Heyst. The combination of unmotivated reversals in Ricardo's adoration and Lena's sudden cleverness may be a low point in Conrad's characterization. The rhetoric follows. Because of Heyst's perseveration, Lena accidentally receives a bullet in the "sacred whiteness" of her breast and dies "with a divine radiance on her lips." We are told her meaning: "the great exaltation of love and self-sacrifice which is woman's sublime faculty."

And we also have Conrad's sublime facilitation of "symbolic readings." Conventional patterns of light-and-dark metaphors: blond Lena-Alma (both names), and the purity of sacrifice and love of day; the three black-hearted and black-haired villains and their nighttime gambling, plotting, corruption, and murder; the dark-light oxymorons of Heyst, with light and shadow, his enterprise of "black diamonds," the combined volcanic smoke and bright fire which mark his hermitage, and other adumbrations of his moral ambivalence between dark evil and light goodness. These patterns, and the bestiary of evil, metaphors of diabolism, and rhetoric about the isolated romantic skeptic are not balanced by the novelist's essential nonrecurrent imagery of tangible life in this self-parodying allegory.

The melodramatic plotting has literally dozens of absurdities which undermine the ostensible theme of willed choice as against romantic skepticism. But perhaps most portentous is the diabolism. Conrad clearly had no religious faith, yet Mr. Jones is patently supernatural. That "insolent spectre on leave from Hades," that "outlaw from the higher spheres," is a nineteenth-century villain, similar to the decayed gentleman who is Ivan Karamazov's devil and to Rigaud in Dickens's *Little Dorrit,* and he evokes the sexual inversion and intellectual ennui of late-romanticism in French literature. He repeatedly provides standard echoes of Satanism. Apparently Heyst's reluctance to acknowledge his pact with the Jones-devil results also from skepticism; the "ill omened chaos of the sky" denies any "Christian virtue," any positive providence. But he has missed the Conradian point that while there may be no absolute good, there is absolute malignancy.

And certain kinds of good become malignant. The parallelism between gentle Heyst and murderous Jones, the romantic skeptic and the diabolical criminal, may be more extreme than Conrad's earlier doublings—Lord Jim and Gentleman Brown, fugitive Leggatt and the young captain, and the others—because both are here treated as intellectuals with "the privileged detachment of a cultivated mind, of an elevated personality." The ironists go in "spectral brothership" to confront the feared female, perfect shot Jones somehow shooting wild, and then, Heyst's demonism done, his devil (Jones) inexplicably drops dead.

Even when Heyst realizes Lena's true sacrifice for him, his too "fastidious soul" (like homosexual Jones's) "kept the true cry of love from his lips in its infernal mistrust of life." His demonic "despair" allows him to declare but not to show active faith in that famous last speech: "woe to the man whose heart has not learned while young to hope, to love—and to put its trust in life." But how could the intellectual, with his denuded consciousness? As Heyst once explained to Lena, "I don't think. Something in me thinks—something foreign to my nature." The self-alienated intellectual, then, cannot be redeemed, only exorcised by Heyst's burning himself in his own house, Lena's funeral pyre, a suicide, yet again, because of self-consciousness.

Some sentimentalist readers of the novel try to see *Victory* as the protagonist's progressive redemption, but clearly his pattern runs from skepticism to demonism to despairing suicide. The only victory was sacrificial Lena's, as Conrad emphasized nine years after writing, when on his celebrity American tour he emotionally read to an American audience his favorite passage, Lena's death scene. Conrad was not about to trust those intellectuals (Heyst, Decoud, and the like) with posthumous life. For "Thinking is the enemy of perfection," wrote Conrad in the later "Author's Note" to *Victory*. But the obsessive anti-intellectualism suffers from excessive intellectualism, including some very bad styling and plotting around allegorical abstractions. Conrad's counterromanticism became a cerebral inversion of the cerebral inversion he set out to expose. The real Conradian irony is the victory of evil over evil, a homeopathic art in which the malady and the medicine have become identical.

It is hard to present *Victory* as other than a bad novel. Still, it has some suggestiveness. Few find even this true of the remaining three fictions. One was the tired finishing of his Malayan saga, *The Rescue*. The other two were simply popular sentimental romances. *The Arrow of Gold* (1919) draws on the author's youthful experiences in Marseilles, though, as recent biographies make clear, with considerable defensive distortion. Covering about a year and a half (in the 1870s), it is the account of an ill-defined young man, M. George, in love with a beautiful and rich ex-courtesan (and ex-Basque

goatgirl), Dõna Rita, who is a conspirator for the supporters of the Spanish royalist pretender in southern France, the Carlists. George coordinates the smuggling of weapons to the Carlist gangs. But the cursory treatment of the gunrunning and politics leaves them vague and largely irrelevant.

The early sections of the novel disproportionately concern minor characters in a mannered account that seems to combine badly Henry James and popular fiction. The George-Rita love affair suffers rhetorical inflation and displacement (typically: "I had the time to lay my infinite adoration at her feet whose white insteps gleamed below the dark edge of the fur out of quilted blue silk bedroom slippers, embroidered with small pearls."). There are scorned lovers, treated with uncertain mock heroics, a piously rapacious sister, a knocked-off indecisive duel, arbitrary symbolic flourishes (the entitling gold hair decoration), the inexplicable decamping of the beloved lady, and other folderol. Embarrassed treatment of politics and sex makes it self-parodying. *The Arrow of Gold* would not make it in the current exploitative romance market because of its inferiority.

The Rover (1923), like several of the novellas discussed above, is a maudlin costume piece in clichéd rhetoric about the Napoleonic era. Peyrol, an ex-pirate and "disinherited soul," sacrifices himself in a fantastic plot for the great English navy, the righteous anti-Jacobins, and an old man's quaint "honor." It also helps unite two young isolatoes in the "unearthly experience" of love so to transcend the humbly wise rover's "disenchanted philosophy." The anxiety of the solitary, suicide, trite prejudices, conservative sentimentalities, and boats, do link it to the rest of Conrad. At his death, Conrad was working on yet another Napoleonic period romance, the incomplete work published posthumously as *Suspense*. Reasonably enough, no serious commentator has spent much time on these fictions, which would no longer be read at all if they were not by the author of "Heart of Darkness" and *The Secret Agent*. Fame and financial ease in his last decade rather confirmed Conrad's role as a commercial entertainer. He seems to have had little awareness of his literary decline.

Perhaps because of the burden of bad writing, Conrad's literary reputation declined markedly in the mid-1920s after his death. A generation later there was a critical-academic revival of interest in Conrad, largely centering on a limited body of works (mostly those written in the decade from 1898 to 1910), which somewhat uncertainly gave his works the status of modern classics. While literary

Joseph Conrad, 1923 (photo by T. R. Annan & Sons)

sity, partly from the anxiously heightened style and partly from the unusually negative view of nature which provides a distinctive malignancy and a grotesqueness of human response. While the ideological insistence on exalting disciplined routines, arbitrary authority, and stupid captains (as in *The Nigger of the "Narcissus"* and "Typhoon") seems a moralistic burden, the peculiarity fascinates authority-yearning readers. The maritime initiation-maturation themes (as in "Youth," the *Patna* section of *Lord Jim,* and *The Shadow-Line*) artistically culminate in the anxious extreme identification with the dark double in "The Secret Sharer," which remains a classic of moral ambivalence.

But Conrad is reported several times as having been upset at being considered primarily a sea writer, though his sea writing accounted for much of his reputation in his lifetime. Certainly both his commercial-popular and artistic-intellectual ambitions went beyond that maritime role. Conrad's seriousness is displayed in his insistent concern with "romantic egoism," from the early Malayan saga through *Lord Jim* and *Nostromo*—those works in which moral ambivalence is exotically tested. In the period of his best writing, from "Heart of Darkness" through *The Secret Agent,* he achieved a distinctive moral resonance and rhetorical intensity. His antipolitical romances of politics sometimes succeeded in disciplining the exoticism and the rhetoric into the cathartic extremity of modernist intellectual probing. He achieved this kind of success in spite of being heavily burdened with some of the worst literary characteristics of his time—including gross sentimentality, shoddy melodrama, chauvinistic moralisms, and sickly repressed eroticism. He achieved some victories over Victorian pathology.

The modernism which Conrad's best work achieved, and upon which his authentic reputation rests, undercut accepted social and other moral values. In modernism, inherited hierarchies and pieties lost their sanctity under extreme explorations and questions. Conrad, rather in spite of himself, also questioned the authority and legitimacy of most values. This may have been less his intention than the inevitable, double-edged outlook of the exilic orphan who did not really have the honor, the solidarity, the patriotism, the simple human faith that he desperately posited. Thus in Conrad we paradoxically see an intellectual anti-intellectualism, a radicalness of tone even when conservative in emphasis, an extremity of imagination which becomes a stern engagement, in spite of the sentimental camouflage, to subterranean denials.

Conrad was simultaneously one of the most

reputations partly depend on extraneous matters (fashion, taste, mythological needs, etc.), they can also sometimes become self-generating when taken up by noted followers. Though the interest in Conrad now may be somewhat less intense than in the 1950s, his centrality to modern fiction is widely accepted and results in a variety of editions, massive studies, cinematic adaptions, specialist journals, and other responses to his writings. His major transitional role between Victorian forms and sentiments and modernist ideologies and perplexities seems well established.

While much of Conrad's fiction is patently poor, even some of that, when compared to other contemporary commercial fiction, is sometimes suggestive and probably retains some historical interest. At a more important level, Conrad's sea stories also have a documentary fascination in their reports of dying nineteenth-century merchant marine sailing experience. Furthermore, some of the maritime accounts display an exceptional inten-

nihilistic and most antinihilistic of fictionists in English, obsessed with finding, and exposing, meanings and meaninglessness. Even as he insisted on the negative process, he deplored it, homeopathically countering alienation, despair, and meaninglessness with doses of the same. A would-be sanctifier of conventionally traditional values, he was yet a drastic doubter—"like most men of little faith," as he described himself in one of his letters, and generally with "scepticism . . . the agent of truth," as he defensively insisted in another. His cosmic doubt often becomes cosmic malevolence, or as a striking phrase of Captain Marlow's in "Heart of Darkness" has it, our world is viewed as a "mysterious arrangement of merciless logic for a futile purpose."

The inverted melodrama of malignant fate in Conrad is not just a popular vice but, at his best, a sense of metaphysical extremity. Fended-off negation was central to his art, with its circling forms, labyrinthine narrative removals, peculiar exaltation of evil chance, mystifying rhetoric, and a defensive ideological insistence overriding human psychology, probability, and decency. He seems driven to the dark "heart of the matter" in which he insistently portrayed failing, suicidal, hollow heroes without sufficient heart. Simple goodness of behavior became the only defense against what he repeatedly called the "cosmic chaos." But as Marlow tells Jewel in *Lord Jim*, "Nobody, nobody, is good enough."

The "simple ideas" with which Conrad wanted to keep desperate faith turn out to be inadequate even when not gross illusions for his solitaries struggling with civilized absurdities as well as oppressive jungle and indifferently tormenting seas. Conrad wanted a "Fidelity" which he did not really possess. He insisted on conventional notions without real faith in them, made even more impossible by extreme situations; in dramatic and dialectical fact, he insisted on harsh skepticism and self-destructiveness. This is true in the best fictions, such as "Heart of Darkness," *Nostromo*, "The Secret Sharer," and *The Secret Agent*, as well as in the more grossly tendentious allegories such as *Under Western Eyes* and *Victory*. For what Conrad often means by his credo of "simple ideas" that informs his fictions is a nihilist's defensive sticking with the limited duties and affirmations of ordinary illusions, in fear of destruction from a malignant world and self. His forced efforts at a positive morality by reversal of radical doubts, which he so obviously had, may remain unpersuasive, not least in their fictional and rhetorical arbitrariness, but may be nonetheless in-

triguing and significant. Conrad is truly read for his perplexity.

As with much of modern moral conservativism, which lacks any transcendent order and organic society, Conrad tried to form a precarious fideistic dialectic from his doubts and fears. His desire for simple virtues and fidelities, on the explicit assumption that "man is a desperately conservative creature," remains poignant. He profoundly recognized that, somehow, values have to be simple or most men will be excluded from them, and thus from purposive life. The unexamined life, Conrad deeply felt, must be worth living because the examined life is suicidally dangerous. Conrad was constitutionally incapable of considering more radically redemptive forms of simple ideas and human fidelities (except as maudlin assertions and tricks). We might therefore respect the unresolvable difficulties of Conrad's moral dilemma of conservative needs versus powerful denials, even when we see that they drove him to pyrrhonistic, and sometimes incoherent and bad, art and ideologies which lacked sufficient humanity. In his best ideological melodramas it is often exemplary the way the nihilist triumphs over the ostensible antinihilist, the villainous intellectual over Conrad's conservative sentiments, the provocative modernist over the mere literary hack and conventional moralist.

Letters:

Joseph Conrad: Life and Letters, 2 volumes, edited by G. Jean-Aubry (Garden City: Doubleday, Page, 1927; London: Heinemann, 1927);

Conrad to a Friend: 150 Selected Letters from Joseph Conrad to Richard Curle, edited by Richard Curle (London: Sampson Low, Marston, 1928; New York: Crosby Gaige, 1928);

Letters from Joseph Conrad, 1895-1924, edited by Edward Garnett (London: Nonesuch, 1928; Indianapolis: Bobbs-Merrill, 1928);

Letters of Joseph Conrad to Marguerite Poradowska, 1890-1920, translated and edited by John A. Gee and Paul J. Sturm (New Haven: Yale University Press, 1940);

Joseph Conrad: Letters to William Blackward and David S. Meldrum, edited by William Blackburn (Durham: Duke University Press, 1958);

Conrad's Polish Background: Letters to and From Polish Friends, edited by Zdzislaw Najder (London & New York: Oxford University Press, 1964);

Joseph Conrad and Warrington Dawson: The Record of a Friendship, edited by D. B. J. Randall (Durham:

Duke University Press, 1968);

Joseph Conrad's Letters to Cunninghame-Graham, edited by C. T. Watts (Cambridge: Cambridge University Press, 1969);

The Collected Letters of Joseph Conrad, volume 1, 23 May 1861-31 December 1897, edited by Frederick R. Karl and Laurence Davies (Cambridge: Cambridge University Press, 1983).

Bibliographies:

Thomas J. Wise, *A Bibliography of the Writings of Joseph Conrad (1895-1921),* revised and enlarged edition (London: Privately printed, 1921; reprinted, London: Dawsons of Pall Mall, 1964);

Kenneth A. Lohf and Eugene P. Streehy, *Joseph Conrad at Mid-Century: Editions and Studies, 1895-1955* (Minneapolis: University of Minnesota Press, 1957);

Theodore G. Ehrsam, *A Bibliography of Joseph Conrad* (Metuchen, N.J.: Scarecrow, 1969);

Bruce E. Teets and Helmut E. Gerber, *Joseph Conrad, An Annotated Bibliography of Writings About Him* (DeKalb: Northern Illinois University Press, 1971).

Biographies:

Ford Madox Ford, *Joseph Conrad: A Personal Remembrance* (Boston: Little, Brown, 1924);

Jessie Conrad, *Joseph Conrad and His Circle* (New York: Dutton, 1935);

Jocelyn Baines, *Joseph Conrad* (New York: McGraw Hill, 1967);

Bernard Meyer, *Joseph Conrad: A Psychoanalytic Biography* (Princeton: Princeton University Press, 1967);

Gustave Morf, *The Polish Shades and Ghosts of Joseph Conrad* (New York: Astra, 1976);

Frederick R. Karl, *Joseph Conrad, The Three Lives* (New York: Farrar, Straus & Giroux, 1979);

Zdzislaw Najder, *Joseph Conrad,* translated by Halina Carroll-Najder (New Brunswick: Rutgers University Press, 1983).

References:

Jeffrey Berman, *Joseph Conrad: Writing As Rescue* (New York: Astra, 1977);

M. C. Bradbrook, *Joseph Conrad: Poland's English Genius* (Cambridge: Cambridge University Press, 1941);

Richard Curle, *Joseph Conrad and His Characters: A Study of Six Novels* (London: Heinemann, 1957);

H. M. Daleski, *Joseph Conrad: The Way of Dispossession* (London: Faber & Faber, 1977);

Avrom Fleishman, *Conrad's Politics: Community and Anarchy in the Fictions of Joseph Conrad* (Baltimore: Johns Hopkins University Press, 1967);

Gary Geddes, *Conrad's Later Novels* (Montreal: McGill-Queens University Press, 1980);

Peter J. Glassman, *Language and Being: Joseph Conrad and the Literature of Personality* (New York: Columbia University Press, 1976);

John Dozier Gordon, *Joseph Conrad: The Making of a Novelist* (Cambridge: Harvard University Press, 1940);

Lawrence Graver, *Conrad's Short Fiction* (Berkeley: University of California Press, 1969);

Albert Guerard, *Conrad the Novelist* (Cambridge: Harvard University Press, 1958);

Eloise Knapp Hay, *The Political Novels of Joseph Conrad* (Chicago: University of Chicago Press, 1963);

Douglas Hewitt, *Conrad: A Reassessment* (Cambridge: Bowes & Bowes, 1952);

Irving Howe, *Politics and the Novel* (New York: Horizon, 1957);

Bruce Johnson, *Conrad's Models of Mind* (Minneapolis: University of Minnesota Press, 1971);

F. R. Leavis, *The Great Tradition: George Eliot, Henry James, Joseph Conrad* (London: Chatto & Windus, 1948);

Thomas Moser, *Joseph Conrad: Achievement and Decline* (Cambridge: Harvard University Press, 1957);

Elsa Nettels, *James and Conrad* (Athens: University of Georgia Press, 1977);

Royal Roussel, *The Metaphysics of Darkness* (Baltimore: Johns Hopkins University Press, 1971);

Norman Sherry, *Conrad's Eastern World* (Cambridge: Cambridge University Press, 1966);

Sherry, *Conrad's Western World* (Cambridge: Cambridge University Press, 1971);

Ian Watt, *Conrad in the Nineteenth Century* (Berkeley: University of California Press, 1979);

Kingsley Widmer, *Edges of Extremity: Some Problems of Literary Modernism* (Tulsa: University of Tulsa, 1980);

Morton D. Zabel, *Craft and Character: Text, Methods, and Vocation in Modern Fiction* (New York: Viking, 1971).

Papers:

The following libraries have collections of Conrad's papers: the Beinecke Library at Yale University, the

New York Public Library, the British Library, the Brotherton Collection at Leeds University, Colgate University Library, Cornell University Library, Dartmouth College Library, the Houghton Library at Harvard University, the Humanities Research Center at the University of Texas at Austin, the Lilly Library at Indiana University, the J. Pierpont Morgan Library, the William T. Perkins Library at Duke University, the Princeton University Library, the Philip H. and A. S. Rosenbach Foundation, the University of Birmingham Library, and the University of Virginia Library.

Marie Corelli
(1 May 1855-21 April 1924)

Margaret B. McDowell
University of Iowa

SELECTED BOOKS: *A Romance of Two Worlds* (London: Bentley, 1886; New York: McNally, 1887);

Vendetta! or, The Story of One Forgotten, 3 volumes (London: Bentley, 1886; New York: Munro, 1888);

Thelma: A Society Novel, 3 volumes (London: Bentley, 1887); republished as *Thelma: A Norwegian Princess* (Chicago: Weeks, 1893);

Ardath: The Story of a Dead Self, 3 volumes (London: Bentley, 1889; New York: Munro, 1895);

My Wonderful Wife (London: White, 1889; New York: Ivers, 1890);

Wormwood, A Drama of Paris, 3 volumes (London: Bentley, 1890; Chicago: Donohue, Henneberry, 1890?);

The Soul of Lilith (London: Bentley, 1892; New York: Lovell, 1892);

The Silver Domino, as Domino (London: Lamley, 1892);

Barabbas: A Dream of the World's Tragedy, 3 volumes (London: Methuen, 1893; Philadelphia: Lippincott, 1894);

The Sorrows of Satan, or The Strange Experience of One Geoffrey Tempest, Millionaire (London: Methuen, 1895; Philadelphia: Lippincott, 1896);

The Silence of the Maharajah (New York: Merriam, 1895);

The Mighty Atom (London: Hutchinson, 1896; Philadelphia: Lippincott, 1896);

Cameos (London: Hutchinson, 1896; Philadelphia: Lippincott, 1896);

The Murder of Delicia (London: Skeffington, 1896; Philadelphia: Lippincott, 1896);

"These Wise Men of Gotham." A "New" Reading of an Old Rhyme (Philadelphia: Lippincott, 1896);

The Distant Voice: A Fact or a Fantasy? (Philadelphia: Lippincott, 1896);

Ziska: The Problem of a Wicked Soul (London: Methuen, 1897; New York: Stone & Kimball, 1897);

Jane: A Social Incident (London: Hutchinson, 1897; Philadelphia: Lippincott, 1897);

The Song of Miriam, and Other Stories (New York: Munro, 1898);

Patriotism or Self-Advertisement? A Social Note on the War (London: Simpkin, Marshall, Hamilton, Kent, 1900; Philadelphia: Lippincott, 1900);

The Greatest Queen in the World (London: Skeffington, 1900);

Boy: A Sketch (London: Hutchinson, 1900; Philadelphia: Lippincott, 1900);

The Master Christian: A Question of Time (London: Methuen, 1900; New York: Dodd, Mead, 1900);

A Christmas Greeting (New York: Dodd, Mead, 1901);

Christmas Greeting of Various Thoughts, Verses, and Fancies (London: Methuen, 1901);

The Passing of the Great Queen (London: Methuen, 1901; New York: Dodd, Mead, 1901);

Temporal Power: A Study in Supremacy (London: Methuen, 1902; New York: Dodd, Mead, 1902);

The Vanishing Gift: An Address on the Decay of the Imagination (Edinburgh: Philosophical Institution, 1902);

The Plain Truth of the Stratford-upon-Avon Controversy (London: Methuen, 1903);

Angel's Wickedness: A True Story (New York: Beers, 1903);

The Strange Visitation of Josiah McNason (London: Newnes, 1904; New York: International News, 1904);

God's Good Man, A Simple Love Story (London: Methuen, 1904; New York: Dodd, Mead, 1904);

Free Opinions, Freely Expressed on Certain Phases of Modern Social Life and Conduct (London: Constable, 1905; New York: Dodd, Mead, 1905);

The Spirit of Work (Edinburgh: Privately printed, 1906);

Faith Versus Flunkeyism, A Word on the Spanish Royal Marriage (London: Rapid Review, 1906);

The Treasure of Heaven: A Romance of Riches (London: Constable, 1906; New York: Dodd, Mead, 1906);

Woman or Suffragette? A Question of National Choice (London: C. A. Pearson, 1907);

Holy Orders: The Tragedy of a Quiet Life (London: Methuen, 1908; New York: Stokes, 1908);

America's Possession in Shakespeare's Town: The Harvard House (Edinburgh: Morrison & Gibb, 1909);

The Devil's Motor: A Fantasy (London: Hodder & Stoughton, 1910);

The Life Everlasting: A Reality of Romance (London: Methuen, 1911; New York: Hodder & Stoughton/Doran, 1911);

Innocent: Her Fancy and His Fact (London: Hodder & Stoughton, 1914; New York: Doran, 1914);

Eyes of the Sea: A Tribute to the Grand Fleet (London: Marshall, 1917);

Is All Well with England? (London: Jarrod's, 1917);

The Young Diana: An Experiment of the Future (London: Methuen, 1918; New York: Doran, 1918);

My "Little Bit" (London: Collins, 1919; New York: Doran, 1919);

The Love of Long Ago, and Other Stories (London: Methuen, 1920; Garden City: Doubleday, 1921);

The Secret Power (London: Methuen, 1921; Garden City: Doubleday, 1921);

Love – and the Philosopher: A Study in Sentiment (London: Methuen, 1923; New York: Doran, 1923);

Praise and Prayer, a Simple Home Service (London: Methuen, 1923);

Open Confession To a Man From a Woman (London: Hutchinson, 1925; New York: Doran, 1926);

Poems, edited by Bertha Vyver (London: Hutchinson, 1925; New York: Doran, 1926).

OTHER: "The Modern Marriage Market," in The Modern Marriage Market, by Corelli and others (Philadelphia: Lippincott, 1900).

Because of the unrivaled popularity of her novels from 1886 to 1924, Marie Corelli (pseudonym for Mary "Minnie" MacKay) demands attention of both social and literary historians. Full and accurate sales comparisons do not exist for the late nineteenth century, but it appears from what sources there are that she ranked as the best-selling writer in the world for about thirty years. Only about half of her novels proved to be best-sellers, but her works succeeded one another so rapidly that she never lost the attention of the public. In his detailed biography of Corelli, Brian Masters reports from his research impressive figures on the sales of several of her works. During every year of her career, her publishers sold over 100,000 copies of her books. (Her nearest competitor, Hall Caine, at the height of his career sold 45,000 copies; Mrs. Humphry Ward, the third most popular novelist, averaged in her best years about 35,000 copies; and H. G. Wells at the height of his career sold about 15,000 copies annually.) Corelli's first three novels—all long—appeared within fourteen months in 1886 and 1887. In the five-year period from 1892 to 1897 Corelli published in rapid succession eight novels, a book of short stories, and two volumes of essays. One of these novels, *The Sorrows of Satan* (1895), broke all records in early sales. It was in its sixtieth edition at her death in 1924, when *Thelma* (1887) was in its fifty-sixth edition and *Barabbas* (1893) its fifty-fourth. Often entire first editions sold in the first week of publication. *Temporal Power* (1902), a novel attacking socialism, in its first week sold the entire first edition of 120,000 copies and 50,000 of a second edition.

In the early years of this century, thousands waited outside the halls where Marie Corelli lectured, and some fought to touch her gown. Even in the 1920s tourists gathered each afternoon to glimpse her as she emerged from her house at Stratford-upon-Avon. Hundreds of parents named their daughters Thelma after the novel by that name. While some churches rang with sermons based on *Barabbas, The Sorrows of Satan, The Master Christian,* and *Holy Orders,* other churches urged that her books be banned.

Corelli's admirers included the famous, and she blatantly publicized every contact with well-known figures, often to their embarrassment. In 1887 she sought out her neighbor, the actress Ellen Terry, even offering her earrings which supposedly once belonged to the actress Mrs. Siddons. Her publisher narrowly prevented her printing of a letter from the queen of Italy, which expressed the queen's enjoyment of *A Romance of Two Worlds* (1886). In 1893 she begged the opera star Adelina Patti to become her friend, addressing her as "*you, who of all women in the world I most admire*" and signing herself "With a kiss on your sweet little singing lips which guard a well of golden melody.... Your friend with entire devotion...." In 1890 Queen Victoria, through the Duchess of Roxburghe, had let it be known that she would accept presentation of a copy of *A Romance of Two Worlds,* a book she had read with pleasure. After

receiving a specially bound edition, she commanded by telegram that copies of all Corelli's books be sent to her at Balmoral Castle. Sales of *The Soul of Lilith* (1892) were said to have doubled the week a newspaper mentioned that the queen was reading the book. Corelli had a long private audience with the widowed Empress Frederick of Germany, daughter of Queen Victoria, at Buckingham Palace; she dined in Hamburg with the Prince of Wales, later returning to London with him in his special train; and she was the only author invited to his coronation as Edward VII. Prime Minister William Gladstone and Prime Minister Herbert Asquith at various times called on her; Oscar Wilde came to say that *Ardath* (1889) "enchanted" him; and Tennyson acknowledged her gift copy of *Ardath* with a letter which ironically congratulated her on her decision not to seek fame.

Curiously, Corelli combined her efforts to seek notoriety with contradictory efforts to maintain personal privacy. In spite of her penchant for publicity, she refused to allow review copies of her books to be distributed after the early years of her career; she pugnaciously dispersed all photographers; she guarded factual evidence regarding her parentage and the date of her birth; and she lied about having extensive training in music and languages. This conflicting behavior in which she both sought and avoided public attention became more evident in the last twenty-five years of her life at Stratford-on-Avon, where she obviously moved to associate her reputation with that of Shakespeare. She tried to monopolize all famous visitors to Shakespeare's birthplace, including William Butler Yeats and Mark Twain; and she led a sensational effort to prevent construction of a public library in Stratford, endowed by Andrew Carnegie.

Corelli's image of herself as a coy and childlike young maiden did not change as she became overweight for her stature, which was only about four feet ten inches. She continued to dress in ruffled, bow-trimmed, pastel clothing. In 1902 she bought two Shetland ponies, Puck and Ariel, in Scotland and a miniature chaise-cart that scarcely bore the weight of herself and her tall, huskily built companion, Bertha Vyver, as they took afternoon rides in Stratford. The cart was decorated with silver lamps and bells, and the tiny ponies had red outfits. In 1905 she indulged another fantasy for her afternoon pleasure after her invariable eight hours of daily writing. She ordered a specially crafted gondola, "The Dream," from Venice and had it delivered with a uniformed gondolier. While the gondolier was soon replaced by her gardener, she and

Corelli and the pony chaise in which she took afternoon rides in Stratford-upon-Avon

Bertha Vyver attracted attention as they floated on the Avon. When she threatened one covert photographer, she said that she wanted to remain to her readers a kind of "veiled prophet."

While Marie Corelli enjoyed popular success and was praised by the famous as well as the masses, the reasons for her success remain, in part, obscure. Her books were outrageously overwritten—every page loaded with adjectives, adverbs, assorted clichés, archaisms, and repetitions. Her novels were far longer than those of her contemporaries, and her readers seemed not to skip the long, unbroken pages of description; in fact, many admirers memorized the passages they found uplifting, poetic, and filled with "lovely pictures." Her scolding rhetoric rose almost to hysteria on such subjects as women who smoked or rode bicycles, Parisians who drank and read cheap novels, socialists, suffragists, and Carnegie libraries.

Her landscapes appeared always with much color and movement—not in static pastoral calm. In *Ardath,* for example, she spends pages on a storm in the mountains:

Night was approaching, though away to the west a broad gash of crimson, a seeming wound in the breast of heaven, showed where the sun had set an hour since. Now and again the rising wind moaned sobbingly through the tall and spectral pines that, with knotted roots fast clenched in the reluctant earth, clung tenaciously to their stony vantage ground; and mingling with its wailing murmur, there came a distant hoarse roaring as of tumbling torrents, while at far-off intervals could be heard the sweeping thud of an avalanche slipping from point to point on its disastrous downward way. . . . Gradually the wind increased, and soon with sudden fierce gusts shook the pine trees into shuddering anxiety—the red slit in the sky closed . . . then—with a swirling, hissing rush of rain—the unbound hurricane burst forth alive and furious. . . . the tempest rolled, thundered and shrieked its way through Dariel.

While readers bought her books by the

Corelli's friend and companion Bertha Vyver (photo by Gabell)

thousands, reviewers ignored or ridiculed them, noting such examples of her writing as "My heart beat thickly" and "that trifling elevation of his countenance called by courtesy a nose." In her religious novels characters used pronouns and verbs from the King James Bible: "Thou wert," "kisseth." Her women "swoon," and they have "brilliant eyes," "orbs," "great sombre dusky eyes," and "eyes reverentially lowered." They tend to be angels or vampires. In *The Sorrows of Satan,* the Devil, appearing as Prince Rimánez, scolds an unfaithful woman: "Your vampire soul leaped to mine at first glance I ever gave you. . . . you deepen folly into crime—with the seduction of your nude limbs and lying eyes you make fools, cowards, and beasts of men." In *Ziska* (1897), Gervase, the French painter, complains of a woman's power: "a woman whose face haunts me; a woman who drags me to her side with the force of a magnet, there to grovel like a brain-sick fool and plead . . . for a love . . . poison to my soul."

The writer's tendency in the passionate love scenes is to picture the woman as one who responds with great passivity—the aggressive passion is in the mind of the man and is fed by the woman's tremulous reactions. For several pages in *Ziska,* Helen's heart is being broken in a love scene, while such passages as these typify her action: "Helen looked at him in speechless despair. . . . Helen, though quiet and undemonstrative, had fine feelings and unsounded depths of passion in her nature. . . . Poor Helen. It was little marvel that she wept as all women weep when their hearts are broken. . . ."

The evasion of explicit physical detail is not surprising in popular novels at the turn of the century, but Corelli's intensity is notable in the long love scenes where emotion is stirred by the woman's agonizing repression. Notable also is Corelli's ability to sustain interest in scenes of passion by placing them in strange—even bizarre—settings, sometimes in remote lands or in other periods of history. Her lovers reach their ecstasy or their moments of heartbreak in an ancient temple in Babylon, amid the confusion of a procession of snake-worshippers in Al-Kyris in 5,000 B.C., at the base of the Great Pyramids in Egypt, on a moonlit beach in Norway, in a darkened mausoleum in plague-swept Naples, and in the artists' studios of Paris. The variety of her sexual appeals even includes, in several of the novels, encounters between lovers where a corpse is present. In *Vendetta!* (1886) Count Fabio takes his hated bride—immediately after the wedding—to the mausoleum and shows her the body of her lover, whom he has slain. (In the following pages she realizes she is trapped; attempts to stab Fabio to death; goes mad and sings a sweet song like Ophelia, which breaks his heart; and just as he repents his punishment of his "hated-beloved," an earthquake hits the underground vault and a section of the rock falls and kills her.) In *Wormwood* (1890) the absinthe addict, who has cruelly spurned his bride before the wedding guests, seeks out her body after she has drowned herself. He looks at her corpse and fantasizes at length about the way the river caressed her:

> I saw the fair, soft, white body of the woman I had loved . . . laid out on the dull hard slab of stone like a beautiful figure of frozen snow. The river had used her tenderly. . . . it had caressed her gently and had not disfigured her delicate limbs or spoilt her pretty face. . . . I fancied the cold and muddy Seine must have warmed and brightened to the touch of her drowned beauty! Yes!—the river had fondled her!—had stroked her cheeks and left them pale and pure—had kissed her lips and closed them in a childlike,

happy smile—had swept all her soft hair back from the smooth white brow just to show . . . the blue veins . . . pencilled under the soft transparent skin—had closed the gentle eyes and deftly pointed the long dark lashes in a downward sleepy fringe. . . .

In *The Sorrows of Satan,* after Prince Rimánez denounces Lady Sibyl, she kills herself. Her husband discovers her seated in a chair before a mirror; he turns the lights up to their brightest, seats himself in another chair, and proceeds to read her suicide message as if they are conversing.

Corelli's narrative voice interrupts or frames her sexual scenes with moralistic generalizations. She found herself unable to use such words as *leg, stomach, bosom,* or *breast.* When in 1899 she had a hysterectomy, she sought out a woman surgeon, apparently from her sense of modesty. From the age of twenty-two until her death at sixty-nine, she had few close male friends and lived with her companion, Vyver, who was one year older. In her middle age, after she had moved to Stratford, she loved

Corelli as Pansy at a Shakespeare fancy-dress ball, Stratford-upon-Avon, 1903 (photo by Gabell)

over a period of several years the artist Arthur Severn, her neighbor. (He illustrated *The Devil's Motor,* 1910, a story in which the devil in smoked glasses drives a huge touring car around the world and is so shocked at human sin that he drives off the cliff with all humankind following his car to utter destruction.)

Severn and his wife Joan had been married for forty years before his "affair" with Marie Corelli, who was fifty-one, began. Her love is recorded in many letters to both Arthur and Joan Severn. The ones to Joan insist that she watch Arthur's diet and that he get enough sleep; Joan is addressed as "Dear Bunch" because of a bunch of flowers she once brought Corelli. The letters to Arthur are often in baby-talk ("Me misses 'oo." "Is 'oo not velly-welly?"). Corelli kept a private journal in poetry in these years, in which one finds such lines as "My breaking heart came throbbing to your feet!" Most important as a record of Corelli's attitude toward Severn and his wife and also as a record of Bertha Vyver's empathy and patience is Corelli's *Open Confession To a Man From a Woman* (1925), which Vyver prepared for publication after her companion's death. Severn's behavior during this period seems to have been characterized by amused tolerance alternating with annoyance, and his amusement was shared by his five grown children. Corelli clearly recognized his attitude toward her and repeatedly expressed her anger and hurt feelings, but the intensity of the fantasy she acted out for years seldom lessened.

On numerous occasions, Marie Corelli expressed anger at suffragist activities. In her essay "The Modern Marriage Market" (published in a book of the same name, 1900) she comments that men try to "make women angels . . . in spite of our cycling mania, our foolish clubs . . . our rough games . . . our general throwing to the winds of all dainty feminine reserve—delicacy and modesty—and we alone are to blame if we shatter their ideals and sit down by choice in the mud when they would have placed us on thrones." Even in her last years she sought to present her image as a childlike, innocent maiden—for example, by choosing a belittling title for the essays describing her action and views related to the war effort, *My "Little Bit"* (1919). A reviewer in the *Nation* further diminished it by commenting: "It is abundantly evident that while the whirlwind raged she did what a woman could—and screamed."

In spite of her statements in *The Sorrows of Satan* that women are born to "lift men a step nearer to glory," one recognizes elsewhere the anger she expresses about the role of women—as when Mary

Mason Croft, Corelli's home in Stratford-upon-Avon (photo by Bertha Vyver)

Magdalene in *Barabbas* rails at men who make woman the scapegoat after they "devour her by selfish lust."

One target of Corelli's anger—which she attacked only obliquely through her fiction—was her half brother's treachery in boasting that he wrote all her best books, while she was actually supporting him totally with her earnings for fifteen years. In both *The Murder of Delicia* (1896) and *The Master Christian* (1900), women are betrayed by lovers who pretend that they have been the creators of the women's artistic achievements. (The description of Delicia's villainous husband reads: "a strong, splendid, bold, athletic, masterful creature.") In the preface to *The Murder of Delicia,* Corelli states boldly that "a great majority of the men of the present day want women to keep them." In spite of her antisuffrage essays and her sentimental presentations of submissive women and dominant men in many novels, Corelli's attitudes toward sex, as expressed in her work, are far more complex than her biographers have suggested.

While rumors surfaced occasionally that Bertha Vyver and Marie Corelli were lesbian lovers, nothing in Corelli's work suggests this, and those who knew the women best did not see the friendship as sexually oriented. Considering the arrogance,

insecurity, eccentric behavior, and virulent disputes that characterized Corelli's life, it seems remarkable that the two women maintained so long and tranquil a companionship. Vyver obviously was awed by Corelli's success and the talent she assumed her friend had. She seems to have been more a mother than a servant, lover, or sister to Corelli, in spite of their similar ages. Corelli's dedication of *Thelma* to Vyver in 1887 was still true in 1924, the year Corelli died: "My dearest friend, in recognition of her sweet companionship, tender sympathy, and most faithful love." Unfortunately, Corelli never presented a woman like Bertha Vyver in her fiction, and in *Open Confession* she complains harshly of the dullness of Vyver. (Bertha Vyver died in poverty in 1941.)

Corelli certainly chose to write religious novels because they were fashionable in her generation, but her interest in religion was genuine. She had been taught as a child of Welsh background that angels surrounded and protected her. She claimed that she changed her plans to be a concert pianist after a mystical experience in which she was directed to make a career of writing. She easily imagined angels, devils, and even Christ appearing visibly and materially to her characters. Satan becomes a prominent character in several of her books, and she sets forth her notion that eventually he will be returned to heaven by the good influence of pure women. In fact, for every human who rejects Satan—as does the millionaire Geoffrey Tempest in *The Sorrows of Satan*—Satan gets an hour in heaven.

At a time when spiritualism was fascinating people in both England and America, Corelli emphasized that she was not a spiritualist. Yet at least ten of her novels focus on the sensational aspects of spiritualist experience: healings by electrical energy, hypnotic trances in which the spirit leaves the body for a time to soar to the center of the universe for healing and insight, and similar journeys of the spirit to another continent, another century, or a previous life. The greatest of her spiritualist wizards, Heliobas, appears in three of her early books (*A Romance of Two Worlds, Ardath,* and *The Soul of Lilith*). Descended from the Wise Men of the East, he is an ancient Chaldean who has been reincarnated in several times and places. In her first book he is a Paris physician; in the other books he appears variously in ancient Al-Kyris, in the Monastery of Lars, in the fields of Ardath ("four miles from the Babylonian ruins"), and in Arabia.

Religious bigotry and prejudice are everywhere in Corelli's work, as is frequently offensive sentimentalism. She attacked Jews ("the fat Jew-spider of several newspaper webs"). When Christ returns as the little child, Manuel, in *The Master Christian,* the Christ-child and the good Abbé in their travels denounce St. Paul's Cathedral as a monument to the Protestant cults that have fragmented the church and placed the teachings of Paul above those of Christ. When they talk to the Pope, they insist, "Command that the great pictures, the tapestries, the jewels, the world's trash of St. Peter's, be sold to the rich. . . . Can you not hear, in the silence of the night, the shrieks of the tortured. . . ." At the end of four pages of such denunciation, the Pope falls senseless to the pavement of the Vatican. Two novels, *Boy* (1900) and *The Mighty Atom* (1896), attack the secular education of children. She urged in her preface to *Wormwood* that parishioners support "temperance preachers" because too often these men are regarded as "sneaks" while people continue to "swill the pernicious drug of all accursed spirits ever brewed to make of man a beast."

Corelli's emphasis on sensational love (accompanied by moralistic judgments on adulterers), her greatly imaginative explorations of spiritualism, her appeals to prejudice, her ambivalent position on the submission of women, her vivid landscapes, and—most of all—her plots, in which credibility never imposes restraints, must be considered in assessing reasons for her success. It is easy to satirize her excesses, but it is difficult to find another notoriously bad writer whose work is fascinating rather than dull. She prefigured the most prominent and successful of the trends of late-twentieth-century popular literature and film—science fiction, futuristic fiction, gothic novels, romance, and satires of education. (Only detective fiction is missing.) Unlike other prolific writers, Corelli stands alone in not repeating plots—seldom even repeating similar scenes or characters. The variety of her plots cannot be equaled. Leonard Woolf's review of *Open Confession* may best suggest the secret of her difference from other popular novelists:

> The ordinary popular novel has something mechanical about it, the expert who examines its surface sees at once that it is machine made; it is written because the author wants to write a popular novel, no real belief in what the typewriter is tapping out. But you have only to read five sentences of Marie Corelli to recognize the passionate conviction with which they are written. . . . Instead of an ancient plot dipped into a thin mixture of sentimentality and bathos, you have a fierce orgy of both. And that goes straight to the heart of the great public.

References:

Eileen Bigland, *Marie Corelli: The Woman and the Legend* (London: Jarrolds, 1953);

Brian Masters, *Now Barabbas Was A Rotter: The Extraordinary Life of Marie Corelli* (London: Hamish Hamilton, 1978).

E. M. Delafield
(Edmée Elizabeth Monica de la Pasture Dashwood)
(9 June 1890-2 December 1943)

Margaret B. McDowell
University of Iowa

SELECTED BOOKS: *Zella Sees Herself* (London: Heinemann, 1917; New York: Knopf, 1917);

The War-Workers (London: Heinemann, 1918; New York: Knopf, 1918);

The Pelicans (London: Heinemann, 1919; New York: Knopf, 1919);

Consequences (London: Hodder & Stoughton, 1919; New York: Knopf, 1919);

Tension (London: Hutchinson, 1920; New York: Macmillan, 1920);

The Heel of Achilles (London: Hutchinson, 1921; New York: Macmillan, 1921);

Humbug: A Study in Education (London: Hutchinson, 1921; New York: Macmillan, 1922);

The Optimist (London: Hutchinson, 1922; New York: Macmillan, 1922);

A Reversion to Type (London: Hutchinson, 1923; New York: Macmillan, 1923);

Messalina of the Suburbs (London: Hutchinson, 1924);

Mrs. Harter (London: Hutchinson, 1924; New York: Harper, 1925);

The Chip and the Block (London: Hutchinson, 1925; New York: Harper, 1926);

Jill (London: Hutchinson, 1926; New York: Harper, 1927);

The Entertainment and Other Stories (London: Hutchinson, 1927; New York: Harper, 1927);

The Way Things Are (London: Hutchinson, 1927; New York: Harper, 1928);

The Suburban Young Man (London: Hutchinson, 1928);

What Is Love? (London: Macmillan, 1928); republished as *First Love* (New York: Harper, 1929);

Turn Back the Leaves (London: Macmillan, 1930; New York: Harper, 1930);

Diary of a Provincial Lady (London: Macmillan, 1930; New York: Harper, 1931);

Women Are Like That (London: Harper, 1930; London: Macmillan, 1931);

Challenge to Clarissa (London: Macmillan, 1931); republished as *House Party* (New York: Harper, 1931);

To See Ourselves: A Domestic Comedy in Three Acts

E. M. Delafield

(London: Gollancz, 1931);

Thank Heaven Fasting (London: Macmillan, 1932); republished as *A Good Man's Love* (New York: Harper, 1932);

The Provincial Lady Goes Further (London: Macmillan, 1932); republished as *The Provincial Lady in London* (New York: Harper, 1933);

The Time and Tide Album (London: Hamilton, 1932);

Gay Life (London: Macmillan, 1933; New York: Harper, 1933);

General Impressions (London: Macmillan, 1933);

The Glass Wall. A Play in Three Acts (London: Gollancz, 1933);

The Provincial Lady in America (London: Macmillan, 1934; New York: Harper, 1934);

Faster! Faster! (London: Macmillan, 1936; New York: Harper, 1936);

Straw Without Bricks: I Visit Soviet Russia (London: Macmillan, 1937); republished as *I Visit the Soviets* (New York: Harper, 1937);

Nothing Is Safe (London: Macmillan, 1937; New York: Harper, 1937);

Ladies and Gentlemen in Victorian Fiction (London: Hogarth Press, 1937; New York: Harper, 1937);

As Others Hear Us. A Miscellany (London: Macmillan, 1937);

When Women Love (New York: Harper, 1938); republished as *Three Marriages* (London: Macmillan, 1939);

Love Has No Resurrection and Other Stories (London: Macmillan, 1939);

The Provincial Lady in Wartime (London: Macmillan, 1940; New York: Harper, 1940);

No One Now Will Know (London: Macmillan, 1941; New York: Harper, 1941);

Late and Soon (London: Macmillan, 1943; New York: Harper, 1943).

OTHER: *The Brontës: Their Lives Recorded by Their Contemporaries,* compiled with an introduction by Delafield (London: Hogarth Press, 1935).

E. M. Delafield (Edmée Elizabeth Monica de la Pasture Dashwood), one of the most prolific writers of fiction in the 1920s and 1930s, published novels, plays, story collections, and volumes of miscellaneous plays and nonfiction. Her more than forty books and numerous essays and sketches in magazines (particularly *Time and Tide* and *Punch*) appeared from World War I to the middle of World War II. In her twenty-six years of writing, hardly a year passed without the publication of at least one new book. Nearly all of her books sold moderately well in both British and American editions and received favorable reviews. In addition to writing novels, Delafield served as a director of the weekly news magazine *Time and Tide*. She was still producing books at her usual rate when, at the age of fifty-three, she collapsed while delivering a lecture at Oxford University and died a few weeks later.

Delafield excelled in the satirical and comic novel, particularly in her five books in the form of rambling diaries by a character known as the Provincial Lady: *Diary of a Provincial Lady* (1930), *The Provincial Lady Goes Further* (1932), *The Provincial Lady in America* (1934), *Straw Without Bricks* (1937), and *The Provincial Lady in Wartime* (1940).

In other works she successfully exploited the popular interest in criminal trials. Usually starting from documented fact, she carefully developed a fictional elaboration in which she analyzed the motivation for the crime, the personalities and social relationships of the people involved in the crime, and the backgrounds of those involved in the trial or the investigation. Several of these fictionalized studies appeared first in magazines, but the best one is *Messalina of the Suburbs* (1924), based on a London murder in autumn of 1922 that resulted in the execution of two people in January 1923. Delafield's position as justice of the peace in Devon whetted her interest in unraveling the truth that is relevant in court and the deeper truth that relates the legal case to human history.

Delafield's father, Count Henry Philip Ducarel de la Pasture, was descended from French nobility who fled to England at the close of the French Revolution. Her mother, popular novelist Elizabeth Lydia Rosabelle, published about twenty novels between 1900 and 1918, her career overlapping with the appearance of the first of her daughter's fiction. She published under two names, Mrs. Elizabeth Bonham de la Pasture and Mrs. Henry de la Pasture and, at her second marriage in 1910, became Lady Clifford. Her novels contrast with her daughter's in that they are highly sentimental rather than satirical, although they are, like her daughter's, often humorous books, comedies of manners.

Delafield worked during the First World War at Exeter and Bristol for the British government and used this background in *The War-Workers* (1918). When she married in 1919, she had already completed four novels. Her husband, Major Arthur Paul Dashwood, the second son of sixth baronet Sir George Dashwood, had just completed military service in the Royal Engineers. The Dashwoods lived in Malaysia in the early 1920s while he built the causeway from Singapore to the mainland. Their son and daughter were the ages of the children of the Provincial Lady in 1930 when that series of books began to appear.

While E. M. Delafield addresses a variety of topics, most of her books focus on the relationship between parents and children, theories of child-rearing, the educational system, the influence of heredity on children, differences in social class, and criminal cases. At the end of her life she seemed to be turning toward historical novels which covered more than one generation of a family.

The books in which she explores the relationships between children and parents or children and education appeared throughout her career and include the Provincial Lady novels as well as several of the criminal case studies. In *The Pelicans* (1919) Delafield analyzes the divergent, and to some degree unpredictable, effects on children of tyranny masked as maternal solicitude. Two of the three girls in the family are foster children. Two of the three rebel—one marries against her mother's will and the other enters a convent. The third finds satisfaction in her life directed by a parent. In this book Delafield emphasizes the effect on the children of the mother's dominance, while in other books she focuses on the mother's needs and the causes of her drive to dominate. In *Consequences* (1919) Delafield subtly and thoughtfully explores the problems of young Alexandra and the tragic inability of a convent school, the Catholic church, and her family to meet her basic need for human warmth throughout her childhood and adolescence. The novel extends the problem to the cold world of London society after Alexandra matures. *Tension* (1920) presents a school torn by gossip and hypocrisy and raises questions about the ability of teachers and intellectuals to communicate values as well as skills and facts to their students. In *Humbug: A Study in Education* (1921) Lily Stellenthorpe, even in adulthood, cannot see reality or express herself freely because her parents foolishly sought to protect her from all contact with evil. They used her upbringing to test their theories of sentimental idealism. In a similar book, *The Optimist* (1922), Canon Marchard adopts an unrealistically sanguine view of the world and overprotects his four children. All but one rebel and abandon him. He approaches death unmoved in his assumption that bad situations yield a modicum of good. In *Challenge to Clarissa* (1931) the author returns to the theme of maternal dominance—this time in a novel of manners with a high-society background. *Nothing Is Safe* (1937) recounts the summer-vacation problems of Terry and Julia, ages ten and twelve, from the children's point of view. Their lives are confused by divorce, remarriage, and moves among the homes of parents, stepparents, and grandparents. While sensitive to their discomfort (at one point Terry is taken to a psychiatrist without warning), generally the children communicate a wry sense of amusement about their disorientation, and the story moves swiftly. Delafield raises questions about family instability but implies no firm conclusions about causes or solutions.

The books in which Delafield considers the deterministic influence of heredity on children's lives lack the satiric and comic strength of most of her other books. In *A Reversion to Type* (1923), she explores the effects of class differences as well as of heredity. Cecil Aviolet's mother, Rose Smith, brings him back to England to his aristocratic grandparents' home after his father, Jim, dies a drunkard's death in India. Rose's anxieties about the weakening of moral fiber in the aristocratic class (she is herself of working-class background) lead to generalizations that barely escape sentimental foolishness. Other books in which Delafield deals with economic and social class differences and their effect on children include: *The Chip and the Block* (1925), in which the father turns from socialism when he gets some money while one of his children remains true to early indoctrination, and *Jill* (1926), in which two branches of the Galbraith family are contrasted and a woman of less-respected status helps an aristocrat disillusioned by his war experience to regain spirit. In these works, as in the historically oriented *Thank Heaven Fasting* (1932), *No One Now Will Know* (1941), and *Late and Soon* (1943), Delafield may have been moving toward a different approach to fiction with emphasis on historical perspective and deeply dramatic clashes of power, envy, and love rather than comedy of manners.

Delafield introduced a family situation in many ways like that of the Provincial Lady in her novel *Faster! Faster!* (1936). Possessing the detachment and dry wit of the Provincial Lady diaries, this book lacks the light humor of the diaries. Although the story is narrated by the angry daughter of a woman named Claudia, one sees into the emotional turmoil of the mother more fully than in the Provincial Lady diaries. Like the Provincial Lady, Claudia gives too much of her life to her husband and children and resents the sacrifice because she wants power and freedom. More than the Provincial Lady, she is able to define her problem and recognize the irreconcilable conflict which exists between her attachment to her family and her desire to be free.

The novel which most strongly prefigures the diaries is *The Way Things Are* (1927). It clearly looks toward the successful ironic comedy of manners that distinguishes the Provincial Lady books. This novel is executed with objectivity and precision, directing its satire at the weaknesses of the upper-middle-class family. Like the Provincial Lady, the protagonist Laura Temple, married seven years, has a stuffy, self-centered husband and thoughtless children. Like the Lady also, Laura blunders inefficiently in her household responsibilities, although she tries to be conscientious. She rambles—often referring to unsatisfactory servants and troublesome neighbor women. She notably exhibits her

"CAN HEAR ROBERT'S NEIGHBOUR . . . TELLING HIM ABOUT
HER CHILBLAINS."

MRS. BLENKINSOP.

THE GARDENER.

"SCHOOLMASTER AND HIS WIFE . . . TALK TO ONE ANOTHER
ACROSS ME."

Illustrations by Arthur Watts for Delafield's Diary of a Provincial Lady

difference from the Provincial Lady in that she engages in a brief, lukewarm love affair—a momentary distraction, of the kind the Lady would never dream of. Four years after *The Way Things Are* appeared, Delafield published a dramatic version of the novel entitled *To See Ourselves: A Domestic Comedy in Three Acts* (1931).

Convincing realistic background, explicit detail, and natural patterns of conversation mark the Provincial Lady volumes, begun by Delafield in response to a request from *Time and Tide* editor Margaret Haig Thomas, Lady Rhondda, for a series that would run for several weeks. The tone and rhythm of the dialogue produce highly effective comedy as the Lady not only records conversations that occur each day but also converses with herself at many points in the entries in the diary.

The Lady is never arrogant about the family's background as members of the British nobility. In spite of her title, she displays a classless attitude. She worries about the family financial situation—as did most readers during the 1930s. Though readers of this period no doubt found a means of escape in Delafield's inside look at the life-style in a mansion with servants on a country estate, they must have sympathetically identified with the Lady because of her small economies and her strategies for making the children feel equal to their more prosperous neighbors. She understands the stress of the young neighbor woman who wants to marry but must also consider her elderly parent—the comically garrulous old Mrs. Blenkinsop.

Perhaps the Lady's sympathetic traits and egalitarian views derive from the models Delafield used in creating her. By the author's account, the Lady is a composite of several governesses who worked for the family when Delafield was a child. The Provincial Lady's success in freeing herself from the hypocrisy and rigidity of titled society enables her to send her diary to a publisher in order to prove its worth—and her own—to her husband and to "Make a Difference" in the financial situation of her family during the Depression. Typical of her disarming self-deprecation is her final entry in the first Provincial Lady book, *Diary of a Provincial Lady.* She has just returned from a dance at the home of the obnoxious Lady B., where everyone was forced at the end of the evening to join hands and shuffle around in a circle singing Auld Lang Syne. She writes in her diary: "Go home and on looking at myself in the glass am much struck with undeniable fact that at the end of the party I do not look nearly as nice as I did at the beginning...."

The antagonism the Lady feels toward her husband and children, which gives a sharpness to her tolerant, patient, self-deprecating life, is found only in *Diary of a Provincial Lady.* In the second volume of the series, *The Provincial Lady Goes Further,* she goes to London, and the family respects her as a professional author. In the third, *The Provincial Lady in America,* she celebrates her fame among American readers. *The Provincial Lady in America* was first published serially in *Punch,* publicizing the second diary and Delafield's lecture trip to America in 1933. Arthur Watts, who illustrated the first two diaries, accompanied and observed Delafield on her tour to provide illustrations for the *Punch* serial.

In *The Provincial Lady in America,* as the Lady travels to New York, Washington, Boston, Chicago, Cleveland, and Toronto, she tries to understand the Army-Harvard football game, sees "extremely nude" dancers in a Harlem nightclub, discovers that all of Canada seems only twenty miles from Niagara Falls, closes her eyes as she walks past an entire wall of large figures with veins, muscles, and nervous systems boldly exposed at the Hall of Science of the Chicago World's Fair, and enjoys the energetic assistance of Alexander Woollcott in gaining entrance to the Alcott house in Concord (ordinarily open to tours only in summer), so that she can daydream about *Little Women* with the right setting.

In the fourth diary, *Straw Without Bricks* (published in the United States as *I Visit the Soviets*), the Lady recounts her adventures as a member of an agricultural commune in Russia, but the anti-Communist slant dulls the exuberance and variety of Delafield's satire. Similarly, in the fifth diary, *The Provincial Lady in Wartime,* Delafield's attention to the plight of wartime England subdues the unpredictable comic spirit of the Lady. In this final diary, the satire of workers at the canteens and workers involved in the resettlement of city children in the provinces curiously returns Delafield to the concerns of her early novel *The War-Workers*—the satire of the sentimental patriotism of volunteers, their bureaucratic inefficiency, and their self-importance.

In the preface to the crime novel *Messalina of the Suburbs,* Delafield explains that, because she believes "causes are more interesting than the most dramatic results," she has tried to "reconstruct the psychological developments that led, by inexorable degrees, to the catastrophe of murder." She addresses what she terms the "real issue" rather than the "sensational accessories." The real issue is to be found on that plane of thought where personalities are dissected, the only plane where true under-

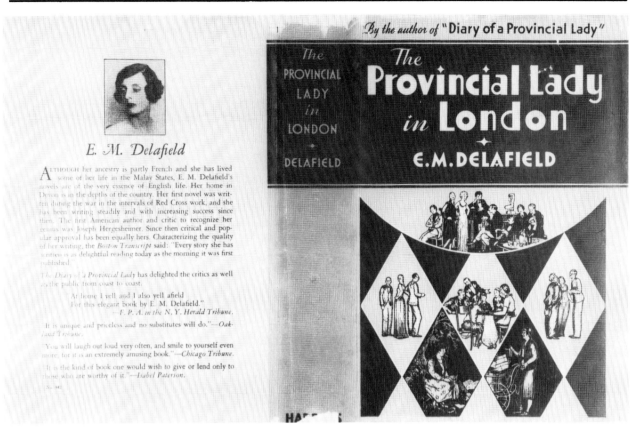

Dust jacket for the American edition of Delafield's second Provincial Lady book (courtesy of Academy Chicago Publishers)

standing of a murder case can emerge. Delafield calls the novel "my story about Elsie Palmer," and for this book the significance of the murder lies in its revelation of Elsie as an ordinary young woman with extraordinarily limited vision, hope, and imagination. The cause of the murder is not passion but complete lack of passion—a matter overlooked in newspaper coverage of the crime and trial.

Elsie is shallow, self-centered, unemotional, and—most important—devoid of imagination. If she cannot imagine the kind of trouble she should avoid, she also cannot imagine experiences which will make her happy. She sneaks off to the movies at the Palatial Picture House with a traveling salesman who boards at her mother's rooming house, but the Russian names on the screen are an effort to follow—is Sergius the villain or the lawyer? Is Olga the vampire? And so she finds herself in the arms of the salesman and feeling bored. She thinks she would be happier if she owned some sheer pink lingerie but gets confused about buying it when her sister says only "tarts" wear it and Irene Tidmarsh, her girl friend, says "women of quality" all own such apparel.

Elsie lacks even enough imagination to understand the principle of cause and effect. She has, at the age of seventeen, been seduced by her first employer, has worried her mother by staying out late at night with a fast crowd, and is wondering whether to go away for a weekend with Mr. Williams, the lawyer for whom she works as a typist. (He is a widower she knows is interested in her mainly because she can smell the shoe polish he is using to dye his few remaining strands of hair to impress her.) At this point, her girl friend startles her by suggesting that sex and pregnancy are related—a cause-and-effect connection that has never occurred to Elsie. Irene suggests that it would be safer to marry Williams than to go away for a weekend.

As she marries him, she feels only how her new shoes hurt and thinks that her new creme-colored hat with a feather makes her look pale. Most telling is the paragraph in which Delafield describes Elsie's indifference to the four years of war. She hums "Tipperary," grumbles about sugar-and-meat-ration coupons, and eagerly listens to anecdotes about Belgian children's hands being cut off.

After ten years of marriage to Williams, she

Advertisement for the first American edition of Delafield's fourth Provincial Lady book

has not matured or enlarged her vision and understanding. She is unable to imagine that having a lover will cause her husband to grow angry, that insulting him beyond a certain point will make him strike her, that showing her bruised arm to her lover will make him want to attack her husband, that the attack on her husband can cause his death, and that her love letters written over the previous year can implicate her in a conspiracy to murder her husband. Because Elsie has not been able to visualize this series of consequences, she can only dimly begin to understand—as Delafield suggests in the closing

sentences—"in the ghastly dawn of a prison-yard, beneath the shadow of the scaffold. . . . Inexorable consequences would be suffered by herself, and she would never know how it was that these things had become inevitable—had happened."

The strength of this novel lies in Delafield's ability to counter sensational newspaper depictions of the accused murderess with a convincing portrayal of Elsie and her family as prosaic working-class people. Rather than showing what makes a murderess different from other people, Delafield concentrates on that which is common (and commonplace) in Elsie and in the other people in her life. The woman, dull in all respects, gradually intrigues the reader, because her ordinary characteristics suggest that murder can take place among people the reader might know.

Messalina of the Suburbs attests to the speed with which Delafield conceived and produced her novels: Percy Thompson (the model for Delafield's Williams) was killed on 5 October 1922, and Edith Thompson and her lover Frederick Bywaters were executed for complicity in his murder on 6 January 1923. Delafield had her book based on the case prepared for publication by August 1923.

Although the dry precision of much of Delafield's satire and her interest in the comedy of manners make many of her characters stylized rather than deeply developed psychologically, she presents the social conditions surrounding them and their institutions without evasion or hypocrisy. Delafield was an incisive interpreter of British life in the 1920s and 1930s and a shrewd and thoughtful analyst of the people she created in her fiction. One nearly always feels, as an anonymous reviewer for the *Times Literary Supplement* said of Delafield's early books, that after reading a few pages "you are deep in realities, gripped by living people."

Norman Douglas
(8 December 1868-9 February 1952)

Ralph D. Lindeman
Gettysburg College

SELECTED BOOKS: *Unprofessional Tales,* by Douglas and Elsa FitzGibbon, as Normyx (London: Privately printed, 1901);

Siren Land (London: Dent, 1911; New York: Dutton, 1911);

Fountains in the Sand: Rambles Among the Oases of Tunisia (London: Secker, 1912; New York: Pott, 1912);

Old Calabria (London: Secker, 1915; New York: Houghton Mifflin, 1915);

London Street Games (London: St. Catherine Press, 1916);

South Wind (London: Secker, 1917; New York: Dodd, Mead, 1918);

They Went (London: Chapman & Hall, 1920; New York: Dodd, Mead, 1921);

Alone (London: Chapman & Hall, 1921; New York: McBride, 1922);

Together (London: Chapman & Hall, 1923; New York: McBride, 1923);

D. H. Lawrence and Maurice Magnus: A Plea for Better Manners (Florence: Privately printed, 1925);

Experiments (Florence: Privately printed, 1925; New York: McBride, 1925; London: Chapman & Hall, 1925);

In the Beginning (Florence: Privately printed, 1927; New York: Day, 1928; London: Chatto & Windus, 1928);

Birds and Beasts of the Greek Anthology (Florence: Privately printed, 1927; London: Chapman & Hall, 1928; New York: Cape/Smith, 1928);

Some Limericks (Florence: Privately printed, 1928; New York: Grove Press, 1967);

Nerinda (Florence: Orioli, 1929; New York: Day, 1929);

One Day (Chapelle-Réanville: Hours Press, 1929);

How About Europe? Some Footnotes on East and West (Florence: Privately printed, 1929; London: Chatto & Windus, 1930); republished as *Good-bye to Western Culture* (New York: Harper, 1930);

Paneros (Florence: Privately printed, 1930; London: Chatto & Windus, 1931; New York: McBride, 1932);

Capri: Materials for a Description of the Island (Florence: Orioli, 1930);

Summer Islands: Ischia and Ponza (London: Harmsworth, 1931; New York: Colophon, 1931);

Looking Back: An Autobiographical Excursion (London: Chatto & Windus, 1933; New York: Harcourt, Brace, 1933);

An Almanac (Lisbon: Privately printed, 1941; London: Chatto & Windus/Secker & Warburg, 1945);

Late Harvest (London: Drummond, 1946);

Footnote on Capri (London: Sidgwick & Jackson, 1952);

Norman Douglas (photo by Islay Lyons)

Venus in the Kitchen or Love's Cookery Book, as Pilaff
    Bey (London: Heinemann, 1952; New York:
    Viking, 1953);
Norman Douglas: A Selection from His Works, edited by
    D. M. Low (London: Chatto & Windus, 1955).

Norman Douglas was a multifaceted man of
letters, having written scientific monographs, descriptive travel literature, memoirs, and several
novels. He is best known in Europe for his travel
writings, which are ranked with those of George
Henry Borrow, Charles Montague Doughty, and
T. E. Lawrence. In America he is best known for
South Wind (1917), a novel which was quite popular
in the 1920s and 1930s and is often called a minor
classic. His erudition and his clear and entertaining
style are almost universally praised. His personality
and philosophy, which show through all his writings, are controversial and provocative. His ostensibly objective tone reflects his characteristic amalgam of aristocratic scorn and humane sympathy.

George Norman Douglas was born in
Thüringen, in the Vorarlberg of the Austrian
Tyrol, of Scottish and German descent. His father,
Sholto Douglass, was the proprietor of a family-
owned cotton mill. His mother, Vanda (Von
Poellnitz) Douglass, was descended from nobility.

His father died in a hunting accident when Douglas
was not quite six, but he had already introduced the
boy to some of the interests which would figure in
his career—topography, geology, mineralogy,
botany, and zoology.

Douglas attended several preparatory schools
in England, but he did not like the narrow-
mindedness, the hazing, and the emphasis on religion. (Throughout his life he was to consider religion the bane of modern culture.) Returning to
the Continent, he attended the Gymnasium at
Karlsruhe from 1883 to 1889 and there completed
his formal education. There he learned the ancient
and modern languages, including French, Italian,
and Russian. (He was bilingual in German and English and published in both languages.) He also
developed an interest in natural science, which was
to persist throughout his life, and made excursions
to various parts of Germany to make observations
and collect specimens. Also during the Karlsruhe
years he learned to admire the philosophy of the
ancient Greeks, especially that before Plato's introduction of idealism, which Douglas, with his interest
in the physical world, was to deplore in any form,
Christian or otherwise.

Douglas in 1892 (photo by Byrne & Co., Richmond)

Falkenhorst, Douglas's birthplace in Thüringen, Austria

In the 1890s Douglas was in London, preparing for a career in the Foreign Office and associating with various young aesthetes. He took more trips, now including the Mediterranean lands, and published monographs on ornithology and herpetology. Shortly after entering the Foreign Office in 1893, he wrote a long paper entitled "On the Darwinian Hypothesis of Sexual Selection," which he regarded as his most important contribution to science. In it he argued that distinctive coloration in male birds and reptiles, along with such habits as nuptial dances and exhibitions of prowess, are not to be explained as simply an attempt to please the female but are rather the result of excessive vitality. This thesis is interesting because Douglas associates it with his belief that "leisure is the key to artistic creation and appreciation," as Constantine FitzGibbon has noted. Thus he favored an aristocratic culture and preferred the Mediterranean lands, where living well required less effort than in northern Europe.

Having served for two and a half years, beginning in 1894, as third secretary of the British embassy in St. Petersburg, Douglas found it necessary, as a result of an affair with a Russian noblewoman,

to "evaporate," as he put it, and left the Foreign Office. In 1896 and 1897 he traveled widely and purchased a villa on the Posilipo. In 1898 he married an Irish-Austrian cousin, Elsa FitzGibbon. Together they produced a volume of short stories, *Unprofessional Tales* (1901), under the pseudonym "Normyx." It was undistinguished, and Douglas took responsibility for only one story and an anacreontic lyric that was included.

The marriage produced two sons but ended in divorce in 1903. Though the details are vague, Douglas was left with some bitterness. After the separation he moved to Capri and began to write seriously about his favorite subjects, the natural histories and antiquities of the Neopolitan region. His sexual interests were henceforth directed mainly toward young people of his own sex. It had always been part of his primitivistic belief that wisdom was more likely to be obtained by talking to people under the age of fourteen, and he doubtless felt that the Mediterranean area, with its centuries-old reputation in these matters, was the best place for the seduction of boys. But his rather open pederasty caused him legal trouble in England and Italy and cost him some close friends.

During the early years of the century Douglas also suffered financial reverses, which made it necessary for him to turn to writing as a source of income. His brother had sold the family's Austrian properties at a low price, and Douglas's share did not enable him to live and travel in the extravagant way to which he had been accustomed. From 1904 to 1907 he lived on Capri, borrowing from acquaintances and tourists and studying the topography, archaeology, and history of the island. He wrote a number of short studies, privately printed. These are heavily annotated works, based on research in the Naples Library, the archives of Capri, and his own collection of rare documents. The latter were sold to an American lady, who doubtless made no use of them, though Douglas kept back some of the choicest items and wrote, "What expert would not do the same?"

During the latter part of the first decade of the century Douglas was living near Nerano, publishing a few articles in respected reviews—*Atlantic Monthly, Putnam's, Cornhill Magazine*—and writing the materials that were to form *Siren Land,* a highly regarded travel book and his first critical success.

In 1910 he moved to London to find employment and to find a publisher for *Siren Land* (1911). This book was put together of material from the Capri studies and some travel pieces about southern Italy which had appeared in the *English Review.* Thus began Douglas's practice of recycling old material rather than producing new. The book finally found a publisher, thanks to the help of Douglas's friends Joseph Conrad and Richard Garnett. A number of chapters were cut, but Douglas was able to include them in *Old Calabria* (1915). Though critics praised *Siren Land* for its erudition, its lucid style, and its fine scornfulness of tone, it did not sell well.

Also in 1910 Douglas spent three months in Tunisia collecting material for a book that he hoped would be more successful than *Siren Land.* He liked the barren regions, with their cleanness of line. (Living in England was, for him "like living in a salad.") The resultant book, entitled *Fountains in the Sand,* was published in 1912 and contains some of Douglas's best descriptive passages. A comparison of sunsets in London and in northern Africa shows his literary use of topography and colors, always important elements in his descriptive style:

> They are fine, these moments of conflagration, of mineral incandescence, when the somber limestone rocks take on the tint of molten copper, their convulsed strata standing out like the ribs of some agonized Prometheus, while the plain, where every little stone casts an inordinate shadow behind it, clothes itself in demure shades of pearl. Fine, and all too brief. For even before the descending sun has touched the rim of the world the colours fade away; only overhead the play of blues and greens continues— freezing, at last, to pale indigo. . . .
>
> And I remembered London at this sunset hour, a medley of tender grey-in-grey, save where a glory of many-coloured lights hovers above some street lantern, or where a carriage, splashing through the river of mud, leaves a momentary track of silver in its rear. There are the nights, of course, with their bustle and flare, but nights in a city are apt to grow wearisome; they fall into two or three categories, whose novelty soon wears off. How different from the starlit ones of the south, each with its peculiar moods and aspirations!

Another comparatively barren region that held attraction for Douglas was the southern tip of Italy, not yet popular with tourists. It was the subject of *Old Calabria,* which some critics consider his best travel book. He loved the austere landscapes and the conversation of the simple and superstitious peasants. The book is long, and rich in its variety of places and subjects. It contains the casual erudition and the salt of cynicism that form much of the appeal of Douglas's work. The vestiges of ancient Greek culture accorded with his tastes and learning. Collecting saints' lives, which he presented with tongue-in-cheek, was a hobby for him, and his chapter on St. Joseph of Copertino, the flying monk, is delightful.

Douglas became an assistant editor on the *English Review* through the auspices of his friend Joseph Conrad, who introduced him favorably to the editor, Ford Maddox Hueffer (later Ford Maddox Ford). Between 1913 and 1916 Douglas wrote a number of articles and reviews for this young journal, which, though short-lived, has come to be thought of as very significant, since it introduced some writers who were to become important. Of the reviews that Douglas wrote for the *English Review,* some were amusing and some sarcastic. Among books that he reviewed favorably were Robert Frost's *A Boy's Will,* H. M. Tomlinson's *The Sea and the Jungle,* and some of D. H. Lawrence's early short stories.

During the years 1910 to 1915 Douglas was also spending time collecting material for *London*

Douglas with Faith Mackenzie, wife of novelist Compton Mackenzie, 1925

Street Games. A strange little book, it was accepted, after a number of rejections, by St. Catherine Press and published in 1916. He enjoyed extracting descriptions of their games from London children and repeating them in their own words. Part of his intention in the book was to show the inventiveness of children and to deprecate the standardizing influence of organized games.

In 1916 things turned bad for Douglas. He was unhappy with the new editor of the *English Review,* Austin Harrison; he had a falling out with Conrad; and it had become clear that he could not find a position in England and that, indeed, the government would like him to leave the country or be subject to arrest as a result of sexual activities with children. It was time for him to "evaporate" again.

The year 1917 was perhaps the darkest of Douglas's career, as it was one of the darkest in the history of modern Europe. But it saw the publication of *South Wind,* which is thought of as his brightest and certainly most popular novel. Planned and begun in England and finished in Italy, its

playfully hedonistic and amoral tone found immediate popularity with a war-weary public. The idea for the novel—setting and theme—were suggested by Conrad.

Of Douglas's three novels, *South Wind* is by far the best known. It is a conversational novel in the manner of Thomas Love Peacock. The setting, the island of Nepenthe, owes a good deal to Capri, as well as to the nearby islands and the mainland. Douglas supplied his fictitious island with a history, an archaeology, a geology, even a local saint. The characters are a diversified lot. The cheerful cynic, Mr. Keith; the innocuous scholar, Mr. Eames; the lovable dipsomaniac, Miss Wilberforce—all were in some ways facets of Douglas's own personality, and their learned and witty conversation was his also.

The theme of *South Wind* was one dear to Douglas's heart—the subtle ability of the sunny Mediterranean atmosphere to "open the moral pores"—in this case those of an amenable but conventional Anglican bishop, who is so affected by the atmosphere and conversations he encounters on Nepenthe that he is finally able to see his cousin push a blackmailer off a cliff and consider it a trivial incident. The "bright young people" of the 1920s loved and lived the characters of *South Wind,* and Douglas became a kind of symbol of the free and pleasure-seeking personality in revolt against Victorian moral standards.

The influence of *South Wind*—in terms of subject, technique, and attitudes—upon the younger writers of Douglas's day is clear. The sharply contrasted and stylized characters, the witty erudition, the lucid paganism, and the derisive tone all reappeared with some frequency in the literature of the period. The practice of bringing together a group of characters with distinctive ideas in order to have them converse in a learned and satirical fashion became a familiar device. The rather brutal humor, the moral deliquescence, the importance of the physical and the pleasurable, and the tropical setting appear variously in the works of Aldous Huxley, Compton Mackenzie, Rose Macaulay, and D. H. Lawrence. So much did this hearty pagan expatriate capture the imaginations of the younger generation of writers that he was a model for characters in several novels—Scrogan in Huxley's *Chrome Yellow* and Argyle in Lawrence's *Aaron's Rod* are examples. Graham Greene has written, "My generation was brought up on *South Wind."*

But Douglas the novelist is still Douglas the travel writer. The descriptive power is there, the ability to create atmosphere, the carefully composed canvas, the clearly defined line and masses moving across mosaics of bright colors in a stylized, almost artificial effect:

> Sirocco mists rose upwards, clustering thickly overhead and rolling in billowy formations among the dales. Sometimes a breath of wind would convulse their ranks, causing them to trail in long silvery pennants across the sky and, opening a rift in the gossamer texture, would reveal far down below, a glimmering of olives shining in the sunlight or a patch of blue sea, framed in an aureole of peacock hues.

In 1919 Douglas returned to Italy and for the next twenty years operated from Florence. His friend Edward Hutton had begun a new journal, and in its brief duration—two volumes—he published four travel pieces by Douglas. All of these were later to become parts of *Alone* (1921), a travel book about Italy, treating Rome, Florence, and the usual varied subjects—topography, history, literature, philosophy.

In 1920 Douglas had a short novel published which some critics have preferred to *South Wind. They Went* is a bizarre tale of the legendary city of Ys, on the misty coast of Brittany during the waning years of the Roman empire. In it, a lovely young princess, cruel but dedicated to beauty in all its forms, is aided in her efforts to beautify the city by a Mephistophelian creature named Theophilus. The book is a kind of allegory of beauty versus morality. The forces of incipient Christianity, deceived in their belief that the ruler of the universe cares about them, foil the forces of beauty. When the city is destroyed by a flood, Theophilus takes the princess off to his own world, where, he promises, "goodness" will be nonexistent and beauty will be everywhere. Some of Douglas's themes—his aestheticism, his anti-Christian and amoral biases—are especially clear in this novel.

Another travel book, *Together* (1923), appeared in the early 1920s, the product of Douglas's tour of his native Vorarlberg with a young Italian friend, René. Written in the informal style introduced in *Alone,* it is marked by autobiographical material. Douglas's brutal humor is exemplified in a passage describing village idiots.

In the Beginning (1927) is somewhat similar in tone to *They Went.* It is a pseudohistorical account of religion, set in a fictitious past in which the earth and heavens are peopled with gods and heroes. Man has been made by the frivolous "great father" out of the dung of a "loathsome fowl" and enjoys cavorting with nymphomaniac goddesses until he

falls victim of the dread disease "goodness." He rejects the advice of the last remaining member of the wise race of satyrs and finally destroys himself. Aroudi, "haunter of outskirts," reclaims the world from the reformers and improvers and turns it back into desert. Douglas's hedonism and primitivism are again apparent here.

Through the 1920s and 1930s Douglas continued to travel and write. He was a well-known figure in Florence and on Capri, his witty conversation much admired. He was a friend of Nancy Cunard and Bryher (Winifred Ellerman) and knew a number of writers—Richard Garnett, Compton Mackenzie, Scott Moncrieff, W. H. Hudson, Charles Doughty, Harold Acton, Ronald Firbank, Michael Arlen—but he didn't like to talk about literature and preferred the conversation of young people or simple farmers or fishermen. He was known as a gourmet and enjoyed harassing waiters in the variety of Italian dialects he knew. (He once made a collection of Florentine oaths and invectives.) He liked to announce that the "dish clout" had obviously been boiled in the *Zuppa di pesche,* and he always maintained that all rabbit served in Italy was actually cat.

In the early 1920s Douglas met Giuseppi Orioli, and there began a long and close relationship. Orioli, an irrepressible little Italian who was liked by everybody, was a buyer and seller of rare books. He was some twenty years younger than Douglas, but they lived in adjoining apartments in Florence, ate together, and made tours together. When Orioli decided to begin a publishing venture featuring little-known writings in attractive bindings, he asked Douglas for something and received the short story "Nerinda," from *Unprofessional Tales.* Thus began the Lugarno series, in which Douglas was virtually a partner. In its short history the company published not only Douglas's work but that of Somerset Maugham, Richard Aldington, D. H. Lawrence, and others whom conventional publishers were chary of. According to Douglas's arrangement with Orioli, his books were put out in limited editions in an expensive format and sold by subscription; when the subscriptions were exhausted, the copyrights were sold to a commercial publisher.

One of the first of Douglas's publications in this series was a pamphlet entitled *D. H. Lawrence and Maurice Magnus: A Plea for Better Manners* (1925). It was a central document in the long-lasting feud between Douglas and Lawrence. Magnus was an American journalist who had escaped from the Foreign Legion. He carried about with him his memoirs, in which Douglas claimed to have collaborated. The two lived together for a time. Lawrence later described Magnus and the relationship disparagingly.

When Lawrence met Magnus, some years after the relationship with Douglas, he paid Magnus's hotel bill and gave him fare to Malta, so that he could escape arrest. Magnus lived extravagantly on Malta, much to Lawrence's chagrin, and eventually committed suicide. His manuscript, *Memoirs of the Foreign Legion,* fell into Lawrence's hands, and he published it, despite the fact that Douglas had been named literary executor. Lawrence's introduction to the book denigrates both Magnus and Douglas. It produced Douglas's response, *A Plea for Better Manners,* a subtle invective which Alexander Woollcott described as having a "come, come, little man" tone. In later books Douglas described Lawrence as "stingy" and "libelous." Some thought Douglas was annoyed by his depiction as Argyle in *Aaron's Rod,* but he denied this charge, claiming that he didn't care about such things.

A Plea for Better Manners was included in *Experiments* (1925), which consisted of some stories from *Unprofessional Tales* and reviews and articles from the *English Review.* It was another instance of Douglas's practice of reprinting old material rather than producing new. His creative energy was becoming depleted. *Birds and Beasts of the Greek Anthology* (1927) was simply a listing, with comments and digressions, of animals mentioned by the early Greek poets, whom Douglas always preferred to later, more romantic poets.

In 1929 Douglas published *One Day,* a short book about Greece. It had originally been an article in *Travel* magazine, begun when a Greek prince commissioned him to write a book about Greece in the manner of *Old Calabria.* Douglas had accepted the advance and made the trip but found the task impossible. There was too much material in the Athens library for him to assimilate in a short time, and he had lost much of his knowledge of Greek. The best he could do was about fifty pages describing the Athens vicinity, along with some comments about the ancient Greek poets and their world view.

The controversial *How About Europe? Some Footnotes on East and West* (republished as *Good-bye to Western Culture*) was also published in 1929. It was an immoderate attack on middle-class values and an ill-humored book and was not well received. More than any other of Douglas's works, *Good-bye to Western Culture* drew charges of fascism and comparisons with the crankiness of the American H. L. Mencken.

Paneros (1930) is a collection and discussion of supposed aphrodisiacs. Written in a pseudoarchaic style and with antiquarian erudition, its tone has a note of the nostalgia of an aging sensualist. Also in 1930 the Capri materials (a series of monographs and offprints previously privately printed from 1904-1915) were collected and published as *Capri: Materials for a Description of the Island,* the largest English-language volume ever published in Italy. *Summer Islands* (1931) was a travel piece written many years before.

Douglas's last attempt to produce something entirely new was *Looking Back* (1933). This is a volume of reminiscences, full of biographical information and amusing anecdotes about friends and acquaintances. The method of its composition was unusual. Douglas claimed to have saved calling cards in an old vase. He supposedly chose them at random and wrote about the memories associated with them. The book, though obviously lacking structure, is pleasantly spontaneous and conversational.

In the 1930s the Lugarno series had trouble with the Italian government. Certain books from the series, such as *Lady Chatterley's Lover,* shocked the public. Complaints were made to the Home Office in London, where a campaign was being waged against what were considered indecent books in English being published abroad. The next book scheduled for prosecution was *Some Limericks* (1928), collected by Douglas, supplied with learned and witty footnotes, and definitely erotic. Defending it before the righteous fascists would not have been easy. Douglas "evaporated" to the south of France, unable to return to Italy until after the war. Orioli, in danger of prosecution for English sympathies, also escaped and died in Portugal in the 1940s. Douglas lived for a time in Lisbon, awaiting an opportunity to return to England. In serious financial straits, he collected epigrams from his books and published them as *An Almanac* in 1941. He was now old and tired and apparently incapable of any more original creative effort.

In London in the early 1940s Douglas prowled the blacked-out streets, his friends almost all gone. He returned to Italy after the war, in 1946, and spent the last years of his life at the villa of his friend Kenneth Macpherson. He haunted his favorite cafés, complained about the food, and tried to shock people with his frank language and iconoclastic opinions. In 1946 he put together a book called *Late Harvest,* which consisted of personal comments on his own books. Photographs by his friend Islay Lyons induced him to do one more small book

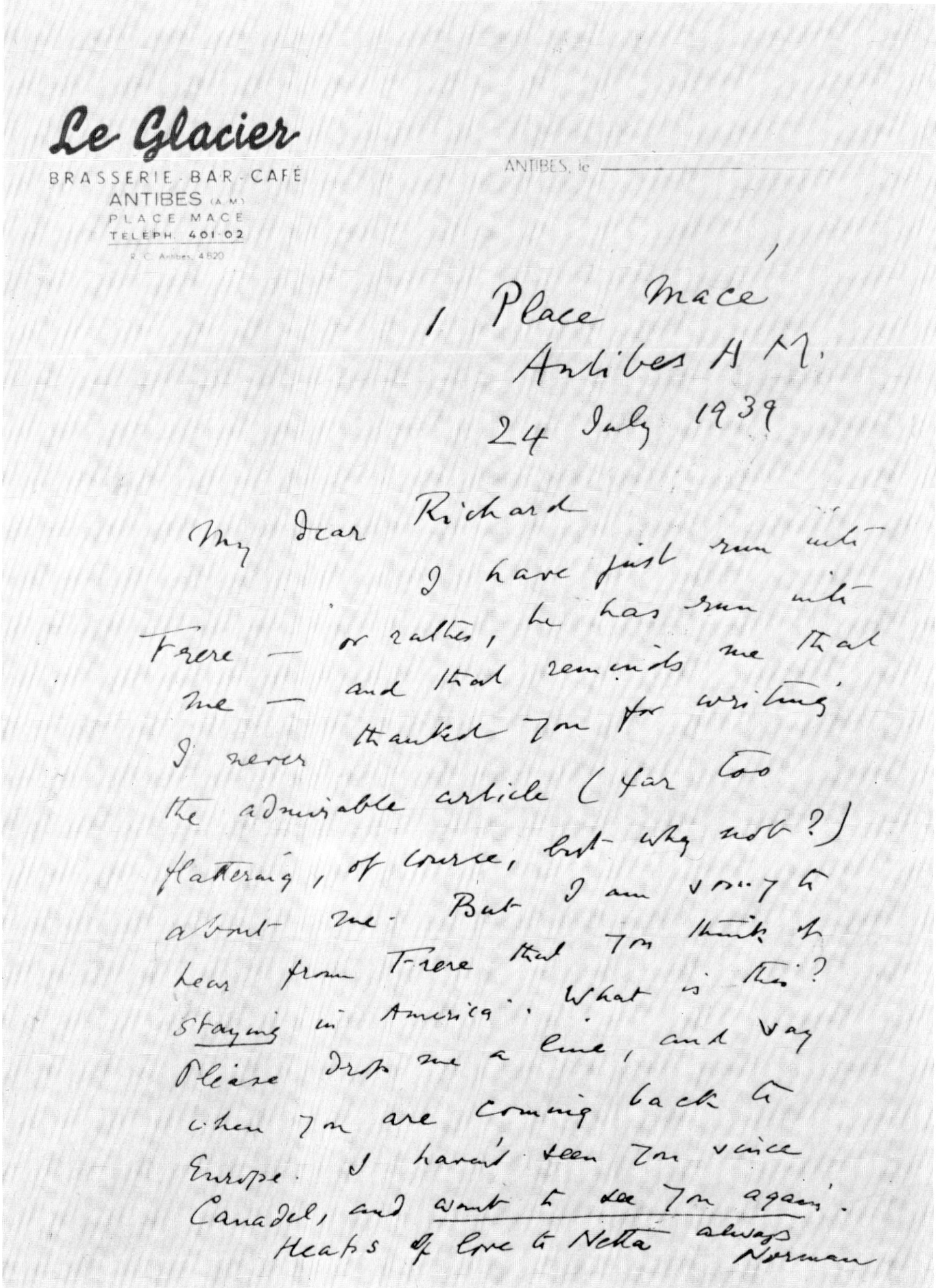

Le Glacier

BRASSERIE · BAR · CAFÉ
ANTIBES (A.M.)
PLACE MACE
TELEPH. 401·02
R. C. Antibes. 4.620

ANTIBES, le

1 Place Mace
Antibes A.M.
24 July 1939

My dear Richard
 I have just run into
Frère — or rather, he has run into
me — and that reminds me that
I never thanked you for writing
the admirable article (far too
flattering, of course, but why not?)
about me. But I am sorry to
hear from Frère that you think of
staying in America. What is this?
Please drop me a line, and say
when you are coming back to
Europe. I haven't seen your voice
Canadel, and want to see you again.
Heaps of love to Netta always
           Norman

Letter from Douglas thanking Richard Aldington for his review-article about Old Calabria, *which had been published in Oxford University Press's World Classics Series (estate of Norman Douglas)*

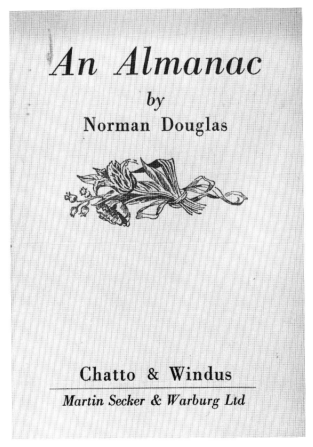

Title page for the British edition of Douglas's 1941 collection of epigrams from his earlier books

about Capri, published posthumously as *Footnote on Capri* (1952).

Douglas's personality was distinctive and somewhat paradoxical. His manners were those of a perfect Victorian gentleman, but he was cantankerous and opinionated, quick to detect and to laugh at any kind of sham or pretension. His conversation has been compared in its effect to that of Dr. Johnson. Constantine FitzGibbon wrote, "Men and women of all classes and many nationalities would travel far out of their way to spend a few hours in his company. The loyalty that he inspired, often in the most unlikely people, was extraordinary. He had the rare and delightful quality of being able to understand without any desire to interfere. His wit was of an infectious variety, so that only the dullest of dogs did not seem more amusing when he was about."

The elderly Douglas deplored the influx into Capri of tourists, cars, and modern music. But not all things modern were subject to his disapproval.

He commented in *Footnote on Capri:* "Now Capri is not the place for moralizing, and even old-fashioned folk like myself will sooner or later be driven to confess that living human thighs and arms and breasts and backs, not to mention certain voluptuous posteriors that would do credit to a Hottentot Venus, are a surprising and delectable sight and one that may presently—who knows?—eclipse the fame of mere terrestrial objects like the blue grotto."

Douglas died in February 1952, apparently from a self-administered overdose of some medication, though the matter is not clear. His last book was a collection of aphrodisiac recipes called *Venus in the Kitchen or Love's Cookery Book* (1952). In the introduction he wrote:

> Not many years ago I met in the South of France a Mr. D. H. Lawrence, an English painter, whom I interested in the subject, and who looked as if his health would have been improved by such recipes as I had gathered together. He became so enthusiastic that he drew for me the frontispiece that adorns this book. I reproduce it because I understand

Douglas with his close friend and literary executor Kenneth Macpherson, circa 1948

For Darling Nancy
with ten thousand good
wishes from
Norman (aged 10
and 83)
Capri
7 Dec 1954

Photograph inscribed to Nancy Cunard, owner of Hours Press

that many of his admirers will be glad to see a new example of his art. For my own part, I must confess that this picture of a fat naked woman pushing a loaf into an oven is not at all my notion of "Venus in the Kitchen." I think such a creature would scare a good many people out of the kitchen, and perhaps out of the house.

Though critics of travel writing have continued to rank Douglas with the best in that genre,

Douglas's reputation declined after the 1930s, especially in the United States, since he wrote no other novel comparable to *South Wind*. A period of political ideology between the wars was antithetical to his conservatism, which was not acceptable to the political left, or to general democratic traditions. Moreover, the tone of his later books was sardonic and cruel, without the attenuating humor of the earlier ones; and the openly erotic aspects of the later novels, probably a deliberate attempt to shock the middle class, were objectionable to many readers. Beyond these problems, there simply was not much genuinely creative activity in the latter part of Douglas's career.

But, at the height of his powers, Douglas was a potent satirist and an effective humorist. His philosophy of healthy naturalism, robust paganism, and unabashed hedonism, though it contained nothing especially new, was popular for a time. His personality shows even through his ostensibly objective writings. Whatever the form or the subject, there was always the leisurely pace, the gratuitous erudition, the disdainful sarcasm, the lush but precise description. Douglas's greatest power lay in his prose style, his descriptive power, and his ability to create atmosphere. His other achievements would have been negligible had his prose style not been the lucid and balanced instrument that it was. It won a place in English letters for a man who was otherwise only an erudite dilettante, a pleasure lover with a keen but rather rigid mind.

References:

Richard Aldington, *Pinorman: Personal Recollections of Norman Douglas, Pino Orioli, and Charles Prentice* (London: Heinemann, 1954);

Nancy Cunard, *Grand Man: Memories of Norman Douglas* (London: Secker & Warburg, 1954);

John Davenport, Introduction to *Old Calabria* (New York: Harcourt, Brace, 1956);

R. M. Dawkins, *Norman Douglas* (London: Hart-Davis, 1952);

Constantine FitzGibbon, *Norman Douglas: A Pictorial Record* (London: Richards, 1953);

R. M. Flint, "Norman Douglas," *Kenyon Review,* 14 (Autumn 1952): 660;

Paul Fussell, *Abroad: British Literary Traveling Between the Wars* (New York: Oxford, 1980);

Ian Greenlees, *Norman Douglas* (London: Longmans, Green, 1957);

Ralph Lindeman, *Norman Douglas* (New York: Twayne, 1965);

D. M. Low, ed., Introduction to *Norman Douglas: A Selection from His Works* (London: Chatto & Windus/Secker & Warburg, 1955);

Kenneth Macpherson, *Omnes Eodem Cogimur* (Naples: Privately printed, 1953);

Edward D. McDonald, *A Bibliography of Norman Douglas* (Philadelphia: Centaur Book Shop, 1927);

H. M. Tomlinson, *Norman Douglas* (New York & London: Harper, 1931; revised, 1952);

H. T. Webster, "Norman Douglas: A Reconsideration," *South Atlantic Quarterly,* 49 (April 1950): 226;

Elizabeth D. Wheatley, "Norman Douglas," *Sewanee Review,* 40 (January 1932): 55;

Cecil Woolf, *A Bibliography of Norman Douglas* (London: Hart-Davis, 1954).

Ford Madox Ford

Richard F. Peterson
Southern Illinois University at Carbondale

BIRTH: Merton, Surrey, England, 17 December 1873, to Francis (formerly Franz) and Catherine Madox Brown Hueffer.

MARRIAGE: 17 May 1894 to Elsie Martindale; children: Christina, Katherine; Esther Julia (by Stella Bowen).

HONOR: Honorary Doctor of Literature, Olivet College, 1938.

DEATH: Deauville, France, 26 June 1939.

BOOKS: *The Brown Owl: A Fairy Story* (London: Unwin, 1891; New York: Stokes, 1891);

The Feather (London: Unwin, 1892; New York: Cassell, 1892);

The Shifting of the Fire (London: Unwin, 1892; New York: Putnam's, 1892);

The Questions at the Well, with Sundry Other Verses for Notes of Music, as Fenil Haig (London: Digby, Long, 1893);

The Queen Who Flew (London: Bliss, Sands & Foster, 1894);

Ford Madox Brown: A Record of His Life and Work (London, New York & Bombay: Longmans, Green, 1896);

Poems for Pictures and for Notes of Music (London: MacQueen, 1900);

The Cinque Ports: A Historical and Descriptive Record (Edinburgh & London: Blackwood, 1900);

The Inheritors: An Extravagant Story, by Ford and Joseph Conrad (New York: McClure, Phillips, 1901; London: Heinemann, 1901);

Rossetti: A Critical Essay on His Art (London: Duckworth/New York: Dutton, 1902);

Romance: A Novel, by Ford and Conrad (London: Smith, Elder, 1903; New York: McClure, Phillips, 1904);

The Face of Night: A Second Series of Poems for Pictures (London: MacQueen, 1904);

The Soul of London: A Survey of a Modern City (London: Rivers, 1905); republished in *England and the English* (1907);

The Benefactor: A Tale of a Small Circle (London: Brown, Langham, 1905);

Hans Holbein the Younger: A Critical Monograph (London: Duckworth/New York: Dutton, 1905);

The Fifth Queen: And How She Came to Court (London: Rivers, 1906);

The Heart of the Country: A Survey of a Modern Land (London: Rivers, 1906); republished in *England and the English* (1907);

Christina's Fairy Book (London: Rivers, 1906);

Privy Seal: His Last Venture (London: Rivers, 1907);

England and the English: An Interpretation (New York: McClure, Phillips, 1907)—*The Soul of London, The Heart of the Country,* and *The Spirit of the People;*

From Inland and Other Poems (London: Rivers, 1907);

An English Girl: A Romance (London: Methuen, 1907);

The Pre-Raphaelite Brotherhood: A Critical Monograph (London: Duckworth/New York: Dutton, 1907);

The Spirit of the People: An Analysis of the English Mind (London: Rivers, 1907); published in *England and the English* (1907);

The Fifth Queen Crowned: A Romance (London: Nash, 1908);

Mr. Apollo: A Just Possible Story (London: Methuen, 1908);

The 'Half Moon': A Romance of the Old World and the New (London: Nash, 1909; New York: Doubleday, Page, 1909);

A Call: The Tale of Two Passions (London: Chatto & Windus, 1910);

Songs from London (London: Elkin Mathews, 1910);

The Portrait (London: Methuen, 1910);

The Simple Life Limited, as Daniel Chaucer (Lon-

Ford Madox Ford, 1939

John Lane, Bodley Head/New York: John Lane, 1911);

Ancient Lights and Certain New Reflections, Being the Memories of a Young Man (London: Chapman & Hall, 1911); republished as *Memories and Impressions: A Study in Atmospheres* (New York & London: Harper, 1911);

Ladies Whose Bright Eyes: A Romance (London: Constable, 1911; revised edition, Philadelphia & London: Lippincott, 1935);

The Critical Attitude (London: Duckworth, 1911);

High Germany: Eleven Sets of Verse (London: Duckworth, 1912);

The Panel: A Sheer Comedy (London: Constable, 1912); revised and expanded as *Ring for Nancy: A Sheer Comedy* (Indianapolis: Bobbs-Merrill, 1913);

The New Humpty-Dumpty, as Daniel Chaucer (London: John Lane, Bodley Head/New York: John Lane, 1912);

This Monstrous Regiment of Women (London: Minerva, 1913);

Mr. Fleight (London: Latimer, 1913);

The Young Lovell: A Romance (London: Chatto & Windus, 1913);

Collected Poems (London: Goschen, 1913);

Henry James: A Critical Study (London: Secker, 1914; New York: A. & C. Boni, 1915);

Antwerp (London: Poetry Bookshop, 1915);

The Good Soldier: A Tale of Passion (London: John Lane, Bodley Head/New York: John Lane, 1915);

When Blood is Their Argument: An Analysis of Prussian Culture (London & New York: Hodder & Stoughton, 1915);

Between St. Dennis and St. George: A Sketch of Three Civilisations (London, New York & Toronto: Hodder & Stoughton, 1915);

Zeppelin Nights: A London Entertainment, by Ford and Violet Hunt (London: John Lane, Bodley Head/New York: John Lane, 1915);

On Heaven and Poems Written on Active Service (London: John Lane, Bodley Head/New York: John Lane, 1918);

A House (Modern Morality Play), The Chapbook no. 21 (March 1921);

Thus to Revisit: Some Reminiscences (London: Chapman & Hall, 1921);

The Marsden Case: A Romance (London: Duckworth, 1923);

Mister Bosphorus and the Muses, or A Short History of Poetry in Britain: Variety Entertainment in Four Acts (London: Duckworth, 1923);

Women & Men (Paris: Three Mountains Press, 1924);

Some Do Not . . . : A Novel (London: Duckworth, 1924; New York: Seltzer, 1924);

The Nature of a Crime, by Ford and Conrad (London: Duckworth, 1924; New York: Doubleday, Page, 1924);

Joseph Conrad: A Personal Remembrance (London: Duckworth, 1924; Boston: Little, Brown, 1924);

No More Parades: A Novel (London: Duckworth, 1925; New York: A. & C. Boni, 1925);

A Mirror to France (London: Duckworth, 1926; New York: A. & C. Boni, 1926);

A Man Could Stand Up—: A Novel (London: Duckworth, 1926; New York: A. & C. Boni, 1926);

New Poems (New York: Rudge, 1927);

New York Is Not America (London: Duckworth, 1927; New York: A. & C. Boni, 1927);

New York Essays (New York: Rudge, 1927);

The Last Post: A Novel (New York: A. & C. Boni, 1928); republished as *Last Post* (London: Duckworth, 1928);

A Little Less Than Gods: A Romance (London: Duckworth, 1928; New York: Viking, 1928);

The English Novel from the Earliest Days to the Death of Joseph Conrad (Philadelphia & London: Lippincott, 1929; London: Constable, 1930);

No Enemy: A Tale of Reconstruction (New York: Macaulay, 1929);

Return to Yesterday: Reminiscences 1894-1914 (London: Gollancz, 1931; New York: Liveright, 1932);

When the Wicked Man (New York: Liveright, 1931; London: Cape, 1932);

The Rash Act: A Novel (New York: Long & Smith, 1933; London: Cape, 1933);

It Was the Nightingale (Philadelphia & London: Lippincott, 1933; London: Heinemann, 1934);

Henry for Hugh: A Novel (Philadelphia & London: Lippincott, 1934);

Provence from Minstrels to the Machine (Philadelphia & London: Lippincott, 1935; London: Allen & Unwin, 1938);

Vive Le Roy: A Novel (Philadelphia & London: Lippincott, 1936; London: Allen & Unwin, 1937);

Collected Poems (New York: Oxford University Press, 1936);

Great Trade Route (New York & Toronto: Oxford University Press, 1937; London: Allen & Unwin, 1937);

Portraits from Life: Memories and Criticisms (Boston & New York: Houghton Mifflin, 1937); republished as *Mightier than the Sword: Memories and Criticisms* (London: Allen & Unwin, 1938);

The March of Literature from Confucius' Day to Our Own (New York: Dial, 1938); republished as *The March of Literature from Confucius to Modern Times* (London: Allen & Unwin, 1939);

Parade's End (New York: Knopf, 1950)—*Some Do Not, No More Parades, A Man Could Stand Up,* and *The Last Post.*

Collections: *The Bodley Head Ford Madox Ford,* 4 volumes (London: Bodley Head, 1962);

Critical Writings of Ford Madox Ford, edited by Frank MacShane (Lincoln: University of Nebraska Press, 1964).

Though a controversial writer and often an easy target for critics because of his literary and personal excesses, Ford Madox Ford played a key role in the development of modern literature. His collaborations with Joseph Conrad, his contributions as editor of the *English Review* and the *transat-*

lantic review, his accomplishments as a novelist, and his defense of the art of fiction rank him among the major writers of his time.

During his lifetime, however, Ford never gained the distinguished reputation his ego craved and often claimed for itself. As a writer of novels, Ford saw himself as fit company for Conrad, his early friend and collaborator, and, as a prose stylist, he believed he was the worthy successor to the master, Henry James. As a man of letters, he was a passionate defender of the tradition of literature, yet he was also a devoted friend—he preferred Dutch uncle—of younger writers, often supporting the most radical writing of his day. In his last years, Ford judged himself as no less than the Dean of English Letters. He firmly believed that he had played a major role in shaping the most important literary movement of the modern age, a movement he termed impressionism, and had been unerring in recognizing and supporting literary genius, including D. H. Lawrence, Ezra Pound, James Joyce, and Ernest Hemingway. He was also proud of the cultural standard he had set for his own career and was convinced that his theory of the small farmer or producer was the bane of modern technology and the salvation of civilized man.

Ford's self-judgment has a good measure of truth to it, but he wrote with an exaggeration about his life and career that still plagues and complicates objective efforts to evaluate his real contributions. Though he wrote thirty-four novels, only one, *The Good Soldier* (1915), stands out as a masterpiece of modern fiction, while four others, the tetralogy Ford titled *Parade's End,* are now regarded as major, if uneven, accomplishments. Ford produced nineteen minor novels—only his collaborations with Conrad are noteworthy—before *The Good Soldier* and never again wrote a single work with the same intensity and control. His literary criticism and reminiscences are often so inflated with his claims for his own genius that these books and essays have been described as more literary invention than an actual record of his time. Jessie Conrad was so enraged at what she believed were Ford's false claims in *Joseph Conrad* (1924) that she wrote a letter to the *Times Literary Supplement* denying emphatically that her husband had "ever *poached* on Mr. Hueffer's vast stock of plots and materials." This public attack haunted Ford the rest of his career, but his megalomania was already well known in literary and publishing circles and played into the hands of his detractors. Those who wanted to think the worst of Ford judged him a literary travesty puffed up with an exaggerated sense of his own importance to other writers, an outrageous womanizer in his personal life who constantly needed female adulation to prop up his male ego, and an intellectual crank whose ideas on culture and civilization were a hopeless muddle of feudalism and liberal posturing.

Whatever the final judgment of Ford, there is little doubt that he was destined to pursue a career in the arts. Ford Madox Ford was born in 1873 and christened Ford Hermann Hueffer. His father, Francis Hueffer, a German, had settled in England in 1869 after receiving his doctorate in philology from Göttingen and beginning his career as a journalist. Author and editor of numerous books, he eventually became music critic for the *Times.* Ford's mother, Catherine Madox Brown Hueffer, was the daughter of the Pre-Raphaelite painter Ford Madox Brown and a talented artist herself. Ford grew up in an artistic circle and played at an early age with the children of William Rossetti and Richard Garnett. Yet he remembered his childhood as a time of emotional and mental oppression. His artistic elders seemed too imposing in their tastes and his father too earnest and demanding. The oldest of three children, Ford never forgot his father's judgment that he was the "stupid donkey" of the family. His early feelings of inadequacy were further complicated by the death of Francis Hueffer in 1889, an event that left the family in financial

Tell's Son, painted in 1877 by Ford Madox Brown using his grandson Ford as the model (courtesy of Sir Frank Soskice, Q.C., M.P.)

difficulty and made it impossible for young Ford to seek a university degree.

Ford's decision in the early 1890s to become a writer was greatly influenced by his affection and deep respect for Ford Madox Brown. From his grandfather, he gained a lifelong faith in the high seriousness and traditional value of art and an unwavering commitment to genius and craftsmanship. With the publication of his first book, the fairy tale *The Brown Owl* (1891), Ford took the literary name Ford H. Madox Hueffer in honor of his grandfather. A few years later, he wrote his grandfather's biography, *Ford Madox Brown* (1896).

In 1892, the year of the publication of Ford's first novel, *The Shifting of the Fire,* a romance described by Conrad as "delightfully young," Ford converted to Catholicism and began what quickly became a turbulent courtship with Elsie Martindale. After the Martindale family refused to recognize their engagement because of Ford's artistic background and his questionable prospects, Ford and Elsie eloped and were married in Gloucester on 17 May 1894. After legal action by Elsie's father failed to dissolve the marriage, the Hueffers entered into a brief period of nervous excitement that gradually deteriorated into a state of depression brought on by financial problems, Ford's failure to establish himself as a serious writer, and his growing restlessness with married life.

At this unsettled and unhappy state in Ford's life and career, he was introduced to Joseph Conrad by Edward Garnett. Ford and Conrad first met in 1898 and for the next decade remained close friends and literary collaborators. The more-established writer even at the time of their first meeting, Conrad had already begun the development of the narrative and thematic strategies of his great fiction. In Ford, however, he gained a devoted admirer, a kindred spirit who also believed in the sacred office of the novelist, and an intellectual companion capable of understanding Conrad's exacting concern with narrative and structure and his constant struggle to find the right word in the manner of Flaubert. For Ford, Conrad provided a new role model, in a sense replacing Ford Madox Brown as Ford's vision of the Great Artist. Even more important, Conrad gave Ford for the first time in his career a clear focus for his writing and definite direction, more modern than Pre-Raphaelite, in his career.

The collaboration between Ford and Conrad produced three undistinguished novels: *The Inheritors* (1901); *Romance* (1903), the best known of the collaborations; and *The Nature of a Crime* (written

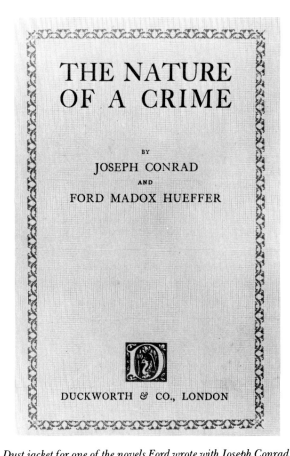

Dust jacket for one of the novels Ford wrote with Joseph Conrad. Through their collaboration the two developed the detached narrative voice that became the hallmark of each writer's finest fiction.

in 1906 and published serially in 1909, but not published as a book until 1924). Though none of the novels has anything more than occasional patches of great writing, the collaboration in itself gave Ford and Conrad the opportunity to develop a common theory of the novel, one that played a major role in shaping Conrad's best work during his ten-year friendship with Ford and later inspired the critical narrative voice in Ford's great novel, *The Good Soldier.* Their theory stressed the importance of a clear and detached narrative voice and a concreteness of character and situation. Essentially, the goal for the novelist was, in Conrad's words in his preface to *The Nigger of the "Narcissus,"* "by the power of the written word, to make you hear, to make you feel—it is, before all, to make you see!" In Ford's fiction, characters ranging from John Kemp in *Romance,* who has to make the court "see things" to save his life, to John Dowell, the narrator of *The Good Soldier,* become obsessed with either seeing things clearly or getting someone else to see things. For Conrad and

Ford in 1900 with his wife, Elsie, and daughters, Katherine and Christina (courtesy of Mr. Jocelyn Baines)

Ford, the narrative of the novel was a journey or quest toward some perceivable truth, evasive but essential for narrator, novelist, and reader.

While Ford's relationship with Conrad brought clarity and purpose to his work, it did not help Ford find financial success or personal happiness. Ford's career continued its uneven course during the 1900s, even though he published several books of fiction, poetry, and criticism, including the *Fifth Queen* trilogy: *The Fifth Queen* (1906), *Privy Seal* (1907), and *The Fifth Queen Crowned* (1908)—three historical novels based on Ford's somewhat idealized interpretation of the life and times of Catherine Howard, the fifth queen of Henry VIII. Beyond his increasing productivity during this period, Ford's most important contributions came through his editorship of the *English Review,* a literary magazine devoted to the most serious and best literature written in England. During Ford's tenure as editor from 1908 to 1910, he published the established writers of his generation, Hardy, Wells, Bennett, Galsworthy, and James, but he also found room for younger writers, including his most important discovery, D. H. Lawrence. Though the *English Review* eventually became a financial disaster—Ford was a poor manager of money throughout his adult life—the excellence of its publication record stands as a tribute to Ford's de-

votion to literature and his ability to recognize and eagerness to support literary genius.

The financial problems of the *English Review* were only a part of the professional and personal difficulties Ford faced during this period in his life. While the review gave him the opportunity and means to act out the man-of-letters role, his own books brought little in the way of either critical or popular success. As a result, Ford constantly fought with his publishers, a pattern that also continued throughout his career, because he firmly believed they were not promoting his books properly and were not paying him sufficiently for his efforts. Plagued by serious money problems, Ford also struggled with a deteriorating marriage, poor physical health, nervous disorders, and a growing frustration at failing to capture his dream of literary glory. Shortly after the birth of his second child in 1900, Ford had a disastrous affair with Mary Martindale, his wife's older sister. By 1903, he had fallen into a deep state of mental depression and, by the following year, plagued by guilt feelings and by agoraphobia, he suffered a nervous breakdown. During the next few years, Ford's marriage worsened, his important friendship with Conrad cooled, and his strong emotional need for attention and praise, especially from attractive women, grew more and more demanding.

In 1908, the same year he started the *English Review,* Ford met the writer Violet Hunt. The daughter of a father who was an Oxford don and a well-known painter and a mother who was a successful novelist, Violet had grown up in the same Pre-Raphaelite circle as Ford and shared his devotion to art. Like Ford, she was also impulsive in her personal life and constantly sought out some form of dramatic or emotional excitement. By 1909, Ford, now completely determined to live with Violet, separated from Elsie and threatened suicide until Violet agreed to become his mistress. Unfortunately for Ford, Elsie refused to grant a divorce. Instead, she began a series of court actions to guarantee her marital rights. At one point, Ford actually spent several days in Brixton Gaol for refusing a court order to give support money to Elsie.

Ford's affair with Violet Hunt cost him Conrad's friendship, and his failure with the *English Review* and his costly legal battles with Elsie reduced him to bankruptcy, periodical bouts of heavy drinking, and another long attack of neurasthenia, complicated by agoraphobia. In the midst of his frustrations, he wrote to an acquaintance: "I see no reason why you should desire to cut my throat, blast my reputation, reveal what you think to be my secrets, or throw vitriol upon me. I never discovered your first work, offered you shelter, food, clothing or encouragement when you were starving. I never lent you money, wrote in praise of your writing or committed against you any of the twenty-seven Nonconformist Deadly Sins." The worst, however, was yet to come for Ford. In 1911, when his false claim that he had gained a German divorce appeared in the *Daily Mirror,* Elsie threatened the newspaper with a lawsuit until they printed a public apology and paid her damages. A year later, Elsie actually went to court when *Throne,* a magazine edited by one of Ford's friends, gave Violet Hunt's name as Mrs. Hueffer. The trial ended in Elsie's favor and brought a humiliating end to Ford's effort to gain public recognition of Violet as his intellectual and emotional companion.

At the age of forty, Ford found himself with little fame and certainly no fortune in spite of the publication of numerous novels, several works of nonfiction, and even three books of poetry. He was trapped in a marriage in name only, had suffered public embarrassment, and now felt betrayed by most of his literary friends. When Ford began experiencing emotional problems with Violet and suffered from a new bout of neurasthenia, he even threatened suicide, as he had done earlier when his marriage with Elsie faltered. Yet, in 1913, at perhaps the emotional and financial low point of his life and career, Ford began his literary masterpiece. Ford's decision to write *The Good Soldier* and the great care and energy he put into his work on the book may well have been caused by his feeling that he had come to the end of his tether, but the result, rather than a literary expression of self-pity, turned out to be the fruition, finally, of all that he had learned from his collaboration with Conrad and his editorship of the *English Review.*

The Good Soldier, finished by Ford in 1914 and published on 17 September 1915, is Ford's one great modern novel, a masterstroke of impressionistic fiction that ranks with James's most complex narratives, Conrad's Marlow stories, and Joyce's *A Portrait of the Artist as a Young Man* (1916) in its perfect balance of point of view, character, and theme. The novel seems especially indebted to James's *The Golden Bowl* (1904) in its compelling study of the destructive intimacy of two couples, "good people" in manner and attitude, torn apart by the contradictory demands of deep passion and loyalty. Indeed, Ford had reread James's fiction, before beginning *The Good Soldier,* for his critical book *Henry James* (1914). No doubt, his critical writing on James brought Ford's similar ideas on the novel into sharper focus and inspired the creation of the book Ford had desperately wanted to write for nearly two decades.

In his "The Art of Fiction," Henry James wrote that the air of reality is the supreme virtue of a novel. For James, reality is defined by experience, and experience is made up of impressions. In other words, an individual cannot experience something unless he perceives the experience, records it in his consciousness. This equation of what is real with what is perceived is at the heart of the fiction writing Ford called impressionism and provides the key to understanding the complex and brilliant narrative design of *The Good Soldier.* The novel's main characters are similar in conception and action to those in Ford's earlier fiction, but the way in which the reader sees the characters through the impressions they have made on the narrator and through the narrator's efforts to get at the truth behind these impressions gives the novel its distinctive quality. Stripped of its narrator, John Dowell, *The Good Soldier,* like Flaubert's *Madame Bovary* when stripped of its ironic perspective, is little more than a tale of false sentiment, sordid passion, and sexual betrayal. What the American Dowell gives to Ford's "tale of passion," his subtitle for the novel, is an air of detachment or objectivity because of his peculiar innocence or lack of passion. Like Conrad's Marlow,

Dowell is not capable of the madness he discovers in those he loves and even grows to hate, but his curiosity and commitment to the truth take him deeper and deeper into the dark heart of passion.

Dowell's main interest as narrator is to write the "real story" of Edward Ashburnham, the finest human being he has ever known and the good soldier of the novel. He tells his tale in "a very rambling way," but he points out, in an explanation of the chronological dislocation that Ford and Conrad had developed earlier as a narrative strategy to draw the reader into the narrator's quest for the truth, that "when one discusses an affair—a long, sad affair—one goes back, one goes forward. One remembers points that one has forgotten and one explains them all the more minutely since one recognizes that one has forgotten to mention them in their proper places and that one may have given, by omitting them, a false impression. I console myself with thinking that this is a real story and that, after all, real stories are probably told best in the way a person telling a story would tell them. They will then seem most real."

As Dowell probes into Ashburnham's character and behavior, he celebrates Ashburnham as the very embodiment of the virtues of the English country gentleman: his sense of saying the right thing, acting publicly in the proper manner, and carrying out his responsibilities to others and performing his duties to his class. Yet Dowell also has to take into account Ashburnham's excessive sentimentality and passion and his need for female approval that compels him into several adulterous relationships, including an affair wth Dowell's wife that ends with her suicide. Dowell never finds the truth of the matter, what makes perfectly good people destroy themselves and the ones they love—even Ashburnham takes his own life—but by novel's end, the narrator of *The Good Soldier* knows that "society can only exist if the normal, if the virtuous, and the slightly deceitful flourish, and if the passionate, the headstrong, and the too-truthful are condemned to suicide and to madness." Yet Dowell also knows in his own heart that he still sympathizes with Ashburnham because those like Ashburnham count—their lives, even if doomed to end tragically, mean something in a world otherwise made up of the drab and the insignificant.

Ford's aesthetic success in *The Good Soldier* was not matched by any critical or financial success immediately after the book's publication. While Rebecca West found the book magnificent, most reviews, like those in the *Times Literary Supplement*, *Athenaeum*, *Saturday Review*, and the *Nation*,

criticized Ford's writing as long-winded, unpleasant, and lacking in focus. Reviewing for the *New Republic*, Theodore Dreiser ridiculed *The Good Soldier* because of its "encrusting formalism." Still plagued by serious difficulties in his public and private life, Ford decided to become the good soldier and enlisted in the British army in August 1915. Before he entered the army, Ford wrote a few propaganda pieces and legally dropped his middle name, Hermann, from his baptismal certificate. (It was only after the war, in 1919, that Ford finally changed his last name from Hueffer to Ford at the instigation of his publisher Duckworth, who claimed: "If only you'd sign your books 'Ford' I might be able to sell the beastly things." The first time he actually used the name Ford Madox Ford as an author was in 1923, with the publication of *The Marsden Case*, his first postwar novel.)

Ford's fortunes in war were not much different from his frustrations and failures as a civilian. Assigned as a company officer in a transportation line, Ford never became engaged in direct combat though his company was assigned near the front

Ford about the time of his enlistment in the British army, August 1915

line. He did, however, have several verbal battles with his commanding officer, who accused Ford of incompetence. When the concussion from a shell explosion knocked him down and damaged some teeth, Ford, his nerves already ragged, suffered another nervous breakdown. After his recovery, Ford returned to France, but he became ill again and returned to England for the duration of the war. Though Ford would later use his war experiences for *Parade's End* and embellish his own war record, he came out of the war still troubled and still uncertain about his future as a writer.

Fortunately for Ford, he had met the Australian painter Stella Bowen during one of his leaves. By the Armistice, he had fallen in love once again and now dreamed of living with Stella in a small cottage in the English countryside. Estranged from Violet Hunt, though she continued to find opportunities to criticize and insult him, Ford finally moved into Red Ford Cottage in April 1919, where he was joined by Stella in June. In *Hugh Selwyn Mauberley* (1920), Ezra Pound mockingly immortalized this new phase in Ford's life, as he and Stella grew their own vegetables and raised pigs and chickens:

> Beneath the sagging roof
> The stylist has taken shelter,
> Unpaid, uncelebrated,
> At last from the world's welter.
>
> Nature receives him;
> With a placid and uneducated mistress
> He exercises his talents
> And the soil meets his distress.
>
> The heaven from sophistications and contentions
> Leaks through its thatch;
> He offers succulent cooking;
> The door has a creaking latch.

During the next few years, while playing at the life of the small farmer or what he called the "Small Producer," Ford tried to re-establish himself as a writer. At the same time, he tried to create in his critical writings the impression that he was a great but sadly neglected literary figure. After finishing *Thus to Revisit* (1921), his survey of the contemporary scene in which he claims that literature has been usurped by pedants, Ford and Stella, now with a baby girl, Esther Julia, born in November 1920, decided to forsake their cottage for the literary scene in Paris, where Ford hoped to fulfill his long frustrated dream of becoming a recognized master of modern letters. By early 1922, Ford had set up

Stella Bowen, the mother of Ford's daughter Esther Julia, born in 1920

his new life with Stella in Paris, but the closest he came to commanding a literary world already dominated by Gertrude Stein and James Joyce and their coteries was his editorship of the *transatlantic review*. Though the magazine lasted for only one year, Ford managed to publish some impressive experimental literature, including poetry by Pound and E. E. Cummings. For his first issue, Ford actually published a fragment, the first to appear in print, of Joyce's *Finnegans Wake*, which appeared in a section called "Work in Progress," a title Joyce quickly adopted for *Finnegans Wake* until its publication in 1939.

While in Paris, Ford began his most ambitious and representative work, the tetralogy *Parade's End*. *Some Do Not*, the first and most important of the four novels, was published in 1924. *No More Parades*, written while Ford was having an unsettling affair with the novelist Jean Rhys, appeared in 1925. *A Man Could Stand Up*, published in 1926, and *The Last*

James Joyce, Ezra Pound, John Quinn, and Ford, Paris, 1923 (courtesy of Miss Jeanne Foster)

Post, published in 1928 and the weakest novel in the tetralogy by Ford's own judgment, were written during a turbulent period when his relationship with Stella Bowen was faltering. Ford spent some of this time in America, where he gave a series of lectures, well received by his own estimation, and discovered more recognition and praise for his novels than he had ever found in England or France. While he entertained the idea of becoming an American writer, he also began another affair, this time with an American, Rene Wright, that finished his relationship with Stella Bowen.

The appearance of *Parade's End* during another time of emotional upheaval in Ford's life sets up an obvious parallel with the similar conditions suffered by Ford when he was writing his masterpiece, *The Good Soldier.* The similarity is particularly intriguing because Christopher Tietjens, the hero of the tetralogy, is very much the good soldier in his Tory belief in the value of duty, loyalty, and propriety. This parallel between *Parade's End* and *The Good Soldier* does not hold, however, beyond Ford's strained emotional state when he wrote his two most important works and his creation in both of a hero representing conservative values dear to Ford's own heart, if not appropriate to his own behavior. While *The Good Soldier,* a tale of passion but also Ford's saddest story, reveals the per-

sonal and tragic side of the Fordian hero irrevocably trapped between duty and feeling, *Parade's End* takes a similar character, but one shaped more by propriety than passion, and examines his Edwardian life-style and beliefs, to determine if he can live in a modern world governed by hypocrisy and treachery. In other words, *The Good Soldier,* Ford's best-written book, probes into the secret heart of the Fordian hero and discovers a conflict that ends in suicide. *Parade's End,* however, portrays with a broad stroke the social struggle of that same hero who tries to make his separate peace with the world that no longer honors his Tory values.

In *Some Do Not,* the first book of *Parade's End,* Ford establishes the Edwardian nature of his hero, the chaotic times in which he lives, and the moral dilemma that will severely test his ability to survive. Christopher Tietjens emerges as the ideal projection of Ford's consciousness, the perfect type of his Tory class, and the final product of England's Edwardian world. His sense of duty and proper behavior is flawless, even in his relationship with his unfaithful wife; his own conscience is clear, and his mind and bloodline first-rate. No matter how difficult or painful, he always does the right thing, expresses the right sentiment, and, without fail, knows the right answer. Tietjens is so good, so perfect, so right in a world falling apart that several critics, including Arthur Mizener and Melvin Seiden, have found his character one of the chief faults in the tetralogy. The amusing irony of this critical reaction to Tietjens is that it matches the frustration experienced by other characters in *Parade's End,* especially Tietjen's wife, who finds her husband intolerably perfect. Tietjens, for his fictive friends and enemies and for Ford's critics, is simply too good to be true, a Christopher who wants to be Christ, an Edwardian saint in search of martyrdom in a modern world.

Ford places his saintly hero in an agonizing emotional situation in which he must tolerate a wife bent on destroying him, a best friend willing to betray him, and authorities who resent his natural superiority and seek to ruin his career. When Tietjens meets and falls in love with Valentine Wallop, a young suffragette, he has the opportunity to satisfy his own needs, but he remains true to his Tory values even though they have isolated him and forced him to play the fool. In a modern world, where most give in to desire, compromise themselves by betraying their principles, some do not— and Tietjens remains in that exclusive company by denying his desire for Valentine and keeping their relationship platonic.

While *Some Do Not* follows Tietjens through the years leading up to World War I and shows him recovering from shell shock and preparing to return to the war at the end of the novel, *No More Parades* and *A Man Could Stand Up* concentrate for the most part on Tietjens at war. In *No More Parades,* Ford actually carries Tietjen's personal problems to him at the front by having his wife, Sylvia, madly pursue him to France, where she deliberately undermines his military position with his battalion and instigates the command decision to send him into battle. It is at the front, however, in *A Man Could Stand Up* that Tietjens discovers his sense of individual will and purpose:

> He had been the Younger Son, loafing, contemptuous, capable, idly contemplating life, but ready to take up the position of the Head of the Family if Death so arranged matters. He had been a sort of eternal Second-in-Command.

> Now what the Hell was he? A sort of Hamlet of the Trenches! No, by God he was not. . . . He was perfectly ready for action. Ready to command a battalion. He was presumably a lover. They did things like commanding battalions and worse!

The worst that Tietjens commits in *A Man Could Stand Up* is to reject his heritage by refusing his family's money and estate. He also makes the decision to become a lover—he has proven himself in battle earlier in the novel—by taking Valentine as his mistress. *The Last Post,* the novel Ford eventually repudiated because it was too weak and unnecessary, closes out the tetralogy by confirming the rightness of Tietjens's decision to seek his separate peace with Valentine, though most of the narrative deals with the unsuccessful efforts of Tietjens's older brother to convince Christopher to take the family's money and estate and Sylvia's last, mad, futile attempts to destroy Christopher's newly found happiness.

If *The Good Soldier,* by Ford's own measurement is his saddest story, then *Parade's End* qualifies as one of his happiest or most optimistic. In his biography of Ford, Mizener describes the subject of the tetralogy as "the inner process by which Christopher and Valentine are gradually transformed from Edwardian to modern people." Since this transformation involves the ideal Ford hero and takes place during the critical years surrounding World War I when the values of Western civilization changed so dramatically, *Parade's End* stands out as Ford's most representative work. Though uneven in conception and execution, the tetralogy is Ford's most ambitious effort to project his own values, his own self-image, upon the pages of his fiction and his most wide-ranging and serious judgment of the failure of the modern world to sustain the essential truths and traditions that most define culture and civilization. It is Ford's judgment of the collapse of Western values that critics and artists ranging from Hugh Kenner to W. H. Auden have found most compelling and convincing in *Parade's End.* Auden actually concluded that Ford's tetralogy "makes it quite clear that World War I was a retribution visited upon Western Europe for the sins and omissions of its ruling class, for which not only they, but also the innocent conscripted millions on both sides must suffer."

While Ford had finally reached the point in his career where he could create a hero capable of reaching a separate peace between himself and society, he found his own life and career as troubled and chaotic as ever. His attempt to reshape his career in America brought some satisfaction with the modest success of *Parade's End,* but the fiction he wrote after the tetralogy was not comparable to his best work. Ford's vision of himself as the undecorated Dean of English Letters remained more myth than reality as the critical and public recognition he had desperately craved for so long still eluded him. Disappointed in his situation in England and France, he seriously entertained the idea of settling permanently in America as part of a scheme to sell himself as an American writer.

Part of Ford's plan for a new life and career in America also included a permanent relationship with Rene Wright, but his failure, once again, to get a divorce from Elsie brought an end to the affair and his plan for the Americanization of Ford Madox Ford. When he returned to Paris in 1930, Ford, with his knack for finding sympathetic and attractive women, met the Polish painter Janice Biala. She soon became Ford's companion and gave him the fierce loyalty and unqualified devotion he always needed from women. Shortly after Ford and Janice moved into the Villa Paul at Cape Brun, he suffered his first heart attack in December 1930. Struggling now with his seriously declining health—he was also badly overweight and out of shape—and still plagued by continuing money problems and periodical attacks of nerves, Ford managed to keep up his writing. He actually planned an American trilogy of novels that he hoped would do for the postwar world what *Parade's End* had done for the World War I generation. He completed two of the novels: *The Rash Act* (1933) and *Henry for Hugh* (1934); but the books are undistinguished and rather improbable in plot and characterization.

Ford's important work in the last decade of his life was his critical writing, especially his literary reminiscences. In much of his writing, he attempted to recreate the literary past and his relationships with the great novelists who had shared his vision of literature. In *Return to Yesterday* (1931), Ford conceives a literary Eden populated by Wells, James, Conrad, and, of course, Ford himself. *It Was the Nightingale* (1933), intended as a sequel to *Return to Yesterday,* darkens Ford's vision, however, as he remembers those in England who had persecuted him throughout his literary career. Both works are entertaining and interesting, but they are plagued by Ford's megalomania, which manifests itself in his exaggerated treatment of literary history to give himself a position of great importance. During this period, Ford also worked on travel guides that turned out to be commentaries on the path of culture and civilization rather than actual aids to travelers. In *Provence* (1935) and *Great Trade Route* (1937), books Ford hoped would contain his message to the world, he evokes those places, ranging from the South of France to the American South, that had given him the most pleasure, as settings for

Ford in the 1930s with Polish painter Janice Biala, his companion during the last nine years of his life

his opinions on the evils of modern life and the virtues of the moderate and simple life of the small farmer or producer. While the travel books are entertaining, they too suffer from intellectual crankery and Ford's megalomania.

Ford spent his last years, in spite of his terrible health, traveling back and forth between Europe and America. In 1937, thanks primarily to the American poet Allen Tate, Ford was invited by the president of Olivet College in Michigan to spend the summer there as a writer and critic in residence. He also accepted an offer from the University of Colorado to direct a writers' conference and, in the fall, returned to Olivet where he taught or, at least, told anecdotes while insisting, as always, on the sacred office of the novelist and the high seriousness of literature. At Olivet, he also worked on his last published work, *The March of Literature* (1938). This last book, Ford's most ambitious attempt to write an intellectual history of literature, has all the virtues and vices of Ford's writing at this time. At its best, *The March of Literature* offers delightfully written portraits of those writers and ages he admires, the great craftsmen of ancient Greece, the middle ages, the seventeenth century, and the impressionists of the modern age. At its worst, the book is riddled with highly personal opinions, sweeping generalities, and judgments that often seem outrageous.

After completing his work at Olivet, Ford returned to Paris, where he suffered another heart

Ford (left) receiving an honorary degree at Olivet College, Michigan, 1938. Beside him is Joseph Brewster, college president.

attack. Once recovered, he returned to Olivet where, in June 1938, he received a Doctor of Literature, his only honorary degree. Delighted by the honor, he began several new projects, including the revival of the *transatlantic review,* but, by the end of the year, he was seriously ill once again. In the spring of 1939, Ford, determined to spend the summer in his beloved South of France, sailed from America, only to suffer another relapse during the voyage. Suffering now from uremia, he was hospitalized at Deauville, where on 26 June 1939 he died of heart failure.

After his death, Ford's reputation survived mainly because of his collaboration with Conrad, his editorship of the *English Review* and the *transatlantic review,* and the notoriety and controversy caused by his exaggerated literary reminiscences. He had written so many mediocre novels, had made so many outrageous claims for his own literary genius, had offered the world so many crank ideas on culture and civilization that he was an easy target for literary critics who saw him as belonging more to the sideshow of modern literature than its main event. For all his efforts as an artist and critic, he appeared in danger of becoming finally judged as a travesty or

eventually ignored altogether.

Since the 1950s, however, Ford has emerged as a major literary figure. The author of so many minor novels, he is now recognized as the writer of one of the true masterpieces of modern literature, *The Good Soldier,* and a tetralogy, *Parade's End,* that is one of the modern period's most imaginative studies of the cultural crisis faced by the Edwardian generation during World War I. As foolish and egocentric as he was in his dealing with people and with literary and business matters, he is now honored as the editor of two reviews that were of major importance because they published the early and later works of some of the most important and experimental writers of the twentieth century. And, while he often failed miserably in his life and career, Ford is now generally perceived as a legitimate member of an exclusive company of artists who shaped modern literature because of their belief in the autonomy of the artist and the primacy of literature in defining the values of civilization. More concretely, Ford's accomplishment as a novelist in *The Good Soldier* and, to a lesser extent, in *Parade's End* places him artistically on a level with Henry James and Joseph Conrad, the two writers he most admired, though he lacked their consistency of technical brilliance or their sustained vision of the novel. As for his dedicated work as an editor, his important role in discovering writers of the genius of a D. H. Lawrence and supporting the literary efforts of Pound and Joyce, even though they ridiculed Ford in return, entitles him to be regarded as one of the main architects of modern literature. An easy and large target for the parodies of friends and critics, Ford was a good and noble soldier in the cause of art. A year after Ford's death, William Carlos Williams wrote:

> I laugh to think of you wheezing in Heaven.
> Where is Heaven? But why
> do I ask that, since you showed the way?
> I don't care a damn for it
> other than for that better part lives besides
> me here so long as I
> live and remember you. Thank God you
> were not delicate, you let the world in
> and lied! damn it you lied grossly
> sometimes. But it was all, I
> see now, a carelessness, the part of a man
> that is homeless here on earth.

Letters:

Letters of Ford Madox Ford, edited by Richard M. Ludwig (Princeton: Princeton University Press, 1965).

Bibliography:

David Dow Harvey, *Ford Madox Ford, 1873-1939: A Bibliography of Works and Criticism* (Princeton: Princeton University Press, 1962).

Biographies:

Douglas Goldring, *The Last Pre-Raphaelite: The Life and Writings of Ford Madox Ford* (London: Macdonald, 1948);

Frank MacShane, *The Life and Works of Ford Madox Ford* (New York: Horizon Press, 1965);

Arthur Mizener, *The Saddest Story: A Biography of Ford Madox Ford* (New York & Cleveland: World, 1971);

Thomas C. Moser, *The Life in the Fiction of Ford Madox Ford* (Princeton: Princeton University Press, 1980).

References:

Robert J. Andreach, *The Slain and Resurrected God: Conrad, Ford, and the Christian Myth* (New York: New York University Press, 1970);

Stella Bowen, *Drawn from Life: Reminiscences* (London: Collins, 1941);

Richard A. Cassell, *Ford Madox Ford: A Study of His Novels* (Baltimore: Johns Hopkins University Press, 1961);

Cassell, ed., *Ford Madox Ford: Modern Judgments* (London: Macmillan, 1972);

Douglas Goldring, *South Lodge: Reminiscences of Violet Hunt, Ford Madox Ford and the English Review Circle* (London: Constable, 1943);

Ambrose Gordon, Jr., *The Invisible Tent: The War Novels of Ford Madox Ford* (Austin: University of Texas Press, 1964);

Robert Green, *Ford Madox Ford: Prose and Politics* (Cambridge: Cambridge University Press, 1981);

Violet Hunt, *I Have This to Say* (New York: Boni & Liveright, 1926);

H. Robert Huntley, *The Alien Protagonist of Ford Madox Ford* (Chapel Hill: University of North Carolina Press, 1970);

Norman Leer, *The Limited Hero in the Novels of Ford Madox Ford* (East Lansing: Michigan State University Press, 1966);

R. W. Lid, *Ford Madox Ford: The Essence of His Art* (Berkeley: University of California Press, 1964);

Frank MacShane, ed., *Ford Madox Ford: The Critical Heritage* (London: Routledge & Kegan Paul, 1972);

John A. Meixner, *Ford Madox Ford's Novels* (Minneapolis: University of Minnesota Press, 1962);

Carol Ohmann, *Ford Madox Ford: From Apprentice to Craftsman* (Middleton: Wesleyan University Press, 1964);

Bernard J. Poli, *Ford Madox Ford* (New York: Twayne, 1968);

Poli, *Ford Madox Ford and the Transatlantic Review* (Syracuse: Syracuse University Press, 1967);

Sondra J. Stang, *Ford Madox Ford* (New York: Unger, 1977);

Stang, ed., *The Presence of Ford Madox Ford* (Philadelphia: University of Pennsylvania Press, 1981);

Paul L. Wiley, *Novelist of Three Worlds: Ford Madox Ford* (Syracuse: Syracuse University Press, 1962).

Papers:

The Violet Hunt and Stella Bowen papers are at Cornell University Library. In addition to major private Ford collections there are lesser deposits at Princeton, Yale, and Virginia.

E. M. Forster

Frederick P. W. McDowell
University of Iowa

BIRTH: London, England, 1 January 1879, to Edward Morgan Llewellyn and Alice Clara (Lily) Whichelo Forster.

EDUCATION: B.A. second class in Classical Tripos, Part I, King's College, Cambridge, 1900; B.A. second class in Historical Tripos, Part I, King's College, Cambridge, 1901; M.A., King's College, Cambridge, 1910.

AWARDS AND HONORS: Tukojirao Gold Medal, Dewas State Senior, India, 1921; Femina/Vie Heureuse Prize for *A Passage to India,* 1925; James Tait Black Memorial Prize for *A Passage to India,* 1925; Fellow, King's College, Cambridge, 1927-1930; Clark Lecturer, Trinity College, Cambridge, 1927; LL.D., Aberdeen University, 1931; Benson Medal, Royal Society of Literature, 1937; Rede Lecturer, Senate House, Cambridge, 1941; W. P. Ker Lecturer, University of Glasgow, 1944; Honorary Fellow, King's College, Cambridge, 1946-1970; Litt.D., Liverpool University, 1947; Litt.D., Hamilton College, 1949; Honorary Corresponding Member, American Academy of Arts and Letters; Litt.D., Cambridge University, 1950; Litt.D., Nottingham University, 1951; Order of Companions of Honor to the Queen, 1953; Litt.D., Manchester University, 1954; Litt.D., University of Leyden, 1954; Litt.D., University of Leicester, 1958; Companion, Royal Society of Literature, 1961; Order of Merit, by Queen Elizabeth II, 1969.

DEATH: Coventry, England, 7 June 1970.

SELECTED BOOKS: *Where Angels Fear to Tread* (Edinburgh & London: Blackwood, 1905; New York: Knopf, 1920);

The Longest Journey (Edinburgh & London: Blackwood, 1907; New York: Knopf, 1922);

A Room with a View (London: Arnold, 1908; New York & London: Putnam's, 1911);

Howards End (London: Arnold, 1910; New York & London: Putnam's, 1910);

The Celestial Omnibus and Other Stories (London: Sidgwick & Jackson, 1911; New York: Knopf, 1923);

The Story of the Siren (Richmond: Leonard & Virginia

E. M. Forster in 1950 (courtesy of R. J. Buckingham)

Woolf at the Hogarth Press, 1920);

The Government of Egypt, Recommendations by a Committee of the International Section of the Labour Research Department, with Notes on Egypt by E. M. Forster (London: Labour Research Department, 1920);

Alexandria: A History and a Guide (Alexandria: Whitehead Morris, 1922; Garden City: Doubleday, 1961; London: Michael Haag, 1982);

Pharos and Pharillon (Richmond: Leonard & Virginia Woolf at the Hogarth Press, 1923; New York: Knopf, 1923);

A Passage to India (London: Arnold, 1924; New York: Harcourt, Brace, 1924);

Anonymity: An Enquiry (London: Leonard & Virginia Woolf at the Hogarth Press, 1925);

Aspects of the Novel (London: Arnold, 1927; New York: Harcourt, Brace, 1927);

The Eternal Moment and Other Stories (London:

Sidgwick & Jackson, 1928; New York: Harcourt, Brace, 1928);

Sinclair Lewis Interprets America (Cambridge, Mass.: Harvard Press, 1932);

Goldsworthy Lowes Dickinson (London: Arnold, 1934; New York: Harcourt, Brace, 1934);

Abinger Harvest (London: Arnold, 1936; New York: Harcourt, Brace, 1936);

What I Believe (London: Hogarth Press, 1939);

England's Pleasant Land, a Pageant Play (London: Hogarth Press, 1940);

Nordic Twilight, Macmillan War Pamphlet, volume 3 (London: Macmillan, 1940);

Virginia Woolf: The Rede Lecture (Cambridge: Cambridge University Press, 1942);

The Collected Tales of E. M. Forster (New York: Knopf, 1947); republished as *Collected Short Stories of E. M. Forster* (London: Sidgwick & Jackson, 1948);

Two Cheers for Democracy (London: Arnold, 1951; New York: Harcourt, Brace, 1951);

Billy Budd: an Opera in Four Acts. Libretto by E. M. Forster and Eric Crozier, Adapted from the Story by Herman Melville (London, New York, Toronto, Sydney, Capetown, Buenos Aires, Paris & Bonn: Boosey & Hawkes, 1951);

The Hill of Devi (London: Arnold, 1953; New York: Harcourt, Brace, 1953);

Marianne Thornton (1797-1887): A Domestic Biography (London: Arnold, 1956; New York: Harcourt, Brace, 1956);

Maurice (London: Arnold, 1971; New York: Norton, 1971);

"Albergo Empedocle" and Other Writings by E. M. Forster, edited by George H. Thomson (New York: Liveright, 1971);

The Life to Come and Other Stories (London: Arnold, 1972); republished as *The Life to Come and Other Short Stories* (New York: Norton, 1972);

The Lucy Novels: Early Sketches for "A Room with a View," edited by Oliver Stallybrass (London: Arnold, 1973; New York: Holmes & Meier, 1973);

The Manuscripts of "Howards End," edited by Stallybrass (London: Arnold, 1973; New York: Holmes & Meier, 1973);

Goldsworthy Lowes Dickinson and Related Writings, edited by Stallybrass (London: Arnold, 1973; New York: Holmes & Meier, 1973);

Aspects of the Novel and Related Writings, edited by Stallybrass (London: Arnold, 1974; New York: Holmes & Meier, 1974);

The Manuscripts of "A Passage to India," edited by Stallybrass (London: Arnold, 1978; New

York: Holmes & Meier, 1978);

Commonplace Book: E. M. Forster (London: Scolar Press, 1978);

Arctic Summer and Other Fiction, edited by Elizabeth Heine and Stallybrass (London: Arnold, 1980; New York: Holmes & Meier, 1980);

The Hill of Devi and Other Indian Writings, edited by Heine (London: Arnold, 1983; New York: Holmes & Meier, 1983).

Collection: *The Abinger Edition of E. M. Forster,* 13 volumes to date, edited by Oliver Stallybrass and Elizabeth Heine (London: Arnold, 1972-1983; New York: Holmes & Meier, 1972-1983).

OTHER: Introduction to *The Longest Journey,* World's Classics Series (London: Oxford University Press, 1960), pp. ix-xiv;

Introduction to *Lord of the Flies,* by William Golding (New York: Coward-McCann, 1962);

Endnote to *Maurice* (New York: Norton, 1971), pp. 249-255;

"Rooksnest," in his *Howards End,* Abinger Edition (London: Arnold, 1973; New York: Holmes & Meier, 1973), pp. 341-351;

"Forster's Programme Note to Santha Rama Rau's Dramatized Version," in his *A Passage to India,* Abinger Edition (London: Arnold, 1978; New York: Holmes & Meier, 1978), p. 328.

PERIODICAL PUBLICATIONS: "Toward a Definition of Tolerance," *New York Times Magazine,* 22 February 1953, p. 13;

"The Art and Architecture of India," *Listener,* 50 (10 September 1953): 419-421;

"The World Mountain," *Listener,* 52 (2 December 1954): 977-978;

"The Blue Boy," *Listener,* 62 (14 March 1957): 444;

"The Charm and Strength of Mrs. Gaskell," *Sunday Times* (London), 7 April 1957, pp. 10-11;

"A View without a Room: Old Friends Fifty Years Later," *New York Times Book Review,* 27 July 1958, p. 4;

"A Presidential Address to the Cambridge Humanists—Summer 1959," *University Humanist Federation Bulletin,* 11 (Spring 1963): 2-8.

During the Edwardian years and into the 1920s, E. M. Forster consolidated his reputation as a novelist of distinction and as a persuasive man of letters. He attained the greatest recognition and authority after World War II when, except for work on *Maurice* (1971; the first draft was completed in

Forster at the age of five with his mother, Alice Whichelo Forster

relevant for them—than his popular and more voluminous contemporaries such as John Galsworthy, H. G. Wells, and Arnold Bennett. Most readers and critics would align him in the quality of his work—though not in breadth and comprehensiveness—with such modern writers as Ford Madox Ford, Joseph Conrad, Virginia Woolf, and D. H. Lawrence.

Edward Morgan Forster was born at 6 Melcombe Place, Dorset Square, London, on 1 January 1879. He represented a divided inheritance. His paternal ancestors, the Thorntons, revealed a seriousness and a moral earnestness that Forster admired but sometimes rebelled against; whereas his maternal ancestors, the Whichelos, revealed an enjoyment of the amenities and an aesthetic responsiveness that attracted him perhaps more strongly. In any event, he owed most to his great-aunt Marianne Thornton, who left him a legacy of £8,000 when she died in 1887. She had thus made it possible for him to receive without strain a university education and to devote himself to a career as a writer without worrying about other employment. His father died a year and a half after the boy's birth, and Forster had to depend upon his mother and the family relatives, who were predominantly women, for his future upbringing and guidance. Over the years the relationship with his mother proved to be at once

1914) and the most important of the short stories that were first published in *The Life to Come and Other Stories* (1972), he had ceased the writing of fiction. Though his repute and influence have suffered since his death in 1970, he still commands the respect and enthusiasm of critics and general readers alike for his many virtues as fiction writer and essayist. His gifts are manifest and manifold: an ability to imagine characters and situations of surpassing aesthetic and human significance; a speculative power and a philosophical acuteness; moral seriousness, sensitivity, and catholic sympathies; a wide aesthetic range both as a perceptive realist in presenting the Edwardian and postwar social scene and as a romancer alive to the mythic and archetypal aspects of human experience; an abundant humor, wit, and irony; an incisiveness of insight, a geniality of temper, and a committed humanism; and a lucid, discerning, and informed intelligence. For most readers Forster now looms larger as a creative force and literary artist—certainly as one who is more

Forster's great-aunt, Marianne Thornton, whose biography by Forster was published in 1956

rewarding and frustrating for Forster as the two were united in sympathy or divided by misunderstanding.

Possibly the most important aspect of his early life was his residence with his mother at Rooksnest, a house in Hertfordshire near Stevenage. Here Forster developed his love for the English countryside, and Rooksnest became the model for Howards End house and farm in *Howards End* (1910). He attended a preparatory school at Eastbourne and then became a day student at Tonbridge School. The family meanwhile had to leave Rooksnest to reside in Tonbridge. These years at school were unhappy for Forster, and he later reflected this disaffection in his depiction of Sawston School in *The Longest Journey* (1907).

In contrast to Tonbridge School, Cambridge University proved to be an inspiring milieu for Forster. At King's College he was conscious that his horizons kept expanding in the congenial company of dons and fellows such as J. E. M. McTaggart with his ethical idealism, Goldsworthy Lowes Dickinson with his charm and his skill as a teacher, Nathaniel Wedd with his love of the classics, Oscar Browning with his colorful personality and knowledge of history, and G. E. Moore with his "realistic" philosophy that was to be a powerful influence upon Cambridge intellectuals at the turn of the century. Forster's closest friend in his undergraduate years was H. O. Meredith, who helped make him conscious of his homosexual inclinations (though the relationship was mostly platonic) and who became the prototype for Clive Durham in Forster's novel *Maurice*.

What Cambridge meant for Forster he revealed directly and by implication in the early chapters of *The Longest Journey* and in *Goldsworthy Lowes Dickinson* (1934), a biography of his Cambridge friend and mentor. In *Goldsworthy Lowes Dickinson* Forster asserted that it was possible in the relaxed but stimulating ambiance at Cambridge for a young man to unite into a meaningful whole the disparate powers of his nature. Through H. O. Meredith's influence Forster became a member of the Cambridge Conversazione Society, otherwise known as the Apostles, a group of young men who discussed passionately moral, intellectual, and aesthetic issues and who were to form the nucleus of the later Bloomsbury coterie. The Apostles during Forster's time at the university and immediately thereafter included Lytton Strachey, John Maynard Keynes, Leonard Woolf, Desmond MacCarthy, and Saxon Sydney-Turner; Roger Fry was a member from an earlier time. Another group of young men,

The Midnight Society, had among its members Strachey, Woolf, Sydney-Turner, Thoby Stephen, and Clive Bell.

All the Cambridge men just mentioned were, upon their removal to London, active in the so-called Bloomsbury Group. The group got under way about 1905 with the informal salons inaugurated by Thoby Stephen's sisters, Virginia Stephen (who became Virginia Woolf in 1912) and Vanessa Stephen (who became Vanessa Bell in 1907). The group was increasingly active after 1910 and achieved a more precise identity with the founding of the Memoir Club in 1920 (it met for the last time in 1956). In London, the original Cambridge set enlarged to include Virginia Stephen, Vanessa Stephen, Adrian Stephen, Molly MacCarthy, and Duncan Grant. Many in the circle were later to become famous: Strachey as critic, historian, and biographer; Leonard Woolf as political activist and theorist and man of letters; Keynes as a political scientist and economist; Bell and Fry as aestheticians and art critics; Grant and Vanessa Bell as painters; and Virginia Woolf and Forster as novelists. The foremost influence, philosophically, upon these intellectuals was that of G. E. Moore, who was both friend and mentor to many in the group. Though Forster claims not to have read G. E. Moore, he nevertheless came under his influence. Moore held in *Principia Ethica* (1903) that the most satisfying states are those deriving from aesthetic experiences and personal relationships. He urged his disciples to value intellectual clarity and common sense, to test their abstract principles empirically, and to regard the tangible world perceived by the senses as the real world. Forster felt a strong affinity with many of the Bloomsbury values, which include friendship, speculative discussion, a persistent questioning of tradition and convention, agnosticism, an advocacy of social change, an appreciation of the innovative in the arts, and a testing of moral values in accordance with the searching premises of a Moorean "realism."

In some sense, Bloomsbury was too intellectual in orientation to gain Forster's complete allegiance. Rather, he valued more fully the visionary and the transcendent than did most of his associates. In any case, his affiliation with the group tended to be tenuous, but it is nevertheless impossible to think of him as essentially apart from it, especially if one remembers his dramatizing so vividly the quintessential Bloomsbury values in the Schlegel sisters in *Howards End,* in Fielding and Adela Quested in *A Passage to India* (1924), and in his own eloquent credo, written later in his career, *What I Believe* (1939; reprinted in *Two Cheers for Democracy,* 1951).

At Cambridge Forster studied under Nathaniel Wedd for the Classical Tripos, Part I, and completed it with a second class in 1900; the next year he studied for the Historical Tripos, Part I, with Oscar Browning and again attained a second class. Upon graduation from Cambridge he traveled for a year with his mother in Italy, Sicily, and Austria, and in 1902 he traveled in Greece. His travels provided him with many of the materials he was to use in the essays, short stories, and novels that he was to be writing shortly thereafter. In 1902 he became an instructor at the Working Men's College in London, an affiliation which lasted for twenty years.

At the suggestion of Nathaniel Wedd, Forster's tutor and friend at Cambridge, he decided to try to become a writer. In his last year at Cambridge and later, he contributed some miscellaneous essays to the Cambridge undergraduate literary journal, the *Basileona,* but his first major writings appeared after his graduation from Cambridge, with the founding in 1903 of the liberal *Independent Review* under Goldsworthy Lowes Dickinson, Wedd, G. M. Trevelyan, and others. Forster's contributions were not political, however, but personal and biographical essays and some of the best of his short stories such as "Albergo Empedocle," "The Road from Colonus," and "The Story of a Panic."

The years from 1903 to 1910 were years of extraordinary creative release for Forster. He wrote four novels of surpassing force and insight, all of them now recognized as Edwardian classics: *Where Angels Fear to Tread* (1905), *The Longest Journey* (1907), *A Room with a View* (1908), and *Howards End* (1910). All of these novels are rooted in Forster's depiction of the life and manners of the upper-middle class that he knew as an insider. He had the insider's love of this society despite its shortcomings, but he also knew its shortcomings as only an insider could. Accordingly, he appreciated its amenities and its graciousness at the same time that he regarded critically its frequent triviality and its materialistic preoccupations. He had the insight, however, to see that people need not be static in a society that was essentially static; it was still possible for the sincere and dedicated individual to achieve salvation, even in unpropitious surroundings. And the finer spirits in this milieu, precisely because they enjoyed at least a modicum of material prosperity, were enabled to appreciate, without undue stress, the resources of culture, the renovating influence of nature, and the potential fullness of the inner life.

Forster's first novel, *Where Angels Fear to Tread,* justifies the opinion that Forster from the first was a literary artist of maturity and power. The book was a notable success with both reviewers and the general public alike, and a pronounced conviction developed that a writer of distinction had appeared. C. F. G. Masterman in the *Daily News* (8 November 1905) hailed the power and strength of Forster's vision, especially in his acute analysis of the conflicts between the Italian and the English cultures, between a vibrant primitivism and an ordered convention. Some readers and critics felt, like the anonymous reviewer in the *Spectator* (23 December 1905), that Forster tended to be overly grim and abrasive in his outlook. In the book Forster contrasts the spontaneous, free, natural life of the village of Monteriano (in reality San Gimignano) in Italy with the conventional, artificial, hypocritical, bourgeois, "civilized" life of Sawston, a suburb of London. Symbolic of these contrasting modes of life are two chief figures in the novel. First, there is Mrs. Herriton, who has warped her son Philip and her daughter Harriet by her domineering personality; she is capable of cruelty, and domestic power has corrupted her. Second, there is Gino Carella, a crude but vital Italian, who becomes the second husband of Lilia Herriton (the widow of Mrs. Herriton's deceased son) and the antagonist of the Herritons.

Through her vulgarity and candor, Lilia embarrasses her in-laws at Sawston, and they send her abroad in the company of Caroline Abbott, a supposedly "safe" woman, who, once away from the influence of Mrs. Herriton, abets Lilia in her marriage to Gino. Mrs. Herriton sends her surviving son, Philip, to prevent the marriage; he arrives too late, although he might have been able to bribe Gino if he had arrived in time. Lilia is weak and unintelligent and cannot manage Gino; her marriage is unhappy, and she mercifully dies in giving birth to a son. Gino soon begins to taunt the respectable Herritons by sending postcards to Lilia's little daughter, Irma (whom Lilia had left with the Herritons in Sawston) to remind her of the existence of her "lital brother" in Italy. In some sense, by challenging Mrs. Herriton, he initiates the action which will finally have tragic consequences for him.

Mrs. Herriton rises to Gino's challenge: hoping to put the best face on things by adopting Lilia's son and thus acknowledging his existence publicly, she sends Philip and Harriet to Italy to bring the child back. Caroline Abbott, also wishing to atone for her laxness as Lilia's former chaperone, decides that she too would like to adopt Gino's son. She travels to Italy with this purpose in mind, but experiences a change of heart when she sees how strong is Gino's adoration of his son. When she offers to wash the baby, she is seemingly transformed from a spinster leading a constricted existence to a protective madonna.

Because Gino's paternal passion has similarly impressed Philip, he and Caroline renounce further interest in the baby. But Harriet, who is grimly self-righteous, decides to take matters into her own hands and kidnaps the child in order to take him back to his Sawston relatives. The baby dies as a result of an untoward accident when he is thrown from the carriage conveying Harriet and her brother to the railway station, in a collision with a carriage conveying Caroline there also.

Philip faces up to his moral responsibilities and brings the news personally to Gino. In a frenzy of despair he cruelly tortures Philip by alternately twisting his broken arm and attempting to suffocate him. Caroline comes upon the men in time to save Philip, and she manages, with her goddesslike dignity, to reconcile the men by having them drink ritually of the milk that the servant had prepared for the now-dead baby.

Despite Gino's cruelty toward Philip, he is preferable, in Forster's view, to Mrs. Herriton and to Harriet, who observe the proprieties but lack considerateness and charity. Both women are fools in their attempts to come between a father and his child. As for Gino, his responses are instinctive rather than intellectual. He is violent and magnanimous, vindictive and openhearted, loving and demonic. The hint of the demonic in him provides a measure not only of his latent violence but also of the depths of life to be found in him. To the extent that he symbolizes Italy, there are some intellectual dimensions of this country that he does not fully embody, but as an archetypal representation of elemental forces he is adequate and impressive.

Both Philip and Caroline are forever changed as a result of having known Gino. The joy and zest for life that the Italians reveal at a performance of *Lucia di Lammermoor* prove to be infectious, so that Philip and Caroline can no longer resist the spell cast over them by the life-infusing Italians, especially Gino (Harriet holds out against the Italians, who only shock her). Philip and Caroline undergo a conversion to the freer and the more spiritually oriented life of Italy; though they cannot remain in Italy at the end of the novel, they will no longer be at ease in the Sawston to which they must return.

Unknown to Philip, Caroline has fallen in love with Gino; she therefore refuses Philip when he proposes to her on the train which takes them back toward England. Philip regards the renewed Caroline as a goddess and feels transformed by her, even though he knows that his love for her will not be requited. He now has a truer perception, too, of Italy's significance: this country unites the disparate facets of experience into a dynamic synthesis. Italy does not evade, he sees, the violent, the evil, and the sinister, but confronts them honestly. By so doing, she can make the influence of the good, the beautiful, and the true more genuine than if no challenges to their supremacy ever existed.

As a symbolic projection of the complications that make up Italian culture, the medieval towers that form the skyline of Monteriano provide the spiritual landscape for the book. They reach up to heaven; they extend down toward the nether regions of the earth; and they are covered, at their bases, with advertisements denoting the mundane concerns and activities of the inhabitants. As Philip Herriton says with discernment, the tower opposite him, as it were, "reaches up to heaven and down to the other place" and becomes, accordingly, "a symbol of the town"; by extension, of the Italian ethos; and, finally, of human life itself.

Forster's novels reveal throughout a characteristic uniting of the real and of the archetype, which George H. Thomson, one of Forster's best interpreters, has defined as "a mythic symbol." On the one side, as a realist and a delightful practitioner of comedy, Forster is in the succession from Jane Austen. On the other side, he is a writer of romance wherein characters and situations expand beyond empiric reality to suggest the general, the archetypal, and the mythic; here the succession is from the Brontës, Meredith, and Hardy, and in this aspect of his work, Forster has affinities also with D. H. Lawrence. In the romance, characters pass beyond their realistic dimensions to attain, openly, a symbolical or even allegorical significance. They attain an elemental dimension as they search for truth, mystical transcendence, visionary experience, and pantheistic immersion in nature; or as they struggle against evil when it is in conflict with the good. Perhaps Forster's chief distinction as a novelist lies in this expert conjoining of realism and romance. Romance involves the active will wherein the protagonist, according to Northrop Frye, engages in a perilous journey, struggles with inimical forces, and attains an infectious exhilaration because he has survived a crucial test of his powers. In

III

Opposite the Volterra gate of Monteriano, outside the city, is a very respectable white mud washed wall, with a coping of red crinkled tiles to keep it from dissolution. It would have give the idea of a gentleman's garden, if there was not a large hole in the middle, which grows larger with every rain storm. Through this hole is visible firstly the iron gate that is intended to close it, which has at last become so small that every one walks round it rather than through; secondly a square piece of ground, which though not quite mud is at the same time not exactly grass: and finally another wall, stone this time, which has a wooden door in the middle, and two wooden shuttered windows each side, apparently forming the façade of a one story house.

This door is always shut and the door-key is a quarter of a... This house is bigger than it looks, for it slides for two stories down the hill behind, and the wooden door, which is always locked, really leads into the attic. The knowing person prefers to follow the presumptuous mule track around the turn of the mud wall, till he can take the edifice in the rear. Then — being now on a level with the cellars — he lifts up his head and shouts if his voice sounds like something light — a letter for example, or some vegetables...

Page from the manuscript for the beginning of the third chapter of Where Angels Fear to Tread, *Forster's first novel (Library of King's College, Cambridge; courtesy of the Provost and Fellows)*

Where Angels Fear to Tread both Philip and Caroline undertake not only a physical journey but, without always realizing it, a spiritual journey as well and reach dimensions of experience that they had not previously known. They emerge with a new knowledge of themselves and their world, and are in fact reborn.

Where Angels Fear to Tread is a remarkable novel which reveals that Forster, from the beginning, had his narrative and his vision under full control. For a short book, it covers much ground. Forster developed in it a contrast in national types; he analyzed a considerable number of middle-class temperaments; he fashioned a witty and perceptive comedy of manners based upon an exposure of the hypocrisies of the middle class; he envisioned a romance in which forces of evil contend with those of good for the mastery of men's souls; and he presented a tragedy resulting from the substitution of convention for charity and imagination. In this novel Mrs. Herriton and those like her use the letter of the law to stifle its spirit.

The Longest Journey is a more complex book than *Where Angels Fear to Tread,* though it displays less assuredness and aesthetic coherence. Upon its first appearance the reactions of readers and reviewers were mixed. The anonymous reviewer for the *Nation* (27 April 1907) praised the book for its witty and philosophical criticism of ordinary life but felt that Forster had made too convenient a use of sudden death. The critic in the *Morning Post* (6 May 1907) also cited as unconvincing the forty-four percent death rate among the major characters. An unnamed reviewer in the *Bookman* (June 1907) praised *The Longest Journey* for its wit and humor, irony, and power of characterization. The most important commentator was again C. F. G. Masterman in the *Daily News* (3 May 1907), who commented upon the unique fusion in the book of the satiric and the visionary and who found it, if not a great book, nevertheless one possessing elements of greatness. Some other brief notices emphasized either its somberness of vision, its preoccupation with "abnormal" characters, or its alleged structural defects. Yet the novel remained Forster's favorite among his own and is perhaps his most deeply felt. His protagonist, Rickie Elliot, is in large part an autobiographical projection, and his other two chief male personages, Stewart Ansell and Stephen Wonham, represent masculine types that attracted Forster. Though no student of Forster has given *The Longest Journey* first place among the novels, it is forceful and exerts a subtle fascination to those attuned to Forster's sensibility and responsive to his universe.

In 1904 on a visit to Wiltshire Forster first conceived his idea of a novel about two half brothers, one of them illegitimate. His discussions with the Wiltshire shepherds led to the conception of Stephen Wonham's character, and the ancient Figsbury Rings became the prototype for the Cadbury Rings. In a 1960 introduction to a World Classics edition, Forster indicated the themes that he had tried to develop, and in doing so he suggested some of the book's richness and fullness: "There was the metaphysical idea of Reality ('the cow is there'); there was the ethical idea that reality must be faced (Rickie won't face Stephen); there was the idea, or ideal, of the British Public School; there was the title, exhorting us in the words of Shelley, not to love one person only; there was Cambridge, there was Wiltshire."

In *The Longest Journey* Forster presented at length an artist-intellectual's pursuit of the truth, Rickie Elliot being a man remarkable both for his sincerity and for his combination of perceptiveness and blindness. The opening scene takes place in Rickie's rooms at Cambridge, where some of his undergraduate friends are discussing the nature of reality. The contest is mainly between Stewart Ansell, a spokesman for G. E. Moore (who is not mentioned in the novel) with his "realistic" philosophy, and Tilliard, a spokesman for the idealism of Plato. For Ansell the cow is there in the actuality, while for Tilliard it is the idea of the cow that constitutes its reality. Rickie himself stays aloof from the discussion and belongs to neither party. Rather, with the help of his imagination, he would place some veils of significance between himself and the actuality and would interpret the cow symbolically.

Rickie's imagination is at once his chief source of strength and his chief source of weakness. His keen imagination is a great strength if one measures by the posthumous success of his short stories, which provide a regular income for his half brother, Stephen Wonham. His imagination is his great weakness if one measures by the disastrousness of his academic career at the bourgeois-oriented Sawston Public School. The facts there are too stark for a man of his disposition to cope with. He also falls in love through his imagination rather than his desires, and the result of his marriage to Agnes Pembroke, the sister of the headmaster of Sawston School, Herbert Pembroke, is calamitous. The Pembrokes visit Rickie at Cambridge and interrupt, physically and symbolically, the discussion of the nature of reality: the Pembrokes are Philistines for whom such discussions are irrelevant, unnecessary, and irritating.

Stewart Ansell, a gifted student of philosophy, who nevertheless fails to get his degree, is a sensitive and sensible mentor for Rickie. Ansell has wisdom and understanding but lacks some degree of comprehensiveness in his views; within his range, however, he judges people and events unflinchingly and unerringly. Incidentally, contact with the earth provided by his friendship with Stephen Wonham enlarges Ansell's views perceptibly. He does not approve of Rickie's interest in Agnes Pembroke, partly out of unadmitted homosexual jealousy but mostly out of distrust for what she represents. For him she does not exist because she is so superficial, and he therefore refuses to take her hand when Rickie introduces her to him. He ascribes, moreover, Rickie's idealizing of her to "a diseased imagination." But she is, in actuality, all too palpably there, and Rickie's imagination is perhaps less diseased than misguided, since he cannot perceive her critically.

Forster derives the title of his novel from Shelley, who in "Epipsychidion" had referred to "the dreariest and the longest journey" as that undertaken in the company of an incompatible mate. The world is sometimes not well lost for love: and this truth is, in essence, the point that Forster dramatizes in the book. Rickie pursues this kind of journey rather than the one for which he might have been better fitted: the journey "beyond right and wrong to a place where only one thing matters—that the Beloved should rise from the dead." He embarks on this second sort of journey when he leaves his wife Agnes, after learning of her duplicity toward Stephen Wonham. In order to insinuate herself into the good graces of Emily Failing (Stephen's and Rickie's well-to-do aunt), Agnes had repeated to Mrs. Failing some derisive comments that Stephen had made about her when he had been riding with Rickie. With Stephen, Rickie attains on this second journey a solid perceptiveness that he had never known before.

Mrs. Failing helps determine Rickie's fate and resembles in her sadism her brother, the father whom Rickie hates and the husband who kills his wife's spirit. Mrs. Failing forgets, Rickie maintains, that people are important, and she experiences much zest in histrionically confronting and shocking them, though she is at heart conventional. She finds satisfaction in exercising power over others and manipulating their fates as if she were a god. She has not seen fit, for example, to divulge to Rickie the fact that Stephen is his half brother, until in a moment of pique she decides to have her petty revenge on him by relaying this information out of

spite. Stephen's coarseness and strong energies repel Rickie, though he feels obliged to acknowledge him as brother. Agnes, to whom Stephen is not so much vital as uncouth, deflects Rickie from so doing, though his instincts tell him that she is wrong.

Stephen displaces Rickie as the hero during the third part of the novel. As a result of his failure to act honestly at a "symbolic moment," Rickie begins to deteriorate spiritually: the light of the truth moves ever further from him, until Ansell exposes him for his moral cowardice in an operatic scene in the dining hall at Sawston School. After Rickie leaves his wife, he revives under the healing influence of his brother. Stephen is a kind of noble savage, rough but forthright and genuine; and he has some of the nobility of spirit and the vitality associated with the Greek gods, some of the serenity also of the Demeter of Cnidus whose picture is in his room at Cadover House in Wiltshire. He is possibly more convincing as an irreverent and superficially irresponsible youth than as an archetypal presence signifying elemental man. Yet he remains impressive also in this role as a primal force and mythic presence and as a touchstone for both Ansell and Rickie of the reality to be found in the spirit of earth.

Rickie feels more positive toward Stephen when he learns that Stephen is his mother's child and not his father's. Stephen is, however, impatient with Rickie's idealizing of him, and in protest he tears in two their mother's portrait, which Rickie had just shown him. The brothers achieve their closest intimacy toward the end of the novel when, on a visit to Mrs. Failing at Cadover, they send lighted paper boats, shaped like roses, under a bridge and down a country stream. Stephen's stays lit longer, and the implication is that the scion of the Greeks and of nature will endure longer than Rickie, the modern, self-conscious intellectual.

The brothers remain united until Rickie becomes disillusioned with Stephen for breaking a promise not to drink. Yet Rickie saves Stephen's life when Stephen lies drunk and inert on the tracks at a railway level crossing; he himself lacks the energy to escape the oncoming train in time. As he is dying Rickie tells Mrs. Failing that she is right in championing the conventions, but by his actions he has, in effect, proved her to be wrong. He survives in his brother's memory, in his brother's child, and in his stories, which become successful with the public after his death.

Rickie is the seeker after the truth which forever seems to elude him. In his quest he becomes an archetypal presence, the hero of romance who is tested by his ordeals in the three milieus of which he becomes part: Cambridge, Sawston, and Wiltshire. It is not so much his failure that matters as his continual efforts to find a reality that will comprehend the intellect, nature, human relationships, and the spirit. Rickie is the man of good intentions and inherent distinction whose occasional blindness about people and whose irresoluteness result in tragedy. Or disaster overtakes him seemingly because he makes a wrong marriage: an unimaginative yet forceful woman regards his strengths as weaknesses, and he accepts her evaluation in order to avert open conflict with her.

Many image patterns exist in the novel, and it becomes something of a pioneer work in the history of modern literature because Forster uses in it so consistently the repeated image as leitmotiv. Symbolic images abound in the book: chalk, flowing water, the constellation of Orion, and the Greek goddess Demeter are only the most vivid. The burden of the nature symbolism suggests that all life is bounded by the contradictory influences of permanence and change. Nature is at once inspiriting and destructive. At the death of his deformed child Rickie realizes how cruel and arbitrary nature can become: he "perceived more clearly the cruelty of Nature, to whom our refinement and piety are but as bubbles, hurrying downwards on the turbid waters." If nature is sometimes harsh and malign, she is never trivial nor less than impressive in her splendor, spaciousness, and energy.

The Longest Journey is perhaps the most difficult of the novels to assess. There are structural weaknesses in the book and some arbitrariness in plot and motivations, but it rises superior to its blemishes. Its scope and frame are perhaps too extended for the resources that Forster had then available to him as creative artist, yet its merits are genuine: a poetic yet concentrated style, a mordant humor, a compelling angle of vision, a refreshing description of both nature and society, an eloquent symbolism, a suggestion of the primordial in the people and the action, an underlying sensitivity to the tragic aspects of human life, and a masterful sense of psychological nuance. If it lacks perfection in the execution, it is nevertheless a brilliant and a highly evocative work.

A Room with a View was the novel that Forster began first. He started writing it in 1902-1903, but he did not finish it until 1908. The most halcyon and direct of his novels, it celebrates the magical time of youth and is his purest social comedy. *A Room with a View* is also Forster's most Jane Austen-like novel in its observations of the minutiae of human behavior

and in its dry, undercut, ironic, aphoristic style. It was a popular book that also earned the immediate and virtually uniform praise of the reviewers, though it was less widely noticed than *The Longest Journey*. The only two important reviews were noteworthy, however. C. F. G. Masterman in the *Nation* (28 November 1908) was enthusiastic about the novel's fusion of a satiric scrutiny of convention with the hidden life of nature and the spirit. In the *Times Literary Supplement* (22 October 1908) Virginia Woolf noted that the book had cleverness, much fun, occasional beauty, originality, and strength but felt that the characters as Forster had envisaged them were not adequate for their functions in the novel.

In *A Room with a View* the question is whether the protagonist, Lucy Honeychurch, will attain self-completion and a sense of the genuine values possible in life or whether she will be a sacrifice to Victorian conventions. Lucy and her companion, Miss Charlotte Bartlett, a chaperone who dominates Lucy completely and who would snuff out her vital sexual instincts if she could, are in a viewless room at a pension in Florence when the novel opens. The elderly Mr. Emerson overhears their complaints and offers them his room with a view, which, after some embarrassment, the ladies accept. Mr. Emerson, who becomes the voice of wisdom in the novel (Forster named him after the American sage, Ralph Waldo Emerson), counters the influence of Charlotte upon Lucy and, in part two of the novel, the influence of her "medieval" fiancé, Cecil Vyse, upon her. In Florence Mr. Emerson is accompanied by his son George, a sexually vital and charismatic young man but inclined to moods of pessimism and discouragement.

An attraction develops between Lucy and George, though Lucy tries not to admit that it has occurred. Chapter four of the novel is crucial because in it Lucy and George witness a quarrel between two Italians which results in a fight and the murder of one of them by the other. So much reality is too much for the gently bred Lucy, who faints in George's arms. Although her experience of intimacy with George changes Lucy's outlook, she tries to deny that anything has happened. In love with George, she will not face the reality of her emotions. In this chapter reality undermines the conventions that have upheld Lucy until now. Blood spatters the prints of some great masters that she is carrying, and George insists upon throwing the soiled prints into the Arno River. They will be washed clean of the blood there, just as Lucy's soul has to be washed clear of the misconceptions that are beclouding it.

Botticelli's *The Birth of Venus* is one of these reproductions. Just as the goddess rises from out of the water to begin her life, so Lucy must now begin a new life for herself, though she is hardly as yet aware of the momentous consequences of her shared experiences with George.

Lucy's mentor, Mr. Emerson, eventually saves her from joining "the vast armies of the benighted," giving her the courage to face the truth about herself, to admit the relevance of Eros as well as Pallas Athene, and to acknowledge that she truly loves his son. The presence of George in Surrey in part two causes her to feel so much discomfort with Cecil Vyse that she breaks her engagement to him, but she is not yet ready to admit her love for George. (George had "insulted" her in Florence by kissing her unexpectedly; she and Charlotte had then left for Rome, where she met Cecil.) But for the intervention of Mr. Emerson she would stay in spiritual darkness. He sweeps away her errors of perception and instructs her about the sanctities of passion. Thus Lucy attains a new "view" of human life.

On the whole, Forster is successful with his characters in *A Room with a View*. George and Lucy are fresh and credible as youthful lovers, and the fervor of their passion is real. The chief weakness of the novel is the imperfect realization of Mr. Emerson, whose wisdom more often registers as perfunctory than as profound. It is with Lucy's antagonists, Charlotte Bartlett and Cecil Vyse, who would each in his or her own way strangle her with propriety, that Forster does best. Although Forster presents them satirically, he also sympathizes with them: while they are hypocrites and repressive individuals, Forster nevertheless imparts to them a monolithic quality that makes them imposing. They are not aware of the troubles that they cause, and for this reason they do not alienate the reader, who is more entertained by them than annoyed with them. They are large-scale figures who fail to develop dynamically, yet they inspire our interest and our dread at what they attempt and almost succeed in accomplishing.

Forster's memorable characters, his wit and stylistic control, his awareness of the nuances of manners and behavior and especially of their comic aspects, his fresh celebration of nature, his satirist's insight into social mores and values, and his open sensibility revealed in *A Room with a View* make of it a memorable novel and a delightful one as well.

Forster attained recognition as a major writer with the publication of *Howards End,* and the book consolidated his reputation as both a comic and a profound novelist. Critics universally praised it, and

Forster and his mother at Rooksnest, near Stevenage, Hertfordshire, around 1885. Rooksnest became the model for Howards End in Forster's 1910 novel.

it was popular with the intelligentsia and the general public alike. Among the most important reviews were those by Edward Garnett in the *Nation* (12 November 1910), Archibald Marshall in the *Daily Mail* (17 November 1910), A. N. Monkhouse in the *Manchester Guardian* (26 October 1910), and R. A. Scott-James in the *Daily News* (7 November 1910). Most people read it enthusiastically, though some readers, including Forster's own mother, thought that he had gone too far in violating the sexual proprieties. It is somewhat ironical, therefore, that more recent readers have criticized him for his reticences. Forster's increasingly wide public was expecting another novel from him shortly, but his followers were to be disappointed, since fourteen years were to elapse and a world war had to be fought and won before *A Passage to India* appeared.

Howards End has an epic quality, since Forster was preoccupied in it with the well-being of an entire society, with the condition-of-England question. He not only analyzed with insight the various strata of the British middle class, but he prophetically discerned that even sincere intellectuals were to encounter great difficulty in attaining wholeness in the fractured modern age. The epigraph of the novel, "Only connect," was therefore more easy to formulate than to put into practice. *Howards End* is also the quintessential Bloomsbury novel with its protagonist, Margaret Schlegel, acting as Forster's spokesperson for Bloomsbury attitudes as she skeptically and rationally tests social and philosophical values and attempts to balance the polarities of the objectively real and the visionary; as she stresses the overriding importance of personal relationships; and as she places high value upon art and culture.

Howards End is a complex work, in which Forster uses a symphonic or dialectical technique to chart the impingement upon each other of two opposing segments of the middle class, represented by the Schlegels and the Wilcoxes. The Schlegels cherish the inner life, personal relationships, culture, and the healing forces to be found in nature. The Wilcoxes represent the outer life of action, empire, business, of "telegrams and anger"; they are often coarse and insensitive but have qualities of persistence and stamina that have made possible the strength of Britain as nation and head of an empire. In this novel Margaret attempts, through her marriage to Henry Wilcox, to connect these two components of the middle class, whereas in *Where Angels Fear to Tread* Forster had presented them as irreconcilable. The Schlegels, in fact, occupy a median position between those in the lower fringe of the middle class, who live close to the abyss of genteel poverty and who are represented in the novel by Leonard and Jacky Bast, and the Wilcoxes, people who are powerful and prosperous as long as they do not concern themselves with the involutions of the inner life. The Wilcoxes are self-centered without being subjective, and they have never learned, or else have forgotten, how to say "I."

Margaret Schlegel is the governing force in the novel, acknowledging the claims both of the lucid intelligence and of the "unseen." She can deal competently with the problems that individuals face in their relationships with each other: her sense of moral reality is firm and assured. But she recognizes that reason can take us only so far when the emotions must be satisfied; then the realm of the spirit exerts its power. If the individual denies its claims, he or she will become impoverished as a person and truncated in his or her development. Margaret is convinced always of the need to attain proportion as the result of actual experience, but she is equally convinced that it is deadening to start out with a formula for reaching proportion. She desires, in short, to connect "the poetry" with "the prose" in our lives, and it is the failure of her husband to do so that leads her to reject him in their quarrel over Helen, her sister, at the end of the novel.

Margaret feels that Helen's idealism is too quixotic at the same time that her husband's materialism is too unimaginative and too monolithic. Margaret has a finer wisdom than either, recognizing the provenance of the "unseen" but feeling that it is "medieval" to brood upon it. She cherishes the inner existence as well as the outer social and political life; and by virtue of her sensibility and imaginative powers, she is paradoxically more aware of the solid realities of the external life than are her "practical" husband and his family.

Henry Wilcox's first wife, Ruth, is more akin to the Schlegels than to the Wilcox family into which she has married. She and Margaret are attracted to one another and become firm friends; and because of the sympathy of spirit that develops between them, Mrs. Wilcox wills to Margaret Howards End, her Hertfordshire house. After her death, in a scene that underscores the deviousness of the Wilcoxes and their disregard of a personal appeal, the Wilcoxes elect to tear up the piece of paper upon which she had written her instructions for the disposal of the house. Ruth Wilcox had indicated her wishes to her family, and they resent her action instead of revealing sympathy for their now-dead wife and mother. One irony in the novel consists in Margaret's coming into final possession of Howards End through her marriage to Henry Wilcox; it is as if she has had to earn demonstrably her right to assume the role of Mrs. Wilcox and the ownership of Howards End, which is a symbol of spiritual value, of the best in national tradition, and, in some sense, of England itself. People like Margaret ought to inherit England, according to Forster, but there are many obstacles in the way of their doing so.

The marriage to Henry Wilcox has struck most critics as improbable and as out of character for Margaret, but a strong element of sexual attraction brings these upholders of opposing values together. Forster views Henry Wilcox, however, as more contemptible than is fitting for him in the role that Forster assigns him in the novel: the conscientious developer of England's and the empire's natural resources. The connection Margaret attains with Henry is imperfect, but perhaps Forster wished to show that such a connection could only be, at best, tentative rather than firm.

Events connected with Leonard Bast impinge upon the Schlegels and the Wilcoxes and contribute much to the tensions dramatized in the remainder of the novel. Through the fallible advice given him by Henry Wilcox, Leonard resigns his position with the Porphyrion Insurance Company and is in danger of sinking into the abyss of poverty. Helen Schlegel decides to take matters in hand and with the Basts storms into Evie Wilcox's wedding ceremony in Shropshire, which Margaret is attending as Henry's fiancée. The impetuous Helen, acting upon the best motives, brings disaster to Leonard. Leonard's wife, Jacky, becomes drunk at the wedding, and it develops that she had been Henry's mistress in Cyprus during his marriage to Ruth Wilcox. Out of resentment against the Wilcoxes' impersonal treatment of Leonard, Helen offers affection to him and they become lovers, at her insistence, for one night. From this liaison Helen becomes pregnant and disappears to the Continent. Margaret is anxious about her sister, and, with Henry's help, lures her back to Howards End under false pretenses. But affection conquers the misunderstandings that promise to develop between the sisters. When Henry finds out that Helen is with child, he pompously refuses to allow the sisters to remain together for one night at Howards End. He cannot afford to have an "immoral" woman on his property, although his own sexual transgression had been more selfish than Helen's. He cannot "connect" his own act with Helen's, but Margaret and Helen defy him and spend a consecrated night at Howards End. They "connect" more deeply than they ever have before, and this connection, most critics agree, is more valuable than the one that the cultured Margaret attempts with the great world as Henry Wilcox represents it. Margaret's marriage to Henry seems to be on the point of breaking up because Henry has been so obtuse and because she has decided to go to Germany to be with Helen while she has her child.

Margaret achieves still another connection of greater importance than that with her husband—a connection with Ruth Wilcox, or with her surviving spirit. As a result of this woman's poised embodiment of the best in the English tradition and her sensitivity to nature, Margaret, who began as a somewhat superficial intellectual, develops a deeply feeling sensibility. At the end of the novel she actually becomes "Mrs. Wilcox," the spiritual heir of her friend as well as the heir to Howards End house and farm.

Unexpectedly, tragic events shape the course of the characters' fates at the end of the novel. Leonard Bast, motivated by remorse, seeks out Margaret at Howards End to confess his "sin" with Helen, but Henry's son Charles has just previously learned from Tibby Schlegel (brother to Helen and Margaret) the identity of the "seducer." Upon his arrival at Howards End, Charles uses the Schlegel family sword to thrash Leonard "within an inch of his life" before the sisters can intervene. Ironically, Leonard is not only thrashed within an inch of his

life, but all the way. He has a weak heart; it fails and he dies, ostensibly from Charles's beating. When Charles is convicted of manslaughter and goes to prison, Henry Wilcox becomes a broken man. Margaret can do nothing other than undertake the cure of her husband at Howards End, and he becomes critical of his long-held values for the first time. On the road to further enlightenment at the end of the novel, he is reconciled to Helen, and he wills Howards End to Margaret. Helen and Leonard's illegitimate child, as the newest heir to Howards End, is symbolic of a classless future when the social rancor of the present day will no longer prevail.

Critics variously judge the concluding sequence. When one considers the complex issues explored in the novel, the spectacle of a subdued Henry and a restored Helen with her healthy child, all dwelling at Howards End under Margaret's aegis, hardly represents an adequate solution to these issues. Such is Wilfred Stone's judgment; yet if one reads this scene as John Edward Hardy does, as a fertility ritual over which the spirit of the departed Ruth Wilcox presides and as a victory of the transcendent powers which she had embodied throughout, it becomes persuasive.

Forster also stressed throughout the novel the stability and the peace of the countryside in contrast to the flux, rootlessness, and mere bigness of London. He criticized directly and by implication the superficial and mechanical aspect of metropolitan "civilization." Mrs. Wilcox, Howards End house, the wych elm and the hayfield there, and Miss Avery (the caretaker at Howards End) are all variously symbols of the vital freshness of earth and of nature, in contrast to the "stinking" motorcar which is emblematic of the impersonality of the modern industrial era.

The novel is to be read not only as social comedy but as a symbolic construct or parable. Margaret, Helen, Leonard Bast, and Ruth Wilcox are all seekers for truth, as are the characters in romance; they attain, on occasion, archetypal dimensions in their various quests to reach a truth viable for themselves. Mrs. Wilcox, in fact, is more convincing seen in her symbolic role than as a real person. As a woman she is a shadowy figure, but as an emblem of the transcendent aspects of tradition and of nature, she is effective. As Margaret says at the end of the novel, all the characters seem to have become "fragments of that woman's mind," though she is no longer alive.

Howards End represents a remarkable fusion of social realism and poetic symbolism, its meaning related at once to human beings as they are and to human beings as they might become, once they acknowledge as authoritative the aspirations of those who can perceive most clearly the ultimate destiny of which mankind is capable. The juxtaposing of the mundane and the transcendent, of the comic mode and the poetic, enables Forster to comment incisively upon the contradictions, complexities, and paradoxes of human experience. While the interplay of the comic and the poetic had also animated Forster's preceding novels, in *Howards End* he achieved the most subtle balancing of these two modes of apprehending realities that are variously social, philosophical, and spiritual. The novel rates highly for its compelling characters; for its merging of character and situation with abstractions; for the interplay of the various segments of the middle class upon one another; for the fusion of the comic and the tragic visions; for the depiction of the romance quest of the truth as taking place in contemporary Edwardian England; for its juxtaposition of the realistic and the archetypal; and for a poet's sensitivity to the beautiful and the ineffable.

After *Howards End* Forster experienced great difficulty in writing fiction. The society that he had known so well had begun to disintegrate even before the great war, his homosexual temperament achieved a dominance greater than it had previously, and he lost interest in writing heterosexually oriented narratives, as his long works up to this time had in large part been. He did try his hand at another novel, *Arctic Summer,* which he could never bring to completion. He had managed to get his antithesis formulated: that between the intellectualized or civilized temperament in Martin Whitby and the heroic or the chivalric in Lieutenant March. But he found it impossible to domesticate March's temperament into the pallid British scene; he could not imagine firmly the climactic event toward which his narrative would move, and he felt thwarted by being unable to explore faithfully the homosexual aspects of the situation.

Arctic Summer in its unfinished form and its variant versions was posthumously published in 1980. What exists of the main version is truly impressive, and it is a loss to contemporary literature that Forster could not complete the novel. The first four chapters of the principal version form a coherent unit, almost as if they were a completely articulated short story. Forster again reveals a misogynist bias, as he had in *The Longest Journey.* Venetia Vorlase is more conscientious and admirable than Agnes Pembroke, but still she intervenes with a heavy hand to thwart the budding relationship between her husband and his new friend. She senses that Lieutenant March will become her rival in Martin's affections, and she invades March's privacy, as it were, by declaring how greatly Martin had been impressed in finding on a fresco at Tramonta Castle (which March has intended to visit) a soldier so similar in appearance to March that he must have been his ancestor. Her curiosity about matters which March regards as his private spiritual concern alienates him, with the result that he turns against Martin as well. These chapters of the fragmentary novel are brilliant and absorbing, but the then-current British mores apparently inhibited Forster as he tried to proceed with it. The result was that he gave over writing this novel in 1912.

In the period before the great war Forster composed most of his short stories except for a handful of tales with homosexual themes that attained posthumous publication. The tales gravitate between the realms of realism and fantasy, the best of them achieving some degree of fusion of these two modes of literary expression. The most notable of the almost purely realistic stories is "The Eternal Moment," which has for protagonist a talented writer, Miss Raby, who had not possessed the courage to seize in the past "the eternal moment" offered to her in the passion of an Italian and who finds that she cannot recapture this lost opportunity. In the opposite mode of pure fantasy, "The Machine Stops" is Forster's most successful venture. It projects an anti-Utopia in which apocalypse occurs when the giant machine that controls all phases of life ceases, without warning, to function.

"Albergo Empedocle," "The Road from Colonus," "Other Kingdom," "The Story of a Panic," "The Story of the Siren," "The Point of It," and "Ralph and Tony" are all stories notable for their fusing of realism and fantasy, of the natural and the supernatural. In "Albergo Empedocle" Harold, the central figure, discovers that he is a modern survivor of a civilization—the Greek—that had been more spiritually meaningful than the modern; and the result is that his life in the present cannot satisfy him and he ostensibly goes mad. Mr. Lucas, the elderly protagonist in "The Road from Colonus," makes a somewhat similar discovery when he realizes that he has a chance to attain a renewed life in modern Greece, only to be prevented from so doing by his peremptory daughter. "Other Kingdom" develops the circumstances leading to the defeat of the unimaginative Harcourt Worters: his insensitivity causes his wife to become a dryad in order to escape his dominion. "The Story of a Panic" somewhat similarly recounts the escape of a

Forster (right) with Syed Ross Masood, who introduced Forster to the culture of India

pagan youth, under the auspices of the great god Pan, from the constrictions of an unsympathetic bourgeois culture. "The Story of the Siren" emphasizes the anger of a siren at the excesses of a materialistic and unimaginative society that causes its potential prophets to be destroyed: a priest pushes from a cliff a woman who is pregnant with a possible savior. "The Point of It" presents a contrast between two friends, Harold and Micky. Harold is in full contact with the cosmic energies, though he dies as a result of overexertion, while Micky lives out a colorless existence as civil servant and achieves salvation only after his death by a recognition of the life-infusing forces that his friend had embodied. "Ralph and Tony" veers toward realism in its contrast between the pagan Tony and the effete Ralph, though Tony has something ineffable about him as an archetypal portrayal of eternal youth, whose very exuberance courts disaster and defeat when heart failure overtakes him. While Forster may lack range in this genre, he more than compensates for such a deficiency by the exquisiteness of his workmanship and by the freshness of his presentation of the "unseen" as it impinges upon the stolidity of

modern middle-class "civilization."

Three events of considerable importance for Forster occurred during the writing of *Howards End* and the years immediately following its publication. First, Forster's friendship with Syed Ross Masood, which was formative upon his development, began in 1906 when Sir Theodore Morison, Forster's neighbor, asked him to become a Latin tutor for Masood, his Indian protégé. By 1910 the friendship had achieved strength and firmness, though the heterosexual Masood could not respond to Forster's declaration of passion for him. Masood enlarged Forster's views and took him beyond the Edwardian drawing room to an absorption in the alien culture of India. Another friend of Forster's from his Cambridge days, Malcolm Darling, who became an English civil servant in India and later tutor to the young Rajah of Dewas State Senior, also aroused Forster's interest in India. Largely as a result of Masood's and Darling's influences, the second major occurrence during these years became possible, a trip to India in 1912-1913 with Goldsworthy Lowes Dickinson and R. C. Trevelyan. The state of Dewas Senior in India (and by extension the whole of India) gave Forster "the greatest opportunity of my life" as he said later, and his fascination with the subcontinent freed him of his insular views and his narcissistic tendencies. It was a truly liberating experience for him with the result that he soon started work on his masterpiece, *A Passage to India,* writing at the time most of the "Mosque" section and mulling over the events to be marshalled in the "Caves" section. The third chief event was a visit in 1913 to Millthorpe to Edward Carpenter, who wrote in behalf of an idealized homosexuality and who had attained a satisfying relationship with George Merrill. During the visit Merrill touched Forster on his posterior. The result was Forster's electrifying realization that he was unmistakably a homosexual. The visit caused a surge of creativity, and Forster wrote quickly his novel about homosexuality, *Maurice,* and finished it in its first form in 1914. He revised it at various times after 1924, particularly the last chapters, and it was posthumously published in 1971.

In *Maurice* the protagonist, Maurice Hall, attains awareness and maturity by acknowledging his homosexual nature and by rejecting, at the same time, the bourgeois values that had, prior to this time, secured his allegiance. His enlightenment occurs in two stages. At Cambridge the intellectual scion of the aristocracy, Clive Durham, declares his love for Maurice but has in mind the spirituality and idealism emphasized by Plato. Maurice at first feels revulsion at Clive's declaration but later admits that his own bent of nature is homosexual. Ironically, Clive loses interest in the love of men after Maurice becomes more deeply involved with him.

The second stage of Maurice's enlightenment occurs when he falls in love, much against the promptings of his own class consciousness, with a gamekeeper, Alec Scudder, who works on Clive's estate. Partly because Maurice is reluctant to form a liaison with a man from the lower class and partly because Alec is uncertain as to whether he wants to love Maurice or to blackmail him, the affair does not proceed smoothly. Finally, Maurice summons the courage to declare to Alec his passion for him and to reject his own class, even though he becomes thereby an outlaw from society.

Maurice is mostly realistic in its mode of presentation, though the mythic "greenwood" to which the lovers retreat assumes an archetypal importance by the end of the novel. The straightforwardness of the presentation means that *Maurice* lacks the tensions and the complications, the richness and the complexity, and the deep-reaching ambiguities of the other novels. Still, Forster is present in the

Dust jacket for Forster's homosexual novel, which was posthumously published in 1971

novel, as one notes the lucidity of its style, the deep feeling for nature found in it, and the sympathy extended to the principal figures as they confront their unusual problems. Forster also writes brilliantly in another mode of expression when he satirizes the aristocracy at Penge, Clive's estate in the country, for the triviality of its existence.

The 1914 war took Forster to Alexandria where he served from 1915 to 1919 with the Red Cross as a "searcher" for missing soldiers, and he achieved a complete sexual fulfillment there for the first time. He formed an ardent attachment with Mohammed el Adl, a tram conductor. The relationship was for Forster a love affair as well as a sexual venture. He returned to England in 1919, after Mohammed had married in 1918. Mohammed's health was poor, and he became progressively more ill and died of consumption in 1922, despite Forster's efforts to save him when he stopped at Alexandria on his way home from his second trip to

Forster in Alexandria during World War I

India. Forster also came to know well the afterward famous Greek poet C. P. Cavafy and tried to forward then and later his reputation in Europe. The sojourn in Egypt helped him to clarify some of his previous experiences in India and to make firm some of the conclusions he had reached on his trip in 1912-1913, especially with respect to the arrogant treatment of the native populations by some British officials; and it helped provide an ambiance that enabled him to complete his greatest work, *A Passage to India.*

The literary fruits of these years were *Alexandria: A History and a Guide* (1922) and *Pharos and Pharillon* (1923). *Alexandria* is a detailed guide to the still-existing monuments and artifacts of the city and to the sites of famous structures that have since disappeared. It also provides in its opening sections a detailed history of Alexandria from the time of Alexander the Great until the consolidation of British power there with the bombardment of 1882. In these pages Forster recreates the historical city by throwing into relief its most colorful personalities and its distinctive cultural traditions.

Forster achieves the same end in the more informally written *Pharos and Pharillon,* which con-

sists of miscellaneous essays mostly collected from the *Egyptian Mail.* Pharos, the great lighthouse now gone from the entrance to the Nile, provides the title for the first half of Forster's book. In this section he focuses upon the older city, its leaders, its culture, or rather, the clashes among cultures that were found there. Among the Alexandrians about whom he writes in "Pharos" are Alexander, Philo, Clement, Saint Athanasius, and Arius. Pharillon was the smaller and less imposing successor to the original great lighthouse at the mouth of the Nile. Under this rubric Forster collects his thoughts about the modern city, from about the seventeenth century to the present. The personalities are altogether less grand than those who graced the ancient city, and its culture is far less rich and various. The outstanding figures in "Pharillon" are the intrepid seventeenth-century traveler Eliza Fay and the twentieth-century poet Cavafy. Forster also writes about the varied life in modern Alexandria, from cotton trading to drug addiction to the present topography of the city: the main thoroughfares, the gates, and Lake Mareotis. In these two books Forster has managed to capture at once the actuality of

Forster in Indian garb

Alexandria and its essence.

Though *The Hill of Devi* dates from 1953, it is relevant to this phase of Forster's career. This book gathers many of the materials from which *A Passage to India* emerged and which Forster transformed in using them for his novel. *The Hill of Devi* consists of Forster's letters sent primarily to his mother and other relatives when he was in India in 1912-1913 and 1921, together with his reminiscences of his life as secretary to the Maharajah (Bapu Sahib) of Dewas State Senior in 1921. (Forster had gotten to know Bapu Sahib on his first journey to India in 1912-1913.)

As in his novels, Forster's sense in *The Hill of Devi* of the distinctive traits which compose human character is strong. The result is that he creates a gallery of portraits of living individuals that have the sharply etched quality of fully wrought characters in a distinguished novel. Among the most memorable of these figures are Sir Malcolm Darling, the capable administrator and civil servant whom Forster had known from his Cambridge years; Colonel Wilson, the paranoid official working for the Maharajah whose place Forster temporarily assumed (and who was actually a Colonel W. Leslie); the Maharajah of Chhatarpur, who had been Forster's great friend on his first Indian trip and who was notable for his consuming intellectual curiosity about European culture; and Bapu Sahib himself, a saint in Forster's view, whose other-worldliness led to striking incompetence in this

world, yet whose reverence for the personal element in his relationships with others was almost beatific. In *The Hill of Devi* Forster recounts experiences that were for him at once intensely rewarding and intensely frustrating: the court of the Maharajah illustrated a marked inefficiency and corruption at the same time that it gave him an insight into the lofty aspects of Hindu culture. Forster's total reactions to his sojourn in Dewas State Senior reveal a deep-thrusting ambiguity, as do his descriptions of the somewhat squalid yet elevating ceremonies depicting the birth of Sri Krishna. Forster recounted further his experiences in India in 1912-1913, including those prior to his visit to Dewas and subsequent thereto, in the recently published "Indian Journal" and relevant family correspondence to be found in the augmented *The Hill of Devi and Other Indian Writings* in the Abinger Edition of E. M. Forster (1983).

The second trip to India in 1921 was necessary, as it turned out, for the completion of *A Passage to India*. Forster's observation in Dewas of the ceremonies connected with the symbolic birth of the Indian savior-god Sri Krishna and his own modified participation in them gave him materials that he was to actualize in the "Temple" section of the novel. As a result, he could now divine the major event toward which his novel had apparently been moving, perhaps even from the beginning, but which had remained inarticulate until the experiences in Dewas in 1921. When Forster returned to England,

Forster (center) with (left to right) W. J. H. Sprott, Gerald Heard, and Lytton Strachey in the early 1920s

Group playing cards in the courtyard of the palace at Dewas during Forster's second trip to India in 1921. The maharaja is third from the left; Forster is fifth from the left.

Leonard Woolf, J. R. Ackerley, and T. E. Lawrence gave him the encouragement that he found so helpful in bringing his novel to a close. Reviewers such as L. P. Hartley (*Spectator,* 28 June 1924), Robert Morss Lovett (*New Republic,* 27 August 1924), Rose Macaulay (*Daily News,* 4 June 1924), Edwin Muir (*Nation,* 8 October 1924), and Leonard Woolf (*Nation and Atheneum,* 14 June 1924) all praised the book and regarded it, generally, as the best novel that Forster had written to date. E. A. Horne in the *New Statesman* (16 August 1924) spoke for those, in the vast minority, who felt that Forster had presented his Anglo-Indians without sympathy and true knowledge. *A Passage to India* was popular both in England and America, and somewhat later in India as well; and in 1925 it earned for Forster two enviable awards, the Femina/Via Heureuse Prize and the James Tait Black Memorial Prize.

In the Chandrapore (based on Bankipore, where Masood lived in 1912-1913) of *A Passage to India* an uneasy truce exists between the English servants of empire and the inhabitants of India, particularly those Indians in the government ser-

vice or in the professional classes. The British, especially those in official positions, are arrogant in their claims to power and in their exercise of it—officials such as the district superintendent of police McBryde, the collector Mr. Turton, and the magistrate Ronny Heaslop, a son of Mrs. Moore's by her first marriage. There are British people in the city of a more positive and humane kind: Mrs. Moore, with her intuitive understanding of other people and of other cultures, and Fielding, the principal of the Government College with his humane values, "good will plus culture and intelligence." Adela Quested has good intentions and is engaged to marry the servant of empire, Ronny Heaslop, and Mrs. Moore is acting as her chaperone. Adela is decent, honest, and sincere but lacks spontaneity, social imagination, and sensitivity to the ineffable.

For the benefit of Adela and Mrs. Moore as newcomers, Collector Turton stages a "bridge party" so that the English ladies can meet the most important Indians in the city. In spite of Fielding's efforts, the party is not a success in bridging the differences between the two races. Aziz, a prominent native Islamic physician, had decided not to go to the party, but Fielding invites him to tea, where he meets the visiting ladies and a Hindu educator, Professor Godbole. Aziz invites the ladies and the rest of the people present to participate in a picnic expedition to the most interesting nearby sight, the Marabar Hills, which are famous for their caves.

In part one of the novel, "Mosque," an atmosphere of serenity prevails, despite the abrasiveness present in the relationships among the Indians and the British. Symbolic of this harmony is the early episode in the moonlit mosque when Aziz first meets Mrs. Moore and is gratified by her tact: she had had the intuitive wisdom, for example, to realize that a visitor to a mosque should remove one's shoes before entering a sacred building. The result is that Aziz with fervor declares that she must be "an Oriental." Despite his subsequent disillusionment with the British, Aziz never loses his respect and love for Mrs. Moore. Some possibilities of rapport between Oriental and Occidental develop at Fielding's tea party, where the atmosphere is benign and cordial until Ronny Heaslop enters. At this party a Hindu educator, Professor Godbole, entertains the guests with a disquieting song whose purport they only vaguely apprehend, an incident

that suggests a rift in understanding even among people of goodwill from the two cultures in surroundings that are pleasant.

In part two of the novel, "Caves," the events presented and the misunderstandings among the characters gather tragic dimensions, especially as racial arrogance extinguishes any display of charitable feeling. The inimical weather prevents any real enjoyment of the picnic at the Caves. Because Godbole has delayed too long at his prayers, he and Fielding miss the train to the Marabar; and Fielding's moderating influence is therefore absent at the Caves. Adela Quested has been indiscreet enough to ask Aziz if he has more than one wife, and she has just had difficulties with her fiancé, Ronny Heaslop: a break with him might well mean a dreaded spinsterhood. The element of sex is on her mind. In the Caves she believes that Aziz has assaulted her: either someone has pushed against her or else she has imagined the attack as a result of her sexual preoccupations at the moment. For her at this point the assault seems real, and she thinks that Aziz has tried to rape her.

Mrs. Moore has had an equally disabling experience in the Caves, perhaps one more truly destroying than Adela's. In seemingly complete isola-

The entrance to the Lomas Rishi Cave, one of the seven Barabar Caves in Bihar Province, India. These caves served as the model for the Marabar Caves in Forster's A Passage to India.

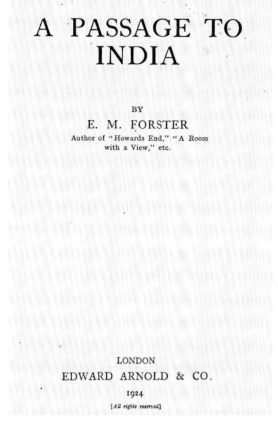

A PASSAGE TO
INDIA

BY

E. M. FORSTER

Author of "Howards End," "A Room
with a View," etc.

LONDON
EDWARD ARNOLD & CO.
1924

*Title page for Forster's best-known novel, which grew out of his experiences in the Indian state of Dewas Senior in 1912-1913 and 1921
(Thomas Cooper Library, University of South Carolina)*

tion within the Caves, she reacts with a total loss of her spiritual self-possession to the annihilating echo that she encounters there. The echo convinces her that all her values and emotions are equal and therefore of no worth at all: the all-encompassing "ou-boum" of the Caves reduces them to nothing: "the echo began in some indescribable way to undermine her hold on life. Coming at a moment when she chanced to be fatigued, it [the echo] had managed to murmur, 'Pathos, piety, courage—they exist, but are identical, and so is filth. Everything exists, nothing has value.'"

As a result of this incident in the Caves, Mrs. Moore loses her hold on life and surrenders to spiritual apathy. Her altruistic Christian emotions and her pantheistic feeling for nature that have sustained her seem irrelevant now in the discordant, disordered, chaotic culture that she finds in India. Her vision of personal despair and cosmic nullity in the Caves is not a Hindu vision; but her experience at the Caves, most critics agree, relates to Hinduism, which is a comprehensive and all-inclusive religion, including all possible philosophi-

cal extremes in its purview and eventually reducing all dichotomies and contradictions and paradoxes to an overall unity. So Mrs. Moore encounters in the Caves a nihilism which suggests that God is no longer present, at least here in the Caves; what she cannot see at this point is that the very absence of God at a given moment or place implies his presence at some other moment or some other place. When she leaves the country, the palms at Asirgarh wave to her and communicate to her the message that the Marabar and its suggestions of nihilism are not all of India.

The Caves are not indeed all of India, for in the cycle of the seasons the healing rains appear, the season for the celebration of the birth of the god, Sri Krishna. The somewhat disorderly rituals in which his devotees participate dominate part three, "Temple," and form a positive spiritual counterpart to the metaphysical blankness and blackness that had emanated to Mrs. Moore from the Caves. Under the aegis of Hindu religious traditions, God, embodied in Sri Krishna, is born again: this Indian god has attributes or lacks them, however he makes his presence felt to the individual worshipper. God is present in "Temple," as he had been absent in "Caves": Mrs. Moore had too quickly surrendered to despair, without realizing that despair, in its intensity, implies that its opposite, hope, exists—or one day can again exist—with an equal intensity.

The majority of Forster's critics such as Louise Dauner, Ellin Horowitz, and Wilfred Stone would subscribe to this interpretation of "Caves." Attempts by other critics to relate the Caves to a specific entity—absolute nihilism (Frederick C. Crews), inhuman rationality (Glen O. Allen), evil and division (Gertrude M. White)—impart to the Caves too specific an identity. They represent, rather, primordial aspects of our experience. There is something elemental in the Marabar Hills—appearing as "fists and fingers" to one viewing them from Chandrapore—and in the Caves which they contain. In addition to suggesting the negative aspect of reality or of God, the Caves seemingly hold within themselves all extreme entities or dichotomies: they are both womb and tomb, a destructive force and a potentially renovating influence. There is no doubt, however, of their shattering effects upon both Mrs. Moore and Adela. Mrs. Moore gives in to a soulless apathy, while Adela gives in to panic. She flees from the scene and goes back to Chandrapore in an automobile which providentially arrives for her and which an Anglo-Indian, a Miss Derek, is driving. Adela reports the alleged rape to the authorities, who arrest Aziz upon his arrival by train from the Marabar.

Equally shattering have been the consequences of this expedition to Aziz. He feels outrage at his arrest, and he is even more outraged possibly in his sexual pride, that someone so sexless (in his view) as Adela should have had the effrontery to feel that she could have had the power to rouse him. By his defense of Aziz, Fielding risks his reputation with the Anglo-Indians at the club, whom the alleged rape incenses, especially since a man from an "inferior" race is the criminal. The members of the Anglo-Indian establishment bring Aziz to trial and believe that he is ipso facto guilty. Adela takes the witness stand: the handsome Indian operator of the fan disturbs her with his equanimity; she is no longer certain that Aziz has assaulted her, particularly since Mrs. Moore has declared him to be innocent; and the crowd's invocation of Mrs. Moore's name as "Esmiss Esmoor" outside the courtroom causes her to perceive in a momentary vision that she has been mistaken. Mrs. Moore thus saves her friend Aziz though she is not physically present to testify in his behalf.

When Adela retracts her charge, she suffers the worst from both worlds: the Indians despise her for the trouble that she has caused, and she is no longer persona grata with the Anglo-Indians who had felt interest in her only as a rallying point for a display of their own racism rather than feeling sympathy with her as a person. Fielding alone befriends her, although this action causes a rift between him and Aziz. Fielding persuades Aziz not to sue Adela for damages; and later, the credulous Aziz accepts the suspicions implanted in him by a friend, that Fielding has married Adela and for this reason had not wanted Aziz to sue her.

The events involving Mrs. Moore are charged with intense symbolic meaning. Her son, Ronny, had hurried her out of India even though the season was unpropitious for travel; he is afraid of her favorable testimony in behalf of Aziz at his trial. Since the traumatic experience at the Marabar, Mrs. Moore's desire to live has diminished and she succumbs to illness, dies, and is buried at sea, much as a dying goddess might be thrown into the waters. The circumstances of her death thereby anticipate the consigning in "Temple" of the image of Sri Krishna to the water at the climax of the festivities in his honor. As a person who dies for others, Mrs. Moore helps bring, through her example, harmony, peace, and prosperity in the third section of the book. She is present in spirit at these ceremonies, having been transformed in the meantime into a minor Indian deity; she is there also in her children Ralph and Stella (who has married Fielding) and in the thoughts of Godbole, the Hindu, who achieves in these ceremonies a mystic identification with the world soul of Hinduism.

Mrs. Moore and the Hindu rituals in honor of the birth of Sri Krishna cause the breach between Aziz and Fielding to be healed, at least for the moment, though it is finally impossible for Aziz and Fielding to be in the present the fast friends that by temperament they ought to be. The cultural differences and the political misunderstandings prevent them from as yet achieving a perfect and lasting accord. As they ride their horses in Mau at the conclusion of the ceremonies, the spirit of the land rises up as the men embrace to say "No, not yet," and the sky replies antiphonally, "No, not there." But if the men cannot achieve their full accord now, the implication is that somewhere at some future time, they may express, without restriction, the love each feels for the other. Hinduism which deifies the spirit of love would include in its dominion the two men of different races who want to love but cannot freely do so. Sometime the infinite love which animates the universe will descend upon them completely, and present hostilities will fade into oblivion. Forster regarded his book as metaphysical rather than social in its impact, since in it he "tried to indicate the human predicament in a universe which is not, so far, comprehensible to our minds." In these words Forster indicates something of the range, scope, and depth of the book that make it so impressive.

Only an individual such as Godbole or Mrs. Moore with developed powers of intuition can grasp the polarities of existence and see them in their true relationships. Since such polarities are continually present to the consciousness of the imaginative and sensitive individual, truth is of necessity paradoxical. The rationalists and the humanists, on the other hand, fail to grasp entirely this comprehensive reality. Aziz, Fielding, and Adela Quested, and, of course, the members of the Anglo-Indian establishment fail to appreciate to the full the ineffable and the irrational, and value too highly the intellect as such. The inner lives of these individuals are, accordingly, incomplete. Without subscribing fully to its doctrines, Forster saw in Hinduism a more inclusive and comprehensive world view than he had found either in Islam or in Christianity.

Professor Godbole is the only character in the book who is imperturbable in his serenity. Such a serenity or luminous spirituality the other characters in the novel are also searching for, as would the characters in romance. Except for the Anglo-Indian bureaucrats, all of them find some further aspect of reality that helps them interpret life. Still, they lack a totality of view (though Mrs. Moore in death does achieve such a view), and they illustrate the difficulty of achieving such wholeness. They are at least discontented with their limitations and with their disabilities of whatever kind that prevent them from attaining a full integration of their powers.

Forster's career as novelist reached a culmination in *A Passage to India,* though he continued writing voluminously as a man of letters. In 1924 he moved to West Hackhurst, Abinger Hammer, Surrey, after he had inherited the lease of this property; he lived there until his mother's death in 1945. He gave up the writing of novels, though he did write from time to time homosexual stories that were not printed until after his death.

Forster was able to consolidate his public reputation in another, but minor, way by delivering the Clark Lectures at Trinity College, Cambridge, in 1927 and then by publishing them as *Aspects of the Novel,* which has since become a standard treatise. It

is important because in it Forster, as an eminent practitioner of the genre, gave us his views of its nature and characteristics and indicated also his own aesthetic preferences. The book helps us understand both the novel as a form and Forster as a writer and sensibility. He does not focus primarily upon the history and traditions of the novel or upon craft and technique. Rather, he is most concerned with the novel as a truthful and perceptive rendition of significant human experience. In *Aspects of the Novel* he not only provided his reader with terms for use in discussing this literary genre (he divided his book into chapters entitled "The Story," "People," "The Plot," "Fantasy," "Prophecy," and "Pattern and Rhythm"), but he also wrote as one who loved literature. In his discussion of abstractions as well as in his judgments of specific books, he revealed a firmness of mind and a depth of sensibility; he understood, moreover, the novelist's practice and the problems associated with creativity. His judgments of specific writers and their works are refreshing and stimulating, sound as well as challenging, sometimes a bit idiosyncratic.

Forster's next work of importance is *Goldsworthy Lowes Dickinson,* a commemorative biography of one of his Cambridge mentors. In this book Forster developed further his biographical impulse which had already surfaced in many of the sketches he was to collect in *Abinger Harvest* (1936). Dickinson emerges in Forster's pages as a vibrant personality and as a dedicated humanist, a man whose true genius lay in his life rather than in his writings. Some measure of Dickinson's charismatic personality animates Forster's book and gives it resonance. Forster's affection for the man gives Dickinson in Forster's account a geniality and a stature that his own books do not quite convey. Forster's admiration for Dickinson and his ideas suffuses the book, which also becomes a mirror of Forster's own temperament, reflecting his own values, his fervent humanism, and his love of Cambridge.

Perhaps Forster's most notable development as writer in the late 1920s and thereafter was as an essayist. As such, Forster wrote commentaries on outstanding individuals of the past and present, on social problems, on political questions, on aesthetics and the arts, on the spell of the past, on the fascination of distant places (including the Orient), on the threat of war, and on the actual cataclysm of the war itself. Forster's point of view was that of the engaged humanist; the stance varied from an objective analysis of a situation, personality, or book to familiar utterances in which his own temperament and preferences predominate. There is no denying

Forster and T. S. Eliot, circa 1930

the depth and sincerity, the freshness and the charm of the essays comprising *Abinger Harvest* and *Two Cheers for Democracy,* as well as their highly personal quality. It is appropriate to consider the two books together since they cover mostly the same range of subjects and since they are successive books in Forster's career, though fifteen years separate them.

The biographical sketches in the two books include presentations of such colorful figures as Gemistus Pletho, Cardan, Voltaire, Gibbon, Coleridge, Keats, Wilfred Blunt, and the Emperor Babur. In each of the portraits Forster reaches beyond known fact toward the establishing of the essence of a personality as he envisioned it. The novelist's ability to discover idiosyncrasy in human behavior, his ability to define the motivations of human beings, his flair for the pungent generalization, his sympathy for individuals of all kinds and classes, his insight into the relationship between individuals and the larger cosmic, historical forces that determine their fates—all these qualities contribute to the excitement and the effectiveness of

these sketches (as they also determine the appeal of Forster's last book, *Marianne Thornton: A Domestic Biography,* 1956).

In *Abinger Harvest* and *Two Cheers for Democracy* Forster is exciting, perceptive, and challenging when he writes about art and literature, books and writers. For him art is at once aesthetic and moral in nature and authority, at once individual and social in its origins and significance. Notable are such discussions as "Anonymity," "Art for Art's Sake," and "Does Culture Matter?" in *Two Cheers for Democracy.* For Forster art is supremely important in its human implications and in its cultural significance, yet art must also be seen in perspective. Art matters tremendously, yet it is not the only activity that matters. The individual's experience with the object of art is central, yet the appreciation of art refines the sensibilities and develops positively the potentialities of the individual; and so art possesses an ultimate social and moral dimension. Notable critiques on individual writers are those on Ibsen, T. S. Eliot, Proust, Sinclair Lewis, and Jane Austen in *Abinger Harvest* and those on Gibbon, Crabbe, Tolstoy,

Proust, Virginia Woolf, and Gide in *Two Cheers for Democracy.*

Several excellent discussions of India in both books supplement significantly Forster's other writings about the subcontinent. "The Emperor Babur," "Adrift in India," and "The Mind of the Indian Native State" (*Abinger Harvest*) and "India Again" (*Two Cheers for Democracy*) are all impressive as renditions of Forster's reactions to Indian culture and politics.

Possibly of greater urgency are the essays commenting upon the condition of England (especially those written as World War II was approaching) or upon the limitations and the possibilities present for human beings in contemporary society. "Notes on the English Character" (*Abinger Harvest*), in which Forster criticizes the British for their failures in emotional responsiveness and imagination, and the first several essays in *Two Cheers for Democracy,* in which Forster comments incisively upon World War II, reveal his abiding social and political preoccupations. The perceptiveness of his ideas and his insight into the problems besetting mankind in the modern age are constantly to the fore in these discussions. Of surpassing interest is the confessional "What I Believe": it expresses Forster's credo, provides the purest summation of his humanist position, and remains a classic formulation of Bloomsbury values. As an essayist of general subjects, Forster is, among modern writers, second in importance only to George Orwell. Like Orwell, he interests his readers immediately; and like Orwell, he conveys simultaneously the excitement of the ideas that he is developing and the essence of a unique personality—that of the writer himself. Forster is perhaps more immediately engaging as an essayist than Orwell but lacks his range and decisiveness.

Forster became more prominent as a public figure in the 1930s and the 1940s than he had been previously partly because his essays kept bringing him before the public. In these public utterances he revealed a deep commitment to values which the Depression, the Nazi threat, and World War II seemed to threaten continually. In 1934-1935, as president of the National Council for Civil Liberties (he was president again in 1942), he was instrumental in discrediting the Sedition Bill and having its provisions modified. He also addressed the International Congress of Writers in Paris in 1935 with a speech, "Liberty in England" (*Abinger Harvest*). The speech was difficult to hear, and the more radical in the audience thought it tepid; but it is an eloquent defense of intellectual freedom in an economic and political climate subtly unfavorable to it. He wrote vigorously against the war in his contributions to *Time and Tide,* for example, and he protested the efforts of the government during the war to impose censorship upon speakers of the BBC.

His friendship in the 1930s with Christopher Isherwood, an active homosexual (though Forster was never involved sexually with him), suggests the other aspect of Forster's life beginning with the 1920s. The facts concerning Forster's homosexuality remained obscure until the appearance of P. N. Furbank's *E. M. Forster: A Life* (1977, 1978). According to this standard source and definitive biography, Forster became sexually active in the London of the 1920s and 1930s when his friends J. R. Ackerley and Sebastian Sprott helped extend his personal life. As a result of Ackerley's efforts, Harry Daley, a rough, brash, and cultured homosexual policeman, became Forster's lover for a few years.

Then, again through Ackerley, Forster about 1931 met another policeman, Bob Buckingham, who in 1953 became a probation officer at Coventry. It is questionable whether he and Forster were

Forster and Bob Buckingham, the policeman who was Forster's friend from 1931 until Forster's death

Goldsworthy Lowes Dickinson, Forster's mentor during his student days at Cambridge and the subject of a biography by Forster in 1934

ever active lovers, since, according to Furbank, Bob evinced surprise when, toward the end of his life, Forster confessed to him that he was an active homosexual. Be that as it may, the two often went on vacation trips together, even after Bob's marriage to May Hockey. May ultimately became Forster's friend, though there was considerable rivalry for Bob's affections following the marriage. Other more casual sexual encounters took place, though Forster rejected for himself the promiscuity of his homosexual friend Ackerley. Concurrently with Forster's somewhat checkered personal existence ran the current of his devotion to the life of the mind and the spirit and his advocacy of humanistic values in a time of economic and political crisis. In 1937 the two Indian friends who had meant so much to him died: Syed Ross Masood and the Maharajah of Dewas State Senior. The loss of these two friends was to Forster irreparable.

World War II was a lackluster time in Forster's life. Throughout the conflict, he continued to live with his mother at West Hackhurst. The owner of the ground rent of the property, Lord Farrer, decided that he wanted the house for his own use when Forster's leasehold expired. Through his own

ineptitude Forster lost whatever chance he may have had of remaining there after the death of his mother in 1945. But the quitting of West Hackhurst was, on the whole, a fortunate occurrence, though Forster might not have thought so at that moment.

At this crucial time, Cambridge University offered him a fellowship at King's College, which he was happy to accept. He became perhaps the best-known figure at the university after he had established residence there, being especially hospitable and cordial to the undergraduates and to his many visitors. The removal coincided with the upsurge in Forster's reputation, as a result of the activities of the wartime intellectuals who had found inspiration in his work and as a result of the publication of Lionel Trilling's *E. M. Forster* in 1943 (London, 1944).

His years at Cambridge were for Forster a time of creativity. He finished one of his best stories, "The Other Boat"; he gave shape to his book of Indian reminiscences, *The Hill of Devi*; he undertook the final revision of *Maurice;* he worked with Eric Crozier on the libretto to Benjamin Britten's *Billy Budd* (1951), an opera based on Melville's novel; he wrote many essays of distinction, as yet uncollected; and he wrote another commemorative biography, this time in honor of his great-aunt Marianne Thornton, who had done so much for him in the past.

In *Marianne Thornton: A Domestic Biography* Forster wrote not only about Thornton but about her extensive family, the members of which are his paternal forebears in the nineteenth century. Affection for the Thorntons tempered his strictures concerning their limitations, and he admired them for their strong qualities, some of them Wilcoxian in kind. He especially admired the vigor, the independence, and the enterprise of the elder Henry Thornton, the founder of the clan. In dealing with the next generation Forster wrote most fully about the second Henry Thornton and his sister Marianne. The Henry Thornton of this newer generation gained Forster's approbation when he defied public opinion and married his deceased wife's sister, a sort of marriage proscribed by Victorian law. Forster also painted, with full attention to all the relevant and colorful details, an authentic portrait of Marianne herself: her domineering nature, her subtle selfishness, her loyalty to her brother in his crisis, her courage and her intrepidity, and her unexpected generosities fuse to form an imposing likeness. If one does not willingly accept this book in lieu of another Forster novel, one still can be grateful that Forster used his skills and his unique talent to write an extended work so close to the end of his career.

At this point one should consider the best of Forster's homosexual stories, all of which date from 1922 through 1958 but which first appeared in print in 1972: "The Life to Come" (1922), "Dr. Woolacott" (1927), "Arthur Snatchfold" (1928), and "The Other Boat" (1957-1958). The composing of these and the other homosexual stories mostly occurred subsequent to the writing of *A Passage to India.* The cited stories have many merits, though they do not rank with Forster's greatest work.

"The Life to Come" traces the disintegrating

MACMILLAN

WAR PAMPHLETS

1. LET THERE BE LIBERTY   A. P. HERBERT

2. WAR WITH HONOUR   A. A. MILNE

3. NORDIC TWILIGHT   E. M. FORSTER

4. THE CROOKED CROSS   THE DEAN OF CHICHESTER

5. NAZI AND NAZARENE   RONALD KNOX

6. WHEN I REMEMBER . . .   J. R. CLYNES

7. FOR CIVILIZATION   C. E. M. JOAD

8. THE RIGHTS OF MAN   HAROLD J. LASKI

NORDIC TWILIGHT
E. M. FORSTER

MACMILLAN WAR PAMPHLETS

NO 3   3d NET

Covers for a pamphlet written by Forster during World War II

effect of the denial of love. A Christian missionary, Mr. Pinmay, becomes by inadvertence the lover for one night of a native African chieftain, Vithobai, but then proceeds to deny, in accordance with Christian tenets, his carnal love for a man. Pinmay has for supporters of his missionary enterprise some modern capitalists who destroy the pastoral beauty of Vithobai's kingdom. Despoiled both of love and political power, Vithobai is desperate. In order to regain his power and his identity, he stabs Pinmay to death before he commits suicide.

The levels of complication in this story give it its distinction, and the same comment can be made for the other three stories. In "Dr. Woolacott" a doctor becomes the agent of death rather than of life. His solicitous efforts would cause his patient Clesant to survive physically for many years but to decay spiritually. A life-enhancing figure, an unknown boy, appears to Clesant and promises deliverance from the heavy-handed doctor and, after this rescue takes place, spiritual salvation. Clesant achieves salvation by choosing the boy rather than the doctor, though the choice entails his physical death. In "Arthur Snatchfold" Forster condemns a society which regards a genuine but casual homosexual encounter as a crime. Snatchfold is a milkman who yields to the advances of a respectable businessman, Sir Richard Conway. Revealing an admirable courage when he is apprehended, Snatchfold refuses to betray his lover, a courage of which Sir Richard finds himself incapable, since to admit his complicity in the act would entail his social and financial ruin.

"The Other Boat" is the best of these stories and has some of the same crispness and starkness as *A Passage to India.* In both works the impact of alien cultures on one another is an underlying theme. Captain Lionel March has by chance fallen into a homosexual liaison with an Indian youth, Cocoa. The youth is extremely possessive and attempts to blackmail March into forming a permanent relationship with him. As the essence of decorum and propriety, Lionel March's mother is a malign influence upon her son; she is a woman whose finer feelings have atrophied and who dominates her son completely as a kind of castrating figure. March is so incensed at the deviousness of Cocoa that he possesses him violently and then strangles him; he then evades the consequences of his murderous passion by jumping into the sea. The close collocation of love and death and the constricting effects of convention upon the free expression of passion are the themes so persuasively dramatized in this distinguished story. This story demonstrates that Forster

had not lost his mastery as a writer of fiction; it was simply that the cultural climate of the early twentieth century made it impossible for him to write on the subjects that most preoccupied him.

Forster continued to write copiously until the early 1960s, when he found that he was unable to concentrate strongly enough to continue in an active manner with his writing and with his career as public sage and cultural arbiter. The 1950s were an active decade for Forster, however. In the celebrated obscenity trial over D. H. Lawrence's *Lady Chatterley's Lover* in 1960 Forster testified eloquently for the defense, a fitting tribute to the writer whom Forster had for so long admired. He was active at Cambridge, particularly with the Humanist Federation there and served for a time as its president. He wrote reviews regularly until 1960-1961, mostly for Ackerley's *Listener,* and he sent many letters to editors of journals and newspapers on such subjects as apartheid, capital punishment, and the Chinese invasion of India. In these utterances and his more private conversations, he expressed a great concern for the consequences of atomic war. He also did much traveling during his later years, the most notable of his excursions being those to America in 1947 and 1949, and in 1945 a third trip to India, where at Jaipur he attended a P.E.N. Conference. The India he had known seemed to be in danger of disappearing, however, and he deplored especially the present obsession among Indian intellectuals with politics, to the exclusion of other interests.

In the years after 1945 he enjoyed international prestige and the homage of the whole world. He suffered his first stroke in 1964 and a more serious one the next year; and his health thereafter deteriorated gradually. He had to give up an active life, though he remained intellectually acute until his death. He suffered a massive stroke on 22 May 1970, and on 2 June, the Buckinghams removed him to their home in Coventry where he died on 7 June.

To the end Forster continued to be an influential voice in the modern cultural scene and an admired presence in Cambridge. Although he conquered by his charismatic personality, it was his fiction that had laid the solid basis for his fame. Despite his later unproductivity as a writer of fiction, it was primarily as the author of universally read and loved novels that the public reverenced him. All of his novels have become classics, and the word Forsterian can alone describe their rich mixture of comedy and poetry, and their luminous, rich, and clear style. The luminous style illuminates the subjects of Forster's fiction as it becomes a mirror of Forster's own luminous temper. Though his canon is a slender one, it is sui generis. No one else ever wrote quite like Forster, and in his case the style is indeed the man and the man is inseparable from the style. The visionary element is strong in Forster and gives his fiction a certain timelessness, as in it he reaches from this world to a kingdom that is mythic and archetypal, to one that partakes not only of the everyday but of the eternal.

Letters:

Selected Letters of E. M. Forster, Volume One 1879-1920, edited by Mary Lago and P. N. Furbank (London: Collins, 1983; Cambridge: Harvard University Press, 1983).

Bibliographies:

B. J. Kirkpatrick, *A Bibliography of E. M. Forster* (London: Hart-Davis, 1965; revised edition, 1968);

Frederick P. W. McDowell, ed., *E. M. Forster: An Annotated Bibliography of Writings about Him* (DeKalb: Northern Illinois University Press, 1977).

Biographies:

P. N. Furbank, *E. M. Forster: A Life, Volume One: The Growth of a Novelist (1870-1914)* (London: Secker & Warburg, 1977); *E. M. Forster: A Life, Volume Two: Polycrates' Ring (1914-1970)* (London: Secker & Warburg, 1978); republished as *E. M. Forster: A Life,* 1 volume (New York: Harcourt Brace Jovanovich, 1978);

Francis E. King, *E. M. Forster and His World* (London: Thames & Hudson, 1978; New York: Scribners, 1978).

References:

Glen O. Allen, "Structure, Symbol, and Theme in E. M. Forster's *A Passage to India,*" *PMLA,* 70 (December 1955): 934-954;

J. B. Beer, *The Achievement of E. M. Forster* (London: Chatto & Windus, 1962; New York: Barnes & Noble, 1962);

Beer, "The Last Englishman: Lawrence's Appreciation of Forster," in *E. M. Forster, A Human Exploration: Centenary Essays,* edited by G. K. Das and Beer (London: Macmillan, 1979; New York: New York University Press, 1979), pp. 245-268;

Elizabeth Bowen, "A Passage to E. M. Forster," in *Aspects of E. M. Forster: Essays and Recollections Written for His Ninetieth Birthday January 1, 1969,* edited by Oliver Stallybrass (London:

Arnold, 1969; New York: Harcourt, Brace & World, 1969), pp. 1-12;

Malcolm Bradbury, "E. M. Forster as Victorian and Modern: *Howards End* and *A Passage to India,*" in his *Possibilities: Essays on the State of the Novel* (London & New York: Oxford University Press, 1973), pp. 91-120;

Bradbury, "*Howards End,*" in *Forster: A Collection of Critical Essays,* edited by Bradbury (Englewood Cliffs, N.J.: Prentice-Hall, 1966), pp. 128-143;

Bradbury, ed., *Forster: A Collection of Critical Essays* (Englewood Cliffs, N.J.: Prentice-Hall, 1966);

Reuben A. Brower, "The Twilight of the Double Vision: Symbol and Irony in *A Passage to India,*" in his *The Fields of Light: An Experiment in Critical Reading* (New York: Oxford University Press, 1951), pp. 182-198;

E. K. Brown, "Expanding Symbols" and "Rhythm in E. M. Forster's *A Passage to India,*" in his *Rhythm in the Novel* (Toronto: University of Toronto Press, 1950), pp. 33-59, 89-115;

Kenneth Burke, "Social and Cosmic Mystery: *A Passage to India,*" in his *Language as Symbolic Action: Essays on Life, Literature, and Method* (Berkeley & Los Angeles: University of California Press, 1966), pp. 223-239;

John Colmer, *E. M. Forster: The Personal Voice* (London & Boston: Routledge & Kegan Paul, 1975);

C. B. Cox, "E. M. Forster's Island," in his *The Free Spirit: A Study of Liberal Humanism in the Novels of George Eliot, Henry James, E. M. Forster, Virginia Woolf, Angus Wilson* (London & New York: Oxford University Press, 1963), pp. 74-102;

Frederick C. Crews, *E. M. Forster: The Perils of Humanism* (Princeton: Princeton University Press, 1962);

G. K. Das, *Forster's India* (London: Macmillan, 1977; Totowa, N.J.: Rowman & Littlefield, 1978);

G. K. Das and Beer, eds., *E. M. Forster: A Human Exploration, Centenary Essays* (London: Macmillan, 1979; New York: New York University Press, 1979);

Louise Dauner, "What Happened in the Cave? Reflections on *A Passage to India,*" *Modern Fiction Studies,* 7 (Autumn 1961): 258-270;

Peter Firchow, "Germany and Germanic Mythology in *Howards End,*" *Comparative Literature,* 33 (Winter 1981): 50-68;

Philip Gardner, *E. M. Forster* (Harlow: Longman, 1978);

Gardner, "E. M. Forster and 'The Possession of England,'" *Modern Language Quarterly,* 42

(June 1981): 166-183;

Gardner, ed., *E. M. Forster: The Critical Heritage* (London & Boston: Routledge & Kegan Paul, 1974);

K. W. Gransden, *E. M. Forster* (Edinburgh & London: Oliver & Boyd, 1962; New York: Grove, 1962);

James Hall, "Forster's Family Reunions," in his *The Tragic Comedians: Seven Modern British Novelists* (Bloomington: Indiana University Press, 1963), pp. 11-30;

John Edward Hardy, "Howards End; the Sacred Center," in his *Man in the Modern Novel* (Seattle: University of Washington Press, 1964), pp. 34-51;

Judith Scherer Herz, "E. M. Forster and the Biography of the Self: Redefining a Genre," *Prose Studies,* 5 (December 1982): 326-335;

Herz and Robert K. Martin, eds., *E. M. Forster: Centenary Revaluations* (London: Macmillan, 1982);

Ellin Horowitz, "The Communal Ritual and the Dying God in E. M. Forster's A Passage to India," *Criticism,* 6 (Winter 1964): 70-88;

Samuel Hynes, "Forster's Cramp," in his *Edwardian Occasions: Essays on English Writing in the Early Twentieth Century* (New York: Oxford University Press, 1972; London: Routledge & Kegan Paul, 1972), pp. 114-122;

Robert Langbaum, "A New Look at E. M. Forster," in his *The Modern Spirit: Essays on the Continuity of Nineteenth and Twentieth-Century Literature* (New York & London: Oxford University Press, 1970), pp. 127-146;

F. R. Leavis, "E. M. Forster," *Scrutiny,* 7 (September 1938): 188-202; republished in his *The Common Pursuit* (New York: Stewart, 1952), pp. 261-267;

June Perry Levine, *Creation and Criticism: "A Passage to India"* (Lincoln: University of Nebraska Press, 1971; London: Chatto & Windus, 1972);

John Lucas, "Wagner and Forster: *Parsifal* and *A Room with a View,*" *ELH,* 33 (March 1966): 92-117;

Rose Macaulay, *The Writings of E. M. Forster* (London: Hogarth Press, 1938; New York: Harcourt, Brace, 1938);

John Magnus, "Ritual Aspects of E. M. Forster's *The Longest Journey,*" *Modern Fiction Studies,* 13 (Summer 1967): 195-210;

John Sayre Martin, *E. M. Forster: The Endless Journey* (Cambridge: Cambridge University Press, 1976);

James McConkey, *The Novels of E. M. Forster* (Ithaca: Cornell University Press, 1957);

Frederick P. W. McDowell, *E. M. Forster* (New York: Twayne, 1969; revised, 1982);

Jeffrey Meyers, "E. M. Forster: *A Passage to India,*" in his *Fiction and the Colonial Experience* (Totowa, N.J.: Rowman & Littlefield, 1973; Ipswich, U.K.: Boydell Press, 1973), pp. 29-54;

K. Natwar-Singh, ed., *E. M. Forster: A Tribute* (New York: Harcourt, Brace & World, 1964);

R. W. Noble, "*A Passage to India:* The Genesis of E. M. Forster's Novel," *Encounter,* 54 (February 1980): 51-61;

Benita Parry, *Delusions and Discoveries: Studies on India in the British Imagination 1880-1930* (Berkeley & Los Angeles: University of California Press, 1972);

Jane Lagoudis Pinchin, *Alexandria Still: Forster, Durrell and Cavafy* (Princeton: Princeton University Press, 1977);

V. S. Pritchett, "Mr. Forster's Birthday," in his *The Living Novel and Later Appreciations* (New York: Random House, 1966), pp. 244-250;

John Crowe Ransom, "E. M. Forster," *Kenyon Review,* 5 (Autumn 1943): 618-623;

Barbara Rosecrance, *Forster's Narrative Vision* (Ithaca & London: Cornell University Press, 1982);

S. P. Rosenbaum, ed., *The Bloomsbury Group: A Collection of Memoirs, Commentary and Criticism* (Toronto & Buffalo: University of Toronto Press, 1975);

Rosenbaum, "*The Longest Journey:* E. M. Forster's Refutation of Idealism," in *E. M. Forster: A Human Exploration,* edited by Das and Beer, pp. 32-54;

Wilfred Stone, *The Cave and the Mountain: A Study of E. M. Forster* (Stanford: Stanford University Press, 1966);

Stone, "E. M. Forster's Subversive Individualism," in *E. M. Forster: Centenary Revaluations,* edited by Judith Scherer Herz and Robert K. Martin, pp. 15-36;

George H. Thomson, *The Fiction of E. M. Forster* (Detroit: Wayne State University Press, 1967);

Edwin Thumboo, "E. M. Forster's *A Passage to India:* From Caves to Court," *Southern Review* (Adelaide), 10 (July 1977): 112-144;

D. A. Traversi, "The Novels of E. M. Forster," *Arena,* 1 (April 1937): 28-40; republished in *E. M. Forster: The Critical Heritage,* edited by Philip Gardner, pp. 387-399;

Lionel Trilling, *E. M. Forster* (Norfolk, Conn.: New

Directions, 1943; London: Hogarth Press, 1944);

Willis H. Truitt, "Thematic and Symbolic Ideology in the Works of E. M. Forster: In Memoriam," *Journal of Aesthetics and Art Criticism,* 30 (Fall 1971): 101-109;

Donald Watt, "The Artist as Horseman: The Unity of Forster's Criticism," *Modern Philology,* 79 (August 1981): 45-60;

Gertrude M. White, "*A Passage to India:* Analysis and Revaluation," *PMLA,* 68 (September 1953): 1-17;

Alan Wilde, *Art and Order: A Study of E. M. Forster* (New York: New York University Press, 1964);

Wilde, *Horizons of Assent: Modernism, Postmodernism,* *and the Ironic Imagination* (Baltimore & London: Johns Hopkins University Press, 1981);

A. Woodward, "The Humanism of E. M. Forster," *Theoria,* 20 (15 June 1963): 17-33;

Virginia Woolf, "The Novels of E. M. Forster," *Atlantic Monthly,* 140 (November 1927): 642-648; republished in her *The Death of the Moth* (New York: Harcourt, Brace, 1942), pp. 104-112.

Papers:

The E. M. Forster Archive is at King's College Library, King's College, Cambridge. The manuscript for *A Passage to India* and some other papers are at the Humanities Research Center, University of Texas.

John Galsworthy

Brian Murray
Youngstown State University

See also the Galsworthy entry in *DLB 10, Modern British Dramatists, 1900-1945.*

BIRTH: Parkfield, Kingston Hill, Surrey, 14 August 1867, to John and Blanche Bartleet Galsworthy.

EDUCATION: B.A., Oxford University, 1889.

MARRIAGE: 23 September 1905 to Ada Cooper Galsworthy.

AWARDS AND HONORS: Membership in the Royal Society of Literature, 1912; membership in the Société des Gens de lettres (France), 1916; knighthood, 1918 (declined); Les Palmes D'Or (Belgium), 1919; first president, International P.E.N. Club, 1921-1933; LL.D., St. Andrews University, 1922; honorary professor of dramatic literature, Royal Society of Literature, 1922; fellowship of the American Academy of Arts and Sciences, 1926; honorary fellow of New College, Oxford, 1926; Litt.D., University of Manchester, 1927; Litt.D., Dublin University, 1929; Order of Merit, 1929; Litt.D., University of Sheffield, 1930; Litt.D., Cambridge University, 1930; Litt.D., and Romanes Lecturer, Oxford University, 1931; Litt.D.,

Princeton University, 1931; Nobel Prize for Literature, 1932.

DEATH: Grove Lodge, Hampstead, London, 31 January 1933.

BOOKS: *From the Four Winds,* as John Sinjohn (London: Unwin, 1897);

Jocelyn, as Sinjohn (London: Duckworth, 1898); as Galsworthy (St. Clair Shores, Mich.: Scholarly Press, 1972);

Villa Rubein: A Novel, as Sinjohn (London: Duckworth, 1900);

A Man of Devon, as Sinjohn (Edinburgh & London: Blackwood, 1901);

The Island Pharisees (London: Heinemann, 1904);

The Man of Property (London: Heinemann, 1906; New York: Putnam's, 1909);

The Country House (London: Heinemann, 1907; New York: Putnam's, 1907);

A Commentary (London: Richards, 1908; New York: Putnam's, 1908);

Fraternity (London: Heinemann, 1909; New York: Putnam's, 1909);

Plays: The Silver Box; Joy; Strife (London: Duckworth, 1909);

A Justification of the Censorship of Plays (London: Heinemann, 1909);

Justice: A Tragedy in Four Acts (London: Duckworth, 1910; New York: Scribners, 1910);

A Motley (London: Heinemann, 1910; New York: Scribners, 1910);

The Spirit of Punishment (London: Humanitarian League, 1910);

"Gentles, Let Us Rest": Reprinted from "The Nation" (London: National Union of Women's Suffrage Societies, 1910?);

The Patrician (London: Heinemann, 1911; New York: Scribners, 1911);

The Little Dream: An Allegory in Six Scenes (London: Duckworth, 1911; New York: Scribners, 1911);

For Love of Beasts (London: Animals' Friend Society, 1912);

The Pigeon: A Fantasy in Three Acts (London: Duckworth, 1912; New York: Scribners, 1912);

Moods, Songs, and Doggerels (New York: Scribners, 1912; London: Heinemann, 1912);

The Inn of Tranquillity: Studies and Essays (New York: Scribners, 1912; London: Heinemann, 1912);

The Eldest Son: A Domestic Drama in Three Acts (London: Duckworth, 1912; New York: Scribners, 1912);

The Fugitive: A Play in Four Acts (London: Duckworth, 1913; New York: Scribners, 1914);

The Dark Flower (London: Heinemann, 1913; New York: Scribners, 1913);

The Slaughter of Animals for Food (London: Royal Society for the Prevention of Cruelty to Animals/Council of Justice to Animals, 1913);

Treatment of Animals: Being a Speech Delivered at the Kensington Town Hall on December 15, 1913, at a Meeting Called to Protest against Cruelties to Performing Animals (London: Animals' Friend Society, 1913);

The Mob: A Play in Four Acts (London: Duckworth, 1914; New York: Scribners, 1914);

The Little Man and Other Satires (New York: Scribners, 1915; London: Heinemann, 1915);

A Bit o'Love: A Play in Three Acts (London: Duckworth, 1915; New York: Scribners, 1915);

The Freelands (London: Heinemann, 1915; New York: Scribners, 1915);

A Sheaf (New York: Scribners, 1916; London: Heinemann, 1916);

"Your Christmas Dinner is Served!" (London: National Committee for Relief in Belgium, 1916);

Beyond (New York: Scribners, 1917; London: Heinemann, 1917);

The Land: A Plea (London: Allen & Unwin, 1918);

Five Tales (New York: Scribners, 1918; London: Heinemann, 1918);

Another Sheaf (London: Heinemann, 1919; New York: Scribners, 1919);

The Burning Spear: Being the Experiences of Mr. John Lavender in Time of War, as A. R. P-M (London: Chatto & Windus, 1919); as Galsworthy (New York: Scribners, 1923);

Addresses in America (New York: Scribners, 1919; London: Heinemann, 1919);

Saint's Progress (New York: Scribners, 1919; London: Heinemann, 1919);

Tatterdemalion (London: Heinemann, 1920; New York: Scribners, 1920);

The Foundations: An Extravagant Play in Three Acts (London: Duckworth, 1920; New York: Scribners, 1920);

The Skin Game: A Tragi-comedy in Three Acts (London: Duckworth, 1920; New York: Scribners, 1923);

In Chancery (London: Heinemann, 1920; New York: Scribners, 1921);

Awakening (New York: Scribners, 1920; London: Heinemann, 1920);

The Bells of Peace (Cambridge: Heffer, 1921);

To Let (New York: Scribners, 1921; London: Heinemann, 1921);

Six Short Plays (London: Duckworth, 1921; New York: Scribners, 1921);

The Forsyte Saga (New York: Scribners, 1922; London: Heinemann, 1922);

A Family Man; in Three Acts (London: Duckworth, 1922; New York: Scribners, 1922);

Loyalties: A Drama in Three Acts (London: Duckworth, 1922; New York: Scribners, 1923);

Windows: A Comedy in Three Acts for Idealists and Others (London: Duckworth, 1922; New York: Scribners, 1923);

Captures (London: Heinemann, 1923; New York: Scribners, 1923);

International Thought (Cambridge: Heffer, 1923);

The Forest: A Drama in Four Acts (London: Duckworth, 1924; New York: Scribners, 1924);

On Expression (London: English Association, 1924);

Memorable Days (London: Privately printed, 1924);

The White Monkey (New York: Scribners, 1924; London: Heinemann, 1924);

Abracadabra (London: Heinemann, 1924);

Old English: A Play in Three Acts (London:

Duckworth, 1924; New York: Scribners, 1925);

Caravan: The Assembled Tales of John Galsworthy (London: Heinemann, 1925; New York: Scribners, 1925);

The Show: A Drama in Three Acts (London: Duckworth, 1925; New York: Scribners, 1925);

Is England Done? (London: Privately printed, 1925);

The Silver Spoon (London: Heinemann, 1926; New York: Scribners, 1926);

Escape: An Episodic Play in a Prologue and Two Parts (London: Duckworth, 1926; New York: Scribners, 1927);

Verses New and Old (London: Heinemann, 1926; New York: Scribners, 1926);

Castles in Spain & Other Screeds (London: Heinemann, 1927; New York: Scribners, 1927);

The Way to Prepare Peace (London: Whitefriars Press, 1927);

Two Forsyte Interludes: A Silent Wooing; Passers By (London: Heinemann, 1927; New York: Scribners, 1928);

Swan Song (New York: Scribners, 1928; London: Heinemann, 1928);

Exiled: An Evolutionary Comedy (London: Duckworth, 1929; New York: Scribners, 1930);

A Modern Comedy (London: Heinemann, 1929; New York: Scribners, 1929);

The Roof (London: Duckworth, 1929; New York: Scribners, 1930);

On Forsyte 'Change (London: Heinemann, 1930; New York: Scribners, 1930);

The Creation of Character in Literature (Oxford: Oxford University Press, 1931);

Maid in Waiting (London: Heinemann, 1931; New York: Scribners, 1931);

Flowering Wilderness (London: Heinemann, 1932; New York: Scribners, 1932);

Candelabra: Selected Essays and Addresses (London: Heinemann, 1932; New York: Scribners, 1933);

Over the River (London: Heinemann, 1933); republished as One More River (New York: Scribners, 1933);

End of the Chapter (New York: Scribners, 1934; London: Heinemann, 1935);

Collected Poems of John Galsworthy (New York: Scribners, 1934);

Forsytes, Pendyces, and Others (London: Heinemann, 1935; New York: Scribners, 1935).

(photo by Pearl Freeman)

During the first decade of the twentieth century, John Galsworthy was widely regarded as one of England's leading writers. As a novelist and a playwright, he was commercially successful and critically esteemed. After the First World War and until his death in 1933, Galsworthy remained one of Britain's most widely read and widely translated authors, even as younger, more experimental writers proclaimed his fiction obsolete. In November 1932 he was awarded the Nobel Prize for Literature. By 1950, however, Galsworthy's reputation had widely and radically declined, especially among academic critics who followed the lead of his earlier detractors—such as Virginia Woolf and D. H. Lawrence—and pointed to his not infrequent lapses into sentimentality and his tendency to "over-write." But as an increasing number of com-

Galsworthy's parents: John Galsworthy, Sr., and Blanche Bartleet Galsworthy (holding the infant John) (courtesy of Mr. Rudolf Sauter)

mentators are pointing out, Galsworthy was much more than an earnest "middlebrow" entertainer. Aside from his impressive accomplishments as a playwright, Galsworthy was the author of a number of novels of considerable literary merit as well as historical worth. As Anthony West put it: "In the context of his time, he was, for his class, a master storyteller."

John Galsworthy's roots, on his father's side, were in Devon. His grandfather, a prosperous Plymstock merchant, came to London in 1833 and quickly increased his wealth by investing shrewdly in local real estate. John Galsworthy III, the novelist's father, was not only a practicing solicitor but a skilled businessman in his own right. "Old John" Galsworthy served as a director of several firms and also bought, sold, and managed a good deal of property in and around London. When he died in 1904 at the age of eighty-seven, he left an estate valued in the six figures, a generous portion of which provided each of his four children with a handsome legacy and a lifelong annuity. Galswor-

thy was devoted to his father, whose relentless business sense was paralleled by the unfailing gentleness he showed his children. In an autobiographical sketch written in 1919, Galsworthy observed that "my father really predominated in me from the start, and ruled my life. I was so truly and deeply fond of him that I seemed not to have a fair share of love left to give my mother." In fact, Blanche Bartleet Galsworthy was not particularly lovable: she was aloof, hypochondriacal, and obsessed with household tidiness. As Alec Fréchet points out, Galsworthy "admitted his mother's charm, elegance, taste, distinction, goodness: in short her nobility of character"; but his novels implicitly show that he could not tolerate her "lack of critical spirit, her dreadful conventionalism in every way, her maternalism." Indirectly, then, says Fréchet, Mrs. Galsworthy exerted a "major influence" by eventually arousing in her son "a reaction against the type of family life she had imposed on him."

With his younger brother and two sisters as his constant companions, Galsworthy's boyhood was happily spent in a series of three spacious homes built by his father on a twenty-four-acre estate near Epsom in suburban London. In his 1919 story "Awakening," Galsworthy sentimentally recreates the well-upholstered leather and mahogany world of his childhood, casting himself as little Jon Forsyte—a hearty boy of eight whose "fancy" is "cooked" by the sea yarns and adventure tales he constantly devours.

In 1876 Galsworthy was sent to Saugeen, a small, family-run prep school in the scenic village of Bournemouth. He participated enthusiastically in a number of school activities even as he impressed his masters with the wide range of his reading. In 1891 Galsworthy entered Harrow, where he became a gymnastics champion, a football captain, and a monitor. In 1886—the same year his parents moved to the Kensington district of London—he went up to New College, Oxford, to study jurisprudence in accord with his father's wishes. Galsworthy was better known at Oxford for the nattiness of his dress—which by this time included lavender gloves and a monocle—than for the brilliance of his mind or for his creativity. Although he took part in, and

wrote, some amateur theatricals, Galsworthy spent considerable time socializing and gambling. He was, then, what he would much later call one of his own fictional creations—"a dyed in the wool Whyte-Melville type."

After graduating with a second class degree in 1889, Galsworthy joined his family in London. Within a year, he was called to the bar at Lincoln's Inn. Galsworthy found the practice of law tedious and confining, and continued to devote much of his energy to the playing of horses and the pursuit of young women such as Sybil Carlisle, a singing instructor who aspired to a career on the stage. Galsworthy's chronic betting and his involvement with a budding actress did not please his propriety-conscious father, who decided that if his son were to mature, he would need to spend a couple of years away from his debilitating distractions. Accordingly, in the summer of 1891 Galsworthy undertook the first in a series of long cruises to inspect the family's far-flung mining investments and to acquire enough experience at sea to prepare him to take up the practice of maritime law. Over the next two years he traveled to Canada, Russia, South Af-

Coombe Warren, the first of three houses Galsworthy's father built on adjoining sites on his twenty-four-acre estate in the London suburbs

Galsworthy in his football uniform at Harrow; Galsworthy at Oxford

rica, and many other places. Initially he was accompanied by his brother Hubert, but he was later joined by his friend Ted Sanderson, whose doctor had prescribed sea air as a cure for fatigue and bad nerves.

In November 1892 Galsworthy and Sanderson sailed to Australia, stopping at assorted exotic ports along the way. For the voyage home they boarded the celebrated clipper *Torrens,* whose first mate was an as-yet-unpublished Polish author who called himself Joseph Conrad. After spending many evenings together on the poop deck of the *Torrens* talking of literature and life, Galsworthy and Conrad formed a friendship that deepened considerably over the next three decades. It was Conrad who eventually brought Galsworthy into a literary circle that included such figures as Ford Madox Ford and Edward Garnett, the eccentric and extraordinarily influential editor whom Ford once described as "London's literary—if Nonconformist—Pope."

Soon after returning from his Far Eastern cruise, Galsworthy established his own modest legal chambers at 3 Paper Buildings, Temple. But the law continued to bore him. Indeed, by the spring of 1895 he was devoting most of his energy not to the scrutiny of legal briefs and the acquisition of clients but to the secret study of the fictional techniques of best-selling authors and to the cultivation of his own writing skills. Galsworthy's literary ambitions finally became known to his family and friends when, in the spring of 1897, he paid for the publication of *From the Four Winds,* a collection of short stories written in heavy-handed imitation of Rudyard Kipling and Bret Harte. In later years, Galsworthy himself called this little volume "vile" and "dreadful" but admitted that the experience of seeing it through print made him "more proud" than did the publication "of any of its successors."

In choosing literature over the law, Galsworthy did not have the immediate support of his parents, for whom respectability—or, as Blanche

FROM THE FOUR
WINDS

BY
JOHN SINJOHN

LONDON: T. FISHER UNWIN
PATERNOSTER SQUARE, 1897

*Title page for Galsworthy's collection of short stories, published at
his own expense and under his pseudonym*

Galsworthy liked to put it, "niceness"—was the preeminent goal of mortal existence. Galsworthy's parents—particularly his father—enjoyed reading and looking at paintings; but, like most members of their class, they apparently assumed that artists were invariably dissolute. For a time, they tried to prevent their daughter Lilian's marriage to Georg Sauter, a Bavarian painter of peasant stock and liberal political views; in his second novel, *Villa Rubein* (1900), Galsworthy tells the story of a sensitive English girl who, despite the objections of her philistine stepfather, falls in love with a rather Byronic Austrian painter. Like others of Galsworthy's transparently autobiographical novels, *Villa Rubein* not surprisingly caused his family considerable unease.

As a neophyte author, Galsworthy did receive immediate support from Ada Cooper Galsworthy, the young wife of his first cousin Arthur, a military man. In turn, Galsworthy consoled Ada, who thought Arthur a bore and a brute and her marriage of convenience to him a hopeless mistake. Galsworthy and Ada had become lovers in September 1895. From the start, Galsworthy's sisters and a few of his closest friends knew of this affair, which at any rate became conspicuous—to everyone except, perhaps, Galsworthy's par-

*Galsworthy's sister Lilian and her husband, Georg Sauter. Their relationship, and Galsworthy's parents' opposition to it,
inspired the plot of* Villa Rubein.

Ada Cooper, who married Galsworthy's cousin, and later Galsworthy (courtesy of Mr. Rudolf Sauter)

ventions of sexual behavior, Galsworthy—notes West—"gave expression to the secret fears and anxieties that revolution aroused in the members of his class."

Galsworthy's first novel, *Jocelyn* (1898), signals his interest in dealing with illicit sexual passion and its consequences. Its "unheroic hero"—as one reviewer called him—is the world-weary Englishman Giles Legard, who for ten years has been living on the Italian Riviera with his tedious wife Irma, a "confirmed invalid" addicted to morphine. When Giles falls in love with Jocelyn Ley—a moody, Ada-like young woman of twenty-two—he finds himself frighteningly alive, and so strongly "under the pressure of the throbbing passion which possessed him" that "conventional morality ceased to be anything to him but a dim, murky shadow falling at times across the path of his longing." Giles is so determined to sate his longing that when he discovers Irma in a drug-induced coma, he does nothing to save her; instead, he spends the day making love to Jocelyn on a picturesque bluff overlooking an appropriately "angry white" sea. Of course, when

ents—during Arthur's two-year tour of duty in the Boer War. Galsworthy and Ada finally married on 23 September 1905, ten months after the death of Galsworthy's father and six months after Ada's divorce.

Ada's role in assisting Galsworthy's career was profound. She was his muse, his amanuensis, and—along with Garnett—his most trusted editor. In 1922 Galsworthy dedicated *The Forsyte Saga* in its entirety to Ada, noting that without her "encouragement, sympathy and criticism, I could never have become such a writer as I am."

Of equal importance was the fact that Ada functioned as the model for many of Galsworthy's heroines and helped him to formulate one of his principal themes. As Anthony West observes, Galsworthy—through his affair with Ada—"became an active participant in the sexual revolution that was transforming the patterns of middle class life in England." By frequently depicting characters who suffer guilt, disrepute, and often destruction as a result of breaking Victorian con-

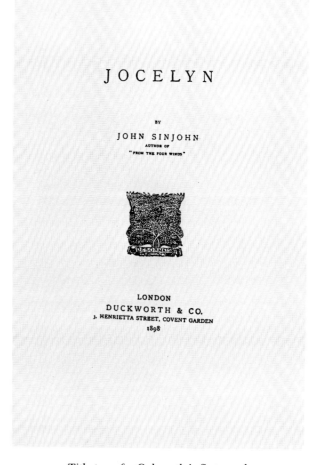

JOCELYN

BY

JOHN SINJOHN

AUTHOR OF
"FROM THE FOUR WINDS"

LONDON
DUCKWORTH & CO.
3. HENRIETTA STREET, COVENT GARDEN
1898

Title page for Galsworthy's first novel

Irma dies, Giles and Jocelyn are overwhelmed by guilt, and they separate. But soon they realize that their passion inextricably links them, and—at the novel's close—they rendezvous once more and vow that they will start anew, wiping out the past.

In later years, Galsworthy thought *Jocelyn* badly written and too emotionally explicit, and he refused to allow its republication. But when the novel first appeared, it drew some encouraging praise. The *Saturday Review* thought it rather too full of "tiresome psychological subtleties" but appraised it as being "above the common run of fiction." Conrad, in one of his avuncular letters to Galsworthy, described *Jocelyn* as "*desperately* convincing" and "inspiring."

Among Galsworthy's new literary friends, *Villa Rubein,* with its Turgenev-like tone, fared even better when it appeared in 1900. H. G. Wells noted that its characters were "finely modelled and drawn." Ford wrote Galsworthy to say that the novel's prose was "lucid and excellent" and quite beyond the ordinary, but that "you are too kind, too deferential to your characters; you haven't enough

Galsworthy around the turn of the century

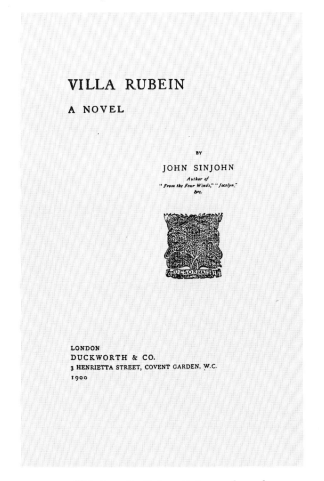

Title page for Galsworthy's second novel

contempt, enough of the *saeva indignatio*." Ford prescribed more "vinegar."

There is plenty of vinegar in Galsworthy's third novel, *The Island Pharisees* (1904), the first of his books to bear his own name instead of the pseudonym John Sinjohn. Its hero, Richard Shelton, is a young Oxford-educated lawyer who has become critical of middle-class materialism and artificiality and generally pained by human nature, which he finds "repulsive." In his blackest moods, Shelton pensively wanders through London's poorest, meanest streets—streets that are "a scandal to the world." He develops a friendship with a French tramp, Ferrand, who adds to Shelton's knowledge of how the have-nots live and offers his own indictments of the indifferent bourgeois.

The Island Pharisees is one of Galsworthy's most autobiographical works. Like Shelton's, Galsworthy's impatience with middle-class life intensified as he became more aware of the plight of London's poor. In the mid-1890s, at about the time he was starting his literary career, he had frequently left his flat on Victoria Street and taken his own excursions through the slums, amazed and angered by what he saw. A few years later, while "among the sparrows in the Champs-Élysées," he had struck up a friendship with a colorful Belgian vagabond, Clermont, with whom he corresponded for years and upon whom he modeled Ferrand. Through Clermont, wrote Galsworthy in 1932, "the world of failures, of the rolling stones, the underworld became disclosed to me."

Galsworthy worked closely with Edward Garnett on the writing of *The Island Pharisees*; in fact, because of Garnett's proddings, Galsworthy utterly recast the book three times before submitting it for publication to Garnett's employer, Gerald Duckworth. In his reader's report, Garnett urged Duckworth to accept *The Island Pharisees*, calling it "a really clever criticism of modern society—a criticism that nobody has yet made so ably." But Duckworth, pointing to the poor sales of *Jocelyn* and *Villa Rubein*, rejected the manuscript, which Joseph Conrad then successfully recommended to his own publisher, William Heinemann. The *Athenaeum* proclaimed *The Island Pharisees* an honest, subtle, and sometimes funny satire, but the *Nation* thought it nothing but a harangue full of "cheap cynicism" and "unconvincing psychology." Other reviews described the novel as too moralistic and too full of boring, predictable characters.

Still, with Garnett's encouragement, Galsworthy pressed on with another novel that would not only blast the upper middle class for its materialism and social apathy but would once again dramatize the agony of lovers who risk the execration of that bourgeois world by breaking social conventions to achieve romantic fulfillment. This was *The Man of Property* (1906), which is set in London and its suburbs in 1886.

Galsworthy spent over two years revising and restructuring *The Man of Property*, often in order to accommodate Garnett's suggestions—or, more frequently, those of Ada. As Dudley Barker notes, Ada virtually stood at her husband's side as he completed *The Man of Property*, "discussing with him every word, every incident, every motive of character; and necessarily, discussing it from the point of view of the woman who knew she was the model for Irene, and whose life was, obliquely, being argued."

Irene is the wife of "flat-shouldered, clean-shaven, flat-cheeked, flat-waisted" Soames Forsyte, a solicitor and prolific investor—"the man of property." Like most of the members of his large, nouveau riche London family, the thirty-one-year-old Soames is opportunistic, arrogant, and mili-

tantly unsentimental. Soames is unable to fully appreciate Irene, who exudes warmth, sweetness, and sensuality; he loves her, but tends to think of her as another piece of property—a portable, highly coveted work of art. Irene loathes Soames and eventually leaves him for Philip Bosinney, the gifted but impecunious architect who has been overseeing the construction of Soames's country mansion. In due course, Soames succeeds in financially ruining Bosinney, who later, in a distracted state after hearing that Soames has asserted his claim to Irene by raping her, is run over in London traffic. Soames also succeeds in breaking Irene, who, after Bosinney's death, is chillingly depicted as "huddled" into the sofa. With nowhere to go, she is pathetically "caged" once again with Soames.

The correlative plot in *The Man of Property* focuses on Old Jolyon Forsyte and his poignant attempts to reestablish intimacy with his son, Young Jolyon, Soames's cousin. Some years earlier, Young Jolyon had horrified the cold-blooded Forsytes by surrendering to honest passion and marrying a mere governess. Unlike the other Forsytes, the two Jolyons are for the most part sympathetically drawn. Young Jolyon, an amateur watercolorist, is blessed with what Galsworthy says is that rarest of all Forsyte traits—the ability to appreciate beauty. Old Jolyon (who is modeled in part on Galsworthy's father) is capable of "tenderness" and "gaiety."

The Man of Property is, on the whole, the most acidic of all Galsworthy's novels: he skewers the Forsytes and displays them pinned and wriggling on the wall. At one point, Soames is described as "carrying his nose with that aforesaid appearance of 'sniff,' as though despising an egg which he could not digest." Elsewhere, soon after Galsworthy describes the Forsytes' greed and usuriousness, he points out that of course they are all members of the Church of England, and even "paid for their pews, thus expressing in the most practical form their sympathy with the teachings of Christ."

Some reviewers were troubled not only by the causticity of *The Man of Property* but by its frank treatment of marital warfare; the *Spectator* said that the novel's "repellent details" rendered it "unacceptable for general reading." But its sales proved steady and brisk, particularly among university students, who, throughout the first decade of the twentieth century, proved receptive to a number of books which savaged the fixations of their parents' generation—books such as Samuel Butler's *The Way of All Flesh* (1903) and Edmund Gosse's *Father and Son* (1907). Thus, wrote Galsworthy in 1924,

Galsworthy (second from left) with fellow playwrights J. M. Barrie and George Bernard Shaw, and producer Harley Granville Barker (photo by E. O. Hoppé)

with *The Man of Property* "my name was made; my literary independence assumed; and my income steadily swollen."

Galsworthy added to his reputation and income when his first completed play, *The Silver Box* (1909), triumphantly debuted at London's Court Theatre on 25 September 1906, just six months after the publication of *The Man of Property*. Produced by Harley Granville-Barker, *The Silver Box* aims to expose a cynical judicial process that inevitably accommodates the rich and the powerful. An unemployed workman is sentenced to a month's hard labor so that the debauched son of a wealthy member of Parliament can escape punishment and the besmirching of the family name. In subsequent plays, Galsworthy again focused on the injustices of the British legal system—perhaps most notably in *Justice* (1910), which dramatizes the horrors that befall a pathetic office clerk sentenced to solitary confinement for doctoring a check. *Justice* proved so potent and so popular that it prompted Home Secretary Winston Churchill to initiate a series of prison reforms.

Over the next twenty-five years Galsworthy wrote at least twenty-five plays, many of which were

successfully produced. Indeed, it is probably safe to say that until the publication of *The Forsyte Saga* in the early 1920s, his fame owed more to his drama than to his fiction. Galsworthy was often described by the critics of his time as a member of the Ibsen-inspired "Theater of Ideas" into which Harley Granville-Barker, George Bernard Shaw, and St. John Hankin were also loosely grouped. Like them, Galsworthy placed a premium on "realism" and dealt with controversial social issues. In *Strife* (1910), he portrayed the tensions and ironies generated by a long, bitter labor dispute at a rural tin plate factory. In what has often been called his best play, *Loyalties* (1922), he sought to shed light on latent anti-Semitism within the English upper crust.

By 1907 Galsworthy had grown uneasy with his reputation as a "revolutionary" and had begun not only to adopt a less acerbic tone in his fiction but to depict more scrupulously upper-class virtue as well as upper-class vice. In *The Country House* (1907), he depicts the tradition-drunk Horace Pendyce as the very symbol of social reaction. Like his spaniel John, "a dog of conservative instincts," Pendyce begins "barking and showing his teeth" at "the approach of any strange thing." But Pendyce's wife, Margery, is a bastion of compassion and common sense.

In *Fraternity* (1909), Galsworthy continued his fictional analysis of the British class system, this time by overtly intermingling characters from the upper class with characters from the slums. Basically, *Fraternity* focuses on the liberal-minded, middle-aged novelist Hilary Dallison and his involvement with Ivy Barton, a slum girl who once modeled for his wife Bianca, a painter. Dallison has not felt a twinge of erotic desire for Bianca for years, but at the mere sound of Ivy's voice he can experience "a sensation as if his bones had been turned to butter." Dallison woos Ivy and wins her love; but in the end, he is unable to commit himself to "the little model" because his attraction to her electric sexuality is checked by his squeamishness in the face of her "traditions, customs, life." Dallison, then, is for Galsworthy typical of his class: he is paralytically self-conscious and terrified of deviating from propriety. But he is not an entirely unsympathetic figure. Unlike the Soames Forsyte depicted in *A Man of Property,* he does have a social conscience of sorts, and he is at least somewhat sensitive to beauty. One reviewer suggested that *Fraternity* proved that Galsworthy's "class hatred had gone mad." In fact, as a more perceptive critic noted with surprise, there is throughout the book "a leaven of humanitarianism."

In his 1923 preface to the Manaton Edition of *The Country House,* Galsworthy explains his belief that "birth, property, position" result from "luck," and that to assume otherwise is simply "ridiculous." "If those who had luck behaved as if they knew it," he argues, "the chances of revolution would sink to zero." These hardly radical notions are at the center of Galsworthy's political philosophy and inform such works as *The Country House* and *Fraternity.* Galsworthy admitted to "a temperamental dislike, not to say horror, of complacency." But like many nineteenth-century gentleman liberals before him, he backed social evolution, not revolution. As he put it elsewhere, "If my work has any mission, it is only a plea for proportion, and for sympathy and understanding between man and man."

Galsworthy himself was remarkably generous and for years donated huge sums to charities designed to help the poor and to numerous groups devoted to such causes as slaughterhouse reform and the abolition of vivisection. Of course, he was wealthy enough to be heroically philanthropic and still live quite comfortably. For years he and Ada kept a residence in London—most notably, from

Galsworthy on his horse, Peggy, at Wingstone, his home in the Devon village of Manaton

1918 on, at Grove Lodge in the London suburb of Hampstead—as well as one in the Devon village of Manaton. They also spent a good deal of time traveling on the Continent and elsewhere. They journeyed to the United States on several occasions, once going as far west as Santa Barbara; they also toured South Africa and Brazil.

Yet every morning, wherever he was, Galsworthy religiously picked up his J-nib and wrote. Between 1910 and 1915 he completed six plays, three novels, and a book of reminiscences. The best of these undistinguished novels is perhaps *The Dark Flower* (1913), which Galsworthy described as an attempt to render the "psychology and the atmosphere of passion." To do so, he follows the sculptor Mark Lennan from young adulthood through middle age, focusing on his love life. At one point, Lennan finds himself desperately in love with his tutor's wife; at another, with Olive Cramier, a woman who—like Ada in her relationship with

Arthur Galsworthy—feels imprisoned by her marriage. Later, when Lennan is forty-seven and contentedly married, he finds himself enamored of Nell Dromore, the lissome, "fiery" eighteen-year-old daughter of an old college friend. Finally, Lennan realizes that his faithful and devoted wife—not Nell—deserves his allegiance, and—more painfully—that he has reached the stage in life at which he must say "good-bye" to "the wild, the passionate, the new," to that "aching" which "never quite dies in a man's heart."

Many reviewers praised *The Dark Flower* for its lyricism, its gusto; but others thought it morbid, mawkish, or plainly immoral. When Sir Arthur Quiller-Couch, writing for the *Daily Mail,* called *The Dark Flower* "fatuous" and "sordid," Galsworthy answered him in a letter which reveals that, eight years after his marriage, he was still quite touchy about the subjects of adultery and divorce: "You can never have looked first hand into the eyes of an unhappy marriage, of a marriage whose soul has gone or never was there, of a marriage that lives on the meanest of all diets, the sense of property, and the sense of convention. . . . My gorge rises within

Margaret Morris, the dancer with whom Galsworthy had an apparently platonic relationship in 1911 (courtesy of Mr. Rudolf Sauter)

me when I encounter that false glib view that the vow is everything, that people do better to go on living together (for nothing else *is* marriage) when one of them, or both, sicken at the other."

It has long been assumed that in describing Lennan's affair with Olive Cramier, Galsworthy gave one of his most exact accounts of his affair with Ada. It is now also known that Nell owed a great deal to Margaret Morris, a beautiful young dancer with whom Galsworthy had an intense but apparently platonic affair in 1911. In her 1967 memoir, Morris wrote of being "startled" by the accuracy with which Galsworthy, in *The Dark Flower,* "quoted almost word for word whole passages of dialogue that actually took place between us." As Galsworthy informed Quiller-Couch, "passion" is "that blind force which sweeps upon us out of the dark and turns us pretty well as it will."

Upon the outbreak of the First World War, Galsworthy began to donate all of his literary earn-

Grove Lodge, Galsworthy's home in Hampstead

Galsworthy in 1911 (photo by E. O. Hoppé)

bedridden soldiers. In April 1918 he assumed editorship of *Reveille,* a journal devoted largely to providing disabled soldiers with information about retraining and rehabilitation. With Galsworthy at its helm, *Reveille* had no trouble attracting pieces from such writers as Conrad, Thomas Hardy, J. M. Barrie, and Ralph Mottram.

The war utterly absorbed Galsworthy and, as his diary shows, depressed him continually. In 1918, in what he called "a revenge of the nerves," he dashed off *The Burning Spear* (1919)—a "comedic satire" and the most curious of all his books. Published under the pseudonym A. R. P-M, *The Burning Spear* features a quixotic hero, John Lavender, who is normally a middle-aged suburbanite of "gentle disposition." But Lavender's wits become "somewhat addled from reading the writings and speeches of public men." As a result, he turns into a Hun-baiting jingoist who stumps the country for the Ministry of Propagation, retching forth the political and journalistic clichés he has fed upon for the past five years. In his preface to a 1923 edition of *The Burning Spear,* Galsworthy underlines his moral: "Was it not bad enough to have to bear the dreads and strains and griefs of the war without having to read day by day the venomous or nonsensical stuff which began pouring from tongues and pens soon after the war began and never ceased till months after the war stopped?" No doubt because his brother-in-law Georg Sauter had been interned throughout the war, Galsworthy found the constant, gleeful "insult to the enemy" especially hard to take.

The second of Galsworthy's books to be completed in the year of the Armistice was *Saint's Progress* (1919), a "legitimate" novel. It evokes the atmosphere of both the battlefield and the home front, and its tone is rather dark. But because *Saint's Progress* is free of the overwrought, perfumed prose style that characterizes much of Galsworthy's work published between 1910 and 1920, it is—like the rest of his later fiction—eminently readable. Its central character is a fifty-year-old Anglican priest, Edward Pierson, whose equanimity is repeatedly tested by Noel, his passionate and eager daughter of eighteen. The earnest Pierson is in some ways a sympathetic figure; but, as Galsworthy makes clear, he has spent too many years suppressing his own "devil of wild feeling" in order to adhere to dogma, and as a result is pathetically prone to misunderstand the sexually impulsive but noble-hearted Noel.

In a later preface to *Saint's Progress,* Galsworthy pointed out that Pierson was a "symbol of the

ings directly to the war effort; his diary reveals that he had already contributed over a thousand pounds to various relief agencies by early August 1914. Indeed, his novel *Beyond,* a monotonous work describing another Ada-like heroine's miseries and ecstasies, was cranked out simply for the healthy sum it yielded in American serial rights—a sum immediately turned over to a soldiers' fund. Galsworthy gave of his time as well as his money to help with the war effort. From the start of the war to its end, he turned out countless "appeal" letters that were run in the popular press: letters, as Ada later remembered, "for refugees, for camp libraries, for vegetables for the fleet, for cigarettes to soldiers, for London horses to be better fed, for Belgians to have a good Christmas dinner. . . ." He spent several months during the winter of 1916-1917 at a military hospital in France providing Swedish massage to

English Church left somewhat high and dry by the receding waters of orthodox faith." The "ebbing" of faith in "orthodox religion" did not pain Galsworthy, who insisted that, like Pierson, the church had for too long "tried to command instead of being content to serve." He thought Christianity true only in "essence," not in fact. He hints at his own religious philosophy near the end of *Saint's Progress* in a scene which shows Pierson, now an army chaplain during the Great War, trying to comfort a dying young soldier. Pierson reminds the boy that he is going to God, and the boy responds with nothing more than "a smile of doubt, of stoic acquiescence." Pierson interprets that smile to mean "Waste no breath on me—you cannot help. Who knows—who knows? I have no hope, no faith; but I am adventuring." And Pierson is horrified. Was it possible, he wonders, to go through life and to confront death "uncertain, yet undaunted"? "Was that, then," he asks himself, "the uttermost truth, was faith a smaller thing?" For Galsworthy, a humanist and agnostic, the answer to both questions was yes.

During the summer of 1918, Galsworthy first conceived of what he hoped would become "the most sustained and considerable piece of fiction of our generation at least": a trilogy based on *The Man of Property* that would follow Soames and certain other Forsytes through the opening decades of the twentieth century. He immediately began work on "The Indian Summer of a Forsyte," the short story which links *The Man of Property* to its sequels, *In Chancery* (1920) and *To Let* (1921). In the beautifully shaped "Indian Summer," the dying Old Jolyon Forsyte strikes up a curious friendship with Irene, whose ill-treatment by Soames has moved him to pity and—as is revealed in *In Chancery*—to provide her with an annuity upon which she can live in France, beyond Soames's reach.

The Soames depicted in *In Chancery* is well into his forties and obsessed with producing an heir. To this end, he divorces Irene and marries Annette Lamotte, the daughter of a Soho restaurant proprietress. But to Soames's disappointment, Annette presents him with a daughter, Fleur. Irene, meanwhile, marries Young Jolyon, by whom she has a son, Jon—the heir Soames will never have.

To Let, which picks up in 1920, is basically the story of how Fleur and Jon fall in love and thus complicate the lives of Soames and Irene, who remain bitterly estranged. Eventually, Soames agrees to sanction Fleur's marriage to Jon. But Jolyon reluctantly writes Jon a letter explaining why Irene would be "utterly destroyed" by Jon's marriage to the daughter of a man who had, twenty years ear-

lier, caused her immeasurable pain. Marry Fleur, writes Jolyon to Jon, and "your children . . . would be the grandchildren of Soames, as much as of your mother, of a man who once owned your mother as a man might own a slave." Jon withdraws his proposal, and a depressed Fleur, "on the rebound," marries Michael Mont, a member of an old-line, landowning family and a future baronet.

When it appeared in one volume in May 1925, the acclaim that greeted *The Forsyte Saga* convinced Galsworthy that he had finally produced his "passport" to "the shores of permanence." Critics praised the trilogy for its sweep and control and proclaimed Galsworthy a modern Thackeray. The book also brought Galsworthy a fortune in royalties. Within months of its publication, over two million copies of *The Forsyte Saga* were sold in Britain and America. Forty-two years later, after being adapted for a television serial by the British Broadcasting Company, *The Forsyte Saga* was back on the British best-seller lists. In late 1969, *The Forsyte Saga* was broadcast in the United States by the National Educational Television network and became the first successful dramatic series ever broadcast on what was soon to be renamed the Public Broadcasting System. As a result of the N.E.T. series, paperback sales of *The Forsyte Saga* soared throughout North America.

Undoubtedly, much of the popularity of *The Forsyte Saga* has stemmed from the public's fascination with Soames, whose role in *The Man of Property* had assured him an exalted place among modern literature's most unsavory characters. In his first incarnation, Soames was basically an easy-to-hate caricature—perhaps the "classical embodiment of the Freudian anal-erotic type, complete with hoarding instinct," as the critic Bernard Bergonzi described him. But as *The Forsyte Saga* progresses, Soames becomes a more intricate, surprising character, even if taxes and interest rates still worry him greatly. By the middle of *To Let,* it is apparent that Soames's self-absorption has lessened as a result of his love for Fleur—that, in the wake of his many disappointments, he has mellowed.

The favorable treatment of Soames continues throughout *A Modern Comedy* (1929), another trilogy of Forsyte novels linked together by a pair of short stories, "A Silent Wooing" and "Passers By." In *The White Monkey* (1924), Soames emerges as a businessman of unusual integrity when he abjures the shady practices of a London insurance company whose board he has joined. In *The Silver Spoon* (1926), Soames dramatically expels from a party at Fleur's house the hedonistic heiress Marjorie Ferrar

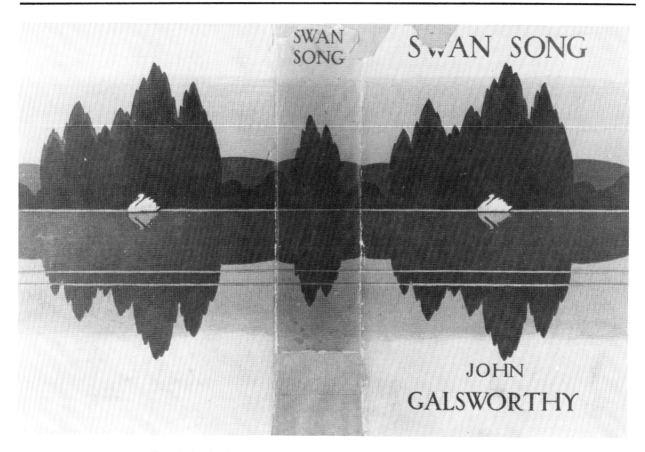

Dust jacket for Galsworthy's novel in which Soames Forsyte meets his end

after hearing her call Fleur a "born little snob." Ferrar takes Soames to court, where he is vindicated. In *Swan Song* (1928), Soames sacrifices his own life rescuing Fleur from a house fire she has accidentally caused. Quite literally, the villain becomes a hero.

Throughout the episodic *A Modern Comedy,* Soames is allowed interior monologues which reveal him to be disarmingly sensitive—even vulnerable. In "Passers By," the seventy-year-old Soames sees Irene for the first time in years and finds himself neither bitter nor angry but sad and full of regret. Automatically, he begins replaying long-buried images of Irene and of "her body crumpled and crushed into the sofa in the dark" on the night of Bosinney's death. "There sits a woman," he realizes, "that I have never known."

Soames is often visited by crystalline recollections of his youth—when his mother called him "Summy"—and by thoughts of his inevitable demise. In *Swan Song,* Soames's meditations on death closely parallel those of Old Jolyon Forsyte in "An Indian Summer of a Forsyte." Like Old Jolyon,

Soames becomes aware that he has been a bit too compulsive in his pursuit of money and property. One afternoon, as he sits in a postprandial glow, smoking a cigar and staring out the window, it occurs to him that, as an adult, he has utterly forgotten about the natural world. "With age," he realizes, "one suffered from the feeling that one might have enjoyed things more. Cows for instance, and rooks, and good smells."

In *The Silver Spoon,* in one of the most affecting passages in all of Galsworthy's fiction, Soames—the man who once "elbowed" his way everywhere—stops along the roadside to tend to a pig struck by his car. The sight of the dying pig, snorting and grunting in a ditch, stirs "a sort of fellow feeling" in Soames and moves him to meditate once more upon death. He resolves to make plans that will insure his burial in some unmarked corner, in the shade of "an apple-tree or something." "The less people remembered him," Soames decides, "the better."

In fact, however, when it was revealed with the July 1928 publication of *Swan Song* that Soames had been killed off, his death was front-page news in several London newspapers. With this kind of publicity, it is not surprising that *Swan Song* quickly went through several editions and that *A Modern Comedy* was a prodigious success when it appeared as an omnibus volume a year later.

The change in Soames's character reflects the change in Galsworthy's own attitude toward English society. He was in his mid-fifties when he began *A Modern Comedy* and had come through the Great War with his sense of citizenship strengthened. He was happily married and had long since become successful enough to settle scores with those among his friends and relatives who once thought him dotty for thinking that he could write novels. Indeed, throughout the 1920s Galsworthy was easily England's most honored author. In 1921 he was elected the first president of the P.E.N. Club, the writers' society that sought world harmony through communication. Between 1920 and 1931 he was awarded honorary Litt.D. degrees by Manchester, Dublin, Sheffield, Cambridge, Oxford, and Princeton universities. In June 1929 he was entered into the Order of Merit.

Ada Galsworthy in 1929 (photo by Fayer, Vienna & London)

Galsworthy leaving St. James's Palace after receiving the Order of Merit in 1929

The authorial voice that informs Galsworthy's later works is often that of the humane but pragmatic public figure: the ex-angry young man turned elder statesman who is eager to offer the breadth of his knowledge. In *A Modern Age*, for example, Michael Mont's parliamentary career—which intersects with the "General Strike" of 1926—enabled Galsworthy to call attention to certain political schemes he favored, including those of Sir James Foggart, who argued that a policy of setting up underemployed young Englishmen in the dominions would reduce the number of British slums while increasing the number of staunch Britons around the world. In *Maid in Waiting* (1931), the first volume of his final trilogy, *End of the Chapter* (1934), Galsworthy again allows Mr. and Mrs. Hilary Cherrell—Michael Mont's aunt and uncle—to champion, as they did in *Swan Song,* the utilization

Bury House, the Sussex mansion Galsworthy purchased in 1926 as a home for his nephew and a country retreat for himself

of the unemployed in a "National Slum Clearance Scheme" that would, as Mrs. Cherrell puts it, "kill the two birds with one stone."

End of the Chapter, which focuses on various members of the Cherrell family, was written largely at Bury House—a fifteen-bedroom Sussex mansion which Galsworthy purchased in 1926 as a residence for his nephew Rudolph Sauter and his wife, and as a country retreat for himself. Galsworthy employed a cook, several maids, and a squad of gardeners at Bury. Predictably, Squire Galsworthy was consistently kind to his employees. He gave them all lifetime security with higher-than-scale wages and for some he built homes in the nearby village.

No doubt Bury House, with its formal gardens and surrounding acreage, provided Galsworthy with an especially conducive atmosphere in which to construct the elegant and civilized world of the Cherrells, to whom Fleur is related through her marriage to Michael Mont. "Seated" since 1217 at Condaford Grange at Oxfordshire, the Cherrells represent—as Galsworthy himself discreetly put it—"the older type of family with more tradition

and sense of service than the Forsytes." According to Galsworthy, this type of family, "much neglected" in modern fiction, deserved scrutiny precisely because it was "dying out."

Galsworthy does not apotheosize the Cherrells, but his treatment of them and of their vanishing world is a good deal less than hostile. James Gindin, one of Galsworthy's most eloquent critics, has suggested that by inventing the Cherrells, Galsworthy "wrote the family he wished he had had, one of gentle anthropologists and radical churchmen who could change and care, one in which aristocracy was not a matter of striving or class superiority, but one of calm responsibility and socialistic concern."

Dinny Cherrell, the central character throughout the trilogy, is certainly sympathetically drawn: she is perhaps, as Catherine Dupré has suggested, "Galsworthy's final portrait of an ideal woman, combining the proud dignity of Ada with the youthful vitality and optimism he had met with in Margaret Morris." In *Maid in Waiting,* Dinny saves her brother Hubert from extradition to Bolivia on a trumped-up murder charge. In *Flow-*

Galsworthy at work on Maid in Waiting, *the first volume of the trilogy* The End of the Chapter

ering Wilderness (1932), she comforts her lover, Wilfred Desert, a well-known agnostic poet. Desert is greatly disliked by some in Dinny's circle because years earlier, while stationed in the Middle East, he had refused to die "for a gesture that I don't believe in." At the point of a pistol, he had renounced Christianity and had pretended to admit to the truth of the Islamic faith. In *One More River* (1933), Dinny supports her sister Clare, who is regularly abused by her husband, a horsewhip-wielding sadist.

Flowering Wilderness is probably the best of these novels—and is certainly one of the better novels in the Galsworthy canon. The "burning tension" and the "classic rigour" that Alec Fréchet finds displayed in *Flowering Wilderness* derive in part from the fact that the novel is refreshingly free of long stretches of ornate prose and contains no meandering subplots. Desert is especially convincing as the intense young veteran whose experience in the war left him, as Dinny puts it, "bitter about the way lives are thrown away, simply spilled out like water at the orders of people who don't know what they're about"; who has both "contempt for convention" and yet enough residual respect for the customs of his class to be wounded deeply when the press and his former comrades accuse him of cowardice and betrayal.

In the *New York Times* of 13 November 1932, Lionel Stevenson proclaimed *Flowering Wilderness* a finer book than *The Man of Property;* but Stevenson

Dust jacket for separate publication of the first volume of Galsworthy's End of the Chapter *trilogy*

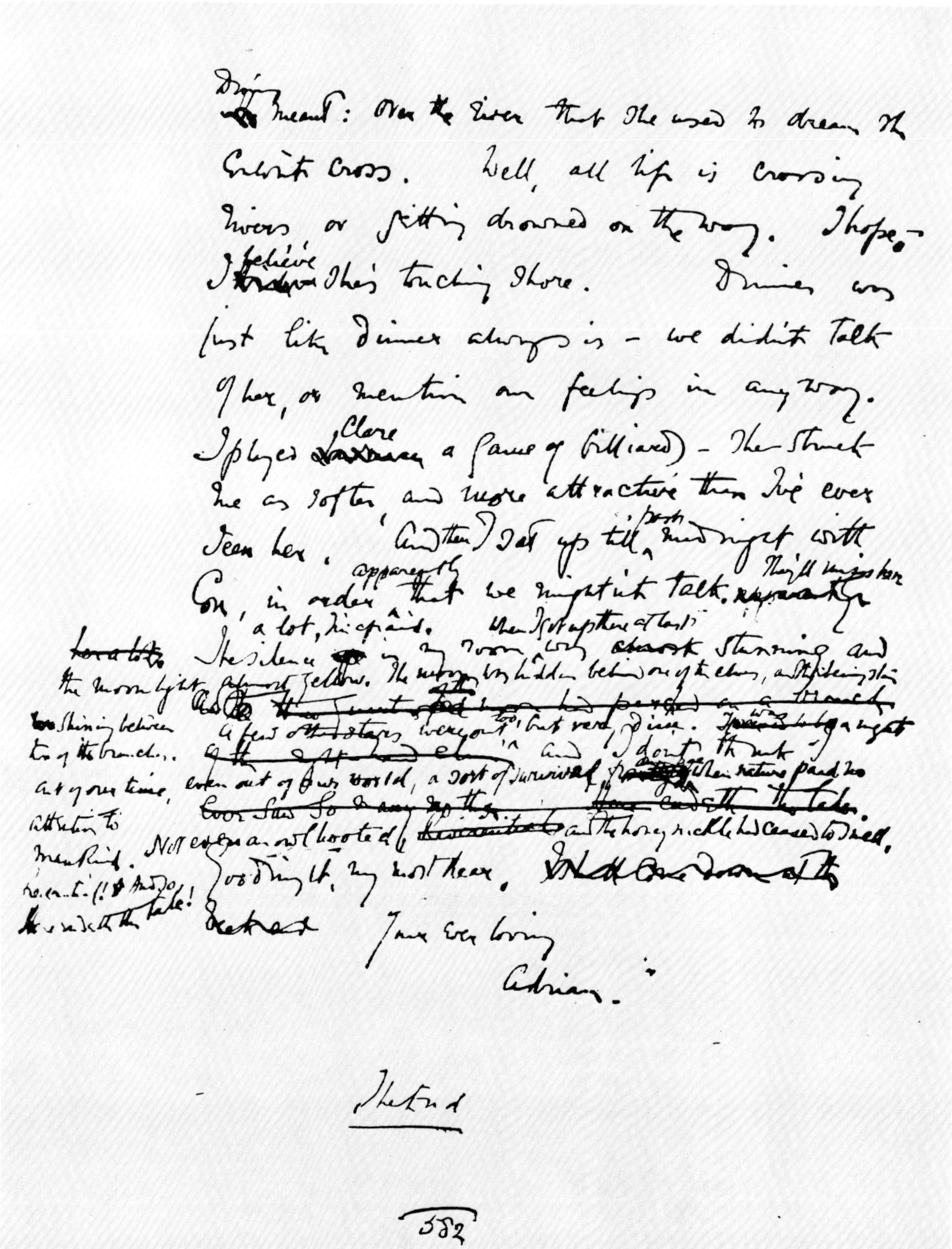

Last page of manuscript for Over the River

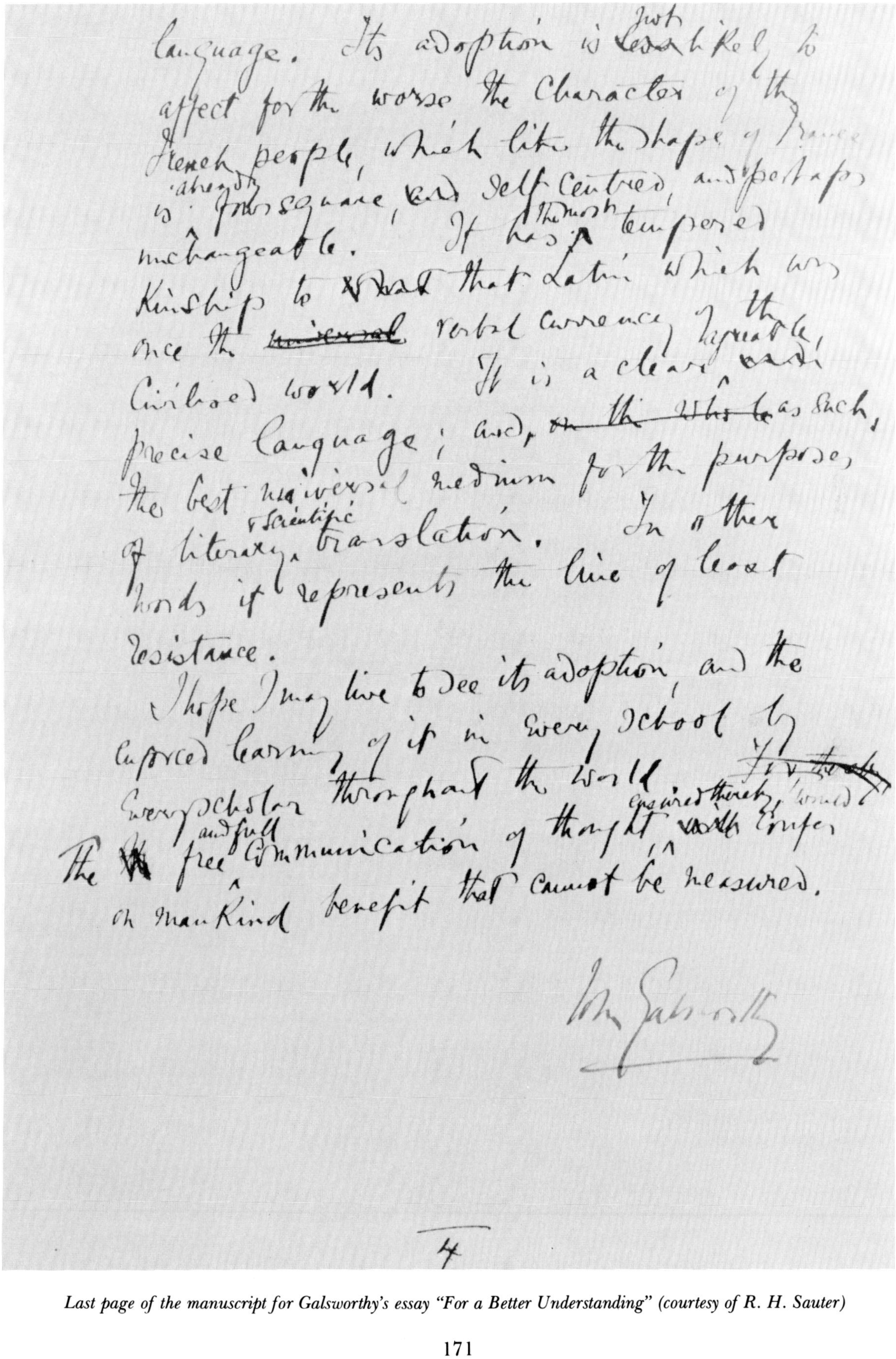

language. Its adoption is just likely to affect for the worse the Character of the French people, which like the shape of France is already four-square, and self-centred, and perhaps unchangeable. It has the most tempered kinship to that Latin which was once the verbal currency figurative, civilised world. It is a clear, precise language; and, as such, the best universal medium for the purpose of literary & scientific translation. In other words it represents the line of least resistance.

I hope I may live to see its adoption, and the enforced learning of it in every school by every scholar throughout the world and full free communication of thought on mankind benefit that cannot be measured.

John Galsworthy

4

Last page of the manuscript for Galsworthy's essay "For a Better Understanding" (courtesy of R. H. Sauter)

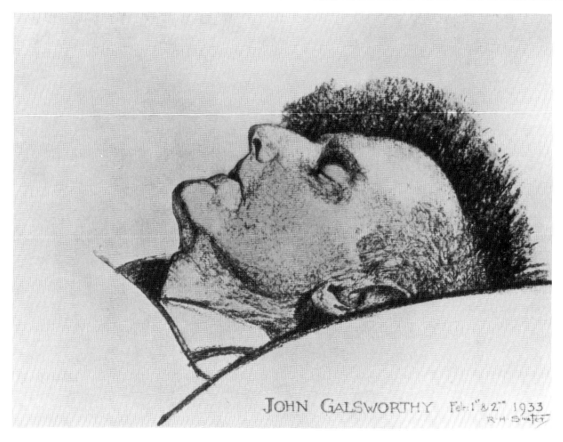

Galsworthy after his death, as sketched by his nephew, Rudolf Sauter

was by then a well-known Galsworthy supporter. Most English and American reviewers regarded *Flowering Wilderness* politely—sometimes warmly—but without real empressement. By the early 1930s Galsworthy's standing within Anglo-American literary circles had become a bit shaky, even though— or perhaps because—his popularity among the reading public had soared. After Galsworthy died of a brain tumor in January 1933, just two months after winning the Nobel Prize, foreign critics hailed his work with a reverence that probably embarrassed many of their English colleagues. One Argentine reviewer favorably compared Galsworthy to Jane Austen and Henry James; an Italian eulogist called him another Proust.

In England, Galsworthy's reputation had been dealt its first truly damaging jolt by Virginia Woolf in her witty 1924 monograph, *Mr. Bennett and Mrs. Brown.* Like Arnold Bennett and H. G. Wells, Galsworthy—argued Woolf—was a well-meaning but superficial writer whose novels were full of predictable, stereotypical characters. Four years later, in an equally influential essay, D. H. Lawrence described Galsworthy as a cynical vulgarian who

poured "a sauce of sentimental savouriness" over everything he wrote, including *The Man of Property.* The "sentimentalising of Old Jolyon Forsyte," complained Lawrence, "fatally blemished" *The Man of Property,* which otherwise "has the element of a very great novel, a very great satire."

But as Galsworthy's career was being reexamined in the 1920s and early 1930s, other British and American critics, while admitting to his weaknesses, called attention to some of his strengths and, in doing so, helped to shape the opinions of later critics. In the *English Journal* of May 1925, J. B. Priestley called Galsworthy a brilliant "critic and historian of contemporary social developments" who managed to forever capture "the established if not decaying middle classes of Edward VII and George V," just as Balzac had immortalized "the insurgent bourgeois of Louis Philippe." Galsworthy lacked Balzac's "creative force and demonic imagination" but was still able to produce his "lively" representation of a period while maintaining "a high standard of sanity, of dignity, and of wit."

Joseph J. Reilly observed in the *Bookman* in 1930 that Galsworthy's mind was essentially "feminine"—a quality which revealed itself in his "smooth, graceful, supple" style. With a "quicker sensitiveness" and a "deeper pity" than his contemporaries, Galsworthy "saw poverty and its attendant evils not primarily as super-scientific questions like Wells . . . not as things to be triumphed over by an imagination, a fairy godmother, or a happy turn of fortune like Barrie, but first of all as objects of human sympathy and after that as intolerable effects of a social and economic situation over which well-to-do Britons must be answerable."

Still, it is not surprising that Lawrence and Woolf should have so roundly thrashed Galsworthy. To advocates of an artistic revolution, he was an antique: an artistic Forsyte unashamedly sticking to "old-fashioned" literary forms. When, in 1920, a young man had asked Galsworthy what writers an ambitious novelist-to-be should read, he was not told to consult Joyce, Mansfield, or even Conrad; read Dickens, instructed Galsworthy, and Stevenson, "and above all, *W. H. Hudson*." In 1915, in a preface to *Green Mansions*, Galsworthy had called Hudson "the most valuable [writer] our age possesses."

Moreover, as John Batchelor notes, Galsworthy's "real strength" was for the sort of "social comedy" he demonstrated in *The Man of Property* and in the plays *The Silver Box*, *Strife*, and *Justice*. These works make their points cleanly, confidently, "without resorting to Shavian 'arias.' " But unfortunately, Galsworthy "did not know his own talent, and was determined to be, like Wells and Shaw, a polymath and prophet, a critic of the age." The result was that he created too many humorless, propagandistic works populated by flat characters who stand too baldly for good or for bad.

But as Galsworthy bibliographers Earl and H. Ray Stevens suggest, one can better assess Galsworthy's stature once one is willing to view him as "the last major Victorian writer." Like many of the very best Victorian novelists, Galsworthy was sometimes facile, prolix, and didactic; but like them, he was also able repeatedly to construct well-built narratives and to invent characters—such as Soames Forsyte and Wilfred Desert—who are subtle and complex enough to intrigue modern readers.

Letters:

Letters from John Galsworthy, 1900-1932, edited by Edward Garnett (London: Cape, 1934; New York: Scribners, 1934);

Margaret Morris, *My Galsworthy Story Including 67*

Hitherto Unpublished Letters (London: Owen, 1967);

John Galsworthy's Letters to Leon Lion, edited by Asher Boldon Wilson (The Hague: Mouton, 1968).

Bibliographies:

H. V. Marrot, *A Bibliography of the Works of John Galsworthy* (London: Mathews & Marrot/New York: Scribners, 1928);

Earl E. Stevens and H. Ray Stevens, *John Galsworthy: An Annotated Bibliography of Writings about Him* (De Kalb: Northern Illinois University Press, 1980).

Biographies:

H. V. Marrot, *The Life and Letters of John Galsworthy* (London: Heinemann, 1935; New York: Scribners, 1936);

M. E. Reynolds, *Memories of John Galsworthy by His Sister* (London: Hale, 1936; New York: Stokes, 1937);

R. H. Mottram, *For Some We Loved: An Intimate Portrait of John and Ada Galsworthy* (London: Hutchinson, 1956);

Dudley Barker, The Man of Principle: A View of John Galsworthy (London: Heinemann, 1963; New York: Stein & Day, 1963);

Rudolf Sauter, *Galsworthy the Man: An Intimate Portrait* (London: Owen, 1967);

Catherine Dupré, *John Galsworthy: A Biography* (London: Collins, 1976; New York: Coward, McCann & Geoghegan, 1976);

James Gindin, *The English Climate: An Excursion into a Biography of John Galsworthy* (Ann Arbor: University of Michigan Press, 1979).

References:

John Batchelor, *The Edwardian Novelists* (London: Duckworth, 1982), pp. 183-202;

William Bellamy, *The Novels of Wells, Bennett and Galsworthy: 1890-1910* (London: Routledge & Kegan Paul, 1971; Totowa, N.J.: Barnes & Noble, 1971);

R. H. V. Bloor, *The English Novel from Chaucer to Galsworthy* (London: Nicholson & Watson, 1935);

Henry Seidel Canby, "Galsworthy: An Estimate," *Saturday Review of Literature,* 9 (18 March 1933): 485-487;

Ford Madox Ford, "Galsworthy," *American Mercury,* 37 (April 1936): 448-459;

Alec Fréchet, *John Galsworthy: A Reassessment* (Totowa, N.J.: Barnes & Noble, 1982);

Richard Gill, *Happy Rural Seat: The English Country*

House and the Literary Imagination (New Haven & London: Yale University Press, 1972);

David Leon Higdon, "John Galsworthy's *The Man of Property:* 'now in the natural order of things,' " *English Literature in Transition,* 21 (1978): 149-157;

David Holloway, *John Galsworthy.* (London: Morgan-Grampion, 1968);

Jefferson Hunter, *Edwardian Fiction* (Cambridge: Harvard University Press, 1982);

Richard M. Kain, "Galsworthy, the Last Victorian Liberal," *Madison Quarterly,* 4 (1944): 84-94;

Sheila Kaye-Smith, *John Galsworthy* (New York: Holt, 1916);

Frank Kermode, "The English Novel, circa 1907," in Reuben A. Brower, ed., *Twentieth Century Literature in Retrospect* (Cambridge: Harvard University Press, 1971), pp. 45-64;

D. H. Lawrence, "John Galsworthy," in Edgell Rickword, ed., *Scrutinies by Various Writers* (London: Wishart, 1928);

J. D. Leavis, *Fiction and the Reading Public* (London: Chatto & Windus, 1932);

Kathryne S. McDorman, "Imperialism Debit and Credit—Some Edwardian Authors' Views," *Illinois Quarterly,* 43 (Summer 1981): 41-50;

Peter McQuitty, "The Forsyte Chronicles: A Nineteenth Century Liberal View of History," *English Literature in Transition,* 23 (1980): 99-114;

R. H. Mottram, *John Galsworthy* (London: Longmans, Green, 1953);

Herman Ould, *John Galsworthy* (London: Chapman & Hall, 1934);

Joseph John Reilly, "John Galsworthy—An Appraisal," *Bookman,* 74 (January-February 1932): 483-493;

William J. Scheick, "Chance and Impartiality: A Study Based on the Manuscript of Galsworthy's *Loyalties," Texas Studies in Language and Literature,* 17 (1975): 653-672;

Leon Schlit, *John Galsworthy: A Survey* (New York: Scribners, 1928; London: Heinemann, 1929);

Earl E. Stevens, "John Galsworthy," in Walter Kidd, ed., *British Winners of the Nobel Prize* (Norman: University of Oklahoma Press, 1973), pp. 130-167;

Harold Ray Stevens, "Galsworthy's *Fraternity:* The Closed Door and the Paralyzed Society," *English Literature in Transition,* 19 (1976): 283-298;

Walter H. R. Trumbauer, *Gerhart Hauptmann and John Galsworthy: A Parallel* (Philadelphia: University of Pennsylvania Press, 1917);

Anthony West, introduction to *The Galsworthy Reader* (New York: Scribners, 1967);

Virginia Woolf, *Mr. Bennett and Mrs. Brown* (London: Hogarth, 1924).

Papers:

Some of John Galsworthy's manuscripts and letters are held by the Bodleian Library, Oxford University; the Houghton Library, Harvard University; and the Firestone Library, Princeton University.

David Garnett

(9 March 1892-17 February 1981)

Roland Dille

SELECTED BOOKS: *Dope-Darling: A Story of Cocaine,* as Leda Burke (London: Laurie, 1919);

Lady into Fox (London: Chatto & Windus, 1922; New York: Knopf, 1923);

A Man in the Zoo (London: Chatto & Windus, 1924; New York: Knopf, 1924);

The Sailor's Return (London: Chatto & Windus, 1925; New York: Knopf, 1925);

Go She Must! (London: Chatto & Windus, 1927; New York: Knopf, 1927);

The Old Dovecote and Other Stories (London: Mathews & Marrot, 1928);

Never Be A Bookseller (New York: Knopf, 1929; London: Chatto & Windus, 1929);

No Love (London: Chatto & Windus, 1929; New York: Knopf, 1929);

The Grasshoppers Come (London: Chatto & Windus, 1931; New York: Brewer, Warren & Putnam, 1931);

A Terrible Day (London: Jackson, 1932);

A Rabbit in the Air: Notes from a Diary Kept While

Learning to Handle an Aeroplane (London: Chatto & Windus, 1932; New York: Brewer, Warren & Putnam, 1932);

Pocahontas; or, the Nonpareil of Virginia (London: Chatto & Windus, 1933; New York: Harcourt, Brace, 1933);

Beany-Eye (London: Chatto & Windus, 1935; New York: Harcourt, Brace, 1935);

War in the Air, September 1939-May 1941 (London: Chatto & Windus, 1941; New York: Doubleday, Doran, 1941);

The Golden Echo (London: Chatto & Windus, 1953; New York: Harcourt, Brace, 1954);

Flowers of the Forest (London: Chatto & Windus, 1955; New York: Harcourt, Brace, 1956);

Aspects of Love (London: Chatto & Windus, 1955; New York: Harcourt, Brace, 1955);

A Shot in the Dark (London: Longmans, Green, 1958; Boston: Little, Brown, 1958);

A Net for Venus (London: Longmans, 1959);

The Familiar Faces (London: Chatto & Windus, 1962; New York: Harcourt, Brace & World, 1963);

Two by Two: A Story of Survival (London: Longmans, 1963; New York: Atheneum, 1964);

Ulterior Motives (London: Longmans, 1966; New York: Harcourt, Brace & World, 1967);

An Old Master and Other Stories (Tokyo: Yamaguchi Shoten, 1967);

The White-Garnett Letters, edited by David Garnett (London: Cape, 1968; New York: Viking, 1968);

First "Hippy" Revolution (Arrilos, N.M.: San Marcos, 1970);

A Clean Slate (London: Hamish Hamilton, 1971);

The Sons of the Falcon (London: Macmillan, 1972);

Plough over the Bones (London: Macmillan, 1973);

Purl and Plain and Other Stories (London: Macmillan, 1973);

The Master Cat: The True and Unexpurgated Story of Puss in Boots (London: Macmillan, 1974);

Up She Rises (London: Macmillan, 1977; New York: St. Martin's, 1977);

Great Friends: Portraits of Seventeen Writers (London: Macmillan, 1980; New York: Atheneum, 1980).

OTHER: T. E. Lawrence, *The Letters of T. E. Lawrence,* edited by Garnett (London & Toronto: Cape, 1938; New York: Doubleday, Doran, 1939); republished as *Selected Letters of T. E. Lawrence* (Westport, Conn.: Hyperion, 1979);

Henry James, *Fourteen Stories,* edited by Garnett (London: Hart Davis, 1946);

David Garnett (photo by Thomas C. Moser, Jr.)

The Novels of Thomas Love Peacock, edited by Garnett (London: Hart Davis, 1948);

The Essential T. E. Lawrence, edited by Garnett (London: Cape/New York: Dutton, 1951);

Dora de Houghton Carrington, *Carrington: Letters and Extracts from Her Diaries,* edited by Garnett (London: Cape, 1970).

TRANSLATIONS: Vincent Alfred Gressent, *The Kitchen Garden and Its Management,* translated by Garnett (London: Selwyn, Blount, 1919);

André Maurois, *A Voyage to the Island of the Articoles,* translated by Garnett (London: Cape, 1928; New York: Appleton, 1929);

T. E. Lawrence, *338171 T. E. (Lawrence of Arabia),* translated by Garnett (London: Gollancz, 1963; New York: Dutton, 1963).

It was perhaps inevitable that David Garnett should spend most of his long life as a novelist, reviewer, and editor. His father, Edward Garnett,

Garnett's parents, Edward and Constance Garnett (photo of Edward Garnett by Fred Holyer; photo of Constance Garnett by David Garnett)

for sixty years a publisher's reader, discovered, encouraged, and assisted many of the most notable and serious writers whose careers began in the early years of the century. His advice seems to have been crucial to Joseph Conrad's development as a novelist and his encouragement of the greatest importance to John Galsworthy and D. H. Lawrence. Garnett's mother, Constance Garnett, translated seventy volumes of Russian literature, making available the great body of nineteenth-century Russian novels and short stories to English writers.

David Garnett was born in Brighton, but he spent his childhood in Sussex, near Kent, where his parents had built a house far enough from London to avoid the fashionable literary life that they disliked. Garnett went to school in London and then to the Imperial College of Science and Technology in London, where he studied zoology.

Garnett had known some of the members of Bloomsbury before World War I, but none of them intimately. When the war began he joined a Quaker relief organization and spent some months in France. He returned to England a pacifist. He declared himself a conscientious objector and was allowed to choose alternative service as a farm laborer, working with Duncan Grant, the two of them living with Vanessa Bell. By the end of the war he was a member of what by then had become, self-consciously, the Bloomsbury Group.

The Golden Echo (1953), Garnett's memoirs, published after most of the members of Bloomsbury had died, is as good a portrait of the group as we have, although its three volumes were published before the age of absolute frankness about sexual matters. The reader of *The Golden Echo* learns a good deal about the friendships that held the group together, and it may be that Garnett's reticence is less distorting than the emphases supplied by the succeeding candor.

In 1921, Garnett married Ray Marshall, an artist who later illustrated his novel *Lady into Fox.* There were two sons by this marriage. He had, by the time of his marriage, become a bookseller in partnership with Francis Birrell, whom he had

Garnett's first wife, Ray Marshall Garnett

Garnett in 1923 (photo by E. O. Hoppé)

known since before the war. In 1923 Garnett and Francis Maynell founded the Nonesuch Press, and they began the publication of their much-admired books. In 1919, using the name of Leda Burke, Garnett had published *Dope-Darling: A Story of Cocaine,* which he claimed to have written deliberately badly. Now, despite his responsibilities to family and business, Garnett completed his first serious novel, *Lady into Fox,* which he had started shortly after his marriage. It was published in 1922.

Lady into Fox tells the story of Mr. Tebrick, whose wife turns into a fox. His love for her is scarcely altered by the metamorphosis and, for a long time, she too resists any change in their relationship. Eventually, however, her animal nature triumphs, and she escapes into the forest. She returns and leads him proudly to her litter; he spends the summer playing with the cubs. In the fall the hunts begin and one day, pursued by the hounds, she dashes out of the forest and leaps into his arms. But the hounds pull her down and kill her. The novel is a perfect, if minor, work in that once the initial impossibility is got past, everything that happens seems probable. Garnett's success in making the ordinary triumph over fantasy is due mostly to his style. In its simple directness, it reminded many reviewers of Defoe, and it is the style that was to serve him all his life: at once graceful and matter-

Francis Birrell, who was Garnett's partner in a London bookshop in the early 1920s (photo by Margaret Bulley)

 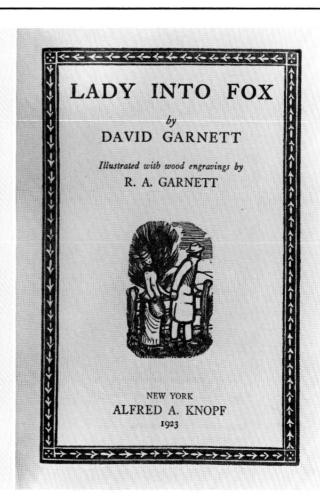

Frontispiece and title page for the American edition of the first novel published under Garnett's own name

of-fact, precise in its descriptions, and apparently effortless. *Lady into Fox* was a remarkable success. It won both the Hawthornden Prize and the James Tait Black Memorial Prize for 1923 and, without ever being a best-seller, has sold more than a half-million copies.

Garnett's next novel, *A Man in the Zoo* (1924), was a far smaller achievement. When Josephine Lackett calls her lover, John Cromartie, an animal because he wants to live with her, he arranges to be exhibited in a zoo. Thus he demonstrates that man in his natural place in the world is unencumbered by the artificialities with which society has surrounded him. Josephine is at first ashamed of the scandal he has created but finally discovers that she loves him, and the story ends happily. In *The Sailor's Return* (1925), Garnett turns to the real world of the nineteenth-century village where the villagers' humanity is tested by a sailor's attempt to settle among them with his black wife. At first things go well, but the villagers are the victims of their ignorance, and

the sailor, who dies in a fight defending his family, leaves his wife to survive as a kitchen drudge far from the African kingdom of her father.

In *Go She Must!* (1927), Anne Dunnock, the daughter of an unpopular clergyman, finds appealing but inadequate both rustic life and the beauties of nature. She goes to Paris, seeking the world of art and culture. She is happy with the world she finds, but she falls in love and marries. She and her husband, who shares her pleasure in Paris, go back to England, where he must take his place in the world of business. They go with small regrets; though Paris is an escape from a stifling life, love is more important still.

Garnett said that he thought that *No Love*, published in 1929, was his best novel. His most autobiographical novel, it is the story of two boys who live in neighboring houses. Benedict grows up in just such a home as Garnett had known, the son of agnostic, tolerant parents, easy with the freedom his parents give him. Simon's family is bound by Victorian pieties, his father determined that his son shall be successful. The two boys grow up and grow apart. Simon marries a woman he cannot love. When Simon's wife and Benedict fall in love, Benedict gives her up believing that he "had no claim on her"; but she cannot return to Simon, for, as Benedict concludes, there is "no love in his heart. He has never learned what it is from other people." It is not, perhaps, so good a novel as Garnett thought, for the contrast between the two friends is too schematic, and in neither are we aware of any emotional struggle to achieve self-knowledge. Simon surrenders his humanity without a fight and Benedict accepts his as a birthright.

If there is in much of Garnett's early work a sharp rejection of the conventional values that restrict human feeling, the judgment he makes of society is balanced by a melancholy that owes less to the losses imposed by the unthinking and the unfeeling than to a regret for death, separation, and the failure of love. Human relationships flounder in compromises with the narrow expectations and unworthy ambitions of society, but neither rural life untouched by bourgeois assumptions nor the intelligent and sophisticated rejection of those assumptions is proof against disappointment.

From 1932 to 1934, Garnett was literary editor of the *New Statesman and Nation*. During those years, and for two years thereafter, he wrote the page "Books in General," reviewing hundreds of books, although only rarely novels and poetry. The range of his interests and knowledge is remarkable. He is interested in how things are done and full of respect for people engaged in many sorts of endeavor. In an earlier novel, *The Grasshoppers Come* (1931), he described a failed attempt to set a long-distance flying record. One of the flyers survives the crash, but Garnett is not so much interested in the less-than-heroic survival as he is in flight itself. T. E. Lawrence told him that it was the only book he had read that caught the exhilaration a flyer feels.

Many of Garnett's reviews reveal his interest in the past, especially as shown in biographies and collections of letters. He is clearly less impressed by a biographer's psychological analysis than by his success in showing his subject in relation to his time. When Garnett made the life of Pocahontas into a novel, his research was obviously thorough. This, the reader feels, is how it really was. *Pocahontas* (1933) is not, however, a very successful novel, for if Garnett avoids sentimentality in his contrast of cultures, he also fails to engage us very deeply in the lives of his characters.

Garnett said later that he regretted that his

Dust jacket for Garnett's realistic novel about racial prejudice

literary journalism had kept him from writing novels. After *Beany-Eye* (1935), a moving account of an episode remembered from his childhood in which a slow-witted farm worker is driven insane by the lack of sympathy of those around him, he gave up the novel for twenty years. They were busy years. The rise of Nazism made pacifism impossible to Garnett, and before the beginning of the Second World War he had enlisted in the Royal Air Force Volunteer Reserve. Called to duty at the start of the war, he served for a year in the intelligence section and then became a planning officer and historian, writing *War in the Air* (1941), an account of the Battle of Britain. His first wife died in 1940 and in 1941 he married Angelica Bell, who was the daughter of Vanessa Bell and Duncan Grant, with whom Garnett had lived during World War I. Following the war he became a partner in the publishing house of Rupert Hart-Davis, edited a number of collections of letters and short stories, and began to put down his reminiscences. His three-volume memoir (*The Golden Echo; Flowers of the Forest*, 1955; and *The Familiar Faces*, 1962) is not only a portrait of

Angelica Bell, who became Garnett's second wife in 1941

to Sir George and Alexis, only a kind of emotional detachment, lacking the personal and loving evolvement that made Mr. Tebrick in *Lady into Fox* at once so absurd and so sympathetic a character. In *A Net for Venus* (1959) and *A Clean Slate* (1971), Garnett again celebrated urbane sexuality and the introduction of the young to a suitable sophistication in the pursuit of love.

Aspects of Love is not a negligible book, but in many of his last novels it is hard not to see Garnett as the writer of a certain kind of popular fiction, with the considerable difference made by a graceful style and a philosophic hedonism. *A Shot in the Dark* (1958), with an Italian setting, a wise bishop, communist plots, gangsters, and Dianic cults, provides almost too heavy a burden of incident for the survival of its serious contrast of reason and mysticism and its celebration of love as the real poetry of life. In *The Sons of the Falcon* (1972), Garnett writes about a Caucasian family, its feuds, its struggles with Kurds, Turks, and tribes of doubtful origin. It is an adventure story, a chronicle without the melodramatic effects of popular adventures, in which Garnett reveals the same concern for showing things as they were that he showed in *Pocahontas*. That sense of the past and the establishment of its reality underlie Garnett's last novel, *Up She Rises* (1977), a great exception to the slightness of most of his later work. It is based on the life of his great-grandmother, but it rises above the limitations imposed by the need to be truthful about real events. The heroine, the ignorant daughter of a poor Scottish crofter, teaches herself to read, marries a man above her own class, walks 500 miles to see him after he has been impressed into the navy, shares his increasingly prosperous life, and never loses her sense of her own worth. The settings, physical and social, are described with care as Garnett achieves the poetic realism that he always claimed he sought. In addition, his imaginative grasp of character here exceeds that in most of his novels. Clementina is a woman of courage, kindness, and understanding, and Garnett's appreciation of these qualities represents a more mature wisdom than does the sophisticated hedonism of many of the books of his last years.

For nearly sixty years Garnett was almost universally praised by reviewers, but critics and literary historians have found little to say about him. His reputation will rest on *Lady into Fox* and on his associations with Bloomsbury. A great deal of modern experience, public and private, lay outside his interests as a novelist; except in his final novel, he

Bloomsbury and one of the best records of literary London between the wars; it is the self-portrait of a man who writes without malice and is revealed as tolerant, wise, and full of sympathy and affection. He had described himself as a libertine, and his memoirs record, with tact and kindness, the kind of full sensual life often ascribed to Bloomsbury, but without the somewhat hysterical quality that love affairs seemed often to induce in his friends.

Aspects of Love (1955), his first novel after twenty years, is almost a personal statement of a man who looks with some pleasure at the life he has led and at what he has become. In the novel, Sir George Dillingham, a man of Garnett's age, tolerantly shares the love of Rose, a French actress, with his nephew, Alexis. Alexis is selfishly ardent, and Sir George must guide him to the higher wisdom of one who believes in passion, but not selfishly, and who accepts all and would change nothing. It is a lesson that Alexis tests in his relationship with several women, but the wisdom seems to the reader, if not

did not deal with life in its complexity; he sought no profound insights into character; of those values that we call enduring, he proclaimed only those that appealed to the fashionable liberalism of the years between the wars. Yet he was, in his life and his work, industrious and productive, reflecting the high seriousness with which his parents had undertaken important tasks. As a writer, editor, publisher, reviewer, critic, and friend, he played a not unimportant part in the literary life of his time. However, he plays almost no part in the literary history of his time.

References:
Walter Allen, *The Modern Novel* (New York: Dutton, 1964), pp. 44-46;

Leon Edel, *Bloomsbury: A House of Lions* (Philadelphia & New York: Lippincott, 1979);

David Gadd, *The Loving Friends: A Portrait of Bloomsbury* (New York & London: Harcourt Brace Jovanovich, 1974);

Carolyn Heilburn, *The Garnett Family* (New York: Macmillan, 1961);

Frank Swinnerton, *The Georgian Scene* (New York: Farrar, Rinehart, 1934), pp. 464-466.

Papers:
Garnett's papers are at the University of Texas Library.

Kenneth Grahame
(8 March 1859-6 July 1932)

Margaret B. McDowell
University of Iowa

SELECTED BOOKS: *Pagan Papers* (London: Mathews & Lane, 1893; Chicago: Stone & Kimball, 1894);
The Golden Age (London: Lane, 1895; Chicago: Stone & Kimball, 1895);
Dream Days (New York & London: Lane, 1898);
The Headswoman (New York & London: Lane, 1898);
The Wind in the Willows (London: Methuen, 1908; New York: Scribners, 1908);
Fun o' the Fair (London & Toronto: Dent, 1929);
First Whisper of 'The Wind in the Willows,' edited by Elspeth Grahame (London: Methuen, 1944; Philadelphia & New York: Lippincott, 1945);
Bertie's Escapade (London: Methuen, 1949; Philadelphia: Lippincott, 1949).

OTHER: Eugene Field, *Lullaby-Land: Songs of Childhood,* edited by Grahame (London: Lane, 1897; New York: Scribners, 1897);
The Cambridge Book of Poetry for Children, edited by Grahame (Cambridge: Cambridge University Press, 1916; New York: Putnam's, 1916);
"Lord" George Sanger, *Seventy Years a Showman,* introduction by Grahame (London & Toronto:

Dent, 1926); introduction republished as *Fun o' the Fair* (London & Toronto: Dent, 1929).

By the late 1890s Kenneth Grahame had established his reputation in England and in the United States as an essayist. In 1898, at the age of thirty-nine, he further distinguished himself by becoming the youngest person to be commissioned secretary of the Bank of England, one of the three top positions in the bank. At this point he surprisingly, but decisively, retired from writing essays, explaining simply that it was his choice to spend more time out-of-doors. Almost by accident several years later he wrote the book on which his current reputation rests—*The Wind in the Willows* (1908), one of the best-known children's classics in the English language. He retired from the Bank of England in 1907 at the age of forty-eight, and though he lived to be seventy-three, he wrote no more books.

Several of Grahame's themes remained constant in both his fiction and nonfiction: the nature of childhood, the need to stimulate the child's imagination between the ages of four and seven, the importance of a positive identification with nature,

Grahame, circa 1919 (photo by J. Russell & Sons)

At the turn of the century, conscientious parents and teachers believed that children must be firmly directed into a world of fact, rationalism, and predictable cause and effect. For them, the larger reality of fairy tales, myths, Santa Claus, and the Easter Bunny was suspect. The "lies" of unrealistic stories might confuse children, and the frivolousness of imaginative literature might precipitate neurotic or lazy daydreaming. Even Theodore Roosevelt, an avid admirer of Grahame, wrote an article opposing Br'er Rabbit stories on the grounds that "confounding animals with human beings is bad natural history and bad literature." Roosevelt at first refused to read *The Wind in the Willows,* because in it Grahame had replaced his favorite character, Harold (who appeared in *The Golden Age* sketches,1895), with four animals who pretended to be people. Similarly, Theodore Dreiser, editing the *Delineator* in 1904, denounced the teddy bear fad that had emerged from Roosevelt's popularity as outdoorsman and hunter. Dreiser contended that giving little girls teddy bears to cuddle, instead of baby dolls, might subtly distort their maternal aspirations.

In assessing Grahame's contribution to children's literature, it is important to recognize that he was not alone in shifting the genre from its traditional didacticism around the turn of the century to a more creative expression, less encumbered by the stress on facts, duty, good manners, and religious precepts. Robert Louis Stevenson, Walter de la Mare, Sir James Barrie, Mark Twain, Joel Chandler Harris, Rudyard Kipling, and Beatrix Potter—like Grahame—emphasized adventure, fantasy, and sheer imaginative pleasure in their books for children. If these writers all maintained that fantasy seldom confuses the immature mind, Grahame alone convinced thousands of devoted adult readers through his essays and sketches that parents and teachers would seriously *damage* their children if they *failed* to expose them to such literature. He disarmed them with his whimsicality even in his meditations with scholarly sounding Latin titles but mostly in sketches involving the partly autobiographical Harold and his siblings. Grahame drew adult readers back to their own childhood adventures and their most private imaginative and intellectual growth by his specific sensory appeals and his consistent reference to the child's perspective on daily living: "It was much too fine a night. . . . Edward and I were still leaning out of the open window in our nightshirts." "Just then, Harold was very proud. The week before he had 'gone into tables' and had been endowed with a new slate, having a

and the psychological necessity for an adult to return continually to the fantasy and memories of childhood, particularly those related to nature and to the warmth of home and family. A child, Grahame asserted, needs a "secret kingdom" within his mind in which to live when under stress or when bored by the rest of the world. Only children between ages four and seven have the full ability to develop imaginatively, because they constantly view the details of life with what he called "wonderment."

Grahame held that if a child receives nurture for his imagination through venturesome experience, stimulating literature, and contact with nature, and if he later defends his imagination against common sense, workaday dullness, and materialistic ambition, he will in adulthood continue to possess a separate world he can enter at will for renewal of spirit. The adult who lacks this inner resource for refreshment and challenge becomes a diminished human being, an "Olympian." Irrevocably damaged, Olympians exist within rigid and limiting societal strictures.

miniature sponge attached. . . . As to tables, nobody knew exactly what they were. . . ." With sophistication and wit, Grahame convinced readers that nature, dreams, fantasy, and memory vitalized a child's mental growth as surely as food and sleep provided for physical health. It is Grahame's insistent articulation of this "anti-Olympian" philosophy in his sketches for adults in the 1890s and his vivid expression of imagination in his fiction for children in the next decade that constitute his principal contribution to intellectual history, to children's literature, and to developmental psychology.

Grahame's understanding of children's sensitivity to nature and their tenacious memory for detail emerged from his generalizations about his own experience. He declared that he remembered all he had felt during the years between the ages of four and seven, but after seven he remembered nothing "particularly." When he returned at forty-six to the rural area where he had lived in these formative years and began exploring it with his small son, he found he accurately recalled every detail and association. "The part of my brain I used from four till about seven can never have altered!" Grahame was born in Edinburgh in 1859 to Cunningham Grahame, an advocate, and Bessie Ingles Grahame. At four he and his family moved into a new home, sustained emotionally by the warmth and vitality of his mother. The week of his fifth birthday his mother gave birth to a fourth child. Within three weeks she died of scarlet fever, and Kenneth, delirious and near death from the disease, could not understand his mother's failure to be near him.

That spring the convalescing Kenneth, the new infant, six-year-old Thomas William (Willie), and eight-year-old Helen went to live with their maternal grandmother in her big, run-down house on the Thames near Cookham Dene. The three older children rambled freely in the meadow and on the river bank. This experience is reflected as a carefree one in the Harold sketches, but Kenneth adjusted to his mother's death and his father's absence by withdrawing into an imaginative world at frequent intervals during the day. Much of his life he impressed people as someone who kept a slight distance from people and events, always observing and listening but seldom talking. The summer he was seven his hopes were raised that his father was about to take the children back home; but the reunion revealed only his father's advanced alcoholism. He soon left for France, abandoning responsibility for the children, who remained out of touch with him until his death in 1887. Kenneth's

grandmother moved the family twelve miles away from the river, so that at the age of seven his hopes for going home again ended, his play on the riverbank was gone, and he was no longer to remember anything "particularly." The following year he and Willie went to St. Edward's School, Oxford, though Willie's health necessitated his returning home in a few months. Willie died in 1875 at the age of sixteen. A few months later, Kenneth's grief for his brother turned to shock when, in spite of his honors in all areas of school and his longstanding assumption that he would enter Oxford University, he was abruptly taken from school by his uncles, who could have afforded to send him to college. At sixteen, he became a clerk in the Bank of London, where for five years he dreamed of Oxford every night. His bitterness against his uncles and their penurious refusal to educate him remained, although he wrote dryly in "The Funeral" (or "On the Obsequies of One's Ambition") of his attempt to bury all his lost hopes: "Let them go. Who cares? . . . The hopes are cold." Ironically, Oxford became the site of Grahame's grave.

In British literary history of the 1880s and 1890s Grahame figures in three groups of consequence. At the close of his first year in London, he met Frederick James Furnivall and became for fifteen years part of the enclave of young intellectuals and established authors who gathered around Furnivall in Soho restaurants or in one of the literary societies he organized—the Early English Text Society, the Chaucer Society, the New Shakespeare Society (of which Grahame was secretary, 1880-1891), the Browning Society, and the Shelley Society. Gregarious and witty, Furnivall possessed remarkable intellectual breadth. He taught British poetry from all periods but had, in the 1860s, focused on medieval poetry and prepared a six-volume edition of *The Canterbury Tales*. He specialized at Cambridge University in mathematics, trained himself in the law, studied music and philosophy, and was closely associated with his friend John Ruskin in his studies in art history for almost fifty years. When Grahame met him, he was preparing the first edition of the New English Dictionary (Oxford). Politically, he advocated Christian Socialism. For the quiet Grahame, the Furnivall groups provided social activity both at society meetings and in the informal evenings in restaurants. Furnivall's enthusiasm for boating on the Thames provided pleasurable weekends for Grahame, who later told a little girl who wrote him about *The Wind in the Willows* that boats were "the most important thing in life!" Furnivall advised

Grahame to leave the writing of poetry in order to concentrate on essays, and he introduced him to important authors—Alfred Tennyson, Robert Browning, John Ruskin, and William Morris.

In the early 1890s Grahame also became one of the "clever young men" who were encouraged by the poet and editor William E. Henley. An article by Grahame in the *St. James Gazette* caught Henley's attention while he was in Edinburgh editing the *Scots Observer,* and after Henley moved to London to edit the *National Observer* (1890-1894) and the *New Review* (1894-1896), he published Grahame's essays regularly. He also persuaded his publisher, John Lane, to print Grahame's collected essays in *Pagan Papers* (1893) and *The Golden Age* (1895). Unfortunately, Henley's advice and editorial additions accounted for some of the overuse of archaic words and phrases in Grahame's prose of the early 1890s.

In 1894 Grahame joined a few others in the establishment of the *Yellow Book,* a much-publicized magazine venture printed by John Lane, edited by Henry Harland, and illustrated by Aubrey Beardsley. Grahame's *The Golden Age* appeared in a bright yellow cover with frontispiece by Beardsley, emphasizing his relationship with the *Yellow Book.* Although founders of this new quarterly probably sought to make it seem more "decadent" than it was, its orientation differed markedly from Henley's political conservatism, militant chauvinism, and vigorous opposition to the "aesthetes."

Pagan Papers, The Golden Age, and *Dream Days* (1898) all went into several editions soon after publication. In the best-known review of *The Golden Age,* Algernon Swinburne exultantly declared that this book might be "too praiseworthy for praise." At various times, Theodore Roosevelt sent his personal copies of all of Grahame's books to England to be autographed by the author, boasting that he and his wife could pass examinations on the works, so thoroughly had they read and reread every word. In letters to the author, the prime minister of Australia expressed similar enthusiasm. Grahame was known internationally before the turn of the century.

Compared with other expository discourse popular in the 1890s, Grahame's essays after *Pagan Papers* are relatively straightforward and free of decorative figures of speech, archaic diction, circumlocutions in sentence structure, and the weighting of the text with classical allusions or long quotations. In *Pagan Papers,* most notable in their wit, fluency, and human interest are the six sketches which focus on nine-year-old Harold and his siblings. "The Olympians," a monologue, is narrated

in the voice of an older Harold looking back to childhood, and it serves as the prologue to *The Golden Age,* a volume in which all of the rest of the Harold essays are reprinted. (In *Dream Days* these children appear only in a prologue-epilogue frame, where they provide the audience for the story, "The Reluctant Dragon.") In "The Olympians" Grahame expresses an exquisite self-pity for the transience of childhood and suggests a fin de siècle nostalgia for lost joy and sensitivity. Essentially, however, he optimistically emphasizes the possible extension of childhood imaginativeness into adulthood, particularly in the characterization of the village curate who shared childlike excitement and fantasy with Harold and the other adventurers.

Achieving a distinctive prose style remained "a sort of hope" for Grahame throughout his life. In 1910 he commented that he hoped to avoid literary fame which would threaten his privacy and simple life, but that he would like to "build a noble sentence that might make Sir Thomas Browne sit up once again in that inhospitable grave of his in Norwich." He used satiric humor in unexpected context, and his anecdotes, witty dialogue, lively characters, and considerable action in many selections give his general discourse the special appeal of short fiction. If his essays now seem mannered and overpolished, even occasionally pedantic in their Latinate phrases and titles, Grahame remains convincingly among England's most eloquent stylists because of his grace, humor, and asperity.

In 1899, forty years old and widely known both as essayist and bank executive, Grahame married Elspeth Thomson, a moderately wealthy woman of thirty-seven. The next year their only child, Alistair (nicknamed Mouse), was born, with impaired sight in one eye and a congenital cataract blinding the other. In 1906 the family moved from London to the area near Cookham Dene on the Thames where Grahame had lived from ages five to seven. The stories that became *The Wind in the Willows* began at bedtime on Mouse's fourth birthday and continued in letters sent during the summer he was seven and away at the seashore. Probably in 1906, Mouse, then six, was "editing" a child's magazine with the help of his governess and a playmate. He wrote an intriguing letter from the seashore at seven: "Dear Daddy. We received the Toad letter. I will send *you* a story. The ship, the Dragon, started at 10 from Portsmouth on a Friday and it was such a fine day that everybody forgot that it was unlucky. From your affectionate, MOUSE."

If the author was encouraged by such evidence of Alistair's imaginative growth and curiosity

Grahame's son, Alastair, for whom he invented the stories that became The Wind in the Willows

about nature in these formative years, the father's anti-Olympian influence did not protect his son from a miserable adolescence when he was confronted by the regimentation and the insensitive "masculinity" of public boys' schools of the time. After two months at Rugby, he had to be withdrawn because of his great unhappiness, and the next year he suffered an emotional breakdown near the end of his first year at Eton. His eyesight had greatly worsened, and he prepared for Oxford University entrance with a tutor. At the university at nineteen he struggled with religious doubts at the time that he faced his undergraduate examinations. He passed the examinations in May 1919, but his committee recommended that the university provide him with the tutoring assistance given totally blind students. A few days later, he was found decapitated by a night train near a crossing in Oxford. Because he suffered poor eyesight, authorities ruled the death accidental, although the nature of the injuries caused persistent suspicion that he had lain across the tracks as the train approached.

In its joyful tone, its little group of adventurous animals led by an impulsive and unwise fellow, its slang-filled dialogue, and its hairbreadth rescue as they flee from pursuers, "Bertie's Escapade," the story Grahame had written for his son's childhood magazine, prefigured *The Wind in the Willows*. The climactic event in this sketch—the singing of Yuletide carols outside a house—Grahame repeated in the "Dulce Domum" section of the novel. All three animal characters are pets of the Grahame family; the Stones, who had a large kennel, are neighbors; and the mole is an animal that fascinated Mouse in his explorations of the meadows. Grahame added a self-portrait, revealed through a nightmare about his embarrassing behavior at a bankers' dinner.

Bertie ("a pig of action, 'Deeds, not grunts' was his motto") yawns in boredom one winter night, takes a running jump, and clears his fence. He then releases the rabbits, Benjie and Peter, and races across the moonlit snow to Christmas carol at the Stones' house. Benjie, too lazy to climb the hill, tries to burrow in the warm snow. Using the slang of 1908, Benjie grumbles: "Hang it all.... I'm not going to fag up that hill tonight for any one." They seek a shortcut through a tunnel and come upon a tiny elevator lit by electric light and operated by Mole. "Good King Wenceslaus" under the Stones' window proves no great success. As Mrs. Stone proposes that her husband loose the dogs to stop "that caterwauling," the singers flee toward the special mushroom, which when pressed makes the elevator appear. The calm, polite gentility of Mole typifies that character as he appears in the novel. He "looked them over and grinned. 'Had a pleasant evening?' he said." Similarly, the picnic lunch they share back in their warm home has all the same foods as one of the meals shared by the animals in the novel.

The Wind in the Willows reflects its origin as a story invented for a particular child. It has characteristics of the oral bedtime story for a child of four, and characteristics of the appeals used in writing to an older, precocious child away for the summer. While the sketches about Harold fail to interest children—although they are *about* children —*The Wind in the Willows* has always succeeded with parents, with preschool children who listen to short selections read aloud, and with older children who can appreciate stylistic variations and the repeated comic devices (for example, the formal polite statement in the midst of disorder; the single inappropriate adjective or adverb that gives satiric twist to an otherwise innocent statement; and the many lists).

16, Durham Villas, Campden Hill, W.

21 June 1907.

My dearest Mouse

No doubt you will be interested to
hear the further adventures of Mr Toad,
after he gallopped away across country on
the bargee's horse, with the bargee shouting
after him in vain. Well presently the
horse got tired of galloping so fast, and
broke from a gallop into a trot, and
then from a trot into a walk, & then he
stopped altogether & began to nibble grass,
and the toad looked round about him &
found he was on a large common. On
the common stood a gipsy tent, and a
gipsy man was sitting beside it, on a bucket
turned upside down, smoking. In front
of the tent a fire of sticks was burning,
& over the fire hung an iron pot, and out
of the pot came steam, & bubblings, and
the most beautiful good smell that ever you
                                        smelt.

When Alastair Grahame spent the summer at the seashore his father sent him stories by mail (courtesy of the Bodleian Library,
Ms. Eng. misc. d. 281).

As in Mark Twain, Grahame's lists evoke humor in their exaggerated specificity, their inclusion of an incongruous item somewhere in the series, their typographical conversion of many words to one very long one (as in the menu that overwhelms the characters by its magnitude and variety) by deleting spaces between words. Often the lists give one a sense of breathlessness or of mindless rattling off of the inconsequential, but at other times the careful detailing becomes an analysis of the experience or a savoring of every detail of an event.

Small children find most appealing the adventures of Mr. Toad, which can be broken into separate short episodes to fit their attention span. Because Toad in some of these sequences is seen apart from his friends—as in his crimes, imprisonment, and escape—a small child can more easily focus on the single character than on several animals at once. Toad's arrogance and foolishness are so exaggerated that even the smallest child recognizes the boaster's penchant for getting himself into difficulty and his refusal to learn from experience. While the other animals manage to rescue him and scold him, they minimize his villainy—if not his foolishness—by celebrating the close of each of his difficulties.

The action provides drama enough to hold the interest of younger children—which was not the case in the Harold sketches Grahame wrote earlier. Considerable dialogue adds to the dramatic interest, and the members of the group are differentiated with some care. A. A. Milne, who adapted parts of the book for the stage in *Toad of Toad's Hall* not long after completing his Winnie the Pooh books, thought that Grahame had so masterfully delineated personalities through dialogue that a playwright needed "merely to listen and record," because "they speak ever after in their own voices." While the slang is outdated, its unfamiliarity adds a comic edge—as Mole gets spring fever and leaves his housecleaning with "Bother," "Oh blow," and "Hang springcleaning." Only in great consternation do the friends go beyond the usual "Oh, my!"—which is often repeated a half dozen times for emphasis. The strongest expression—used only in warnings to Toad—is "Stop being an ass."

Older children enjoy Grahame's appeal to their superior wisdom, as when Ratty, the wisest of the talkers, gives up in frustration, because he cannot convince Toad and Badger that we must "Teach 'em" instead of "Learn 'em." They also enjoy the humor in the ambivalent nature of the characters—part animal, part human. Although they live underground or on the riverbank, Mole

has a neat house with whitewashed walls, Rat's house in the Wild Wood has a fireplace and a large dining room, and Toad lives in an elegant mansion with a banquet hall and stylish wicker chairs. Toad wears suits with pockets for money, watches, and keys. They eat from a carefully packed picnic basket. They cuddle under warm blankets when chilly or afraid. Mr. Toad can drive a car—although in 1908 few motorcars appeared on the streets—and he can disguise himself with the washerwoman's dress given him by the daughter of the jailer. The disguise fools the Barge Woman only for a time; she knows—as do all readers—that he is "A HUMBUG!" All his dignity of class and swaggering manner disappear when he is seen as a "slippery" animal tossed into the canal, but one knows that Rat will be there to rescue him with "friendly paw" and soon Toad will be again the jaunty character who "walked as he sang and sang as he walked. . . . Ho! ho! I am the Toad, the handsome, the popular, the successful Toad!"

Grahame's appeals to the senses are strong—the sky changes color gradually or suddenly, bird songs differ between morning and evening and each bird has a distinctive voice; water is glassy clear or greasy or thick with mud; hearth fires warm the air, are heard to crackle and roar, and flicker, flare up, and die down to embers; blankets are warm but also amazingly soft to the touch; and some two dozen foods are carefully specified in the book. Meals become rituals which mark the times of preparation, peacemaking, fellowship, consolation, or celebration.

Some critics have addressed the possibility that satire directed to adult readers underlies *The Wind in the Willows,* as in *Gulliver's Travels.* A sustained satirical structure, however, does not exist here. Grahame described this book as one "for youth." Satire only for sophisticated adult readers appears rarely, and when it does, it is whimsical rather than organized and purposeful. Clearly appealing to adults with a background in literature are sections of varying length in which Grahame imitates or parodies other authors. Most obvious of these is the mock-epic comedy in "The Return of Ulysses." In this chapter Grahame introduces exaggerated similes characteristic of epic style, and he opens with a ritualistic preparation of Toad's men for the siege which will remove the "wooers" who have in his absence abused his noted hospitality and "laid waste" to his hall. Toad, who was arrested for car theft when he went joyriding, has, after an escape from jail, journeyed slowly and circuitously over land and water, venture by venture. The animals from the Wild Wood who occupy his home—stoats, weasels, and ferrets—are hardly barbarian invaders. Their outrages have been simple violations of conservative middle-class norms: "lying in bed half the day, and breakfast at all hours—and the place in such a mess." In this new version of the *Odyssey,* after the mock-slaying of the wooers, the victors led by Toad force the vanquished to clean up the messy house and make all of the beds neatly. They then receive warm buns and tea and are sent back to the Wild Wood where they belong.

Some writers also have questioned the degree to which Grahame, through his portrayal of certain characters and situations in the novel, implicitly introduced serious arguments about society and social change—for example, his negative attitude toward urbanization of rural areas. He makes only a vague reference to the Wild Wood existing on the ruins of a decadent city; the idea is not developed, and the residents of the Wild Wood are hardly villainous. Rat's fine home is, in fact, in the Wild Wood—even if he criticizes his neighbors and if the members of the quartet fear those "different" animals they have not met.

Others have suggested that Grahame's treatment of the motorcar indicates his antagonism toward increased industrialism and privately owned transportation. In Toad's infatuation with cars, Grahame may satirize the enthusiasts in the motorcar "cult," much as E. M. Forster derogated the Wilcox family's orientation around that symbol of material wealth and efficiency in *Howards End.* Toad's joyriding—in stolen cars—can scarcely be construed as an attack on modern commitment to progress in industry and transportation, especially when in this fantasy Toad's cars start without cranking and he needs no lesson in driving. In 1908 few of the readers of this book had even ridden in a motorcar, much less owned one. While Grahame was creating the stories that became *The Wind in the Willows,* people lined the roads in rural Massachusetts not to see Edith Wharton and her famous passenger, Henry James, drive by, but just to get a glimpse of Wharton's car. Toad's dust coat and goggles annoy his buddies not because they oppose the invention of cars but because Toad looks silly and his behavior is ostentatious once he puts on the touring uniform.

Still other readers suggest that Grahame commented implicitly on the caste system in a capitalist society by making Toad—who lived on inherited wealth—a foolish and slightly decadent character. But the animal friends do not seem aware of a class barrier. He is one of them. Nagging him

Kenneth Grahame, circa 1895

for his mischief and foolhardiness, Rat exclaims to Toad that his behavior "is getting *us animals* a bad name," that "*we animals* never allow our friends to make fools of themselves beyond a certain limit."

Two chapters inserted into this work, but planned as separate sketches, hold special interest for adult readers: "The Piper at the Gates of Dawn" and "Wayfarers All." Similar to his sketches in *Dream Days* ten years earlier, these chapters unfold as highly descriptive, meditative, almost mystical reveries. The experience in "The Piper at the Gates of Dawn" strikes Ratty dumb; the experience in "Wayfarers All" lures him into a hypnotic trance. Though they are unlike the rest of the novel, which grew from the bedtime stories and letters for Mouse, these sections do show adequate adaptation to the personalities of the characters in the novel and to the landscape in which it is set. They provide quiet interludes between the more adventure-filled episodes without weakening the unity of the book.

"The Piper at the Gates of Dawn" possesses a poetic eloquence. In it the narrator recounts an existential experience in which Rat becomes "utterly possessed" by the transient beauty in the silence between night and dawn—the moment before the first bird song. In this silence he perceives a sound beyond normal sensory acuity. He is overcome by joy—and then by sadness because this ecstasy cannot be kept. Only his tears communicate to his companion in the boat, Mole, his awe and his sense of vulnerability in abandoning himself to nature. Mole hears nothing at all, but he is deeply moved by his friend's unexpressed rapture.

In "Wayfarers All" an Old Seafarer encounters Rat when he is vulnerable to wanderlust because of domestic difficulties. (Elsewhere in the book Rat appears to live alone.) As the reader enjoys the varied stories the Seafarer tells of ports around the world, the Seafarer's voice hypnotizes Rat, and all of the cities become for him one idyllic place in "the South." In a waking dream, Rat moves compulsively toward the land which does not exist. "Today the unseen was everything; the unknown the only real fact of life."

Badger gently breaks the spell by encouraging Rat to write poetry about his great vision. Rat writes, sucks his pencil, and writes again. Gradually, he sucks his pencil more than he writes, and the fever of wanderlust subsides. "Wayfarers All" won back Theodore Roosevelt's heart because Grahame expressed in it Roosevelt's own compulsive wanderlust. Both of these chapters provide a superb bonus for the adult who reads *The Wind in the Willows.*

Kenneth Grahame's only novel remains one of the most memorable and popular books for children in both England and America, and through its translations it is widely read in other countries. Its appeal seems timeless. The literary world is fortunate that Grahame's young son enticed him into the creation of this final book, but it must regret that he wrote no other fiction in the last twenty-five years of his life.

References:

Patrick Chalmers, *Kenneth Grahame: Life, Letters, and Unpublished Work* (London: Methuen, 1933);

Eleanor Graham, *Kenneth Grahame* (New York: Walck, 1963);

Peter Green, *Kenneth Grahame, A Biography* (London: Murray, 1959; Cleveland: World, 1959).

Maurice Hewlett
(22 January 1861-15 June 1923)

Ann Adams Cleary
University of Tulsa

SELECTED BOOKS: *Earthwork Out of Tuscany* (London: Dent, 1895; revised, London: Dent, 1899; New York: Putnam's, 1899; revised again, London & New York: Macmillan, 1901);

A Masque of Dead Florentines (London: Dent, 1895; Portland, Maine: Mosher, 1911);

Songs and Meditations (Westminster: Constable, 1896);

The Forest Lovers (New York & London: Macmillan, 1898);

Pan and the Young Shepherd (London & New York: Lane, 1898);

Little Novels of Italy (London: Chapman & Hall, 1899; New York & London: Macmillan, 1899);

The Life and Death of Richard Yea-and-Nay (London & New York: Macmillan, 1900);

The New Canterbury Tales (New York & London: Macmillan, 1901);

The Road in Tuscany, 2 volumes (New York & London: Macmillan, 1903);

The Queen's Quair (London & New York: Macmillan, 1904);

Fond Adventures: Tales of the Youth of the World (London: Macmillan, 1905; New York & London: Harper, 1905);

The Fool Errant (London: Heinemann, 1905; New York & London: Macmillan, 1905);

The Stooping Lady (London: Macmillan, 1907; New York: Dodd, Mead, 1907);

The Spanish Jade (London: Cassell, 1908; New York: Doubleday, Page, 1908);

Half-way House: A Comedy of Degrees (London:

Maurice Hewlett.

Chapman & Hall, 1908; New York: Scribners, 1908);

Letters to Sanchia (London: Privately printed, 1908; revised, London: Macmillan, 1910; New York: Scribners, 1910);

Open Country: A Comedy with a Sting (London: Macmillan, 1909; New York: Scribners, 1909);

Artemision: Idylls and Songs (London: Mathews, 1909; New York: Scribners, 1909);

Rest Harrow: A Comedy of Resolution (London: Macmillan, 1910; New York: Scribners, 1910);

Brazenhead the Great (London: Smith, Elder, 1911; New York: Scribners, 1911);

The Song of Renny (London: Macmillan, 1911; New York: Scribners, 1911);

The Agonists: A Trilogy of God and Man (London: Macmillan, 1911; New York: Scribners, 1911);

Mrs. Lancelot: A Comedy of Assumptions (London: Macmillan, 1912; New York: Century, 1912);

Bendish (London: Macmillan, 1913; New York: Scribners, 1913);

Lore of Proserpine (London: Macmillan, 1913; New York: Scribners, 1913);

Helen Redeemed and Other Poems (London: Macmillan, 1913; New York: Scribners, 1913);

A Lover's Tale (London & Toronto: Ward, Lock, 1915; New York: Scribners, 1915);

The Little Iliad (London: Heinemann, 1915; Philadelphia & London: Lippincott, 1915);

Frey and His Wife (London: Ward, Lock, 1916; New York: McBride, 1916);

Love and Lucy (London: Macmillan, 1916; New York: Dodd, Mead, 1916);

Gai Saber: Tales and Songs (London: Mathews, 1916; New York: Putnam's, 1916);

The Song of the Plow (London: Heinemann, 1916; New York: Macmillan, 1916);

Thorgils (London: Ward, Lock, 1917; New York: Dodd, Mead, 1917);

Gudrid the Fair (London: Constable, 1918; New York: Dodd, Mead, 1918);

The Village Wife's Lament (London: Secker, 1918; New York & London: Putnam's, 1918);

The Outlaw (London: Constable, 1919; New York: Dodd, Mead, 1920);

The Light Heart (London: Chapman & Hall, 1920; New York: Holt, 1920);

Mainwaring (New York: Dodd, Mead, 1920; London: Collins, 1921);

Flowers in the Grass (London: Constable, 1920);

In a Green Shade (London: Bell, 1920);

Wiltshire Essays (London & New York: Oxford University Press, 1921);

Extemporary Essays (London & New York: Oxford University Press, 1922);

Last Essays of Maurice Hewlett (London: Heinemann, 1924; New York: Scribners, 1924).

"I have often wished that I could write a novel in which, as mostly in life, thank goodness, nothing happens," wrote Maurice Hewlett near the end of a literary career devoted to the intrigues of medieval romance and swashbuckling historical drama. He had just finished reading with approval one of Dorothy Richardson's experimental "mental process" fictions. Hewlett, who wrote nothing but legal briefs until age thirty, was a reluctant, if prolific, novelist. "The truth is," he explained, "I write everything and approach everything as a poet—history, psychology, romance, novels, everything. It was by an accident, and an unfortunate one for me, that I was tempted to write prose." The critical and popular success of his first novel, *The Forest Lovers* (1898), had condemned him, he thought, to turning out "potboiling fancies imbued with pothouse realism" in order to satisfy the expectations of his readers. Although Hewlett's published work is varied—short stories, translations of Dante, travelogues, scholarly articles on Italian Renaissance painters, essays, lyrics and narrative poetry, verse drama, literary criticism, newspaper columns, contemporary thesis novels, and even a filmscript—his name is most often associated with fair damsels, dark deeds, and other clichés of popular romantic fiction. Hewlett was ever the facile stylist in search of a satisfying genre.

Maurice Henry Hewlett was born on 22 January 1861, at Oatlands Park, Weybridge, Surrey, to Henry Gay Hewlett and Emmeline Mary Knowles. His mother was the daughter of an architect. Hewlett's father, the author of half a dozen books on English history and poetry, was an expert in antiquarian law. He held a civil-service post in the Land Revenue Records Office; Maurice Hewlett was appointed to the same position following his father's death in 1897.

Describing himself in *Lore of Proserpine* (1913) as a "moody, irresolute, and hatefully reserved" child, Hewlett (eldest of eight children) wrote that "To my father I could not speak, to my mother I did not; the others, being my juniors all, hardly existed." Hewlett lived a "thronged and secret" fantasy life: "At nine years old, I knew Nelson's ardour and Wellesley's phlegm; I had Napoleon's egotism, Galahad's purity, Lancelot's passion, Tristram's melancholy. I reasoned like Socrates and made Phaedo weep. . . . I was by then Don Juan and Don Quixote, Tom Jones and Mr. Allworthy, Hamlet and his uncle, young Shandy and his. You will gather that I was a reader."

The young reader was an indifferent student. He attended day schools in Surrey and Kent and, at age thirteen, spent a year boarding at the Palace School in Enfield. In 1875, accompanied by a younger brother, Hewlett began attending the experimental International College at Spring Grove, Isleworth. The three years Hewlett spent there were predictably unhappy ones for the shy young man who entertained himself by winning class prizes in English literature and by publishing a paper entitled the *Saturday Review, A Weekly Journal of Politics, Literature and the Drama,* featuring strong Conservative political views and news about fictitious members of the peerage. Hewlett left college without a degree in December 1878 and began the study of antiquarian law in his cousin's legal firm at Gray's Inn. After his family moved to the village of

Addington in 1882, Hewlett took his own apartment in London. He was still a reader.

A self-styled "jaded novel-monger," his tastes now included Kant, Fichte, and Dante. Hewlett was never to edge far from the influence and examples of his early reading. As his contemporary critics noted, Hewlett's books, more than most, were made from other books. Some praised his ability to evoke a sense of time and place. Others, less kind, dismissed his work as tediously derivative, because Rosalind, Falstaff, Cyrano, Patient Griselda, Lancelot, and Sir Gawain kept appearing under assumed names.

In 1888, after a two years' courtship, Hewlett married Hilda Beatrice Herbert, a vicar's daughter who became a pioneer aviatrix and designer of pre-World War I aircraft. In 1911, she became the first British woman to gain a pilot's certificate. A son, Cecco, was born in 1890, and a daughter, Pia, in 1895. Although the Hewletts held very different professional interests, they shared a passion for travel and for gardening at Broad Chalke, the fourteenth-century former rectory near Salisbury they acquired in 1903 as a country home.

During the early years of his marriage, Hewlett continued his study of law. On 30 April 1890 Hewlett was called to the bar by the Inner Temple and became a partner in his cousin's legal firm. In 1889, he made the first of his many journeys abroad; while in Tangiers recuperating from nervous strain, Hewlett began writing. As he commented in a letter to his wife, "I have a lot of poetical stuff floating about me; not easy to catch and fix on paper; but it makes one live in a dream which is a pleasant thing." Hewlett's first books were influenced by his travels in Italy. *Earthwork Out of Tuscany* (1895), a collection of "imaginary portraits" of Botticelli and other Renaissance figures, was in the manner of Walter Pater. In *Athenaeum* one critic noted that "the impressions and translations are not interesting, and his style is frequently affected and disagreeable. The best that can be said of the book is that it shows a very proper sympathy with much that is good in art; but this will not make the book a good one. In one place, the author modestly speaks of his writings as watered wine, and we must confess his modesty is not unbecoming." Hewlett's earliest volume of poetry, *A Masque of Dead Florentines* (1895), was mercifully ignored by reviewers.

In 1892 Hewlett decided to give himself seven years to prove whether he could retire from the legal profession and support his family by writing. He lectured on medieval subjects at South Kensington University and began publishing journal articles and reviews. In addition to essays, stories, and poems about Renaissance Italy, Hewlett began working on classical Greek themes, spending two years writing a trilogy in the Sophoclean vein (published in revised form as *The Agonists* in 1911). He also wrote *Pan and the Young Shepherd* (1898), a mythological drama peopled, according to one critic, "with peasants of today labeled with Greek names." (The peasants, Pan, and seven Daughters of the Earth reside in the Cheviot hills along the English-Scottish border and occasionally lapse into Chaucerian diction.) In 1897 Hewlett was appointed keeper of the land revenue records and enrollments; the trial period he had allowed himself for becoming an author was almost over. After mining Shakespearean sonnets for *Songs and Meditations* (1896), Hewlett decided to write a romance drawing on Sir Thomas Malory and the Middle Ages. The success of this first novel, *The Forest Lovers,* enabled Hewlett to retire from the Records Office in 1900 and devote the rest of his life to writing.

The Forest Lovers met immediately with popular and critical acclaim and established Hewlett's reputation as a romance writer. In the company of Joseph Conrad (whose *Tales of Unrest* was also awarded a prize), Hewlett's romance was hailed by the *Academy* as the best novel of 1898. Years later, Jean Rhys would remember *The Forest Lovers* as the only book she could bear to read during her early years in England. In her memoirs, she recalls that she and the other touring chorus girls had endless conversations about how and why the young couple in Hewlett's book slept with an unsheathed sword between them.

Hewlett begins his romance: "My story will take you into times and spaces alike rude and uncivil. Blood will be spilt, virgins suffer distresses; the horn will sound through woodland glades; dogs, wolves, deer, and men, Beauty and the Beasts will tumble each other, seeking life or death with their proper tools. There should be mad work, not devoid of entertainment.... You will know something of Morgraunt Forest and the Countess Isabel; the Abbot of Holy Thorn will have postured and schemed (with you behind the arras); you will have wandered with Isoult and will know why she was called La Desirous, with Prosper le Gai, and will understand how a man may fall in love with his own wife."

In *The Forest Lovers,* Prosper le Gai, a heedless young knight bent on having the usual gallant adventures involving the rescue of distressed damsels and gaining justice through jousting, marries a poor, ragged girl, Isoult La Desirous, in order to save her from the gallows. She excites his pity, then his respect, and finally his love, by serving him humbly, faithfully, and at great personal risk. When Isoult and Prosper eventually consummate what had been a white marriage of convenience, "It was as in a field of blood that the rod of love thrust into flower at last."

The Forest Lovers exhibits all of the strengths and most of the weaknesses found in Hewlett's subsequent novels. It is frankly escapist fiction and gave fin-de-siècle readers of romance exactly what they expected: improbable characters speaking quaintly as they were propelled from one fantastic turn of the plot to another. Hewlett added to these conventional elements touches of humor and spiced the whole with a bizarre eroticism. The narrator cautions early on that "Your romancer must be neither a lover of his heroine nor (as the fashion now sets) of his chief rascal; . . . he must be a jigger of strings." Hewlett manages to jiggle almost every string attached to sexual desire, including bestiality and bondage. The novel serves as a literary paradigm of the varieties of love—deviations on a theme.

In his second novel, *The Life and Death of Richard Yea-and-Nay* (1900), Hewlett bases a portrayal of Richard Coeur de Lion on the conflicting passions of secular love and religious fervor. In order to gain financing for his crusade, the twelfth-century king must make a loveless marriage with a wealthy sovereign; but in order to marry, he has to give up his true love, the French girl Jehane. Hewlett, drawing on an extensive knowledge of medieval matters gained by his legal work with the Domesday Book and other records, presents meticulous historical details of dress and daily life. He then adds a realistically earthy heroine and a gloss of occult mysticism to his psychological romance. Unlike Sir Walter Scott, who relegated historical personages to peripheral places in his romances, Hewlett put them center stage. Unlike Thackeray, who never tampered with historical fact, Hewlett adjusted, ignored, and invented in order to work out the machinations of his plot. *The Life and Death of Richard Yea-and-Nay* was well received, and Hewlett began another historical romance—about Mary, Queen of Scots. He felt that her need for love had never been properly understood or acknowledged and that he was the writer who could remedy that lack.

In 1902 Hewlett left off his work on *The Queen's Quair* (he later referred to this novel as a disguised "symphony of sounds, very artfully done and never discovered by the critics") and made a two-month trip to Italy. Out of this journey came *The Road in Tuscany* (1903).

When his book on Mary Stuart finally appeared in 1904 (*The Queen's Quair* first ran in serial form in *Pall Mall*), it sold 15,000 copies the first month. Irritated that critics failed to take the work seriously, Hewlett complained to a friend: "They say it is a Romance, confound them. I say it is History. I haven't had one single review by a man who knows anything whatever about the woman or her times—beyond what he has got out of me. But I am sure my notion of giving *real* history in this form—of illuminating history from within—is a sound one—and perhaps one of these days I shall get people to agree with me." Hewlett was especially irked because he had refrained from using any fictional characters; neither had he altered any "significant" episodes in his study of the Scottish queen.

Following the publication of *The Fool Errant* in 1905, Hewlett noted that the book (a picaresque psychological romance set in eighteenth-century Italy) "has brought me much money, but no credit from myself." He thought that his "novel-writing epoch" might have been at an end: "Prosperity no doubt has killed that form of letters. No doubt I have done well, no doubt I have also increased my style of living; no doubt that has meant I *must* write novels; and that involves that I do them not so well, for what I do of necessity I do as an exercise."

In 1905 Hewlett took a month's holiday in Spain that resulted in *The Spanish Jade* (1908), a recasting of characters from Cervantes's *Don Quixote* in 1860s dress. The novel begins with the comic presentation of a staid English traveler confronting the perils of Spanish deserts and denizens; the traveler is armed with nothing more than a toothbrush, a copy of *Don Quixote,* and an unflappable compulsion to do what is proper and befitting a gentleman. The inconsistencies of style and tone that mar much of Hewlett's work are apparent: good-natured parody, social realism, and romantic idealism are impossible to meld—the work loses focus.

A trilogy of contemporary novels of manner "in the modern tack" (*Half-way House,* 1908; *Open Country,* 1909; and *Rest Harrow,* 1910) was Hewlett's last effort to write novels of substance. Senhouse, the peripatetic hero of the trilogy, is highly reflective of Hewlett's own philosophical beliefs: divorce should not be censured and women's rights should be supported. Underlying the novels is his rather Tolstoyan concept that the virtues of the agricultural peasant class could be the salvation of modern England.

Caricature of Hewlett in 1908 by Max Beerbohm (© Eva Reichmann; courtesy of Ashmolean Museum, Oxford)

Although Hewlett consistently abhorred any publicity about his private life (to the point of considering his public a "dirty feeder"), he was working as early as 1909 on a series of autobiographical essays (published as *Lore of Proserpine*). This odd volume is indispensable to any serious study of Hewlett. Freudian metaphors and frank reminiscences about his school years give way mid-book to a catalogue of fairy sightings in Edwardian England. During this self-searching period, Hewlett also wrote to his early biographer and admiring critic, Milton Bronner, to defend himself against the charge of being a "fleshly" writer: "The characters of my novels are men and women, and when I see them doing things which men and women do— kissing and mating, as well as praying and fighting, I say so, and make no bones. I have never in my life been 'suggestive' for the sake of lust, and never prurient. But I don't see why I should leave out half of life, when I am writing for men and women who are alive. That's all I have to say about that."

The onset of World War I coincided with Hewlett's return to poetry and classical themes. Even for his novels, Hewlett explained, "I use the poetic method entirely—stuff myself with the subject, drench myself, and then let it pour out as it will. I used once to re-write over and over (*Pan*, about five times; *The Queen's Quair*, four times)—but can't do that now. Twice is as much as I can manage. I am not sure it's a good plan. You get richness, but stickiness too, I think. What I mean about method is, that I trust to intuition or what is called inspiration, absolutely. I never put conscious or deliberate brainwork into a book. Such as there may be of that is done in sleep. Now, when I was at the Bar, I used to get up my cases in exactly the same way, and all the close searching and arrangement of evidence was the result of inspiration and brainwork done unconsciously. I know no other way of doing anything. If I were Prime Minister of England I would do the same." Although Hewlett continued to turn out novel after potboiling novel, often drawing now on Norse mythology, his major commitment lay in fashioning an epic portrayal of the English peasant class, tracing in verse the deeds of Hodge (traditional nickname for a farmworker). This "Hodgiad" was published as *The Song of the Plow* in 1916.

In 1917 Hewlett was asked to stand as the Labour candidate, but he decided instead to devote his time to the bureaucratic job of housing inspector, a position he served for several years. His novels had not been selling well for some time, even in America, where he had earlier enjoyed great popularity. Hewlett, in financial difficulties, wrote to his friend E. V. Lucas that he was tempted to lease his home and live in a cottage: "That is my only way of escaping the degrading occupation of writing bad novels—novels in which I don't myself for one moment believe."

During the last three years of his life, Hewlett turned to literary journalism. His magazine and newspaper essays were collected for the final four volumes of his publishing career (*In a Green Shade*, 1920; *Wiltshire Essays*, 1921; *Extemporary Essays*, 1922; and *Last Essays*, 1924). Often cited as a writer whose work never quite measured up to his talent, Hewlett did exhibit sound critical perceptions. His assessments of early modernists such as Dorothy Richardson and Virginia Woolf are worthwhile, though after reading James Joyce's *A Portrait of the Artist as a Young Man*, Hewlett wrote to a friend that he wished "that Joyce had been limited some more, unless it is really true that undergraduates in Dublin *do* catch lice on their necks (because if it is really true I suppose we ought to know it). I have been hunting on mine since. Do you really think it is a good book? It seems to me shoddy in parts and pose in other parts—yet I can't deny I read it—partly because I wanted to see what other words besides 'bloody' (which is stale now) he would use. He has a good record. . . . Nobody since Swift has been so good at urinals as this Egoist."

Hewlett, the novelist in spite of himself, took scant interest in the literary and social scene of London, though he corresponded regularly with several minor figures of the time: Laurence Binyon, Robert Bridges, E. V. Lucas, and Sir Henry Newbolt. His collected correspondence, heavily edited by Binyon, discloses Hewlett's generosity in giving advice to aspiring authors. In contrast to his mannered fiction style (parodied in 1912 by Max Beerbohm in *A Christmas Garland*), Hewlett's letters are remarkably casual and forthright. Hewlett was active in literary matters until his death on 15 June 1923. A hope he once voiced for the 1898 novel *The Forest Lovers* that so irrevocably set him on his professional course can serve as comment on his place in literature: "It will be a piece of myself—neither modern nor antique, but a queer composite, rather bewildering to those who love to classify and label what they read."

Letters:
The Letters of Maurice Hewlett, edited by Laurence Binyon (Boston: Small, Maynard, 1926).

References:
Milton Bronner, *Maurice Hewlett: Being a Critical Review of His Prose and Poetry* (Boston: Luce, 1910);
Jean Rhys, *Smile, Please: An Unfinished Autobiography* (New York: Harper & Row, 1979).

James Hilton
(9 September 1900-20 December 1954)

Lauren H. Pringle
Ohio State University

BOOKS: *Catherine Herself* (London: Unwin, 1920);

Storm Passage (London: Unwin, 1922);

The Passionate Year (London: Butterworth, 1923; Boston: Little, Brown, 1924);

The Dawn of Reckoning (London: Butterworth, 1925);

The Meadows of the Moon (London: Butterworth, 1926; Boston: Small, Maynard, 1927);

Terry (London: Butterworth, 1927);

The Silver Flame (London: Butterworth, 1928);

And Now Goodbye (London: Benn, 1931; New York: Morrow, 1932);

Murder at School, as Glen Trevor (London: Benn, 1931); republished as *Was It Murder?* (New York: Harper, 1933);

Contango (London: Benn, 1932); republished as *Ill Wind* (New York: Morrow, 1932);

Rage in Heaven (New York: King, 1932);

Knight Without Armour (London: Macmillan, 1933); republished as *Without Armor* (New York: Morrow, 1934);

Lost Horizon (London: Macmillan, 1933; New York: Morrow, 1933);

Good-bye, Mr. Chips (London: Macmillan, 1934; Boston: Little, Brown, 1934);

We Are Not Alone (London: Macmillan, 1937; Boston: Little, Brown, 1937);

To You, Mr. Chips (London: Hodder & Stoughton, 1938);

To You, Mr. Chips: A Play, by Hilton and Barbara Burnham (London: Hodder & Stoughton, 1938);

Random Harvest (London: Macmillan, 1941; Boston: Little, Brown, 1941);

The Story of Dr. Wassell (Boston: Little, Brown, 1943; London: Macmillan, 1944);

So Well Remembered (Boston: Little, Brown, 1945; London: Macmillan, 1947);

Nothing So Strange (Boston: Little, Brown, 1947; London: Macmillan, 1948);

Twilight of the Wise (London: St. Hugh's Press, 1949);

Morning Journey (London: Macmillan, 1951; Boston: Little, Brown, 1951);

Time and Time Again (London: Macmillan, 1953; Boston: Little, Brown, 1953);

James Hilton (photo by Robert Disraeli)

H.R.H.:The Story of Philip, Duke of Edinburgh (London: Müller, 1956; Boston: Little, Brown, 1956).

SCREENPLAYS: *Camille,* by Hilton, Z. Akins, and F. Marion, M-G-M, 1936;

We Are Not Alone, with Milton Krims, Warner Bros., 1939;

The Tuttles of Tahiti, adapted by Hilton, RKO, 1942;

Mrs. Miniver, by Hilton, A. Wimperis, G. Froeschel, and C. West, M-G-M, 1942;

Forever and a Day, by Hilton and twenty others, RKO, 1944.

PERIODICAL PUBLICATIONS: "What Mr. Chips Taught Me," *Atlantic Monthly,* 162 (July 1938): 28-40;

"Literature and Hollywood," *Atlantic Monthly,* 178 (December 1946): 130ff.

James Hilton, best-selling novelist, screen-writer, journalist, and short-story writer, was born at Leigh, Lancashire, England, on 9 September 1900. His father, John Hilton, was a schoolmaster as was his wife before their marriage, and in 1902 the family moved to London where John Hilton became headmaster of an elementary school. After grammar school, James Hilton entered Leys School, a public school in Cambridge where he encountered the Chipsian "world of the ablative absolute and toasted crumpets for tea, of Greek verses and cricket." At Leys he dabbled in "pacifist and revolutionary poetry" and served as editor of the school magazine. He continued his education at Christ's College, Cambridge.

Hilton's professional writing career began during his undergraduate years at Cambridge. At seventeen, he had published an article in the *Manchester Guardian* and had begun his first novel, *Catherine Herself*, which was published with little reaction in 1920. He graduated in 1921, receiving a B.A. in history and English. Entering a job market affected by the postwar economic slump, he was unable to find a steady salaried job and spent eleven harried years as an instructor at Cambridge, a biweekly pseudonymous columnist for Dublin's *Irish Independent,* and fiction reviewer for the London *Daily Telegraph*. Meanwhile, his career as a novelist dragged on: during the 1920s six of Hilton's books were published, including *Storm Passage* (1922) and *The Passionate Year* (1923), but none received much attention.

It was not until the appearance of *And Now Goodbye* (1931) that he realized any significant monetary return from his novel writing. Critics called this study of an English minister's near-breakdown and recovery an "absolutely satisfying story," "sentiment without sentimentality," "a delicate and moving book." Also in 1931, under the snappy pseudonym "Glen Trevor," Hilton published a thriller called *Murder at School*. Reprinted in the United States as *Was It Murder?*, it received generally favorable reviews. Oddly enough, over half a century later it is the only Hilton work still in print, with the natural exception of his two blockbusters, *Lost Horizon* and *Good-bye, Mr. Chips*.

Contango (1932), *Rage in Heaven* (1932), and *Knight Without Armour* (1933) enjoyed the same moderate success as his other novels of the early 1930s. *Lost Horizon* (1933) earned him the coveted Hawthornden Prize, awarded annually to the most imaginative work by a young British author. At this time, however, the novel had little effect on increasing his audience.

The year 1934 marked the turning point of Hilton's career. Late in 1933 Hilton agreed to complete within two weeks a long short story for the *British Weekly*'s special Christmas issue. Half of his allotted time slipped by as he sought in vain for inspiration. Finally an early morning bicycle ride led him to reminiscences about his school days—and in four days *Good-bye, Mr. Chips* was created. The story stirred favorable but muted critical mentions in England; its extraordinary success was due almost wholly to America's enthusiastic reception. It appeared in the April 1934 *Atlantic Monthly* and soon afterwards was published as a book in the United States.

Good-bye, Mr. Chips became an overnight best-seller as a direct result of media promotion. Alexander Woollcott recommended it in the *New Yorker* and devoted a "Town Crier" broadcast to praise of Hilton's new work. There was such "a run on bookstores all over the country [that] the publishers had difficulty filling the reorders as they came streaming in." The book was a smash success, placing fourth on the 1934 best-seller list and fifth in 1935.

This tale of an old schoolmaster's reminiscences did, as predicted in a *Commonweal* review, "hit almost every soft spot in the reading public." *Mr. Chips*'s popularity was not limited to this single novelette, however. Hilton adapted the story for a radio special in March 1935, which was received enthusiastically and rebroadcast. He also capitalized on the Chips fad by writing six short stories about his hero's further exploits, first published in magazines and collected as *To You, Mr. Chips* (1938). *Good-bye, Mr. Chips* won him sterling reviews and became a successful 1939 film.

The Chips craze sparked popular interest in the earlier Hilton novels, most of which were immediately reprinted. The motion picture *Knight Without Armor* was released in 1937, and a dramatization of *And Now Goodbye* played in New York the same year. Of all Hilton's novels, however, *Lost Horizon* was revived most successfully, becoming in time even more popular than *Good-bye, Mr. Chips*. It too was lauded by Woollcott and placed eighth on the 1935 best-seller list: Hilton enjoyed the rare honor of having two books among the top ten sellers that year—*Good-bye, Mr. Chips* was fifth. Frank Capra, enraptured by *Lost Horizon*'s cinematic potential, made it a lavish Hollywood spectacle starring Ronald Colman as Conway, the introspective diplomat-adventurer. "Shangri-La," the name of the hidden Tibetan valley where moderation reigns and time slows down, became a household equiva-

Dust jacket for Hilton's 1937 novel; he also wrote the scenario for
the 1939 film version

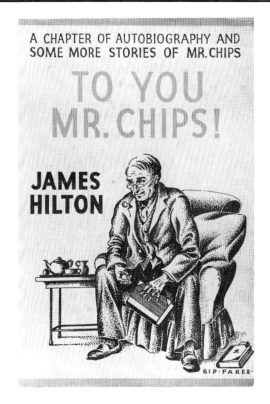

Dust jacket for Hilton's collection that includes short stories about
a kindly old schoolmaster

Dust jacket for the British edition of Hilton's novel set in a
Midlands industrial town before and during World War II

Dust jacket for the novel in which Hilton drew upon his Hollywood experiences for the story of an actress and a producer

Chapter VII.

Conway was calm, behind calm their eagerness that grew in intensity as he accompanied Chang across the empty courtyards. If the words of the Chinese meant anything, he was on the threshold of discovery : soon he would know whether his theory, still half-formed, were less impossible than it appeared. it would be interesting to meet Conway had met many potentates in his time ; he took a detached interest in them, and was shrewd as a rule in his conscious, he also had the valuable knack of being able to say polite things in languages of which he knew very little indeed.

Conway reflected

A Bicycle Ride Inspired Him

JAMES HILTON

IN the autumn of 1933 the author of "Good-bye, Mr. Chips" and "We Are Not Alone" was living at Wanstead, an old part of London, "in a house that dates from 1780 or so, in a district that is charming, quiet and unfashionable." It was quite close to Epping Forest where Hilton walked his burly Alsatian and tiny Pekingese, which in winter evenings rather inadequately balanced the Hilton hearthrug.

James Hilton was born in 1900 in Lancashire. At an early age he was taken to live in London, where he attended various schools. Too young for service in the War, he was in the Cambridge O.T.C. when the War ended.

Hilton had been writing since his boyhood. His first article was accepted by none other than the *Manchester Guardian* when he was only seventeen. His first novel, "Catherine Herself," was written also when he was seventeen, and published two years later (1920) while he was still an undergraduate.

What he calls his "real stroke of good luck" came when he was commissioned by the editor of the *British Weekly* to write a long short story for a special Christmas supplement to be completed in a fortnight. Inspiration would not come. Mr. Hilton says he never suffered so much in his life, and spent the whole of the first week in a blue funk. Then while he was bicycle-riding one foggy winter morning the idea came, "Good-bye, Mr. Chips" was finished in four days, within a year was a best-seller on two continents, and Mr. Hilton was established, at the age of thirty-three, at the top of his profession.

Recently Mr. Hilton has been writing for the movies in Hollywood. He is one of the few authors to do so with no complaints about the temperaments of movie executives.

Publisher's advertisement for We Are Not Alone, *telling the story of how Hilton got the idea for* Good-bye, Mr. Chips

lent for Utopia, as well as the designation for the base of Jimmy Doolittle's 1942 Tokyo raid and a 27,000-ton aircraft carrier christened in 1944.

Hilton and his wife, Alice Brown Hilton, arrived in the United States in November 1935 for a few months' stay to aid in the filming of *Lost Horizon* and *Knight Without Armor*. Upon his arrival, a *New York Times* interviewer elicited from him some views on his work: "I don't mind being called a sentimentalist so long as it is not used in a derogatory sense. A lot of modern books have come out of the icebox and not out of the oven. They are cold cerebration.... All great novels of the world have been sentimental." In a 1936 interview, he objected "to being classed as an 'escapist,' " while admitting that "the idea for *Lost Horizon* was germinated out of anxiety over the European situation and a desire to stage a conception of a world as far removed from this sort of thing as possible."

Hilton took up permanent residence in California in 1937 and became an American citizen in 1948. He filed for a Mexican divorce from his wife, which was granted 13 April 1937; seven days later he married Galina Kopineck, an actress with whom he had been associated for some time. She divorced him in 1945. Hilton became a popular screenwriter, among the highest paid in Hollywood; he was involved in writing scenarios for several films, including *Camille* (1936), his own *We Are Not Alone* (1939), *The Tuttles of Tahiti* (1942), and the excellent *Mrs. Miniver* (1942), for which he won an Academy Award. He collaborated with Robert Benchley on the dialogue for Alfred Hitchcock's *Foreign Correspondent* (1940) and narrated *Madame Curie* (1943). Eight of his own novels were made into motion pictures, generally with his supervision.

Hilton's last big success was *Random Harvest,* which, except for A. J. Cronin's *The Keys of the Kingdom,* was the best-selling novel of 1941. The sales of this story of a successful industrialist's struggle to recapture three years of his life spent in shellshock amnesia were in no way hindered by cynical reviewers who called it "implausible," "dullish," and "a bore." *Random Harvest* went through twenty-two printings in three years and in 1942 was made into a sentimental M-G-M film starring Ronald Colman and Greer Garson.

Hilton had a long-standing interest in communications. The *Atlantic Monthly* of December 1946 featured an article, "Literature and Hollywood," in which he expressed his views on popular literature's relation to other media and the incorporation of all forms of entertainment, literature included, into "a highly lucrative Frankenstein," the "Entertainment Machine." His successful career in screenwriting gave way to one in radio: beginning in 1948, he served as host and editor of the "Hallmark Playhouse," a weekly broadcast.

After *Random Harvest,* Hilton published five novels, none of which matched the success achieved by *Good-bye, Mr. Chips; Lost Horizon;* or *Random Harvest,* although two, *So Well Remembered* and *Time and Time Again,* were top-ten best-sellers. His reputation as a popular novelist had been made with the first of these, and the other four novels, as speculated by a 1937 reviewer, did "leap on the best seller list just in tribute to Mr. Chips." Hilton had his own ideas on what made his books sell: a mixture of media promotion and genuine coincidence with the tastes of the general public, not necessarily the tastes of the professional critics. He was, as he once said, a "novelist who sells the reader a good time." A *Saturday Review of Literature* critic suggested that Hilton's novels were popular because of their aloofness to "the intellectual ferment of the times"—he "gave the public a glimpse of escape into philosophical reflection, a sight of a man who made peace and quiet in his own mind." Many of his books wistfully evoke a rosy image of Victorian and Edwardian life, what he calls in his autobiographical essay "What Mr. Chips Taught Me" "the English illusion": that humane, genteel, balanced atmosphere which Hilton—and his readers—felt was destroyed in the ferocity and barbarism of the world war.

James Hilton died of cancer of the liver on 20 December 1954 after a long hospital stay. His novels and movies had made him quite wealthy, and he left an estate of over $250,000 in trust to his first wife and his father. *Time* summed up his thirty-five-year career thus: "Millionaire Novelist Hilton served up a mellow blend of worldly wisdom and well-bred British morality that delighted the book clubs, Hollywood producers, and the general public, but alienated first-line critics."

Constance Holme

(7 October 1880-17 June 1955)

Charlotte Stewart
University of North Carolina

BOOKS: *Crump Folk Going Home* (London: Mills & Boon, 1913);
The Lonely Plough (London: Mills & Boon, 1914);
The Old Road from Spain (London: Mills & Boon, 1916); republished as *The Homecoming* (New York: McBride, 1916);
Beautiful End (London: Mills & Boon, 1918);
The Splendid Fairing (London: Mills & Boon, 1919);
The Trumpet in the Dust (London: Mills & Boon, 1921);
The Things Which Belong (London: Mills & Boon, 1925);
He-who-came? (London: Chapman & Hall, 1930);
Four One-Act Plays (Kirby Lonsdale: Wolfenden, 1932);
The Wisdom of the Simple, and Other Stories (London: Oxford University Press, 1937).

Edith Constance Holme was born in Milnthorpe, Westmorland, where, except for brief periods at school in Birkenhead and Blackheath, she remained for the rest of her life. Her eight novels are infused with her deep attachment to this region—to the traditions of her forebears, who were chiefly land agents, to the values of the ruling classes; and increasingly in her later work, to the lives, struggles, and values of the region's ordinary folk. She wrote well and carefully about what she knew, and although her novels can be classified as regional, they strike universal themes, for Holme was concerned above all with the continuity of human life, traditions of work and service, and the mysteries of human character as it unfolds amid natural and social constraints. Sir Humphrey Milford, for years the chairman at the Oxford University Press, expressed his admiration of Holme's work by publishing all eight of her novels and one book of short stories in the Oxford World's Classics series. Holme was the only twentieth-century English author to be so honored.

Constance Holme was the youngest of the fourteen children born to John Holme and his wife Elizabeth (née Cartmel). Her first two novels, *Crump Folk Going Home* (1913) and *The Lonely Plough* (1914), reflect the traditions of her father's family.

Constance Holme

John Holme, himself a land agent, was descended from land agents, lawyers, and farmers who had settled in South Westmorland, a corner of Cumbria bounded on the east by the Pennine Mountains, on the north and west by the Lakeland fells, and on the south by Morecambe Bay. Holme married a Westmorland land agent, Frederick Burt Punchard, in 1916, when she was thirty-five. Punchard was agent to the Underley Hall estates at Kirkby Lonsdale, where the couple lived, ten miles from Milnthorpe, until Punchard's retirement in 1937.

As critic Glen Cavaliero points out, Holme's "attitude to her work was serious (she was a slow and careful writer) and her outlook conservative." She once wrote Sir Humphrey Milford (26 January 1939) that she had "tried to crystallise the loveliness of England before it departed." Holme's early novels concentrate on the lives and fortunes of members of the upper class—landed gentry like her own forebears—and evoke life as it was when the Edwardian era waned.

Crump Folk Going Home is a brisk, somewhat stagy novel, in which the details of country life are lovingly and carefully observed. Its heroine, Deborah Lyndesay, is the only surviving daughter of a respected land agent, who would like to assume her father's post but cannot because she is a woman. The novel chronicles Deborah's struggle to maintain her hold upon the land she loves and considers her own by right of birth.

Holme's second novel, *The Lonely Plough,* is the work for which she is most widely known. Like *Crump Folk,* it gives a view of country life in which class distinctions play an accepted role—not so much for the honor they confer but for the sense of order and purpose they bring to human life. The drama here is provided by the threat, which looms throughout the novel, of a disastrous flood, and by the way the novel's hero (the land agent Lancaster) and the region's farmers pull together when the flood arrives. Indeed, the novel shows in plenary fashion "an ancient system working at its best . . . , a triangular relationship which needed the right men in each department to keep the bearings smooth."

Holme's third novel, *The Old Road from Spain* (1916), was her favorite. It was published the year she was married and is imbued with the traditions of her mother's folk. The Cartmel family legend held that a castaway from an Armada galleon, wrecked in Morecambe Bay, had entered the family line, endowing it with a recurring exotic strain. In *The Old Road from Spain,* the Huddleston family, like the Cartmel family, carries a restless Spanish strain, which sits like a curse upon the novel's hero, Luis Huddleston. To reinforce the human legend, a flock of sheep descended from Spanish sheep that came from the old Armada galleon periodically descend from the fell to the grounds of Thorns, the family estate, to warn the Huddlestons of impending death. Although Holme stated in her introduction to the Oxford World's Classics edition, "the 'sheep-doom' . . . is entirely my own fabrication," she managed to weave this odd, supernatural element plausibly into the novel's plot.

Holme's first three novels are all cast in a form conventional to the novels of her time, with the action extending over a lengthy period. And although each is in its way a convincing chronicle of family and regional traditions, her best work lay ahead.

According to Alan L. Brown, 1918 was a watershed year in Holme's life: "Her personal scrapbook . . . contains many newspaper cuttings concerning local boys who fought, and especially who fell, in the Great War. Under the impact of the carnage from the Somme onwards her writing changed. She now became preoccupied with the mystery of suffering; turned afresh to Greek tragedy on which she meditated deeply in these war years."

Holme's new preoccupation resulted in her major achievement—four novels which she and her family called her "Greek novels": *Beautiful End* (1918), *The Splendid Fairing* (1919), *The Trumpet in the Dust* (1921), and *The Things Which Belong* (1925). These novels represent a deepening of Holme's sympathies for the lives and hardships of ordinary folk—the people whose labor made possible the comfort of the upper classes. Each novel is a kind of meditation upon the nature of tragedy. And each, in keeping with Holme's attention to the Greek unities, takes place within the space of a single day.

As Glen Cavaliero has observed, each of these books "centres round a dream and the nature of its fulfilment and as such comments obliquely on the rural novelist's confrontation of change." In *Beautiful End,* Christopher Sill, an impoverished old fiddler, dreams of returning to his old marsh home, which he had earlier lost through his own improvidence. His dream sustains him through a long, hard sojourn in the home of his elder son, whose shrewish wife rules their lives with petty cruelties. But when old Kit finally can go home, at the bidding of his kindly younger son and his good wife, who have bought the old farm and fixed it up, he finds the place so changed, so uncomfortably bright and new, that it destroys his dream of the shabby home that nourished him. The only way he can regain his dream, and his tenuous hold on life, is to return to the home of the elder son, where hardship kept his vision alive.

In *The Splendid Fairing* (for which Holme received the Femina-Vie Heureuse award in 1919), Simon and Sarah Thornthwaite have grown old and bitter trying to eke out a life on a poor marsh farm. Their only comfort is to dream that someday their son, Geordie, who ran away to Canada, will come back. On the day that Simon and Sarah decide that they must give up their farm and throw themselves upon the mercy of Simon's younger brother, Geordie does in fact return with a fortune that could make their final years comfortable. But for some perverse reason, Geordie pretends to be his look-alike cousin, Jim, son of their prosperous sister-in-law, Eliza, whom Sarah hates. Sarah, blinded by her own bitterness, turns Geordie out into the night,

Dust jacket for Holme's 1925 novel about a woman unable to realize her dream

where she knows he will drown on the marsh when the tide comes in.

In *The Trumpet in the Dust,* an elderly charwoman, Ann Clapham, dreams of retiring to a comfortable almshouse which had been promised to her years before. Toward the end of the day on which Ann actually acquires her house, she learns that her daughter has died in a distant town, and she gives up her new home so she can take care of her grandchildren, even though it means she must continue her old work of scrubbing floors.

Mattie Kirkly, in *The Things Which Belong,* has always felt confined by life on the estate whose beautiful gardens her husband has tended for years. Mattie yearns to go to Canada, where her children live, and weaves an elaborate vision of life "on the other side of the pond." When at last her dream is about to come true, Mattie finds that her age, her husband's needs, and her own fear of the long ocean voyage make it impossible for her to go.

In each of these four novels, the tragic dimension arises from the interplay between character formed by hardship and loyalty to traditional values, and the demands of external reality. Kit Sill must retreat once more into his dream because there is no other refuge for him in the changed and changing world; Mattie Kirkly undergoes genuine disillusionment and is able to accept her fate; and Ann Clapham, under a different set of constraints, reaffirms the pattern of her life. Only Sarah Thornthwaite attempts to deny her fate, by refusing to acknowledge the fulfillment of her dream, and the tragedy that befalls her and Simon is thus darker and more profound than that which strikes the characters in the other works.

Constance Holme had a fine ear for local patterns of speech and an excellent eye for the details of village and country life, and in her "Greek novels" she penetrated more deeply than before her characters' hearts and minds. As Cavaliero suggests, her later works "present a fuller and more satisfactory picture of the life of the region, perhaps because in them the human element interprets the regional and not the other way round."

Holme's last published novel, *He-who-came?* (1930), is a departure from the rest. It is a fanciful tale of good Aunt Martha, who cares for her dead sister's children. Martha is gifted with second sight and can commune with animals and natural things. The novel coyly builds to a concluding anecdote about a night when Martha misapplies her magic powers.

Except for *The Wisdom of the Simple, and Other Stories,* first published in 1937 in the World's Classics series, and *Four One-Act Plays* (1932), Holme's publishing career seems to have ended with *He-who-came?* And today, as Margaret Crosland suggests, "Outside Cumbria . . . there are few people . . . who know the work of Constance Holme well." Perhaps real fame always eluded her, despite the evidence of a letter to the editor of *Saturday Review* (19 February 1938) by Ruth G. Brown of the Oxford University Press, which states, "[Constance Holme] happens to be one of our most popular authors. . . . Sales on 'The Lonely Plough' up to October, 1937, were over 35,000 in England and America." The letters column in which Brown's letter appeared was subtitled "Crusaders for Constance Holme" and consisted of responses to an earlier editorial comment (22 January 1938) that "We are still hunting for someone who has actually read Constance Holme's novels." Eleven enthusiastic readers replied.

Alan L. Brown notes that Holme's later books, despite a kind reception from the critics, did not sell well: "She had made only 'pin money' and she was discouraged." A final novel, "The Jasper Sea," remains unpublished.

Holme suffered from diabetes and increasingly led a reclusive life until her death in 1955 at age seventy-four. She died in the village of Arnside, where she had moved the previous fall. Her husband had died in 1946, after they had returned to the home of Holme's birth above Milnthorpe, Owlet Ash. They had no children.

Constance Holme wrote her finest novels during the years when Dorothy Richardson, Virginia Woolf, and James Joyce were extending the frontiers of the form. Although her achievement was more modest and remains more hidden from public view, she nevertheless deserves recognition for the authenticity of her vision, her serious craftsmanship, and her celebration of the dignity of human life.

References:
Alan L. Brown, "Constance Holme," *The Serif,* 1 (1964): 21-24;

Glen Cavaliero, "A Land of One's Own: Constance Holme," *The Rural Tradition in the English Novel* (London & New York: Macmillan, 1977), pp. 157-172;

Margaret Crosland, "Devolving (1)," *Beyond the Lighthouse: English Woman Novelists in the Twentieth Century* (New York: Taplinger, 1981), pp. 120-123.

Jerome K. Jerome

(2 May 1859-14 June 1927)

Ruth Marie Faurot
University of the Pacific

See also the Jerome entry in *DLB 10, Modern British Dramatists, 1900-1945.*

SELECTED BOOKS: *On the Stage—and Off* (London: Field & Tuer, 1885; New York: Holt, 1891);

The Idle Thoughts of an Idle Fellow (London: Field & Tuer/New York: Scribner & Welford, 1886; New York: Holt, 1890);

Barbara (London & New York: French, 1886);

Sunset (New York: French, 1888?);

Fennel (London & New York: French, 1888);

Stage-land (London: Chatto & Windus, 1889; New York: Holt, 1890);

Three Men in a Boat (To Say Nothing of the Dog) (Bristol: J. W. Arrowsmith/London: Simpkin, Marshall, 1889; New York: Holt, 1889);

Diary of a Pilgrimage (and Six Essays) (Bristol: J. W. Arrowsmith, 1891; New York: Holt, 1891);

Told after Supper (London: Leadenhall Press, 1891; New York: Holt, 1891);

Novel Notes (London: Leadenhall Press, 1893; New York: Holt, 1893);

John Ingerfield and Other Stories (London: McClure,

1894; New York: Holt, 1894);

The Prude's Progress, by Jerome and Eden Phillpotts (London: Chatto & Windus, 1895);

Biarritz, by Jerome and Adrian Ross, with music by F. O. Carr (London: Francis, Day & Hunter/ New York: T. B. Harms, 1896);

Sketches in Lavender, Blue and Green (London: Longmans, Green, 1897; New York: Holt, 1897);

The Second Thoughts of an Idle Fellow (London: Hurst & Blackett, 1898; New York: Dodd, Mead, 1898);

Three Men on the Bummel (London: Arrowsmith, 1900); republished as *Three Men on Wheels* (New York: Dodd, Mead, 1900);

The Observations of Henry (Bristol: J. W. Arrowsmith, 1901; New York: Dodd, Mead, 1901);

Paul Kelver (London: Hutchinson, 1902; New York: Dodd, Mead, 1902);

Miss Hobbs (New York & London: French, 1902);

Tea-table Talk (London: Hutchinson, 1903; New York: Dodd, Mead, 1903);

Tommy and Co. (London: Hutchinson, 1904; New York: Dodd, Mead, 1904);

Woodbarrow Farm (New York & London: French, 1904);

Idle Ideas in 1905 (London: Hurst & Blackett, 1905);

The Passing of the Third Floor Back, and Other Stories (London: Hurst & Blackett, 1907; New York: Dodd, Mead, 1908);

The Angel and the Author and Others (London: Hurst & Blackett, 1908);

Fanny and the Servant Problem (New York & London: French, 1909);

They and I (London: Hutchinson, 1909; New York: Dodd, Mead, 1909);

The Passing of the Third Floor Back: An Idle Fancy in a Prologue, A Play and an Epilogue (London: Hurst & Blackett, 1910; New York: Dodd, Mead, 1921);

When Greek Meets Greek (Philadelphia: Penn, 1910);

The Master of Mrs. Chilvers (London: Unwin, 1911; New York: Dodd, Mead, 1911);

Robina in Search of a Husband (New York: French, 1913);

Malvina of Brittany (London & New York: Cassell, 1916);

All Roads Lead to Calvary (London: Hutchinson, 1919; New York: Dodd, Mead, 1919);

Anthony John (London & New York: Cassell, 1923; New York: Dodd, Mead, 1923);

A Miscellany of Sense and Nonsense (London: J. W. Arrowsmith, 1923; New York: Dodd, Mead, 1924);

The Soul of Nicholas Snyders (London: Hodder & Stoughton, 1925);

The Celebrity (London: Hodder & Stoughton, 1926; New York & London: French, 1927);

My Life and Times (London: Hodder & Stoughton, 1926; New York & London: Harper, 1926).

PLAYS: *Barbara,* London, Globe Theatre, 19 June 1886;

Sunset, adapted from Alfred Tennyson's "The Two Sisters," London, Comedy Theatre, 13 February 1888;

Fennel, adapted from François Coppée's *Le Luthier de Crémone,* London, Novelty Theatre, 31 March 1888;

Woodbarrow Farm, London, Comedy Theatre, 18 June 1888; produced again as *The Master of Woodbarrow,* New York, Lyceum Theatre, 26 August 1890;

Pity is Akin to Love, London, Olympic Theatre, 8 September 1888;

New Lamps for Old, London, Terry's Theatre, 8 February 1890;

Ruth, by Jerome and Addison Bright, Bristol, Prince's Theatre, 20 March 1890;

What Women Will Do, Birmingham, Theatre Royal, 17 September 1890;

Birth and Breeding, adapted from Hermann Sudermann's *Die Ehre,* Edinburgh, Theatre Royal, 18 September 1890;

The Councillor's Wife, by Jerome and Eden Phillpotts, New York, Empire Theatre, 6 November 1892; produced again as *The Prude's Progress,* London, Comedy Theatre, 22 May 1895;

The Rise of Dick Halward, London, Garrick Theatre, 19 October 1895;

Biarritz, by Jerome and Adrian Ross, music by F. O. Carr, London, Prince of Wales's Theatre, 11 April 1896;

The MacHaggis, by Jerome and Phillpotts, London, Globe Theatre, 25 February 1897;

Miss Hobbs, New York, Lyceum Theatre, 7 September 1899; London, Duke of York's Theatre, 18 December 1899;

Susan in Search of a Husband, London, Scala Theatre, 16 March 1906; produced again as *Robina in Search of a Husband,* London, Vaudeville Theatre, 16 December 1913;

Sylvia of the Letters, London, Playhouse, 15 October 1907;

The Passing of the Third Floor Back, London, St. James's Theatre, 1 September 1908;

Fanny and the Servant Problem, London, Aldwych Theatre, 14 October 1908; produced again as

The New Lady Bantock, New York, Wallack's
Theatre, 8 February 1909;

The Master of Mrs. Chilvers, London, Royalty
Theatre, 26 April 1911;

Esther Castways, London, Prince of Wales's Theatre,
21 January 1913;

The Great Gamble, London, Haymarket Theatre, 21
May 1914;

Poor Little Thing, adapted from Jules Lemaître's
play, New York, Bandbox, 22 December 1914;

The Three Patriots, London, Queen's Theatre, 27
July 1915;

Cook, London, Kingsway Theatre, 18 August 1917;
produced again as *The Celebrity,* London,
Playhouse, 25 June 1928;

Man or Devil, New York, Broadhurst Theatre, 21
May 1925; produced again as *The Soul of
Nicholas Snyders,* London, Everyman Theatre,
13 December 1927.

Jerome K. Jerome was a familiar name at the
turn of the nineteenth century and in the first
quarter of the twentieth. He was a humorist, who,
under the pose of "the Idler," made his reputation
as an essayist, the editor of two magazines (the *Idler,*
1892-1897, and *To-day,* 1893-1897), and the author
of *Three Men in a Boat (To Say Nothing of the Dog)*
(1889). His plays were successes, none more so than
The Passing of the Third Floor Back (first produced in
1908), performed the world over. Contemporary
reviewers compared his novels favorably to Dickens's. Their subjects vary; their tone runs from
comical to polemical. They are all, in a sense, autobiographical.

Jerome was born in Walsall, Staffordshire, on
2 May 1859, of Devonshire and Welsh parents,
Jerome Clapp Jerome and Margaret Jones Jerome,
both Nonconformists. His father, who was a trained
architect with a strong inclination to the ministry,
lost the family wealth in a coal-mining venture in
Staffordshire. In his move to London, where he
became an ironmonger and solicitor, he was equally
unlucky. The boy grew up in East London with the
family's striving to maintain their genteel heritage
and their Puritan faith. Through scholarships
Jerome acquired a good early education, but the
death of both his father and his mother when he was
in his mid-teens left him desolate and poor. After
various clerking jobs, he took to the stage for three
years, touring the provinces. It gained him little
money but much experience, which he used in his
humorous but accurate portrayal of the East End
theater and the traveling companies. Publication of
On the Stage—and Off (1885), *The Idle Thoughts of an*

Jerome K. Jerome (© Strand Magazine)

Idle Fellow (1886), and *Stage-land* (1889) gave him
courage. At the insistence of Georgina Henrietta
Stanley, whom he married on 21 June 1888, he
decided to live by his writing.

Three Men in a Boat, begun in the year of his
marriage, became an enormous success, subsequently going into many printings. Selling more
than a million copies in Jerome's lifetime, it was
translated into twenty-seven languages and became
a student's English-language reader. It was a
Time-Life reprint in 1964; in 1977 it was presented
as a BBC television special seen worldwide. Its 1981
adaptation as a one-man show in London and a
1982 edition, annotated by Christopher Matthew
and Benny Green, attest to its timelessness. Presenting the universal experience of the amateur's
camping trip along with the exuberance and nonsense of young office workers on holiday, it could,
Jerome ruefully reflected, apparently have been
written by anybody; but it was written with the
Jeromian wit. Already his earlier works had earned
the label "the new humor" (*Punch* condescendingly
referred to him as " 'Arry K. 'Arry").

The collapse of Jerome's weekly newspaper, *To-day,* in November 1897 as a result of a lawsuit left him in a reflective mood. He began, then, his major novel, the autobiographical *Paul Kelver* (1902), a maturation novel poignantly capturing the family life of a poverty-ridden father, mother, and only son in their working-class neighborhoods in East London. The novel's close reflection of Jerome's actual life is verified by his book *My Life and Times* (1926), published one year before his death. Certainly his parents' personalities come through, the father with the high ethical standards, who seemed "one of the unlucky ones," and the dreamy, gentle, and pious mother. Paul is fictionalized as an only child. In truth, Jerome's two sisters, older by eleven years, could scarcely be playmates. Narrated in first person, the novel depicts the loneliness of the hero's childhood, his unpopularity among school friends, and his wry recognition that his humor and droll wit are what his school friends like about him. This quality strikes him as unworthy, beneath his potential. Yet constant in Jerome's writings is the reassurance to the clowns that there is merit in their gift of making the world laugh.

True to Jerome's own life, the early death of the parents forces Paul, at fourteen, to make his own way. The struggle for companionship and purpose in living is poignant. Necessity and inclination lead him to the theater, where he aspires to be a second Irving and finds himself playing multiple parts, traveling the provinces, even writing some plays. It is a hard life, far from the boy's dreams, and, after three years, he walks out of the theater. At the threshold of adulthood he seeks the persons influential in his childhood, the kind but cynical young doctor and the woman he now loves, and the beautiful Barbara Hasluck, who had always been Paul's own romantic ideal. He is disturbed at the failure of his youthful idols to maintain their idealism.

After amusing and realistic scenes of boardinghouse life, the novel ends with Paul's love for a girl of contrasting qualities from Barbara's. Norah, daughter of an artist, offers friendship and will be a helpmeet. She assures him that his ability to create a "fortress of laughter" may help right the wrongs and sorrows of this world. *Paul Kelver* was well received, though one critic, James Douglas of the *Bookman,* felt it was a rewrite of *David Copperfield.*

In *Tommy and Co.* (1904), Jerome, drawing from his days as editor of *The Idler* and *To-day,* wrote one of the earliest novels about the staff of a paper. Loosely plotted, this novel is structured on the slow buildup of Peter Hope's periodical, with chapter headings indicating the progress. The central figure is Tommy, the gamin who has decided to "do for" the widower, Peter Hope. The two take to each other, the ragamuffin girl reminding Peter of the infant son who, had he lived, would have been her age. Tommy develops into almost an adopted daughter. This relationship leads to much talk of "the new woman," educated and independent. The others who come to the office form gradually an association. Each has his own story and eventually some niche to fill in the publication group. The final chapter tells of Tommy's love for Dick Danvers, one of the staff, a tale with a happy ending but not without suffering. Jerome often uses the theme of the dual nature of man and the need for woman to be understanding. A great deal of witty, lifelike dialogue marks the book, though the *Times Literary Supplement* called it an "unexacting and amusing book, capital companion for an hour or so on a hot afternoon."

A novel with a modern appeal, *They and I* (1909) deals with the generation gap and the dream and reality of a house in the country. The narrator, a writer not unlike Jerome, tells of his decision to choose a house in the country for the benefit of his children: Dick, nineteen, down from the university; Robina, seventeen and pretty; Veronica, eleven, who most strongly feels the generation gap. Not exactly roughing it, the writer and his children set out to oversee the remodeling of the house while living in the nearby cottage, with the young people in charge of the housekeeping and the ailing mother coming only for visits. Comic incidents include discussions over architecture with the opinionated children, troubles with the chimney—and Veronica's method of cleaning it—milking a cow, and being introduced to the neighborhood. Long colloquies between the father and the children and some matchmaking among the young people make light reading. It is an amusing novel, quite timeless, but it received little critical attention and had poor sales.

Jerome's last two novels were written after World War I, in which he served with the French as an ambulance driver. In both books Jerome belabored his interpretation of Christianity, based on Tolstoy, in which an imperfect God needs man's aid to bring about a better world. In both novels the humor is gone; the characters are deeply committed to solving their own religious doubts and society's problems with the poor.

In *All Roads Lead to Calvary* (1919), the protagonist is a young journalist, neither poor nor piously reared. Enlisting in various movements—

woman's suffrage, the reform of journalism, opposition to warmongering—Joan Allway's search for truth finally invades her private life, her involvement with the young politician from the lower classes, whose wife fails to rise with his social promotion. Joan finds she must sacrifice her own desires if she is to expect others to act altruistically. There are some good, brief realistic war scenes in the novel, but though the topics discussed are not outdated, the main character lacks the appeal of either Paul Kelver or Tommy. "I felt sad when I wrote it," said Jerome. The *Times Literary Supplement* reviewer spotted the weaknesses in the plotting and thought it would have made a good lecture.

Anthony John (1923) again confronts Paul Kelver's problem: Why do the idealists lack power to fulfill their dreams, and why do the powerful lose their idealism? *Anthony John* portrays, as does *Paul Kelver,* a young boy's maturing amid poverty. The setting, in the industrial North, is more grim than the London scene, but the protagonist, unlike Paul, is an aggressive young lad. Winning community respect and riches, he marries into an aristocratic family, but having gained the world, he renounces it, leaving his fine home to establish himself as a solicitor for the poor. In these last two novels, Jerome introduces the mysterious stranger, a device employed most successfully in his *The Passing of the*

Third Floor Back. In *All Roads Lead to Calvary,* this stranger appears as a peasant encouraging the wounded soldiers and Joan, who has become a nurse. In *Anthony John,* Wandering Peter appears at moments of crises, encouraging and strengthening those around him. His function in both novels is to bring out the finest qualities in man and to reassure the individual that he is needed by God.

Reviewing his life in his memoir, Jerome described himself as having a melancholy, brooding disposition: "I can see the humorous side of things and enjoy the fun when it comes; but look where I will, there seems to me always more sadness than joy in life." His later plays and novels reflect the serious side. Nevertheless, his particular skill is in depicting fun and humor. His autobiographical novel, *Paul Kelver,* which combines both humor and pathos, is likely to survive.

References:

Joseph Connolly, *Jerome K Jerome* (London: Orbis Publishing, 1982);

Ruth Marie Faurot, *Jerome K. Jerome* (New York: Twayne, 1974);

Alfred Moss, *Jerome K. Jerome* (London: Selwyn & Blount, 1928);

V. S. Pritchett, "The Tin-openers," *New Statesman and Nation* (15 June 1957): 783-784.

Rudyard Kipling
(30 December 1865-18 January 1936)

Mary A. O'Toole
University of Tulsa

See also the Kipling entry in *DLB 19, British Poets, 1880-1914.*

SELECTED BOOKS: *Schoolboy Lyrics* (Lahore: Privately printed, 1881);

Echoes, by Kipling and Alice Kipling (Lahore: Privately printed, 1884);

Departmental Ditties and Other Verses (Lahore: Privately printed, 1886; enlarged edition, Calcutta: Thacker, Spink/London & Bombay: Thacker, 1890);

Plain Tales from the Hills (Calcutta: Thacker, Spink/London: Thacker, 1888; New York:

Lovell, 1890; London & New York: Macmillan, 1890);

Soldiers Three: A Collection of Stories Setting Forth Certain Passages in the Lives and Adventures of Privates Terence Mulvaney, Stanley Ortheris, and John Learoyd (Allahabad: Wheeler, 1888; London: Low, Marston, Searle & Rivington, 1890);

The Story of the Gadsbys: A Tale Without a Plot (Allahabad: Wheeler, 1888; Allahabad: Wheeler /London: Low, Marston, Searle & Rivington, 1890; New York: Lovell, 1890);

In Black and White (Allahabad: Wheeler, 1888; Al-

(H. Roger-Viollet, Paris)

lahabad: Wheeler/London: Low, Marston, Searle & Rivington, 1890);

Under the Deodars (Allahabad: Wheeler, 1888; Allahabad: Wheeler/London: Low, Marston, Searle & Rivington, 1890; New York: Lovell, 1890);

The Phantom 'Rickshaw and Other Tales (Allahabad: Wheeler, 1888; Allahabad: Wheeler/London: Low, Marston, Searle & Rivington, 1890);

Wee Willie Winkie and Other Child Stories (Allahabad: Wheeler, 1888; Allahabad: Wheeler/London: Low, Marston, Searle & Rivington, 1890);

Soldiers Three [and *In Black & White*] (New York: Lovell, 1890);

Indian Tales (New York: Lovell, 1890)—includes *The Phantom 'Rickshaw and Other Tales* and *Wee Willie Winkie and Other Child Stories*;

The Courting of Dinah Shadd and Other Stories (New York: Harper, 1890);

Departmental Ditties, Barrack-Room Ballads, and Other Verses (New York: United States Book Company, 1890);

The Light That Failed (London: Ward, Lock, Bowden, 1891; Philadelphia: Lippincott, 1891; revised edition, London & New York: Macmillan, 1891);

The City of Dreadful Night and Other Places (Allahabad: Wheeler, 1891; Allahabad: Wheeler/London: Low, Marston, 1891; New York: Ogilvie, 1899);

The Smith Administration (Allahabad: Wheeler, 1891);

Letters of Marque (Allahabad: Wheeler, 1891; republished in part, London: Low, Marston, 1891);

American Notes (New York: Ivers, 1891);

Mine Own People (New York: United States Book Company, 1891);

Life's Handicap: Being Stories of Mine Own People (New York: Macmillan, 1891; London: Macmillan, 1891);

The Naulahka: A Story of West and East, by Kipling and Wolcott Balestier (London: Heinemann, 1892; New York & London: Macmillan, 1892);

Barrack-Room Ballads and Other Verses (London: Methuen, 1892); republished as *Ballads and Barrack-Room Ballads* (New York & London: Macmillan, 1892);

Many Inventions (London & New York: Macmillan, 1893; New York: Appleton, 1893);

The Jungle Book (London & New York: Macmillan, 1894; New York: Century, 1894);

The Second Jungle Book (London & New York: Macmillan, 1895; New York: Century, 1895);

Out of India: Things I Saw, and Failed to See, in Certain Days and Nights at Jeypore and Elsewhere (New York: Dillingham, 1895)—includes *The City of Dreadful Night and Other Places* and *Letters of Marque*;

The Seven Seas (New York: Appleton, 1896; London: Methuen, 1896);

"Captains Courageous": A Story of the Grand Banks (London & New York: Macmillan, 1897; New York: Century, 1897);

An Almanac of Twelve Sports, text by Kipling and illustrations by William Nicholson (London: Heinemann, 1898; New York: Russell, 1898);

The Day's Work (New York: Doubleday & McClure, 1898; London: Macmillan, 1898);

A Fleet in Being (London & New York: Macmillan, 1898);

Kipling's Poems, edited by Wallace Rice (Chicago: Star Publishing, 1899);

Stalky & Co. (London: Macmillan, 1899; New York:

Doubleday & McClure, 1899);

Departmental Ditties and Ballads and Barrack-Room Ballads (New York: Doubleday & McClure, 1899);

From Sea to Sea and Other Sketches, 2 volumes (New York: Doubleday & McClure, 1899; London: Macmillan, 1900);

The Kipling Reader (London: Macmillan, 1900; revised, 1901);

Kim (New York: Doubleday, Page, 1901; London: Macmillan, 1901);

Just So Stories: For Little Children (London: Macmillan, 1902; New York: Doubleday, Page, 1902);

The Five Nations (London: Methuen, 1903; New York: Doubleday, Page, 1903);

Traffics and Discoveries (London: Macmillan, 1904; New York: Doubleday, Page, 1904);

Puck of Pook's Hill (London: Macmillan, 1906; New York: Doubleday, Page, 1906);

Collected Verse (New York: Doubleday, Page, 1907; London: Hodder & Stoughton, 1912);

Letters to the Family (Toronto: Macmillan, 1908);

Actions and Reactions (London: Macmillan, 1909; New York: Doubleday, Page, 1909);

Rewards and Fairies (London: Macmillan, 1910; Garden City: Doubleday, Page, 1910);

A History of England, by Kipling and C. R. L. Fletcher (Oxford: Clarendon Press/London: Frowde/London: Hodder & Stoughton, 1911; Garden City: Doubleday, Page, 1911);

Songs from Books (Garden City: Doubleday, Page, 1912; London: Macmillan, 1913);

The New Army, 6 pamphlets (Garden City: Doubleday, Page, 1914); republished as *The New Army in Training,* 1 volume (London: Macmillan, 1915);

France at War on the Frontier of Civilization (London: Macmillan, 1915; Garden City: Doubleday, Page, 1915);

The Fringes of the Fleet (London: Macmillan, 1915; Garden City: Doubleday, Page, 1915);

Sea Warfare (London: Macmillan, 1916; Garden City: Doubleday, Page, 1917);

A Diversity of Creatures (London: Macmillan, 1917; Garden City: Doubleday, Page, 1917);

The Eyes of Asia (Garden City: Doubleday, Page, 1918);

Twenty Poems (London: Methuen, 1918);

The Graves of the Fallen (London: Imperial War Graves Commission, 1919);

The Years Between (London: Methuen, 1919; Garden City: Doubleday, Page, 1919);

Rudyard Kipling's Verse, Inclusive Edition, 1885-1918 (3 volumes, London: Hodder & Stoughton, 1919; 1 volume, Garden City: Doubleday, Page, 1919);

Letters of Travel (1892-1913) (London: Macmillan, 1920; Garden City: Doubleday, Page, 1920);

Selected Stories From Kipling, edited by William Lyon Phelps (Garden City & Toronto: Doubleday, Page, 1921);

A Kipling Anthology: Verse (London: Methuen, 1922; Garden City: Doubleday, Page, 1922);

A Kipling Anthology: Prose (London: Macmillan, 1922; Garden City: Doubleday, Page, 1922);

Kipling Calendar (London: Hodder & Stoughton, 1923; Garden City: Doubleday, Page, 1923);

Land and Sea Tales (London: Macmillan, 1923; Garden City: Doubleday, Page, 1923);

Songs for Youth (London: Hodder & Stoughton, 1924; Garden City: Doubleday, Page, 1925);

A Choice of Songs (London: Methuen, 1925);

Debits and Credits (London: Macmillan, 1926; Garden City: Doubleday, Page, 1926);

Sea and Sussex (London: Macmillan, 1926; Garden City: Doubleday, Page, 1926);

Songs of the Sea (London: Macmillan, 1927; Garden City: Doubleday, Page, 1927);

Rudyard Kipling's Verse, Inclusive Edition, 1885-1926 (London: Hodder & Stoughton, 1927; Garden City: Doubleday, Page, 1927);

A Book of Words: Selections from Speeches and Addresses Delivered Between 1906 and 1927 (London: Macmillan, 1928; Garden City: Doubleday, Doran, 1928);

The Complete Stalky & Co. (London: Macmillan, 1929; Garden City: Doubleday, Doran, 1930);

Poems 1886-1929, 3 volumes (London: Macmillan, 1929; Garden City: Doubleday, Doran, 1930);

Limits and Renewals (London: Macmillan, 1932; Garden City: Doubleday, Doran, 1932);

Souvenirs of France (London: Macmillan, 1933);

Rudyard Kipling's Verse, Inclusive Edition, 1885-1932 (London: Hodder & Stoughton, 1933; Garden City: Doubleday, Doran, 1934);

Something of Myself for My Friends Known and Unknown (London: Macmillan, 1937; Garden City: Doubleday, Doran, 1937);

Rudyard Kipling's Verse, Definitive Edition (London: Hodder & Stoughton, 1940; New York: Doubleday, Doran, 1940).

Collection: *The Sussex Edition of the Complete Works of Rudyard Kipling,* 35 volumes (London: Macmillan, 1937-1939); republished as *The Collected Works of Rudyard Kipling, The Burwash Edition,* 28 volumes (Garden City: Doubleday, Doran, 1941).

Rudyard Kipling is better known as a poet and short-story writer than as a novelist. He wrote only three novels and collaborated with Wolcott Balestier on another, highly forgettable one. The shorter forms were his métier, and after the publication of *Kim* in 1901, Kipling never attempted another novel.

Joseph Rudyard Kipling was born in Bombay, India, on 30 December 1865, to John Lockwood Kipling and Alice Macdonald Kipling. His father at this time was professor of architectural sculpture in the School of Art in Bombay. Kipling had a pampered early childhood surrounded by servants. At the age of five and a half, however, along with his sister, two years younger, Kipling was taken to live with a family in Southsea to begin his "anglicization" and early schooling. The next five years were, in the main, years of misery. In addition to feelings of bewilderment and abandonment, Kipling had to suffer bullying by the woman of the house and her son. His poor eyesight slowed his progress in school. His only relief during these years was an occasional holiday visit to his aunt, who was married to the painter Edward Burne-Jones. There Kipling played with his cousins, enjoyed the company of William Morris, and fortified his spirit for the re-

Lorne Lodge, the "House of Desolation" in Southsea where Kipling and his sister Trix endured five years of misery (Roger Lancelyn Green)

Kipling's parents, John Lockwood Kipling and Alice Macdonald Kipling (Bateman's, Burwash, Sussex)

turn to Southsea and the "house of desolation."

From 1878 to 1882 Kipling attended the United Services College in Westward Ho!, Devon, a fairly new institution established primarily for, but not limited to, the sons of military officers. Kipling's stories in *Stalky & Co.* (1899) grew out of this experience. At the age of almost seventeen, obviously unsuited for a military life, Kipling returned to India as reporter, assistant editor, and general factotum for the *Civil and Military Gazette* in Lahore; later he moved to Allahabad to work on the newspaper, the *Pioneer*. He fell in with the pace of Indian life as though he had never left the country. His observation of the British civil, diplomatic, and military establishment in India resulted in 1886 in his first published book of poems, *Departmental Ditties*. Kipling's *Plain Tales from the Hills* (1888) was a collection of stories based on the lives of the British at their summer mountain retreat, Simla. These stories had previously been published in the *Civil and Military Gazette*.

Six more collections of his stories were published as part of the Indian Railway series in 1888: *Soldiers Three, The Story of the Gadsbys, In Black and White, Under the Deodars, The Phantom 'Rickshaw and*

Simla, the summer retreat of the British in the Himalayan foothills, the setting for Kipling's Plain Tales from the Hills *(Radio Times Hulton Picture Library, London)*

Other Tales, and *Wee Willie Winkie and Other Child Stories.* These, along with *Departmental Ditties and Other Verses* and *Plain Tales from the Hills,* paved the way for his burgeoning reputation when he moved to London in 1889. His poems and stories elicited strong reactions of love and hate from the start—almost none of his advocates and detractors were temperate in praise or in blame. Ordinary readers liked the rhythms, the cockney speech, and the imperialist sentiments of his poems and short stories; critics generally damned the works for the same reasons. His novels, however, were less controversial.

Kipling's first novel, *The Light That Failed* (1891), is partly autobiographical, especially in its depiction of the "house of desolation," where the orphan Dick Heldar has been sent to be raised by the widow Mrs. Jennett. After the arrival of another orphan, Maisie, an independent girl, Dick finds solace in her company. The two are separated when they are sent away to school, and both become artists. Dick eventually becomes a war correspondent as well, and, while covering the Gordon relief expedition in the Sudan, he is discovered sketching by Torpenhow, of the Central Southern Syndicate. Dick's pictures of soldiers and battles (subjects similar to those of Kipling's stories and poems) are published by the syndicate and achieve such popularity that Torpenhow calls Dick back to London, where prints of his sketches bring him financial success. Yet despite his popularity with the public there is the suggestion that Dick has compromised his artistic integrity.

In London he once again meets Maisie, still

Covers of seven of Kipling's collections of stories in the Indian Railway series (Grenville Taylor Collection)

the line of fire and is killed.

In the early 1890s, a number of Kipling's poems were published in W. E. Henley's *National Observer* and then collected into *Barrack-Room Ballads* (1892). This collection was immensely popular and contains some of the poems for which he is most famous—"Danny Deever," "Gunga Din," and "Mandalay." He also collaborated on *The Naulahka: A Story of West and East* (1892) with Wolcott Balestier, a young American publisher who died on 6 December 1891, shortly before work on the book was completed.

The Naulahka is not even discussed in Kipling's reticent autobiography, *Something of Myself for My Friends Known and Unknown* (1937). It reads more like one of Kipling's travel books than like a novel; the depiction of the Indian scene is not as well done as it is in *Kim*. The main characters are an American man and woman. The man, through a certain naiveté and boldness, wins the rajah's treasure, only to be persuaded by the woman to return it. The ending is ambiguous as the sheer diversity of Indian life prevails over the Americans' efforts. The novel seems rather hastily and opportunistically concocted and suffers from lack of unity and design, perhaps as a result of the unwieldy nature of joint authorship.

independent (and perhaps a lesbian). She is dissatisfied with her work, and, as Dick tries to help her (while unsuccessfully entreating her to marry him), it becomes apparent to the reader that she is essentially shallow. Dick also begins the painting that he hopes will be his masterpiece, a conception of Melancholia; but in the Sudan he had received a sword cut over one eye, a serious wound that took months to heal, and his eyesight begins to deteriorate rapidly. Struggling heroically, he completes the painting before the onset of total blindness, but a vengeful former model defaces the painting—a fact that his friends keep from him at first. He has been too proud to tell Maisie about his condition, but Torpenhow seeks her out in Paris, where she had gone to study, and brings her back to London.

Two versions of the novel were published in 1891. For *Lippincott's Monthly Magazine* (January 1891), Kipling wrote a happy ending; but he preferred the other ending, in which Maisie displays her weak character by refusing to stand by Dick, and the heartbroken young man, who has also discovered the fate of his masterpiece, returns to the battlefield, where he deliberately places himself in

Wolcott Balestier, coauthor with Kipling of the novel The Naulahka *(by permission of the Harvard College Library)*

Caroline Balestier, who married Kipling in 1892

Kipling wrote more stories during these years, including some of his best, such as "Without Benefit of Clergy." Shortly after Balestier's death, Kipling married his sister, Caroline Balestier, on 18 January 1892. They moved to Brattleboro, Vermont, close (too close, as it turned out) to Caroline's other brother, Beatty. Kipling loved his life in New England at first. He wrote more poems and short stories there, had the two *Jungle Books* (1894, 1895) published, and began work on *Kim*. A daughter, Josephine, was born in December 1892; another daughter, Elsie, came along two years later.

The Kiplings left America in 1896 after Kipling's ne'er-do-well brother-in-law, Beatty, threatened him, and Kipling pressed charges. An inconclusive public hearing was held during which Kipling's testimony was contradictory. He was ridiculed and his poems were parodied in the American press. (Kipling was unpopular with reporters because of his refusal to grant interviews.) Before the trial itself took place, the Kiplings left for England.

Kipling's novel *"Captains Courageous"* (1897), published shortly after the return to England, is based on his observation of life in New England fishing ports. The profusion of technical detail in the novel illustrates Kipling's lifelong respect for competence, and, while the novel is marred by sentimentality, its depiction of brave men who undertook the dangerous task of fishing the Grand Banks off the coast of Newfoundland in the days before

steam-powered fishing boats has won *"Captains Courageous"* admirers. Emphasizing the value of hard work in the development of character, the novel is the story of Harvey Cheney, a wealthy and spoiled fifteen year old who one May is washed overboard from an ocean liner bound for Europe, rescued by a fisherman, and taken aboard the schooner *We're Here,* captained by Disko Troop. The fishing season having just begun, Troop is unwilling to risk his season's profits by immediately taking the boy to port. Harvey insists that his father is a millionaire who would pay handsomely for his immediate return to New York, but Troop, doubting the boy's tale of his father's wealth, refuses and says that instead he will hire Harvey as a member of his crew until they return to Gloucester in September. When the arrogant young man becomes insulting, Troop punches him in the nose, beginning his education about the harsh discipline aboard ship. Because of such treatment and because he is an intelligent young man, Harvey learns quickly and earns the respect and friendship of the crew. He especially values their acceptance because it is based on his merits as a crewman, rather than on

Kipling in his study at Naulahka, the home he built in Vermont (Library of Congress)

year of the Queen's Jubilee, he wrote the well-known "Recessional," with its familiar phrases "the tumult and the shouting," "the Captains and the Kings," and "lest we forget." As early as 1897-1898 Kipling foresaw the dangers posed by Germany; during these years, as later in the 1930s, he urged his countrymen to take the German threat seriously and to arm and train and prepare to meet it. Both in the 1890s and in the 1930s, his countrymen ignored him.

The Kiplings' daughter Josephine died in 1899 during the family's last visit to America. Kipling himself was gravely ill at the time, and news of his daughter's death was kept from him until he began to regain his health. He was devastated by the loss.

After Josephine's death and until 1908, the Kiplings traveled each winter to South Africa. During the Boer War (1899-1902), Kipling helped to edit a newspaper for the troops, wrote the *Just So Stories* (1902), became acquainted with Cecil Rhodes, and observed the mismanagement of the war. His attraction to the common soldier, as evidenced in his poetry and early Indian stories, and his disgust with the ineptitude of those in command were heightened by what he observed in South Africa and were dominant themes in much of what he

Illustration for Kipling's sea novel, "Captains Courageous," which he later dismissed as a "boy's story"

his father's wealth, the stories of which only two, the captain's son Dan and the Negro cook, believe. After the ship has docked in Gloucester and Harvey's parents have come to take him home, his father, a self-made man, is pleased to see that his son has grown from a snobbish boy to a self-reliant young man who has learned how to make his own way through hard work and to judge people by their own merits rather than by their bank balances. While *"Captains Courageous"* has the elements of a good sea tale and novel of maturation, it is flawed by episodic plotting, shallow characterization, and sometimes-dubious psychologizing. Kipling eventually rejected the novel as simply a "boy's story."

Upon their return from America, the Kiplings settled for a time in Rottingdean, Sussex, where their son, John, was born in 1897. (John Kipling was to die in the Battle of Loos in 1915.) Kipling went often to London to visit his clubs and traveled quite extensively to other parts of the world. In 1897, the

Kipling's daughter Josephine, whose death in 1899 devastated Kipling (courtesy of Howard C. Rice, Jr.)

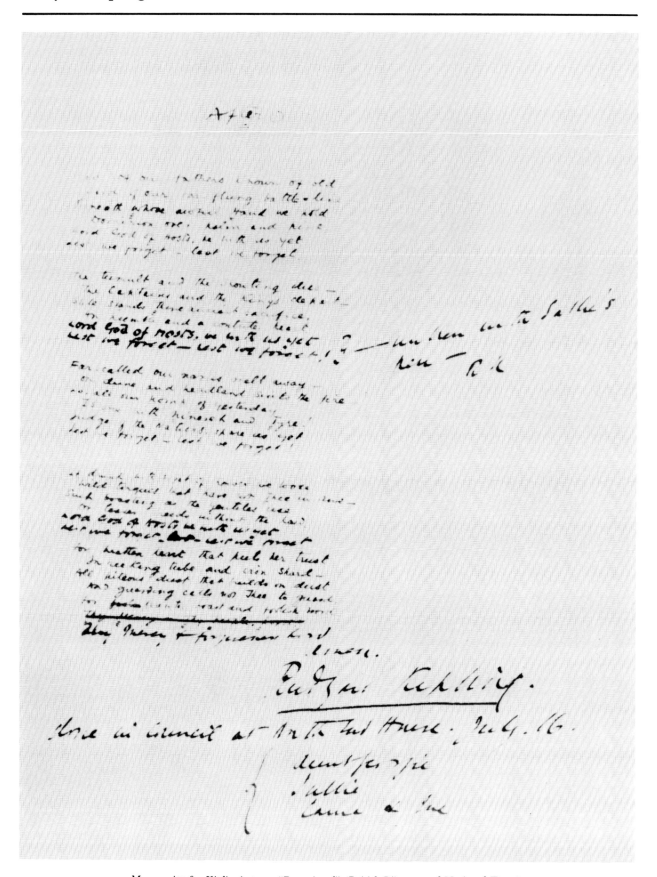

Manuscript for Kipling's poem "Recessional" (British Library and National Trust)

Illustration by Kipling for "The Cat That Walked by Himself" in
Just So Stories

wrote and said in these years. When America acquired the Philippines and Cuba, Kipling wrote "The White Man's Burden" and dedicated it to Theodore Roosevelt. This poem, this phrase, and this sentiment turned many people against Kipling and continue to do so today. Later Kipling pleaded with Roosevelt to try to effect America's entry into World War I.

Kipling's best novel, *Kim*, was published in 1901. The glory of *Kim* lies not in its plot nor in its characters but in its evocation of the complex Indian scene. The great diversity of the land—its castes; its sects; its geographical, linguistic, and religious divisions; its numberless superstitions; its kaleidoscopic sights, sounds, colors, and smells—are brilliantly and lovingly evoked. The British are less sympathetically portrayed, as one character says, "the Sahibs have not all this world's wisdom," and they are wrong to try to change the ineluctably Indian nature of the country. Kim, "the little friend of all the world," represents a union of both cultures and ignores religious and caste prejudices. Kim was

born Kimball O'Hara to an Irish mother who died giving birth to him and an Irish father, formerly a member of a regiment called the Mavericks, who died of drinking and drugs leaving his young son in the care of a half-caste woman. Growing up in the streets of Lahore, Kim becomes so tanned by the sun that he looks like an Indian boy, and, on meeting an old Tibetan lama searching for the River of the Arrow, which will wash away all sin, he decides to accompany the lama on his quest. Kim is also befriended by Mahbub Ali, a horse trader who, at first unknown to Kim, belongs to the British secret service.

Kim has been told that his life will change when he sees a red bull in a green field, and in their travels Kim and the lama come upon the Mavericks, whose regimental flag is a red bull on a green background. After a regimental chaplain opens an amulet Kim has worn around his neck and discovers Kim's baptismal certificate and a letter from his father asking that his son be cared for, it is decided Kim should be sent to school. The lama agrees and obtains the money from his order to pay for Kim's

Illustration by Kipling's father for the first edition of Kim

217

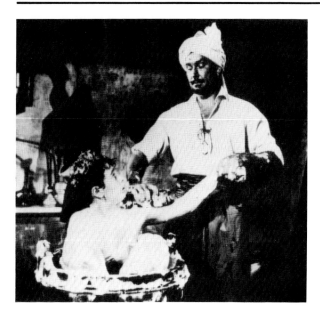

Errol Flynn as Mahbub Ali bathes Dean Stockwell as Kim in the 1950 film version of Kipling's novel

education at St. Xavier's, a school for British colonials. Kim dislikes his lack of freedom, but he is a good student and remains at the school for three years, traveling in the summer with Mahbub Ali, who, with other members of the secret service, educates Kim to play the "great game," as they call their work.

After leaving school, Kim, once again dressed as a street boy, travels with the lama to aid in his quest, while at the same time he uses their journey as a cover for his clandestine activities on behalf of the British, uncovering the existence of Russian spies in the north of India. The novel ends with the dying lama believing that he has found his river on the estate of a wealthy old woman who has aided them in the past, and with the assurance that Kim has performed well in the great game. This enigmatic ending (it is not made clear how Kim resolves the conflict between the Indians and the Sahibs) suggests a compromise between the pragmatic and the otherworldly, between the imposed British organization and the myriad, sprawling, resistant realities of India. As Kim realizes that his collaboration with the British contributes to the bondage of the native people he feels so close to, he faces a dilemma of allegiance. Although he has favored the native life-style that he slips into whenever he can, the lure of the civilization through the British also appeals to him.

Kipling has been rebuked for his sympathy with British foreign policy, a stand which also sur-

faces in *Kim,* although to a lesser extent than many of his other works. ("*Kim* is the answer to nine-tenths of the charges levelled against Kipling and the refutation of most of the generalizations about him," Mark Kinkead-Weekes contends.) Edmund Wilson denounced the novel's "imperialistic strain"—although he admitted it is "enchanting, almost a first-rate book"—and Boris Ford remarked that "this novel is so disarmingly superficial that even its less pleasant features, those relating to the colour conflict, fail to give any sharp offence." Yet Kipling's gentle warmth seems to overshadow ideological issues for a great many critics. "*Kim* is the profoundest expression of Kipling's creative talent," Vasant A. Shahane suggests. "It is not only the climax of his artistic development, but also a culmination of the process of Becoming which is woven into the texture of his work." *Kim* was Kipling's last novel. In the remaining thirty-five years of his life, he devoted himself to poetry and the short story.

In 1902 the Kiplings moved permanently to Bateman's in Burwash, Sussex. In the years after the move Kipling for the most part turned away from the types of stories he had written early in his career and explored new subjects and techniques. He wrote allegories, fables, futuristic fiction, historical tales for young people, tales of fairies and devils—an enormous variety of stories; he included verses in the collections of his stories, most importantly his well-known and often quoted "If," which appeared in *Rewards and Fairies* (1910). Some of the stories are obscure to the point of unintelligibility; others, such as "Mary Postgate" in the collection *A Diversity of Creatures* (1917), contain the kind of cruelty and desire for vengeance that his detractors detested and that eventually caused him to lose much of his audience. Another cause of Kipling's falling popularity was his insistence, through both the spoken and written word, that Britain institute compulsory military service.

Critical opinion on Kipling is still divided. Early critics such as Robert Buchanan denounced him as a "hooligan"; George Orwell grudgingly conceded that he could be called a "good bad poet"; Edmund Wilson misread and therefore disliked *Kim* because Kim did not take a stand against the British ruling classes; T. S. Eliot, who was a vice president of the Kipling Society, defended Kipling's verse in his preface to a collection of Kipling's poetry. Critics have attacked and defended him; only in recent years have they attempted to analyze his work. His political stance has finally been deemphasized and his artistry and craftsmanship have

Front page of a London newspaper for 18 January 1936, showing report of Kipling's death overwhelmed by news of the king's illness. King George V died two days later.

been recognized. Critical opinions are contradictory because Kipling was a man of contradictions. He had enormous sympathy for the lower classes, both military and civilian, yet distrusted all forms of democratic government. He would not accept any of the honors that were offered him by the British government throughout his life, yet he accepted a number of honorary doctorates from universities, and in 1907 he was awarded the Nobel Prize for literature.

Kipling's health was never good, and after a long and painful illness, he died on his forty-fourth wedding anniversary, 18 January 1936; his death was overshadowed by that of King George V. Kipling's ashes are buried in Westminster Abbey. He remains an intriguing personality and writer. In the summer of 1984, a one-man show, *Kipling,* written by Brian Clark and performed by Alec McGowan at the Mermaid Theatre in London, did nothing to resolve the antithetical elements in the man and his work.

Bibliographies:
Flora V. Livingston, *Bibliography of the Works of Rudyard Kipling* (New York: Wells, 1927);
Catalogue of the Works of Rudyard Kipling Exhibited at the Grolier Club from February 21 to March 30, 1929 (New York: Grolier Club, 1930);
Ellis Ames Ballard, *Catalogue Intimate and Descriptive of My Kipling Collection* (Philadelphia: Privately printed, 1935);
Livingston, *Supplement to Bibliography of the Works of Rudyard Kipling* (Cambridge: Harvard University Press, 1938);
James McG. Stewart, *Rudyard Kipling: A Bibliographical Catalogue,* edited by A. W. Yeats (Toronto: Dalhousie University Press/University of Toronto Press, 1959).

Biographies:
C. E. Carrington, *The Life of Rudyard Kipling* (Garden City: Doubleday, 1955);
Kingsley Amis, *Rudyard Kipling and His World* (London: Thames & Hudson, 1975);
Angus Wilson, *The Strange Ride of Rudyard Kipling* (New York: Viking, 1978);
Lord Birkenhead, *Rudyard Kipling* (London: Weidenfeld & Nicolson, 1978).

References:
Bonamy Dobrée, *Rudyard Kipling: Realist and Fabulist* (London: Oxford University Press, 1967);
T. S. Eliot, preface to *A Choice of Kipling's Verse* (London: Faber & Faber, 1941);
Elliot L. Gilbert, ed., *Kipling and the Critics* (New York: New York University Press, 1965);
James Harrison, *Rudyard Kipling* (Boston: Twayne, 1982);
Andrew Rutherford, ed., *Kipling's Mind and Art: Selected Critical Essays* (Stanford, Cal.: Stanford University Press, 1964);
J. I. M. Stewart, *Rudyard Kipling* (New York: Dodd, Mead, 1966);
J. M. S. Tompkins, *The Art of Rudyard Kipling* (London: Methuen, 1959).

Papers:
The Kipling Papers are the property of the National Trust, London.

Compton Mackenzie
(17 January 1883-30 November 1972)

Brian Murray
Youngstown State University

BOOKS: *Poems* (Oxford: Blackwell/London: Simpkin, Marshall, Hamilton, Kent, 1907);

The Passionate Elopement (London: Secker, 1911; New York: John Lane, 1911);

Carnival (London: Secker, 1912; New York: Appleton, 1912);

Kensington Rhymes (London: Secker, 1912);

Sinister Street, volume 1 (London: Secker, 1913); republished as *Youth's Encounter* (New York: Appleton, 1914);

Sinister Street, volume 2 (London: Secker, 1914; New York: Appleton, 1914);

Guy and Pauline (London: Secker, 1915); republished as *Plashers Mead* (New York & London: Harper, 1915);

The Early Life and Adventures of Sylvia Scarlett (London: Secker, 1918; New York: Harper, 1918);

Sylvia & Michael: The Later Adventures of Sylvia Scarlett (London: Secker, 1919; New York: Harper, 1919);

Poor Relations (London: Secker, 1919; New York & London: Harper, 1919);

The Vanity Girl (London & New York: Cassell, 1920; New York & London: Harper, 1920);

Rich Relatives (London: Secker, 1921; New York & London: Harper, 1921);

The Altar Steps (London & New York: Cassell, 1922; New York: Doran, 1922);

The Parson's Progress (London & New York: Cassell, 1923; New York: Doran, 1924);

Gramophone Nights, by Mackenzie and Archibald Marshall (London: Heinemann, 1923);

The Seven Ages of Woman (London: Secker, 1923; New York: Stokes, 1923);

The Heavenly Ladder (London: Cassell, 1924; New York: Doran, 1924);

The Old Men of the Sea (London: Cassell, 1924; New York: Stokes, 1924); republished as *Paradise for Sale* (London: Macdonald, 1963);

Santa Claus in Summer (London: Constable, 1924; New York: Stokes, 1925);

Coral: A Sequel to "Carnival" (London & New York: Cassell, 1925; New York: Doran, 1925);

Fairy Gold (London: Cassell, 1926; New York: Doran, 1926);

Compton Mackenzie, 1907

The Life and Adventures of Sylvia Scarlett (London: Secker, 1927);

Mabel in Queer Street (Oxford: Blackwell, 1927);

Rogues and Vagabonds (London: Cassell, 1927; New York: Doran, 1927);

Vestal Fire (London: Cassell, 1927; New York: Doran, 1927);

Extraordinary Women: Theme and Variations (London: Secker, 1928; New York: Macy-Masius, 1928);

Extremes Meet (London: Cassell, 1928; Garden City: Doubleday, Doran, 1928);

The Unpleasant Visitors (Oxford: Blackwell, 1928);

Gallipoli Memories (London: Cassell, 1929; Garden City: Doubleday, Doran, 1929);

The Adventures of Two Chairs (Oxford: Blackwell, 1929);

The Three Couriers (London: Cassell, 1929; Garden City: Doubleday, Doran, 1929);

April Fools: A Farce of Manners (London: Cassell, 1930; Garden City: Doubleday, Doran, 1930);

The Enchanted Blanket (Oxford: Blackwell, 1930);

Told (Oxford: Blackwell, 1930; New York: Appleton, 1930);

First Athenian Memories (London: Cassell, 1931);

Buttercups and Daisies (London: Cassell, 1931); republished as *For Sale* (Garden City: Doubleday, Doran, 1931);

The Conceited Doll (Oxford: Blackwell, 1931);

Our Street (London: Cassell, 1931; Garden City: Doubleday, Doran, 1932);

The Fairy in the Window-Box (Oxford: Blackwell, 1932);

Address . . . Delivered in the St. Andrew's Hall on January 29th, 1932, on the Occasion of His Installation as Rector (Glasgow: Jackson, Wylie, 1932);

Greek Memories (London: Cassell, 1932);

Prince Charlie (de jure Charles III, King of Scotland, England, France and Ireland) (London: Davies, 1932; New York: Appleton, 1933);

Unconsidered Trifles (London: Secker, 1932);

The Dining-Room Battle (Oxford: Blackwell, 1933);

Literature in My Time (London: Rich & Cowan, 1933);

Water on the Brain (London: Cassell, 1933; Garden City: Doubleday, Doran, 1933);

The Lost Cause: A Jacobite Play (Edinburgh: Oliver & Boyd, 1933);

Reaped and Bound (London: Secker, 1933);

The Darkening Green (London: Cassell, 1934; Garden City: Doubleday, Doran, 1934);

The Enchanted Island (Oxford: Blackwell, 1934);

Marathon and Salamis (London: Davies, 1934);

Prince Charlie and His Ladies (London & Toronto: Cassell, 1934; New York: Knopf, 1935);

Figure of Eight (London: Cassell, 1936);

Catholicism and Scotland (London: Routledge, 1936);

The Naughtymobile (Oxford: Blackwell, 1936);

The East Wind of Love: Being Book One of 'The Four Winds of Love' (London: Rich & Cowan, 1937); republished as *The East Wind* (New York: Dodd, Mead, 1937);

The South Wind of Love: Being Book Two of 'The Four Winds of Love' (London: Rich & Cowan, 1937; New York: Dodd, Mead, 1937);

The Stairs that Kept on Going Down (Oxford: Blackwell, 1937);

Pericles (London: Hodder & Stoughton, 1937);

The Windsor Tapestry (London: Rich & Cowan, 1938; New York: Stokes, 1938);

A Musical Chair (London: Chatto & Windus, 1939);

The West Wind of Love: Being Book Three of 'The Four Winds of Love' (London: Chatto & Windus, 1940; New York: Dodd, Mead, 1940);

West to North: Being Book Four of 'The Four Winds of Love' (London: Chatto & Windus, 1940; New York: Dodd, Mead, 1941);

Aegean Memories (London: Chatto & Windus, 1940);

The Monarch of the Glen (London: Chatto & Windus, 1941; Boston: Houghton Mifflin, 1951);

The Red Tapeworm (London: Chatto & Windus, 1941);

Calvary, by Mackenzie and Faith Compton Mackenzie (London: John Lane, 1942);

Keep the Home Guard Turning (London: Chatto & Windus, 1943);

Mr. Roosevelt (London: Harrap, 1943; New York: Dutton, 1944);

Wind of Freedom: the History of the Invasion of Greece by the Axis Powers, 1940-1941 (London: Chatto & Windus, 1943);

The North Wind of Love, Book One: Being Book V of 'The Four Winds of Love' (London: Chatto & Windus, 1944; New York: Dodd, Mead, 1945);

The North Wind of Love, Book Two: Being Book V of 'The Four Winds of Love' (London: Chatto & Windus, 1945); republished as *Again to the North* (New York: Dodd, Mead, 1946);

Dr. Benes (London & Toronto: Harrap, 1946);

Whiskey Galore (London: Chatto & Windus, 1947); republished as *Tight Little Island* (Boston: Houghton Mifflin, 1947);

The Vital Flame (London: Published for the British Gas Council by F. Muller, 1947);

All Over the Place (London: Chatto & Windus, 1949);

Hunting the Fairies (London: Chatto & Windus, 1949);

The Adventures of Sylvia Scarlett (London: Macdonald, 1950)—*Sylvia and Michael* and *The Life and Adventures of Sylvia Scarlett;*

Eastern Epic: Volume 1, Defence (London: Chatto & Windus, 1951);

The House of Coalport, 1750-1950 (London: Collins, 1951);

I Took a Journey: A Tour of National Trust Properties (London: Published for the National Trust by Naldrett Press, 1951);

The Rival Monster (London: Chatto & Windus, 1952);

The Queen's House: A History of Buckingham Palace (London: Hutchinson, 1953);

The Savoy of London (London: Harrap, 1953);

Ben Nevis Goes East (London: Chatto & Windus, 1954);

Echoes (London: Chatto & Windus, 1954);

Realms of Silver: One Hundred Years of Banking in the East (London: Routledge & Kegan Paul, 1954);

My Record of Music (London: Hutchinson, 1955; New York: Putnam's, 1956);

A Posy of Sweet Months (London: Privately printed, 1955);

Thin Ice (London: Chatto & Windus, 1956; New York: Putnam's, 1957);

Rockets Galore (London: Chatto & Windus, 1957);

Sublime Tobacco (London: Chatto & Windus, 1957; New York: Macmillan, 1958);

The Lunatic Republic (London: Chatto & Windus, 1959);

Cats' Company (London: Elek, 1960; New York: Taplinger, 1961);

Greece in My Life (London: Chatto & Windus, 1960);

Mezzotint (London: Chatto & Windus, 1961);

Catmint (London: Barrie & Rockliff, 1961; New York: Taplinger, 1962);

On Moral Courage (London: Collins, 1962); republished as *Certain Aspects of Moral Courage* (Garden City: Doubleday, 1962);

Look at Cats (London: Hamilton, 1963);

My Life and Times, 10 volumes (London: Chatto & Windus, 1963-1971);

Little Cat Lost (London: Barrie & Rockliff, 1965; New York: Macmillan, 1965);

The Stolen Soprano (London: Chatto & Windus, 1965);

Paper Lives (London: Chatto & Windus, 1966);

The Strongest Man on Earth (London: Chatto & Windus, 1968);

Robert Louis Stevenson (London: Morgan-Grampian, 1968; Cranbury, N.J.: A. S. Barnes, 1969);

The Secret Island (London: Kaye & Ward, 1969).

Compton Mackenzie was one of the most prolific British authors of the twentieth century. His first book was published when he was in his mid-twenties and his last when he was nearly ninety. In fact, between 1907 and 1971 Compton Mackenzie produced at least 100 books, nearly half of which are novels. Most of these fictions are frothy "entertainments," but some deserve far more serious critical attention than they have received. Although Mackenzie wrote compulsively and for money, he was a writer of consistent integrity who, "at his best," as Edmund Wilson once noted, was also "a fine artist."

Mackenzie's was a privileged childhood, a charmed life. He was the eldest son of Edward Compton and the stunning Virginia Bateman, two

of the most successful and respected actors of the late Victorian era. As a child, he exhibited a Macaulay-like precocity: he read at two and a half and studied Latin at four, Greek at nine. By his own account he had, at thirteen, read "every play of major and minor importance written and produced by the year 1830." And yet, he was also an extrovert. Mackenzie's mentors at St. Paul's School described him as the most promising boy in his class, but also ranked him the most mischievous.

Mackenzie entered Magdalen College, Oxford in 1901, where he read modern history and quickly established himself as perhaps the handsomest, cleverest, and busiest young man on campus. He not only acted and debated, but edited the *Oxford Point of View*—a literary review he founded. In his last year at Oxford, Mackenzie suddenly informed his friends that he had decided to become a writer and that he would therefore need to adopt a less hectic way of life. Accordingly, he and another novelist-to-be, Christopher Stone, moved to a cottage in the Cotswold Hills. A year later Mackenzie emerged with a verse drama on Joan of Arc he could not finish and a book of forgettable Rossettian poems that he published at his own expense.

By the time he was twenty-four, Mackenzie had married his friend's sister, Faith Stone (on 30 November 1905), and had written an amusing play called *The Gentleman in Grey,* which his father's troupe—the Compton Comedy Company—successfully produced. Buoyed, Mackenzie turned the play into his first novel, *The Passionate Elopement* (1911), which for three years passed rudely from editor to editor before being brought out by Martin Secker's fledgling firm. Within three weeks *The Passionate Elopement* was in a second edition, and Compton Mackenzie, at twenty-eight, was a literary star.

The Passionate Elopement, which tells of various debaucheries at an eighteenth-century spa, has the rompish quality of an Anthony Hope romance. But Mackenzie's second novel, the more controlled and realistic *Carnival* (1912), employs what Mackenzie described as "the Flaubertian method of never allowing the chief character off the stage." The chief character, Jenny Pearl, is a nineteen-year-old ballerina from Islington's narrow and proper lower-middle class who settles for a job in the chorus line of the "Orient Palace of Varieties" in London. She is unsophisticated as well as highly principled: In a pseudoartistic milieu where sex is easy, she resolves to remain chaste. Unfortunately, the young man she loves, a self-proclaimed dilettante called Maurice Avery, wearies of what he calls her "old

Max Beerbohm and Compton Mackenzie in Rapallo, 1913
(photo by Florence Beerbohm)

in Britain and America alone. It was adapted for the stage twice and, though much revised, filmed three times. In 1929 it was turned into a widely acclaimed BBC radio play that ran for more than two hours at a time when any radio play that went beyond thirty minutes was thought unusually ambitious and daring.

The protagonist in Mackenzie's 1913 novel, *Sinister Street* (volume two appeared in 1914), is Michael Fane, an upper-middle-class boy from West Kensington who attends an elite London prep school before moving on to Oxford and London and a life filled with romantic infatuations and spiritual crises. Once again Mackenzie sought to "avoid," as he put it, "anything outside the ken of my chief figure, Michael Fane." But he also sought to avoid "psychologizing" over Fane's thoughts and behavior, as he had with Jenny Pearl's. He wanted to "omit any suggestion or comment, direct or implied by myself as author," and so compel the reader to see life exactly as Fane sees it as he learns and

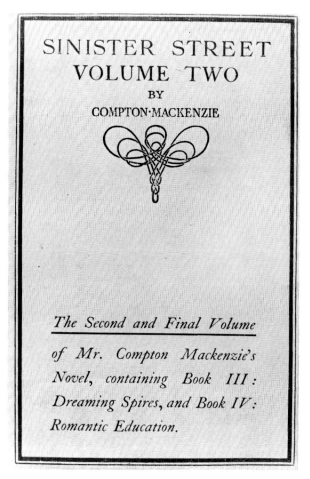

Dust jacket for the second volume of the 1132-page novel in which, according to one reviewer, Mackenzie included "everything he had experienced from the age of three or thereabouts"

women's notion of morality" and deserts her. In anger and despair, she first sleeps with a bounder and then marries an obtuse but doting farmer who proudly carts her back to Cornwall. Though most of *Carnival* is unsentimental and ironic, it ends perhaps a bit too melodramatically with a repentant Avery's pilgrimage to Cornwall and Jenny's shocking death.

Carnival was praised by the popular press and by some of the most esteemed writers of the day. W. B. Yeats and J. M. Barrie sent Mackenzie congratulatory letters, and so did Henry James, even though, as Mackenzie admitted, James "doubted whether the figure of a ballet girl was substantial enough to sustain so much centralization." *Carnival* was, moreover, an enormous financial success and for the first time proved that Mackenzie—in Kenneth Young's words—"always had hunches for writing what the public swiftly discovered it had been waiting for." Before fizzling out of print in the 1930s, *Carnival* had been translated into nearly a dozen languages, and its sales totaled half a million

Publisher's ads in part one of Sinister Street

PUBLISHER'S NOTE

SINISTER STREET: VOLUME Two is not a sequel. It is the second and final instalment of a single novel.

The First Volume, published in September 1913, narrates Michael Fane's experience of life from earliest childhood till the time when he leaves St. James' School. His first memories are of life in Carlington Road with his sister Stella, who is however soon parted from him by her musical studies. Mrs. Fane, his mother, seems to be continually travelling, and the two children are usually left in the care of their nurse and of their governess Miss Carthew, who afterwards marries Captain Ross, uncle of Michael's great school friend Alan Merivale. Captain Ross dies in the South African War, as does also Lord Saxby : and it is only then that Mrs. Fane reveals to her children the fact that Lord Saxby was their father.

Michael's earliest religious experiences centre round a stay at Clere Abbey, where also he makes the acquaintance of the man, temporarily known as Brother Aloysius, who later re-appears at Earl's Court as Henry Meats, and by his repulsive familiarity with evil, exercises over Michael an unholy fascination.

Other school holidays Michael spends with schoolmasters in Brittany, with Alan at Eastbourne, with Stella at Compiègne, with Miss Carthew and her mother at Cobble Place, their home in Hampshire ; or wandering from London bookshops into Kensington Gardens. Here, when he is seventeen years old, he first meets Lily Haden, whom he immediately adores. But his young dream is shattered when, from the house of a neighbour and schoolfellow, Drake, he sees her in her garden kissing another boy ; and he tries to forget her in the excitement of Stella's first public concert, which takes place when he is preparing to go up to Oxford.

This note in part two of Sinister Street *explains the relationship of the two volumes*

matures. Thus, in the novel's opening pages, the reader sits with the three-year-old Michael in his crib and with him establishes "an intimacy with the various iron bars of his cage." As Michael affixes personalities and primitive motives to these variously nicked and bent bars, the reader remembers the almost mystical intensity of a child's perception, much as he does when reading the opening pages of Joyce's *A Portrait of the Artist as a Young Man,* which the *Egoist* started serializing five months after the publication of *Sinister Street.*

But if *A Portrait of the Artist as a Young Man* is one of the most tightly constructed major novels of the twentieth century, the 1132-page *Sinister Street,* which Young aptly places within "the rambling rose tradition of much English fiction," is one of the

loosest. A reviewer for the *Daily Mail,* for one, observed that *Sinister Street* appeared as though it had been written "with no particular scheme in mind"; that Mackenzie had simply spewed forth "everything he had experienced from the age of three or thereabouts."

Yet *Sinister Street* is rarely dull, for it is filled with dozens of effectively drawn and colorful minor characters, some of whom—like Guy Hazelwood and Sylvia Scarlett—assume key roles in subsequent Mackenzie novels. On virtually every page of *Sinister Street,* moreover, Mackenzie displays his skill as a descriptive writer of photo-realistic brilliance. At Leister Square's seedy Cafe d'Orange, for example, Michael—searching for a cocotte he thinks he loves—catches sight of "a leaden-lidded girl, ivory white and cloying the air with her heavy perfume" who "was arguing in low passionate tones with a cold-eyed listener who with a straw was tracing niggling hieroglyphics upon a moist surface of cigarette ash." In the background, "a quartette of unkempt musicians in seamy tunics of beer-stained scarlet frogged with debilitated braid were grinding out ragtime."

Sinister Street proved to be exceptionally popular among prep school and university students, who not only readily identified with the sensitive, intelligent, and truth-seeking Michael, but who relished Mackenzie's graphic descriptions of urban low life—descriptions that so shocked some British and American librarians that they refused to allow *Sinister Street* a place on their shelves. George Orwell would later recall that when he and Cyril Connolly were adolescent students together at St. Cyprian's, they were given a caning simply for owning a copy of *Sinister Street*. F. Scott Fitzgerald freely admitted that he was very much under the spell of *Sinister Street* while he wrote his autobiographical first novel, *This Side of Paradise* (1920). According to Edmund Wilson, the influence of the early Mackenzie on the early Fitzgerald "can't be overestimated."

Mackenzie was thirty-one and suffering from acute sciatic pain when, in 1914, war broke out in Europe. He was thus considered "unfit for service," but insisted anyway on obtaining a commission in the Royal Marines and being sent to an area of combat. He wound up in the Dardanelles, partaking in the disastrous Gallipoli expedition. From there, in 1916, he went to Athens and to a high-level position in the British Secret Service. Mackenzie's breezy and at the time controversially candid war memoirs, *Greek Memories* (1932) and *Aegean Memories* (1940), reveal that while in Greece he worked assiduously and covertly to bring about the abdication of the pro-German King Constantine and the return to the prime ministry of Eleutherios Venizelos, a staunch supporter of the Allied cause. These activities often put Mackenzie in extreme danger, but also led to his becoming for several months the titular governor of the Cyclades Islands when, in early 1917, Venizelos established a provisional government at Salonika.

Before the end of the war Mackenzie had managed to complete two other novels of Balzacian sweep, *The Early Life and Adventures of Sylvia Scarlett* (1918) and its closely related sequel *Sylvia & Michael* (1919). Mackenzie later admitted that he produced these works primarily because—not for the first time and certainly not for the last—he was desper-

ately short of cash. His military salary was far from enough to maintain Casa Solitaria, the stylish villa on the Isle of Capri that he had purchased in 1913. Thus, while on leave on Capri during the winter of 1917, he worked twelve hours a day for one hundred and eighty days to produce the three-hundred-thousand-word chronicle of Sylvia Scarlett, a beautiful young woman, who, after being orphaned at sixteen, fends for herself as an actress, a cabaret singer, and—when absolutely necessary—a prostitute. Her wanderings take her to three continents, to such exotic locales as Petrograd, Bucharest, Nish; to, of all places, Sulphurville, Indiana. Along the way she falls in and out of love with numerous men, including—in the end—an older and wiser Michael Fane.

Not surprisingly, the hastily produced Sylvia Scarlett novels are flawed. They contain too many soap-operatic coincidences, too many superfluous scenes and overly long conversations. But they also contain many remarkably well-written passages—passages that prove that at his most disciplined Mackenzie was as gifted a prose stylist and dialogist as any novelist of his generation. Certainly they show that he was an astute and sympathetic observer of women; that he could without condescension invest a character such as Sylvia Scarlett with considerable dignity as well as charm. Sylvia never appears as the silly scatterbrain or as the dainty little woman-child who must turn to a man for help with her problems. She is not only compassionate and refreshingly free of egocentricity; she is energetic, intelligent, independent. Her thoughts and opinions are every bit as interesting—and as well informed—as Michael Fane's. She is very probably one of the best drawn, most appealing heroines in modern British literature.

Like the Michael Fane of *Sinister Street*, Sylvia eventually undergoes a profound spiritual reawakening that leads her to embrace Christianity. Indeed, near the conclusion of *Sylvia & Michael* she proclaims that without God, "I am nothing, I am nothing, I am nothing." Mackenzie himself converted to Roman Catholicism in 1914, and much of his fiction does argue for the viability of the Christian message, though by no means heavy-handedly. Only Mackenzie's trilogy of meandering Mark Lidderdale novels—*The Altar Steps* (1922), *The Parson's Progress* (1923), and *The Heavenly Ladder* (1924)—concern themselves overtly with religious issues, and these in fact should be viewed within the tradition of such didactic "novels and faith and doubt" as Cardinal Newman's *Loss and Gain* (1848) and Lady Georgina Fullerton's *Ellen Middleton* (1849). The

Lidderdale novels feature many spirited exchanges between Lidderdale, a "High Churchman," and other less "Popish" Christians over matters of ritual and theology. Lidderdale ultimately leaves the Anglican church and becomes a Roman Catholic.

During the 1920s, Mackenzie continued to live primarily on Capri and to spend money compulsively. He collected suits, cats, flowers, and phonograph records. He assumed long-term leases on two small islands in the Channel group, Herm and Jethou; he bought outright the Shiant Islands in the Outer Hebrides. He continued thus to write, unrelentingly. Between 1923 and 1930, Mackenzie wrote fourteen books while simultaneously cranking out book reviews for assorted newspapers and articles on classical music for the *Gramophone*—a journal he founded in 1923. During this period, Mackenzie's reputation as a bon vivant and raconteur soared even as his reputation as a novelist plunged. Reviewers routinely described Mackenzie as a man who had squandered his talents; they chided him for constructing potboilers and for occasionally dropping—as in the case of *The Vanity Girl* (1920)—an absolute bomb. These critics were not far off the mark. Mackenzie's *Santa Claus in Summer* (1924) is a delightful children's book that has often been reprinted. But the "serious" novels Mackenzie wrote during this period are awkwardly constructed and do suffer from what Katherine Mansfield described as a "general jamminess and stickiness." Mackenzie's *Vestal Fire* (1927) and *Extraordinary Women* (1928) are exceptions. As literary historian Martin Seymour-Smith notes, these wry studies of life among Capri's eccentric sophisticates and pseudointellectuals are among the funniest "light novels" of their time.

In 1930, Mackenzie moved to Scotland, and in 1931 he was elected rector of Glasgow University—a position he held until 1934. During the early 1930s, he began work on a long series of separately published novels collectively titled *The Four Winds of Love*. The first of these, *The East Wind of Love* (1937), opens in 1900 and introduces the protagonist of the series, John Pendarves Ogilvie, here a seventeen-year-old student whose intelligence and eagerness to discuss public issues bring him several well-read and politically aware friends, including Edward Fitzgerald, a fervent Irish nationalist. Covering the years 1912 to 1917, *The South Wind of Love* (1937) portrays Ogilvie as a successful dramatist who joins the British Secret Service upon the outbreak of war and travels to Greece, where he falls in love with a beautiful Greek girl and with the courage and exuberance of the Greek

people. *The West Wind of Love* (1940) chronicles Ogilvie's affair, during the 1920s, with Athene Langbridge, an unhappily married American living in Italy; *West to North* (1940) dramatizes his conversion to Catholicism and his increasing involvement in the movement for home rule for Scotland. *The North Wind of Love* (two volumes, 1944-1945) covers the 1930s and in part follows Ogilvie as he travels to a beleagured Poland and broods over the "moral and mental laziness which infects this post-war age."

As Edmund Wilson pointed out on several occasions, *The Four Winds of Love* is a remarkable achievement that is too often overlooked by critics of modern British literature. Its passionate advocacy of democracy and autonomy for all nations—however small—is admirable and relevant. Several of its principle characters—such as Fitzgerald and the multifaceted, increasingly crotchety Ogilvie—are ably drawn, believable. By Mackenzie's own estimation, *The Four Winds of Love* runs to nearly one million words, but thanks largely to its liberal use of lively dialogue and its artful display of comic relief, it rarely bogs down utterly.

Still, *The Four Winds of Love* is by no means free of technical and stylistic problems. Perhaps most of its secondary characters are quite flat; in fact, several—including P. J. Kelley, a loud, cigar-

Compton Mackenzie and Eric Linklater, 1930s

Mackenzie on the train to Bangkok, 1947

chomping American tycoon—are little more than "B" movie stereotypes. Worse, *The Four Winds of Love* also contains more than a few purplish passages. As Cuthbert Wright noted in his 1945 review of *The North Wind of Love,* reading Mackenzie had for him become merely "a tradition or an irresistible habit like smoking Turkish cigarettes, or sipping creme de menthe every night after dinner. The. comparison is not too inept," wrote Wright, "since the Mackenzian style has always been marked by a slightly cloying opulence which, amid much that is humorous, virile and arresting in this writer remains its chief defect."

During the postwar years and until his death, the peripatetic Mackenzie lived primarily in Edinburgh and continued to involve himself closely with Scottish political issues, particularly with the movement for Scottish nationalism. He also continued to produce at least one book a year, including the very popular 1947 comic novel *Whiskey Galore* (published in America as *Tight Little Island*). Set on the Scottish island of Little Todday during the time of the Second World War, *Whiskey Galore* depicts a group of stouthearted but constantly parched Scotsmen struggling through life on the home front on greatly reduced allotments of their beloved Scotch

whiskey. Mackenzie wrote the screenplay for, and briefly acted in, director Alexander Mackendrick's 1949 film version of *Tight Little Island,* which did fairly well at the box office while earning much critical praise.

Mackenzie's best novel of this period is probably *Thin Ice* (1956), a relatively brief, cleanly written, and widely praised account of the personal and political life of Henry Fortescue, an ambitious English politician who attains considerable influence while concealing his homosexuality; but who, as he gets older, decides to "let discretion go hang," especially after he is rejected for a key cabinet post he has long desired. Fortescue thus develops what his sister-in-law describes as a "mania for young men"—a mania which brings him considerable pain as well as pleasure, and which in due course makes him an easy mark for blackmailers and other unsavory characters. Through the comments of his narrator George Gaymer, Mackenzie makes clear his own distaste for homosexuality; nevertheless he portrays the aging but ever-vital and adventuresome Fortescue with sympathy. In fact, the proper but fusty, ever-nervous Gaymer is, by comparison, quite bland.

Mackenzie's first wife, Faith, died in 1960. In

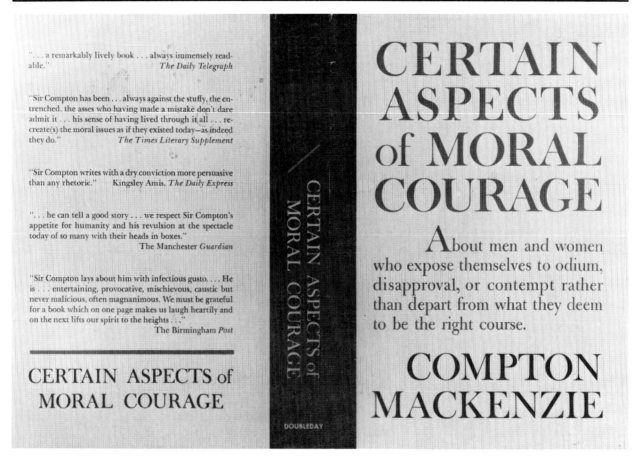

Dust jacket for the American edition of Mackenzie's 1962 book, which praises those who rebel against prevailing opinion for the sake of personal integrity. Mackenzie finds such courage in the actions of Socrates, Oscar Wilde, Conan Doyle, and D. H. Lawrence.

1962 he married Christina MacSween, who died two years later. Mackenzie married Christina's sister Lillian in 1965. Throughout the 1960s, Mackenzie devoted himself primarily to the completion of his autobiography, *My Life and Times,* which he brought out in yearly "Octaves" from 1963 to 1971. Though sometimes a bit too self-indulgent, these widely praised volumes are in the main as readable and entertaining as the best of Mackenzie's novels. They contain delightful, detailed portraits of Henry James, D. H. Lawrence, Norman Douglas, and dozens of other prominent figures whom Mackenzie counted among his acquaintances and friends.

Mackenzie's status remains uncertain. Several of his books remain in print; indeed sales of *Sinister Street* — the *Catcher in the Rye* of its day — have been steady in Britain for more than sixty years. Literary critics and historians continue to ignore him, however — a fact which greatly puzzled Edmund Wilson, who at the time of his death in 1972 was planning his own, largely favorable analysis of Mac-

kenzie's work. In 1962 Wilson remarked that at least among English critics Mackenzie was slighted because as a "professed Scot" and "something of a crypto-American," he was always at an off-putting "angle to English society." English critics, Wilson suggested, "don't understand him or don't want to understand him." But as D. J. Dooley has more recently pointed out, Mackenzie did his own reputation little good by regarding his writing as simply "day-to-day work" to be kept at "whether or not he had something worthwhile to say." The consequence, notes Dooley, was "vast overproduction" and work "so uneven and so variegated" that the task of categorizing Mackenzie "is almost impossible." Still, as Kenneth Young suggests, there are in Mackenzie's canon at least half a dozen novels "built to last," and much to move, fascinate, and amuse.

References:

D. J. Dooley, *Compton Mackenzie* (New York: Twayne, 1974);

Leo Robertson, *Compton Mackenzie* (London: Richards, 1954);

Edmund Wilson, *The Bit Beneath My Teeth* (New York: Farrar, Straus & Giroux, 1965);

Wilson, *Letters on Literature and Politics: 1912-1972* (New York: Farrar, Straus & Giroux, 1974);

Kenneth Young, *Compton Mackenzie* (London: Longmans, Green, 1968).

Papers:

The University of Texas has a major collection of Mackenzie's manuscripts.

Charles Morgan
(22 January 1894-6 February 1958)

Maureen Modlish

SELECTED BOOKS: *The Gunroom* (London: A. & C. Black, 1919);

My Name Is Legion (London: Heinemann, 1925; New York: Knopf, 1925);

First Love (New York: Knopf, 1929);

Portrait in a Mirror (London: Macmillan, 1929; New York: Knopf, 1929);

The Fountain (London: Macmillan, 1932; New York: Knopf, 1932);

Epitaph on George Moore (London: Macmillan, 1935; New York: Macmillan, 1935);

Sparkenbroke (London: Macmillan, 1936; New York: Macmillan, 1936);

The Flashing Stream: A Play, with An Essay on Singleness of Mind (London: Macmillan, 1938; New York: Macmillan, 1938; revised edition, London: Macmillan, 1948);

The Voyage (London: Macmillan, 1940; New York: Macmillan, 1940);

The Empty Room (London: Macmillan, 1941; New York: Macmillan, 1941);

The House of Macmillan, 1843-1943 (London: Macmillan, 1943; New York: Macmillan, 1943);

Reflections in a Mirror (London: Macmillan, 1944; New York: Macmillan, 1945);

The Artist in the Community: The Sixth W. P. Ker Memorial Lecture (Glasgow: Jackson, 1945);

Reflections in a Mirror. Second Series (London: Macmillan, 1946; New York: Macmillan, 1947);

The Judge's Story (London: Macmillan, 1947; New York: Macmillan, 1947);

The Liberty of Thought and the Separation of Powers: A Modern Problem Considered in the Context of Montesquieu (Oxford: Clarendon Press, 1948);

The River Line (London: Macmillan, 1949; New York: Macmillan, 1949);

A Breeze of Morning (London: Macmillan, 1951; New York: Macmillan, 1951);

Liberties of the Mind (London: Macmillan, 1951; New York: Macmillan, 1951);

The River Line: A Play (London: Macmillan, 1952);

The Burning Glass: A Play. With a Preface: On Power Over Nature (London: Macmillan/New York: St. Martin's, 1953);

Dialogue in Novels and Plays (Aldington, Kent: Hand and Flower Press, 1954);

On Learning to Write (London: Oxford University Press, 1954);

Challenge to Venus (London: Macmillan, 1957; New York: Macmillan, 1957);

The Writer and His World: Lectures and Essays (London: Macmillan, 1960).

Charles Landbridge Morgan was born in Bromley, Kent, the youngest of the four children of Sir Charles Morgan, a civil engineer, and Mary Watkins Morgan. When he was thirteen, he entered the Royal Navy as a cadet and was educated later at naval colleges in Osborne and Dartmouth. After serving in China and the Atlantic from 1911 to 1913, he left the navy. "It appears he is happy in his present work, and all his surroundings," his father wrote to the Secretary of the Admiralty. "The reason he gives for desiring to retire from the Service is that he wishes to follow a literary career." A year later, however, with the outbreak of World War I, he reentered the navy, and by October 1914 he was a prisoner in Holland, following the retreat from Antwerp (an internment which lasted until 1917). During these years in Holland he was paroled and allowed to live with the de Pallandt family at Rosendsal in Guelderland. (He used Rosendsal

Castle as the background for his 1932 novel, *The Fountain.*) In 1918 he began three years of study at Brasenose College, Oxford. Following his university training, he worked as an assistant drama critic for the *Times* (London) for five years, marrying another writer, Hilda Vaughan, in 1923. In 1926 he was promoted to principal drama critic, a job he performed until 1939, while also contributing weekly articles to the *New York Times.* He served at the Admiralty from 1939 to 1944, with stays in France and the United States. Following the war, he lectured at the University of Glasgow and at Oxford. He died on 6 February 1958 in London.

Morgan's writing demonstrates a preference for the essay form, although his eleven novels are better known, and he also wrote plays and poetry. With the exception of *The Gunroom* (1919) his novels contain extended philosophical perorations, and to each of his three plays he appended an essay, one of whose titles indicates a recurring theme in his writing, "Transcending the Age of Violence" (published in *The River Line,* 1952). For example, his novel *Portrait in a Mirror* (1929), which received the Femina/Vie Heureuse Prize and initiated Morgan's popularity in Europe, particularly in France, presents entrapment and death as unavoidable but asserts that transcendence is possible, a view of the human condition that appealed to French critics. English critics were also drawn to Morgan's optimism, reflected in the triumphs of the good and the beautiful in his novels. Yet Henry C. Duffin, the author of the only book-length study in English of Morgan's novels, observes that Morgan's work has been snubbed by academics because his optimistic point of view is uncharacteristic of modern fiction. Morgan's novels were widely reviewed, with reviewers' opinions radically divided as to the books' literary merits.

Morgan would not allow his first novel, *The Gunroom,* to be reprinted during his lifetime, "Not because it was anything but deadly true about the Navy as I knew it, but because I think the love story was weak and therefore the novel not very good as a novel." This love element was not in the first version, which more closely resembled a documentary than a novel. Unfortunately, this manuscript sank along with the ship that was torpedoed while transporting back to England Morgan from his internment in Holland in 1917. After being rescued by a British destroyer and returned to England, Morgan rewrote the novel twice, adding the love story. The happy resolution of this love story does not lead to transcendence of the issues as it does in his other novels, but of all Morgan's novels *The Gunroom* is

Charles Morgan (photo by Roland d'Ursel)

probably the most interesting to readers who admire realism in fiction. It is the only one of his novels that may be described as documentary fiction.

Like Morgan, John Lynwood, the protagonist of *The Gunroom,* begins his career in the Royal Navy at age thirteen. The novel opens with Lynwood's assignment to a ship, the *King Arthur,* four years later. As one of six midshipmen, he is subject to abuse in accordance with naval traditions and with the whims of the sublieutenant (or "sub"), the officer in charge of the midshipmen. Not even the gunroom, where the midshipmen relax in off-duty hours, is a sanctuary. Through its direct confrontation of the British navy, *The Gunroom* is an energetic confrontation of Western institutions. The abuses designed to break and dehumanize the midshipmen are perpetuated in the name of tradition and are foiled only sporadically by the actions of a few individuals, such as the sublieutenant and the captain of the *Pathfinder,* the ship to which Lynwood transfers. The upholders of tradition are men who have been broken in some way—Krame, the sublieutenant on the *King Arthur,* who relieves his boredom by abusing the midshipmen; Aggett, the sadistic engineer on the *Pathfinder;* and Ordith, an arms manufacturer's son, who enlisted with an eye to future business contacts. Morgan characterizes the traditionally accepted gain for the few at the expense of the many as a net in which people are caught, and from which one may escape only through love and through transcendence. Lynwood dodges the net by leaving the navy to attend Oxford and to pursue a vocation as a poet and a career in journalism. Margaret Ibble, his love, eludes the net with her refusal to marry Ordith, a marriage which would have joined two competing arms manufacturers under one name. But the novel ends with Lynwood, having matriculated at Oxford, reenlisting in the navy at the beginning of World War I, as Morgan himself did.

Never again was Morgan to confront the power of institutions as convincingly as he did in *The Gunroom,* but his distrust of institutions seems to have been the motivating force behind his advocacy of transcendence and his preference for writing about the society of the pastoral countryside, where the war was less intrusive. In *The Gunroom* nature is described by reference to its absence: "In a ship there is neither bud nor fallen leaf. There is no ploughing of furrows, no scattering of seed. . . . Nothing flowers or goes to rest; nothing is ever born again." In subsequent novels Morgan rhapsodizes about nature for paragraphs, frequently smothering the delicacy of transitory appreciation with layers of images and verbiage. These novels deny the power of institutions implicitly, rather than directly, advocating transcendence over adherence to tradition, valuing individual acts of goodness over collective evil, and subtly suggesting that sexual attraction is the most powerful force in the lives of human beings. Such a sensibility is neo-Romantic, avowedly so in *Sparkenbroke* (1936), tempered by an emphasis on the value of the contemplative life. While *The Gunroom* demonstrates that Morgan had all the makings of a radical, he lacked the disposition to be one and developed what a detracting reviewer described as a propensity for writing guides to spiritual behavior.

My Name Is Legion (1925), published after Morgan joined the staff of the *Times,* was followed by *Portrait in a Mirror* (1929), the story of a first love. *The Fountain* (1932), which was awarded the Hawthornden Prize in 1933, deals with his experiences during internment and is the first of his novels to be dominated by the theme of contemplation. Its protagonist, Lewis Allison, looks forward to his internment as an opportunity for the solitude and time he

needs to write a history of contemplative lives in England. The novel ends with Allison's vow to continue his "battle for spiritual independence," but to continue it in the company of Julie: "As she depended on him, so he on her. . . . to whatever issue, he and she were staked finally on each other." *Sparkenbroke* was both admired and detested for its Byronic protagonist, Piers Tenniel, Seventh Viscount and Twelfth Baron of Sparkenbroke, poet and storyteller. *The Voyage* (1940), set in rural France, received a James Tait Black Memorial Prize in 1941. Several novels followed after Morgan left the *Times* and went to work at the Admiralty.

The Empty Room (1941) involves the redemption of a difficult woman who lacks strength and intelligence and taxes the generosity of her husband, who has to deal with her problems. Duffin says that of all Morgan's novels, this is "the one novel written on a lower level, and more than one scene reads unsatisfactorily." But the book does convey Morgan's sense of society's overwhelming influence on the individual—one of his most common themes.

A more satisfactory story line is developed in *The Judge's Story* (1947), which describes several characters who give in to temptation and their reactions to the strife that follows. The characterizations of the retired judge, the solicitor, and the scheming millionaire contribute to a moral complexity which saturates the novel.

The River Line (1949), which Morgan later adapted as a play in 1952, examines the uncertain identities of several closely connected people. The novel explores the strong influence of a dead man on his half sister, as she is involved in a love relationship with a man who has traveled to America to satisfy certain unanswered questions from his past. Morgan's gradual revelation of past events demonstrates his narrative skills as well.

A Breeze of Morning (1951) describes a young teenage boy's unconsummated passion for a slightly older woman, who is almost twenty. A combination of the boy's unbridled imagination and his love for classical poetry allows him to indulge himself in admiring his love's beauty without the unnecessary intrusion of sex. The attraction of other young men to this woman and to the boy's sister offers a counterbalance for his platonic romance. The teenager himself asserts that he has "a boy's view of the love of others older than himself."

Challenge to Venus (1957), Morgan's last novel, focuses on a good-looking, self-confident man who believes he can foretell events (through flashes of "abrupt certainty"). He casually enters into a re-

Dust jacket for Morgan's 1932 novel based on his internment during World War I

lationship which turns out to have fiery consequences when he begins to think about marrying the woman. The attraction between the two characters seems to be purely physical, and their relationship is rife with disagreements which separate them, draw them back together, and separate them again.

Although Morgan is charged with creating a world "too good" and paradoxically too often dwelling on sexual relationships and stilted philosophical discourse, his moral intent and significant narrative skill prove his literary merit. "There is hardly one of the novels in which we do not feel that what is happening has a higher significance, a profounder importance than it would have in the trammelled and inhibited space-time of actuality," Duffin suggests. Differences in literary taste have also contributed to the critical disagreement over Morgan's work. "His central characters pursue their ideal of 'singleness of mind,' as Morgan also calls this spiritual freedom from the claims and conflicts of everyday life, with the zeal and discipline of mystics," Margaret Willy contends. "Their struggles with the varied distractions from its achievement

form the absorbing theme of work whose integrity of purpose, however frequently flawed its expression, cannot fairly be disputed."

The principal objection to all Morgan's writing is that it is stifling. Reviewers, admiring his seriousness and noble intent, frequently expressed an annoyance whose source is difficult to place. The inadequacies of Morgan's novels are best described as lack of proportion. When he concentrates on realistic description, on dialogue, and on immediate situations his stories engage interest, but when the narrator's reflections take over in long, sequential narrative paragraphs the reader loses interest. Intended to inspire, the reflections tend to be redundant, as when the boy-narrator in *A Breeze of Morning* comments on the significance of a conversation after its significance has been adequately established in the conversation itself: "That trivial conversation remains in my mind as the recollection of a battle remains, perhaps, in the mind of a private soldier who, at the time, understood little of it and yet felt the great yawn of history at the passion of mortal fools." Lush images and allusions to eternity and the gods have the effect of trivializing what Morgan did well, which was to convey relationships through conversation and briefly observed gestures, as well as trivializing what he did less well, which was to philosophize. Such philosophizing is usually left to the narrator, who is mainly interested in his own thoughts and seems for the most part a vehicle for Morgan's ideas rather than a character.

The weaknesses in Morgan's narrative technique help to explain the obscurity to which his work has been relegated; yet his books were popular with many of his contemporaries. Attempting to deal with the experience of World War I, he created a philosophy that established the possibility of transcendence to a state of mind in which joy and dignity would again be possible, an optimism that struck a responsive chord with his readers.

Letters:

Selected Letters of Charles Morgan, edited, with a memoir, by Eiluned Lewis (London & Melbourne: Macmillan, 1967).

References:

Henry Charles Duffin, "Charles Morgan's Novels," *Contemporary Review,* 193 (March 1958): 123-128;

Duffin, *The Novels and Plays of Charles Morgan* (Cambridge: Bowes & Bowes, 1959);

Eiluned Lewis, Preface to *The Gunroom* (London: Chatto & Windus, 1968).

H. H. Munro
(Saki)
(18 December 1870-14 November 1916)

Maureen Modlish

BOOKS: *The Rise of the Russian Empire* (London: Richards, 1900);

The Westminster Alice (London: Westminster Gazette, 1902; New York: Viking, 1929);

Reginald (London: Methuen, 1904; New York: McBride, 1922);

Reginald in Russia, and Other Sketches (London: Methuen, 1910);

The Chronicles of Clovis (London & New York: John Lane, 1912; New York: Viking, 1927);

The Unbearable Bassington (London & New York: John Lane, 1912; New York: Viking, 1928);

When William Came: A Story of London under the Hohenzollerns (London & New York: John Lane, 1914; New York: Viking, 1929);

Beasts and Super-Beasts (London & New York: John Lane, 1914; New York: Viking, 1928);

The Toys of Peace, and Other Papers (London & New York: John Lane, 1919; New York: Viking, 1928);

Reginald and Reginald in Russia (London: John Lane/Bodley Head, 1921; New York: Viking, 1928);

The Square Egg, and Other Sketches, With Three Plays (London: John Lane, 1924; New York: Viking, 1929).

Collection: *The Works of Saki,* 8 volumes (London: John Lane/Bodley Head, 1926-1927; New York: Viking, 1927-1929).

H. H. Munro (photo by E. O. Hoppé)

Hector Hugh Munro (Saki), one of many British writers to die during World War I, is thought to have died before his writing attained its full potential. While he wrote short stories throughout his career, he eventually turned to writing novels and plays as well, seeking a genre with a larger scope than that of the short story, which, as he conceived it, was too limited to allow either for character development or for the sustained treatment of issues, particularly the issue of Britain's national survival. The single situation that engages attention through clever plot turns and witticisms in his short stories becomes in his novels one of a series whose variety allows for more extensive development of character and theme in the novels.

Hector Hugh Munro was born in Akyab, Burma, the third child of Charles Augustus Munro, a career officer in the British army, and Mary Frances Mercer Munro, who died in winter 1872. Deciding that it was impossible to raise three small children in Burma, C. A. Munro left Ethel, Charles, and Hector with his widowed mother and two unmarried sisters at Broadgate Villa, a large house that he rented in Pilton, near Barnstaple in Devonshire. Broadgate's comforts, which included servants, a governess, gardens, and access to the coast of North Devon, were overshadowed for Hector by his sickliness and the presence of his aunts, from whose bickering and strict governance there was little relief.

By comparison to his childhood at Broadgate, Munro's attendance at Pencarwick, a boarding school in Exmouth, was pleasant. He "was very happy there," his sister wrote, but a year later at the age of fourteen he was sent to Bedford Grammar School in Bedfordshire, which was stricter but acceptable to Munro, who attended the school for four terms. Yet his public-school education, which confirmed his membership in the English upper class, did not modify his skepticism about its pretenses. Rather, his schooling contributed to a facility with language, which would enable him to cast his skepticism into stories the upper class would read. As J. C. Squire observed, "he polished his sentences with a spinsterish passion for neatness and chose his words as the last of the dandies might choose his ties." In his fiction, through deft turnings of plot and phrase, Munro assures that his upper-class characters will be found wanting in generosity, honesty, and common sense.

Having retired from service in the East, C. A. Munro took his children on several trips to Europe during the years 1887-1890, and in late 1890 the rest of the family went to live at Heanton Court, in Devonshire, where, for the next two years, after their brother had left to join the Burmese police, Munro and his sister were tutored by their father. In June 1893, Munro went to Burma, where his father had procured a post for him in the military police. He seems to have been as unenthusiastic about it as the cynical young dandy, Comus, is about his West African post in *The Unbearable Bassington* (1912). After contracting malaria Munro resigned his post and in August 1894 returned to Devonshire for a lengthy convalescence, during which he had the leisure to consider the idiocies of colonial bureaucrats, who were destined to number among his characters, and to become more acquainted with the lore and superstitions of Devonshire, which influenced him in writing stories such as "The Music of the Hill." These features, together with his estimation of propriety as pragmatic rather than moral in motive, and his ferocious irony are prominent in many of his short stories.

In 1896 he left for London to become a writer. By 1899, after several false starts, he had begun his first project, a history of medieval Russia, an indication of his youthful ambitions as well as of his capacity for hard work. He wished to be acknowledged as a professional historian by other historians. Subsidized by his family, he spent hours reading books in Russian in the British Museum Reading Room, completing the history in 1899. But *The Rise of the Russian Empire* (1900), while well-enough received by lay reviewers, was dismissed by the professionals as confused, flippant about religion, and sarcastic, in short, bad historiography. It was his first and last venture into history, but from it he gained knowledge which would be useful to him when he became a foreign correspondent for the London *Morning Post*.

The heresies noted by the historians were to be turned on the class to which the historians belonged in the satires he began to write in 1900 to accompany the illustrations of the political cartoonist F. Carruthers Gould for the *Westminster Gazette*. For these satires he adopted the pen name Saki, the name of the cupbearer to the gods in the *Rubáiyát of Omar Khayyám*.

The *Westminster* Alice sketches, published in the *Gazette* in 1900 (eleven were collected in a book in 1902), were followed by another, less successful, series. The "Not So Stories," a series published in the *Gazette* in 1902, parodied Parliament by imitating the form of Rudyard Kipling's *Just So Stories*. Midway through the series, the title was changed to "The Political Jungle Book," further strengthening the connection with Kipling. In 1903 Munro began the Reginald series. Reginald comments extend from political satire to broader criticisms of the upper class, but the Reginald sketches are remembered more for their witticisms than for their satire: "Why are women so fond of raking up the past? They're as bad as tailors, who invariably remember what you owe them for a suit long after you've ceased to wear it." As in his short stories, the wit of the satirist diverts attention from the objects of criticism to the cleverness of the critic. Saki's novels suffer less from this circumstance.

The Reginald sketches appeared in the *Gazette* while Munro was a foreign correspondent for the *Morning Post*, an assignment which took him to the Balkans in late 1902, to Serbia and Poland in 1904, and then to St. Petersburg in autumn 1904. Remaining there until late 1906, he was a witness to the Bloody Sunday massacre in St. Petersburg on 22 January 1905 and to political intrigues of the kind he dramatized in his play *The Death Trap* (posthumously published in *The Square Egg*, 1924). On 10 May 1906 he reported on the first session of the Russian Duma, the newly constituted governing body of Russia, formed in the wake of the 1905 rebellion, before his transfer to Paris. The Balkans and Russia remained a part of his imagination, re-

Munro with his sister, Ethel; sister-in-law, Muriel; niece, Felicia; and brother, Charles, 1908

curring through characters with Russian and Slavic names, and forming the substance of *Reginald in Russia* (1910).

After returning briefly to England in May 1907 to be at his father's deathbed, he went back to France, but in 1908 he resigned to become a freelance writer. His stories became regular features in the *Gazette*, the *Morning Post*, and the *Bystander* until 1914. *The Chronicles of Clovis* (1912), one of several collections of his short stories, was followed by his first novel, *The Unbearable Bassington* (1912). The title refers to Comus Bassington, and aptly describes him. Like many of Saki's upper-class characters, he is clever, cynical, self-indulgent, and self-destructive. The source of his decadence is suggested by the characterization of his widowed mother, Francesca Bassington, who "if pressed in an unguarded moment to describe her soul would probably have described her drawing-room." To assure her continued financial security, as well as her son's, she twice attempts to arrange suitable marriages for Comus, but each time his misbehavior

ruins the match. She then attempts to find him suitable employment. A post is procured for him in West Africa, where he dies. Toward the end of the novel both Comus and his mother become dimly aware that their values have betrayed them, have undermined whatever potential there might have been for them to discover their importance to one another. In a final blow, Francesca learns that her Van der Meulen painting, the most prized of all the possessions in her drawing room, is a copy. Saki's critics, such as Charles H. Gillen, tend to regard this ending as gratuitously cruel.

When William Came (1914), while peopled with Saki's bores, politicos, cynics, and socially ambitious women, is distinctive among his works for its directness and seriousness. The malice with which Saki assails the English upper class seems less gratuitous in *When William Came* than in his short stories, in which the petty consequences of blundering and selfishness seem too unimportant to warrant Saki's violence. In this novel, however, the same upper-class proclivities have resulted in tragedy, the ac-

Munro in the enlisted-man's uniform of the 22nd Battalion, Royal Fusiliers

the boy scouts who are supposed to honor the new king with a parade, but who do not appear. With England's involvement in World War I only a year away, the observation of a young clergyman, one of the novel's few heroic characters, seems appropriate: "I have learned one thing in life, and that is that peace is not for this world. Peace is what God gives us when He takes us into His rest. Beat your sword into a ploughshare if you like, but beat your enemy into smithereens first." For all its strengths *When William Came* is propaganda, and its causes and prejudices, which Saki forwards without question, are those of the upper class. His disagreement was not with the existence of the upper class, but with the failure of its members to take social responsibility more seriously than they took their privileges.

In 1914 he finished a collaboration with Cyril Maude on a play, *The Watched Pot,* a surprisingly

E whom this scroll commemorates was numbered among those who, at the call of King and Country, left all that was dear to them, endured hardness, faced danger; and finally passed out of the sight of men by the path of duty and self-sacrifice, giving up their own lives that others might live in freedom.
Let those who come after see to it that his name be not forgotten.

L/Serjt. Hector Hugh Munro
Royal Fusiliers

Memorial scroll sent by the king to Munro's family

quiescence of Britain to Germany. It is as if prior to its writing, Saki observed the inadequacies of the upper class but was unable to attribute dire consequences to them, at least unable to do so with conviction. The novel is set in the near future. Its upper-class protagonist, Murrey Yeovil, returns from Russia to England to learn the significance of England's conquest by Germany to language, art, daily activities, and to his own life. His wife, Cicely, as socially ambitious as ever, has begun to cultivate the conquerors. Her rationalizations and Yeovil's own apologies for retiring to the country rather than fighting the Germans are more subtly realized than anything else in Saki's writing. The Tory slant of the book is reminiscent of Tory arguments against financial interests and Tory anxieties about the decline of taste which surfaced during and after the accession of William and Mary in 1688. The novel has several minor heroic figures, each of whom gives to Yeovil his account of the conquest and response to it, and ends with unnamed heroes,

lighthearted comedy of manners in the tradition of Richard Brinsley Sheridan, and fired a parting shot at George Bernard Shaw with *Beasts and Super-Beasts,* a collection of short stories. When war was declared in August 1914, Munro enlisted. He was killed in action on 14 November 1916.

Although he is best known for his fiction, drama seems to be the genre best suited to Munro's abilities. His plays show his strengths—witty dialogue, complexity of plot, and energetic pace—to advantage, while his weaknesses, which appear in his fiction as gratuitous witticisms and pompous asides in the narrative, are absent from his plays. In the traditional dramatic form there is no place for such weaknesses, and his extant plays give no indication that he was inclined to make a place for them. Had he survived the war, he might have been better known as a playwright than as a short-story writer.

Biographies:

Ethel Munro, "Biography of Saki," in *The Square Egg, and Other Sketches* (London: John Lane, 1924; New York: Viking, 1929);

A. J. Langguth, *Saki: A Life of Hector Hugh Munro with Six Short Stories Never Before Collected* (London: Hamilton, 1981).

References:

Noel Coward, Introduction to *The Complete Works of Saki* (Garden City: Doubleday, 1976);

Charles H. Gillen, *H. H. Munro (Saki)* (New York: Twayne, 1969);

J. C. Squire, Introduction to *The Complete Novels and Plays of Saki* (New York: Viking, 1945).

J. B. Priestley
(13 September 1894-14 August 1984)

A. A. DeVitis
Purdue University

SELECTED BOOKS: *The Chapman of Rhymes* (London: Moring, 1918);

Brief Diversions: Being Tales, Travesties, and Epigrams (Cambridge: Bowes & Bowes, 1922);

Papers from Lilliput (Cambridge: Bowes & Bowes, 1922);

I for One (London: John Lane, 1923);

The English Comic Characters (London: John Lane, 1925; New York: Dodd, Mead, 1925);

George Meredith (London: Macmillan, 1926; New York: Macmillan, 1926);

Talking (London: Jarrolds, 1926; New York & London: Harper, 1926);

Adam in Moonshine (London: Heinemann, 1927; New York: Harper, 1927);

Benighted (London: Heinemann, 1927); republished as *The Old Dark House* (New York: Harper, 1928);

The English Novel (London: Benn, 1927; revised edition, London: Nelson, 1935; Folcroft, Pa.: Folcroft Editions, 1974);

Open House: A Book of Essays (London: Heinemann, 1927; New York & London: Harper, 1927);

Thomas Love Peacock (London: Macmillan, 1927; New York: Macmillan, 1927);

Apes and Angels: A Book of Essays (London: Methuen, 1928);

The Balconinny, and Other Essays (London: Methuen, 1929; New York & London: Harper, 1930);

English Humour (London: Longmans, Green, 1929);

Farthing Hall, by Priestley and Hugh Walpole (London: Macmillan, 1929; Garden City: Doubleday, Doran, 1929);

The Good Companions (London: Heinemann, 1929; New York: Harper, 1929);

Angel Pavement (London: Heinemann, 1930; New York: Harper, 1930);

The Town Major of Miraucourt (London: Heinemann, 1930);

Self-Selected Essays (London: Heinemann, 1932; New York: Harper, 1932);

Faraway (London: Heinemann, 1932; New York: Harper, 1932);

I'll Tell You Everything: A Frolic, by Priestley and Gerald Bullett (New York: Macmillan, 1932; London: Heinemann, 1933);

Albert Goes Through (London: Heinemann, 1933; New York: Harper, 1933);

Wonder Hero (London: Heinemann, 1933; New York: Harper, 1933);

English Journey (London: Heinemann/Gollancz, 1934; New York & London: Harper, 1934);

They Walk in the City: The Lovers in the Stone Forest (London: Heinemann, 1936; New York: Harper, 1936);

Midnight on the Desert (London: Heinemann, 1937; New York & London: Harper, 1937);

The Doomsday Men (London: Heinemann, 1938; New York: Harper, 1938);

Let the People Sing (London: Heinemann, 1939; New York: Harper, 1940);

Rain upon Godshill (London: Heinemann, 1939; New York & London: Harper, 1939);

Britain Speaks (New York & London: Harper, 1940);

Postscripts (London: Heinemann, 1940);

Out of the People (London: Collins/Heinemann, 1941; New York & London: Harper, 1941);

Black-out in Gretley: A Story of and for Wartime (London: Heinemann, 1942; New York & London: Harper, 1942);

Britain at War (New York & London: Harper, 1942);

British Women Go to War (London: Collins, 1943);

Daylight on Saturday: A Novel About an Aircraft Factory (London: Heinemann, 1943; New York: Harper, 1943);

Three Men in New Suits (London: Heinemann, 1945; New York: Harper, 1945);

Bright Day (London: Heinemann, 1946; New York: Harper, 1946);

Jenny Villiers, A Story of the Theatre (London: Heinemann, 1947; New York: Harper, 1947);

Theatre Outlook (London: Nicholson & Watson, 1947);

Delight (London: Heinemann, 1949; New York: Harper, 1949);

Festival at Farbridge (London: Heinemann, 1951); republished as *Festival* (New York: Harper, 1951);

The Other Place, and Other Stories of the Same Sort (London: Heinemann, 1953; New York: Harper, 1953);

Low Notes on a High Level: A Frolic (London: Heinemann, 1954; New York: Harper, 1954);

The Magicians (London: Heinemann, 1954; New York: Harper, 1954);

Journey Down a Rainbow, by Priestley and Jacquetta Hawkes (London: Heinemann-Cresset, 1955; New York: Harper, 1955);

The Writer in a Changing Society (Aldington, Kent: Hand & Flower Press, 1956);

J. B. Priestley, 1961

The Art of the Dramatist (Melbourne: Heinemann, 1957);

Thoughts in the Wilderness (London: Heinemann, 1957; New York: Harper, 1957);

Topside; or, The Future of England (London: Heinemann, 1958);

The Story of Theatre (London: Rathbone, 1959); republished as *The Wonderful World of the Theatre* (Garden City: Doubleday, 1959; London: Macdonald, 1969);

Literature and Western Man (London: Heinemann, 1960; New York: Harper, 1960);

William Hazlitt (London: Longmans, Green, 1960);

Charles Dickens (New York: Viking, 1961);

Saturn Over the Water (Garden City: Doubleday, 1961; London: Heinemann, 1961);

The Thirty-First of June; A Tale of True Love, Enterprise, and Progress, in the Arthurian and Ad-atomic Ages

(London: Heinemann, 1961; Garden City: Doubleday, 1962);

Margin Released: A Writer's Reminiscences and Reflections (London: Heinemann, 1962; New York: Harper & Row, 1962);

The Shapes of Sleep: A Topical Tale (Garden City: Doubleday, 1962; London: Heinemann, 1962);

Man and Time (Garden City: Doubleday, 1964; London: Aldus, 1964);

Sir Michael and Sir George (London: Heinemann, 1964; Boston: Little, Brown, 1965);

Lost Empires (London: Heinemann, 1965; Boston: Little, Brown, 1965);

The Moments, and Other Pieces (London: Heinemann, 1966);

Salt is Leaving (London: Pan/Heinemann, 1966);

It's an Old Country (London: Heinemann, 1967; Boston: Little, Brown, 1967);

All England Listened: The Wartime Broadcasts of J. B. Priestley (New York: Chilmark, 1967);

The Image Men (2 volumes, London: Heinemann, 1968; 1 volume, Boston: Little, Brown, 1969);

Trumpets Over the Sea (London: Heinemann, 1968);

The Prince of Pleasure and His Regency, 1811-20 (London: Heinemann, 1969; New York: Harper & Row, 1969);

Anton Chekhov (London: International Textbook, 1970);

The Edwardians (London: Heinemann, 1970; New York: Viking, 1970);

Snoggle (London: Heinemann, 1971);

Victoria's Heyday (London: Heinemann, 1972; New York: Harper & Row, 1972);

Over the Long High Wall (London: Heinemann, 1972);

The English (London: Heinemann, 1973; New York: Viking, 1973);

A Visit to New Zealand (London: Heinemann, 1974);

Outcries and Asides (London: Heinemann, 1974);

The Carfitt Crisis and Two Other Stories (London: Heinemann, 1975);

Particular Pleasures: Being a Personal Record of Some Varied Arts and Many Different Artists (London: Heinemann, 1975);

Found, Lost, Found; or, The English Way of Life (London: Heinemann, 1976; New York: Stein & Day, 1976);

The Happy Dream: An Essay (Andoversford: Whittington Press, 1976);

Instead of the Trees (London: Heinemann, 1977; New York: Stein & Day, 1977).

Born in the wool-merchandizing city of Bradford, Yorkshire, John Boynton Priestley is the author of more than four score works. These include literary criticism, novels, plays, collected short stories, essays, illustrated accounts of social and literary history, and books of autobiographical and historical recollection.

After his mother's early death the boy Priestley was reared by a stepmother who, he has observed in *Margin Released* (1962), defied tradition by being kind and loving. His father, Jonathan Priestley, a schoolmaster, was, as Priestley has described him, the kind of man socialists have in mind when they write about socialists. Priestley was educated in Bradford, a city that provided a remarkable cultural ambiance for an imaginative boy who wanted to be a writer. Bradford not only offered drama, serious music, and the music hall, but also the Yorkshire Dales just a tram ride away. Priestley has acknowledged that Bradford from 1911-1914 did more for his education than Cambridge did several years later.

Priestley during World War I

At the age of twenty, in 1915, Priestley enlisted in the West Riding Regiment, was sent to France where he was wounded, then invalided home, and later gassed on his return to the front. Significantly, World War I serves as immediate locale for only one of Priestley's fictional pieces, a haunting short story entitled *The Town Major of Miraucourt,* published in 1930. His entire creative output may, however, be a means of placing war in a meaningful long-range perspective. Priestley's contribution to England at war in the period of World War II was a series of radio broadcasts, widely heralded, making him, as some admirers have observed, a national hero equal to Winston Churchill.

In 1919, the war over, Priestley married Pat Tempest, who died in 1925; he enrolled in Cambridge University to study literature, political science, and history. With the collection of undergraduate pieces entitled *Brief Diversions* (1922), he had embarked on a literary career. In 1926 he married Mary Holland Wyndham Lewis, from whom he was divorced in 1952. In 1953 he married the noted anthropologist Jacquetta Hawkes. Priestley had six children. He traveled extensively in Europe, the United States, Australia, Mexico, New Zealand, and other countries; and he often used the places he visited as locales for both his novels and his dramas. He served as a delegate to UNESCO, and as a member of the board of Britain's National Theatre. He refused a knighthood and a life-peerage, but accepted membership in the Order of Merit and the conferment of the Freedom of the City from his native Bradford. "I started as J. B. Priestley and I'll finish as J. B. Priestley," he said to a *New York Times* reporter in 1974.

In his novels Priestley portrays an essentially optimistic view of man in nature. They are for the most part romances, although there are exceptions to this general rule, and fall naturally into three categories: the romantic escapade, which includes his novels of intrigue and espionage; the farcical romp; and the seriously conceived and executed novel that makes use of symbolical structures and essays characterizations of depth. Priestley never considered himself a novelist only, although it was a novel, *The Good Companions* (1929), that gave him a popular success that has never waned. In the 1930s he began writing innovative and challenging plays and then directing and producing these often commercially successful dramas, upon which his reputation as a writer is also based. Although he disliked the term, Priestley can rightly be called a "Man of Letters" in the eighteenth-century tradition.

In the majority of his works Priestley exemplifies a theory of time derived from his reading of J. W. Dunne's *An Experiment with Time* (1927) and *The Serial Universe* (1934), and P. D. Ouspensky's *A New Model of the Universe* (1931). Briefly stated, the time theory as illustrated in such plays as *I Have Been Here Before* (1931) and such novels as *Jenny Villiers* (1947) and *It's an Old Country* (1967) proposes a means of transcendence. Explaining his adaptation of Dunne's Serialism to his created world, Priestley wrote, "There had always been something bewildering to me about the idea of self-consciousness, we observe something, and we are conscious of our observation, and we are conscious of the observation of the observation and so forth." This awareness of self in space and time allowed Priestley to deal with character creatively; i.e., many of his characters reexperience themselves as they were in the past, usually in moments of decision; and occasionally they anticipate the future. Through an effort of the sympathetic imagination these characters are sometimes able, through "tunnels" of time, to communicate directly with others who lived in the past. This moment of transcendence is sometimes referred to as "time alive." From Ouspensky Priestley took the notion that time, like space, has three dimensions, but that these three dimensions can be regarded as a continuation of the dimensions of space, i.e., as the fourth, fifth, and sixth dimensions of space. Priestley believed with Ouspensky that time, wavelike and spiral, provides for eternal "recurrence," yet recurrence not to be confused with Nietzsche's "eternel retour" or with reincarnation, or Bergsonian durée. It is the aspect of recurrence or "recreation" that chiefly interested Priestley in his fiction and drama. Ouspensky provided him the possibility of "intervention" in space and time through inner development of self. In other words, self-conscious observation of self in past time can recreate the past in the present; sympathetic recreation of self and others in "time alive" can give new meaning to the present and offer hope for the future. Ultimately, despite the fact that certain seers into the past are motivated by selfishness or greed and are categorically evil in Priestley's created universe, this concept allowed for an optimistic view of humanity inasmuch as it provides for a rectification of evil done in past time; many of these ideas are illustrated in his book called *Man and Time* (1964). For Priestley, the artist, whether he be a writer or painter or musician or the organizer of a festival, or even a butler in a country house, is the character who looks imaginatively into the past and by doing so helps reshape the present and thereby create the future. The organizer or shaper is, consequently, his most forceful character.

In matters of politics Priestley has, consistent with his generally optimistic view, called himself a Liberal Socialist, which meant to him that the less government interference the better, but only after the material needs of the individual have been assured. He was opposed to communism because of its insistence on the material. His great theme is England and the English character, and many of his best drawn characters are ordinary citizens, who in their insistence on fair play and right action make a better world. Priestley's world view, although primarily romantic, demonstrates shrewdness and perception of human failure which keeps his work from being sentimental or Pollyannish.

Priestley's first novel, *Adam in Moonshine* (1927), is a romantic farce, "all fine writing and nonsense, a little coloured trial balloon . . . creaking with self-consciousness," as he himself described it. The novel is notable chiefly for the presentation of two characters who appear in later fictions under various guises. Adam Stewart is the romantic seeker and Baron Roland the charismatic organizer. They are brought together in an implausible attempt to return the Stuarts to the English throne, but the novel's chief charm lies in the description of the Yorkshire Dales, presented with fervor and devotion. This beguiling farce was followed by *Benighted* (1927), a Gothic tale given psychological resonance through the character of Roger Penderel, through whom Priestley examined the postwar malaise in the uprooted younger middle class, a theme he would return to following World War II in two novels, *Three Men in New Suits* in 1945 and *Bright Day* in 1946.

Farthing Hall (1929), a collaboration with Hugh Walpole, the older writer kindly securing for Priestley a publisher's advance so that the younger might have time to do his more serious writing, was followed the same year by *The Good Companions*, a runaway best-seller that established Priestley both artistically and financially.

The Good Companions is a robust, picaresque account of a group of stranded music-hall entertainers who are transformed from the down-and-out Dinky Doos into the successful Good Companions by the organizing ability and determined efforts of Elizabeth Trant, who has spent the last several years caring for an ailing parent. Her father's death and a small inheritance permit Elizabeth to escape from the weary tedium of provincial life into the romantic world of gypsy entertainers. She is aided in her efforts by Mr. Oakroyd, a gentle Yorkshireman seeking refuge from a termagant wife, and, among others, by Inigo Jollifant, a schoolteacher on retreat from a rural classroom, who has a rare talent for composing songs. *The Good Companions* makes use of collective effort as a plot device, a device that Priestley employed with fair regularity in both his novels and his plays. A group of disparate people are united in a common endeavor to secure the betterment of the whole. The psyche is freed as a result of the successful effort to do other and better work. Democratic action is portrayed as a means of securing a brighter future. The Good Companions—most of them, at any rate—realize that the entertainment they offer has no future in an increasingly mechanized world; the motion pictures will soon replace the flesh-and-blood itinerant entertainers. Elizabeth leaves the Good Companions to marry an old admirer, Mr. Oakroyd leaves to live in Canada with his daughter Lily, and Inigo Jollifant follows Miss Susie Dean, the ingenue, to London's West End, where he will yearn for her as an unfulfilled promise of youth.

The following year, 1930, Priestley published *Angel Pavement,* almost as great a success as *The Good Companions* but in many ways very different. The novel, best in its description of a large metropolis on the brink of economic disaster, presents through Golspie, a balding middle-aged adventurer, another aspect of the organizer represented by Baron Roland in Priestley's first novel and, in a more sentimental vein, by Elizabeth Trant in *The Good Companions*. Golspie, somewhat sinister, brings to Twigg and Dersingham, a firm located in Angel Pavement, just off the main road, a mysterious and seemingly inexhaustible supply of Baltic veneers, which he offers to the firm well below the current market price. Golspie breathes new life into the business for a while, but when he leaves, as mysteriously as he had arrived, the company is all but bankrupt. The novel is remarkable for its portrayal of men and women at their jobs, as it reiterates Priestley's belief in the common man. *Angel Pavement,* furthermore, gives evidence of Priestley's maturing craftsmanship in that it makes use of telling image patterns and provocative symbols that characterize the city.

The decade of the 1930s was for Priestley a busy time inasmuch as it marked his entry into the British theater. *Dangerous Corner* appeared in 1932 and firmly established Priestley as a dramatist of note. He is, in fact, the only British dramatist of importance (if Sean O'Casey, an Irishman, and James Bridie, a Scot, are excluded) who bridges the gap between Shaw and John Osborne, who with the

Graham Cunningham, Priestley, and John Galsworthy, circa 1936 (Radio Times Hulton Picture Library)

production of his *Look Back in Anger* (1955) revitalized the British theatre. The 1930s saw the production of such enduring plays as *Eden End* (1934), *Cornelius* (1935), and *Time and the Conways* (1937). The novels of the 1930s, however, failed to sustain the promise of Priestley's first works.

Faraway (1932), a symbolical treasure hunt for pitchblende, presents Priestley's protagonist, William Dursley, confronting an unscrupulous profiteer called Garsuvin. The adventure, though largely predictable, is, nevertheless, remarkable for its shrewd portrayal of the United States in the prohibition era, its descriptions of far-off places, notably Tahiti and Easter Island, and the emphasis placed at the novel's conclusion on England as a force for tradition and honor in an increasingly materialistic world. One character in the novel, Ramsbottom, is given a comic moment in "time alive" when he encounters Maggie Armitage, the dream of his youth. Revisiting the past is, however, given a poignant as well as memorable poetic expression in the brief fantasy called *The Town Major of*

Miraucourt, in which the invalided soldier-narrator enters a time tunnel and glimpses at its end the comic characters of Shakespeare's *Henry IV* plays, all named Smith, in the quiet moment that the piece describes. The moment in past time recreates an oasis distilled from the immediate pressures of war and submerged memories of pain and loss. It is one of Priestley's best fictional treatments of his reading of Dunne and Ouspensky.

Albert Goes Through (1933), a lighthearted satirical fantasy, makes farcical comment on the notion of serial time and recurrence as Albert crashes through a motion picture screen to enter into the life of the film, which repeats the same episode. Albert escapes the life of the film and his pursuit by Felicity Storm within the film to find himself content to accept the homelier charms of Nellie Weedon. *Wonder Hero* (1933) and *They Walk in the City* (1936), also satirical, comment in a dogmatic and journalistic fashion on the social and moral injustice of the Depression era. More successful than either *Faraway* or *Wonder Hero* or *They Walk in the City* is *The Doomsday Men* (1938), which is set in the Mojave Desert in California. Its theme, allegorically projected, concerns the successful attempt of London architect Malcolm Darbyshire to thwart the detonation of a doomsday apparatus; the novel, in fact, anticipates Priestley's novels of the 1960s, his international espionage thrillers entitled *Saturn Over the Water* (1961) and *The Shapes of Sleep* (1962), in which conspiracies to thwart the best intentions of the free world figure prominently. In these two later novels the concept of time transcendence is an important plot device.

The advent of the Second World War found Priestley a very busy, energetic, and concerned Englishman. Besides chairing a committee on war aims, writing semipropaganda pieces such as *Britain at War* (1942) and *British Women Go to War* (1943), and speaking regularly over the BBC to and for the English conscience in his "Postscripts," Priestley continued his professional work. Such plays as *Good Night Children* (1942) and *They Came to a City* (1943) appeared in the years of war. His novels of the period also illustrate his commitment not only to England at war but to the cause of democratic success. *Let the People Sing* (1939) celebrates within a

Dust jacket for the 1946 novel that is generally considered Priestley's finest

Dust jacket for Priestley's 1939 novel celebrating English tradition and commitment to the democratic cause during World War II

contrived and lackluster plot the great English traditions: love of liberty, toleration of others, public service, love of England itself, English humor, depth of sentiment. *Black-Out in Gretley: A Story of and for Wartime* (1942) deals with traitors at home who would betray England to the Nazis, and *Daylight on Saturday: A Novel About an Aircraft Factory* (1943) with the effects of war on the men and women who work in shops and factories for democratic victory. *Daylight on Saturday,* one of Priestley's finest novels despite its obvious aim of propaganda, indicates by means of point of view and modified stream of consciousness his ability to draw forceful characters and create symbolical structures. The factory within which the action is set becomes itself a symbol of the common cause of England at war. The works manager Cheviot, one of Priestley's organizers, acknowledges his own responsibility for the war by having sold machinery to the Germans, and, like a reluctantly enlightened deity, grieves for himself and for others who, like his son, have been forced to pay for earlier mistakes. The novel also presents Bob Elrick, who anticipates the angry young men of the postwar 1950s: ". . . he's angry inside all the time," says Cheviot. "The trouble in him joins up with any trouble outside."

In 1946 Priestley published what is generally considered to be his finest novel, *Bright Day,* a work that earned for him the praise of Carl Jung. As Priestley's searcher—this time a disenchanted film scriptwriter called Gregory Dawson—remembers his past, the reader becomes aware that Dawson is conceived of as a symbolical character whose movements between two world wars represent a rite of passage. The time shifts in *Bright Day,* relying perhaps more on Bergson and Proust than on Dunne and Ouspensky, allow the character to revisit and learn from the past. He comes to understand that what happened to him in the past is both present and future, and that his knowledge of self in time is a necessary preliminary to his forgiveness of self and society.

The late 1940s and early 1950s saw the publication of two full-scale treatments of the time theme, *Jenny Villiers, A Story of the Theatre,* originally

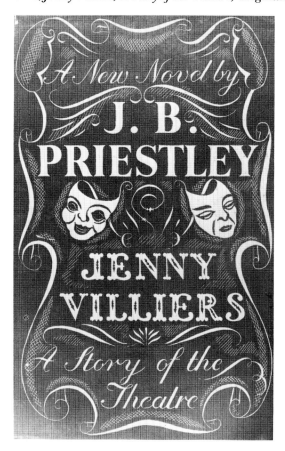

Dust jacket for Priestley's 1947 novel based upon his theory of time

written as a play for the Bristol Old Vic in 1946, and *The Magicians* (1954), the latter employing Priestley's version of the Wandering Jew. Both novels stress the notions of recurrence and intervention, as had such Priestley plays of the late 1930s as *Time and the Conways* (1937) and *The Long Mirror* (1940). In 1951 *Festival at Farbridge* was published. It is one of Priestley's longest novels and one that demonstrates his deftness in deploying a large number of comic and grotesque characters in a delightful and kaleidoscopic frenzy of action. The novel's action hinges on the organization and presentation of a festival for the Midlands town of Farbridge to celebrate the 1951 Festival of Britain. *Low Notes on a High Level* (1954), a frolic or farce, pokes good-natured fun at pomposity in high places within a musical milieu, allowing Priestley to demonstrate a keen awareness of musical values.

Saturn Over the Water and *The Shapes of Sleep* appeared, respectively, in 1961 and 1962. These works, in the tradition of Priestley's earlier *The Doomsday Men,* can be called international conspiracy thrillers, employing as they do the paraphernalia of mystery stories; both novels give evidence again of Priestley's belief that man can learn from his past mistakes by "intervening" in the present to keep the errors of the past from recurring. *Salt is Leaving* (1966) is set in the English Midlands, and it too, within the framework of the thriller, stresses the dangers to the world of a seemingly paternalistic power force. Two more farces, *The Thirty-First of June* (1961) and *Sir Michael and Sir George* (1964), good-naturedly satirize advertising and governmental intervention in the arts.

Three seriously conceived and executed novels of the same time, however, distinguish Priestley's last efforts in the genre of the novel: *Lost Empires* (1965), *It's an Old Country* (1967), and Priestley's longest novel, and his favorite, *The Image Men,* published in two volumes in 1968 and in one volume in 1969. *Lost Empires* is in some ways a return to a romantic past, the English music hall in its period of decline immediately before World War I. Dick Herncastle, as an apprentice to his uncle Nick Ollanton, a magician and mesmerizer on the halls, learns that the true adventure of life is to strive for permanence in art. The action of the novel loosely allegorizes the politics of a world destined for global war, and Dick's choice of profession, as a watercolorist, suggests strongly that through art alone can man gain immortality.

It's an Old Country, elaborately plotted and symbolically structured, centers on Tom Adamson's search for the father who abandoned him and his

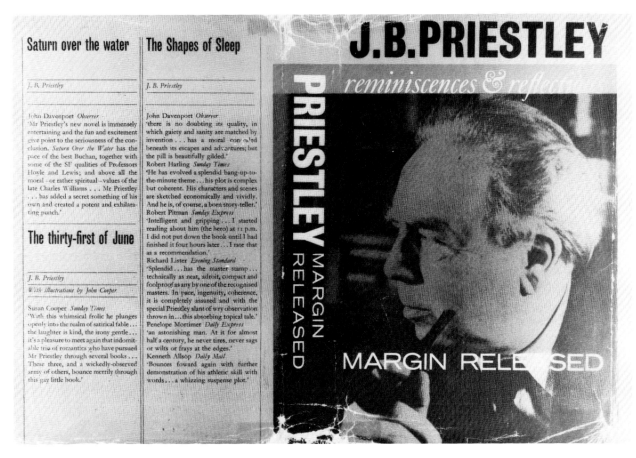

Dust jacket for Priestley's literary reminiscences, titled, as he notes in the preface, for the typewriter key "labelled 'Margin Release' " to suggest that "something . . . has escaped from that narrow frame which has a conceited reticence at one end and a diffident humility at the other and . . . has found release in these pages"

mother thirty years before the novel's action begins. In finding his father Tom Adamson finds himself, forgives the past, and moves into a meaningful future. A symbolical character in the novel, Professor Firmius, indicates to Tom the real possibility of contributing to a "Third Time," thus making it possible for Tom to devote himself to "the whole bedevilled human race, for a global civilization."

"Out of Town," the first part of *The Image Men,* presents two down-and-out academics combining forces to make a living; Cosmo Saltana and Owen Tuby are logical descendants of Baron Roland and Adam Stewart from Priestley's first novel, *Adam in Moonshine.* They band together and form the Institute for Social Imagistics; together they make war, and profit, on the world of false illusion of mass media. "Out of Town" largely concerns their attempt to find academic backing, and "London End," the second part of the novel, their successful attempts to sell their wares. A mixture of broad farce and seriously intended satire, *The Image Men*

belongs to the same picaresque traditions of Priestley's *The Good Companions,* but here Priestley gives his wit full reign as he directs his barbs at the parvenus, the bullies, deceivers, racketeers, and exploiters of the media milieux. In *Journey Down a Rainbow* (1955), an exchange of observations between himself and Jacquetta Hawkes, Priestley coined the word "Admass," his name for "high-pressure advertising and salesmanship, plus mass communications . . . and the creation of the mass mind." The world of *The Image Men* is a successful portrayal of Admass.

Priestley himself pointed out in *Outcries and Asides* (1974) that Owen Tuby and Cosmo Saltana are not to be seen as antiheroes but as true heroes, for they represent worthwhile values and qualities, those to which Priestley dedicated himself through a long and fruitful career as a professional writer. They are, as he himself admitted, aspects of himself dramatically projected, as were Adam Stewart and Baron Roland of his first novel. The ending of *The*

Publisher's ad, Bookseller, *4 August 1984*

Image Men, furthermore, emphasizes, in a stern manner, an optimism that largely remained undimmed in one of our century's most prolific and entertaining novelists.

As a novelist Priestley has been largely ignored by the more intellectually oriented critics. Walter Allen finds no place for him in *Tradition and Dream,* but Anthony Burgess in *The Novel Now* warns against overlooking his achievement, saying that it would be foolish to disparage his vast creative energy. And Colin Wilson has pointed out that Priestley's works can best be read as a continuation of the great tradition of popular entertainment, placing him alongside Dickens, Hardy, and Trollope.

Priestley's best critics are, in fact, his readers. The great majority of his novels have remained in print through five decades. His plays are frequently revived, most recently *Time and the Conways* in 1983, *Dangerous Corner* in 1982, and *Eden End* in 1974.

Ultimately this is the kind of criticism all writers strive for.

References:
John Braine, *J. B. Priestley* (London: Weidenfeld & Nicolson, 1978);
Ivor Brown, *J. B. Priestley. Writers and Their Work,* No. 84 (London: Longmans, Green in association with the British Council, 1957);
Susan Cooper, *J. B. Priestley: Portrait of an Author* (London: Heinemann, 1970);
A. A. DeVitis and A. E. Kalson, *J. B. Priestley* (Boston: Twayne, for G. K. Hall, 1980);
J. W. Dunne, *An Experiment with Time* (London: A. & C. Black, 1927);
David Hughes, *J. B. Priestley: An Informal Study of His Work* (London: Rupert Hart-Davis, 1958);
P. D. Ouspensky, *A New Model of the Universe* (London: Kegan Paul, 1931);
Colin Wilson, "A Hell of a Talent," *Books and Bookmen,* 21 (January 1975): 26ff.

Frederick William Rolfe
(Baron Corvo)
(22 July 1860-23 October 1913)

Maureen Modlish

SELECTED BOOKS: *Tarcissus* (N.p., 1880);
Stories Toto Told Me (London & New York: Lane, 1898);
The Attack on St. Winefride's Well, anonymous (N.p., 1898?);
In His Own Image (London & New York: Lane, 1901);
Chronicles of the House of Borgia (London: Richards/New York: Dutton, 1901);
Hadrian the Seventh (London: Chatto & Windus, 1904; New York: Knopf, 1925);
Don Tarquinio (London: Chatto & Windus, 1905);
Don Renato (London: Francis Griffiths, 1909);
The Weird of the Wanderer, cowritten by Rolfe and Harry Pirie-Gordon as Prospero & Caliban (London: Rider, 1912);
The Bull Against the Enemy of the Anglican Race (London: Privately printed, 1929);
The Desire and Pursuit of the Whole (London: Cassell, 1934; New York: New Directions, 1953);

Hubert's Arthur, by Rolfe and Pirie-Gordon as Prospero & Caliban (London: Cassell, 1935);
Nicholas Crabbe (London: Chatto & Windus, 1958; New York: New Directions, 1958);
The Armed Hands and Other Stories, edited by Cecil Woolf (London: Cecil & Amelia Woolf, 1972);
Collected Poems, edited by Woolf (London: Cecil & Amelia Woolf, 1972).

OTHER: *The Rubaiyat of Umar Khaiyam,* translated by Corvo (London & New York: Lane, 1903);
Owen Thomas, *Agricultural and Pastoral Prospects of South Africa,* ghostwritten by Corvo (London: Constable, 1904);
The Songs of Meleager, translated by Rolfe (London: The First Edition Club, 1937).

Frederick William Serafino Austin Lewis Mary Rolfe (Baron Corvo), born in Cheapside, London, projected almost as many personae as he

Frederick Rolfe at Oscott (photo by William Wort)

had names. In *Hadrian the Seventh* (1904) George Arthur Rose, first rejected for the priesthood and later elevated to Pope, asserts: "my pseudonimity has been misunderstood by the stupid. . . . That a man should split his [personality] into four or more, and should develop each separately and perfectly, was so abnormal that many normals failed to understand it." None of his personae was to achieve the recognition Rolfe felt he deserved except for Rose, and then only in *Hadrian the Seventh* and only to be recognized by a few readers.

The literary career of "Fr. Rolfe," as he insisted his name should appear on his books, began in earnest when he was thirty-eight with the publication of *Stories Toto Told Me* (1898) in the *Yellow Book,* an appropriate beginning for one who, like another of the journal's contributors, Aubrey Beardsley, was known for his personal eccentricities as much as for his technical ability Corvo published the first Toto stories in *The Yellow Book*; they met with such popular acclaim that they were repub-

lished by Bodley Head in *Bodley Booklets.* The success of these stories encouraged Corvo to write twenty-six more Toto stories, which were published with the original ones as *In His Own Image* (1901). (A twenty-six-story edition culled from both sets of stories was published in 1969 as *Stories Toto Told Me.*) In his preface to this later edition, Christopher Sykes comments that "One should perhaps think of the stories as being greatly extended and greatly sophisticated versions, contrived by a writer who had something of real genius in him, of those tales which are the subject of demure merriment among pious people, and have for long been commonplace in clergy houses and behind convent walls." Indeed, the mixture of legend, theology, and myth produces a certain buoyancy among the interrelated stories. "Each is a fraction of a large and colourful panorama of saints and sinners, the pagan past intermingled with the reverent present," Donald Weeks suggests. All of the stories are fashioned around Toto—"an uneducated peasant," as Corvo called him—as the storyteller. "No school board had defiled him; and hence his exquisiteness," Corvo remarked.

Chronicles of the House of Borgia, also published in 1901, is a collection of loosely connected monographs in which Corvo tried to demonstrate the unlikelihood that the Borgias were responsible for all of the more extreme accusations charged against them. Although Corvo admitted the errors of Roderigo Borgia, Pope Alexander VI, he tried to portray him as a grand figure capable of recognizing his own flaws. In addition to the attempt at verisimilitude by choosing the monograph format, Corvo also adopted spelling and syntax of the period to further reinforce the effect. Henry Harland describes the work as being "like a magnificent series of tapestry pictures of the fifteenth century," and that is certainly true. But at the same time, Corvo's technical ability is overshadowed by his penchant for the unusual, which is largely responsible for his individuality as a writer. "It was Rolfe's obsession and research for weird detail rather than his character-drawing that made the *Chronicles of the House of Borgia* interesting," Shane Leslie asserts.

As Corvo wrote in *Nicholas Crabbe* (1958), he produced the *Chronicles of the House of Borgia* and two other romances—*Don Tarquinio* (1905) and *Don Renato* (1909)—during a time when he "lived in the British Museum, studying, discovering unknown Medici MSS. and some unpublished holographs, following clues, and generally collecting the atmosphere and the background on which to place his figures 'vividly and picturesquely to suit the Library

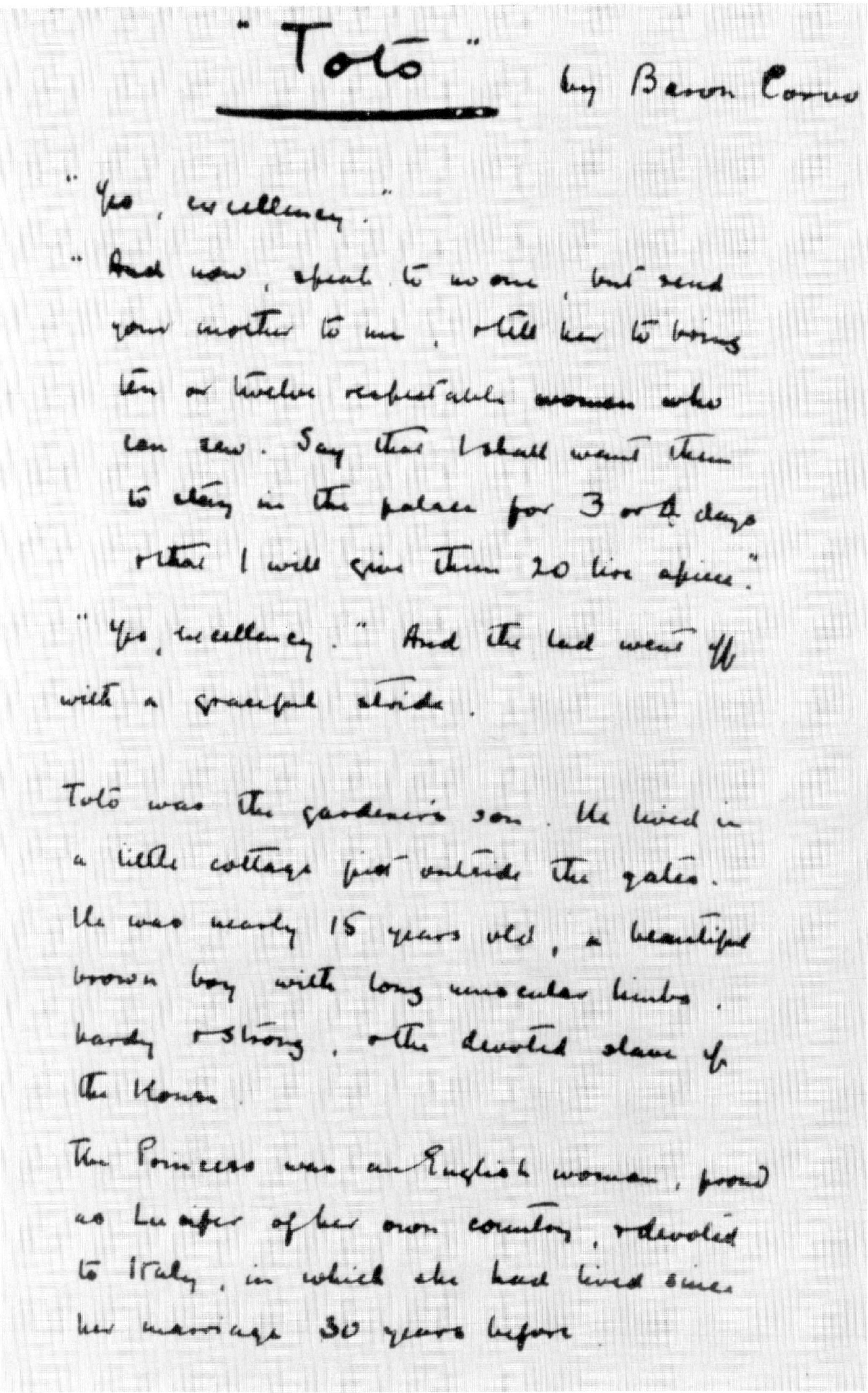

"Toto"
by Baron Corvo

"Yes, excellency."

"And now, speak to no one, but send your mother to me, & tell her to bring ten or twelve respectable women who can sew. Say that I shall want them to stay in the palace for 3 or 4 days & that I will give them 20 lire apiece."

"Yes, excellency." And the lad went off with a graceful stride.

Toto was the gardener's son. He lived in a little cottage just outside the gates. He was nearly 15 years old, a beautiful brown boy with long muscular limbs, hardy & strong, & the devoted slave of the House.

The Princess was an English woman, proud as Lucifer of her own country, & devoted to Italy, in which she had lived since her marriage 30 years before.

First page of the manuscript for Rolfe's first Toto story (Donald Weeks, Corvo, 1971)

Public' (whatever that chimaera might be)."

His work includes *Hubert's Arthur* (1935, co-authored with Harry Pirie-Gordon), a speculative history set in the time of the Crusades, short stories, and six novels whose heroes strongly resemble their author. Even in his book about the Borgias, Rolfe may be identified with his protagonists. Like his painting of the translation of the body of St. William of Norwich, in which he reproduced more than one hundred images of himself in a variety of vestments, his stories depict him and his life in the colorations of late medieval and early Renaissance Italy and allow him to render his life as heroic, particularly in *Hadrian the Seventh*. The self-absorption evident in his work; the neologisms, which are as often annoying as they are surprising ("tygendis," "technikrym," "contortuplication," "fumificables," "zaimph," "aseity," and "banaysically," for example); his idiosyncratic spellings; and punctuation in the style of Joseph Addison combine with his arcane subjects to alienate many readers. But those readers at first enthusiastic about his work tend soon to become obsessed with it and, necessarily, with

Rolfe's life. Obsessions with Rolfe, in addition to inspiring the book collecting and searches for lost manuscripts that literary preoccupations usually inspire, have resulted in two works more widely known and generally admired than are any of Rolfe's works: A. J. A. Symons's *The Quest for Corvo* (1934), a biography written with the energy and some of the conventions of a good detective story, and Peter Luke's play *Hadrian VII* (produced in 1968), acknowledged as one of the best plays of the 1960s.

Rolfe's intensity, his peculiarities which were initially part of his charm, and his ability, in his conversation as well as in his stories, to give events from his life the aura of mythological significance, drew friends and patrons no less ardent in their attentions than the "Corvinists" among his readers. However, almost every one of his supporters was unable to sustain the attention, financial and otherwise, that Rolfe demanded. Some came to feel that he was more a con artist than a literary artist; while others simply became tired. Having exhausted his friends and patrons, Rolfe died in debt and social

Covers designed by Rolfe

disgrace in Venice on 23 October 1913.

While the influence of his work is difficult to estimate, the value of it, at least to present-day Corvinists, seems to be the degree to which it renders Rolfe's madness as well as his brilliance. Pamela Hansford Johnson, who has based one of her own characters on Rolfe, writes of "the fascination of the paranoid personality" which "very often has the power to give a significant, penetrating quality to literary expression." Rarely has a work been so clear an expression of delusions of grandeur and yet so riveting as *Hadrian the Seventh*. In a letter to Maurice Hewlett, Corvo wrote that *Hadrian the Seventh* is "a modern and simple psychology, deliberately written for the many." Still, the intensity of the novel derives from its improbable yet irresistible story in which justice runs amok. The life of Rose, the protagonist, parallels Rolfe's to a point. Like Rose, Rolfe was rejected for the priesthood, but, unlike Rolfe's existence from patron to patron and hand to mouth, Rose's life of poverty ends triumphantly. Rose is recalled by representatives of the Church, who acknowledge the Church's wrongs. In recognition of Rose's virtue as well as to resolve a political deadlock, they appoint him Pope, whereupon he scandalizes the Church with actions such as selling the Vatican jewels to raise money for the poor. It was A. J. A. Symons's fascination with *Hadrian the Seventh*, particularly with its idealism, which initiated his quest; Symons's subsequent perusal of Rolfe's letters, with details of Rolfe's debaucheries in Venice, stimulated his interest.

Neither Symons's nor subsequent quests have yielded much information about Rolfe's childhood. Rolfe was born into circumstances ill-suited to the ambitions he was to conceive: his father was not only a piano maker, thus of the artisan class, but was also a religious dissenter. Rolfe attended North London Collegiate School in Camden Town, leaving at age fourteen. Although he was not a matriculated student, he spent several months at Oxford and was to return there on a regular basis to read exams for one of the few friends he retained throughout his life. Indeed he seemed to want desperately to belong to the elite, but his class background precluded the possibility. Vincent O'Sullivan, a contemporary at Oxford, wrote to Symons that Rolfe "had what used to be known as the 'Oxford accent' in the extreme." From 1874 to 1886 he made his living by teaching at a succession of schools. While he apparently performed to the headmaster's satisfaction at each, he stayed no more than a few terms at any one.

On 3 January 1886 he was received into the Catholic church at St. Aloysius, Oxford. Soon after his conversion, Rolfe decided he had a vocation for the priesthood. Symons speculates that Rolfe's temperament, artistic and scholarly, inclined him to the Church. One might also speculate, as does Johnson, that his desire for power and status led him there, that Rolfe "wanted less to be priest than to be Pope." He had no patience with the impositions of clerical training. His career as a cleric spanned three years, from 1887 to mid-1890, during which he left one seminary, Oscott, and was expelled from another, Scots College in Rome, after having been initially well received in both.

Disappointed in his attempt to realize his vocation, he took up residence in Rome with the Sforza-Cesarini family for a little less than a year. According to Rolfe, the Duchess Sforza-Cesarini, in accordance with privileges of patronage allowed to Italian nobility, conferred on Rolfe the title of Baron Corvo as well as providing him with an allowance which continued for some time after his return to Britain. Other commentators speculate that the title was part of a joke which evolved from Rolfe's

Frederick Rolfe, circa 1908 (courtesy of Julian Symons)

fetish for ravens, or that Rolfe conferred it on himself to compensate for his dismissal from Scots College. *Corvo* means raven, or, as one of Rolfe's Scottish detractors claimed, crow, derived from the Scots "corbie," and the raven became Rolfe's emblem even after he no longer insisted on his aristocratic title.

From 1898 to 1908 Rolfe wrote most of his books and letters, many of them denunciations of the friends, patrons, and publishers who circulated through his life at this time. Rolfe was so convinced of the reality of his delusions about himself that he was not only able to convince others of their reality, but was able to make business agreements on the basis of them. Indeed, he had abilities, but he treated them as if they were real estate on which a second mortgage might be taken out. When his books became successful, he promised, he would repay the lenders, but his books never became successful enough. When they failed and his patrons and creditors grew tired of supporting him, he mounted campaigns against them, claiming breach of faith. After an unsuccessful lawsuit against one of his former associates, Rolfe took up travels with a new patron, a Professor Dawson who was struck by Rolfe's "personal intensity and singularity."

Because Rolfe intended to repay Dawson, he could justify his "elaborate idleness," as Symons records it, and indulge himself in luxuries which his new patron found too expensive. Dawson finally left Rolfe in Venice with some money which he soon spent. Throughout the period from 1907 until his death in 1913, Rolfe sent solicitations for money to former friends and patrons, but he was to acquire only one new patron able to support him adequately. Rolfe, who was by this time in poor health and filled with the venom of a disappointed prima donna, was unable to make use of the funds as he might have—or at least as he claimed he might have—to write much more than the letters which detailed his miseries and resentments. Unknown to the new patrons with whom he was residing, he spent the money in high living and debauchery. He was writing his last book, *The Desire and Pursuit of the Whole* (posthumously published in 1934), a book which was to lose him these patrons when they dis-

covered that it ridiculed many of their friends and acquaintances. The fictionalized people and events from his own experiences in Venice from 1909 to 1910 involve a romance between a maid and a man and a test of Nicholas Crabbe's (a persona for Corvo) faith. Not alone among those who praised this work, Stuart Gilbert, in his *James Joyce's Ulysses,* commented that Corvo's hero—Crabbe—"had a good deal in common with Stephen Dedalus." Gilbert added that "Indeed, had the Fates been kinder, that unhappy genius might have moved parallel, if on a somewhat lower plane, to Joyce's."

This satire on twentieth-century Venice also completes his semiautobiographical tetralogy which is initiated with *In His Own Image.* The series continues with *Hadrian the Seventh,* which details his involvement with Roman Catholicism from 1886 to 1902, then shifts back to *Nicholas Crabbe* to the miserable beginning of his career as a writer in London from 1900 to 1903. The final entry of the tetralogy covers his first year in Venice. He died in 1913 in a wretched condition.

Fascination with Rolfe seems to be a fascination with a phenomenon as much as with an individual author and his works. He exemplified an artistic type, to which Wilde and Huysmans also belong. Beyond that the fascination may be with the paranoid personality, as it is for Johnson, with the number and variety of contradictions a single human being can contain, as it was for Symons; or with questions his life and art raise, such as how much should genius be indulged before its claims cease to be legitimate?

References:

Pamela Hansford Johnson, "The Fascination of the Paranoid Personality," in *New Quests for Corvo,* edited by Cecil Woolf and Brocard Sewell (London: Icon Books, 1965);

Peter Luke, *Hadrian VII* (New York: Knopf, 1969);

A. J. A. Symons, *The Quest for Corvo: An Experiment in Biography* (New York: Macmillan, 1934);

Donald Weeks, *Corvo* (London: Joseph, 1971);

Cecil Woolf, *A Bibliography of Frederick Rolfe, Baron Corvo* (London: Rupert Hart-Davis, 1957).

V. Sackville-West
(9 March 1892-2 June 1962)

Priscilla Diaz-Dorr
University of Tulsa

SELECTED BOOKS: *Poems of West and East* (London & New York: John Lane, 1917);

Heritage (London: Collins, 1919; New York: Doran, 1919);

The Dragon in Shallow Waters (London: Collins, 1921; New York & London: Putnam's, 1922);

Orchard and Vineyard (London & New York: John Lane, 1921);

The Heir: A Love Story [one story] (London: Privately printed, 1922);

The Heir: A Love Story [five stories] (London: Heinemann, 1922; New York: Doran, 1922);

Knole and the Sackvilles (London: Heinemann, 1922; New York: Doran, 1922; revised edition, London: Benn, 1958);

Challenge (New York: Doran, 1923);

Grey Wethers: A Romantic Novel (London: Heinemann, 1923; New York: Doran, 1923);

Seducers in Ecuador (London: Leonard & Virginia Woolf, 1924; New York: Doran, 1925);

Passengers to Teheran (London: Leonard & Virginia Woolf, 1926; New York: Doran, 1927);

The Land (London: Heinemann, 1926; Garden City: Doubleday, Doran & Coy, 1927);

Aphra Benn: The Incomparable Astrea (London: Howe, 1927; New York: Viking, 1928);

Twelve Days: An Account of a Journey across the Bakhtiari Mountains in South-Western Persia (London: Hogarth Press, 1928; Garden City: Doubleday, Doran, 1928);

Andrew Marvell (London: Faber & Faber, 1929);

King's Daughter (London: Leonard & Virginia Woolf, 1929; Garden City: Doubleday, Doran, 1930);

The Edwardians (London: Leonard & Virginia Woolf, 1930; Garden City: Doubleday, Doran, 1930);

All Passion Spent (London: Leonard & Virginia Woolf at the Hogarth Press, 1931; Garden City: Doubleday, Doran, 1931);

Family History (London: Leonard & Virginia Woolf at the Hogarth Press, 1932; Garden City: Doubleday, Doran, 1932);

Thirty Clocks Strike the Hour and Other Stories (Garden City: Doubleday, Doran, 1932);

The Death of Noble Godavary and Gottfried Künstler (London: Benn, 1932);

Collected Poems (London: Leonard & Virginia Woolf at the Hogarth Press, 1933; Garden City: Doubleday, Doran, 1933);

The Dark Island (London: Leonard & Virginia Woolf at the Hogarth Press, 1934; Garden City: Doubleday, Doran, 1934);

Saint Joan of Arc (London: Cobden-Sanderson, 1936; Garden City: Doubleday, Doran, 1936; revised edition, London: Joseph, 1948);

Joan of Arc (London: Leonard & Virginia Woolf, 1937; New York: Stackpole, 1938);

Pepita (London: Leonard & Virginia Woolf, 1937; Garden City: Doubleday, Doran, 1937);

Some Flowers (London: Cobden-Sanderson, 1937);

Solitude: A Poem (London: Hogarth Press, 1938; Garden City: Doubleday, Doran, 1939);

Country Notes (London: Joseph, 1939; New York & London: Harper, 1940);

Country Notes in Wartime (London: Hogarth Press, 1940; New York: Doubleday, Doran, 1941);

Selected Poems (London: Hogarth Press, 1941);

Grand Canyon: A Novel (London: Joseph, 1942; Garden City: Doubleday, Doran, 1942);

The Eagle and the Dove, A Study in Contrasts: St. Teresa of Avila. St. Thérèse of Lisieux (London: Joseph, 1943; Garden City: Doubleday, Doran, 1944);

The Women's Land Army (London: Joseph, 1944);

The Garden (London: Joseph, 1946; Garden City: Doubleday, Doran, 1946);

Devil at Westease: The Story as Related by Roger Liddiard (Garden City: Doubleday, 1947);

Nursery Rhymes (London: Dropmore Press, 1947);

In Your Garden (London: Joseph, 1951);

The Easter Party (London: Joseph, 1953; Garden City: Doubleday, Doran, 1953);

In Your Garden Again (London: Joseph, 1953);

More for Your Garden (London: Joseph, 1955);

Even More for Your Garden (London: Joseph, 1958);

A Joy of Gardening: A Selection for Americans, edited by Hermine I. Popper (New York: Harper, 1958);

Daughter of France: The Life of Anne Marie Louise d'Orleans, Duchesse de Montpensier, 1627-1693,

Victoria and Vita Sackville-West (courtesy of Nigel Nicolson)

La Grande Mademoiselle (London: Joseph, 1959; Garden City: Doubleday, 1959);

No Signposts in the Sea (London: Joseph, 1961; Garden City: Doubleday, 1961).

OTHER: *The Diary of Lady Anne Clifford,* introduction and notes by Sackville-West (London: Heinemann, 1923);

Rainer Maria Rilke, *Duineser Elegien: Elegies from the Castle of Duino,* translated by Sackville-West (London: Hogarth Press, 1931).

V. Sackville-West was born into one of the oldest families of England, the Sackvilles, whose ancestral estate, Knole, was a gift to poet and dramatist Thomas Sackville (1536-1608) from his cousin Elizabeth I. Sackville-West's family history is so vivid and complex that she wrote two volumes on the subject, and Knole was for her a living symbol of the continuity of history, an emblem of an ordered world. Yet, at the same time, this British novelist felt herself an alien in the Edwardian aristocracy that was her heritage.

Victoria Mary Sackville-West was born at Knole on 9 March 1892, the only child of Victoria Josepha Dolores Catalina Sackville-West and Lionel Sackville-West, who became the third Lord Sackville in 1908 after the death of Lionel Sackville-West, the second Lord Sackville, his uncle and his wife's father. The child was called Vita to distinguish her from her unpredictable and high-spirited mother, a former hostess in Washington diplomatic

circles and a lion in British and European societies, who included among her friends Renoir, Rodin, and Queen Victoria. Victoria Sackville-West was the eldest daughter of an English diplomat and Pepita, a beautiful and internationally famous Spanish dancer of humble birth, whose real name was Josefa Duran. V. Sackville-West's *Pepita* (1937) explores the life of this unusual woman from whom the novelist inherited her passionate nature, as she so often said.

As a child Sackville-West was frequently miserable and lonely. In a society where personal appearance counted for a great deal, she was neither popular nor beautiful. She felt herself to be a source of disappointment to her mother, unable to fulfill the roles she was constantly placed in. Of her mother's influence in the writer's early childhood Sackville-West wrote: "My principal recollection of her then is that I used to be taken to her room to be 'passed' before going down to luncheon on party days, when I had had my hair crimped; and I was always wrong and miserable, so that parties used to blacken my summer." There were two consolations for the child: her friendship with her grandfather, with whom she stayed when her mother was away on her frequent trips; and her many solitary hours spent roaming the grounds and halls of Knole, a house alleged to have fifty-two staircases and 365 rooms, including The King's Bedroom with sterling-silver furnishings prepared for the reception of King James I.

Sackville-West's education was typical for girls

of her era: she was instructed by governesses until in her teens and then was enrolled as a day pupil at Miss Woolf's School, a girls' school in London. She found educational achievement to be a source of recognition and worked eagerly to receive prizes and honors: "if I couldn't be popular, I would be clever," she wrote in her manuscript autobiography (written in 1920). Shy and intensely emotional Sackville-West turned to reading and writing in rebellion against her social class, and during her teens she wrote historical novels, poetry, and plays.

In 1910, when she was eighteen, Sackville-West was required to participate in the social ritual of coming out, a process which she found distasteful. However, at one of the parties she met Harold Nicolson, a twenty-three-year-old diplomat, whom she married on 1 October 1912.

After a honeymoon in Italy and Egypt, the couple went to live in Constantinople, where Nicolson had been posted. In spite of her dislike for social functions, she assumed the role of "the correct and adoring wife of the brilliant young diplomat." They were recalled to England in June 1914; and on 6 August 1914 their first son, Benedict, was born. In

1915 Sackville-West delivered a stillborn child, an event which had a profound effect on her emotional health. Her distress was further agitated by a confession, by her husband, that he had a male lover who had infected him with venereal disease. Feelings of discontent that she had been suppressing for years emerged. She was confronted with an inner conflict over her own sexuality, what she called her "dual nature." She was no longer content with playing a role.

In 1917, the year in which her son Nigel was born, John Lane accepted for publication her *Poems of West and East.* She was ready to embark on a career as a serious author, confident in a new power of artistic insight and sure of her facility in the craft of writing. Wanting recognition not as a *woman*-poet but as a serious writer, she devised the signature V. Sackville-West, which she used for the rest of her life. By 1918 she was involved in a serious love affair with a childhood friend, Violet Keppel (later Violet Trefusis). While this affair placed severe stress on her marriage, it marked the beginning of a highly passionate and inspired period in her writing career.

Vita Sackville-West and Harold Nicolson, 1919 (courtesy of Nigel Nicolson)

Sackville-West's career as a novelist was launched in 1919 with *Heritage,* published with the help of George Moore, a member of the Bloomsbury group who was the Nicolsons' London neighbor. Moore also introduced the couple to some of the members of Bloomsbury, but Sackville-West did not meet Virginia Woolf until 1922.

Heritage introduces several themes that are characteristic of all Sackville-West's early novels, including the role of heredity and the influence of foreign blood. Convinced that her Spanish blood was the more vehement strain and the source of her creative talent, Sackville-West also believed that it was the source of a wild and irresponsible impulse and that it conflicted with the stability she coveted. Her second novel, *The Dragon in Shallow Waters* (1921), also treats this theme, as well as the existence of the dual nature, the mirror image of male and female within the single self.

By 1920 Sackville-West's affair with Violet Keppel had escalated into a scandal. The affair was a way of expressing a romantic ideal that was frequent among the British middle and upper class at this time, what Violet called "the all too small fraternity of the adventurers, the reckless, the enterprising, the free." This fraternity of adventurers sought to rebel against the conventions of the British social codes by living a secret life in France. The affair between the two women was marked by a role-playing situation: Sackville-West, acting out the masculine side of her dual nature, would dress in men's clothing and assume the role of "Julian," a tall slender young man who escorted Violet as "Lushka" to dinner and dancing in Paris. When passing as a man, Sackville-West felt most free.

The affair is riddled with complex detail. Sackville-West was receiving pressure from both her mother and her husband to end the liaison. In the midst of it all Violet married Denys Trefusis with whom Sackville-West corresponded regarding the match. It was as though they were trying to intellectualize that which they were romanticizing. An account of the affair, which lasted about three years, was written in Sackville-West's confessional autobiographical fragment and was not published until after the deaths of those involved. From it we learned about the end of the liaison.

The two women finally eloped to France with plans of settling there and buying a house. Even though they were eloping together, Sackville-West wrote to her husband on a regular basis to advise him of their whereabouts, and in the end the two men came to retrieve their wives. The crowning blow for Sackville-West was when Denys confessed that he and Violet had had sexual relations. The crux of the conflict between the two Nicolsons had been that Violet made Vita promise not to have any relations with her husband: it was part of their Sapphic vow to one another. When Vita found out that Violet had lied to her, her passions were cooled. Although after the two women were returned to England they still saw one another, the romantic ideal they had constructed was no longer operative, and gradually their involvement waned.

The result of this affair, however, was the novel *Challenge* (1923), a romantic novel about the conflict of love and duty, set on a Greek island. Julian Davenant, a wealthy vine grower on the island of Herakleion who becomes involved in the revolution there, is torn between his love for his country and the love of a beautiful woman, Eve. Eve is patterned after Violet Keppel Trefusis and Julian is obviously Sackville-West. A great deal of the novel was written while they were traveling together, and the likenesses and the underlying Sapphic philosophy were apparent enough that the families of these two women suppressed its publication in England.

Grey Wethers (1923) demonstrates Sackville-West's skill in portraying British countryside society. It is the story of Clare Warrener, the daughter of a scholarly squire, and her tragic love for Nicholas Lovel, a Gypsy. The setting is important to the story because it evokes a supernatural quality: Wiltshire Downs, a little village, is entirely surrounded by a prehistoric earthwork, and in the village are the mystical stones, the Grey Wethers. As representations of the dual nature, Clare and Lovel together form a perfect unity, but due to the circumstances of life and of heritage, they cannot be together.

What gives this novel its strength is the strong poetic prose, clear imagery, and the author's strong affinity for detail. Sackville-West's talent for careful observation is demonstrated by a small incident when Clare receives a negative response to a message she has sent Lovel: "At that Clare flamed into anger. . . . She was all the angrier with him because she was angry with herself for having sent a verbal message . . . , the story conceivably, would be repeated . . . , in which case it would be all over the village; she ought to have written Lovel a note." The subtle juxtaposition of the social and the individual impulse, a continuous and ongoing antagonism, plagued Sackville-West's characters as it plagued her. Her careful chronicle of social detail is a great virtue of all her novels. As her own concerns pervade the text, the nature of the society that surrounds her becomes clearly evident and carefully preserved.

In 1922 Sackville-West met Clive Bell, and through him she made the acquaintance of Virginia Woolf. From January to March 1923 the two women exchanged letters, books, and occasional social calls. Woolf was fascinated by Sackville-West's aristocratic manner and her family background. The two women had much in common, especially their love for writing and their intense individual natures. However, it was not until 1924 that their personal relationship developed further.

In July 1924, the Nicolsons took a walking tour in the Dolomites, and each night Sackville-West worked on *Seducers in Ecuador*. She wrote to Woolf: "You asked me to write a story for you. On the peaks of mountains, and beside green lakes, I am writing it for you. I shut my eyes to the blue of gentians, to the coral of androsace; I shut my ears to the brawling of rivers; I shut my nose to the scent of pines; I concentrate on my story." The story, or short novel, was published by Leonard and Virginia Woolf at the Hogarth Press in November 1924 and contributed to the growing bond between the two women. One of Sackville-West's most experimental works, with a surrealist quality, it is written sparsely, avoiding for the most part the traditional elements of scene, setting, and dialogue, substituting a narrator who tells swiftly of an interlude in Arthur Lomax's life.

Lomax begins to look at the world through colored glasses while in Egypt, a stopover on his Mediterranean Sea journey with the three other characters in the novel, Bellamy, the captain, Artivale, the scientist, and Miss Whitaker, a mysterious woman who writes letters to a man in Ecuador. Lomax's glasses literally change his view of the world and are symbolic of his own desire to change the way he administers his affairs. He becomes an adventurer, making decisions on the spur of the moment as the options are presented to him.

On the journey he makes two decisions which have unexpected consequences and ultimately lead to his death. After Miss Whitaker, whom he has just met, declares that she is pregnant by the man in Ecuador, he secretly marries her in order to save her honor. As a result he is unable to fulfill his long-held desire for Marian Vane when her husband dies unexpectedly. After he poisons Bellamy, at the captain's request, because he is dying and cannot face the pain of his terminal disease, Bellamy wills his fortune to Lomax. For Lomax, the "murder," as he calls it later in the book, is a humane action. However, the police investigation of Bel-

lamy's death leads to the accusation and conviction of Lomax. The resolution of the plot, built on a series of unusual circumstances, prefigures Camus's *L'Etranger*. Lomax goes to his death explaining that "we are all condemned, you know."

Virginia Woolf's response to the book was typical of her usual mixed review: "I like the story very very much . . . being full of a particular kind of interest which daresay has something to do with its being the sort of thing I should like to write myself." She goes on to include a critical comment: "I like its obscurity so that we can play about with it— interpret it different ways, and the beauty and fantasticallity of the details. . . . This [the details] is all quite sincere, though not well expressed." By 26 December 1924 the book had sold 899 copies, and in January 1925 Woolf wrote in a letter to Sackville-West: "We are making money very comfortably out of *Seducers*. I am very pleased, not only commercially, but I think it to people's credit, considering how out of the way it is, in size and price and meaning and everything."

The publication of *Seducers*, an increased correspondence, and more visits signaled the intensification of this relationship which has been analyzed

This photograph of Sackville-West was published in Virginia Woolf's Orlando *(1928), a fictional "biography" of a character based on Sackville-West, with the caption "Orlando about the year 1840."*

in several works on both authors. For Sackville-West it was the most important event in her life except her marriage, giving her warm companionship, literary stimulus, and, as she once told Harold Nicolson, it was "a treasure and a privilege." In 1928, as the affair began to wane, Virginia Woolf published *Orlando,* inspired by her fascination with Knole, the Sackvilles, and Sackville-West herself. Nigel Nicolson described it as "her most elaborate love-letter, rendering Vita androgynous and immortal: it transformed her story into a myth, gave her back to Knole."

From 1925 to 1929 Sackville-West devoted her time to writing poetry and nonfiction. She was prompted to write her long poem *The Land* (1926) by a realization of the increasing threat of progress to traditional English rural life. The poem was awarded the Hawthornden Prize in 1927. During this time Sackville-West also wrote two travel books on Persia, *Passengers to Teheran* (1926) and *Twelve Days: An Account of a Journey across the Bakhtiari Mountains in South-Western Persia* (1928), as a result of two visits there to stay with her husband, who, still in the foreign service, was posted in Persia. Tension had been developing in their marriage over their continuous partings, and these two visits only amplified the problem.

In 1929 Harold Nicolson began to have health problems and considered leaving the foreign service in order to be closer to home. Sackville-West encouraged him in this decision, stressing his literary talents, suggesting he take up a literary career. In 1921 Nicolson had started writing books, and by 1927 he had published one novel, four works of literary biography on Paul Verlaine, Tennyson, Byron, and Swinburne, and *The Development of English Biography* (1927). Moreover, friends in England, notably Leonard and Virginia Woolf, had told him that he was wasting his talents in diplomacy; he should be a writer or enter politics. Then in June 1929 Nicolson was offered a job on the *Evening Standard,* to write for and edit a page called the "Londoner's Diary," and he accepted it.

The Nicolsons' purchase of Sissinghurst Castle in 1930 marked a new period in Sackville-West's life. In the English countryside she could have the seclusion and stability she had long desired. She spent a great deal of time developing the gardens at Sissinghurst, a hobby that would sustain her for the rest of her life, and wrote: "How fortunate we both are to have both indoor and outdoor occupations. If we can't garden, we can write." The Sissinghurst style of gardening became known all over the country. Through the years the gardens were

Dust jacket for the first of Sackville-West's best-selling novels

opened to tourists, and Sackville-West was to write a number of columns on the subject in the years after World War II. In later years it was through her writing about gardening that she acquired a new and different kind of renown.

In 1930 the Woolfs published the first of her three best-selling novels, *The Edwardians.* The novel shows a change in the mood of her works. The mysterious view of the early works is replaced by a clearer and more direct kind of storytelling. The focus on social mores is more pronounced. The setting is the country homes of the British aristocracy, where Sackville-West is more assured in her descriptions and characterizations. In *The Edwardians,* the manners and situations of the two young characters, Sebastian and Lucy, are close to the childhood and young adult life of their author. The Edwardians are without doubt Sackville-West's mother's friends. Sebastian and Lucy, who are a more relaxed rendition of Sackville-West's theme of the dual nature, are presented with a new option in life by the arrival of Leonard Anquetil, a genuine adventurer. In the end, when they both decide to give up their social position for individual fulfillment and experience by following in Anquetil's footsteps instead of the Edwardians', there is something natural in their decision, which precludes the kind of suffering the author experienced to get to the same point.

Sackville-West's novels also introduce a new theme during this period: equal rights for women. On the radio broadcasts she and Nicolson did for the BBC, she had become more vocal on the issue of the independence of women, independence being inherent in the individualism she had always written about. Their talks on marriage emphasized the importance of a woman's right to pursue a career. This same theme is implicit in *The Edwardians* when Lucy, as well as her brother, has an equal opportunity to pursue her wanderlust. The feminist theme is also apparent in her 1931 novel, *All Passion Spent*.

Published by the Hogarth Press and also a best-seller, *All Passion Spent* tells the story of the final years of Lady Slane, who sets out to spend her widowhood pursuing the goals of individual expression that she gave up in her youth in order to fulfill her social obligations as the wife of a public figure. There is a strong connection between the ideas in this novel and those in Virginia Woolf's two nonfiction books about women, *A Room of One's Own* (1929) and *Three Guineas* (1938). Built into the novel is Sackville-West's lifelong anger about the way society distorts and inhibits the individual, particularly if that individual is a woman. Nowhere is this idea better portrayed than in the character of Lady Slane, who has "had enough of bustle and competition and of one set of ambitions writhing to circumvent another."

In 1932 Sackville-West wrote *Family History*, also a best-seller, which continues the portraits of Edwardian manners for which Sackville-West is best known. She also published *Thirty Clocks Strike the Hour*, which was a collection of short stories that for the most part had appeared in British magazines.

In 1933, Sackville-West had gained enough popularity due to her recent works that she and Harold Nicolson undertook a lecture tour of the United States. Both writers had American followings, although hers was greater. Sackville-West, whose reputation for her theories on independence of women preceded her, gave lectures on literary figures such as D. H. Lawrence and Virginia Woolf, and she also spoke on her travels through Persia and changes in English social life. They arrived in New York in January 1933. Her first lectures at Springfield and Yale went well. They worked their

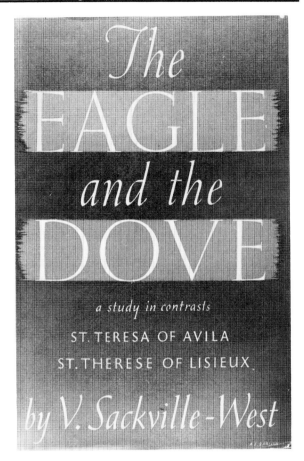

Dust jacket for Sackville-West's examination of the contrasting personalities of two saints

way across the country, being shown around Hollywood by Gary Cooper. She spent some time in New England and met Robert Frost. Between them, Nicolson calculated, they visited fifty-three different cities, made seventy-two different journeys, spent sixty-three nights in the train, and covered 33,527 miles. Greatly inspired by the American experience, Sackville-West planned to write a novel with America as its setting. Although it was not published until 1942, *Grand Canyon* was in part the result of this trip.

From 1933 to 1941 Sackville-West wrote several books, including a novel, *The Dark Island* (1934), which was not well liked by her friends because of its somewhat cruel and secretive manner. It also received mixed reviews from critics. During this time she also wrote two biographies, *Saint Joan of Arc* (1936) and *Pepita* (1937). Her poems were collected in 1933. She published a long poem, *Solitude*, in 1938 and *Selected Poems* in 1941.

On 28 March 1941 Virginia Woolf committed suicide by drowning. The death of her closest friend

Low sinks the sun, and long the shadows fall.
The sun-clock, faithful measurer of time,
Fixed to man's dwelling on his flimsy wall
Or tabled flat on curving pedestal
Amongst his dying flowers, tells the last
Hours of the year (and also of my rhyme.)
Now is the sunlight ebbing, faint and fast
In intermittent gleams that seldom cut
Throughout the day the quadrant of our fate
With the slow stroke that says TOO SOON ... TOO LATE ...
BEWARE, THE OPEN GATE WILL SOON BE SHUT.
The stroke that turns our present to our past.

November sun that latens with our age,
Filching the zest from our young pilgrimage,
Writing old wisdom on our virgin page.
Not the hot ardour of the summer's height,
Not the sharp-minted coinage of the spring
When all was but a delicate delight
And all took wing and all the bells did ring;
Not the spare winter, clothed in black and white,
Forcing us into fancy's eremite,
But gliding time that slid us into gold
Richer and deeper as we grow more old
And see some meaning in this dying day;
Travellers of the war, who faintly say
Thank God that beauty walks the common way.

AMEN.

30.10.1945

Last page of the manuscript for The Garden *(courtesy of Nigel Nicolson)*

Sackville-West and her dog Rollo at Sissinghurst, 1956. Her writing room was on the first floor of the tower, built circa 1565.

and the outbreak of World War II caused a decline in her creative output. During the war Sackville-West agreed to be involved in the local administration, recruitment, and publicity of the Women's Land Army. She stockpiled straw as bedding for refugees, was designated as an ambulance driver in case of air-raid injury, and wrote "a propaganda book" for the Women's Land Army tracing its history, but she did not consider it real writing.

In 1947, in the midst of a personal literary crisis, Sackville-West received significant literary recognition. Her long poem *The Garden* (1946) was awarded the Heinemann Award for Literature, and she was made a Companion of Honor for her services to literature. Her 1953 novel, *The Easter Party,* did not meet with popular success, but she continued her work, writing a number of articles on

gardening, and constructing a biographical account of Anne Marie Louise d'Orléans (1627-1693), *Daughter of France.* It was not completed until 1959. In the last decade of her life she wrote no poetry.

Her later years are portrayed in her correspondence with an American writer, Andrew Reiber. In this collection of letters, her personality, her life as member of the Queen's inner circle, her love for gardening and writing, and her need for solitude come through with an unusual clearness.

Her last novel, *No Signposts in the Sea,* was published in the year before her death from cancer in 1962. Written on cruise ships, it was begun in January 1959 while she and her husband were journeying to Tokyo and Saigon, and the bulk of the writing was done on a cruise, in January and February 1960, to South Africa. It was completed in the fall of 1960. The themes of aloneness and the difficulty of communication between two people are presented through the device of the diary. It is a record of Edmund Carr's last journey, a cruise to the Far East. The diarist reflects on his approaching death and on his last weeks, which he has chosen to spend with the woman he loves. *No Signposts in the Sea* was written, like all her other works, in complete secrecy, its contents unknown even to her family and friends, until it came into print. The novel was well received by critics.

In general, critical response to Sackville-West's writing has been mixed. When her novels are evaluated by the prevailing code of modernist aesthetics, they fall short of critical expectations. But Sackville-West was a reactionary to modernist tendencies and, for the most part, wrote in a traditional mode. However, her themes are anything but traditional, and their real meanings are sometimes deeply embedded in the text, dependent on a symbolic or allegorical interpretation to illuminate, for example, her concept of the dual nature, a subject that was not allowed direct treatment during her lifetime.

Sackville-West wrote novels that concentrated on story and theme more than technique. She revised little, assuming that the first thought put down on paper was the best. Occasionally her books begin strangely with unnaturally elevated diction, unnecessary for the storytelling which is to follow. There are sprinklings of literary and structural devices which have no real purpose and distract the reader. These flaws do not detract from the overall effect of her natural poetic style and her vivid and clear descriptions. Her sense of narrative is always very strong.

Recent criticism indicates a renewed interest in Sackville-West's works. When placed in the tradition of twentieth-century British women novelists, her writings contribute to the history of women's thought during the turbulent years after emancipation when British women were seeking a new identity. The enduring value of her works comes from the honesty with which she portrays the emotional turmoil created by the changing social and intellectual environment of the 1920s and 1930s in England. She renders, carefully and precisely, the need to reconcile the inner will with the external world; her strong belief in the sanctity of the individual spirit and the right to freedom of thought and expression pervades each of her works. For the student of the novel her works offer a meaningful counterpoint to the modernist text: the use of the traditional style with modern subjects and the quiet, almost private, resolution of the dualistic life.

Letters:
Dearest Andrew: Letters from V. Sackville-West to Andrew Reiber, 1951-1962, edited by Nancy MacKnight (New York: Scribners, 1979).

Biographies:
Sara Ruth Watson, *V. Sackville-West* (New York: Twayne, 1972);
Michael Stevens, *V. Sackville-West: A Critical Biography* (London: Joseph, 1973);
Nigel Nicolson, *Portrait of a Marriage* (New York: Atheneum, 1973);
Victoria Glendinning, *Vita: The Life of Vita Sackville-West* (New York: Knopf, 1983).

Reference:
The Letters of Virginia Woolf: Volume III 1923-1928, edited by Nigel Nicolson and Joanne Trautmann (New York: Harcourt Brace Jovanovich, 1977).

Papers:
V. Sackville-West's papers are at Lilly Library, Indiana University.

Frank Swinnerton
(12 August 1884-6 November 1982)

Douglas M. Catron
Iowa State University

SELECTED BOOKS: *The Merry Heart: A Gentle Melodrama* (London: Chatto & Windus, 1909; Garden City: Doubleday, Doran, 1929);

The Young Idea: A Comedy of Environment (London: Chatto & Windus, 1910; New York: Duffield, 1911);

The Casement: A Diversion (London: Chatto & Windus, 1911; New York: Duffield, 1911);

George Gissing: A Critical Study (London: Secker, 1912; New York: Kennerley, 1912);

The Happy Family (London: Methuen, 1912; New York: Doran, 1912);

On the Staircase (London: Methuen, 1914; New York: Doran, 1914);

R. L. Stevenson: A Critical Study (London: Secker, 1914; New York: Kennerley, 1915);

The Chaste Wife (London: Secker, 1916; New York: Doran, 1917);

Nocturne (London: Secker, 1917; New York: Doran, 1917);

Shops and Houses (London: Methuen, 1918; New York: Doran, 1918);

Women, anonymous (London: Secker, 1918; New York: Knopf, 1919);

September (London: Methuen, 1919; New York: Doran, 1919);

Coquette (London: Methuen, 1921; New York: Doran, 1921);

The Three Lovers (New York: Doran, 1922; London: Methuen, 1923);

Young Felix (London: Hutchinson, 1923; New York: Doran, 1923);

The Elder Sister (London: Hutchinson, 1925; New York: Doran, 1925);

Summer Storm (London: Hutchinson, 1926; New York: Doran, 1926);

Tokefield Papers (London: Secker, 1927; New York: Doran, 1927); enlarged as *Tokefield Papers, Old and New* (London: Hamilton, 1949; Garden City: Doubleday, 1949);

A Brood of Ducklings (London: Hutchinson, 1928; Garden City: Doubleday, Doran, 1929);

A London Bookman (London: Secker, 1928);

Sketch of a Sinner (Garden City: Doubleday, Doran, 1929; London: Hutchinson, 1930);

Frank Swinnerton

Authors and the Book Trade (London: Howe, 1932; New York: Knopf, 1932);

The Georgian House: A Tale in Four Parts (Garden City: Doubleday, Doran, 1932; London: Hutchinson, 1932);

Elizabeth: A Story in Six Parts (London: Hutchinson, 1934; Garden City: Doubleday, Doran, 1934);

The Georgian Scene: A Literary Panorama (New York: Farrar & Rinehart, 1934); republished as *The Georgian Literary Scene: A Panorama* (London & Toronto: Heinemann, 1935);

Swinnerton: An Autobiography (Garden City: Doubleday, Doran, 1936; London: Hutchinson, 1937);

Harvest Comedy: A Dramatic Chronicle (London: Hutchinson, 1937; Garden City: Doubleday, Doran, 1938);

The Reviewing and Criticism of Books (London: Dent, 1939; New York: Oxford University Press, 1939);

The Two Wives: A Tale in Four Parts (London: Hutchinson, 1940; New York: Doubleday, Doran, 1940);

The Fortunate Lady: A Dramatic Chronicle (London: Hutchinson, 1941; Garden City: Doubleday, Doran, 1941);

Thankless Child (London: Hutchinson, 1942; Garden City: Doubleday, Doran, 1942);

A Woman in Sunshine (London & New York: Hutchinson, 1944; Garden City: Doubleday, Doran, 1945);

English Maiden: Parable of a Happy Life (London: Hutchinson, 1946);

The Cats and Rosemary (New York: Knopf, 1948; London: Hamilton, 1950);

A Faithful Company: A Winter's Tale (London & New York: Hutchinson, 1948; Garden City: Doubleday, 1948);

The Doctor's Wife Comes to Stay (London & New York: Hutchinson, 1949; Garden City: Doubleday, 1950);

Arnold Bennett (London: Published for the British Council by Longmans, Green, 1950);

A Flower for Catherine (London & New York: Hutchinson, 1950; Garden City: Doubleday, 1951);

The Bookman's London (London: Wingate, 1951; New York: Doubleday, 1952; revised, London: Baker, 1969);

Londoner's Post: Letters to Gog and Magog (London: Hutchinson, 1952);

Master Jim Probity (London: Hutchinson, 1952; republished as *An Affair of Love* (Garden City: Doubleday, 1953);

A Month in Gordon Square (London: Hutchinson, 1953; Garden City: Doubleday, 1954);

The Sumner Intrigue (London: Hutchinson, 1955; Garden City: Doubleday, 1955);

The Adventures of a Manuscript, Being the Story of "The Ragged-Trousered Philanthropists" (London: Richards Press, 1956);

Authors I Never Met (London: Frederick Books, Allen & Unwin, 1956);

Background with Chorus: A Footnote to Changes in English Literary Fashion Between 1901 and 1917 (London: Hutchinson, 1956; New York: Far-

rar, Straus & Cudahy, 1957);

The Woman from Sicily (London: Hutchinson, 1957; Garden City: Doubleday, 1957);

A Tigress in Prothero (London: Hutchinson, 1959); republished as *A Tigress in the Village* (Garden City: Doubleday, 1959);

The Grace Divorce (London: Hutchinson, 1960; Garden City: Doubleday, 1960);

Death of a Highbrow (London & New York: Hutchinson, 1961; Garden City: Doubleday, 1962);

Figures in the Foreground: Literary Reminiscences 1917-1940 (London: Hutchinson, 1963; Garden City: Doubleday, 1964);

Quadrille (London: Hutchinson, 1965; Garden City: Doubleday, 1965);

A Galaxy of Fathers (London: Hutchinson, 1966; Garden City: Doubleday, 1966);

Sanctuary (London: Hutchinson, 1966; Garden City: Doubleday, 1967);

The Bright Lights (London: Hutchinson, 1968; Garden City: Doubleday, 1968);

Reflections from a Village (London: Hutchinson, 1969; Garden City: Doubleday, 1969);

On the Shady Side (London: Hutchinson, 1970; Garden City: Doubleday, 1971);

Nor All Thy Tears (London: Hutchinson, 1972; Garden City: Doubleday, 1972);

Rosalind Passes (London: Hutchinson, 1973; Garden City: Doubleday, 1973);

Some Achieve Greatness (London: Hamilton, 1976; Garden City: Doubleday, 1976);

Arnold Bennett: A Last Word (London: Hamilton, 1978; Garden City: Doubleday, 1978).

OTHER: *An Anthology of Modern Fiction,* edited by Swinnerton (London: Nelson, 1937);

Arnold Bennett, *Literary Taste,* edited by Swinnerton (London: Cape, 1937);

William Hazlitt, *Conversations of James Northcote,* edited with an introduction by Swinnerton (London: Müller, 1949);

The Journals of Arnold Bennett, selected and edited by Swinnerton (London: Penguin, 1954).

In 1978 Frank Swinnerton published his sixty-first book, *Arnold Bennett: A Last Word.* Two years earlier, at the age of ninety-two, he published his forty-first novel, *Some Achieve Greatness.* It is clear that he was one of the most prolific of British novelists. His career as a novelist spans nearly seven decades, beginning with *The Merry Heart* (1909). As a contemporary not only of Joseph Conrad, Arnold Bennett, H. G. Wells, and John Galsworthy but also of the "second" generation of novelists Virginia

Woolf mentions in her now-famous essay "Mr. Bennett and Mrs. Brown," Swinnerton's work spans the entire history of what is often called the modern novel.

Frank Swinnerton was born in Wood Green, a suburb of London, on 12 August 1884, the youngest son of Charles and Rose Cottam Swinnerton. According to Swinnerton's autobiography, both the elder Swinnertons and Cottams were fiercely independent artisans "totally outside class." His father was a copperplate engraver. That same spirit of independence is reflected in Swinnerton's continuing examination in his novels of conventional attitudes toward class distinctions; the craftsmanship is expressed in his sense of proportion, clarity of purpose, and economy of plot in the best of his novels.

Swinnerton's early life was marked by frequent periods of near poverty, particularly after the death of his father. Swinnerton and his older brother Philip, both of whom were already working, became responsible for the household. Frank Swinnerton, in fact, began working at the age of fourteen as a clerk at Hay, Nisbet and Company, a newspaper office on Fleet Street, for six shillings per week. Here he got his first taste of journalism and even produced his own little journal on the side, a monthly entitled *Jottings*. Swinnerton would remain active in the world of publishing for more than a quarter-century, first as a confidential clerk to Hugh Dent at J. M. Dent and Company from 1902 to 1907 and later as reader and eventually editor at Chatto and Windus from 1907 to 1926. The teenager's desire to write blossomed quite easily in this atmosphere of ideas and books.

Swinnerton's first novel, *The Merry Heart,* developed in response to a competition announced by Fisher Unwin in 1908. Although Swinnerton's entry did not win the prize of one hundred pounds offered for this best "first novel," a friend at Chatto and Windus, Lee Warner, asked to look at it and within a few weeks agreed to publish it. Thus, with his first novel (by the author's later estimation a juvenile effort) in print, Swinnerton was encouraged to continue writing novels, almost annually, for the next several decades. *The Merry Heart,* which sold barely seven hundred copies that first year, was nevertheless a harbinger of considerable future success.

With his second novel, *The Young Idea* (1910), Swinnerton established a pattern that would serve him effectively in half a dozen later novels. His strategy is to focus in these novels on the interactions between siblings—usually sisters—recording

what, in Swinnerton's hands, seems a remarkable balance of tension and loyalty. The three central characters in *The Young Idea* (Bertram, Hilda, and Gladys Verrens) try to make a home for themselves after the death of their parents. Bertram, the eldest, is twenty-four, Hilda twenty-two, and Gladys eighteen as the novel opens. The two eldest work, while Gladys keeps house and tries to write stories for publication. Maintaining a household becomes increasingly difficult on their very small wages, especially after Bertram becomes entangled with a married woman and Hilda must leave her job to evade the attentions of her boss, Percy Temperton, a partner in the firm where she is a clerk.

Sorting out these and other domestic difficulties becomes the task of Eric Galbraith, a young man who moves in next door to the Verrenses and who becomes immediately attracted to Hilda. Swinnerton describes him at several points in the novel as a "protector," and indeed he becomes just that for the Verrens family.

Although *The Young Idea* sold fewer copies than Swinnerton's first novel, it received many good critical reviews, including enthusiastic praise from Arnold Bennett, to whom Swinnerton had sent a copy shortly after publication. Just being noticed by one of Bennett's stature, said Swinnerton, made him feel "rich in praise." The critical success of *The Young Idea* led to widespread acclaim both in England and America. By 1912, Swinnerton had gotten contracts with two new publishers (Methuen and Doran) through the efforts of J. B. Pinker; he had been introduced to a literary circle including such notables as Compton Mackenzie, Gilbert Cannan, John Middleton Murry, and Katherine Mansfield; and he had finished two more novels.

The first of these, *The Casement* (1911), is a story of two sisters—Olivia and Loraine—and of the men in their lives. First there is Robert Burton, Olivia's husband of five years; next, Paul Trevell, a former admirer of Olivia's and now Robert's business partner; finally, there is Michael Reay, a passionate and thoroughly silly younger man whom readers first encounter as a burglar at Paul's flat and who, three weeks later, is an aspiring confidential clerk at Burton and Trevell's firm. The book received mixed reviews. One critic in the *New York Times* called it "a pleasant book for a lazy hour." Another referred to it as "a story of temperaments, all of which are very effectively delineated and none of which are very attractive." Swinnerton's next novel, *The Happy Family,* is a more effective and ambitious study of English life through the contrast between two family groups. One reviewer's comment on *The Happy Family* reflects the character of many of Swinnerton's novels: "Swinnerton's style is controlled, ironic, sometimes vivid, always unemotional." These same qualities pervade Swinnerton's work, whatever his theme.

From 1912 throughout the war years, Swinnerton continued to write his novels, while at the same time serving as a reader at Chatto and Windus. He also wrote two critical works, *George Gissing: A Critical Study* (1912) and *R. L. Stevenson: A Critical Study* (1914), for Martin Secker's monograph series. The former was highly praised by H. G. Wells, who called it "a model for such monographs." The latter was not so well received, partly because Swinnerton was unaffected by the popular adoration of Stevenson and his works.

It was also during the war years that Swinnerton wrote what has become perhaps his most famous novel, *Nocturne* (1917). Although Swinnerton dismissed it as something of a "stunt" composed in barely six weeks, the critics did not. In fact, *Nocturne* became for many critics the measure by which they evaluated later novels. "This fine work," H. G. Wells writes in his introduction to the American edition, "ends a brilliant apprenticeship and ranks Swinnerton as Master. This is a book that will not die. It is perfect, authentic, and alive." Such high praise from Wells perhaps accounts in part for the book's success. According to the author's own estimates, *Nocturne* sold ten thousand copies within a few weeks of its release in the United States and continued to sell well here—perhaps as many as fifty thousand copies—over the next several years.

The idea to write a novel in which the action takes place during a single night came from Nigel de Grey of Heinemann. Originally, Swinnerton wanted to call the novel "In the Night." While the novel was being set in type, however, Ronald Gorell Barnes published one with the same title. Swinnerton then chose *Nocturne* as the title for his novel. In spite of Swinnerton's disclaimer, the novel he produced for Martin Secker in less than two months is a very tightly knit and artistically executed work. For the drama of *Nocturne* Swinnerton again chose two sisters, Emmy and Jenny Blanchard. Torn between the loyalty they feel for one another and for their invalid father and the desperate hope for something better in their rather hopeless lives, Emmy and Jenny eagerly, if guiltily, clutch at the fleeting opportunity to realize their respective dreams. Emmy, the elder sister at twenty-eight, has seen her youth fade in the ten years since her mother's death when she assumed the responsibility for the household and her increasingly dependent father. Her

Caricature of Swinnerton by Nicolas Bentley (Gale International Portrait Gallery)

dream is a modest one—marriage, a home, children. Jenny's dream is the stuff of romance. She refuses to become a willing prisoner to the convention that seems to govern other girls like herself: "get up at six, eat so much a day, have six children, do what you're told." Jenny will not be governed, not even by her lover Keith, a captain on a small yacht. Coincidentally, on the same night Jenny manages to trick Alf Rylett, her suitor, into taking Emmy to the theater, she receives a note from Keith asking her to join him on the yacht. She goes even though she feels she should stay with her father. Pa Blanchard's fall from a chair shortly before Emmy and Alf return from the theater is not critical, but it reinforces Jenny's sense of guilt.

Swinnerton's skillful characterization and economical rendering of this conflict of personalities was almost universally praised by reviewers. H. W. Boynton's response was typical: "Mr. Swinnerton is after, not a slice of life, but a distilled and golden drop of life. . . . As for the meaning or moral of the story, it is inherent, not appended." Like many novelists before him, Swinnerton had some difficulty living up to such success and such reviews. In their reviews of later works several critics compared them unfavorably with *Nocturne*.

In his next novel, *Shops and Houses* (1918), Swinnerton returned to the theme of class differences. William Vechantor, a small grocer, comes to the suburban town of Beckwith with his family, not knowing that the leading family in Beckwith society, the Emanuel Vechantors, are distant cousins. By taking over the long-established grocery business of Mr. Peel, William Vechantor has unwittingly brought chaos to the unruffled lives of his upper-crust relatives. Louis Vechantor is the first of the Beckwith family to seek out his newly discovered cousins, an action that not only estranges him initially from his family but also from nearly all of Beckwith society. Eventually Louis will succeed in bringing the two families together. He and Dorothy Vechantor, the eldest daughter of William, fall in love and are married. Swinnerton's portrait of Beckwith society won high praise from several critics. A few reviewers, however, criticized the pace of the novel, pointing out that the later chapters are marred by "dull types" and "stage-worn accidents." Such a criticism must be granted, especially if one compares *Shops and Houses* with *Nocturne,* as many reviewers did. The later novel lacks the artistry of the earlier one, and because it has a larger cast of characters and a more overtly expressed thesis, Swinnerton tends to overstate his vignettes of gossips and busybodies in his portrait of Beckwith society.

Throughout the war years and into the 1920s Swinnerton continued to have success at Chatto and Windus and with his novels. His growing reputation as a novelist/editor brought several writers to Chatto and Windus, among them Aldous Huxley, whose first volume of short stories, *Limbo* (1920), was sent in manuscript to Swinnerton for consideration. After this first work was published by the firm, Huxley continued to publish with Chatto and Windus for many years. Other writers who offered Swinnerton works for Chatto and Windus included A. A. Milne, Arnold Bennett, Sir Harry Johnston, and H. G. Wells. Many of the comments of Arnold Bennett and others in *Frank Swinnerton,* published in 1920 by Doran, reflect Swinnerton's growing reputation. Here is Bennett commenting on Swinnerton's style: "I read a sketch of his of a commonplace crowd walking round a bandstand which brought me to a decision as to his qualities. The thing was like life, and it was bathed in poetry."

The 1920s and 1930s were very productive years for Swinnerton, not only in terms of his novels but also in nonfiction. *The Georgian Scene: A Literary Panorama* (1934) and *Swinnerton: An Autobiography* (1936) offer both reminiscences about and critical

insights into dozens of writers of the period. As both successful novelist and respected editor, Swinnerton was uniquely qualified to review the literature of the Georgian era. Other works which focus more pointedly on the publishing world include *Authors and the Book Trade* (1932) and *The Reviewing and Criticism of Books* (1939). All are useful to students of the modern novel or those interested in particular authors of the Georgian period.

Swinnerton's novels of the 1920s include three produced in rapid succession: *Coquette* (1921), *The Three Lovers* (1922), and *Young Felix* (1923). Two others, *The Elder Sister* (1925) and *Summer Storm* (1926), followed after a brief American tour early in 1924 during which Swinnerton spoke at Yale, Princeton, and Columbia and traveled from New York to Los Angeles, across the Midwest, and along the Pacific coast. Swinnerton speaks fondly of his recollections of the tour in his *Autobiography.* Shortly after his return to England, Swinnerton married Mary Dorothy Bennett, his second wife, and began a brief vacation in Rome with his new bride. Swinnerton's first wife was the poet Helen Dircks, author of a volume of poems entitled *Passenger* (1920) for which Swinnerton had written the preface.

The themes of the 1920s and 1930s were not unlike those in Swinnerton's early novels—the anxiety of youth, the conflict between family loyalties and personal identity, the demands of love and marriage. They are present in all the novels just mentioned and in several others, including *The Georgian House* (1932) and *Elizabeth* (1934). In *Coquette*, for instance, Swinnerton traces the misadventures of a determined young woman named Sally Minto from first infatuation to an unfortunate marriage that ends in tragedy. Bent on rising above her lower-class origins, Sally charms the son of her employer into an ill-fated marriage, while at the same time continuing her affair with a younger man of her own class. In a twist of fate she loses them both. Several reviewers praised Swinnerton's realistic portrayal of Sally, some even comparing the novel favorably with *Nocturne*.

Although *The Three Lovers* is thematically similar to *Coquette,* it does not engage the reader in quite the same way. Like Sally, the protagonist Patricia Quin strives to sort out her suitors, but she and the three central male characters in the novel remain flat compared to those of *Coquette*. Even Edgar Mayne, the man who eventually wins Patricia after her fling with the two others, is a figure one finds hard to believe in or to accept wholeheartedly. The best of the 1920s series of five novels is *The Elder Sister,* a story of two sisters, Anne and Vera

Treacher, in love with the same man. Here Swinnerton explores again the effects of the love triangle on family loyalties. Since Anne and Vera both unwittingly fall in love with Mortimer Scott, a bank clerk and longtime friend, the conflict is set. Mortimer's hasty marriage to Anne can only end badly, for Swinnerton makes clear early in the novel that the differences in their personalities will eventually cause a split. When Mortimer and Vera run away together, one is not surprised, so carefully has Swinnerton developed his characters. Anne, the elder sister in more than years, has the strength not only to forgive the wrong she has suffered but also to pity Mortimer and Vera, who have, true to their natures, grasped at what can only be a fleeting love affair, filled with remorse and shame.

By 1927, Swinnerton had "retired" to a country home in Surrey, yet he still remained active in several publishing ventures beyond his own novels. From 1929 to 1932, he was literary critic for the *London Evening News*; shortly thereafter, from 1937 to 1943, he served as novel critic for the *London Observer*. His "John O'London" series (1949-1954) for the weekly of the same name reflects his zest for life—especially the literary life—his humor, and his wit as an essayist. Still in his forties at retirement from Chatto and Windus, Swinnerton scarcely paused before beginning a new series of novels and nonfiction works.

As his early works indicate, Swinnerton was particularly interested in the cultural restrictions placed on women in England. Several of his later novels reflect the social barriers many women faced in simply earning a living. Four of his later novels in particular were designed, according to the author, "to suggest changes which have taken place during the past half-century in the outlook of women as it relates to men." In these four novels—*The Woman from Sicily* (1957), *A Tigress in Prothero* (1959), *The Grace Divorce* (1960), and *Quadrille* (1965)—Swinnerton traces four generations of a single family. The resulting chronicle of the Grace Family gives an unusual glimpse of life in modern London and of the characters who inhabit the wealthy and artistic world Swinnerton creates in the novels.

Swinnerton was almost never idle, as his bibliography indicates. Even in his seventies and eighties, when most would be happy to sit by the fireside, he was busily writing novels and assembling earlier essays for book-length collections. His last few novels reflect the same attention to character, scene, and elements of plot one finds in the best of his early work. As he grew older he did allow himself older characters, such as Graham Stanhope,

Dust jacket for Swinnerton's book about Thomas Hardy, Henry James, Joseph Conrad, Norman Douglas, George Saintsbury, and D. H. Lawrence

aging poet and critic, and his lifelong friend Thomas Curtal in *Death of a Highbrow* (1961). But frequently, even with his older characters, Swinnerton liked to review the life either using interior monologue or through an opening chapter, as in *The Bright Lights* (1968), the story of an aging actress, Constance Rotherham, who recalls in the novel her lifelong competition domestically and as professional actress with her younger sister Penelope.

Swinnerton's last two novels, published when he was in his nineties, might easily be classed as early twentieth-century in spite of their publication dates, but the themes of *Rosalind Passes* (1973) and of *Some Achieve Greatness* (1976) are indeed timeless—beauty, evil, love, courage, death. In the earlier novel, Rosalind, a beautiful young girl, passes through the lives of Clarissa and Henry Maynard, at first creating a tension in their already shaky marriage but later becoming a source of strength, especially for Clarissa. Rosalind's death, midway through the novel, serves as focal point for

Swinnerton (photo by Bernard Grover)

Clarissa's growth. In the closing chapter, the courage and strength she has developed throughout the novel enable her to save her child, her husband, and herself from certain death following an automobile accident.

Swinnerton's last novel seems appropriately titled. *Some Achieve Greatness* might almost be a comment on Swinnerton's career itself. Indeed, Florence Marvell, the central figure in the novel, is a writer of children's stories and something of a healer of other characters in the novel—one of Swinnerton's "protectors," like Eric Galbraith of *The Young Idea*. Florence, like many of Swinnerton's women, chose to give up the man she loved. Thirty years later, as the novel opens, she again meets Rod (now Sir Roderick Patterson), an important M.P. and possible contender for prime minister. Swinnerton's irony, of course, is that it is Florence, not Roderick, as we might suspect for most of the novel,

who achieves greatness. At the end of the novel, she wins a coveted book award, the Spencer Prize for the best juvenile book of the year, and is nominated as one of the Women of the Year.

Like Florence Marvell, Swinnerton led a quiet life, one devoted to his books, his cats, and his gardening. Within the literary community he received few accolades, though his books were widely read. It is difficult to sum up a career that spanned most of the twentieth century, though perhaps Swinnerton's own words, recorded in 1972, will serve: "My grandfathers were both what are called 'Master Craftsmen'; and while not claiming to be a master I do regard myself as, first of all, a craftsman. That is, I love my work, regardless of reward."

References:

Arnold Bennett and others, *Frank Swinnerton* (New York: Doran, 1920);

Richard Church, "Frank Swinnerton," in *British Authors: A Twentieth-Century Gallery* (London, New York & Toronto: Longmans, Green, 1948), pp. 95-98;

Joseph Collins, "Mr. Frank Swinnerton and His Books," in his *Taking the Literary Pulse: Psychological Studies of Life and Letters* (New York: Doran, 1924), pp. 190-206;

Claude Louis Gibson, "An Annotated Index to the Frank Arthur Swinnerton Correspondence," Ph.D. dissertation, University of Arkansas, 1976;

Jesse F. McCartney, "The Frank Arthur Swinnerton Collection: A Special Literary Collection at the University of Arkansas," *English Literature in Transition*, 18, no. 4 (1975): 248-253;

Ruth Capers McCay, *George Gissing and His Critic, Frank Swinnerton* (Philadelphia: Folcroft, 1932);

Grant Martin Overton, "Frank Swinnerton: Analyst of Lovers," in his *Authors of the Day* (New York: Doran, 1924), pp. 327-343.

Papers:
The manuscript collection at the University of Arkansas Library, Fayetteville, includes correspondence, typescripts or proof copies of many works, working notes for *The Georgian Literary Scene,* and clippings from periodicals to which Swinnerton contributed.

Hugh Walpole
(13 March 1884-1 June 1941)

Mary A. O'Toole
University of Tulsa

SELECTED BOOKS: *The Wooden Horse* (London: Smith, Elder, 1909; New York: Doran, 1915);

Maradick at Forty (London: Smith, Elder, 1910);

Mr. Perrin and Mr. Traill (London: Mills & Boon, 1911); republished as *The Gods and Mr. Perrin* (New York: Century, 1911);

The Prelude to Adventure (London: Mills & Boon, 1912; New York: Century, 1912);

Fortitude (London: Secker, 1913; New York: Doran, 1913);

The Duchess of Wrexe, Her Decline and Death: A Romantic Commentary (London: Secker, 1914; New York: Doran, 1914);

The Golden Scarecrow (London & New York: Cassell, 1915; New York: Doran, 1915);

The Dark Forest (London: Secker, 1916; New York: Doran, 1916);

Joseph Conrad (London: Nisbet, 1916; New York: Holt, 1917; revised, London: Nisbet, 1924);

The Green Mirror (New York: Doran, 1917; London Macmillan, 1918);

The Secret City (London: Macmillan, 1919; New York: Doran, 1919);

Jeremy (London & New York: Cassell, 1919; New York: Doran, 1919);

The Art of James Branch Cabell (New York: McBride, 1920);

The Captives (London: Macmillan, 1920; New York: Doran, 1920);

The Thirteen Travellers (London: Hutchinson, 1921; New York: Doran, 1921);

The Young Enchanted (London: Macmillan, 1921; New York: Doran, 1921);

The Cathedral (London: Macmillan, 1922; New York: Doran, 1922);

Jeremy and Hamlet (London & New York: Cassell, 1923; New York: Doran, 1923);

The Crystal Box (Glasgow: Printed for the author by R. Maclehose, 1924);

The Old Ladies (London: Macmillan, 1924; New York: Doran, 1924);

The English Novel: Some Notes on its Evolution (Cambridge: The University Press, 1925);

Portrait of a Man with Red Hair (London: Macmillan, 1925; New York: Doran, 1925);

Hugh Walpole (photo by Abraham, Keswick)

Harmer John (London: Macmillan, 1926; New York: Doran, 1926);

Reading: An Essay (London: Jarrolds, 1926; New York & London: Harper, 1926);

Jeremy at Crale (London: Cassell, 1927; New York: Doran, 1927);

Anthony Trollope (London: Macmillan, 1928; New York: Macmillan, 1928);

My Religious Experience (London: Benn, 1928);

The Silver Thorn (London: Macmillan, 1928; Garden City: Doubleday, Doran, 1928);

Wintersmoon (London: Macmillan, 1928; Garden City: Doubleday, Doran, 1928);

Farthing Hall, by Walpole and J. B. Priestley (London: Macmillan, 1929; Garden City: Doubleday, Doran, 1929);

Hans Frost (London: Macmillan, 1929);

Rogue Herries (London: Macmillan, 1930; Garden City: Doubleday, Doran, 1930);

Above the Dark Circus (London: Macmillan, 1931); republished as *Above the Dark Tumult* (Garden City: Doubleday, Doran, 1931);

Judith Paris (London: Macmillan, 1931; Garden City: Doubleday, Doran, 1931);

The Apple Trees (Waltham, Saint Lawrence, Berkshire: Printed by the Golden Cockerel Press, 1932);

The Fortress (London: Macmillan, 1932; Garden City: Doubleday, Doran, 1932);

A Letter to a Modern Novelist (London: Leonard & Virginia Woolf at the Hogarth Press, 1932);

All Souls' Night (London: Macmillan, 1933; Garden City: Doubleday, Doran, 1933);

Vanessa (London: Macmillan, 1933; Garden City: Doubleday, Doran, 1933);

Extracts from a Diary (Glasgow: Printed for the author by R. Maclehose, 1934);

Captain Nicholas (London: Macmillan, 1934; Garden City: Doubleday, Doran, 1934);

The Inquisitor (London: Macmillan, 1935; Garden City: Doubleday, Doran, 1935);

A Prayer for My Son (London: Macmillan, 1936; Garden City: Doubleday, Doran, 1936);

The Cathedral: A Play in Three Acts (London: Macmillan, 1937);

John Cornelius (London: Macmillan, 1937; New York: Doubleday, Doran, 1937);

Head in Green Bronze (London: Macmillan, 1938; Garden City: Doubleday, Doran, 1938);

The Joyful Delaneys (London: Macmillan, 1938; New York: Doubleday, Doran, 1938);

The Haxtons: A Play in Three Acts (London: Deane/ Boston: Baker International Play Bureau, 1939);

The Sea Tower (London: Macmillan, 1939; New York: Doubleday, Doran, 1939);

Roman Fountain (London: Macmillan, 1940; New York: Doubleday, Doran, 1940);

The Bright Pavilions (London: Macmillan, 1940; New York: Doubleday, Doran, 1940);

The Blind Man's House (London: Macmillan, 1941; Garden City: Doubleday, Doran, 1941);

Open Letter of an Optimist (London: Macmillan, 1941);

The Killer and the Slain (London: Macmillan, 1942; Garden City: Doubleday, Doran, 1942);

Katherine Christian (Garden City: Doubleday, Doran, 1943; London: Macmillan, 1944);

Mr. Huffam (London: Macmillan, 1948).

OTHER: *The Waverley Pageant: Best Passages from the Novels of Sir Walter Scott,* edited by Walpole (London: Eyre & Spottiswoode, 1932).

Hugh Walpole was one of the most prolific writers of his day. He lived the sophisticated life of London to the fullest, yet retained throughout his life a certain boyish enthusiasm and naiveté that are reflected in his writings. He was born the first of three children of George Henry Somerset and Mildred Barham Walpole on 13 March 1884 in New Zealand, where his father was a vicar of St. Mary's Church, Parnell, Auckland. His family soon moved to New York, where his father taught at the General Theological Seminary, and in 1893, Walpole was sent to England to begin an English public school education, first in Truro, then in Marlow and at King's School, Canterbury. In 1898, his family returned to Durham from the United States, and Walpole became a day student at Durham School, a place he heartily disliked.

He was an avid reader and was early influenced by Nathaniel Hawthorne and his ideas of evil. (Walpole said later in life that there were "two strands—say Hawthorne and Trollope—from which I am derived.") He attempted to write historical romances in his teens and seems to have been a born storyteller, although later in life he resented this designation and thought that he was stronger as a creator of intriguing characters than as a spinner of tales.

In October 1903, Walpole went up to Emmanuel College, Cambridge, as a subsizar (receiving a yearly stipend because his parents could not pay the full fee); in September 1906, after graduation, he went reluctantly to Liverpool as a lay missioner on the staff of the Mersey Mission to Seamen. It soon became apparent that he was not cut out to be a lay missioner and certainly not a cleric as his father was. He seems to have had little doubt that he wanted a career in letters, and he began supporting himself by teaching in Germany and England until the publication of his first novel, *The Wooden Horse,* in 1909. When the novel was published, Walpole was on the threshold of the London literary world—reviewing books for the *London Standard,* seeing Henry James, and communicating with other literary figures. He came to know many of the most prominent members of that world: James, Joseph Conrad, John Galsworthy, Arnold Bennett, Virginia Woolf, John Buchan, Maurice Hewlett, J. B. Priestley, Dorothy Richardson (who called him "eminently a humanist, a collector of people"), and many others.

From 1909 until a few years after his death, his novels appeared almost at the rate of one per year, and during those years when a novel did not appear, a book of short stories or a critical study was published. Most of his novels were well received, and each one sold better than the one before. Of course, Walpole had his detractors, with some of whom he argued via letters, but most of whom he dismissed as "modern" and therefore coldhearted and incapable of understanding a good story well told.

With his novel *Fortitude* (1913) Walpole achieved widespread recognition in the literary world of London. The novel is a Bildungsroman of sorts with a slow but steady narrative pace and a deadly serious tone. Its young hero, Peter Westcott, is a writer who achieves some measure of attention in literary London, but the early scenes of Peter's trials and triumphs in the public school are most intriguing. Peter's toughness in facing bullies and his emergence as a victor in school struggles suggest a bit of wishful thinking on Walpole's part—what he himself may have wished to accomplish in his unhappy days at school. This and some later novels (*The Green Mirror,* for instance) contain mystical elements to which some critics objected. In *Fortitude,* Peter hears voices enumerating a new set of beatitudes at the end of the novel. Walpole saw no problem with the inclusion of the mystical in an otherwise realistic novel.

In 1914 *The Duchess of Wrexe* was published to generally favorable reviews. This book is discussed by Henry James in his essay on "The Younger Generation." He praises Walpole's enthusiasm but looks forward to the time when "form" or "a process" will be manifest in Walpole's writings. Indeed, this kind of criticism—that he was careless and failed to impose upon his novels some controlling sense of form—was made of Walpole's work throughout his career. He himself realized his lack of a distinguished style, but he recognized and emphasized his strong points—his goodwill, enthusiasm, and verve in storytelling. In a letter to Arnold Bennett (one of the many mutually chiding letters that these two wrote), Walpole says, "I know that I am sentimental, romantic and slipshod," but, he insists, this combination of traits represents the essential Hugh Walpole, take it or leave it. He had extraordinary vigor. He was caught up in the sheer pleasure of storytelling; polishing the style was a secondary consideration. He was apparently never afflicted with writer's block. He wrote fast, rarely revised, and, upon the completion of one novel, always had another novel in his head. At times he doubted the value of his novels because of the ease with which he wrote them.

Just after the start of World War I, Walpole went to Russia to write newspaper articles for the *London Daily Mail.* Soon he was put in charge of the British propaganda bureau in Petrograd, but the enterprise degenerated into a rather farcical operation in which all secrecy was lost and the office of propaganda became almost useless. He witnessed the first revolution of 1917 in Petrograd and left Russia just as the Bolsheviks were taking over in November 1917. The material for two novels came out of Walpole's Russian experiences—*The Dark Forest* (1916) and *The Secret City* (1919), both wonderfully atmospheric and the latter the winner of the first James Tait Black Memorial Prize for the best work of fiction in 1919.

Back in London, Walpole worked for a short time in the Foreign Office of the Department of Information under novelist John Buchan and was awarded the C.B.E. (Commander of the Order of the British Empire) after the war. *The Green Mirror* was published in England in 1918, again to generally good reviews and only one or two dissenting voices. In 1919 *Jeremy,* the first of a series of books, was published, and Walpole left on the first of several lecture tours of America. On these tours, over the years, he met many American writers. In 1921, *A Hugh Walpole Anthology* was published with a short prefatory note by Joseph Conrad, one of Walpole's close friends.

In 1922, the year of the publication of T. S. Eliot's *The Waste Land* and James Joyce's *Ulysses,* Walpole produced *The Cathedral,* in which his claim to be a creator of intriguing characters rather than a storyteller only is partially justified. The antagonists, Archdeacon Brandon and Canon Ronder, are skillfully drawn and balanced one against the other, although the author gives Brandon more than his share of punishment for the sin of pride. Walpole's biographer, Sir Rupert Hart-Davis, suggests that in this novel Walpole hits back at the cathedral clique and the snobbishness of which he and his family were the victims in their years in Durham. *The Cathedral* is more assured than earlier novels. It has an unobtrusive, gentle irony in the early parts. It is well plotted and paced with less description merely for its own sake, fewer authorial asides, and good character studies. The fictional town of Polchester in this novel is also the setting for *Jeremy, Harmer John* (1926), and *The Inquisitor* (1935).

In 1924, Walpole purchased Brackenburn, a home in Cumberland. He also kept a flat in London

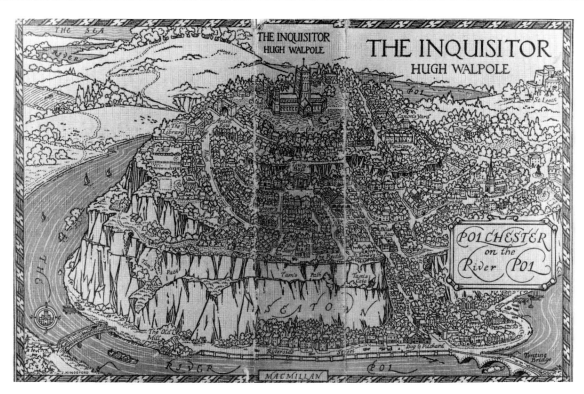

Dust jacket for Walpole's fourth novel set in the fictional town of Polchester

Walpole and J. B. Priestley, 1930 (Mansell Collection, London)

and divided his time between the two locations for the rest of his life. Throughout his career, Walpole felt a simultaneous respect for and distrust of the modernists. In 1928 he produced *Wintersmoon,* in which he sets forth his ideas on the new "modern" temperament as opposed to the traditional English one and, by extension, his ideas on modernist writers as opposed to traditionalist writers. The coldness, detachment, and scorn for traditional values—personal, societal, literary—that Walpole believed characterized the moderns are manifested in *Wintersmoon*'s characters Rosalind and Ravage. Their antitheses are Janet Grandison and the members of her husband's aristocratic family. The novel is skillfully plotted, steadily paced, and the characters are fairly well realized. *Wintersmoon* is more a thesis novel than most of Walpole's other works, but apart from the thesis Walpole, as usual, tells a good story.

Walpole was acquainted with Virginia Woolf and knew T. S. Eliot slightly. He wrote a pamphlet, *A Letter to a Modern Novelist* (1932), for Leonard and Virginia Woolf's Hogarth Press; and he was gratified when Eliot asked him to contribute a work for serialization in his *Criterion*. (Walpole selected *The Old Ladies* for this honor; it was subsequently published in book form in 1924.) Walpole acknowledged what he considered the superior genius of

Virginia Woolf and contrasted it with his own mere talent. Sometimes he felt that he would like to be a more modern writer but realized that he was hopelessly old-fashioned: "verbose, over-emphasized, unreal in many places, sometimes very dull" was his self-evaluation on one occasion. He felt that his connection with Virginia Woolf helped him "to get over a little of my sententiousness and sentimentality"—a change he welcomed while at the same time not wanting to surrender too much to her influence.

It is difficult to see any change in his writing because of his friendship with Virginia Woolf, though two years after *Wintersmoon* he departed from traditional realistic fiction with an escape into historical romance. Over the years Walpole had become something of an authority on Sir Walter Scott, and it is Scott that is reflected in some of his best-known works, not Woolf and her circle. The Herries novels, beginning with *Rogue Herries* in 1930 and continuing with *Judith Paris* (1931), *The Fortress* (1932) and *Vanessa* (1933), reflect something of Walpole's interest in Scott and his own adopted Cumberland. *Rogue Herries* is about an outcast from society. The novel is set around Cumberland, and its action skirts the events of the 1745 rebellion. The novel is lively but promises more than it delivers. Walpole develops the tic of saying "he would remember this incident years later," and then allows allegedly unforgettable events to come to nothing. But *Rogue Herries* is a good story (Virginia Woolf herself enjoyed it); and the four novels were gathered into one volume in 1939, *The Herries Chronicle,* and were popular for years. Walpole's own evaluation of the series might be applied to his fiction as a whole: "It carries the English novel no whit further but it *sustains* the tradition and has vitality."

During the 1920s and 1930s Walpole supported himself comfortably on the income from his writing. He enjoyed his country home in Cumberland as well as the cosmopolitan life of London. Among his activities were founding the Society of Bookmen and holding the chairmanship of the selection committee for the Book Society. In 1934 Walpole went to Hollywood, where he wrote the scenario for the film version of *David Copperfield* (1934). He became friends with George Cukor and David Selznick and had a small part in *Copperfield.* He also wrote the scenarios for his own novel *Vanessa* (1934) and for *Little Lord Fauntleroy* (1936) and *Kim.* In 1936 he began his last lecture tour of America. In March 1941 he produced a war pam-

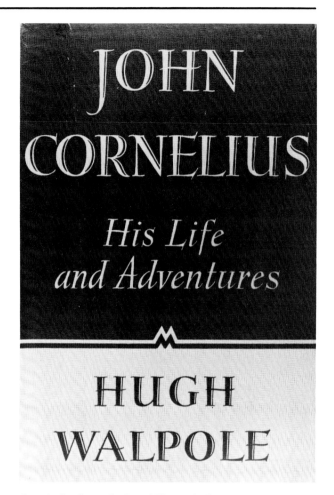

Dust jacket for Walpole's 1937 novel whose writer-protagonist resembles Hans Christian Andersen

phlet, *Open Letter of an Optimist,* and deliberately left his Cumberland refuge and endured the blitz in London. He made some broadcasts on the BBC, and in 1940 during the blitz, *The Bright Pavilions,* his fifth Herries novel, was published and enjoyed good sales. After its publication a reviewer commented that Walpole might have been a serious artist but had settled instead for being "a very good entertainer." Walpole answered, "This is the old regular 'highbrow' attack. How sick I am though of this long-continued attempt to make the novel a solemn, priggish, intellectual affair, removed from the ordinary reader. Surely the novel should *entertain* first, and then let all else be added unto it!"

Hugh Walpole never married. He was knighted in 1937, died at Brackenburn, his Cumberland home, on 1 June 1941, and was buried in St. John's churchyard, Keswick, Cumberland.

Biography:

Rupert Hart-Davis, *Hugh Walpole, A Biography* (London & New York: Macmillan, 1952).

References:

Elizabeth Steele, *Hugh Walpole: His World of Fiction* (Ann Arbor: University Microfilms, 1967);

Steele, *Hugh Walpole* (New York: Twayne, 1972);

L. A. G. Strong, *Personal Remarks* (London: Nevill, 1953).

Sylvia Townsend Warner
(6 December 1893-1 May 1978)

Barbara Brothers
Youngstown State University

BOOKS: *The Espalier* (London: Chatto & Windus, 1925; New York: Dial, 1925);

Lolly Willowes; or, The Loving Huntsman (London: Chatto & Windus, 1926; New York: Viking, 1926);

Mr. Fortune's Maggot (London: Chatto & Windus, 1927; New York: Viking, 1927);

The Maze: A Story to Be Read Aloud (London: Fleuron, 1928);

Time Importuned (London: Chatto & Windus, 1928; New York: Viking, 1928);

Some World Far From Ours; and "Stay, Corydon, Thou Swain" (London: Mathews & Marrot, 1929);

The True Heart (London: Chatto & Windus, 1929; New York: Viking, 1929);

Elinor Barley (London: Cresset, 1930);

This Our Brother (London: Cambridge, 1930);

Opus 7 (London: Chatto & Windus, 1931; New York: Viking, 1931);

A Moral Ending and Other Stories (London: Jackson, 1931); enlarged as *The Salutation* (London: Chatto & Windus, 1932; New York: Viking, 1932);

Rainbow (New York: Knopf, 1932);

Whether a Dove, or Seagull, by Warner and Valentine Ackland (New York: Viking, 1933; London: Chatto & Windus, 1934);

More Joy in Heaven, and Other Stories (London: Cresset, 1935);

Summer Will Show (London: Chatto & Windus, 1936; New York: Viking, 1936);

After the Death of Don Juan (London: Chatto & Windus, 1938; New York: Viking, 1939);

24 Short Stories, by Warner, Graham Greene, and James Laver (London: Cresset, 1939);

Sylvia Townsend Warner, 1936

The Cat's Cradle-Book (New York: Viking, 1940; London: Chatto & Windus, 1960);

The People Have No Generals (London: Newport, 1941);

A Garland of Straw and Other Stories (London: Chatto & Windus, 1943); republished as *A Garland of*

Straw; Twenty-Eight Stories (New York: Viking, 1943);

Two Poems (Derby: Hopkins, 1945);

The Museum of Cheats (London: Chatto & Windus, 1947; New York: Viking, 1947);

The Corner That Held Them (London: Chatto & Windus, 1948; New York: Viking, 1948);

Somerset (London: Elek, 1949);

Jane Austen, 1775-1817 (London & New York: Published for the British Council and the National Book League by Longmans, Green, 1951; revised, London & New York: Longmans, Green, 1957);

The Flint Anchor (London: Chatto & Windus, 1954; New York: Viking, 1954); republished as *The Barnards of Loseby* (New York: Popular Library, 1974);

Winter in the Air, and Other Stories (London: Chatto & Windus, 1955; New York: Viking, 1956);

Boxwood (London: Privately printed, 1957; enlarged, London: Chatto & Windus, 1960);

A Spirit Rises (London: Chatto & Windus, 1962; New York: Viking, 1962);

Sketches from Nature (Wells & London: Clare, 1963);

A Stranger with a Bag, and Other Stories (London: Chatto & Windus, 1966); republished as *Swans on an Autumn River* (New York: Viking, 1966);

T. H. White: A Biography (London: Cape with Chatto & Windus, 1967; New York: Viking, 1968);

King Duffus and Other Poems (Wells: Clare, 1968);

The Innocent and the Guilty: Stories (London: Chatto & Windus, 1971; New York: Viking, 1971);

Kingdoms of Elfin (London: Chatto & Windus, 1977; New York: Viking, 1977);

Azrael and Other Poems (Newbury: Libanus, 1978); republished as *Twelve Poems* (London: Chatto & Windus, 1980);

Scenes of Childhood (London: Chatto & Windus, 1981; New York: Viking, 1982);

Collected Poems, edited by Claire Harman (Manchester: Carcanet, 1983; New York: Viking, 1983);

One Thing Leading to Another: And Other Stories (London: Chatto & Windus, 1984; New York: Viking, 1984).

OTHER: *Alleluia, Anthem for Five Voices,* score by Warner (London: Oxford, 1925);

"Notation; the Growth of a System," the introductory volume of *The Oxford History of Music* (London: Oxford, 1929), pp. 66-84;

The Week-End Dickens, edited with an introduction by Warner (London: Machelose, 1932; New York: Lorring & Mussey, 1932?);

The Portrait of a Tortoise: Extracted from the Journals of Gilbert White, introduction and notes by Warner (London: Chatto & Windus, 1946; Toronto: Oxford University Press, 1946);

T. H. White, *The Book of Merlyn,* prologue by Warner (Austin: University of Texas Press, 1977).

TRANSLATIONS: Marcel Proust *(Contre Sainte-Beuve) By Way of Saint-Beuve,* translated by Warner (London: Chatto & Windus, 1958); republished as *On Art and Literature* (New York: Meridian, 1958);

Jean René Huguenin, *A Place of Shipwreck,* translated by Warner (London: Chatto & Windus, 1963).

Sylvia Townsend Warner's first novel, *Lolly Willowes; or, The Loving Huntsman* (1926), was the first selection of the Book-of-the-Month Club, her second novel, *Mr. Fortune's Maggot* (1927), an early selection of the Literary Guild. In spite of such an auspicious beginning as a popular novelist, Warner's next five novels received only cursory reviews. Readers more likely will recognize her name as a short-story writer. She contributed 144 stories to the *New Yorker* from 1936 until her death in 1978 and produced ten collections of short stories. A critical assessment of her fiction has not been made, though there have been some appreciative essays, such as John Updike's, on her short stories. The republication of *Lolly Willowes,* with an introduction by Anita Miller, by Academy Chicago Limited in 1979 indicates, however, that Warner's fiction may be worthy of a closer look.

Warner was born in Harrow, Middlesex, England, the daughter of a Harrow House master, George Townsend Warner. Taught to read by her mother, Nora Hudleston, Warner continued her education at home under the tutelage of a French governess and her father who gave her informal instruction in history. By age ten, according to William Maxwell, she was reading books from her father's extensive library; *Vanity Fair* and works on witchcraft were among her favorites. Her interest in music was fostered by Dr. Percy Buck, music master at Harrow, and she would have studied composing with Arnold Schönberg if her plans had not been interrupted by the outbreak of World War I. After her father died in 1916, she went to London to pursue a career as a musicologist, serving on the editorial committee for *Tudor Church Music* (1923-1929).

Warner claimed her career as a writer of literature began accidentally when she decided to cover a blank sheet of paper with a poem. Through Stephen Tomlin, a Harrow boy and London friend, she met T. F. Powys and David Garnett. Powys would later write an introduction for her first collection of short stories, *A Moral Ending,* and Garnett would send her poems to Chatto and Windus, who published them in 1925 under the title *The Espalier.* In spite of making her writing debut as a poet and wishing to be known as one, Warner produced only one more significant collection of poems, *Time Importuned* (1928), before her death. *Opus 7* (1931) was a long narrative poem; *Rainbow* (1932) was published as number two of the Borzoi Chap Books; *Boxwood* (1957) contained verse illustrations for Reynold Stone's woodcuts; *Whether a Dove, or Seagull* (1933) was a volume of untitled and unattributed poems by Valentine Ackland and Warner; and *Two Poems* (1945), *King Duffus* (1968), and *Azrael* (1978) were privately printed and circulated. In addition to fiction and poetry, Warner wrote a biography (*T. H. White,* 1967), a travel guidebook (*Somerset,* 1949), and a volume of criticism (*Jane Austen,* 1951). She edited a portion of the journals of the naturalist Gilbert White (*The Portrait of a Tortoise,* 1946), translated two works from French into English, and had three of her poems set to music in John Ireland's *Songs Sacred and Profane* (1934). She was a fellow of the Royal Society of Literature and an honorary member of the American Academy of Arts and Letters.

In *Lolly Willowes,* Warner exhibits the heretical spirit that characterizes all her writing: she chooses as her heroine an unmarried woman who has no desire to play a role in a romantic drama; she mixes the fantastic and the realistic in telling her story; she assumes no moral stance (that is, she likes those who are not good in society's eyes rather more than those who are). Nearly thirty when her father dies, Laura Willowes moves from the family home in the country to the London home of her brother and sister-in-law and their two daughters. As Aunt Lolly, she is "indispensable"; as Miss Willowes she is a "redundant" woman. Is the devil responsible for her waywardness in choosing at forty-seven to live her own life in a remote country village to no other end than her own enjoyment of botany, brewing, and the magical arts? (Warner herself was said to be an expert on mysticism, the black arts, and cooking.) The novel, with the wit, humor, and deft, precise phrasing characteristic of Warner's prose, probes the problem of identity and the conventions of society which, in Warner's view, sanction busyness and good manners to the detriment of genuine respect

for the mysteries of life and the uniqueness of other human beings.

In *The Espalier,* Warner's first volume of poetry, she includes a short narrative poem about a man who is captured by the spell of a wildflower and tills no more, losing his job and becoming a wanderer. In *Mr. Fortune's Maggot* she tells the story of Rev. Timothy Fortune who goes to a remote South Sea island to bring Christianity to the natives. But through the love he develops for the natives, particularly for a young boy Lueli, and the understanding he gains of the insignificance of man before the powerful forces of nature, he is the one who is saved—heathenized and humanized. As one reviewer said, the novel is "a whimsical fancy at once ridiculous, satirical and true."

The True Heart (1929) is written in the same vein. The setting is England; the heroine, Sukey Bond, is an orphan who, while working as a hired girl on a remote farm in the marshes, falls in love with Eric Seaborn, a retarded boy of gentle and loving spirit who makes his home with the farm owners because his mother finds him an embarrassment. The fairy-talelike narrative is enriched by delightfully comic scenes and episodes which make Sukey's goodness and purity believable as presences in the human spirit. In one of these episodes, Sukey seeks shelter in what she considers a "disorderly house," actually a house of ill repute.

In 1930, Warner moved to the country to live with Valentine Ackland, her companion until Ackland's death in 1969. Warner's first collection of short stories, *A Moral Ending,* appeared in 1931 and included *Elinor Barley,* a novelette which had been published separately the preceding year. The stories of *A Moral Ending,* along with twelve more, were included in *The Salutation,* a collection published in 1932. Her short stories, including those in *More Joy In Heaven* (1935), her poems, and her novels published between 1925 and 1936 reflect her eye for those thought to be too insignificant to have a real story to tell and her love of nature, though Warner's nature is no idyllic pastoral world.

Summer Will Show (1936), treated by most reviewers as a historical romance, is a novel of social protest—feminist and economic. Unlike Warner's first three novels, it has never been reprinted, though it is one of her best. In this novel set in the mid-nineteenth century, Sophia Willoughby is a member of the English gentry, running the estate that had been her family's and rearing her two children after she has dismissed her fop of a husband to lead his own life in Paris. But the death of her children from smallpox sends her to Paris

Tom Mooney, Warner, and Dr. Edward Benes at an American Writers' Congress dinner, New York, 1939 (photo by Robert Disraeli)

where she becomes involved with the Paris Revolution of 1848. Not only is the novel, as Mary McCarthy said of it in the *Nation*, "the most sure-footed, sensitive, witty piece of prose yet to have been colored by left-wing ideology," but also it is a historically accurate depiction of the multiple forces at work in the revolution.

After reading the novel one is not surprised to learn that Warner was active in left-wing politics in the 1930s: she joined the Communist party in 1935 and in 1936 served with Ackland for three months as a Red Cross volunteer in Barcelona, Spain. Nor is one surprised that in her next novel, *After the Death of Don Juan* (1938), she examines the plight of the Spanish peasant. Like all of her novels, *After the Death of Don Juan* is a serious fantasy which reveals that love, like power, is basically a selfish desire and that education without the power and will to effect change is hollow. Warner's short stories in *A Garland of Straw* (1943) are about the Spanish civil war and about England during World War II. As in her two novels of this period, Warner exhibits less of the spirit of comic acceptance and more of the anger of satiric rejection than she had previously.

In *The Corner That Held Them* (1948) Warner creates the story of a convent which she calls Oby, sketching its founding in 1163 and tracing its history through the Black Death of 1349 to the peasant uprising of 1382. Events unfold as in an annal,

emphasizing the vagaries of fate which control men's lives and the interweavings of fact and fiction which pass as history. In one of the many mini-narratives that make up the novel, Dame Lilias believes herself touched by St. Leonard to be anchoress when she falls at the altar. Actually she was shoved by Dame Dorothy who despises her. Is this God working through man? Or man looking for signs where there are none but the ones created by the tales of his own imagination? While most reviewers liked the book immensely for its ribald spirit and for the panoramic display of human nature, the critic for *Catholic World* was offended and called it a "dreary book." In Warner's view, organized religion and the Christian faith in particular offer not hope but hypocrisy. As she comments at the end of one of her *Scenes of Childhood* (1981), she, like "The Young Sailor," eventually left the church.

The Flint Anchor (1954) is the story of John Barnard (1790-1863) and his family. As in her other novels she finds the English too stern and rule-bound, too dominated by the bourgeois values of church and work, too filled by a guilty need for self-punishment to develop the self-understanding that recognizes the need each human creature has to be loved. This is the only novel of Warner's that does not flaunt to some extent the conventions of the realistic novel, but in its themes and in its finely hewn prose it is still recognizably hers.

After *The Flint Anchor,* Warner produced five more volumes of short stories: *Winter in the Air* (1955); *A Spirit Rises* (1962); *A Stranger with a Bag* (1966); *The Innocent and the Guilty* (1971); *Kingdoms of Elfin* (1977). Two more collections were published after her death: *Scenes of Childhood* and *One Thing Leading to Another* (1984). No assessment of Warner's stature as a poet, novelist, or short-story writer has yet been made. Louis Untermeyer was an early champion of her poetry and Claire Harmon has written a fine introduction to Warner's *Collected Poems* (1983). In addition Harmon edited a special supplementary section of *PN Review 23,* "Sylvia Townsend Warner 1893-1978: A Celebration." The supplement included some of Warner's poetry, personal reminiscences of her by friends, an inter-view, and short critical essays on her work. Certainly Warner's fiction merits a full-length critical study, and Harmon makes a good case for one on her poetry as well.

Letters:
Letters, edited by William Maxwell (London: Chatto & Windus, 1982; New York: Viking, 1983).

References:
Claire Harmon, ed., "Sylvia Townsend Warner 1893-1978: A Celebration," *PN Review 23,* 8, no. 3 (1981-1982): 30-61;
John Updike, "The Mastery of Miss Warner," *New Republic,* 154 (5 March 1966): 23-25.

Mary Webb

(25 March 1881-8 October 1927)

Margaret B. McDowell
University of Iowa

BOOKS: *The Golden Arrow* (London: Constable, 1916; New York: Dutton, 1935);
Gone to Earth (London: Constable, 1917; New York: Dutton, 1917);
The Spring of Joy (London & Toronto: Dent/New York: Dutton, 1917; New York: Dutton, 1937);
The House in Dormer Forest (London: Hutchinson, 1920; New York: Doran, 1921);
Seven for a Secret, A Love Story (London: Hutchinson, 1922; New York: Doran, 1923);
Precious Bane (London: Cape, 1924; New York: Dutton, 1926);
Poems, and The Spring of Joy (London: Cape, 1928; New York: Dutton, 1929);
Armour Wherein He Trusted (London: Cape, 1929; New York: Dutton, 1929);
The Chinese Lion (London: Bertram Rota, 1937);
Fifty-one Poems Hitherto Unpublished in Book Form (London: Cape, 1946; New York: Dutton, 1947);
Mary Webb: Collected Prose and Poems, edited by Gladys Mary Coles (Shropshire: Wildings, 1977).
Collection: *The Collected Works of Mary Webb,* 7 volumes (London: Cape, 1928-1929).

Between 1916 and her early death in 1927, Mary Webb produced novels which portrayed in realistic detail the people, customs, and superstitions of rural Shropshire. In her vivid descriptions she created not only the beauty of the Shropshire plains and the overwhelming presence of the high rock formations but also the mystery and spiritual power the region held for her—power that she portrayed as both bane and blessing in the lives of her characters. Webb's fascination with psychology and mysticism emerges in all her fiction and poetry. She explores intuitive apprehension of truth, rural superstitions and legends, prototypical myths that recur in many literatures and religions, and the creative—or destructive—interaction between nature and the innermost being of the sensitive individual. Mary Webb's prose possesses the symmetry, the complex symbolism, and the compression of thought and symbol which one associates with poetry. In remarking on the aesthetic effect of Webb's peculiar intensity, G. K. Chesterton wrote: "The light in the stories . . . is a light not shining on things but through them."

Already seriously ill at twenty of Graves' disease (characterized by hyperthyroidism, bulging eyes, and external goiter), Mary Webb produced in

Mary Webb

dogs and horses for hunting, she despised the hunting of animals for sport and had by adolescence become a committed vegetarian. Except for two years at a private school in Southport, she was educated at home, and by the time she began writing novels, she had read William James's writings on religious experience and had studied the works on mysticism by Evelyn Underhill, whom she later met in London through their mutual friend, novelist and mystic May Sinclair.

All Webb's novels have similar themes and express the principles which dominated the highly self-conscious mental and spiritual orientation of her personal life. She saw love as the vital power in the universe and attaining "the apocalypse of love" as the highest human goal. For her, the spiritual aspect of love, more than the physical, determines its quality, strength, and endurance. However, since sex must be included in a harmonious perspective of nature, she also recognized that no one can reasonably separate physical love from devotion to the spirit of the beloved. She gradually realized that love of nature prepares one for love of humankind, although nature is destructive as well as benevolent. While love for nature prepares one to love others, it also draws the human spirit to a plane where it can apprehend the divine force. Webb believed in her early career that God reveals himself to those who cling to the beauty of nature as to the "garment of God."

After her first attack of Graves' disease in 1901—which kept her in bed most of the time for two to three years—Mary Webb developed an anxious preoccupation with the transient nature of joy. Having prayed since childhood for a spirit sensitive to the full experience of life, she realized that such sensitivity makes one as vulnerable to extreme pain, fear, and despair as to extreme joy. In the essays she wrote during her recovery (collected sixteen years later in *The Spring of Joy,* 1917) she reflected often on the closeness between pain and deep spiritual satisfaction, and she began to come to terms with her protruding eyes and disfigured neck, which so suddenly and markedly had changed her appearance. In 1909 she suffered great grief at the loss of her father early in the year, but that spring she met Henry Webb, a Cambridge graduate, who was—like her father—a teacher and scholar. They became engaged in the summer of 1911 and married in June 1912 in an unconventional ceremony. The bridesmaid was the gardener's three-year-old daughter, and the seventy guests were mostly the aged and destitute residents of a nearby workhouse.

her brief career five novels and a substantially completed sixth, a book of poetry, and a sequence of meditative essays, in addition to about forty stories, sketches, and review articles published in periodicals. While Rebecca West, reviewing the second novel, declared that Webb was "a genius," the general recognition of her literary talent came, ironically, the year after her death in October 1927. Following a laudatory address by Stanley Baldwin, Prime Minister of England, before the Royal Literary Fund Society in April 1928 (the Archbishop of York and Professor G. M. Trevelyan responded with toasts), Webb's novel *Precious Bane* (1924) went through five editions in six months and continued for a decade to be a best-selling novel. The book remained popular as late as 1961, when readers of the *Sunday Times* (London) voted to add it to the *Times "100 Books,"* ranking it in their acclaim just above George Orwell's *Nineteen Eighty-Four* (1949).

Born in Leighton-under-the-Wrekin, Shropshire, to George Edward Meredith, who conducted a private school for boys, and his wife, Sarah Alice Scott, Mary Gladys Meredith developed most of her basic convictions through sharing her father's Christian mysticism. Unlike her father who raised

Webb's birthplace, Leighton Lodge in Shropshire

For the rest of her life, the more intense her love for her husband, the deeper her terror became that their love might vanish. In her poetry she repeatedly fused joy and pain as concurrent emotional experience ("Let me inherit/Agony-wonder"; "a joy like pain possesses the soul"; "joy as keen as pain"). Even the impressive, sweeping winds that stirred her sense of beauty also aroused fear in her: "Come, like ravens with wide black wings,/To waken me with their screaming." Like their creator, the characters in Webb's fiction, mostly simple country folk, live with intense closeness to nature and at the edge of extreme emotion.

In *The Golden Arrow* (1916), Mary Webb's first novel, she based her portrait of the shepherd John Arden on her schoolteacher father. A realistically portrayed countryman, Arden is described unsentimentally, even in the depiction of his idyllic relationship with his daughter, Deborah, who shares his devotion to nature. Patty, John's wife, works as a midwife and has the sharp and domineering tendencies that Mary Webb found difficult in her mother. Deborah falls in love with Stephen South-ernwood, a former preacher who has mentally rejected the conventional dogma of his youth, including belief in marriage, but emotionally feels empty without faith. The lovers live together in the shadow of a great black rock formation, the Devil's Chair. Deborah, who is secretly pregnant, pressures Stephen into marriage; and she then begins to urge him to quit his job as a miner and to become a shepherd so that he can remain near her each day.

Feeling entrapped by her anxious, smothering love, Stephen perceives the Devil's Chair as an ominous symbol of the implacable and unchanging forces in society and abandons Deborah on St. Thomas Day—the day that honors a disciple who expressed doubts. Many of the local superstitions—particularly about the gathering of ghosts at the Devil's Chair—center on this day, and that night Deborah—yielding hysterically to her pain from Stephen's rejection, her bewilderment in the maze of superstitions surrounding her, her fear of the ghosts gathering about the Devil's Chair and her house, and her hostility toward the enormous black Devil's Chair—burns the house to the ground.

Wandering all night in the snow, she is saved from freezing only because she sees the lantern of her father, who guides her back to the family cottage. In June, after her child is born, Stephen returns, and Deborah, though expressing no anger, draws herself and the child away from the deserter; but her father gently maneuvers the two toward a gradual reconciliation. They unite not in a joyous reunion of romantic lovers but out of loneliness and pity. Stephen's loss of religion left a void, deepening his need for human ties. Love provides some consolation and encouragement for both Stephen and Deborah before each must encounter alone "the infinite void." Stephen's spiritual development, then, is not a religious renewal, but an ability to pity the imperfections in one other human being and to love the spirit and the body of that human being. If Stephen and Deborah find what Webb terms "the apocalypse of love," such experience will be born of the weakness of the beloved, weakness which evokes pity in the heart of the lover. In the apocalypse of love, the people embrace both suffering and joy in their full acceptance of the human condition and human sensitivity.

A subplot in the novel deals with the marriage of Deborah's brother, Joe, to Lily Huntbatch, a superficial, self-centered, and deceptive woman, who derides Deborah's conviction that lovers must love in spirit in order to experience full ecstasy in sexual love. Ironically, the marriages of the harsh Patty and the deceptive Lily appear stronger than that of the idealistic Deborah, who hopes for a more complete physical and spiritual union in love. In her pairing of two strongly contrasting personalities in each of the marriages, in her use of three parallel marriages, and in her analysis of the higher and lower characteristics of the six individuals, Mary Webb used conventional plotting she had learned from the great Victorians. Webb also creates intense and memorable scenes, even if she may have fallen short of creating a fully unified novel; and at every point, the natural background causes or heightens the emotional force of her work.

Webb's psychological autobiography runs close beneath the surface of this novel—in the portraits of her parents as John and Patty, in John's pantheistic mysticism taught to Deborah, in Stephen's sense of emptiness after his rejection of orthodox Christianity, and in Deborah's anxiety to have her husband constantly near her. Deborah's negative reaction to the rock formation and her narrow escape from freezing hint at Webb's doubts about the benevolence of nature and its basically benign spirit—doubts which become stronger in her next novel.

In 1915, as Mary Webb awaited the publication of her first novel and brooded over her plans for *Gone to Earth,* she found an activity which provided for her a positive involvement with World War I, whose cruelty she was about to allegorize in her second novel. She and Henry Webb had planted a large victory garden, and she was eager to use it to assist those troubled by high costs of food. She also believed, as she remarked in *The Golden Arrow,* in the "beauty of common transactions." Although her mother, sister, and mother-in-law thought Webb had disgraced them by renting a stall in Shrewsbury market and selling vegetables, fruits, and flowers, she saw herself helping others relate to "the large dignity of Nature itself." She and her husband rose at 3:00 A.M. or 4:00 A.M. to pick vegetables and arrange flowers (she sold roses for a half-penny a bouquet). Henry Webb seldom accompanied her to the market. In spite of her fragile health, she enjoyed sitting all day in the midst of the country women minding their stalls, and she talked in country dialect with simple people. After her day's work, she walked nine miles home and seldom earned over five shillings for the entire day's effort; but Henry Webb later recalled that she seemed "brighter" and always satisfied. "She felt she had done something beautiful."

At first Mary Webb worked on *Gone to Earth* only on weekends, when she and Henry Webb returned to Shropshire, after spending weekdays unhappily in Chester, where they were living with Mary's mother and sister. The war seemed more oppressive to them in the city, and Mary Webb felt even greater distress than might be expected over her three brothers on the Western front because of her mother's apparently casual attitude toward their danger. On weekends she wrote with compulsive speed, hardly sleeping, and letting each page simply fall to the floor as she rushed on to the next page. Fearing that Mary Webb's health might again collapse under her stress, Henry Webb resigned his position at Chester after three months and found another at Shrewsbury. Mary Webb finished her allegory of the war in a cottage at Lyth. When it was published, no reviewer noted that, on one level at least, the book addressed the war. Although reviews and sales were sparse, all reviews were favorable. Rebecca West not only declared that Mary Webb was a genius but also informally nominated the novel as "book of the year." In 1917 Mary Webb's book of essays was published as was Henry Webb's epic poem, *The Everlasting Quest,* which expresses a view of love similar to hers—the belief that deep love inevitably is a fusion of joy and pain. *Gone to Earth* carried the simple dedication to her husband: "To him whose presence is home."

At its simplest, *Gone to Earth* is a story of seduction, but it is also a statement about war and forces of power exploiting the powerless. While depicting the struggle between two men—the Reverend Edward Marston, a man of spirit, and Squire Jack Reddin, a man of physical lust—for one woman, it also deals with the conflict between the forces of nature and the forces of civilization which misuse nature. A Gothic story that includes a haunted hall, a decaying and beautiful garden, and a place of torture, it is also a fairy tale about a girl, Hazel Woodus, who lives close to nature and can sing hypnotic songs to the birds and beasts of the forest and who talks to the bees and the rocks. It is a psychological study in which a pet fox becomes a totem or "externalized soul" for a woman, so that the animal and the human react to each other's suffering or pleasure, and when one must die the other dies. It is a story in which many questions are raised, and not all are answered.

The novel is laid in the Borderland Welsh country about 1870. Its themes emerge mainly through dramatic incident and dialogue, rather than through narrative comment (on which Webb had depended too heavily in her first book). The plot possesses clear direction and inevitability. As in her first novel, Mary Webb questions the survival of marriage where only physical attraction vitalizes the relationship and also questions the possibility of true marriage where spiritual love is unnaturally separated from sexuality. The primitive individual who sympathizes with natural creatures is superior to the "righteous" believers in abstract theology or social respectability. Superstitions touch the book on every page and deepen the allegorical and mythical levels of the novel.

The early pages present a pastoral life with benign and comforting aspects, although it is not idealized and romantic. Hazel Woodus's parents were eccentric—her mother, now dead, sat looking into the distances of the landscape and sky through her open door and forgot about the little child who needed a mother's love. Her father, Abel, a recluse who gives harp concerts on occasion, raises bees and makes all the coffins for the area. Hazel "tells the bees" about each coffin ordered, but her father believes one needs to share with them only the news of death in one's own house. He views his coffin-

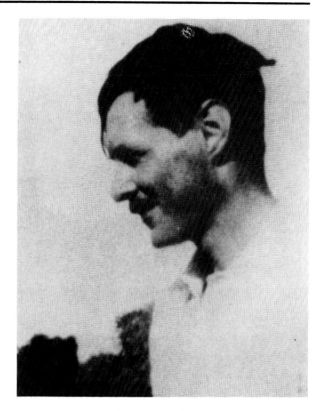

Henry Webb, 1924

making only as craft, not as a sharing of the grief of others. Hazel, on the other hand, responds to the joy and sorrow of every creature she contacts. Understanding an inarticulate man's grief, Webb tells of Abel Woodus's response to his wife's death: "He had gone out on that vivid June morning to his hives, and had stood watching the lines of bees fetching water, their shadows going and coming on the clean white boards. Then he had stooped and said with a curious confidential indifference, 'Maray's dead.' He had put his ear to the hive and listened to the deep, solemn murmur within; but it was the murmur of the future, and not of the past, the preoccupation with life, not with death, that filled the pale galleries within."

After this scene (in which nature holds the forces of life and comfort and in which young Hazel Woodus can fully express her extraordinary tenderness for living things and enjoy her gentle, wild, and impulsive life in a household that includes her pet fox, a blind bird, a rabbit, and a one-eyed cat), Webb describes Undern Hall, where Squire Reddin almost rapes Hazel and later seduces her. Beauty and horror are oddly fused: "Even in May, when the lilacs frothed into purple, paved the lawn with shadows, steeped the air with scent; when soft leaves lipped each other consolingly; when blackbirds sang, fell in their effortless way from the green height to the green depth, and sang again—still, something that haunted the place set the heart fluttering . . . the smell of the mud tainted the air—half sickly, half sweet. . . . The cattle drowsed in the meadows, birds in the heavy trees; the golden day-lilies drooped like the daughters of pleasure; the very principle of life seemed to slumber . . . narcotic, aphrodisiac."

If in the sinister atmosphere of Undern Hall nature takes on an ominous mask, it is even more disturbing that the minister, Edward Marston, a man of great kindness and gentleness, finds that nature's beauty does not lead him to God, as romantics and even psalmists have assumed should happen. Instead, he confides to his mother that, since he has come to the chapel at God's Little Mountain, he sees nature as a frightening force. Nature has, not through its beauty, but through its potential for terror and cruelty, driven him toward God—and made him fear that God who expresses himself in nature: "on winter nights at the mountain, when the tingling stars sprang in and out of their black ambush and frost cracked the tombstones; in summer, when lightning crackled in the woods and ripped along the hillside like a thousand devils, the need of a God grew ever more urgent . . . [he wondered] why the cry of a sheep from an upper slope was so forlorn."

Early in the novel, the wealthy resident of Undern Hall, Jack Reddin, attempts to seduce Hazel, but she slips from him "as a fish escapes the net." Later, Marston marries Hazel but decides that she is too childlike and unsophisticated for the marriage to be consummated, and he prays for power to wait for sexual satisfaction. Hazel, however, grows bored and finds Reddin's appeals to go with him to Undern Hall intriguing. She returns to Marston—pregnant—after she is repulsed by Reddin's encouraging his servant to flog a horse, trap a rabbit, torture a hedgehog, burn Hazel's beehive, and train his hounds to be "the death pack." Marston, angry and bitter, decides to care for Hazel as Christ would care for the one lamb that wandered away: "And darkly on his dark mind loomed his new and bitter creed, There is no Christ!" He now thinks of Christ as "not God, but only a brave, loving heart hunted to death."

Marston's mother had once communicated to her son in a shocked whisper that his wife was not Christian, because Hazel had said—in their talk about theology—that she "refused to be died for."

Now his judgmental mother and the Marstons' "respectable" woman servant abandon the minister rather than live with a "fallen woman." At this point, Hazel is praying to the black cloudy sky that *Whoever* is there will be good to Foxy, who has been crying at night.

Hazel, the character most pantheistic and with the greatest insight into the secrets of the forest and the animals, also believes that nature conspires to entrap her. She tells her husband, Edward Marston, that Jack Reddin lured her to Undern Hall but not totally through his own power. She was "druv" to him, as a rabbit would be driven to mate in the grass, by "Summat strong and drodsome as druvs us all." Throughout the book Hazel fears the mythical Black Huntsman and his "death-pack." At the close of the book she is driven over the wall of the quarry to her death far below, as she tries to save her pet Foxy from pursuing hounds led by a huntsman she never sees.

The dramatically powerful final scene is preceded by an idyllic one that concentrates the effect of the last scene and adds depth of human experience to the book. Awaiting the birth of Reddin's child, Hazel and Edward find their tenderness toward each other increasing in the midst of their suffering and look forward to the future with hope. As Hazel says to Edward, "going out of a May morning, you and me—and maybe Foxy on a string—and looking nests, and us with cobwebs on our boots, and setting primmy-roses, red and white and laylac, in my garden as you made, and then me cooking the breakfast, and you making the toast and burning it along of reading some hard book, and maybe us laughing over a bit o' fun. And then you off to read to somebody ill, and me waiting outside, pleased as a queen, and harkening to your voice coming quiet through the window. And picking laylac, evenings, and going after mushrooms at the turn of the year. Them days be coming, Ed'ard, inna they?"

The horror of the final scene contrasts bitterly with this idyllic dream. As the hounds close in on Foxy, Hazel grasps him to her and attempts to run, but Reddin's child in her womb slows her as much as the convulsive struggling of Foxy. Recognizing that she cannot climb the steep green turf "which rose before her like the ascent of Calvary" and that she cannot give Foxy to the huntsmen and the shrieking hounds, she faces what she has always most feared—falling into the quarry—and allows herself to be driven over the rocky wall and hurtles through space. The silence is followed by the echoes of the traditional cry of the hunt as the prey is brought down by the hounds: "Gone to earth!"

The deaths of Hazel, of Foxy, of Christ, and of soldiers in the war are all indictments of the injustice and cruelty implicit in power. Forces of evil triumph over the loving and simple individuals. These conclusions are implicit in the action, but Mary Webb's statement stops short of such conclusiveness: "For all our tears and prayers and weary dreaming, we cannot know."

By the time she wrote this book, Mary Webb's nature mysticism seems to have been no longer related to Christian mysticism. She questions the dominant benignity of nature. Her suspicion that there exists no control over nature or that the force that dominates nature is cruel leads her toward despair, particularly as she relates such suspicions to the principles that drive nations to war.

Mary Webb spent a long time meditating over her next book, *The House in Dormer Forest* (1920). As she wrote it, she was celebrating the safe return of many soldiers from the war, but she also contemplated the forces that had led nations to war and the apparent uselessness of the conflict. In *The House in Dormer Forest* she considers Jasper Darke's rejection of Christian faith, which horrifies his family and causes his dismissal from the university where he has pursued theological studies. But Webb treats his rebellion as positive—the first step toward a difficult, but vitalizing, exploration of the unconscious and toward acceptance of the influence of myth upon the unconscious. Jasper, though his isolation is stressed, receives support from three other mystics—his former teacher, Michael Hallowes, who comes to visit him in the second part of the book; his sister, Amber, a love mystic, whose insights derive from nature and are expressed in maternal love, nurturing protection of others, and a spirit of laughter; and Enoch Gale, an earth mystic and seer, who is the gardener and handyman for the Darke family. It is Enoch who prophesies the destruction not only of the house but of the oppressive history and laws which it symbolizes. Evidence of Webb's humorous satire in this novel appears in her naming Rose Darke's husband the Reverend Ernest Swyndle.

In the early 1920s Mary Webb's non-Christian mysticism had become less exclusively dependent upon constant contact with nature, although her "passionate identification" with nature remained. She now saw nature as a neutral force, totally separate from human welfare. She no longer questioned, as in her first two novels, whether nature was beneficent or malignant. She wrote of the popular "fondness" for nature as foolish sentimentality: the nature mystic derived strength from a passionate involvement with nature, which deepened the "well of the unconscious," or the source of energy, vitality, and creativity in the human spirit. Rather than focusing upon the external landscape, she now emphasized the internal landscape of the mind and the exploration of that landscape through introspection, meditation, and recall of deeply hidden memory—the echoes that come from both personal experience and "race memory." As early as *Gone to Earth,* she had referred to the echoes we all hold in our minds: "echoes of the past, reflex echoes of the future, and echoes of the soil."

The Gothic background of Dormer Old House, Dormer forest, the brook, the steep cliff that insures the remoteness of the haunted house, the Four Waters, the Beast Walk, the Grotto of Suffering, and the "cuplike valley" all must be seen as the dark and hidden places of the mind. The experiences of the four searchers differ in kind and occur in different parts of the Dormer landscape or house. Amber finds deep understanding through the intuitive wisdom she receives in the Upper Woods and in Birds' Orchard. Her experience appears to reflect most closely that of Mary Webb and she reflects, as well, the maternal longings that distressed the childless author at this period in her marriage. Jasper achieves mental and emotional transformation through a symbolic drowning in the "opaque and fathomless pool lying within his own being." His former teacher, Michael, prevents his death after Jasper has jumped into the brook in despair over his foolish attempt to "invent a god" that would satisfy his sweetheart and family. Enoch finds his source of strength in the soil and the garden; earth mystics grasped a "wilder" intuition.

Most dramatic are the torturing experiences of suffering the characters undergo in the grotto and the testing they receive through terror as they walk through the Beast Walk. In this terrible avenue of their unconscious instincts, secret desires, and repressed urges, they are surrounded by the distortions and crooked shapes of yew trees (traditional symbols of death) that have been trimmed over the years into the shape of beasts. (This sort of topiary in formal gardens was not uncommon in Shropshire.) The "monsters" encountered in the Beast Walk may represent the threatening aspects of world history as well as the fearsomeness of the individual psyche. The Gothic atmosphere builds through allusions to rodents, bats, death-watch beetles, and cobwebs. The remoteness of the house, high on a cliff—even beyond the sweep of the winds—is emphasized in such vivid sentences as this: "When the bats slipped from their purlieus in the cobwebby outbuildings and climbed towards this rim, they had to ascend step after grey step of the windless air, and only attained their ambition after long flying."

Once she began to write *The House in Dormer Forest,* she worked compulsively—writing through a whole night rather than stopping the ideas and words pouring freely from the recesses of her mind. For some readers, her vivid and detailed elaborations of landscape or mood distract one from the relatively slight action in the novel. Others resent her preaching and excessive use of the narrative voice. Her many characters and fragmented subplots confuse readers. Reviewers noted these weaknesses, and they failed to recognize the significance of Webb's symbolism or the impressive intensity of the struggle undertaken by Amber and Jasper Darke, Michael Hallowes, and Enoch Gale to achieve fuller mystic understanding and hold back repressive forces of the past. The sales of the book disappointed Mary Webb—who had thought the end of the war would bring her commercial success. The new experience of receiving negative reviews so distressed her that it may have precipitated a greater thyroid imbalance. She suffered a major recurrence of Graves' disease and an extended and serious depression.

The relative shallowness of *Seven for a Secret* (1922) probably resulted from Webb's disappointment at the critical response to *The House in Dormer Forest. Seven for a Secret,* the first novel she was able to complete away from the Shropshire setting, was dedicated "To the illustrious name of Thomas Hardy, whose acceptance of this dedication has made me so happy." He not only agreed to accept her dedication but delighted her by praising her work and inviting her to visit him. The visit never occurred because both became more gravely ill, and their deaths occurred at about the same time. Although she still suffered from depression and her health had greatly worsened, Mary Webb now found new, stimulating friendships with May Sinclair, Walter de la Mare, Rebecca West, and Evelyn Underhill.

The plot of *Seven for a Secret,* the configuration of characters, and the themes all recall *Gone to Earth,* although the selfish Gillian Lovekin is far less interesting than Hazel Woodus. Just as Hazel for a time chose Jack Reddin over Edward Marston, Gillian chooses the less worthy Ralph Elmer for mere physical attraction and later returns to the poetmystic, Robert Rideout. Another Gothic house of

evil, this time called Mermaid's Rest, provides the place for the woman's seduction.

The story ostensibly takes place on the Welsh border. The people remain flat characters as in a fable, but the message of the fable is deliberately withheld: Is there further meaning in life than the paltry revelation of bitter experience? "One cannot be sure . . . except perhaps in death." The secret remains secret in this fable. The book, like Webb's others, is distinguished by fine descriptions and graceful style.

Webb wrote *Precious Bane,* usually considered her best book, in autumn 1923 at Hampstead, near London, depending on her acute memory of the Shropshire milieu for her evocation of the landscape. The setting is further north than those of her other novels—in the rocky lake lands near the Welsh border—but her characters still use the dialect of the South. She controlled every part of the book with a new assurance, and her poetic rhythms and imagery clearly reflect her favorite sections of the Bible—the Song of Solomon and Revelation—as well as the medieval mystics. The dialect has an easy naturalness, and she employs carefully balanced repetition and parallelism, as in this description of the smell of the golden corn: "There is summer in it, and frost. There is water in

The cottage in Hampstead where Webb wrote Precious Bane
(drawing by Gladys Mary Coles)

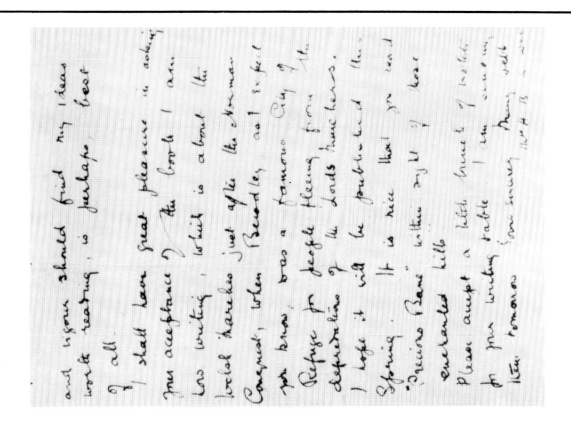

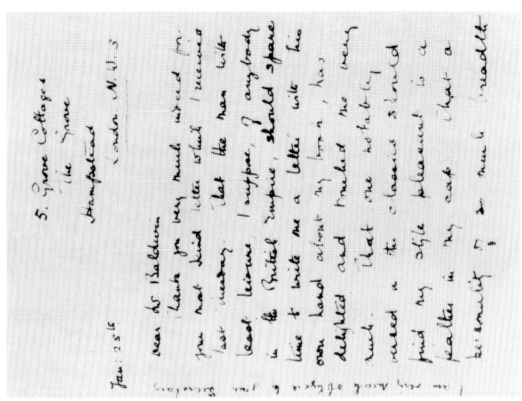

After Stanley Baldwin wrote Webb to praise Precious Bane, *Webb responded gratefully and asked that she be allowed to dedicate* Armour Wherein He Trusted *to the prime minister (Gladys Mary Coles,* The Flower of Light: A Biography of Mary Webb, *1978).*

it, and the heart of the flint which the corn has taken up into its hollow stalks. There is bread in it, and life for man and beast."

Webb found the title for her novel in the first book of *Paradise Lost:* "Let none admire / That riches grow in Hell; that soyle may best / Deserve the pretious bane." The "precious bane" in Prudence Sarn's life has been her harelip, since it has given her an inner "blessedness." Because of it, she learned to accept life patiently and thoughtfully, and she became fully grateful for the love of Kester, the town weaver. The deformity, however, is baneful as well as precious, because she has worked like a slave for her brother, Gideon Sarn, in return for his promise of money for the curing of the defect, and the deformity has marked her as a witch in the sight of the community. It is baneful also to her mother, who feels guilty for bearing her. Her father cruelly taunted her mother for causing the defect. Prue cannot understand the power of the hare that had crossed her mother's path and set the spell on her.

Gideon also has a precious bane, and his story is interwoven with hers. His precious possession is the gold he craves, and for which he sacrifices all else—the gold that comes from the golden corn. The baneful effects of the gold appear most poignantly when, because of his greed, he betrays the golden-haired Jancis.

Prudence's first-person narration sets a tone of patient acceptance. An old woman, she is ready to "say good night to the world" as soon as she tells the story: "Well, it is all gone over now, the trouble and the struggling. It be quiet weather now, like a still evening with the snow all down, and a green sky, and lambs calling." The web of superstition that entraps the characters emphasizes the ominous aspects of the story. (Webb is said to have included more than two hundred allusions to country superstitions and local legends in this novel.) At his father's funeral Gideon becomes the "sin-eater," who takes communion over the casket so that the corpse will not restlessly rise from the grave and wander back. Since the "sin-eater," ordinarily a beggar, would have been paid, Gideon at the point of his father's burial forces his mother to give him title to the farm in return for what she wants most at the moment—the peaceful rest of the dead man. Gideon's lust leads him next to demand Prue's work without pay—except for the written promise of up to fifty pounds to fix her lip when he can afford it. Greed leads him to poison his mother to save money, and eventually it leads him to reject Jancis, the lovely daughter of the wizard, Beguildy, to avoid the expense of a wife. When, out of love for

Mary Webb during her last years

him, she begs him to reconsider his decision, he promises to marry her if the harvest is good. In the meantime, he impregnates her. Beguildy avenges the dishonor of his daughter by setting fire to Gideon's ricks, and the equipment and harvest are destroyed.

Jancis drowns herself and her baby in the mere, and Gideon, crazed by the ghosts of the girl and the baby, drowns himself there also. Prudence prepares to leave the farm, but as she takes the livestock to the fair to sell, a crowd of villagers attacks her, believing she is a witch who has caused the deaths of father, mother, brother, Jancis, and the baby. In the "testing" Prue herself is almost drowned, but in a romantic ending, Kester sweeps her up into his saddle, and as they ride away, he kisses her "full on the mouth."

If the many deaths and Gideon's exaggerated greed strain credibility, the close web of superstition, the force of the natural imagery, and the remoteness in time as Prudence talks of her youth from the distance of age give the story a sense of inevitable doom, as in a folk ballad. The story also gains credibility through Mary Webb's projection of her own experience of physical handicap and of love on Prue's experience. She saw her growth in mystical understanding and her gratitude for Henry Webb's love as closely related to her adjustment to the disease which had made people stare at her and isolated her from others.

Mary Webb expressed concern about what she saw as a weakness in the book—an inadequate portrayal of the Christ-like, but inarticulate, Kester Woodseaves. She feared that she had made him abstract rather than realistic but acknowledged that she could not have done otherwise. While Mary Webb was working on her last two books, she was separated for considerable periods of time from her husband. The marriage had deteriorated in part because of the effect of her illness on her emotional control and in part because of her husband's interest in one of his students, who became his wife two years after Mary Webb's death. Though her dedication of *Precious Bane* to her husband is unusually formal and short—compared to earlier dedications to him—the simple "To my dear H.B.L.W." is augmented by the idealized presentation of Kester, who is based on Henry Webb.

Webb's unfinished novel, *Armour Wherein He Trusted* (posthumously published in 1929), is far different from her other novels. A historical novel set in the Middle Ages, it demanded accommodation to another time and place. The Shropshire landscape is absent, and she made the style formal and artificial in her attempt to approximate the speech of an earlier time. In this novel the love of Christ has won over an earthly love, but earthly love is also good; and one might expect the chief character to return to the beloved whom he temporarily abandons. The fragment ends with Gilbert of Polrebec leaving to follow Peter-the-Hermit on the First Crusade. Gilbert has left "those three beloved, one weeping and groaning," but he looks up to see that the figure of Christ on the cross has ceased weeping, and his expression appears to show satisfaction.

Mary Webb's great fame arrived six months after her death with the recognition of *Precious Bane* by Stanley Baldwin. The most important recognition during her lifetime came in 1926, when she received the Femina/Vie Heureuse prize for *Precious Bane*. The presentation at the Institut Français in July 1926 honored her for "the best imaginative work in prose or verse descriptive of English life by an author who has not gained sufficient recognition." One of the speakers at the ceremony, Arthur St. John Adcock, saw in her work "A feeling for the magic of words, a beauty of style that none of her contemporaries surpassed."

Bibliography:
Charles Sanders, "Mary Webb: An Introduction" and "An Annotated Bibliography," *English Literature in Transition,* 9 (1966): 115-136.

Biographies:
Hilda Addison, *Mary Webb: A Short Study of the Life and Work* (London: Palmer, 1931);
Thomas Moult, *Mary Webb: Her Life and Work* (London: Cape, 1932);
Dorothy P. Wrenn, *Goodbye to Morning: A Biographical Study of Mary Webb* (Shrewsbury: Wilding, 1964);
Gladys Mary Coles, *The Flower of Light, A Biography of Mary Webb* (London: Duckworth, 1978).

References:
Ronald Butler, *The Relations of Art to Thought in the Novels of Mary Webb,* M.A. Thesis, University of Kentucky, 1957; Kentucky Microcard Series A, Modern Language Series, no. 78 (Lexington: University of Kentucky Press, 1961);
W. Byford-Jones, *The Shropshire Haunts of Mary Webb* (Shrewsbury: Wilding, 1948);
W. Reid Chappell, *The Shropshire of Mary Webb* (London: Palmer, 1930);
Gladys Peake, "The Religious Teaching of Mary Webb," *Congregational Quarterly,* 11 (January 1933): 41-50;
Charles Sanders, "The Golden Arrow: Mary Webb's 'Apocalypse of Love,'" *English Literature in Transition,* 10 (1967): 1-8;
Sanders, "Webb's Precious Bane, Book III, Chapter 2," *Explicator,* 25 (October 1966): 10;
Evelyn Underhill, *Mysticism* (London: Methuen, 1911; revised, 1945).

H. G. Wells

Michael Draper

BIRTH: Bromley, Kent, England, 21 September 1866, to Joseph and Sarah Neal Wells.

EDUCATION: B.S., Normal School of Science, London, 1890.

MARRIAGES: 31 October 1891 to Isabel Mary Wells; divorced 1895. 27 October 1895 to Amy Catherine Robbins; children: George Philip, Frank Richard, Anna-Jane White (by Amber Reeves), Anthony Panther West (by Rebecca West).

AWARDS AND HONORS: International president, P.E.N. Clubs (1934-1946).

DEATH: London, 13 August 1946.

SELECTED BOOKS: *Text-book of Biology*, 2 volumes (London: Clive, 1893);

Honours Physiography, by Wells and R. A. Gregory (London: Hughes, 1893);

Select Conversations with an Uncle, Now Extinct, and Two Other Reminiscences (London: Lane, 1895; New York: Merriam, 1895);

The Time Machine: An Invention (London: Heinemann, 1895; New York: Holt, 1895);

The Wonderful Visit (London: Dent, 1895; New York: Macmillan, 1895);

The Stolen Bacillus, and Other Incidents (London: Methuen, 1895);

The Island of Dr. Moreau (London: Heinemann, 1896; New York: Stone & Kimball, 1896);

The Wheels of Chance: A Holiday Adventure (London: Dent, 1896); republished as *The Wheels of Chance: A Bicycling Idyll* (New York: Macmillan, 1896);

The Plattner Story, and Others (London: Methuen, 1897);

The Invisible Man: A Grotesque Romance (London: Pearson, 1897; New York: Arnold, 1897);

Thirty Strange Stories (New York: Arnold, 1897);

Certain Personal Matters: A Collection of Material, Mainly Autobiographical (London: Lawrence & Bullen, 1897);

The War of the Worlds (London: Heinemann, 1898; New York: Harper, 1898);

When the Sleeper Wakes: A Story of the Years to Come (London & New York: Harper, 1899); revised as *The Sleeper Awakes* (London: Nelson, 1910);

Tales of Space and Time (London: Harper, 1899; New York: Doubleday, McClure, 1899);

A Cure for Love (New York: Scott, 1899);

Love and Mr. Lewisham (London & New York: Harper, 1900);

The First Men in the Moon (London: Newnes, 1901; Indianapolis: Bowen-Merrill, 1901);

Anticipations of the Reaction of Mechanical and Scientific Progress upon Human Life and Thought (London: Chapman & Hall, 1901; New York: Harper, 1902);

The Discovery of the Future: A Discourse Delivered to the Royal Institution on January 24th, 1902 (London: Unwin, 1902; New York: Huebsch, 1913);

The Sea Lady: A Tissue of Moonshine (London: Methuen, 1902); republished as *The Sea Lady* (New York: Appleton, 1902);

Mankind in the Making (London: Chapman & Hall, 1903; New York: Scribners, 1904);

Twelve Stories and a Dream (London: Macmillan, 1903; New York: Scribners, 1905);

The Food of the Gods, and How It Came to Earth (London: Macmillan, 1904; New York: Scribners, 1904);

A Modern Utopia (London: Chapman & Hall, 1905; New York: Scribners, 1905);

Kipps: The Story of a Simple Soul (London: Macmillan, 1905; New York: Scribners, 1905);

The Future in America: A Search after Realities (London: Chapman & Hall, 1906; New York: Harper, 1906);

Faults of the Fabian (London: Fabian Society, 1906);

Reconstruction of the Fabian Society (London: Privately printed, 1906);

Socialism and the Family (London: Fifield, 1906);

In the Days of the Comet (London: Macmillan, 1906; New York: Century, 1906);

The So-Called Science of Sociology (London: Macmillan, 1907);

This Misery of Boots (London: Fabian Society, 1907; Boston: Ball, 1908);

Will Socialism Destroy the Home? (London: Independent Labour Party, 1907);

New Worlds for Old (London: Constable, 1908; New

H. G. Wells (photograph by Howard Coster)

York: Macmillan, 1908);

The War in the Air, and Particularly How Mr. Bert Smallways Fared while It Lasted (London: Bell, 1908; New York: Macmillan, 1908);

First and Last Things: A Confession of Faith and Rule of Life (London: Constable, 1908; New York: Putnam's, 1908; revised and enlarged, London: Cassell, 1917);

Tono-Bungay (New York: Duffield, 1908; London: Macmillan, 1909);

Ann Veronica: A Modern Love Story (London: Unwin, 1909; New York: Harper, 1909);

The History of Mr. Polly (London: Nelson, 1910; New York: Duffield, 1910);

The New Machiavelli (New York: Duffield, 1910; London: Lane, 1911);

Floor Games (London: Palmer, 1911; Boston: Small, Maynard, 1912);

The Country of the Blind, and Other Stories (London & New York: Nelson, 1911);

The Door in the Wall and Other Stories (New York: Kennerley, 1911; London: Richards, 1915);

Marriage (London: Macmillan, 1912; New York: Duffield, 1912);

The Great State: Essays in Construction, by Wells, Frances Evelyn Warwick, L. G. Chiozza Money, E. Ray Lankester, C. J. Bond, E. S. P. Haynes, Cecil Chesterton, Cicely Hamilton, Roger Fry, G. R. S. Taylor, Conrad Noel, Herbert Trench, Hugh P. Vowles (London: Harper, 1912); republished as *Socialism and the Great State* (New York: Harper, 1914);

The Labour Unrest (London: Daily Mail, 1912);

War and Common Sense (London: Daily Mail, 1913);

Liberalism and Its Party: What Are the Liberals to Do? (London: Good, 1913);

Little Wars: A Game for Boys from Twelve Years of Age to One Hundred and Fifty and for that More Intelligent Sort of Girls Who Like Boys' Games and Books (London: Palmer, 1913; Boston: Small, Maynard, 1913; revised, London: Palmer, 1931);

The Passionate Friends (London: Macmillan, 1913; New York: Harper, 1913);

An Englishman Looks at the World: Being a Series of Unrestrained Remarks upon Contemporary Matters (London: Cassell, 1914); republished as *Social Forces in England and America* (New York: Harper, 1914);

The End of the Armament Rings (Boston: World Peace Foundation, 1914);

The World Set Free: A Story of Mankind (London: Macmillan, 1914; New York: Dutton, 1914);

The Wife of Sir Isaac Harman (London & New York: Macmillan, 1914);

The War That Will End War (London: Palmer, 1914; New York: Duffield, 1914);

Boon, The Mind of the Race, The Wild Asses of the Devil, and The Last Trump: Being a First Selection from the Literary Remains of George Boon, Appropriate to the Times. Prepared for Publication by Reginald Bliss with an Ambiguous Introduction by H. G. Wells, as Reginald Bliss (London: Unwin, 1915; New York: Doran, 1915);

Bealby: A Holiday (London: Methuen, 1915; New York: Macmillan, 1915);

The Research Magnificent (London & New York: Macmillan, 1915);

The Peace of the World (London: Daily Chronicle, 1915);

What Is Coming? A Forecast of Things after the War (London: Cassell, 1916); republished as *What Is Coming? A European Forecast* (New York: Macmillan, 1916);

The Elements of Reconstruction: A Series of Articles Contributed in July and August 1916 to the Times

(London: Nisbet, 1916);

Mr. Britling Sees It Through (London: Cassell, 1916; New York: Macmillan, 1916);

The Soul of a Bishop: A Novel (with Just a Little Love in It) about Conscience and Religion and the Real Troubles of Life (London: Cassell, 1917; New York: Macmillan, 1917);

War and the Future: Italy, France and Britain at War (London: Cassell, 1917); republished as *Italy, France and Britain at War* (New York: Macmillan, 1917);

God, The Invisible King (London: Cassell, 1917; New York: Macmillan, 1917);

A Reasonable Man's Peace (London: Daily News, 1917);

In the Fourth Year: Anticipations of a World Peace (London: Chatto & Windus, 1918; New York: Macmillan, 1918);

British Nationalism and the League of Nations (London: League of Nations Union, 1918);

Joan and Peter: The Story of an Education (London: Cassell, 1918; New York: Macmillan, 1918);

The Undying Fire: A Contemporary Novel (London: Cassell, 1919; New York: Macmillan, 1919);

History Is One (New York: Ginn, 1919);

The Idea of a League of Nations, by Wells, Lord Grey, L. Curtis, W. Archer, H. W. Steed, A. F. Zimmern, J. A. Spender, Lord Bryce, G. Murray (London: Oxford University Press, 1919; Boston: Atlantic Monthly Press, 1919);

The Outline of History, Being a Plain History of Life and Mankind (24 parts, London: Newnes, 1919-1920; 1 volume, London: Newnes, 1920; 2 volumes, New York: Macmillan, 1920);

Frank Swinnerton, Personal Sketches: Together with Notes and Comments on the Novels of Frank Swinnerton, by Wells, Arnold Bennett, and G. M. Overton (New York: Doran, 1920);

Russia in the Shadows (London: Hodder & Stoughton, 1920; New York: Doran, 1921);

The Salvaging of Civilisation (London: Cassell, 1921; New York: Macmillan, 1921);

The New Teaching of History: with a Reply to Some Recent Criticisms of The Outline of History (London & New York: Cassell, 1921);

The Secret Places of the Heart (London: Cassell, 1922; New York: Macmillan, 1922);

Washington and the Hope of Peace (London: Collins, 1922); republished as *Washington and the Riddle of Peace* (New York: Macmillan, 1922);

What H. G. Wells Thinks about "The Mind in the Making" (New York: Harper, 1922);

University of London Election: An Electoral Letter (London: Finer, 1922);

The World, Its Debts, and the Rich Men: A Speech (London: Finer, 1922);

A Short History of the World (London: Cassell, 1922; New York: Macmillan, 1922);

Socialism and the Scientific Motive (London: Co-operative Printing Society, 1923);

To the Electors of London University General Election, 1923, from H. G. Wells, B. Sc., Lond. (London: Craig, 1923);

The Labour Ideal of Education (London: Craig, 1923);

Men Like Gods (London: Cassell, 1923; New York: Macmillan, 1923);

The Story of a Great Schoolmaster: Being a Plain Account of the Life and Ideas of Sanderson of Oundle (London: Chatto & Windus, 1924; New York: Macmillan, 1924);

The P. R. Parliament (London: Proportional Representation Society, 1924);

A Year of Prophesying (London: Unwin, 1924; New York: Macmillan, 1925);

The Dream: A Novel (London: Cape, 1924; New York: Macmillan, 1924);

The Atlantic Edition of the Works of H. G. Wells, 28 volumes (London: Unwin, 1924-1927; New York: Scribners, 1924-1927);

Christina Alberta's Father (London: Cape, 1925; New York: Macmillan, 1925);

A Forecast of the World's Affairs (London: Encyclopaedia Britannica, 1925);

The World of William Clissold: A Novel at a New Angle (3 volumes, London: Benn, 1926; 2 volumes, New York: Doran, 1926);

Mr. Belloc Objects to The Outline of History (London: Watts, 1926; New York: Doran, 1926);

The Essex Collected Thin Paper Edition of the Works of H. G. Wells, 24 volumes (London: Benn, 1926-1927);

Meanwhile: The Picture of a Lady (London: Benn, 1927; New York: Doran, 1927);

Democracy under Revision: A Lecture Delivered at the Sorbonne, March 15th, 1927 (London: Woolf, 1927; New York: Doran, 1927);

Experiments on Animals: Views for and Against, by Wells and G. B. Shaw (London: British Union for the Abolition of Vivisection, 1927);

Playing at Peace (London: National Council for the Prevention of War, 1927);

The Short Stories of H. G. Wells (London: Benn, 1927; Garden City: Doubleday, Doran, 1929);

The Way the World Is Going: Guesses and Forecasts of the Years Ahead (London: Benn, 1928; Garden City: Doubleday, Doran, 1929);

The Open Conspiracy: Blue Prints for a World Revolution (London: Gollancz, 1928; Garden City:

Doubleday, Doran, 1928; revised, London: Woolf, 1930);

Mr. Blettsworthy on Rampole Island (London: Benn, 1928; Garden City: Doubleday, Doran, 1928);

The King Who Was a King: The Book of a Film (London: Benn, 1929); republished as *The King Who Was a King: An Unconventional Novel* (Garden City: Doubleday, Doran, 1929);

The Adventures of Tommy (London: Harrap, 1929; New York: Stokes, 1929);

The Common Sense of World Peace: An Address Delivered to the Reichstag at Berlin, on Monday, April 15th, 1929 (London: Woolf, 1929);

Imperialism and the Open Conspiracy (London: Faber & Faber, 1929);

The Science of Life: A Summary of Contemporary Knowledge about Life and Its Possibilities, by Wells, Julian Huxley, and G. P. Wells (31 parts, London: Amalgamated Press, 1929-1930; 3 volumes, London: Amalgamated Press, 1929-1930; 4 volumes, Garden City: Doubleday, Doran, 1931);

The Autocracy of Mr. Parham: His Remarkable Adventure in this Changing World (London: Heinemann, 1930; Garden City: Doubleday, Doran, 1930);

Points of View: A Series of Broadcast Addresses, by Wells, G. Lowes Dickinson, Dean Inge, J. B. S. Haldane, Sir Oliver Lodge, and Sir Walford Davies (London: Allen & Unwin, 1930);

The Way to World Peace (London: Benn, 1930);

The Problem of the Troublesome Collaborator: An Account of Certain Difficulties in an Attempt to Produce a Work in Collaboration, and of the Intervention of the Society of Authors Therein (Woking, U.K.: Privately printed, 1930);

Settlement of the Trouble between Mr. Thring and Mr. Wells: A Footnote to The Problem of the Troublesome Collaborator (Woking, U.K.: Privately printed, 1930);

Divorce as I See It, by Wells, Bertrand Russell, Fannie Hurst, Theodore Dreiser, Warwick Deeping, Rebecca West, André Maurois, and Lionel Feuchtwanger (London: Douglas, 1930);

What Are We to Do with Our Lives? (London: Heinemann, 1931; Garden City: Doubleday, Doran, 1931);

The New Russia: Eight Talks Broadcast, by Wells, H. R. Knickerbocker, Sir John Russell, Sir Bernard Pares, Dr. Margaret S. Miller, B. Mouat-Jones, Stafford Talbot, and Frank Owen (London: Faber & Faber, 1931);

The Work, Wealth and Happiness of Mankind (2 volumes, Garden City: Doubleday, Doran, 1931;

1 volume, London: Heinemann, 1932);

After Democracy: Addresses and Papers on the Present World Situation (London: Watts, 1932);

What Should Be Done—Now: A Memorandum on the World Situation (New York: Day, 1932);

The Bulpington of Blup: Adventures, Poses, Stresses, Conflicts, and Disaster in a Contemporary Brain (London: Hutchinson, 1932; New York: Macmillan, 1933);

The Shape of Things to Come: The Ultimate Revolution (London: Hutchinson, 1933; New York: Macmillan, 1933);

Experiment in Autobiography: Discoveries and Conclusions of a Very Ordinary Brain (Since 1866), 2 volumes (London: Gollancz & Cresset, 1934; New York: Macmillan, 1934);

Stalin-Wells Talk: The Verbatim Record, and a Discussion by G. Bernard Shaw, H. G. Wells, J. M. Keynes, Ernst Toller and Others (London: New Statesman & Nation, 1934);

The New America: The New World (London: Cresset, 1935; New York: Macmillan, 1935);

Things to Come: A Film Story Based on the Material Contained in His History of the Future "The Shape of Things to Come" (London: Cresset, 1935; New York: Macmillan, 1935);

The Croquet Player: A Story (London: Chatto & Windus, 1936; New York: Viking, 1937);

The Man Who Could Work Miracles: A Film Story Based on the Material Contained in His Short Story (London: Cresset, 1936; New York: Macmillan, 1936);

The Anatomy of Frustration: A Modern Synthesis (London: Cresset, 1936; New York: Macmillan, 1936);

The Idea of a World Encyclopaedia (London: Woolf, 1936);

The Informative Content of Education (London: British Association, 1937);

Star Begotten: A Biological Fantasia (London: Chatto & Windus, 1937; New York: Viking, 1937);

Brynhild (London: Methuen, 1937); republished as *Brynhild; or, The Show of Things* (New York: Scribners, 1937);

The Camford Visitation (London: Methuen, 1937);

The Brothers: A Story (London: Chatto & Windus, 1938; New York: Viking, 1938);

Apropos of Dolores (London: Cape, 1938; New York: Scribners, 1938);

World Brain (London: Methuen, 1938; Garden City: Doubleday, Doran, 1938);

Travels of a Republican Radical in Search of Hot Water (Harmondsworth, U.K.: Penguin, 1939);

The Fate of Homo Sapiens: An Unemotional Statement of

*the Things That Are Happening to Him Now, and
of the Immediate Possibilities Confronting Him*
(London: Secker & Warburg, 1939); republished as *The Fate of Man: An Unemotional
Statement of The Things That Are Happening to
Him Now, and of the Immediate Possibilities Confronting Him* (New York: Alliance, 1939);

The Holy Terror (London: Joseph, 1939; New York:
Simon & Schuster, 1939);

Babes in the Darkling Wood (London: Secker & Warburg, 1940; New York: Alliance, 1940);

*The New World Order: Whether It Is Attainable, How It
Can Be Attained, and What Sort of World a World
at Peace Will Have to Be* (London: Secker &
Warburg, 1940; New York: Knopf, 1940);

The Rights of Man; or, What Are We Fighting For?
(Harmondsworth, U.K. & New York: Penguin, 1940);

*The Common Sense of War and Peace: World Revolution
or War Unending?* (Harmondsworth, U.K. &
New York: Penguin, 1940);

All Aboard for Ararat (London: Secker & Warburg,
1940; New York: Alliance, 1941);

Two Hemispheres or One World? (N.p., 1940);

*Guide to the New World: A Handbook of Constructive
World Revolution* (London: Gollancz, 1941);

You Can't Be Too Careful: A Sample of Life 1901-1951
(London: Secker & Warburg, 1941; New
York: Putnam's, 1942);

*The Outlook for Homo Sapiens: An Amalgamation and
Modernization of Two Books,* The Fate of Homo
Sapiens *and* The New World Order, *Published
Severally in 1939 and 1940* (London: Secker &
Warburg, 1942);

*Modern Russian and English Revolutionaries: A Frank
Exchange of Ideas between Commander Lev Us-
pensky, Soviet Writer, and H. G. Wells* (London:
Privately printed, 1942);

Science and the World-Mind (London: New Europe,
1942);

*Phoenix: A Summary of the Inescapable Conditions of
World Reorganization* (London: Secker & Warburg, 1942);

*A Thesis on the Quality of Illusion in the Continuity of
Individual Life of the Higher Metazoa, with Par-
ticular Reference to the Species Homo Sapiens*
(London: Privately printed, 1942);

*The Conquest of Time, by H. G. Wells: Written to Replace
His* First and Last Things (London: Watts,
1942);

The New Rights of Man (Girard, Kans.: Haldeman-
Julius, 1942);

*Crux Ansata: An Indictment of the Roman Catholic
Church* (Harmondsworth, U.K. & New York:
Penguin, 1943);

The Mosley Outrage (London: Daily Worker, 1943);

*'42 to '44: A Contemporary Memoir upon Human Be-
haviour during the Crisis of the World Revolution*
(London: Secker & Warburg, 1944);

*Reshaping Man's Heritage: Biology in the Service of
Man,* by Wells, J. S. Huxley, and J. B. S. Haldane (London: Allen & Unwin, 1944);

The Happy Turning: A Dream of Life (London:
Heinemann, 1945); with *Mind at the End of Its
Tether* (New York: Didier, 1946);

Mind at the End of Its Tether (London: Heinemann,
1945); with *The Happy Turning* (New York:
Didier, 1946);

The Desert Daisy, edited by Gordon N. Ray (Urbana,
Ill.: Beta Phi Mu, 1957);

Hoopdriver's Holiday, edited by Michael Timko (West
Lafayette, Ind.: Purdue University Press,
1964);

The Wealth of Mr. Waddy: A Novel, edited by Harris
Wilson (Carbondale: Southern Illinois University Press, 1969; London: Feffer & Simons,
1969);

*H. G. Wells: Early Writings in Science and Science Fic-
tion,* edited by Robert M. Philmus and David Y.
Hughes (Berkeley & London: University of
California Press, 1975);

H. G. Wells's Literary Criticism, edited by Patrick Parrinder and Philmus (Brighton, Sussex: Har-
vester, 1980; Totowa, N.J.: Barnes & Noble,
1980);

H. G. Wells in Love, edited by G. P. Wells (London &
Boston: Faber & Faber, 1984).

OTHER: Catherine Wells, *The Book of Catherine
Wells,* edited by Wells (London: Chatto &
Windus, 1928; Garden City: Doubleday,
1928).

H. G. Wells's earlier works of science fiction
have retained their popularity for nearly a century.
In recent years they have also won academic regard
for integrating the fantastic with the realistic to
produce challenging alien perspectives. The influence of Wells's science fiction—virtually inescapable for writers who specialize in the *genre*—
extends to such distinguished authors as Yevgeny
Zamyatin, George Orwell, Jorge Luis Borges, and
William Golding. Wells's two outstanding comic
novels possess a vitality and social awareness akin to
those of Dickens. His social novels, the most substantial of which is *Tono-Bungay* (1908), offer an

Wells's parents, Joseph and Sarah Wells

ambitious account of their period, incorporating many imaginative and journalistic insights. In addition to works of fiction, he produced a large number of discursive books, pamphlets, and articles: notably, the best-selling *Outline of History* (1919-1920). He has been described as the most serious of the popular writers and the most popular of the serious writers of his time.

Wells's lower middle-class origin and scientific training made him unique among contemporary novelists, enabling him to introduce new subject matters into English fiction. As a personality, he attracted additional attention for his dynamism, his adventurous love life, and his controversial repudiations of aesthetic principles. He has remained in the popular mind, above all, through his slightly inflated reputation as a forecaster of scientific developments and human destiny. Wells is an author whose achievement is as impossible to ignore as it is difficult to fit into readily assessed categories.

Herbert George Wells began life in Bromley, Kent, as the youngest son of a former lady's maid and a former gardener. His father had turned storekeeper and professional cricketer, but still found it difficult to support his family. When Mrs.

Wells took the post of housekeeper at a country house in Sussex in 1880, she decided that thirteen-year-old Bertie should also go out to work. The boy, who had been a promising pupil, found himself relegated to menial jobs.

Drudgery was relieved by visits to his mother's work place. Throughout Wells's formative years, the occasional freedom to roam the house and grounds of Up Park deeply stimulated his imagination. In the library there he explored books by Swift, Voltaire, Johnson, Paine, and Plato which encouraged him to look critically at society and which eventually became models for his own writings. Plato's *Republic* merged in his mind with the orderly world of Up Park to suggest a utopia which might be realized through the growth of science and socialism. Such an ideal appeared to offer a plausible secular alternative to heaven as a goal capable of conferring meaning and coherence on his life. Wells rebelled early against his mother's piety and maintained a lifelong hostility to Christianity as the official mythology of a social order which had denied him education and almost condemned him to dispense dry goods for his livelihood.

Wells's chance of escape from this fate came in

Wells at about age ten

biology by Wells appeared in 1893; one of these was a collaboration. In the same year another hemorrhage brought him close to death.

With the determination of one who feared he had little time to live, the twenty-seven-year-old Wells decided to remake his life. Shortly after moving to Sutton, Surrey, he ran off with one of his students, Catherine Robbins. They set up home near Euston in north London, and Wells embarked on a new career as a professional writer. Like his earlier threat of suicide, this fresh beginning helped confirm his faith in the revolutionary power of will, which he was later to proclaim in *The History of Mr. Polly* (1910): "If the world does not please you, *you can change it.*"

During 1894 he exchanged educational journalism for book reviews; speculative articles on science; and light essays, the best of which were collected as *Certain Personal Matters* (1897). More important, he started to produce distinctive short stories which have remained in print ever since.

Just as science was exploding the nineteenth-century frames of reference which had once bound

1882 when, nearing sixteen years of age, he was offered a student assistantship at Midhurst Grammar School, Sussex. After arguments with his parents and a threat of suicide, he succeeded in having his apprenticeship to the Southsea Drapery Emporium canceled. From his new post he unexpectedly obtained a scholarship to the Normal School of Science in South Kensington, London (now Imperial College, part of London University), where he attended the lectures of Darwin's champion, T. H. Huxley. Wells neglected the study of science after a successful first year and turned in preference to the role of "philosophical desperado." He read Blake and Carlyle, openly committed himself to socialism, and involved himself in the college's magazine and debating society.

After leaving college in 1887 he taught for a time at private schools in Wales and London, but suffered recurrent lung hemorrhages; he also received a damaged kidney when he was kicked in the back while refereeing a football game at the school in Wales. The belated acquisition of his degree in 1890 enabled him to become a correspondence-course tutor in biology. With this secure income, he married his cousin Isabel in 1891, settled in Wandsworth, southwest London, and expanded his career in educational journalism. Two textbooks of

Isabel Mary Wells, Wells's cousin, in 1886. She and Wells were married in 1891.

Amy Catherine Robbins in 1893, two years before she became Wells's second wife

Wells, so in these stories fantastic events erupt into the commonplace Victorian world and demonstrate the unrecognized precariousness of that world. Inventions threaten to radically disrupt human existence in "The New Accelerator" and "The Land Ironclads"; hostile creatures emerge from the sea or jungle in "The Sea Raiders" and "The Empire of the Ants"; people's perceptions suddenly come adrift from their bodies in "Under the Knife" and "The Remarkable Case of Davidson's Eyes"; man-made objects are mistaken for gods and even receive human sacrifice in "Jimmy Goggles, the God" and "The Lord of the Dynamos." Wells wrote the majority of these stories as pure entertainment, but through their imaginative exuberance an underlying conviction emerges that, as science reveals more and more of reality, our world and our ways of thinking will be radically transformed.

While temporarily resident in Sevenoaks, Kent, during the later part of 1894, Wells composed his first substantial fiction, *The Time Machine*. This novella recounts the claim of an anonymous inventor to have traveled into the distant future. He reaches the goal that nineteenth-century progress is tending toward only to find that, in the absence of any further challenge to initiative, its inhabitants

have devolved into puny and unintelligent creatures known as Eloi. Worse still, these descendants of the ruling class have now become the meat supply of the descendants of the working class, the subterranean Morlocks. After he and an Eloi girl, Weena, have various adventures which end with her death, the Time Traveller presses on to a period when all trace of human life has been annihilated by the meaningless processes of nature. None of the Time Traveller's friends believe his accounts, and he sets off on a further voyage in time, from which he does not reappear. The primary appeal of the book lies in a persuasive unfolding of fantastic events, rendered in some of Wells's most careful prose. The Time Traveller is the prototypical Wellsian hero, who defies established notions of reality for a greater one revealed through science. His secular prophecies parody both Christian and Marxist beliefs, while satirizing the nature and aims of industrial civilization. The Time Traveller's adventures implicitly endorse the view of T. H. Huxley that man's ethical progress must be limited and finally destroyed by an indifferent cosmic process, with which man must nonetheless continue to battle. Critics now regard *The Time Machine* as Wells's most flawless and quintessential work. It was received

Wells about 1895, the year The Time Machine *was published (Frank Wells)*

Yvette Mimieux as Weena and Rod Taylor as the Time Traveller in a scene from the 1960 film version of Wells's
The Time Machine *(M-G-M)*

favorably on its publication in 1895, selling 6,000 copies in five months. It was filmed by George Pal in 1960 with Rod Taylor as the Time Traveller and Yvette Mimieux as a rather more feminine Weena than the one described in the book.

The Wonderful Visit (1895), written on Wells's return to London, is a more openly satirical tale of similar brevity. A vicar accidentally shoots down an angel. The angel, a naive refugee from a fourth-dimensional Land of Dreams, at first struggles to understand natural suffering and social injustice, but is himself contaminated by human emotions, and eventually dies for love. Although it is a slight production beside the originality and imaginative power of *The Time Machine,* this comic fable mocks both worldliness and sentimentality with an engaging double irony.

Wells's second science-fiction classic, *The Island of Dr. Moreau* (1896), describes the adventures, while marooned on a tropical island, of Edward Prendick, a former student of T. H. Huxley. The island's owner, Moreau, is working on a series of gruesomely unsuccessful attempts to turn beasts into people by surgery. Moreau is both a misguided

exponent of progress and a personification of natural evolution. His doctrines challenge the traditional view of man as a distinct creation; his actions burlesque Christian mythology. The Beast People he has created worship him in a vain attempt to appease his wrath and preserve their unstable human qualities. Eventually Moreau and his assistant Montgomery are killed and the Beast People degenerate. Prendick escapes to civilization, only to find that he can no longer distinguish between the human beings he finds there and Moreau's travesties. The book grotesquely illustrates Huxley's observation that nature tends always to subvert man's order, from without and from within. *The Island of Dr. Moreau* is now regarded as one of Wells's finest works, but few contemporary reviewers discerned the serious implications beneath its horror. It has never quite achieved the degree of fame enjoyed by Wells's other early scientific romances. It has been filmed twice: first in 1932 as *The Island of Lost Souls,* with Charles Laughton as Moreau; and in 1977, under its original title, with Burt Lancaster as the mad scientist.

In 1895 Wells and Isabel were divorced, and

Claude Rains as Dr. Griffin, the title character in the 1933 film version of Wells's The Invisible Man *(Universal Pictures)*

Wells married Catherine (later to be known by the nickname Jane). The couple moved to Woking, Surrey, where Wells wrote his first comic novel, *The Wheels of Chance* (1896). Hoopdriver, a draper's apprentice, lacking the good fortune of Wells to escape the servile life, is able to live fully only in his fantasies. On a cycling vacation, he chances to rescue Jessie Milton, a girl of emancipated views, from her unscrupulous companion, Bechamel. He enjoys her friendship and temporarily becomes the spirited figure he has longed to be, but in due course has to return to the repressive life of the drapery. Less obviously than the Eloi, the Morlocks, and the Beast People, Hoopdriver is a victim of natural and social forces which humanity has failed to master. The book can still be read with pleasure, although it lacks the assurance of Wells's later comic novels.

The Invisible Man (1897) brings together comedy and science fiction. An outcast scientist who has made himself invisible disrupts the quiet village of Iping. After being deserted by his highly reluctant assistant, a tramp named Marvel, he is shot; he takes refuge in the house of Dr. Kemp, to whom he reveals himself as a former colleague named Griffin.

He plans to terrorize the nation, but Kemp betrays him, and he is finally killed. Although the book implicitly questions whether scientific knowledge and the power it brings are ultimately compatible with human sympathy, it is a less complex, more melodramatic work than the two earlier scientific romances. It is an absorbing narrative, however, and has remained a favorite with readers. The 1933 motion picture version, directed by James Whale and starring Claude Rains—whose face is never seen until the last scene, after he has been killed—as Griffin, is a minor film classic.

The most celebrated of all Wells's ventures into science fiction is *The War of the Worlds* (1898), the history of a Martian invasion. The action is located in actual places in southern England and is developed with remarkably persuasive attention to detail. Embedded in the vivid sequence of events, perhaps a little too unobtrusively, is a sustained assault on human self-regard. Wells repeatedly compares the Martians' brutal treatment of their victims to civilized man's treatment of animals and supposedly inferior races. The overdeveloped brains, lack of emotions, and artificial bodies of the

Martian spaceships on the attack in a scene from the 1953 film version of Wells's The War of the Worlds
(Paramount Pictures Corporation)

Martians parody the characteristics of modern man and suggest his evolutionary destiny. Having overcome the human race with ease, the Martians are fortuitously killed by bacteria, against which they possess no resistance. In the cosmic perspective which the Martians' presence opens up, man seems impotent, fate arbitrary, good and evil relative. The book is slightly marred by a clumsily contrived husband-and-wife reunion at its conclusion, but otherwise deserves its reputation as one of Wells's most gripping and imaginative creations. The updated, realistic radio dramatization of *The War of the Worlds* by Orson Welles's Mercury Theater on Halloween, 1938—in which the Martians land in New Jersey instead of suburban London—threw many listeners into a panic. The novel was updated again for the George Pal movie version in 1953, which had spectacular special effects for that time.

The War of the Worlds marks the end of the first, most satisfactory phase of Wells's literary career. With his move, late in 1897, to a larger house in Worcester Park, Surrey, where he could exercise his remarkable talent for entertaining guests, Wells began trying to live up to what he saw as his responsibilities as a public figure. His fiction shows an increased concern to supply positive conclusions for the issues it raises.

By the time he moved, Wells was already working on *When the Sleeper Wakes* (1899). In this, the first scientific romance of his second phase, a nineteenth-century radical who has fallen into a coma wakens after two centuries to find that the actions of the stock market have made him the owner of the world. This future seems to be a stage in the development of the nightmarish world depicted in *The Time Machine*. Unlike the Time Traveller, however, the Sleeper, Graham, has the opportunity to inspire and direct a revolution against the constricting social categories which sustain waste and exploitation. The book fails because, unable to furnish Graham with a coherent vision of an alternative society, Wells resorts to crude messianic fantasy. Graham's death in an aerial battle against the forces of the tyrant Ostrog evades the difficulties of formulating an explicit conclusion. *When the Sleeper Wakes* is more notable for its influence on later narratives, such as Orwell's *1984* (1949), than in its own right. Recognizing some deficiency, Wells revised it in 1910 as *The Sleeper Awakes,* but without improving it. The story line remains one of Wells's best-known to the general public, but neither version of the book has won the admiration of critics.

Tales of Space and Time (1899), Wells's most ambitious collection of shorter fiction, is more impressive. The future society of *When the Sleeper Wakes* is again depicted in "A Story of the Days to Come"; it is cleverly juxtaposed to the life of the past through "A Story of the Stone Age," although to less final effect than might have been hoped. "The Man Who Could Work Miracles" is one of Wells's most engaging comic tales: a contemporary variation on the Midas theme, it describes the problems which ensue when a store assistant, Fotheringay, suddenly acquires omnipotence. In the haunting tale of "The Crystal Egg" a storekeeper named Cave withdraws from business pressures and his scolding family to peer at the landscape of Mars, visible to him in a mysterious crystal. Perhaps the most remarkable of all Wells's short stories, however, is "The Star." A wandering planet passing through the solar system kills millions and alters the geography of the earth. Wells vividly depicts the catastrophe by cutting

Wells's friend, the novelist George Gissing, in 1901

from one particular experience to another, building up a global vision adequate to the scale of the action.

Ever resistant to classification, Wells was tiring of his reputation as a writer of scientific romances by the time this collection appeared. His thoughts had already turned to the realistic novel when he moved for health reasons to Sandgate, on the Kentish coast, in September 1898. He had already made literary friendships with Arnold Bennett and George Gissing; in Sandgate he became friendly with several writers who were his neighbors—in particular, Henry James and Joseph Conrad, both of whose work he had singled out for praise when reviewing novels. He also met and felt a strong affinity for two visitors from the United States, William James and Stephen Crane.

In Sandgate, Wells finished *Love and Mr. Lewisham* (1900), a novel which plainly draws on his own experiences. George Lewisham is an impoverished student at the Normal School of Science who has delivered an enthusiastic lecture on socialism to the college debating society. Love for Ethel Henderson, the stepdaughter of a fraudulent medium, distracts him from his studies. After he impetuously marries Ethel, her conventional outlook and their increasing need for money cause him to relinquish his long-standing ambition of contributing to scientific and political progress. Wells—surprisingly, in view of his own career— presents this resignation as a victory for maturity. Yet he also leaves no doubt that it entails submission to an unjust social order. In effect, Lewisham is Wells as he might have been if he had stayed with Isabel. The rogue medium, Chaffery, who abandons his wife, seems to represent Wells's fear of what he might yet become if he lost his faith in utopia: a high-spirited maker of fictions who sees through the collective beliefs on which social reality depends, only to manipulate them purely selfishly. Like most of Wells's realistic novels, *Love and Mr. Lewisham* has gained respect rather than detailed attention from critics. It is impaired by the heavy-handed tone Wells employs, but is otherwise successful in combining a conventional love story with autobiographical material.

Wells returned to the scientific romance with *The First Men in the Moon* (1901), which contains a number of highly memorable passages but does not achieve the imaginative unity of his early science fiction. It begins as a comic novel, with Bedford, an opportunistic bankrupt, befriending the eccentric scientist Cavor. The mood shifts to one of wonder as they employ a gravity-repelling substance to fly to the moon in a sphere. Under the lunar surface they discover the civilization of the insectlike Selenites, which furnishes Wells an opportunity for social satire. The Selenites' way of life parodies our own by its excessive specialization of labor, but contrasts with ours in having achieved unity and rationality. Bedford escapes to Earth, where his account of his adventures is supplemented by fragmentary radio messages from the doomed Cavor. The implicit suggestion that our own society may develop in ways comparable to the Selenites' indicates Wells's increasing preoccupation at the turn of the century with the potential character of twentieth-century life. *The First Men in the Moon* was adapted for the screen twice: first in a silent version in 1919, and again in 1964.

By December 1900, when he moved into Spade House, Sandgate—designed for him by C. F. A. Voysey—Wells was a firmly established writer. Some of his works had already been translated into French and Italian. He decided to offer his growing public a nonfictional expression of his ideas in a volume of speculations on man's future. The result, *Anticipations* (1901), sold as well as a novel in Britain and was keenly received in France, Germany, and Italy. Much of the book now seems naive, and there are places where its sweeping proposals become uncomfortably fascistic. It does, however, put forward an idea which was to inform nearly all of Wells's later work: that the growth of communication and transport facilities, which lies behind modern social tensions and conflicts, might in the longer term, under the direction of a technocratic elite, make possible a just, efficient world order. Encouraged by public interest, Wells began to produce further volumes of future-oriented social comment—*The Discovery of the Future* (1902), *Mankind in the Making* (1903), and *New Worlds for Old* (1908)—plus numerous pamphlets and articles, the best of which he collected as *An Englishman Looks at the World* (1914), which was republished in the United States as *Social Forces in England and America*. At this stage Wells regarded such work as an occasional and temporary diversion from fiction. Only at the time of the Great War did it come to supplant fiction as his main literary occupation.

In conjunction with his increasing output of social comment, he took on himself a more active involvement in public affairs. He became a borough magistrate. In 1903 he joined the socialist Fabian Society, two of whose leading members, George Bernard Shaw and Graham Wallas, were already friends of his. *The Sea Lady* (1902), an inferior fantasy about the fatal love of the politician Harry Chatteris for a mermaid, reflects a sense of conflict between political commitment and the world of intuition and imagination. This conflict also informs two of Wells's best short stories: "The Country of the Blind" (1904), in which Nunez, a sighted man, is rejected as ruler by a blind race in a South American valley; and "The Door in the Wall" (1906), in which a government minister, Wallace, is haunted and destroyed by a vision from his childhood.

Wells wished to harness his literary talent to his new political preoccupations; but he found this extremely difficult, since his imagination was essentially subversive and concerned with the particular, while his political goal was general and authoritarian. *The Food of the Gods* (1904) attempts unsuccessfully to symbolize the power of science—initially disruptive, finally therapeutic—through a growth-inducing drug called Herakleophorbia. The enlarged wild creatures in the first part of the book are convincingly frightening, but the race of giant children in the second part, intended to be heroic symbols of mankind's future, seem both pitiful and sinister.

A Modern Utopia (1905) tries to overcome the conflict by an experiment in literary form, which is ultimately indebted to Plato's dialogues. The narrator begins by considering abstract ideas about utopia, yet also takes on the role of a powerless outsider suddenly transported to an ideal world, whose features he is struggling with limited success to comprehend. He is accompanied by a conventionally minded botanist, who refuses to endorse his idealism and finally dispels the utopian vision. This shifting, inconsistent framework allows a measure of uncertainty and openness to offset the book's totalitarian bias, but the final effect is evasive rather than genuinely complex. The foregrounding of skeptical, liberal attitudes does not fundamentally alter the nature of the Platonic, one-party state envisaged, with its ruling elite, the Samurai. *A Modern Utopia* is a fascinating document for understanding Wells, and occupies a significant place in the history of literary utopias, but few read it now for political enlightenment or for pleasure.

This could certainly not be said of the other book Wells published in 1905. *Kipps* remains one of the best loved of Edwardian novels. The book traces the career of Artie Kipps through a playful childhood, an apprenticeship in a drapery, and the sudden liberation which follows an inheritance of £26,000. Kipps's clumsy attempts to adapt to the demands of ruling-class custom under the instruction of the earnest Chester Coote, together with his ill-advised engagement to Helen Walsingham, who had formerly patronized him as a pupil in her wood-carving class, satirize contemporary social values. Abandoning pretension by stages, Kipps finds true happiness with his childhood sweetheart, Ann Pornick; and after losing much of his fortune, he settles down as a storekeeper. Wells takes the opportunity to make general social comments, but minimizes their disruptive effect by using two minor characters as mouthpieces: Ann's socialist brother Sid and his lodger, the thwarted and consumptive revolutionary Masterman. A more immediate challenge to the constrictions of society is offered by Harry Chitterlow, an actor-dramatist whose overflowing vitality is associated with rule-breaking and intoxication. Wells succeeds in persuading readers to identify with an unprecedentedly lower-class character, but does not always avoid reducing Kipps to a mere comic object. Nor was Wells able to devise a framework which would thoroughly integrate the liberation of Kipps with the plight of society as a whole. Nonetheless, the book is a remarkable achievement: a rags-to-riches romance, structurally modified to accord with Wells's experience and native skepticism, and told

with great verve and invention. *Kipps* was a commercial success, selling 12,000 copies in the first two months of its publication. It has been filmed three times; in a silent version in 1922; in a sound version directed by Carol Reed and starring Michael Redgrave as Kipps in 1941; and as a musical, *Half a Sixpence,* in 1967.

Wells's work had by this time appeared in eight European languages; it was especially popular in Russia, where his fiction seems to have been translated directly from serialization in British periodicals. Wells arranged for his next novel to be simultaneously published in English, French, German, Italian, and Dutch. The first part of *In the Days of the Comet* (1906), narrated by a young clerk, Willy Leadford, presents conflicts between individuals, social classes, and nations. The second half is a romance in which all of these conflicts are overcome when a comet discharges a sanity-inducing gas into the Earth's atmosphere. Willy and his high-born rival Edward Verrall agree to share the love of Nettie Stuart, an unorthodox relationship that caused much controversy when the book appeared. The novel is more successful than *The Food of the Gods* because the realistic and fantastic elements are not

Tommy Steele as Artie Kipps in a scene from Half a Sixpence, *the 1967 musical film based on Wells's novel* Kipps
(Paramount Pictures Corporation)

allowed to conflict so openly; but again Wells's metaphor is inadequate to sustain the burden placed on it, which tends only to discredit his vision of apocalyptic change.

In early 1906 Wells made a two-month visit to the United States, where he interviewed Theodore Roosevelt and befriended the exiled Russian author Maxim Gorki. *The Future in America* (1906), some of which was written before his departure, records his hopes and fears not only for the U.S.A. but for the "creative mind of man" in general. The tour gave the Fabian Society a rest from Wells's prolonged attempt to convert it into a mass movement for social revolution. Balked at the end of the year, he gradually withdrew from Fabian activities. However, some lectures delivered to Fabian students at Cambridge in the fall of 1907 did become the basis of Wells's *First and Last Things: A Confession of Faith and Rule of Life* (1908), a compact statement of his fundamental beliefs.

It was during 1907 also that Wells wrote *The War in the Air* (1908), his only scientific romance to combine tendentiousness and artistic success. It follows the adventures of Bert Smallways, a former bicycle dealer who is accidentally carried from Britain to Germany in a balloon. Briefly mistaken for the inventor of a coveted new flying machine, Bert is taken to the United States aboard an invading German airship fleet. The Chinese and Japanese intervene in the conflict, and soon a world war and the collapse of industrial civilization are underway. After shooting the German leader, Prince Karl Albert, at Niagara Falls, Bert makes his way back to Britain and is reunited with his sweetheart, Edna. As a witness to key events, Bert provides a subjective view to which Wells is able to add clarification and polemic, balancing the particular and the general as he criticizes the Edwardian arms race and its likely outcome. The book depicts global warfare and aerial bombardment with remarkable foresight, but also repays reading as a highly enjoyable adventure story. Critics have tended to ignore it, since it does not fit the obvious pattern "early scientific romances good, later ones bad," but it has continued to attract readers.

In the summer of 1908 Wells was involved in the launching of the *English Review,* which was to include among its contributors such diverse writers as Thomas Hardy and D. H. Lawrence. Its opening numbers serialized Wells's most determined effort to produce a serious novel, *Tono-Bungay* (1908). The novel is narrated by George Ponderevo, whose early life is modeled on Wells's. George's Up Park is a country house called Bladesover. To George,

Bladesover represents the decayed traditional order, for which some replacement must soon be found if social fragmentation and unenlightened commercialism are not to undermine civilization. Despite his ideals, George agrees to quit college to assist his uncle Edward in the marketing of Tono-Bungay, a worthless patent medicine. Its enormous commercial success reveals the inadequacies of contemporary society, an unhealthy body politic whose members tend to be in poor physical condition, anxious, and ill-educated. George feels he is himself in such a state after the breakup of his marriage. He is unable to accept the artistic detachment of his friend Ewart and seeks an alternative, more authentic order. At times he appears to glimpse one through the scientific truth and personal integrity which his aeronautical researches produce. Even these are called into question, however, by a radioactive mineral, quap, which subverts the laws of physics and mysteriously causes George to commit murder. Eventually the Ponderevos' fraudulent business empire collapses, Edward dies in squalor, and George, deserted by his aristocratic lover Beatrice Normandy, is left to reflect on the significance of his life. In a final attempt to affirm some transcendent ideal, the precise implications of which remain controversial, George builds and tests a destroyer. Of all Wells's writings, *Tono-Bungay* has provoked the most critical debate. The consensus of opinion is that the book ultimately fails to supply an adequate perspective for its abundant and intractable subject matter, but is such a resourceful performance that it must nonetheless be reckoned a modern classic.

Wells, with his wife's knowledge and acquiescence, had enjoyed casual affairs with women for many years. In early 1909 an unusually serious relationship with Amber Reeves, a young Fabian, culminated in her pregnancy and a brief elopement to France. Wells and Amber eventually agreed to part, although Amber was later to be virtual coauthor of Wells's *The Work, Wealth and Happiness of Mankind* (1931). Wells, Jane, and their two sons, George Philip ("Gip") and Frank, moved to West Hampstead, London, amid much controversy. People were scandalized less by Wells's adultery, which was unknown to the public at large, than by his latest novel, *Ann Veronica* (1909), which draws on his relationships both with Jane and Amber. Young Ann Veronica Stanley fights for her personal independence, becomes involved with militant feminists, and successfully courts a married biology teacher, Godwin Capes. Her alleged immorality led to a wave of criticism of Wells and caused many libraries to ban the novel, but for the same reason the book achieved unexpectedly high sales. Apart from a clumsily evasive and sentimental conclusion, *Ann Veronica* is an accomplished minor novel. Continued interest in it largely derives from its historical significance as an index of women's changing place in society.

Amid all the turmoil of this period, Wells somehow found time to compose his comic masterpiece, *The History of Mr. Polly*. Alfred Polly, an insolvent storekeeper, reviews his life, which after occasional early joys has dwindled to a quarrelsome marriage and a failed career. He decides to kill himself and burn down his store, disguising the two crimes as a single accident so that his wife, Miriam, will receive the insurance money. Instead, he turns the aimless life of Fishbourne into a comic chaos and for rescuing an old lady from the mysterious blaze becomes a public hero. This unaccustomed success rouses him from despair, and he abandons his old life for the freedom of the road. After defending the landlady of the Potwell Inn from her delinquent nephew Jim in a series of slapstick battles, he at last finds a congenial home there. With his cheerful mispronunciation of words and innocent yearning for a richer life, Mr. Polly is Wells's most memorable and vital character. The book's appeal comes from Wells's success in transforming a realistic world into a gratifying one of romance without denying the inevitability of conflict, suffering, and individual limitation. His attempts to construe Polly as a socially typical figure are forced, but sufficiently marginal that they do not interfere with the book's imaginative unity. Although *The History of Mr. Polly* received little praise from reviewers, it is now recognized as one of Wells's finest achievements. It was adapted for a 1949 film directed by Anthony Pellisier and starring John Mills as Polly.

The scandal surrounding *Ann Veronica* made it difficult for Wells to find a British publisher for *The New Machiavelli* (1910). Its narrator, a politician named Richard Remington, traces the conflict between idealism and passion which has led him to abandon both his wife Margaret and his political ambition in favor of his mistress, Isabel Rivers. The book draws heavily on Wells's own experience for its plot and on his acquaintances for its characters. Oscar and Altiora Bailey, for instance, are caricatures of the Fabian leaders Sidney and Beatrice Webb. The autobiographical element gives the book vitality, and probably aided its sales (17,000 copies in three months), yet it is marred by lengthy passages of incoherent discussion and overidentification of author with narrator. Wells seems less concerned to create a character than to set up a public persona whose discursiveness can conceal the inconsistencies in his creator's thinking. Since the trend toward unproductive argument continues in Wells's subsequent works, *The New Machiavelli* may be taken to mark the end of the second phase of Wells's literary career and the beginning of his artistic decline.

In "The Scope of the Novel," a lecture of 1911, Wells suggests that fiction is valuable to a liberal society because it can probe received views and explore the moral dilemmas brought about by social change. He champions a capacious, discursive ideal of fiction in the tradition of Dickens, Sterne, and Rabelais, implicitly defying his friend Henry James's conception of the novel as a rigorous and critical presentation of an individual's moral consciousness. Wells turned down James's offer the following year of membership in the Academic Committee of the Royal Society of Literature; this refusal was consistent with his mission to challenge accepted beliefs and standards, but was also a sign that he was beginning to lose patience with the category of "literature" itself. Like George Ponderevo in *Tono-Bungay*, Wells seems to have felt guilty that he had abandoned science, and the idealism he associated with it, in order to create mere fiction. He repudiated Christianity, but retained a puritanical conscience which insisted that a worthwhile piece of writing should be a secularized prophecy, a contribution to the growing Mind of the Race.

Early in 1912 the Wells family took up residence at Easton Glebe, Essex, a Georgian house which proved a fine setting for frequent weekend parties. (Wells held on to the West Hampstead house as his town base until 1913, when it was replaced by a flat in Westminster.) The books he wrote during the Easton Glebe period are uneven and generally of limited artistic value. *Joan and Peter* (1918), *The Research Magnificent* (1915), *Marriage* (1912), *The Wife of Sir Isaac Harman* (1914), and *The Passionate Friends* (1913)—here listed in roughly descending order of merit—all depict central characters who seek a new, "Wellsian" outlook on life. Although the protagonists travel widely and undergo striking experiences, these are usually presented in a rather cursory fashion. Action is subordinate to long and poorly focused discussion. *The Undying Fire* (1919), closely modelled on the Book of Job, pursues this tendency still further.

The World Set Free (1914) is a vigorous but crude history of the future, distinguished by Wells's brilliant prediction of atomic warfare. *Little Wars*

Easton Glebe, the converted rectory in Essex where Wells lived after 1912 (Frank Wells)

(1913), an entertaining guide to war-gaming with models, stands apart from the main body of Wells's writings, but was seminal in its field and is still available in facsimile editions. *Bealby* (1915) is the most entertaining work of this period. In its subplot a Captain Douglas questions the established order through the application of science, while in the main plot young Arthur Bealby defiantly runs away from home and has lively adventures. Bealby's escapades recall Mr. Polly's, but lack an underlying theme to give them comparable significance. The tacit assumption that Bealby and Douglas are engaged in complementary rebellions is never substantiated.

Boon (1915) is a revealing collection of stories, jottings, dialogues, and drawings, supposedly written by George Boon and edited posthumously by Reginald Bliss (both fictitious characters). The book's subject is the social function of the author, examined in a playful, fragmentary way, and it is chiefly remembered for Wells's notorious criticism and parody of Henry James. Having virtually relinquished artistic ambition, Wells failed to establish in the book, or in his subsequent correspondence with the aggrieved and dying James, that he had earlier been practicing a variety of fiction distinct from James's. Instead, Wells categorized his own work as

journalism with some accidental artistic qualities, an affectation which has given valuable ammunition to his detractors. Wells's artistic apostasy never became total philistinism, as can be seen from his pioneering review in 1917 of James Joyce's *Portrait of the Artist as a Young Man*. Wells was able to approve of Joyce's novel as a radical challenge to the social consensus, even though that challenge took such a different form from his own and concerned a different kind of outsider.

The year 1914 was a memorable one for Wells. As a public figure he visited Russia; as a private man he gained a third son, Anthony, born to the writer Rebecca West on the day war with Germany broke out. To Wells, as one of his book titles proclaims, the eruption of international conflict seemed *The War That Will End War* (1914): a challenge that would tend to promote collectivization, solidarity, and social justice, preparing the way for a secure world order once the conflict ceased. His gradual disillusionment is charted in his last outstanding novel, *Mr. Britling Sees It Through* (1916), which under a thin disguise offers a portrait of life at Easton Glebe. Hugh Britling, a highly successful author, presides over a lively household in the Essex village of Matching's Easy, which the reader gradually explores through the eyes of an American visitor,

Wells about 1915 (Frank Wells)

a "telepherage" system to move supplies at the battlefront and, with the aid of Winston Churchill, sought unsuccessfully to have it implemented. During 1918 he was for a time in charge of the Policy Committee for Propaganda in Enemy Countries; but he resigned, impatient with British xenophobia and unsatisfactory war aims. He campaigned lengthily for a League of Nations to prevent new wars, only to ridicule the impotent assembly which finally emerged. After the war, in late 1919, he and his son Gip went to inspect the new Communist regime in Russia. While there, Wells argued with Lenin, befriended Pavlov, and addressed the Petersburg Soviet. The visit was recorded in a series of largely sympathetic newspaper articles, collected as *Russia in the Shadows* (1920).

The war had convinced Wells that history had become "a race between education and catastrophe." Unless militant nationalism was replaced by a global outlook, more world wars with increasingly destructive weapons would be bound to follow. To encourage the growth of cosmopolitanism, Wells produced his *Outline of History* (1919-1920), a supranational history of the world and mankind, written with the help of several distinguished ad-

Mr. Direck. At the outbreak of war Britling writes an optimistic pamphlet entitled "And Now War Ends," but as the conflict drags on he becomes increasingly critical of the Allies' conduct, abroad and at home. His spirit is nearly shattered by the deaths in battle of his son Hugh and the family's German tutor, Herr Heinrich. The book ends on a forced note of uplift as Britling composes a letter to Heinrich's parents proclaiming that their sons live on as part of God. Wells had often suggested that human culture amounted to an emergent collective mind, in an attempt to guarantee the integrity of his future utopia and to reconcile religious idealism with science. Now he personified the Mind of the Race in an effort to find meaning in individual suffering. *God, the Invisible King* (1917), a nonfictional treatment of these ideas, marks Wells's temporary desire to help create a new religion. The public was understandably bewildered by this departure, but they were moved by the novel's portrait of life on the home front. In Britain *Mr. Britling Sees It Through* was reprinted a dozen times in three months, and its popularity was almost as great in the United States.

Despite a chronic state of anxiety which was causing his hair to fall out, Wells maintained a variety of public activities throughout the war years, including a high output of journalism. He designed

Rebecca West with Anthony West, her son by Wells, in about 1916

Wells, Maxim Gorki, and their interpreter, Marie Budberg, on Wells's visit to Russia in 1920 (Frank Wells)

visors. He expected it to lose money, but in Britain alone the serial parts attained a printing of 100,000 copies. In Britain and the U.S.A. together, the completed work sold over two million volumes. Sales in translation around the world were enormous. Despite inevitable criticism of details, the book was praised by such eminent historians as H. A. L. Fisher, Arnold Toynbee, and Carl Becker. The compact version which followed two years later, *A Short History of the World* (1922), remains in print as a standard popular account.

In 1922 Wells joined the Labour party (for which he was unsuccessfully to stand for Parliament several times as a candidate for London University) and began to write a syndicated newspaper column, later published in book form as *A Year of Prophesying* (1924) and *The Way the World Is Going* (1928). In contrast to his shorter-term preoccupations, two minor works of fiction from this period, *Men Like Gods* (1923) and *The Dream* (1924), juxtapose our stubbornly unregenerate world with a remote utopia, located in another dimension in the first book and in the distant future in the second,

peopled by beautiful nudists with names like Sunray and Crystal.

Following the departure of Rebecca West for the United States in October 1923, Wells found a new mistress in Odette Keun and a new home at Grasse in the south of France, to which he moved in the fall of 1924. His most strenuous attempt to produce a substantial work of fiction while in this new residence was the three-volume *The World of William Clissold,* the longest novel published in 1926. Unfortunately, the book consists almost entirely of opinions on rather abstract issues, poorly coordinated by the framework of Clissold's autobiography. The novel received sharply dismissive reviews, including one from D. H. Lawrence, who contrasted it unfavorably with *Tono-Bungay.*

A novel Wells had written during a convalescence in Portugal shortly before moving to France gives evidence of continuing literary talent, however, and perhaps suggests some subconscious discomfort with the role of social prophet. *Christina Alberta's Father* (1925) tells of a retired laundry owner, Albert Preemby, who comes to believe himself the reincarnation of Sargon, King of Kings, charged to wipe out poverty, emancipate women, and abolish war. This mission, both heroic and absurd, leads to his imprisonment in an insane asylum. After being rescued, he is taught by the intellectual Wilfred Devizes that the only true King of Kings is the human race, whose collective potential must be released through educational and political reform. Devizes, not Preemby, is secretly the real father of Christina Alberta, a liberated young woman seeking a more meaningful life. This amusing but neglected work attempts to reconcile imaginative and intellectual rebellion in favor of the latter, but presents the former far more convincingly. Wells seems to admit this at the end, when Christina Alberta defers working for the collective good until she has fulfilled herself as an individual.

Mr. Blettsworthy on Rampole Island (1928) also tries to proceed from an imaginative criticism of the world to a supposedly rational program for its improvement, and again it is the imaginative part of the book which is much the more compelling. The sheltered Arnold Blettsworthy has a nervous breakdown after his first experience of injustice and immorality. He goes to sea to recuperate, but is taken prisoner by natives from Rampole Island, whose primitive culture parodies the hypocrisy and destructiveness of contemporary civilization. Eventually Blettsworthy realizes that the island is actually New York, which his distraught mind has disguised with hallucinations in order to protect itself from the horror of the modern world. In recent years several critics have recognized *Mr. Blettsworthy on Rampole Island* to be one of Wells's most accomplished minor works.

In October 1927 Jane died of cancer. Wells edited a collection of her stories and verse, with a sensitive introduction. The celebrity he continued to enjoy during these years is evident in invitations to lecture at the Sorbonne in 1927 and the Reichstag in 1929. During 1929 he moved back to London and took a flat near Baker Street. His major project of the period was a pair of encyclopedic works designed to expand the *Outline of History* into an educational trilogy: *The Science of Life* (1929-1930) on biology, written in collaboration with Julian Huxley and Gip Wells, and *The Work, Wealth and Happiness of Mankind* (1931) on economics. Although they were remarkable examples of intellectual synthesis and popularization, neither had the wide appeal of *The Outline of History*. Wells supplemented these histories of the past with a "history" of the future, *The Shape of Things to Come* (1933), which purports to

offer glimpses of a history as yet unwritten, revealed to one of Wells's friends in a series of dreams. Wells foresees a second world war in 1939, initiating the gradual collapse of civilization, which is only checked when a global dictatorship of airmen imposes a utopian world state.

By 1933 Wells had parted with Odette Keun, and Moura Budberg had succeeded her as the chief companion of his later years. Despite his age, Wells remained extremely active, not only as a lover but as a public figure. In 1934 he became international president of the PEN Clubs, which help to promote authors' freedom of expression; also, having developed a diabetic condition himself, he became founding president of the British Diabetic Association. He interviewed Franklin D. Roosevelt in May and Joseph Stalin in July, trying to persuade both men that they led state-capitalist societies of a potentially similar nature, where the true revolutionaries were the technical intelligentsia. While in the U.S.S.R. he was dismayed to discover his old friend Gorki supporting Stalin's suppression of birth control and freedom of expression, both of which Wells strongly advocated.

On return, he completed a masterful two-volume *Experiment in Autobiography* (1934), his last substantial contribution to literature. Wells describes his early life with candor and perceptiveness, and gives a vigorous account of his ideas. (A third volume, concerning his love life, was deferred for posthumous publication; it appeared in 1984.) Toward the end of 1934 he moved into his final home, 12A Hanover Terrace, at the edge of Regent's Park, London. He renumbered it 13, with characteristic scorn for superstition.

Wells had a long-standing interest in the cinema. In 1925 he had helped to found the Film Society; in 1928 he supplied the scenario for three silent shorts, *Bluebottles, The Tonic,* and *Daydreams,* directed by Ivor Montagu, which offered Charles Laughton his first screen roles. Now he wrote the script for what was to prove one of the most memorable British films of the 1930s, *Things to Come* (1936). Arthur Bliss furnished its musical score. At one time or another Le Corbusier, Gropius, Léger, and Moholy Nagy were brought to England to work on the artistic design, although most of their suggestions were finally rejected. Wells's script sadly coarsens his utopianism to the point of self-parody in a misguided attempt to simplify his ideas for a mass audience, but the film's impressive integration of images and music reputedly owed much to his intervention.

Throughout the 1930s he continued to produce books both fictional and nonfictional, most of which may be ignored. One novel, *The Bulpington of Blup* (1932), is of interest to students of Wells's development, since it tries to show that literary culture can pose a threat to self-knowledge and social progress, and to offer scientific culture as an alternative. The artistic Theodore Bulpington indulges in poses and fantasies until he irretrievably reduces himself to a ridiculous persona. His gradual self-destruction is contrasted with the constructive, scientific outlook of his childhood friends Margaret and Teddy Broxted. Bulpington is partly intended as a satirical caricature of Ford Madox Ford, but paradoxically he is also a successor to such earlier comic characters as Hoopdriver, Lewisham, and Preemby, with whose eccentricities the reader was expected to sympathize. Wells admits in the *Experiment in Autobiography* that even his own persona, that of an "originative intellectual worker," is a "pose" open to reassessment by others, so that the conflicts between fantasy and reality presented in *The Bulpington of Blup* and other books of this period are very much a simplification of Wells's considered views. A similar false polarization may be seen in *Apropos of Dolores* (1938), which some critics have claimed represents a resurgence of Wells's comic talent. The novel recasts Wells's quarrels with Odette Keun as a conflict between a progressive publisher, Stephen Wilbeck, and his malicious, reactionary wife Dolores, whom he eventually kills.

Wells made donations to various left-wing organizations in the 1930s, including the Communist Party's Unity Theatre. The growth of fascism increased his suspicion of any organization that could be considered reactionary, leading to outspoken attacks on the Roman Catholic church. In 1936 he became vice-president of the Abortion Law Reform Society. Wells's stand as a controversialist at this time is accurately indicated by the title of his 1939 book, *Travels of a Republican Radical in Search of Hot Water* (that is, of trouble), a collection of essays published after an Australian voyage on which his critical attitudes toward Zionism, the British monarchy, and Hitler all provoked hostility.

When World War II began, Wells once more sought to establish what kind of world the Allies intended to set up, which led to his involvement in the formulation of a doctrine of human rights. He wrote a "Penguin Special" on the subject, *The Rights of Man* (1940), and was a key figure behind *The Sankey Declaration of the Rights of Man* published in 1940.

Wells's literary talents were still not completely spent. *You Can't Be Too Careful* (1941) offers a final, negative portrait of a "little man," this time a small-minded, self-seeking reactionary, Edward Tewler, who demonstrates what a good citizen should not be. The parable *All Aboard for Ararat* (1940) includes some amusing dialogue between the writer Noah Lammock and Almighty God, who dispatches Noah in a new ark to escape the war.

At the age of seventy-six Wells began work on a D.Sc. thesis, arguing that humanity could only achieve mental coherence on a collective basis. The thesis was accepted by London University in 1943, but did not earn him a fellowship in the Royal Society, his final ambition. The mental texture of Wells's life in declining years is agreeably expressed in *The Happy Turning* (1945), a short book made up of reflections, reminiscences, and whimsical fantasies. That he proclaims the imminent end of human life in his last book, *Mind at the End of Its Tether* (1945), is often seized upon as an admission that his commitment to social change had been altogether ill-founded. This is a misleading interpretation. Wells never believed progress to be inevitable. Against the dark background of the interwar years, he cham-

Wells during the final year of his life ("Illustrated")

pioned it as a necessary goal, but his assessment of its actual likelihood swung between extremes of optimism and pessimism. These were irrationally related to the successes and failures of his own career. In the year of his death he painted a mural of evolution on a wall behind his house, placing beneath man the caption "Time to go." His last published article, in contrast, assumes a comparatively optimistic view of mankind's prospects.

Wells had always held that the desire to be remembered by posterity, whether through tombstones or works of literature, was unhealthy and, in the perspective of cosmic time, absurd. After his death in August 1946, his body was cremated and the ashes scattered over the sea off the south coast.

Van Wyck Brooks's acute introduction to Wells's writings, *The World of H. G. Wells* (1915), had appeared thirty-one years previously. No study of comparable seriousness was to appear for another fifteen years. During the intervening period, informed readers came to regard Wells as at best a peripheral figure, at worst a discredited one — although most of them remained familiar with his best fiction, which they had read in their youth. The reputation Wells had established for himself, as a hasty and obsessive writer, reiterating impractical ideas with little concern for literary elegance, inhibited appreciation of his earlier, more substantial writings.

Positive discussions of these did exist, but were occasional in nature and undeveloped. It was more common for critics to belittle or dismiss Wells. To Virginia Woolf in two essays of 1924, "Modern Fiction" and "Mr. Bennett and Mrs. Brown," Wells seemed the practitioner of a wholly external realism who failed to give his characters' inner life the kind of sensitive rendering the modern age (and Virginia Woolf) demanded. Even George Orwell, who recognized Wells to be one of his own formative influences, saw him as one who undervalued the importance of the irrational and traditional in human life, a deficiency which caused his work to be overconfident and superficial. When in 1948, in the widely read essay "Technique as Discovery," Mark Schorer pronounced Wells (along with Defoe and Lawrence) formally inadequate, and therefore deprived of necessary self-knowledge, it seemed that Wells had been classified as an inferior writer against objective criteria.

However, an obituary tribute by Jorge Luis Borges — "The First Wells" — reprinted in Parrinder's *H. G. Wells: The Critical Heritage* (1972) — had already opened the way for later revaluation by politely dismissing Wells the social thinker and singling out for praise Wells the creator of engrossing, disturbing fantasies. An article of 1957 by Wells's son Anthony West, reprinted in Bernard Bergonzi's *H. G. Wells: A Collection of Critical Essays* (1976), insists that this early Wells wrote with unflinching skepticism. West argues that the later commitment to utopianism was a comforting delusion which Wells imposed on himself at the cost of crippling his intelligence and artistic integrity. West's case is slightly overstated, in suggesting that Wells ever wholeheartedly adopted social pessimism or optimism. There was always a tension between the two outlooks, most clearly in the second phase of his career. However, the basic point West makes is now generally accepted: that Wells's most lasting literary achievement is the comparatively detached, open fiction he wrote up to the time of World War I.

The approach of Borges and West was endorsed by Bernard Bergonzi's major reassessment of Wells's scientific romances, *The Early H. G. Wells* (1961). Bergonzi challenges received views of Wells by placing these early writings in the context of the fin de siècle era and drawing attention to their symbolistic qualities. Since Bergonzi's study gave Wells academic respectability, works of criticism have steadily accumulated. The most important to date is Patrick Parrinder's *H. G. Wells* (1970), which examines all of Wells's most important works of fiction as expressions of alternating "hope and despair. . . . release and submission." Despite the constraints of being part of a publisher's series, Parrinder's book stands second only to Wells's autobiography as a source of insight into his fiction and thought.

The West-Bergonzi-Parrinder consensus has been supported by other studies, consolidated by many articles in the *Wellsian* (the annual journal of the H. G. Wells Society), and given an institutional basis by the establishment in 1981 of an important center for Wells Studies at the Polytechnic of North London.

Future criticism of Wells's work may bring new shifts of emphasis. Wells was certainly a pioneer in global, interdisciplinary, and future-oriented thought, and it may be that this aspect of his work has been taken too much for granted since his death. No matter how much this side of Wells is rehabilitated, it remains unlikely that the bulk of his discursive work will ever again be consulted except as historical documentation. Wells was undeniably an expert publicist, but as a thinker he relied too much on simplistic antitheses, such as "future versus past," "responsibility versus subjectivity," and "science versus politics or art." Because he was unable to resolve ambivalences or intellectual issues explicitly, the books where he was most in earnest are generally his worst. The writings Wells himself valued the most are uneven, incoherent, and carelessly phrased, faults which even *Tono-Bungay,* the finest of them, does not entirely avoid.

The books which do fullest justice to Wells's vision are those primarily intended as entertainments: the early scientific romances and the two comic novels, *Kipps* and *Mr. Polly.* To some readers, these books will seem slight, and it is true that they have little to offer those who seek verbal sophistication or profound characterization. Nonetheless, they have genuine merits which should not be undervalued. The cosmic despair and painful social change Wells experienced were transformed in his imagination into brisk, colourful narratives which, however chilling their implications, are first-rate entertainment, powered by the voice and indomitable personality of their author. Their appeal to a wide variety of readers, from professors to schoolboys, seems likely to endure for a long time—a development which, despite all his foresight in other fields, would probably have greatly surprised Wells himself.

Letters:

Henry James and H. G. Wells, edited by Leon Edel & Gordon N. Ray (Urbana: University of Illinois Press, 1958; London: Hart-Davis, 1958);

Arnold Bennett and H. G. Wells, edited by Harris Wilson (Urbana: University of Illinois Press, 1960; London: Hart-Davis, 1960);

George Gissing and H. G. Wells, edited by Royal A. Gettmann (Urbana: University of Illinois Press, 1961; London: Hart-Davis, 1961).

Bibliographies:

Geoffrey H. Wells, *The Works of H. G. Wells, 1887-1925: a Bibliography, Dictionary and Subject-Index* (London: Routledge, 1926);

H. G. Wells Society, *H. G. Wells: A Comprehensive Bibliography* (London: H. G. Wells Society, 1972);

J. R. Hammond, *H. G. Wells: An Annotated Bibliography* (New York & London: Garland, 1977).

Biographies:

Geoffrey West, *H. G. Wells: A Sketch for a Portrait* (London: Howe, 1930);

Vincent Brome, *H. G. Wells: A Biography* (London & New York: Longmans, Green, 1951);

Lovat Dickson, *H. G. Wells: His Turbulent Life and Times* (London: Macmillan, 1969; New York: Atheneum, 1969);

Norman and Jeanne MacKenzie, *The Time Traveller* (London: Weidenfeld & Nicolson, 1973; New York: Simon & Schuster, 1973);

Gordon N. Ray, *H. G. Wells & Rebecca West* (New Haven: Yale University Press, 1974);

Frank Wells, *H. G. Wells: A Pictorial Biography* (London: Jupiter, 1977);

J. R. Hammond, *H. G. Wells: Interviews and Recollections* (London: Macmillan, 1980);

Anthony West, *H. G. Wells: Aspects of a Life* (London: Hutchinson, 1984; New York: Random House, 1984).

References:

Bernard Bergonzi, *The Early H. G. Wells* (Manchester: Manchester University Press, 1961; Toronto: Toronto University Press, 1961);

Bergonzi, ed., *H. G. Wells: A Collection of Critical Essays* (Englewood Cliffs, N.J.: Prentice-Hall, 1976);

Van Wyck Brooks, *The World of H. G. Wells* (New York: Kennedy, 1915; London: Unwin, 1915);

J. R. Hammond, *An H. G. Wells Companion* (London: Macmillan, 1980);

Mark R. Hillegas, *The Future as Nightmare: H. G. Wells and the Anti-Utopians* (New York: Oxford University Press, 1967);

Samuel Hynes, *The Edwardian Turn of Mind* (Princeton: Princeton University Press, 1968; London: Oxford University Press, 1968);

Peter Kemp, *H. G. Wells and the Culminating Ape* (London: Macmillan, 1982; New York: St. Martin's Press, 1982);

David Lodge, "Assessing H. G. Wells" and "Utopia and Criticism," in his *The Novelist at the Crossroads* (London: Routledge & Kegan Paul, 1971; New York: Cornell University Press, 1971);

George Orwell, "Wells, Hitler and the World State" and "The Rediscovery of Europe," in his *Collected Essays, Journalism and Letters,* volume 2 (London: Secker & Warburg, 1968; New York: Harcourt, Brace, 1968);

Patrick Parrinder, *H. G. Wells* (Edinburgh: Oliver & Boyd, 1970; New York: Putnam's, 1977);

Parrinder, ed., *H. G. Wells: The Critical Heritage* (London & Boston: Routledge & Kegan Paul, 1972);

Gordon N. Ray, "H. G. Wells Tries to be a Novelist," in *Edwardians and Late Victorians,* edited by· Richard Ellmann (New York: Columbia University Press, 1960);

Darko Suvin and Robert M. Philmus, eds., *H. G. Wells and Modern Science Fiction* (Lewisburg, Pa.: Bucknell University Press, 1977; London: Associated University Presses, 1977);

W. Warren Wagar, *H. G. Wells and the World State* (New Haven: Yale University Press, 1961);

Alan Wykes, *H. G. Wells in the Cinema* (London: Jupiter, 1977).

Papers:

The Wells Archive (Wells's books, letters, and papers) is preserved in the Rare Book Room, University of Illinois Library, Urbana-Champaign. The most extensive collection of Wells material in Britain is that held by Bromley Central Library, London.

Oscar Wilde

Robert Boyle, S. J.
Marquette University

See also the Wilde entries in *DLB 10, Modern British Dramatists, 1900-1945,* and *DLB 19, British Poets, 1880-1914.*

BIRTH: Dublin, 16 October 1854, to Dr. William Robert Wills Wilde and Jane Francesca Elgee Wilde.

EDUCATION: Trinity College, Dublin, 1871-1874; B.A., Magdalen College, Oxford University, 1878.

MARRIAGE: 29 May 1884 to Constance Lloyd; children: Cyril, Vyvyan.

DEATH: Paris, 30 November 1900.

BOOKS: *Newdigate Prize Poem: Ravenna, Recited in the Theatre, Oxford 26 June 1878* (Oxford: Shrimpton, 1878);

Vera; or, The Nihilists: A Drama (London: Privately printed, 1880);

Poems (London: Bogue, 1881; Boston: Roberts, 1881);

The Duchess of Padua: A Tragedy of the XVI Century, Written in Paris in the XIX Century (New York: Privately printed, 1883);

The Happy Prince and Other Tales (London: Nutt, 1888; Boston: Roberts, 1888);

The Picture of Dorian Gray (London, New York & Melbourne: Ward, Lock, 1891);

Intentions (London: Osgood, McIlvaine, 1891; New York: Dodd, Mead, 1891);

Lord Arthur Savile's Crime & Other Stories (London:

Osgood, McIlvaine, 1891; New York: Dodd, Mead, 1891);

A House of Pomegranates (London: Osgood, McIlvaine, 1891; New York: Dodd, Mead, 1892);

Salomé: Drame en un Acte (Paris: Librairie de l'Art Indépendant/London: Mathews & Lane, Bodley Head, 1893); republished as *Salome: A Tragedy in One Act,* translated into English by Alfred Douglas (London: Mathews & Lane/ Boston: Copeland & Day, 1894);

Lady Windermere's Fan: A Play about a Good Woman (London: Mathews & Lane, Bodley Head, 1893);

The Sphinx (London: Mathews & Lane, Bodley Head/Boston: Copeland & Day, 1894);

A Woman of No Importance (London: Lane, Bodley Head, 1894);

The Soul of Man (London: Privately printed, 1895);

The Ballad of Reading Gaol, as C.3.3. (London: Smithers, 1898);

The Importance of Being Earnest: A Trivial Comedy for Serious People (London: Smithers, 1899);

An Ideal Husband (London: Smithers, 1899);

The Portrait of Mr. W. H. (Portland, Maine: Mosher, 1901); edited by Vyvyan Holland (London: Methuen, 1958);

De Profundis (London: Methuen, 1905; New York & London: Putnam's, 1905);

Impressions of America, edited by Stuart Mason (Sunderland, U.K.: Keystone Press, 1906);

First Collected Edition of the Works of Oscar Wilde, edited by Robert Ross (volumes 1-11, 13-14, London: Methuen, 1908; Boston: Luce, 1910;

volume 12, Paris: Carrington, 1908);

Second Collected Edition of the Works of Oscar Wilde,
edited by Ross (volumes 1-12, London: Methuen, 1909; volume 13, Paris: Carrington,
1910; volume 14, London: Lane, 1912);

The Suppressed Portion of "De Profundis" (New York:
Reynolds, 1913);

To M. B. J., edited by "Stuart Mason" (C. S. Millard)
(London: Privately printed, 1920);

For Love of the King: A Burmese Masque (London:
Methuen, 1923);

Complete Works of Oscar Wilde, edited by Vyvyan
Holland (London: Collins, 1948);

Essays of Oscar Wilde, edited by Hesketh Pearson
(London: Methuen, 1950);

Literary Criticism of Oscar Wilde, edited by Stanley
Weintraub (Lincoln: University of Nebraska
Press, 1968);

The Artist as Critic: Critical Writings of Oscar Wilde,
edited by Richard Ellmann (New York: Ran-
dom House, 1969).

Oscar Wilde brightened up, for the English-
speaking world at least, the stiff and somber final
years of the nineteenth century. Like the other
magnificent Irishmen, Joyce and Beckett, who
would cast brilliant light on the dark and bloody
twentieth century, he was born in Dublin. On 16
October 1854, the second son of Dr. William Robert
Wills Wilde and Jane Francesca Elgee Wilde
sounded his first human cry in No. 21, Westland
Row, and soon was christened Oscar Fingal
O'Flahertie Wilde; he later added "Wills" as a third
middle name.

Wilde's first name, which means "champion"
in Gaelic, celebrates two Oscars: the ancient Irish
warrior, son of the third-century warrior-poet Os-
sian, son of Fingal; and Oscar I, king of Sweden, a
patient of Dr. Wilde and godfather of Oscar Wilde.
Jane Wilde, under the pen name "Speranza," wrote
florid battle cries to advance the cause of Irish freedom. She followed the example of her granduncle,
the Reverend Charles Maturin, author of *Melmoth
the Wanderer* (1820), one of the longest, most perfer-
vid, morbidly imaginative, savagely anti-Catholic of
the Gothic novels; he also wrote, to his own Anglo-
Irish detriment, in favor of Irish freedom. As
Speranza settled into maturity, she recorded Irish
folklore and conducted well-attended literary salons in Dublin and in London.

Oscar's older brother, Willie, who became a
lawyer and later a journalist, had been born in 1852.
Speranza's fervent desire for a daughter, temporarily frustrated by the birth of Oscar, was ful-

Oscar Wilde

filled in 1856 by the birth of Isola Francesca Wilde.
Family interest centered in Isola until her death at
the age of ten. How deeply her death affected her
brother Oscar can be guessed from the lifelong
intensity with which he treasured an elaborately
decorated envelope as a shrine for a lock of her hair.
What is perhaps his most popular lyric, "Requies-
cat," expresses his profound affection for his sister
and his lasting sorrow over her death. Philip K.
Cohen has probed, with most interesting and illuminating speculations, the psychological influence of Isola's life and death on the works of her
brother.

As an Anglo-Irish Protestant, Wilde was sent
at the age of ten to the prestigious Portora Royal
School in Enniskillen, Fermanagh, where he excelled in Greek studies. In October 1871 he entered
Trinity College in Dublin, where he roomed with
his brother Willie and was tutored in Greek and
given a passion for ancient Greek culture by the
Reverend John Mahaffy. After Wilde went to Mag-

dalen College, Oxford, on a scholarship in 1874, Mahaffy invited his former student to accompany him in viewing the treasures of Italy. In the Easter vacation of Wilde's third year at Oxford the two marveled at Greek loveliness in Athens and Mycenae; Wilde, going back through Rome to see the pope, with difficulty resisted the Catholicism which tugged at him for years.

In 1878 Wilde achieved the prestigious Newdigate Prize for Poetry with imitative verses praising Ravenna, a city he had visited with Mahaffy and had seen, perhaps, with a personal interest: his mother claimed, through her Italian ancestry, some family connections with Dante, who was entombed in Ravenna.

Wilde learned much at Oxford from John Ruskin and Walter Pater, especially the latter. Pater's move away from Matthew Arnold's objectivity in art into the subjective realm of one's own interior had a large, healthy influence on Wilde's critical thought. Pater, perhaps fearing social disapproval, wavered in his urge to find the ultimate realm of art within human experience; but Wilde, having ac-

Wilde as a student at Oxford (courtesy of Mrs. Muriel Sherard)

cepted the Paterian gospel, went all the way. In one of his best critical essays, "The Critic as Artist" (1890) Wilde explicitly (in the person of his character Gilbert) rejects Arnold's theory: "It has been said by one whose gracious memory we all revere . . . that the proper aim of Criticism is to see the object as in itself it really is. But this is a very serious error, and takes no cognizance of Criticism's most perfect form, which is in its essence purely subjective, and seeks to reveal its own secret and not the secret of another." Gilbert's theory is that the aim of criticism is "to see the object as in itself it really is not."

In his efforts to express this principle, "to reveal [his] own secret" in his book reviews, critical articles, and above all in his own creative works, Wilde did a great service for many subsequent artists, as a number of them have acknowledged. Wilde was thus an influence in breaking up the smothering didacticism of the established canons on literature, and in enabling literary art to shake off the trammels of a conventional moral code.

Wilde received his B.A. from Oxford in 1878, stayed on for a fifth year, then went to London, aiming at some profitable career worthy of a man who could tame words. First he essayed a play: in the fall of 1880 *Vera; or, The Nihilists* was published, perhaps at Wilde's own expense. British interest in affairs in Russia, where the play is set, had been increased by the assassination of Czar Alexander II in March; and, under the auspices of the actress Mrs. Bernard Beere, the play was scheduled for performance at the Adelphi Theatre on 17 December 1881. However, the production was canceled three weeks before the premiere out of deference to the feelings of the Princess of Wales, whose sister was the newly widowed czarina.

Vera, an attempt to deal seriously with important political problems, has high points of dramatic interest in spite of its generally turgid progress and its clumsy construction. Vera the revolutionary is, like Shaw's Saint Joan, an interesting if imperfect depiction of a passionate woman involved in idealism and violence; and Prince Paul Maraloffski, surely based on the poseur Wilde, haltingly foreshadows the wit and glitter of *The Importance of Being Earnest.*

For two years Wilde had dressed in outlandish outfits, courted famous people—strewing lilies before Sarah Bernhardt, waiting upon Lillie Langtry—and built his public image. Since he had built one that fitted Bunthorne the Aesthete in Gilbert and Sullivan's *Patience* (1881), he was hired by the producer, Richard D'Oyly Carte, to advertise the opera in America. The six-feet-three-inch

Wilde, dressed in black velvet and carrying a lily, was to lecture in American cities on the new aestheticism. On 24 December 1881 Wilde embarked for New York, taking copies of *Vera* with him.

He succeeded brilliantly, even in Leadville, Colorado. He liked America, in spite of what he saw as its vulgarity, and even enjoyed the abuse that was heaped on him by many newspapers. During his year-long tour, he visited Henry Wadsworth Longfellow, Oliver Wendell Holmes, Louisa M. Alcott, Charles Eliot Norton, Walt Whitman, and Jefferson Davis. He attempted to secure a producer for *Vera,* but failed. He returned to London, where his *Poems,* which had appeared in June 1881, had done little to advance his reputation.

He went, therefore, to Paris to mingle with such literary figures as Victor Hugo, Emile Zola, and Paul Verlaine and with such painters as Edgar Degas, Camille Pissarro, and Henri de Toulouse-Lautrec. He also managed, through the American actress Marie Prescott, to find a producer for *Vera.* He began as well to compose another play for the American actress Mary Anderson, and on 15 March 1883 he sent her a copy of *The Duchess of Padua.*

In *The Duchess of Padua,* a five-act blank verse drama with bloody echoes of *Hamlet* and of John Webster's *The Duchess of Malfi* (circa 1613), Wilde turned from current political tangles to sixteenth-century Italy. In the melodramatic final scene the well-cloaked duchess enters the prison cell of her condemned lover Guido. She orders him to escape in her clothing, drinks poison, and "falls back dead in a chair." Guido promptly stabs himself, and, as the stage directions demand, "as he falls across her knees, clutches at the cloak which is on the back of the chair. Then down the passage comes the tramp of soldiers; the door is opened, and the Lord Justice, the Headsman, and the Guard enter and see this figure shrouded in black, and Guido lying dead across her. The Lord Justice rushes forward and drags the cloak off the Duchess, whose face is now the marble image of peace, the sign of God's forgiveness." It was a dangerous effort indeed to aim, through such tricky athletics, to achieve the sacred calm of the Pietà scene. And at the end of such a play, the presumption of God's forgiveness must depend on a thoroughly sentimental notion of God's cosmic amiability. The play is, nevertheless, better constructed than was *Vera* and is more interesting in style and characterization; and Wilde learned from it that blank verse was not his proper element. He turned thereafter from social and historical themes to social comedies.

Wilde was present when *Vera* opened in New York in 1883 and closed after a week. The dejected playwright returned home to lecture in England and Ireland on his American experiences. In November, lecturing in Dublin, he encountered Constance Lloyd, the lovely, fairly well-to-do daughter of a deceased barrister; he had first met her in London two years previously. They were married on 29 May 1884 in an aesthetic glow of yellow costumes and moved into a sternly commercial house at 16 Tite Street, Chelsea, in London. With the expensive assistance of his friend James McNeill Whistler, Wilde transformed the prim house into a peacock's delight, with oriental and Greek decor and all his precious books and art objects carefully enshrined.

In the following two years he produced several reviews, essays, and lectures, and he and his wife produced two children, Cyril on 5 June 1885 and Vyvyan on 3 November 1886. In 1886 Wilde met a young Canadian, Robert Ross, and according to fairly well-accepted opinion began his involvement in the disordered, destructive homosexual life-style so luridly suggested in *The Picture of Dorian Gray* (1891) and catalogued in his sensational trials. In April 1887 Wilde became the editor of *The Lady's World* magazine. He stated that his aim was to pro-

Wilde's wife, Constance Lloyd Wilde

Cover of the magazine Wilde edited from April 1887 until July 1889

literary art. Victorian criticism subjected literature to the demands of morality and utility; Matthew Arnold was the best, and thus the worst, of such critics. Wilde strove to dislodge that burden.

Wilde was dismissed as editor of *The Woman's World* in July 1889; the same month saw the appearance of "The Portrait of Mr. W. H.," a brilliant commentary on Shakespeare's sonnets. In this story Wilde created a character so vivid and alive that Shakespeare scholars, a solemn crew, still feel obliged to devote a footnote or two to killing him off—Willie Hughes. Wilde perceptively satirizes Matthew Arnold's "touchstone" approach to literature in developing from sonnet twenty a theory about Hughes. Cyril Graham, the central character in Wilde's story, which skillfully affects a documentary realism, intuits "on a kind of spiritual and artistic sense" that Willie was the sonnets' "Onlie Begetter," the "Mr. W. H." of the title page of Shakespeare's work. Many kinds of artistic trickery in poetry and in painting complicate the plot. There is no more detailed, more illuminating, and perhaps more eerily degenerate analysis of those glorious sonnets in all of the vast critical writing dealing with them.

"The Portrait of Mr. W. H.," usually classified with Wilde's critical essays, could equally well be approached as a story or novella. Its structure, involving a beautiful youth (Willie Hughes), two older men (Shakespeare and the Rival Poet), and a homosexual ambience (slightly disturbed by an interfering Dark Lady) foreshadows Wilde's only novel. The revised "Mr. W. H." of 1893 in turn shows a considerable influence of *The Picture of Dorian Gray* in its stressing of an intellectual nobility in the love of man for boy, in adverting to the influence of the unconscious, and in the development of a Platonic idealism in the fruitful "marriage of true minds."

The first version of *The Picture of Dorian Gray* appeared in July 1890 in *Lippincott's Monthly Magazine*. In his essays, Wilde had preached Pater's doctrine with glib grace and triumphant success. In his novel, that eloquent doctrine, mixing with human realities, ran into considerable trouble.

Wilde posited quite a simple plot. A remarkably attractive twenty-year-old, upper-class Englishman faces his future, and after the passage of time—twelve years in the short *Lippincott* version, eighteen years in the longer version published in book form the following year— concludes his development in abrupt and destructive fashion.

The *Lippincott* version has only three main characters; three others appear briefly. The novel

vide "for the expression of women's opinions on all subjects of literature, art, and modern life" and changed the name to *The Woman's World*.

In 1887 some of his best short stories appeared, notably "Lord Arthur Savile's Crime" in the 11, 18, and 25 May issues of *Court and Society Review*. In this story the moral complications resulting from efforts to conform to the demands of a stagnant and corrupt society are grimly and satirically understated, with the spooky, suprarational involvement of a "Professional Cheiromantist." *The Picture of Dorian Gray* would develop a similar suprarational situation with far deeper and more complex personal and social effects. In 1888 his fairy tales *The Happy Prince and Other Tales* and "The Young King," revealing another approach to moral situations and human relationships, interested and delighted adults as well as children—and puzzled some, as they still do.

In 1889 the first of his critical essays, so deeply influential for some great artists of the twentieth century, appeared. All his most important critical essays were published on 2 May 1891 under the title *Intentions*. This collection forms one of the profoundest, healthiest, and most graceful nineteenth-century investigations into the nature of

begins with the artist Basil Hallward painting a portrait of Dorian; Lord Henry Wotton, an elegant man-about-town, a "Prince of Paradox," comes in to meet the subject of the picture. Basil fears that he is putting too much of his intense love for the young man into the painting; Lord Henry sees in the youth an opportunity to observe the higher life, the welcoming of every sensation, the fullest development of soul and sense in a beautiful human being.

The homosexual undertones of Wilde's development of his plot roused a critical eruption, mostly of indignation and vilification. The plot was reputedly (but probably not actually) based on an experience Wilde had had in the studio of Basil Ward, an artist friend, where Wilde expressed regret that a beautiful young man in one of Ward's paintings should ever grow old. (Another version places the incident in the studio of a woman painter who painted Wilde's portrait.) In the Gothic tone of his mother's granduncle, Charles Maturin—author of the model of all Gothic novels, *Melmoth the Wanderer*—Wilde introduces a painting which, after the subject of the painting offers his soul for the miracle, takes on the signs of age and moral decay while its lovely, criminal original remains unchanged.

The main characters, according to Wilde's later account, are three aspects of Wilde himself. Hallward is the suffering and sacrificed artist; Dorian is the youthful aesthete-about-town; Lord Henry is the mature philosopher and wit. Their tortuous and fascinating wanderings in obscure psychological depths have kept readers, viewers of movies, psychiatrists, and critics mildly agog for a hundred years—and will no doubt continue to do so, in the company of Hamlet, Balzac's *Peau de Chagrin,* Mary Shelley's *Frankenstein,* Edgar Allan Poe's Usher family, Bram Stoker's *Dracula,* and James Joyce's Stephen Dedalus.

Turning the *Lippincott* version of the novel into a book required more bulk, better balance, and tighter unity. Wilde added six chapters and other characters, increased the scope and depth of the second half (Dorian's mature experience, James Vane's return), and toned down the homosexual implications of the first version. He also added a preface, to meet some of the charges made against the first version and to set forth some of the Paterian bases for the doctrine involved.

The preface upholds Pater's view of art as a reflecting function independent of the strictures of conventional morality. The surface of art, that smooth and lovely skin that all can see, conceals human experience; the symbol, the hidden meaning, of art expresses what the partaker of art finds beneath the surface if he dares to penetrate it—his own face confronting him. Those who rage and howl, like the critics of Wilde's novel, suffer from seeing their own savage faces reflected in the artist's creation. For the artist morality is of interest only as subject matter; ethics should not constrict his scope, nor does he concern himself with encouraging or discouraging moral behavior. The work of art is totally useless; it finds its goal within itself, a beautiful creation reflecting all things human. It should be contemplated for itself, and aims at no other use. Thus the critics who condemn it as having evil effects should look inside themselves for the causes of those effects, not in the work.

In his arrangement of the twenty chapters of his book, Wilde devotes ten chapters to the twenty-year-old Dorian, one remarkable bridge chapter to the eighteen following years, and nine chapters to Dorian at the age of thirty-eight. The ten chapters of the first section are divided into three groups. Chapters 1 through 3 establish the relationships among the three central characters. Chapters 4 through 7 set forth the effect of Sibyl Vane on the three men. Chapters 8 through 10 deal with the portrait—the change in it, the painter's attitude, the hiding of the picture.

Chapter 11 carries the reader by a most effective narrative device over eighteen years of Dorian's sybaritic life. Chapters 12 through 14 deal with Basil's murder, chapters 15 through 18 with James Vane's return. Chapter 19 echoes, in the talk of Henry and Dorian, the Paterian idealism of the early chapters, now with a sinister tonality. In the final chapter, Dorian kills his conscience.

Each chapter has a calculated task in the carefully planned whole. Chapter 1 sets forth, in the conversation of Basil Hallward and Lord Henry, their views on the aim of the artist, on the effect on the artist of his work of art, and on the danger for a young man of Henry's teaching of the value of the fullest possible self-development. Henry preaches "a new Hedonism" in which the doctrine of Pater is central. In his *Studies in the History of the Renaissance* (1873), Pater urged response to all sensations, intense concern for keeping always burning the "hard gem-like flame" of self-fulfillment. Lord Henry's advice to Dorian in chapter 2 echoes Pater: " 'Yes,' continued Lord Henry, 'that is one of the great secrets of life—to cure the soul by means of the senses, and the senses by means of the soul.' " The mature Dorian of chapter 16 finds those words ringing in his ears, continuously repeats them with savage intensity as if they were a talismanic formula, and desperately wonders whether or not his senses could, after a life of total self-indulgence, cure his sick soul.

In chapter 2 the twenty-year-old Dorian finds Henry's words a clarion call to a brave new world. An apprehensive Basil moves to destroy the picture, but Dorian stops him. At the end of the chapter, Dorian leaves Basil to join Lord Henry.

Chapter 3, the first of the new chapters added to the *Lippincott* version, develops Henry's growing control of both Dorian and Basil. He preaches Plato's reality, the intellectually perfect form which gives reality to shadows. Thus style, the surface, is of prime importance to every artist—to Michaelangelo in stone, to Shakespeare in sonnets. So Henry, as an artist, in living aims to dominate and fashion Dorian. Echoing the attacks on the first version of the novel, Wilde introduces the proper Sir Thomas, who condemns with "tight lips" Henry's Paterian advocacy of freedom from conventional moral restraints. Henry defends his idea, and the narrator describes Henry's method (which is also Wilde's) of using fancy and language in his campaign to repel mere facts: "He played with the idea, and grew willful; tossed it into the air and transformed it; let it escape and recaptured it; made it iridescent with fancy, and winged it with paradox. The praise of folly, as he went on, soared into a philosophy, and Philosophy herself became young, and catching the mad music of Pleasure, wearing, one might fancy, her wine-stained robe and wreath of ivy, danced like a Bacchante over the hills of life, and mocked the slow Silenus for being sober. Facts fled before her like frightened forest things. Her white feet trod the huge press at which wise Omar sits, till the seething grape-juice rose round her bare limbs in waves of purple bubbles, or crawled in red foam over the vat's black, dripping, sloping sides. It was an extraordinary improvisation." Again, and more definitely, Dorian deserts Basil to follow Henry.

In chapter 4, Dorian has acquired "a passion for sensations." He has "collected" Sibyl Vane, who resembles Wilde's wife Constance (as Wilde described his fiancée in a letter to Lillie Langtry in December 1883). Sibyl, Dorian thinks, escapes time; she is full of mystery, sacred. She is all great heroines, never an individual. Dorian seems to have persuaded himself that by joining her he, too, will exist in the world of art, the world created by Shakespeare. She seems divine to him, since she will lift him out of the crass world where imagination must be subject to animal necessities. Henry attempts to discourage Dorian: "Good artists exist simply in what they make, and consequently are perfectly uninteresting in what they are." Henry decides, however, to watch the situation as an experiment, to achieve "scientific analysis of the passions."

Chapter 5 is the second added chapter, and its mean style fits the situation—Sibyl's poverty-ridden and melodramatically sterile home life. The reader is told about her romantic dream, her mother's overacted apprehensions, her brother James's sincere concern and his violent threats to anyone who should harm her. In soap-opera tonality, the reader learns, as James now finally does, that Sibyl's children are bastards, since the "highly connected" gentleman she had loved could not marry her. Mother and brother have listened to Sibyl declare her passion for a Prince Charming whose real name she does not know.

In chapter 6, Lord Henry and Basil discuss Dorian's determination to marry, and after his arrival, Dorian describes his infatuation. Henry doubts the quality of Dorian's "selfless" love, and asserts the superiority of selfish pleasure: "I should fancy that the real tragedy of the poor is that they can afford nothing but self-denial." They drive off to the theater, Basil gloomy and apprehensive.

Chapter 7 reveals that Sibyl's power of acting has deserted her. Dorian's love evanesces, his friends leave, he berates Sibyl as she sobs. She flings herself at his feet (people fling themselves throughout the novel). He coldly leaves her and wanders through the night. At dawn, returning home, he notes a new expression of hard cruelty on the face in the portrait. But maybe it is not so; maybe he can yet love Sibyl.

In the third subsection of the first half of the novel, chapter 8 sees Dorian, with Lord Henry's tutelage, transforming Sibyl's suicide into a triumph of art, a further help to his own self-development: "It has been a marvelous experience. That is all." The picture still mirrors his cruelty, bears "the burden of his shame: that was all." In chapter 9 Basil arrives at Dorian's house; they exchange views; Basil confesses the intense love he had expressed in the picture, the motive for his effort to destroy it. Dorian resolves to hide it away safely. He takes the painting in chapter 10 to the unused old schoolroom at the top of the house, where he had spent much of his childhood. Then he turns to the book Henry had sent to him, a volume resembling J. K. Huysmans's *A Rebours* (1884), a book written in "that curious jeweled style" which Wilde himself had admired. Here the voice of the narrator strongly suggests that he is Wilde himself; it is almost, but not quite, identical with the voice of Lord Henry: "There were in it [the book Lord Henry had sent to Dorian] metaphors as monstrous as orchids, and as subtle in color. The life of the senses was described in terms of mystical philosophy. One hardly knew at times whether one was reading the spiritual ecstasies of some medieval saint or the morbid confessions of a modern sinner. It was a poisonous book." This view of the operation of a work of art does not at all seem in accord with Wilde's preface.

For his bridge chapter, chapter 11, Wilde hit upon the effective device of merging Dorian's experience for the next eighteen years with the vast historical background, mostly deviously evil, of the beautiful objects he collects—manuscripts depicting sensual adventures and mystical theologies; perfumes; music of savage as well as of civilized traditions; exquisite jewels; embroideries, tapestries, and vestments; paintings; literature; poisons. Thus Wilde gives the effect of many passing years, bringing Dorian to the point at which he can look "on evil as a mode through which he could realize his conception of the beautiful." The chapter brilliantly deals with time on two levels: general human historical experience with beautiful and poisonous things, and Dorian's shifting interest in those same things.

The last half of the novel begins in chapter 12, on the eve of Dorian's thirty-eighth birthday. On his way home through the fog from a party at Lord Henry's, Dorian passes the hurrying figure of Basil Hallward, and attempts to avoid speaking to him. But Basil turns and requests an interview. He confronts Dorian with the stories of his moral corruption and urges him to reveal the truth. Dorian furiously agrees and invites Basil upstairs.

In chapter 13, Basil, horrified, sees the picture. He urges repentance. Dorian stabs him to death, then goes outside and rings the bell to establish an alibi (his valet had previously sent Basil on his way, and was unaware of his return with Dorian). Dorian looks into the Blue Book, a listing of notable persons, to find the address of Alan Campbell, a scientist.

In chapter 14 Dorian blackmails Campbell into destroying Basil's body, apparently by reducing it to its elements. The florid style of these chapters continues the atmosphere of the elegantly evil bridge chapter, chapter 11.

In the four following chapters, added to the *Lippincott* version, Wilde fleshes out the lean earlier ending, particularly by bringing back Sibyl's brother James to attempt to carry out his threat of

Hurd Hatfield, as Dorian Gray, looks at his portrait in the 1945 film version of Wilde's novel (National Film Archive)

vengeance. Wilde achieves far greater unity, as well, by reviving Dorian's first vicious cruelty and depicting the cowardice and fear of Sibyl's Prince Charming in his maturity.

In chapter 15 Dorian, fresh from his gruesome crime (or "tragedy," as the narrator puts it) goes to a party at Lady Narborough's. The narrator's voice here is closer than ever to Lord Henry's, and the narrator literally quotes Henry's statements. Lord Henry arrives late, notes something changed in Dorian, and amuses the company with a series of paradoxes: "She is very clever, too clever for a woman. She lacks the indefinable charm of weakness. It is the feet of clay that makes the gold of the image precious. Her feet are very pretty, but they are not feet of clay. White porcelain feet, if you like. They have been through the fire, and what fire does not destroy, it hardens. She has had experiences." The image has its application to Dorian, as does much of Henry's persiflage. (Wilde refers to this image in *De Profundis,* his long letter from prison to Alfred Douglas: "When I wrote, among my aphorisms, that it was simply the feet of clay that made the gold of the image precious, it was of you that I was thinking.")

After the party, Dorian returns home, disquieted and craving forgetfulness. He collects some drugs and takes a hansom for the opium dens of Chinatown. When, in chapter 16, Dorian enters the squalid den, he sees a sailor "sprawled over a table." An old crone, a woman Dorian had corrupted many years ago, calls after him, "Prince Charming." The sailor, who by strange coincidence turns out to be James Vane, hears the name his sister had called the man she loved. He follows Dorian, threatens him, and Dorian steps into light to reveal the face of "a lad of twenty summers." Vane subsides in confusion, and Dorian departs. The crone, creeping up, informs Vane that that "lad" had ruined her "nigh on eighteen years since. . . ." Vane stares at empty streets.

In chapter 17, a week later, at a hunting party in the country, Lord Henry is entertaining the guests, earning the title of "Prince Paradox" from Dorian. There are hints of the future *Importance of Being Earnest:* "That is the reason I hate vulgar realism in literature. The man who would call a spade a spade should be compelled to use it. It is the only thing he is fit for." Then Dorian, having seen through a window the white, staring face of James Vane, faints. In chapter 18, Dorian, though ill, goes out on the hunt. Over Dorian's protest, since he was charmed by the hare's grace of movement, Sir Geoffrey shoots into the bush—and kills the hiding James Vane. Dorian weeps with relief that he is now safe.

Chapter 19 returns to the material of the *Lippincott* version. Henry and Dorian return to the Paterian atmosphere of the first chapters, now without Basil. Dorian's determination to reform and be good, evidenced by his refraining from corrupting altogether a village maid who reminded him of Sibyl, meets with tolerant incredulity from Lord Henry: "Crime belongs exclusively to the lower orders. . . . I should fancy that crime was to them what art is to us, simply a method of procuring extraordinary sensations." They discuss Basil's disappearance, his possible murder, Dorian's life, the loss of the soul. For Dorian, Henry tells him, "Life has been your art." As he leaves, Dorian hesitates, as if he had left something important unsaid. "Then he sighed and went out."

In the final chapter, Dorian for the last time "throws himself" down on the sofa and thinks. The past overwhelms him. He determines to be good. Having accomplished one minor triumph by resisting a sexual urge, he goes to see if the picture looks better. It is more disgusting. He stabs it with the knife that had killed Basil. When the servants break in, they find a picture of an exquisite youth and an old, withered, loathsome corpse with a knife in its heart.

This second version of *The Picture of Dorian Gray* is a well-balanced and unified novel, expressed in a musical, clear, and flowing style, if flowery and overstuffed like stylish Victorian furniture. The imagery well serves the central insight, which contemplates the goal of existence in human beings involved with art. Wilde formally disavows a moral aim, but his book frustrates that disavowal. The human who serves only self, as a perfect work of art may do, may end murdered in horror like Basil, suicidal like Dorian stabbing his conscience, or vapidly mouthing entertaining aphorisms like the seemingly self-sufficient Lord Henry.

Wilde's reputation as a novelist has to rest on this one work, but that is not a trivial base. The novel's solid structure and other virtues have kept it alive for a century, tempting filmmakers and playwrights, as well as a steady stream of interested critics and readers.

James Joyce understood why Wilde failed to achieve the highest literary merit and fell short of revealing the ultimate human secret in his novel. In a letter to his brother in 1906 after reading *The Picture of Dorian Gray,* Joyce laid his critical finger on Wilde's literary fatal flaw: "Wilde seems to have some good intentions in writing it—some wish to put himself before the world—but the book is rather crowded with lies and epigrams. If he had had the courage to develop the allusions in the book it might have been better." Wilde, in what he and Joyce both recognized as the goal of the literary artist—to express human experience in all its psychic complexity—lacked courage. In the young Joyce's view, Wilde feared self-revelation.

An illustration of the difference as well as the likeness between the flawed artist and the toweringly successful one might be discerned in a comparison of artistic achievement in the creation of the somewhat similar characters of Dorian Gray and Stephen Dedalus. For example, in chapter 11 the young Dorian contemplates the sinister transformation of his portrait: "He grew more and more enamoured of his own beauty, more and more interested in the corruption of his own soul. He would examine with minute care, and sometimes with a monstrous and terrible delight, the hideous lines that seared the wrinkling forehead or crawled around the heavy sensual mouth, wondering sometimes which were the more horrible, the signs of sin or the signs of age." In chapter 3 of *A Portrait of the Artist as a Young Man* (1916), Joyce says of Stephen Dedalus: "He stooped to the evil of hypocrisy with others, sceptical of their innocence which he could cajole so easily. . . . If ever his soul, re-entering her dwelling shyly after the frenzy of his body's lust had spent itself, was turned towards her whose emblem is the morning star, 'bright and musical, telling of heaven and infusing peace,' it was when her names were murmured softly by lips whereon there still lingered foul and shameful words, the savour itself of a lewd kiss." Joyce could powerfully and unashamedly depict hypocrisy; Wilde, according to Joyce, crippled his art by a concern for concealing his own hypocrisy.

Probably in January 1891 Wilde met Lord Alfred Douglas, the third son of the eighth Marquis of Queensberry. For the nine years that Wilde had yet to live, "Bosie" Douglas would be the "fidus Achates" who, as Wilde cries in *De Profundis* (1905), would thrust Wilde into Hades. When he was brought to meet Wilde, Douglas was a twenty-one-year-old Oxford student. According to his own unlikely account, he, a youthful innocent, was debauched by the worldly-wise, thirty-eight-year-old playwright. Wilde would give a different version in *De Profundis*.

Other events of 1891 included the production in New York of *The Duchess of Padua* (under the title *Guido Ferranti*), and the publication of the essay "The Soul of Man under Socialism"; *Lord Arthur Savile's Crime & Other Stories*, a book of stories and essays; and *A House of Pomegranates*, a second book of fairy stories. (James Joyce obtained permission to translate "The Soul of Man under Socialism" into Italian, but never did so. Its Shelleyan or softheaded treatment of human society in an ownerless world probably had some influence on Joyce's youthful socialism, "compounded of his own simples," as Richard Ellmann aptly puts it.)

In November and December, Wilde, in Paris, finished the composition in French of his sinuously sensual *Salomé*. The Bible, long outlawed on the English stage because of Reformation antipathy to Catholic mystery plays, provided an excuse for the lord chamberlain to suppress the elaborate production planned by Sarah Bernhardt in June 1892. Wilde managed to get a good deal of publicity through his widely disseminated elegant and witty indignation.

Lord Alfred Douglas ("Bosie"), whose relationship with Wilde led to Wilde's ruin (by courtesy of the William Andrews Clark Library, Los Angeles)

Wilde's next play, *Lady Windermere's Fan* (1893), comments on the society of the 1890s with wit and humor. Wilde plotted this play with great care. Unlike the large, unwieldy themes of his earlier plays, the focus here is on one important aspect of the society of which he was a part. Wilde bares the morally questionable choices of his characters with an almost honest vision and with literary and dramatic skill. As Alan Bird says: "That kind and tolerant humour for which he was famous embraces all his characters without, however, sugaring their weaknesses. That is why *Lady Windermere's Fan* must be considered with respect: it is an indirect indictment of a heartless and mercenary society of which the fan, an extravagant and useless toy, is so accurate a symbol." The play opened at St. James's Theatre on 20 February 1892 for a run of five months, then went on tour; it reopened in London on 31 October. It opened in America on 6 February 1893 and ran for several months.

A Woman of No Importance (1894) stresses the moral optimism of Wilde's socialist doctrine to the point of absurdity. The heroine is, like Hardy's Tess, "A Good Woman" who does any number of formally evil deeds but remains pure. Wilde's attitude is less grimly hardheaded than Hardy's; and his moralizing, surrounded with sparkling epigrams and graceful, melodramatic Irish flow, is easier to take. But it is equally vapid in its aftertaste. Hester Worsley, denouncing society for its hypocrisy toward women, later learns that "God's law is only Love." The same lesson emerges from the self-pitying sufferer of *De Profundis*. In both cases, how much of such rich piety emerges from hypocrisy is not easy to determine.

A Woman of No Importance contains a grim humor which, as Robert Keith Miller points out, foreshadows the more perfect treatment of human decay and death in *The Importance of Being Earnest* (and which also lays a basis for the stylized, cosmic humorous treatment of human suffering in Beckett's *Waiting for Godot* and *Endgame*). *A Woman of No Importance* however, chokes on its lumpy moralizing in spite of its saucy humor. As Miller puts it, "Each act becomes more didactic than the last, and by the end of the play, the comic is abandoned for the maudlin." The play was performed at the Haymarket Theatre in London from 19 April to 16 August 1893; it opened in New York on 11 December for a short run.

An Ideal Husband was written in 1894-1895 and produced in London in 1895, but was not published until 1899. In this play Wilde again reveals the hypocrisy rife in society, evident especially in the willingness to achieve good ends through evil means, and applies his revelation pointedly to English society. He improves greatly on his previous play, keeping an ironic distance from the weavings of selfish crimes and noble standards. Alan Bird notes, "There is here a subtle twisting together of personal and public morality, both of them shams," and believes that Wilde contrived these turns of events with "his tongue prominently in his cheek." Christopher S. Nassaar, on the other hand, supposes that Wilde was in total earnest, and that *An Ideal Husband* demonstrates a triumph over "the demon universe" and finds the guilty husband and forgiving wife "entering a state of higher innocence." Bird presupposes a wider context, including a catholic Christianity, that Nassaar seems innocent of. Nassaar projects as Wilde's view a simple choice between God and devil; Bird sees Wilde's view as the complex necessity of balancing many elements in the face of ultimately incomprehensible mystery.

Bird also demonstrates the operation of a complex basic hypocrisy throughout *An Ideal Husband*. There are strained plot contrivances in the play, but none are so damaging as the inept moral symbols of Wilde's previous plays. *An Ideal Husband* reveals how much Wilde had learned about revealing the complexities in human choices and about the limits of the dramatist's art.

An important event of 1895, and the climax of Wilde's artistic career, was the production of *The Importance of Being Earnest*, which opened on 14 February at the St. James's Theatre in London and was wildly cheered by the first-night audience. Written at Worthing in August and September 1894, the play is described by W. H. Auden as "perhaps the only pure verbal opera in English" and is called by Alan Bird "the only work that Wilde wrote which is worthy of his genius."

Having illustrated in his previous plays the difficulties of balancing conventional moral norms with the realities of human behavior, Wilde finally leaves that effort behind, and, as Auden said, creates "a verbal universe in which the characters are determined by the kinds of things they say, and the plot is nothing but a succession of opportunities to say them." Words for the first time in Wilde's work achieve complete autonomy—words as words, not words doing something useful outside a verbal universe.

Not that moral interests do not operate in the words of *The Importance of Being Earnest*—there are analogies in the play to the dark orgies of *The Picture of Dorian Gray*, and there are faint overtones of such real horrors as child abandonment, of valuing literature (especially in three volumes) more than the life of a baby, and of other moral aberrations—but they operate here wholly inside the delighted imagination. Judgments need not be made, sides need not be chosen. One can laugh freely because words as words give as much delight in expressing objective evil as they do in expressing objective good, as in *The Pirates of Penzance* or *The Mikado*. This joy in words reaches its highest point in the twentieth century in *Finnegans Wake* (1939); and those Joycean swaggering, many-leveled words, shining with something of Dante's depth and music, learned much from the stylized perfection of Wilde's words in *The Importance of Being Earnest*. Robert Keith Miller discusses *The Importance of Being Earnest* under the heading "Exploring the Absurd," and in his final summing up of Wilde's work he perceptively observes that *"The Importance of Being Earnest* anticipates the world of Samuel Beckett."

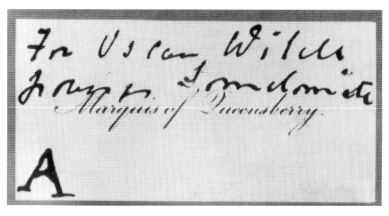

The Marquis of Queensberry's calling card, with the inscription accusing Wilde of being a "Somdomite." It is marked as Exhibit "A" in Wilde's trial (Public Record Office, London, and Mrs. Mary Hyde).

A few days after the opening of *The Importance of Being Earnest,* the Marquis of Queensberry, Bosie's boisterous father, publicly accused Wilde of "posing as Somdomite"—he had intended to write *sodomite,* but the crude old peer was not much of a speller. Urged on by Bosie, Wilde sued for libel; the trial opened on 3 April 1896. The cross-examination of Wilde by Edward Carson, a former fellow student and academic rival at Trinity College, has all the fascination of court dramas—the sparkle of brilliant language, the human interest of observing the conflict in a talented artist between an aesthetic construct and human lust, the posturing of a hypocritical society upholding a traditional morality in judging Wilde harshly while it protected guilty members of its own favored group, and the painful sight of the public disintegration of a true "lord of language." Wilde, basing himself on the construct of beauty he had long preached, stated that he had not kissed a certain boy because he was "unfortunately, extremely ugly." Carson focused on this and, in forcing Wilde to face up to the contradiction in himself between his aesthetic construct and a loving human attitude, reduced Wilde to stumbling confusion. Wilde was thus trapped into realizing clearly that he had indeed used other human beings selfishly, far more grossly than had the Selfish Giant in his own fairy tale; and that under the guise of beauty he had, like an animal, ingested the appetizing and rejected the repulsive. That he was not alone in such activity did not save him from his own inner hell.

Although he had ample opportunity to escape abroad, he chose to remain in London to face up to arrest and trial on charges of offenses to minors under Section 11 of the Criminal Law Amendment Act, 1885. Two trials followed: the first, from 26 April to 1 May 1895, ended in a hung jury; in the second, from 20 May to 25 May, he was found guilty and given the maximum sentence of two years at hard labor. (*The Importance of Being Earnest* ran until 8 May despite Wilde's disgrace.)

Wilde served the first five months of his sentence in Wandsworth prison, where a fall during a fainting fit caused an ear injury which would contribute to his death five years later. He suffered at learning that his treasured possessions were to be sold at public auction on 24 April and after the sale he was pained that almost none of his friends, most of all Bosie, had attempted to salvage any of them. Constance visited him in what she described as "the saddest meeting of my life," at which, she reported, Wilde said that he would shoot Bosie if he ever saw him again.

In an effort to improve Wilde's circumstances, R. B. Haldane, a member of the Prison Commission, arranged to have him transferred to Reading Gaol, which had a library and a garden. There Wilde was known as "C.3.3.," the number of his cell, and the name he would use on *The Ballad of Reading Gaol* (1898). In February 1896 Constance, who had gone into exile with their children and changed their name to Holland, made the long journey from Genoa to tell Wilde the bitter news of his mother's death.

Salomé was finally produced in Paris on 11 February 1896; news of this event came to Wilde in Reading Gaol, bringing him some comfort but not much badly needed profit. Alan Bird outlines the play's star-crossed, painful history. Notable of

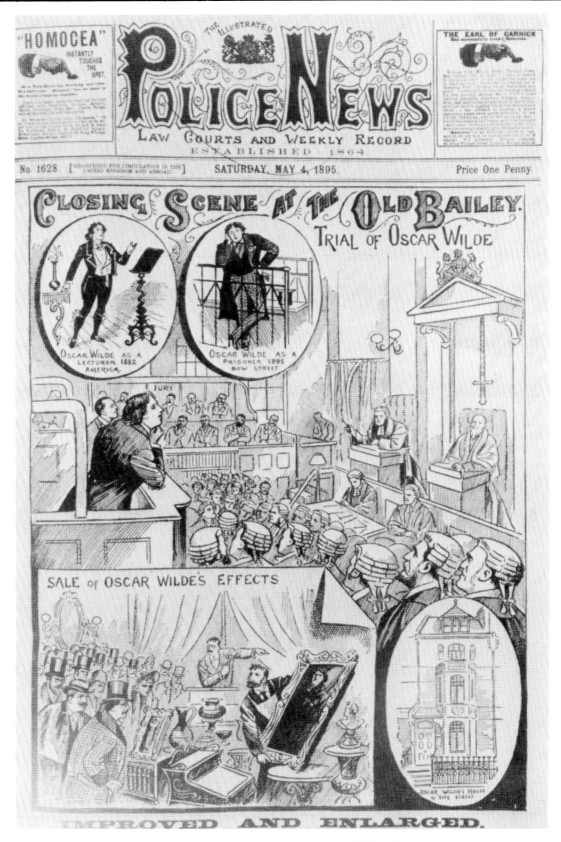

Cover of a magazine published during Wilde's trial

Part of the first page of Wilde's manuscript for De Profundis *(British Museum)*

course was its union, in its German translation, with the musical genius of Richard Strauss in 1905 to produce the great opera.

After a kinder warden, Major Nelson, had taken charge, it became possible for Wilde to write, from January through March of 1897, on paper furnished and removed one sheet at a time, the long letter to Bosie which came to be known as *De Profundis*. In an accompanying letter to the faithful Robbie Ross, Wilde compared his letter to the encyclicals of the popes and suggested that his work should be called "Epistola: In Carcere et Vinculis." Thus Wilde, by means of literature, could carry out his threat to shoot Bosie. (This episode is referred to in *Finnegans Wake* in many-leveled Joycean fashion: ". . . and fire off, gheol ghiornal, foull subustioned mullmud, his farced epistol to the hibruws." Here Wilde's message to the highbrows of England—his daily journal from a hellish "gaol"—and his vicarious shooting of Bosie are united to St. Paul's *Letter to the Hebrews*. "Subustioned mullmud" refers to Sebastian Melmoth, the name Wilde adopted after his release, and also implies a "busted" felon mulling over his miseries, like the Prodigal Son, in the mud.)

No objective criticism is possible in treating of *De Profundis*. While not formally a work of art, it displays both Wilde's personal feelings and the array of imagery and music with which he strove to conceal and to display those feelings. It is a profoundly interesting human document, moving or disgusting according to the attitude the reader brings to it. It has suffered severe injury, as a document, from its publishing history—rushed into fragmentary publication by Ross to protect the copyright; published in a chopped-up version in 1905 by Methuen with all references to Bosie excised, so that it made little sense and destroyed Wilde's aim; published in supposedly complete but actually still cut and botched condition in 1949 by Wilde's son Vyvyan Holland; and finally published in full and well edited by Rupert Hart-Davis in *The Letters of Oscar Wilde* (1962).

Wilde's efforts to probe his own psyche and his relationship to Bosie reveal the religious urges which, under calculated control and never dominant in his serious artistic products, here surge almost unrestrained into the artist Wilde-Christ undergoing sacrificial suffering on account of and on behalf of Bosie-Judas. The beauty of the Christ aspect and the perversion of the devil aspect mingle in a weird, phantasmagoric fashion. The unsatisfied tensions left by *The Picture of Dorian Gray* are released, according to one critic, in Wilde's final great effort to express his human vision. Philip K. Cohen judges that under Pater's tutelage, Wilde had, like Basil Hallward, confused the goal of human life with the goal of the artist. The artist aims at a perfect work, and orders all his artistic endeavors to this end. The good of the work is, in the realm of art, supreme. But the artist controls the work and all that goes into it. If the work of art were to take over and the human being, like the breathless Dorian when the Paterian Lord Henry "awakened" him in the second chapter, were to become the work of art while the picture became the moral human, making the "conscience" visible, a hideous morass might open up. Basil Hallward permits the barrier between life and art to break down. Philip Cohen expresses it thus: "Before he painted the fateful portrait, Basil had adhered to a mode of existence prescribed in 'The Critic as Artist.' He had treated life as though it were art, had kept between it and himself the 'mist or veil' of mythology and the dress, literal and metaphorical, of past ages. Filtered through this protective medium, life had served as raw material to be reshaped under the complete control of imagination. In the preliminary portraits, Basil could vicariously multiply his personality, could imaginatively assume and configure a number of identities without losing his own. But then he cast aside the veil to find in life, and to render in its own terms, the ideal he had previously imposed upon it. The Barrier having fallen, he surrendered that control which, according to 'The Critic,' shields one from life's agonies. Dominance shifted from artist to sitter, and Basil began to suffer. But he knows, and the other characters agree, that the portrait is his greatest achievement. And, on the last page of the novel, though without even a hint of explanation, Wilde restores the painting to its original perfection. Just as he acknowledges that one must enter life in order to be fully human, so he vaguely suggests that great art must somehow encompass reality. But he did not know how this could be achieved positively at the time of *Dorian Gray,* when, though he knew that separations between art and life are morally wrong, he could discover no benefit from their union. Only in *De Profundis,* after he recognized the value of suffering itself, could he celebrate a unified vision in which the artist's life becomes the supreme work of art precisely because it encompasses and expresses reality." If Cohen is

right, he explains why *De Profundis* itself has claimed a constant and growing public during its checkered career. When *De Profundis* is better understood, *The Picture of Dorian Gray* may be revealed to be a more profound searching of human experience than has yet been recognized, and a solid basis for a novelist's reputation.

Sebastian Melmoth, the name Wilde chose for himself after his release on 19 May 1897, is deeply revealing. He took the name Melmoth from his mother's granduncle's book *Melmoth the Wanderer,*

Wilde in Naples after his release from prison (Radio Times Hulton Picture Library)

the story of a man who had sold his soul to the devil and is condemned to wander the earth for centuries, seeking someone who would agree to exchange his soul to release Melmoth. William F. Axton, in his introduction to a 1961 edition of the novel, describes Maturin's theme in words that fit one aspect of *De Profundis:* "the tragic human perversion of a religion of love into a means of self-torment and torture of others." Axton notes an aspect of Melmoth that fits Wilde: "Melmoth becomes almost forgivable because of his tormented awareness of his own evil." The significance of the name Sebastian is less clear, although it is known that homosexuals in Wilde's day liked the painting of St. Sebastian pierced by arrows.

Wilde's story after his release from prison is brief and sad. He linked up with the miserable Bosie again, moved here and there in France and Italy, picked up and paid boys when he could afford them, had *The Ballad of Reading Gaol* published in February 1898, learned that Constance had died in April 1898, was operated on for an ear infection on 10 October 1900, and, having been received into the

Catholic church, died in his bleak hotel room on Friday, 30 November 1900.

Most critics, at least in their tone, reveal their judgments on Wilde as a good or as a bad man. Some of the best seem to feel that he was fairly rotten; when they come to that deathbed conversion, they tend to treat it either as the babblings of a frightened, semiconscious, and demonstrably superstitious Irishman, or as the revival of a youthful enthusiasm without sufficient basis to be taken seriously. But to render judgment on Wilde as a man is not an act befitting any human creature, even a literary critic. It is wiser, surely, to enjoy the living Wilde in his own words; for the dead Wilde, to award him the treatment he urged for the "wretched man" of *The Ballad of Reading Gaol:* "And there, till Christ call forth the dead/In silence let him lie."

Letters:

The Letters of Oscar Wilde, edited by Rupert Hart-Davis (New York: Harcourt, Brace & World, 1962).

Bibliographies:

Stuart Mason, *Bibliography of Oscar Wilde* (London: Laurie, 1914);

Ian Fletcher and John Stokes, "Oscar Wilde," in *Anglo-Irish Literature: A Review of Research,* edited by Richard J. Finneran (New York: Modern Language Association, 1976), pp. 48-137;

E. H. Mickhail, *Oscar Wilde: An Annotated Bibliography of Criticism* (London: Macmillan, 1978).

Biographies:

Hesketh Pearson, *The Life of Oscar Wilde* (London: Methuen, 1946); republished as *Oscar Wilde: His Life and Wit* (New York: Harper, 1946);

Vyvyan Holland, *Oscar Wilde: A Pictorial Biography* (London: Thames & Hudson, 1960); republished as *Oscar Wilde and His World* (New York: Scribners, 1960);

W. H. Auden, "An Improbable Life," preface to *De Profundis* (New York: Avon, 1964);

Richard Ellmann, Introduction to *The Artist as Critic: Critical Writings of Oscar Wilde* (New York: Random House, 1969), pp. ix-xxviii;

Rupert Croft-Cooke, *The Unrecorded Life of Oscar Wilde* (New York: McKay, 1972);

H. Montgomery Hyde, *Oscar Wilde: A Biography* (New York: Farrar, Straus & Giroux, 1975);

Sheridan Morley, *Oscar Wilde* (New York: Holt, Rinehart & Winston, 1976).

Wilde's tomb, designed by Jacob Epstein, in Père Lachaise Cemetery, Paris. Wilde was buried here in 1909, after having lain for nine years in a temporary grave at Bagneux (photo: Jacqueline Hyde, Paris).

References:

Karl Beckson, ed., *Oscar Wilde, The Critical Heritage* (New York: Barnes & Noble, 1970);

Alan Bird, *The Plays of Oscar Wilde* (New York: Barnes & Noble, 1977);

Philip K. Cohen, *The Moral Vision of Oscar Wilde* (London: Fairleigh Dickinson University Press, 1976);

Richard Ellmann, ed., *Letters of James Joyce,* volume 2 (New York: Viking, 1966), p. 150;

H. Montgomery Hyde, *The Trials of Oscar Wilde* (New York: Dover, 1973);

Ellsworth Mason and Richard Ellmann, eds., *The Critical Writings of James Joyce* (New York: Viking, 1959), p. 205;

Stuart Mason, *Oscar Wilde: Art and Morality* (New York: Haskell House, 1971);

Robert Keith Miller, *Oscar Wilde* (New York: Ungar, 1982);

Christopher S. Nassaar, *Into the Demon Universe: A Literary Exploration of Oscar Wilde* (New Haven: Yale University Press, 1974);

Rodney Shewan, *Oscar Wilde: Art and Egotism* (New York: Barnes & Noble, 1977).

Papers:

The largest collection of Oscar Wilde's manuscripts and letters is at the William Andrews Clark Memorial Library of the University of California at Los Angeles. Other collections are at the New York Public Library; the J. Pierpont Morgan Library; the Beinecke Library, Yale University; the British Library; the Humanities Research Center, University of Texas, Austin; the Houghton Library, Harvard University; the University of Edinburgh Library; The Rosenbach Museum, Philadelphia; and Magdalen College, Oxford University.

P. G. Wodehouse
(15 October 1881-14 February 1975)

Richard J. Voorhees
Purdue University

SELECTED BOOKS: *The Pothunters* (London: A. & C. Black, 1902; New York: Macmillan, 1902);

A Prefect's Uncle (London: A. & C. Black, 1903; New York: Macmillan, 1903);

Tales of St. Austin's (London: A. & C. Black, 1903);

The Gold Bat (London: A. & C. Black, 1904; New York: Macmillan, 1923);

William Tell Told Again (London: A. & C. Black, 1904; New York: Macmillan, 1904);

The Head of Kay's (London: A. & C. Black, 1905; New York: Macmillan, 1922);

Love Among the Chickens (London: Newnes, 1906; New York: Circle, 1909);

The White Feather (London: A. & C. Black, 1907; New York: Macmillan, 1922);

The Globe By the Way Book, by Wodehouse and Herbert Westbrook (London: *Globe* Publishing, 1908);

Not George Washington (London, Paris, New York, Toronto & Melbourne: Cassell, 1909);

The Swoop! (London: Alston Rivers, 1909);

Mike: A Public School Story (London: A. & C. Black, 1909; New York: Macmillan, 1910); chapters 30-59 republished as *Enter Psmith* (London: A. & C. Black, 1935; New York: Macmillan, 1935) and as *Mike and Psmith* (London: Jenkins, 1953); chapters 1-29 republished as *Mike at Wrykyn* (London: Jenkins, 1953);

The Intrusion of Jimmy (New York: Watt, 1910); republished as *A Gentleman of Leisure* (London: Alston Rivers, 1910);

Psmith in the City (London: A. & C. Black, 1910; New York: Macmillan, 1910);

The Prince and Betty (New York: Watt, 1912; London: Mills & Boon, 1912);

The Little Nugget (London: Methuen, 1913; New York: Watt, 1914);

The Man Upstairs and Other Stories (London: Methuen, 1914);

Psmith, Journalist (London: Black, 1915; New York: Macmillan, 1915);

Something New (New York: Appleton, 1915); republished as *Something Fresh* (London: Methuen, 1915);

Uneasy Money (New York: Appleton, 1916; London: Methuen, 1917);

Piccadilly Jim (New York: Dodd, Mead, 1917; London: Jenkins, 1918);

The Man With Two Left Feet and Other Stories (London: Methuen, 1917; New York & Chicago: A. L. Burt, 1933);

My Man Jeeves (London: Newnes, 1919);

Their Mutual Child (New York: Boni & Liveright, 1919); republished as *The Coming of Bill* (London: Jenkins, 1920);

A Damsel in Distress (New York: Doran, 1919; London: Jenkins, 1920);

The Little Warrior (New York: Doran, 1920); republished as *Jill the Reckless* (London: Jenkins, 1921);

Indiscretions of Archie (London: Jenkins, 1921; New York: Doran, 1921);

The Clicking of Cuthbert (London: Jenkins, 1922); republished as *Golf Without Tears* (New York: Doran, 1924);

Three Men and a Maid (New York: Doran, 1922); republished as *The Girl on the Boat* (London: Jenkins, 1922);

The Adventures of Sally (London: Jenkins, 1923); republished as *Mostly Sally* (New York: Doran, 1923);

The Inimitable Jeeves (London: Jenkins, 1923); republished as *Jeeves* (New York: Doran, 1923);

Leave It to Psmith (London: Jenkins, 1923; New York: Doran, 1924);

Ukridge (London: Jenkins, 1924); republished as *He Rather Enjoyed It* (New York: Doran, 1925);

Bill the Conqueror (London: Methuen, 1924; New York: Doran, 1925);

Carry On, Jeeves! (London: Jenkins, 1925; New York: Doran, 1925);

Sam the Sudden (London: Methuen, 1925); republished as *Sam in the Suburbs* (New York: Doran, 1925);

The Heart of a Goof (London: Jenkins, 1926); republished as *Divots* (New York: Doran, 1927);

The Small Bachelor (London: Methuen, 1927; New York: Doran, 1927);

Meet Mr. Mulliner (London: Jenkins, 1927; Garden City: Doubleday, Doran, 1928);

Money for Nothing (London: Jenkins, 1928; Garden City: Doubleday, Doran, 1928);

Mr. Mulliner Speaking (London: Jenkins, 1929; Garden City: Doubleday, Doran, 1930);

Fish Preferred (Garden City: Doubleday, Doran, 1929); republished as *Summer Lightning* (London: Jenkins, 1929);

Very Good, Jeeves (Garden City: Doubleday, Doran, 1930; London: Jenkins, 1930);

courtesy of Barrie & Jenkins

Big Money (Garden City: Doubleday, Doran, 1931; London: Jenkins, 1931);

If I Were You (Garden City: Doubleday, Doran, 1931; London: Jenkins, 1931);

Louder and Funnier (London: Faber & Faber, 1932);

Doctor Sally (London: Methuen, 1932);

Hot Water (London: Jenkins, 1932; Garden City: Doubleday, Doran, 1932);

Mulliner Nights (London: Jenkins, 1933; Garden City: Doubleday, Doran, 1933);

Heavy Weather (Boston: Little, Brown, 1933; London: Jenkins, 1933);

Thank You, Jeeves (London: Jenkins, 1934; Boston: Little, Brown, 1934);

Right Ho, Jeeves (London: Jenkins, 1934); republished as *Brinkley Manor* (Boston: Little, Brown, 1934);

Blandings Castle (London: Jenkins, 1935; Garden City: Doubleday, Doran, 1935);

The Luck of the Bodkins (London: Jenkins, 1935; revised, Boston: Little, Brown, 1936);

Young Men in Spats (London: Jenkins, 1936; revised, Garden City: Doubleday, Doran, 1936);

Laughing Gas (London: Jenkins, 1936; Garden City: Doubleday, Doran, 1936);

Lord Emsworth and Others (London: Jenkins, 1937);

The Crime Wave at Blandings (Garden City: Doubleday, Doran, 1937);

Summer Moonshine (Garden City: Doubleday, Doran, 1937; London: Jenkins, 1938);

The Code of the Woosters (New York: Doubleday, Doran, 1938; London: Jenkins, 1938);

Uncle Fred in the Springtime (New York: Doubleday, Doran, 1939; London: Jenkins, 1939);

Eggs, Beans and Crumpets (London: Jenkins, 1940; New York: Doubleday, Doran, 1940);

Quick Service (London: Jenkins, 1940; New York: Doubleday, Doran, 1940);

Money In the Bank (New York: Doubleday, Doran, 1942; London: Jenkins, 1946);

Joy in the Morning (Garden City: Doubleday, 1946; London: Jenkins, 1947);

Full Moon (Garden City: Doubleday, 1947; London: Jenkins, 1947);

Spring Fever (Garden City: Doubleday, 1948; London: Jenkins, 1948);

Uncle Dynamite (London: Jenkins, 1948; New York: Didier, 1948);

The Mating Season (London: Jenkins, 1949; New York: Didier, 1949);

Nothing Serious (London: Jenkins, 1950; Garden City: Doubleday, 1951);

The Old Reliable (London: Jenkins, 1951; Garden City: Doubleday, 1951);

Barmy in Wonderland (London: Jenkins, 1952); republished as Angel Cake (Garden City: Doubleday, 1952);

Pigs Have Wings (Garden City: Doubleday, 1952; London: Jenkins, 1952);

Ring for Jeeves (London: Jenkins, 1953); republished as The Return of Jeeves (New York: Simon & Schuster, 1954);

Bring on the Girls!, by Wodehouse and Guy Bolton (New York: Simon & Schuster, 1953; London: Jenkins, 1954);

Performing Flea (London: Jenkins, 1953); revised as Author! Author! (New York: Simon & Schuster, 1962);

Jeeves and the Feudal Spirit (London: Jenkins, 1954); republished as Bertie Wooster Sees It Through (New York: Simon & Schuster, 1955);

French Leave (London: Jenkins, 1956; New York: Simon & Schuster, 1959);

America, I Like You (New York: Simon & Schuster, 1956); republished as Over Seventy (London: Jenkins, 1957);

Something Fishy (London: Jenkins, 1957); republished as The Butler Did It (New York: Simon & Schuster, 1957);

Cocktail Time (London: Jenkins, 1958; New York: Simon & Schuster, 1958);

A Few Quick Ones (New York: Simon & Schuster, 1959; London: Jenkins, 1959);

How Right You Are, Jeeves (New York: Simon & Schuster, 1960); republished as Jeeves in the Offing (London: Jenkins, 1960);

The Ice in the Bedroom (New York: Simon & Schuster, 1961; London: Jenkins, 1961);

Service With a Smile (New York: Simon & Schuster, 1961; London: Jenkins, 1962);

Stiff Upper Lip, Jeeves (New York: Simon & Schuster, 1963; London: Jenkins, 1963);

Biffin's Millions (New York: Simon & Schuster, 1964); republished as Frozen Assets (London: Jenkins, 1964);

The Brinkmanship of Galahad Threepwood (New York: Simon & Schuster, 1965); republished as Galahad at Blandings (London: Jenkins, 1965);

Plum Pie (London: Jenkins, 1966; New York: Simon & Schuster, 1967);

The Purloined Paperweight (New York: Simon & Schuster, 1967); republished as Company for Henry (London: Jenkins, 1967);

Do Butlers Burgle Banks? (New York: Simon & Schuster, 1968; London: Jenkins, 1968);

A Pelican at Blandings (London: Jenkins, 1969); republished as No Nudes Is Good Nudes (New York: Simon & Schuster, 1970);

The Girl in Blue (London: Barrie & Jenkins, 1970; New York: Simon & Schuster, 1971);

Much Obliged, Jeeves (London: Barrie & Jenkins, 1971); republished as Jeeves and the Tie that Binds (New York: Simon & Schuster, 1971);

Pearls, Girls and Monty Bodkin (London: Barrie & Jenkins, 1972); republished as The Plot That Thickened (New York: Simon & Schuster, 1973);

Bachelors Anonymous (London: Barrie & Jenkins, 1973; New York: Simon & Schuster: 1974);

Aunts Aren't Gentlemen (London: Barrie & Jenkins, 1974); republished as The Cat-Nappers (New York: Simon & Schuster, 1974);

Quest (London: Privately printed, 1975);

Sunset at Blandings (London: Chatto & Windus, 1977; New York: Simon & Schuster, 1978).

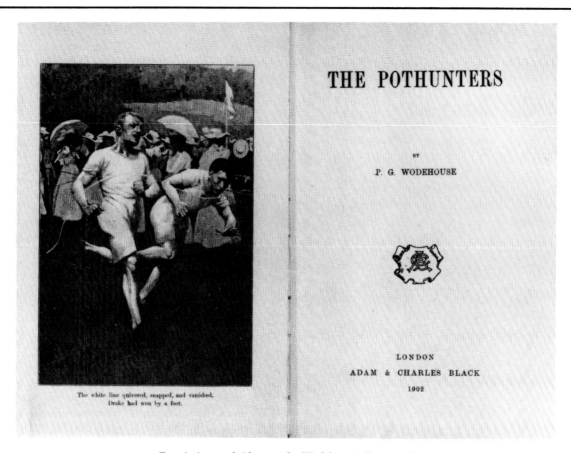

Frontispiece and title page for Wodehouse's first novel

P. G. Wodehouse was born in Guildford, the suburb of London to which Dickens retired Mr. Pickwick, and educated at Dulwich College, one of England's best public schools. After graduating, Wodehouse worked briefly in a bank and then turned to full-time writing. In 1914 he married Ethel Rowley, and thereafter the Wodehouses lived mostly in the United States and England, though they also had a house in France, at Le Touquet. Between World War I and World War II, Wodehouse was by far the most prolific and popular writer of fiction in the English-speaking world. In *America, I Like You* (1956) he says that he has already written "ten books for boys, one book for children, forty-three novels, if you can call them novels, three hundred and fifteen short stories, four hundred and eleven articles, and a thing called *The Swoop.*"

Wodehouse arrived at a turning point in his career in 1914, when the *Saturday Evening Post* serialized *Something Fresh* (1915), the first of twenty-one of his novels to appear in the magazine. His amusing romances, such as *A Damsel in Distress* (1919), his sentimental romances, such as *The Little Warrior* (1920), and his pure comedies, such as *Right*

Ho, Jeeves (1934), *The Code of the Woosters* (1938), and other books about Bertie Wooster and his man Jeeves, were best-sellers in England and America and translated into all the major languages and a few obscure ones. His short stories also had an immense audience.

Wodehouse's work for the theater was no less abundant and successful than his fiction. *America, I Like You* informs us, "I have also been author or part author of sixteen plays and twenty-two musical comedies." Wodehouse wrote original plays, alone or with others, including *Brother Alfred* (by Wodehouse and Herbert Westbrook), first produced in 1913, and *Her Cardboard Lover* (by Wodehouse and Valerie Syngate), staged in 1927. He turned his own novels into plays; for example, *A Gentleman of Leisure* was produced in 1911, *A Damsel in Distress* in 1928. He adapted the work of Continental playwrights, including *The Play's the Thing* (1926) from Ferenc Molnar and *Candle-Light* (1929) from Siegfried Geyer.

Among the stars of the era who were pleased to appear in Wodehouse's plays were Douglas Fairbanks, John Barrymore, Beatrice Lillie, and Stanley

Holloway. Wodehouse liked actors, found no more vanity in them than he did in other people, and was modest enough himself to be willing to learn from them. He believed that when they suggested lines for their parts, they usually did so because they thought that the additions would emphasize a point in the play.

Wodehouse wrote lyrics and books for the music of Jerome Kern, Victor Herbert, Rudolf Friml, Sigmund Romberg, and George Gershwin. His brightest lyrics were those he did for musicals with Guy Bolton, a former architect, who, alone or with Wodehouse, wrote the books, and Jerome Kern. Today Wodehouse's best-known lyrics are those which he wrote for the song "Bill," dropped from the Wodehouse-Bolton-Kern show *Oh, Lady! Lady!* (1918) but used in the much more famous musical *Show Boat* (1927).

Leave It to Jane (1917), with book by Bolton and Kern, lyrics by Wodehouse, transformed the Broadway musical. Earlier musical shows in America were imported from Europe or were strongly influenced by European models. Actually more operettas than musical comedies, they were set in Graustarkian kingdoms and featured princes

Cover of the libretto for the Wodehouse-Bolton-Kern collaboration that opened at New York's Princess Theatre on 1 February 1918

giving up the barmaids they loved and submitting to royal marriages arranged by ministers of state; hussars swaggering around in foppish uniforms; peasants dancing on village greens; gypsies singing at campfires. Wodehouse, Kern, and Bolton had the happy idea of using George Ade's play *The College Widow* (1904) to make a musical which was really American and really comic. *Leave It to Jane* is set on a college campus, most members of the cast are students, the results of a football game figure in the intrigue, and the leading lady is neither princess nor barmaid. Once overwhelmingly popular, the Wodehouse-Bolton-Kern shows no longer enjoy frequent revivals or long runs. The great exception is *Leave It to Jane,* which, when it was revived Off-Broadway in 1971, ran for a fabulous 928 performances.

Wodehouse fared much less well in Hollywood, where (as he might have put it himself) he did two stretches. In 1930 M-G-M paid him well for a year but gave him few significant assignments. Naively he told a reporter for the *Los Angeles Times* that he regretted that he did nothing for two thousand dollars a week. When the reporter's story appeared, bankers charged apoplectically from the East Coast to the West, anglophobes all over the country were infuriated, studio policies were revised, and Wodehouse left Hollywood under a cloud.

Wodehouse, however, had made good friends in Hollywood, for example, Maureen O'Sullivan and her husband the director John Farrow. He therefore returned in 1936, this time to work for RKO, which he found more agreeable than M-G-M. He liked George Stevens and Edmund Goulding, the directors for whom he worked, and he was especially pleased to do the script for the 1937 remake of *A Damsel in Distress*, with Fred Astaire and Joan Fontaine and with music by George Gershwin. But in less than a year he left Hollywood again, because he preferred fiction to writing scripts, and he was eager to do a novel which he had already blocked out. Most of the movies made from his novels were scripted by other writers. Had Hollywood been wiser, it would have tried hard to retain Wodehouse. He wrote excellent dialogue, and because of his experience in the theater, he had come to think always in scenes, even when he wrote novels and short stories.

Aside from the interludes in Hollywood, the 1920s and 1930s were a happy period for Wodehouse. He did the work he loved and was handsomely paid for it. Literary critics did not bother their heads about him, but the reviews he

Wodehouse, 1928

received were a great chorus of enthusiasm and gratitude. In 1939 Oxford University made him Doctor of Letters, an honor which the *London Times* promptly sanctioned in a leading article.

A year after Oxford's tribute there began a series of events in Wodehouse's life beside which the Hollywood flap was nothing at all. When in the summer of 1940 the Germans arrived at Le Touquet, Wodehouse was living in his house there. He thought that they would not intern British nationals, but in fact he was held in prison camps for forty-nine weeks. On 26 June 1941 he was released, because it was the policy of the Germans not to hold British civilians over sixty years of age. He gave an interview to Harry Flannery, the CBS man in Berlin, and later recorded five talks which were broadcast, not over CBS but on the German network. The result was outrage in England: indignant letters to newspapers, angry editorials, questions in Parliament, and a BBC broadcast that denounced Wodehouse as a Quisling and Hitler-worshipper.

The truth is that accusing Wodehouse of treason made as much sense as accusing him of rum-running or witchcraft. He was, to be sure, foolish to make recordings for the Germans. On the other hand, the German censors were extremely stupid to pass everything that he said. All five talks combine two important characteristics of his writing, clarity of exposition and narrative and a keen perception of the absurd. He does not make his German captors beasts (he was not treated with great cruelty, but he slept on hard beds and cold floors and was put on short rations), but he makes them idiots. When, for example, they try to count their prisoners, they run around like actors in a Hollywood farce. Obviously, they do not know a damned thing about running a prison camp.

Still, someone is likely to ask, how could Wodehouse have been so indiscreet as to do the broadcasts? One may ask in turn, how could he have have been so indiscreet as to tell a reporter that he was paid two thousand dollars a week for doing nothing? His own mental world was almost as distant from the real world as the world of his fiction. And after forty-nine weeks in prison camps he was completely out of touch with military and political

Wodehouse and his stepdaughter, Leonora, arriving in Hollywood, 1930

ordeal, and it left its mark on him, though not on his work. It was not in his nature to hold a grudge, but he had been made to feel unwelcome in England. After the Liberation of France, the Wodehouses lived there until 1947, when they came to the United States; they became American citizens in 1955. Wodehouse died in Southampton, New York, on 14 February 1975, shortly after he had been knighted by Elizabeth II.

Writing was Wodehouse's life. He wrote some of his best novels in his last ten years and at the time of his death was working on one. Although the bulk of his stage work is now only a footnote in the history of the theater, his fiction still has a huge audience, and there is a growing group of biographers and critics.

Wodehouse produced so many volumes of fiction that it is impossible to deal even briefly with all of them. The best course is probably to describe the kinds of fiction that he wrote and to give some examples. The school novels for boys, published in the first decade of the century, have been republished many times in England, most recently in the late 1970s. The first of them, *The Pothunters* (1902), is a conventional specimen of the public-school novel, with its "code" and cult of games, its conscious and unconscious snobbery. But irony appears in the second, *A Prefect's Uncle* (1903), in which Wodehouse goes so far as to make jokes about the school hierarchy, cricket, and the stereotypes of school fiction. In *Mike* (1909) one boy asks another whether he is the pride of the school, the bully, or the fellow who takes to drink in chapter five. Wodehouse's style and some of his typical characters evolve as the school novels progress. In the novels after *The Pothunters,* there is a great deal of literary quotation and allusion, including some favorite lines of Bertie Wooster quoted from Hood's ballad about Eugene Aram: "And Eugene Aram walked between, with gyves upon his wrists." The schoolboy Psmith is the precursor of two later kinds of adult characters: the brash, fast-talking heroes of the romances and the unheroic clowns of the comedies, who, like Psmith, are very fluent and allusive but, unlike him, muddled in their metaphors and their sources.

With two school books still to come, Wodehouse made an excursion into adult fiction. The hero of *Love Among the Chickens* (1906) is, like Wodehouse himself, a young man making his way as a writer, and the heroine is the first grown girl in Wodehouse's fiction. Their love affair is naive and sentimental; its environment is an idyllic Devonshire of sheep bells in the dusk, duets after dinner,

developments and with the feelings of the British people. Besides, in the 1920s and 1930s he had spent so much time in the United States that in some ways he thought of himself as an American citizen. When Flannery told him that doing anything on the German radio, even playing the violin, would be propaganda, he said, "We're not at war with Germany."

Wodehouse was the victim of a great war—a convenient scapegoat when England was fighting for its life, a suspect when the war was won, and a figure in vague disrepute in the years following. At last, in 1961, the BBC broadcast an apology to him, in which it declared that it had been forced by the Ministry of Information into an affair for which it had always felt disgust. Some of Wodehouse's persecutors did not apologize; William Connor, who wrote the BBC attack, argued that it had been necessary. Today the number of people who assume that Wodehouse was a traitor is probably not small. But the full texts of the five talks for the German network are available in *Encounter* (October and November 1954) and in *Wodehouse at War* (1981), by Iain Sproat.

Wodehouse was deeply wounded by his

Dust jacket for a 1930 story collection and a 1934 novel featuring Wodehouse's famous gentleman's gentleman, Jeeves

and the use of Christian names only after engagements. Into this pastoral, however, farce intrudes: the love story is entwined with the story of Ukridge, Wodehouse's first antihero. Cadger, crook, liar, but forever self-righteous, Ukridge is a picaresque character without enough brains to play the part well. Raising chickens is only the first of his lunatic schemes to get rich quickly, all of which fall flat. Since he learns nothing from experience, he serves Wodehouse well as the protagonist of further misadventures in a series of short stories. Wodehouse has already found the right idiom for Ukridge (everybody, including bishops, is "old horse" to him) and the invariable costume: old gray flannel suit, beat-up sneakers, and mackintosh.

The light novels that follow *Love Among the Chickens*—for example, *The Intrusion of Jimmy* (1910, published the same year in England as *A Gentleman of Leisure*) and *Something New* (1915, in Great Britain, *Something Fresh*)—are sentimental but in a less naive, obvious, and dated way. The romance of *Love*

Among the Chickens clearly derives from the Victorian novelette; that of the light novels derives from musical comedy. The rigid distinction between sentimental hero and clown is breached, and the lover himself is put through the paces of the farceur.

Through his apprenticeship of writing light novels, Wodehouse arrived at the pure comedy which is his greatest achievement. For the comic novels and short stories he invented his best plots, created his best characters, and perfected his style. Wodehouse is one of the most ingenious plotters in the history of comic writing. Before he ever touched his typewriter, he planned his novels and short stories in penciled "scenarios," which ran to as many as seventy pages for the novels. Short summary of the plots is impossible, and in *America, I Like You* Wodehouse jokes that when working out their complexities he often feared that his brain would "come unstuck." But once the story or novel was neatly blocked out, he typed the manuscript rapidly, and no trace of effort remains.

Like the characters in Restoration comedy and in Dickens, Wodehouse's comic characters have good names to begin with, for example, Oofy Prosser, Bingo Little, Sir Roderick Glossop, Bertie Wooster, Sir Watkyn Bassett. None of the many young men is notable for intelligence; each has the world view of the schoolboy. Fascinated by gambling, overfond of food and drink, harassed by aunts, they stumble from one imbroglio to another. Freddie Threepwood, who first appears in *Something Fresh,* has already been expelled from Eton, sent down from Oxford, and rejected by the army. Charles Edward Biffen, who appears in *Carry On, Jeeves!* (1925), *Biffen's Millions* (1964), and other novels and stories early and late, has such a short memory span that he actually forgets the name of a girl to whom he has proposed. The dramatis personae also include numerous older characters. Lord Emsworth is the owner of Blandings, the country house which is the scene of *Blandings Castle* (1935) and other novels and stories in the Blandings cycle. He is a dotty old party whose only desire is that his prize pig, the Empress, should go on winning prizes. Uncle Fred, a citizen of the world who frequently visits Blandings, is well stricken in years but has not lost his passion for schoolboy pranks, practical jokes, and stirring up affairs in general.

Wodehouse's greatest accomplishment in comic character is Bertie Wooster, the hero and narrator of *The Inimitable Jeeves* (1923), *Stiff Upper Lip, Jeeves* (1963), and other Bertie and Jeeves novels and stories. Unlike the heroes of the school novels and the romances, Bertie is not athletic. The football field and even the golf course are no more to him than distant memories. His London club is, appropriately, the Drones, where his most strenuous activity is throwing bread in the dining room with like-minded members. He has entered the swimming pool on only one occasion: on a bet, he tried to swing across on the gym rings, but they had been tied back by some rotter, so that he was immersed fully clothed.

Bertie is a bachelor, though he is highly susceptible to beautiful girls. He is wise in his bachelorhood, for all the girls he knows are sentimentalists who communicate with small animals in excruciating baby talk; or intellectuals who are determined that he should read Nietzsche or Bergson; or holy terrors who force him into lunatic and dangerous schemes.

Two aunts are formidable figures in Bertie's life: Dahlia, whom he always identifies as "my good and deserving aunt," and Agatha, whom he refers to as "the werewolf," or "the one who eats broken

Wodehouse and his wife, Ethel, Paris, 1945 (photo by Compix)

glass," or "the one who wears barbed wire next to the skin." There is a lot of amiable pip-pipping between Bertie and Dahlia, whom he addresses as "aged relative," a variation on Wemmick's "aged parent" or "aged P." in Dickens's *Great Expectations.* But both aunts, like the wild girls, forever find reasons for getting Bertie "in the soup" or "beneath the harrow."

It is the function of Jeeves, not only a model of the gentleman's gentleman but also a fellow of infinite resource and flexible ethics, to rescue Bertie from the traps of aunts, girls who want to marry him, and assorted menaces like Sir Watkyn Bassett (a retired magistrate who is convinced that Bertie is a habitual thief) and Sir Roderick Glossop (a "loony doctor" who is convinced that he is a madman). But Jeeves himself exerts an auntlike authority over Bertie, who must pay for each rescue by sacrificing a suit, hat, or tie which does not come up to Jeeves's high standards. Though never disrespectful to Bertie, Jeeves has a low opinion of his intelligence. But he also knows, as the reader does, Bertie's virtues: gratitude, modesty, magnanimity. Bertie has a code, if only the schoolboy code, and can always be

Page of notes from the many papers Wodehouse bequeathed to his alma mater, Dulwich College (courtesy of Dulwich College)

counted on to run a risk or take a rap for an old school friend or a kind uncle.

Wodehouse's comic style is not without antecedents in British literature, but it is without parallel in the twentieth century. In a sense (though not a sense that a linguist would admit), Wodehouse invented a new language. Its sources lie in Wodehouse's omnivorous reading and in his sharp ear for spoken language. He was educated in the classics at Dulwich, and in his free time there he began to acquire his wide knowledge of later literature. From the time he left school, he read constantly, for the most part in British literature, but also in American and French. He read the plays of Shakespeare annually and took an edition of Tennyson's complete works with him when he was imprisoned by the Germans. He also knew the minor poets, including Thomas Hood and, for that matter, Felicia Hemans. Although he read the great English novelists, he probably knew more about Victorian-Edwardian trash or, as he called it, "bilge literature," than anybody but those who actually wrote the stuff.

Wodehouse's style is a bright mosaic in which literary quotations and allusions, slang phrases and scientific terms, and the shop talk of trades and professions are some of the pieces. The first principle of the style is disparity. For example, Mrs. Cream, the popular American novelist in *Jeeves in the Offing* (1960), writes thrillers that always harrow her readers with pity and terror—as if they were Greek tragic dramas. And when, in the course of farcical adventures, Bertie and Jeeves are obliged to separate for a time, they take leave of each other with a solemn farewell from *Julius Caesar:* "We shall meet at Philippi."

Wodehouse happily borrows for his comedy the clichés of the sentimental novel. In "Sundered Hearts," one of the stories collected in *Golf Without Tears* (1924), the heroine must confess to her fiancé that she is not a champion golfer but only a champion croquet player: "A faint blush of shame mantled her cheek, and into her blue eyes there came a look of pain, but she faced him bravely." Monomania is endemic on the golf course. When in "The Heart of a Goof," the first story in *Divots* (1927), the hero has at last won his girl, Wodehouse concludes, "He folded her in his arms, using the interlocking grip."

Always a pleasure, the style suits the character of Bertie Wooster perfectly. Wooster demonstrates in *The Code of the Woosters,* and the other novels and stories that he narrates, the inspired hyperbole of it. He is grateful for Jeeves's "tissue-restorer," an un-

Wodehouse one week before his death in February 1975 (©BBC)

failing mixture for hangovers, but the initial effect is that "of having the top of the skull fly up to the ceiling and the eyes shoot out of their sockets and rebound from the opposite wall like raquet balls." He illustrates Wodehouse's marvelous stylistic amalgam as he opens *Stiff Upper Lip, Jeeves:* "I marmaladed a slice of toast with a flourish . . . for I was feeling in mid-season form this morning. God, as I once heard Jeeves put it, was in His heaven and all right with the world. He added, I remember, some guff about larks and snails, but that is a side issue and need not detain us."

In 1941 an article by John Hayward was published in the annual *Saturday Book,* demonstrating the extent to which Wodehouse's early novels anticipated the later ones. In a 1945 issue of *Windmill* George Orwell pointed out that the atmosphere of Wodehouse's novels had not changed since 1925 and that his best-known characters had appeared even earlier. In *New Statesman* in 1953 A. P. Ryan observed that Wodehouse (like Jane Austen) had wisely confined himself to a convention that suited him perfectly. In a 1958 piece in *New World Writing* John Aldridge called Wodehouse the best writer of light comedy in the twentieth century. In the autumn 1959 *Arizona Quarterly* Lionel Stevenson traced Wodehouse's antecedents in English literature from Ben Jonson to Oscar Wilde. In the 1960s books on Wodehouse began to appear, and since then there has been no lack of commentators and biographers. It is now abundantly clear that Wodehouse is one of the funniest and most productive men who ever wrote English. He is far from being a mere jokesmith: he is an authentic craftsman, a wit and humorist of the first water, the inventor of a prose style which is a kind of comic poetry.

Bibliography:

Dave A. Jasen, *A Bibliography and Reader's Guide to the First Editions of P. G. Wodehouse* (Hamden, Conn.: Archon Books, 1970).

Biographies:

Benny Green, *P. G. Wodehouse: A Literary Biography* (London: Joseph, 1981);

Frances Donaldson, *P. G. Wodehouse: A Biography* (New York: Knopf, 1982).

References:

Robert A. Hall, *The Comic Style of P. G. Wodehouse* (Hamden, Conn.: Archon Books, 1974);

James H. Heineman and Donald R. Benson, eds., *P. G. Wodehouse: A Centenary Celebration 1881-1981* (New York & London: Pierpont Morgan Library/Oxford University Press, 1981);

Richard Usborne, *Wodehouse at Work* (London: Jenkins, 1961); revised and enlarged as *Wodehouse at Work to the End* (London: Barrie & Jenkins, 1976);

Richard J. Voorhees, *P. G. Wodehouse* (New York: Twayne, 1966).

Supplementary Reading List

Aldridge, John W., ed. *Critiques and Essays on Modern Fiction: 1920-1951.* New York: Ronald, 1952.

Baker, Ernest A. *The History of the English Novel,* volume 10. New York: Barnes & Noble, 1939.

Beach, Joseph Warren. *The Twentieth-Century Novel: Studies in Technique.* New York: Appleton, 1932.

Bellamy, William. *The Novels of Wells, Bennett, and Galsworthy: 1890-1910.* New York: Barnes & Noble, 1971.

Bergonzi, Bernard. *The Situation of the Novel.* Pittsburgh: University of Pittsburgh Press, 1970.

Bergonzi. *The Turn of the Century: Essays on Victorian and Modern English Literature.* New York: Barnes & Noble, 1973.

Bradbury, Malcolm. *Possibilities: Essays on the State of the Novel.* New York: Oxford University Press, 1973.

Brewster, Dorothy, and Angus Burrell. *Modern Fiction.* New York: Columbia University Press, 1934.

Bridgwater, Patrick. *Nietzsche in Anglosaxony: A Study of Nietzsche's Impact on English and American Literature.* Leicester: Leicester University Press, 1972.

Brown, Edward K. *Rhythm in the Novel.* Toronto: University of Toronto Press, 1950.

Bufkin, E. C. *The Twentieth-Century Novel in English: A Checklist.* Athens: University of Georgia Press, 1967.

Bullett, Gerald. *Modern English Fiction.* London: Jenkins, 1926.

Chapple, J. A. V. *Documentary and Imaginative Literature, 1880-1920.* New York: Barnes & Noble, 1970.

Chevalley, Abel. *The Modern English Novel,* translated by B. R. Redman. New York: Knopf, 1927.

Cooper, Frederic Taber. *Some English Story Tellers: A Book of the Younger Novelists.* New York: Holt, 1912.

Cox, C. B. *The Free Spirit: A Study of Liberal Humanism in the Novels of George Eliot, E. M. Forster, Virginia Woolf, Angus Wilson.* London: Oxford University Press, 1963.

Cross, Wilbur J. *Four Contemporary Novelists.* New York: Macmillan, 1930.

Cunliffe, J. W. *English Literature in the Twentieth Century.* New York: Macmillan, 1934.

Daiches, David. *The Novel and the Modern World.* Chicago: University of Chicago Press, 1939; revised, 1960.

Drew, Elizabeth. *The Modern Novel: Some Aspects of Contemporary Fiction.* New York: Harcourt, Brace, 1926.

Dyson, A. E., ed. *The English Novel: Select Bibliographical Guides.* London: Oxford University Press, 1974.

Eagleton, Terry. *Exiles and Emigres: Studies in Modern Literature.* New York: Schocken, 1970.

Edel, Leon. *The Psychological Novel: 1900-1950.* Philadelphia: Lippincott, 1955. Republished as *The Modern Psychological Novel.* New York: Grove, 1959.

343

Fleishman, Avrom. *The English Historical Novel: Walter Scott to Virginia Woolf.* Baltimore: Johns Hopkins University Press, 1971.

Follett, Helen Thomas, and Wilson Follett. *Some Modern Novelists: Appreciations and Estimates.* New York: Holt, 1918.

Ford, Boris, ed. *The Modern Age.* Harmondsworth: Penguin, 1961.

Forster, E. M. *Aspects of the Novel.* London: Arnold, 1927.

Fraser, G. S. *The Modern Writer and His World,* revised edition. London: Deutsch, 1964.

Friedman, Alan W. *The Turn of the Novel.* New York: Oxford University Press, 1966.

Friedman, ed. *Forms of Modern British Fiction.* Austin: University of Texas Press, 1975.

Frierson, William C. *The English Novel in Transition, 1885-1940.* Norman: University of Oklahoma Press, 1942.

Garrett, Peter K. *Scene and Symbol from George Eliot to James Joyce: Studies in Changing Fictional Mode.* New Haven: Yale University Press, 1969.

Gill, Richard. *Happy Rural Seat: The English Country House and the Literary Imagination.* New Haven: Yale University Press, 1972.

Gillie, Christopher. *Movements in English Literature, 1900-1940.* Cambridge: Cambridge University Press, 1975.

Gindin, James. *Harvest of a Quiet Eye: The Novel of Compassion.* Bloomington: Indiana University Press, 1971.

Hampshire, Stuart N. *Modern Writers and Others: Essays.* New York: Knopf, 1970.

Hardy, Barbara. *The Appropriate Form: An Essay on the Novel.* London: University of London Press, 1964.

Hardy, John Edward. *Man in the Modern Novel.* Seattle: University of Washington Press, 1964.

Harper, Howard M., and Charles Edge, eds. *The Classic British Novel.* Athens: University of Georgia Press, 1972.

Hoare, Dorothy M. *Some Studies in the Modern Novel.* London: Chatto & Windus, 1938.

Hoffman, Frederick J. *The Mortal No: Death and the Modern Imagination.* Princeton: Princeton University Press, 1964.

Hough, Graham. *Image and Experience: Studies in a Literary Revolution.* Lincoln: University of Nebraska Press, 1960.

Humphrey, Robert. *Stream of Consciousness in the Modern Novel.* Berkeley & Los Angeles: University of California Press, 1954.

Hynes, Samuel. *Edwardian Occasions: Essays on English Writing in the Early Twentieth Century.* London: Routledge, 1972.

Hynes. *The Edwardian Turn of Mind.* Princeton: Princeton University Press, 1968.

Jackson, Holbrook. *The Eighteen Nineties: A Review of Art and Ideas at the Close of the Nineteenth Century.* London: Richards, 1913.

Johnstone, J. K. *The Bloomsbury Group: A Study of E. M. Forster, Lytton Strachey, Virginia Woolf, and Their Circle.* New York: Noonday, 1954.

Josipovici, Gabriel. *The World and the Book: A Study of Modern Fiction.* Stanford: Stanford University Press, 1971.

Kenner, Hugh. *Gnomon: Essays on Contemporary Literature.* New York: McDowell, Obolensky, 1958.

Kermode, Frank. "The English Novel, circa 1907," in *Twentieth-Century Literature in Retrospect,* edited by Reuben A. Brower. Cambridge: Harvard University Press, 1971, pp. 45-64.

Kettle, Arnold. *An Introduction to the English Novel,* volume 2, *Henry James to the Present.* London: Hutchinson, 1951.

Knight, Grant C. *The Novel in English.* New York: Smith, 1931.

Lauterbach, Edward S., and W. Eugene Davies. *The Transitional Age in British Literature, 1880-1920.* Troy, N.Y.: Whitston, 1973.

Leavis, Q. D. *Fiction and the Reading Public.* London: Chatto & Windus, 1932.

Lesser, Simon O. *Fiction and the Unconscious.* Boston: Beacon, 1957.

Lovett, Robert M., and Helen S. Hughes. *The History of the Novel in England.* Boston: Houghton Mifflin, 1932.

Lubbock, Percy. *The Craft of Fiction.* London: Cape, 1921.

Maurois, André. *Prophets and Poets,* translated by Hamish Miles. New York: Harper, 1935.

McCullogh, Bruce. *Representative English Novelists: Defoe to Conrad.* New York: Harper, 1946.

Muir, Edwin. *The Structure of the Novel.* London: Hogarth Press, 1928.

Nicholson, Norman. *Man and Literature.* London: Macmillan, 1943.

Paterson, John. *The Novel as Faith: The Gospel According to James, Hardy, Conrad, Joyce, Lawrence and Virginia Woolf.* Boston: Gambit, 1973.

Phelps, Gilbert. *The Russian Novel in English Fiction.* London: Hutchinson, 1956.

Phelps, William L. *The Advance of the English Novel.* New York: Dodd, Mead, 1916.

Rice, Thomas Jackson. *English Fiction, 1900-1950,* 2 volumes. Detroit: Gale Research, 1979, 1983.

Schorer, Mark. "Technique as Discovery." *Hudson Review,* 1 (Spring 1948): 67-87.

Schorer, ed. *Modern British Fiction.* New York: Oxford University Press, 1961.

Scott-James, Rolfe A. *Fifty Years of English Literature, 1900-1950; With a Postscript, 1951-1955.* London: Longmans, Green, 1956.

Stade, George, ed. *Six Modern British Novelists.* New York: Columbia University Press, 1974.

Stang, Richard. *The Theory of the Novel in England, 1850-1870.* New York: Columbia University Press, 1959.

Stewart, J. I. M. *Eight Modern Writers.* Oxford: Clarendon Press, 1963.

Swinnerton, Frank. *The Georgian Scene: A Panorama.* New York: Farrar & Rinehart, 1934.

Temple, Ruth Z., and Martin Tucker. *Twentieth Century British Literature: A Reference Guide and Bibliography.* New York: Ungar, 1968.

Tillyard, E. M. W. *The Epic Strain in the English Novel.* London: Chatto & Windus, 1963.

Tindall, William York. *Forces in Modern British Literature, 1885-1956.* New York; Knopf, 1956.

Van Ghent, Dorothy. *The English Novel: Form and Function.* New York: Rinehart, 1953.

Verschoyle, Derek, ed. *The English Novelists: A Survey of the Novel by Twenty Contemporary Novelists.* London: Chatto & Windus, 1936.

Wagenknecht, Edward. *Cavalcade of the English Novel.* New York: Holt, 1954.

Ward, Alfred C. *The Nineteen-Twenties: Literature and Ideas in the Post-War Decade.* London: Methuen, 1930.

Ward. *Twentieth-Century English Literature, 1900-1960.* London: Methuen, 1964.

Watt, Ian. *The Rise of the Novel.* Berkeley & Los Angeles: University of California Press, 1957.

West, Paul. *The Modern Novel,* volume 1, revised edition. London: Hutchinson, 1965.

Weygant, Cornelius. *A Century of the English Novel.* New York: Century, 1925.

Wiley, Paul L. *The British Novel: Conrad to the Present.* Northbrook, Ill.: AHM, 1973.

Williams, Raymond. *The English Novel from Dickens to Lawrence.* London: Chatto & Windus, 1970.

Zabel, Morton Dauwen. *Craft and Character: Text, Methods, and Vocation in Modern Fiction.* New York: Viking, 1957.

Contributors

Robert Boyle, S.J. ....*Marquette University*
Barbara Brothers...*Youngstown State University*
Barbara B. Brown ....*Marshall University*
Douglas M. Catron...*Iowa State University*
Ann Adams Cleary...*University of Tulsa*
A. A. DeVitis ....*Purdue University*
Priscilla Diaz-Dorr ....*University of Tulsa*
Roland Dille...*Moorhead, Minnesota*
Michael Draper ....*London, England*
Ruth Marie Faurot...*University of the Pacific*
Peter M. Irvine...*University of Tulsa*
Ralph D. Lindeman ....*Gettysburg College*
Frederick P. W. McDowell ....*University of Iowa*
Margaret B. McDowell ....*University of Iowa*
Anita Miller...*Chicago, Illinois*
Maureen Modlish ....*Tulsa, Oklahoma*
Brian Murray...*Youngstown State University*
Mary A. O'Toole ....*University of Tulsa*
Richard F. Peterson ....*Southern Illinois University at Carbondale*
Lauren H. Pringle...*Ohio State University*
Charlotte Stewart ....*University of North Carolina*
Richard J. Voorhees ....*Purdue University*
Kingsley Widmer ....*San Diego State University*

Cumulative Index
Dictionary of Literary Biography, Volumes 1-34
Dictionary of Literary Biography Yearbook, 1980-1983
Dictionary of Literary Biography Documentary Series, Volumes 1-4

Cumulative Index

DLB before number: *Dictionary of Literary Biography*, Volumes 1-34
Y before number: *Dictionary of Literary Biography Yearbook*, 1980-1983
DS before number: *Dictionary of Literary Biography Documentary Series*, Volumes 1-4

C

G

H

I

N

O

Q

R

U

V

W